PEARSON CUSTOM BUSINESS RESOURCES

Consumer Behavior 10th edition
Author: Michael Solomon
BA 492/592 Consumer Behavior

PEARSON

This special edition published in cooperation with Pearson Learning Solutions.

Please visit our website at *www.pearsonlearningsolutions.com*.

Attention bookstores: For permission to return any unsold stock, contact us at *pe-uscustomreturns@pearson.com*.

Pearson Learning Solutions, 501 Boylston Street, Suite 900, Boston, MA 02116
A Pearson Education Company
www.pearsoned.com

Printed in the United States of America.
V3NL

ISBN 10: 1-256-61053-4
ISBN 13: 978-1-256-61053-3

PEARSON

Table of Contents

1. Buying, Having, and Being
Michael R. Solomon

1

2. Perception
Michael R. Solomon

41

3. Learning and Memory
Michael R. Solomon

81

4. Motivation and Global Values
Michael R. Solomon

117

5. The Self
Michael R. Solomon

167

6. Personality and Psychographics
Michael R. Solomon

217

7. Attitudes and Persuasion
Michael R. Solomon

253

8. Decision Making
Michael R. Solomon

301

9. Buying and Disposing
Michael R. Solomon

343

10. Organizational and Household Decision Making
Michael R. Solomon

379

11. Groups and Social Media
Michael R. Solomon

415

Glossary
Michael R. Solomon

455

Index

469

Buying, Having, and Being

Buying, Having, and Being

Chapter Objectives

When you finish reading this chapter you will understand why:

1. We use products to help us define our identities in different settings.

2. Consumer behavior is a process.

3. Marketers need to understand the wants and needs of different consumer segments.

4. The Web is changing consumer behavior.

5. Our beliefs and actions as consumers strongly connect to other issues in our lives.

6. Many different types of specialists study consumer behavior.

7. There are two major perspectives on consumer behavior.

MyMarketingLab

Visit **www.mymktlab.com** to find activities that help you learn and review in order to succeed in this chapter.

Gail has some time to kill before her Accounting class, so she pulls out her trusty iPhone to see what's going on in her social networks. Between studying for her Accounting and Marketing exams, she hasn't checked out anything interesting in days—even her Facebook friends around campus have been quiet. Enough of the serious stuff, she decides. It's time for some *really* educational surfing.

So, where to go first? Gail figures she'll start at one of the popular women's portals and see what happens. She goes to iVillage.com, where she quickly scans a feature on the top 10 virtual makeovers. At Oxygen .com she watches a streaming video preview about a new reality show and some scenes from the latest episode of Bad Girls Club. She flicks over to HerCampus ("a collegiette's guide to life^SM") to quickly check out the male students they're featuring in today's Eye Candy section. Just then Gail gets a text from Jewelmint.com to notify her that the site has a new jewelry option for her that's based on the profile she filled out when she registered—and it's recommended by actress Kate Bosworth. Wow, a gorgeous pendant for only $29.99! With her PayPal account, it doesn't take Gail long to throw it in the cart and order it—and to share a photo of her haul on Facebook. As Gail glances at the clock, she realizes she'd better come back to the real world or she'll miss her exam. OK, enough time for one quick post before she runs to catch the campus shuttle: Gail logs on to Ratemyprofessors.com and writes a quick but glowing paragraph about how great her Consumer Behavior professor has been this semester . . . not to mention that awesome textbook they've been using.[1]

Consumer Behavior: People in the Marketplace

This text is about people like Gail—and *you*. It concerns the products and services we buy and use, and the ways these fit into our lives. This chapter describes some important aspects of the field of consumer behavior and some reasons why it's essential to understand how people interact with the marketing system. For now, though, let's return to one "typical" consumer: Gail, the business major. The preceding vignette allows us to highlight some aspects of consumer behavior.

Gail is a consumer, so let's compare her to other consumers. For some purposes, marketers find it useful to categorize her in terms of her age, gender, income, or occupation. These are descriptive characteristics of a population, or **demographics**. In other cases, marketers would rather know something about Gail's interests in clothing or music, or the way she spends her leisure time. This sort of information comes under the category of **psychographics**, which refers to aspects of a person's lifestyle and personality. Knowledge of consumer characteristics plays an extremely important role in many marketing applications, such as defining the market for a product or deciding on the appropriate techniques to employ when a company targets a certain group of consumers.

Gail's sorority sisters strongly influence her purchase decisions. The conversations we have with others transmit a lot of product information, as well as recommendations to use or avoid particular brands; this content often is more influential than what we see on television commercials, magazines, billboards, or even MySpace. The growth of the Web has created thousands of online **consumption communities** where members share opinions and recommendations about anything from Barbie dolls to iPhone apps. Gail forms bonds with fellow group members because they use the same products. There is also pressure on each group member to buy things that will meet with the group's approval. A consumer may pay a steep price in the form of group rejection or embarrassment when she doesn't conform to others' conceptions of what is good or bad, "in" or "out."

As members of a large society, such as the United States, people share certain cultural values, or strongly held beliefs about the way the world should function. Members of subcultures, or smaller groups within the culture, also share values; these groups include Hispanics, teens, Midwesterners, and even Lady Gaga's "Little Monsters."

As she surfed around to different Web sites, Gail was exposed to many competing *brands*. Numerous sites did not capture her attention at all, whereas she noticed but rejected others because they didn't relate to products, people, or ideas with which she identified or to which she aspired. The use of **market segmentation strategies** means targeting a brand only to specific groups of consumers rather than to everybody—even if it means that other consumers who don't belong to this target market aren't attracted to that product.

Brands often have clearly defined images, or "personalities," created by advertising, packaging, branding, and other marketing strategies. The choice of a favorite Web site is very much a *lifestyle* statement: It says a lot about a person's interests, as well as something about the type of person she would like to be. People often choose a product because they like its image or because they feel its "personality" somehow corresponds to their own. Moreover, a consumer may believe that if she buys and uses the product or service, its desirable qualities will "magically" rub off onto her. When a product or service succeeds in satisfying our specific needs or desires, we may reward it with many years of *brand loyalty*, a bond between product and consumer that is very difficult for competitors to break.

The appearance, taste, texture, or smell of the item influences our evaluations of products. A good Web site helps people to feel, taste, and smell with their eyes. We may be swayed by the shape and color of a package, as well as by more subtle factors, such as the symbolism in a brand name, in an advertisement, or even in the choice of a cover model for a magazine. These judgments are affected by—and often reflect—how a society feels people should define themselves at that point in time. If she were asked, Gail might not even be able to say exactly why she considered some Web sites and rejected others. Many product meanings are hidden below the surface of the packaging and advertising; we'll discuss some of the methods marketers and social scientists use to discover or apply these meanings.

Like Gail, our opinions and desires increasingly are shaped by input from around the world, which is becoming a much smaller place as a result of rapid advancements in communications and transportation systems. In today's global culture, consumers often prize products and services that "transport" them to different places and allow them to experience the diversity of other cultures—even if only to watch others brush their teeth on YouTube.

OBJECTIVE 1
We use products to help us define our identities in different settings.

What Is Consumer Behavior?

The field of **consumer behavior** covers a lot of ground: *It is the study of the processes involved when individuals or groups select, purchase, use, or dispose of products, services, ideas, or experiences to satisfy needs and desires.* Consumers take many forms, ranging from an 8-year-old child begging her mother for a Webkinz stuffed animal to an executive in a large corporation deciding on a multimillion-dollar computer system. The items we consume can include anything from canned peas to a massage, democracy, Reggaeton music, or a celebrity like Lady Gaga. The needs and desires we satisfy range from hunger and thirst to love, status, and even spiritual fulfillment. Also, people can get passionate about a broad range of products. Whether it's vintage Air Jordans, that perfect yoga mat, or the latest laptop, there's no shortage of brand fans who will do whatever it takes to find and buy what they crave.

MyMarketingLab
Visit **www.mymktlab.com** to test your understanding of chapter objectives.

The expanded view of consumer behavior embraces much more than the study of what and why we buy; it also focuses on how marketers influence consumers and how consumers use the products and services marketers sell. In this case, a hotel in Dubai promotes responsible behavior.
Source: Courtesy of Marco Polo Hotel/Dubai; Brandcom Agency.

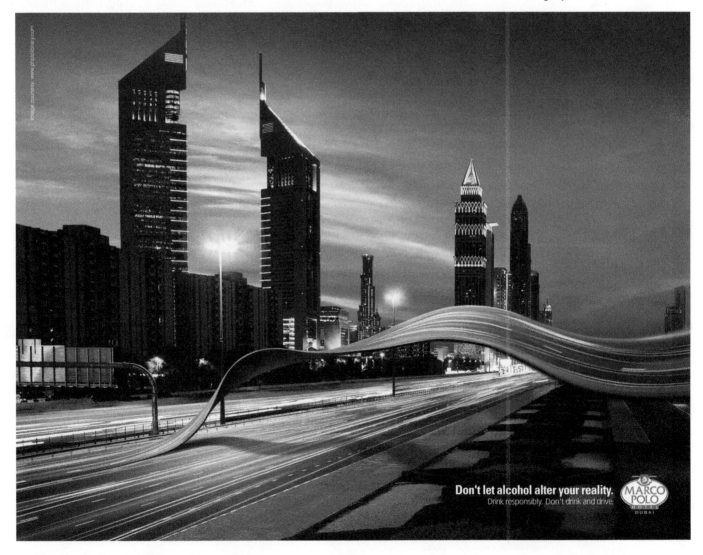

Don't let alcohol alter your reality.
Drink responsibly. Don't drink and drive.

MARCO POLO
HOTEL
DUBAI

Consumer Behavior Is a Process

In its early stages of development, researchers referred to the field as *buyer behavior;* this reflected an emphasis on the interaction between consumers and producers at the time of purchase. Most marketers now recognize that consumer behavior is in fact an ongoing *process*, not merely what happens at the moment a consumer hands over money or a credit card and in turn receives some good or service.

The **exchange**, a transaction in which two or more organizations or people give and receive something of value, is an integral part of marketing.[2] Although *exchange theory* remains an important part of consumer behavior, the expanded view emphasizes the entire consumption process, which includes the issues that influence the consumer before, during, and after a purchase. Figure 1 illustrates some of the issues that we address during each stage of the consumption process.

A **consumer** is a person who identifies a need or desire, makes a purchase, and then disposes of the product during the three stages of the consumption process. In many cases, however, different people play a role in this sequence of events. The purchaser and user of a product might not be the same person, as when a parent picks out clothes for a teenager (and makes selections that can result in "fashion suicide" in the view of the teen). In other cases, another person may act as an *influencer,* providing recommendations for or against certain products without actually buying or using them. A friend's grimace when you try on that new pair of pants may be more influential than anything your mother might say.

Finally, consumers may take the form of organizations or groups. One or several persons may make the decisions involved in purchasing products that many will use, as when a purchasing agent orders the company's office supplies. In other organizational situations, a large group of people may make purchase decisions: for example, company accountants, designers, engineers, sales personnel, and others—all of whom will have a say in the various stages of the consumption process. One important type of organization is the family, where different family members play pivotal roles in making decisions regarding products and services that all will use.

Figure 1 STAGES IN THE CONSUMPTION PROCESS

Consumers' Impact on Marketing Strategy

Surfing cool Web sites is a lot of fun. But, on the more serious side, why should managers, advertisers, and other marketing professionals bother to learn about consumer behavior? Very simply, *understanding consumer behavior is good business*. The basic marketing concept states that firms exist to satisfy needs. Marketers can satisfy these needs only to the extent that they understand the people or organizations who will use the products and services they sell.

The Sony Walkman is a good example of a successful product that needed to update its image and consumer marketing strategy—especially since the company faces fierce competition from the incredibly popular Apple iPod. Although Sony revolutionized the mobile music experience and sold almost 300 million Walkmans in the process, today's teens see portable cassette players as dinosaurs (assuming they've even heard of cassettes!). The company's advertising agency followed 125 teens to see how they use products in their day-to-day lives. Based on this consumer research, Sony relaunched the product with a removable "Memory Stick" instead of a cassette player so it works with MP3 files. The new S Series plays video and instantly creates channels based on a user's listening preferences.[3] Too little, too late to catch up with Apple? That's a verdict only customers can deliver.

As Sony discovered, consumer response is the ultimate test of whether a marketing strategy will succeed. Thus, a marketer should incorporate knowledge about consumers into every facet of a successful marketing plan. Data about consumers help organizations to define the market and identify threats to and opportunities for a brand. And, in the wild and wacky world of marketing, nothing is forever: This knowledge also helps to ensure that the product continues to appeal to its core market.

OBJECTIVE 3
Marketers need to understand the wants and needs of different consumer segments.

Consumers Are Different! How We Divide Them Up

Our society is evolving from a mass culture in which many consumers share the same preferences to a diverse one in which we have almost an infinite number of choices. This change makes it more important than ever to identify distinct market segments and to develop specialized messages and products for those groups.

Consider, for example, how one of the world's largest food chains is adapting to changing times: McDonald's now devotes a third of its U.S. marketing budget to television, compared with two-thirds a few years ago. The company uses that leftover money to sponsor closed-circuit sports programming piped into Hispanic bars and for ads in *Upscale*, a custom-published magazine distributed to barber shops that cater to African American consumers. McDonald's advertises on Foot Locker's in-store video network to reach young men, and it zeroes in on mothers through ads in women's magazines such as *O: The Oprah Magazine* and Web sites such as iVillage.com. McDonald's even sponsored one of the first global **alternate reality games (ARGs)**, called *The Lost Ring*. An ARG integrates multiple media channels, ranging from TV, email, SMS, and even snail mail to engage a community of players who collaborate to solve a complex puzzle. *The Lost Ring* was the story of six amnesiac Olympians who competed in an ancient, lost Olympic sport: labyrinth running. Gamers from all over the world found clues hidden both online, in places like YouTube and Flickr and story microsites, as well as in offline locations. McDonald's strategically placed 27 game artifacts in the United States, Germany, Australia, China, France, Spain, Switzerland, Japan, Canada, Argentina, England, Singapore, Korea, South Africa, Sweden, Italy, the Netherlands, and Mexico; the final story lines were not revealed until the final artifact was discovered. By the end of the campaign, the game's Web site had received 4.8 million visits, and almost 3 million people in 110 countries participated.[4] Unlike most McDonald's advertising, which makes it clear that you need to buy a burger, there was no mention of the company's sponsorship in the campaign

The woman in this Danish ad is fed up with bad financial news. Whether we like it or not, the global recession has affected all of us. Marketers are scrambling to adjust their strategies to this glum economic environment.

Source: Courtesy of Bianco Footwear & Co.

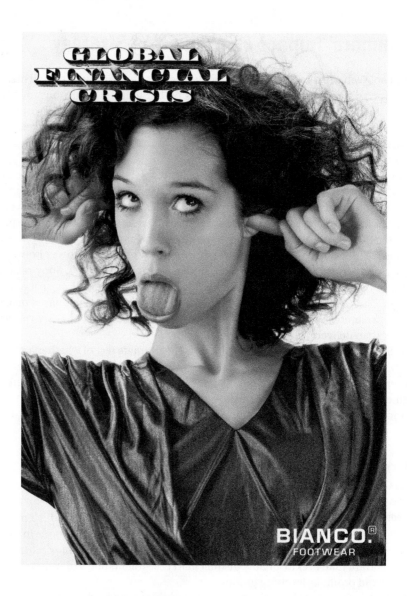

(this is known as a "dark-play ARG"). Still, the chain benefited from a substantial boost in favorability ratings when people learned who was behind the global game.[5]

Building loyalty to a brand is a very smart marketing strategy, so sometimes companies define market segments when they identify their most faithful customers or **heavy users**. As a rule of thumb, marketers use the **80/20 rule**: 20 percent of users account for 80 percent of sales. This guideline often holds up well, and in some cases even this lopsided split isn't big enough: A recent study of 54 million shoppers reported that only 2.5 percent of consumers account for 80 percent of sales for the average package-goods brand. The 1 percent of pet owners who buy 80 percent of Iams pet food spend $93 a year on the brand, and the 1.2 percent of beer drinkers who account for 80 percent of Budweiser sales spend $170 on Bud each year. Of the 1,364 brands the researchers studied, only 25 had a consumer base of more than 10 percent that accounted for 80 percent of volume.[6] In the fast-food industry, the heavy user (no pun intended) accounts for only one of five customers but for about 60 percent of all visits to fast-food restaurants. Taco Bell developed the Chalupa, a deep-fried and higher-calorie version of its Gordita stuffed taco, to appeal to its heavy users. The Checkers burger chain describes *its* core customer as a single male under age 30 who has a working-class job, loves loud music, doesn't read much, and hangs out with friends.[7] To attract the same customer, Hardee's unveiled its Monster Thickburger that weighs in at 1,418 calories—comedian Jay Leno joked that the burger comes in a cardboard box shaped like a coffin.[8] Finally, Burger King aims a lot of its promotions (including its weird but popular King character) to its "Super Fans"—mostly young men who pop into fast-food restaurants 16 times a month on average.[9]

Aside from heavy usage of a product, we use many other dimensions to divide up a larger market. As we've already seen, *demographics* are statistics that measure observable aspects of a population, such as birth rate, age distribution, and income. The U.S. Census Bureau is a major source of demographic data on U.S. families, but many private firms gather additional data on specific population groups as well. The changes and trends that demographic studies reveal are of great interest to marketers because they can use the data to locate and predict the size of markets for many products, ranging from home mortgages to brooms and can openers. Imagine trying to sell baby food to a single male, or an around-the-world cruise to a couple making $15,000 a year!

In this text we explore many of the important demographic variables that make one consumer the same as or different from others. We also consider other important characteristics that are a bit more subtle, such as differences in consumers' personalities and tastes that we can't objectively measure yet may be tremendously important in influencing product choices. For now, let's summarize a few of the most important demographic dimensions.

Age

Consumers of different *age groups* obviously have very different needs and wants. Although people who belong to the same age group differ in many other ways, they do tend to share a set of values and common cultural experiences that they carry throughout life.[10] In some cases, marketers initially develop a product to attract one age group and then try to broaden its appeal later on. That's what the high-octane energy drink Red Bull does. The company aggressively introduced it in bars, nightclubs, and gyms to the product's core audience of young people. Over time, it became popular in other contexts, and the company began to sponsor the PGA European Tour to broaden its reach to older golfers (who probably aren't up partying all night). It also hands out free cans to commuters, cab drivers, and car rental agencies to promote the drink as a way to stay alert on the road.[11]

Gender

We start to make gender distinctions at a very early age—even diapers come in pink versions for girls and blue for boys. Many products, from fragrances to footwear, target either men or women. An all-female marketing team at Procter & Gamble (P&G), who jokingly call themselves "chicks in charge," introduced Crest Rejuvenating Effects, the first mass-market toothpaste positioned just for women. P&G communicates that this product is feminine when the company packages it in a teal tube nestled inside a glimmering "pearlescent" box. The toothpaste is sparkly, teal-toned, and tastes like vanilla and cinnamon.[12]

Family Structure

A person's family/marital status is yet another important demographic variable, because this has a huge effect on consumers' spending priorities. Not surprisingly, young bachelors and newlyweds are the most likely to exercise; go to bars, concerts, and movies; and consume alcohol (enjoy it while you can!). Families with young children are big purchasers of health foods and fruit juices, whereas single-parent households and those with older children buy more junk food. Older couples and bachelors are most likely to use home maintenance services.[13]

Social Class and Income

People who belong to the same *social class* are approximately equal in terms of income and social standing in the community. They work in roughly similar occupations, and they tend to have similar tastes in music, clothing, leisure activities, and art. They also tend to socialize with one another, and they share many ideas and values regarding the

The Redneck Bank takes a unique approach to social class segmentation (yes, this is a real bank).
Source: Courtesy of www.redneckbank.com.

way life should be lived.[14] The distribution of wealth is of great interest to marketers because it determines which groups have the greatest buying power and market potential.

Race and Ethnicity

African Americans, Hispanic Americans, and Asian Americans are the three fastest-growing ethnic groups in the United States. As our society becomes increasingly multicultural, new opportunities develop to deliver specialized products to racial and ethnic groups and to introduce other groups to these offerings. For example, when Reebok introduced its RBK shoe line, it signed popular urban artists like 50 Cent to promote that line.

Geography

Many national marketers tailor their offerings to appeal to consumers who live in different parts of the country. Some southerners are fond of a "good ol' boy" image that leaves others scratching their heads. Although many northerners regard the name "Bubba" as a negative term, businesses in Dixie proudly flaunt the name. Bubba Co. is a Charleston-based firm that licenses products such as Bubba-Q-Sauce. In Florida, restaurants, sports bars, nightclubs, and a limousine firm all proudly bear the name Bubba.[15]

Lifestyles

Consumers also have very different *lifestyles,* even if they share other demographic characteristics such as gender or age. The way we feel about ourselves, the things we value, the things we like to do in our spare time—all of these factors help to determine which products will push our buttons, or even those that make us feel better. Procter & Gamble developed its heartburn medicine Prilosec OTC with an ideal customer in mind based on a lifestyle analysis. Her name is Joanne, and she's a mother over the age of 35 who's more likely to get heartburn from a cup of coffee than from an overdose of pizza and beer. A P&G executive observed, "We know Joanne. We know what she feels. We know what she eats. We know what else she likes to buy in the store."[16]

Marketers carefully define customer segments and listen to people in their markets as never before. Many of them now realize that a key to success is building relationships between brands and customers that will last a lifetime. Marketers who believe in this philosophy, called **relationship marketing**, interact with customers on a regular basis and give them reasons to maintain a bond with the company over time. A focus on relationships is even more vital during the tough economic conditions we've been experiencing—when times are tough, people tend to rely on their good friends for support!

Another revolution in relationship building is brought to us courtesy of the computer. **Database marketing** involves tracking specific consumers' buying habits very closely and crafting products and messages tailored precisely to people's wants and needs based on this information. Walmart stores massive amounts of information on the 100 million people who visit its stores each week, and the company uses these data to fine-tune its offerings. For example, when the company analyzed how shoppers' buying patterns react when forecasters predict a major hurricane, it discovered that people do a lot more than simply stock up on flashlights. Sales of strawberry Pop-Tarts increase by

This Italian ad for a yacht company appeals to people who have money—or who dream they will someday have enough to buy a yacht.

Source: Courtesy of Azimut Yachts.

CAPTURE THE DREAM.

WWW.AZIMUTYACHTS.COM

AZIMUT
YACHTS

Many products help to define our identities. Are you what you drive?
Source: Courtesy of Automobile Magazine, Source Interlink.

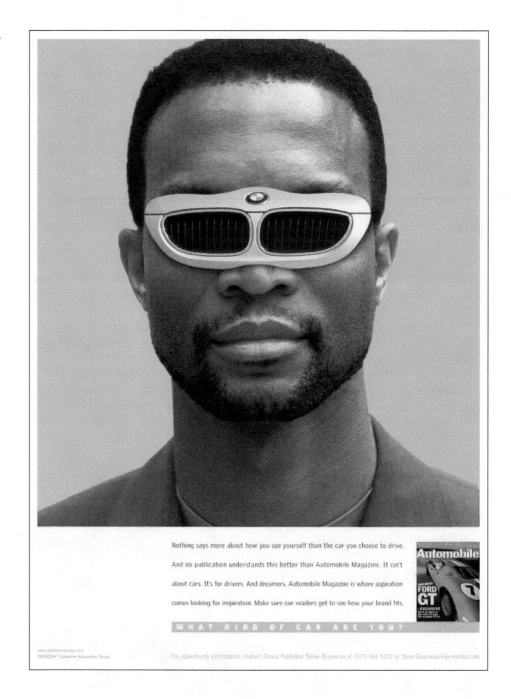

Nothing says more about how you see yourself than the car you choose to drive. And no publication understands this better than Automobile Magazine. It isn't about cars. It's for drivers. And dreamers. Automobile Magazine is where aspiration comes looking for inspiration. Make sure our readers get to see how your brand fits.

WHAT KIND OF CAR ARE YOU?

about 700 percent, and the top-selling product of all is . . . beer. Based on these insights, Walmart loads its trucks with toaster pastries and six-packs to stock local stores when a big storm approaches.[17]

Marketing's Impact on Consumers

Does marketing imitate life, or vice versa? After the movie *The Wedding Crashers* became a big hit, hotels, wedding planners, and newlyweds reported an outbreak of uninvited guests who tried to gain access to parties across the United States.[18] For better or for worse, we all live in a world that the actions of marketers significantly influence.

Popular Culture

Marketing stimuli surround us as advertisements, stores, and products compete for our attention and our dollars. Marketers filter much of what we learn about the world, whether through the affluence they depict in glamorous magazines or the roles actors play in commercials. Ads show us how we should act with regard to recycling, alcohol consumption, the types of houses and cars we might wish to own—and even how to evaluate others based on the products they buy or don't buy. In many ways we are also at the mercy of marketers, because we rely on them to sell us products that are safe and that perform as promised, to tell us the truth about what they sell, and to price and distribute these products fairly.

Popular culture, consisting of the music, movies, sports, books, celebrities, and other forms of entertainment that the mass market produces and consumes, is both a product of and an inspiration for marketers. It also affects our lives in more far-reaching ways, ranging from how we acknowledge cultural events such as marriage, death, or holidays to how we view social issues such as global warming, gambling, and addictions. Whether it's the Super Bowl, Christmas shopping, national health care, newspaper recycling, body piercing, cigarette smoking, tweeting, or online video games, marketers play a significant role in our view of the world and how we live in it.

This cultural impact is hard to overlook, although many people do not seem to realize how much marketers influence their preferences for movie and musical heroes; the latest fashions in clothing, food, and decorating choices; and even the physical features that they find attractive or ugly in men and women. For example, consider the product icons that companies use to create an identity for their products. Many imaginary creatures and personalities, from the Pillsbury Doughboy to the Jolly Green Giant, at one time or another have been central figures in popular culture. In fact, it is likely that more consumers could recognize such characters than could identify past presidents, business leaders, or artists. Although these figures never really existed, many of us feel as if we "know" them, and they certainly are effective spokescharacters for the products they represent.

What Does It Mean to Consume?

What's the poop on Peeps? Every year, people buy about 1.5 billion of these mostly tasteless marshmallow chicks; about two-thirds of them sell around Easter. They have no nutritional value, but they do have a shelf life of 2 years. Maybe that's why not all Peeps get

We are surrounded by elements of popular culture—the good, the bad, and the ugly. This ad for the Museum of Bad Art reminds us of that.

Source: With permission of Museum of Bad Art.

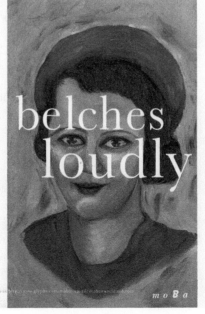

Some art speaks to you. Some just belches loudly in your face.

Visit the permanent collection at 580 High Street, Dedham, Massachusetts · 617-325-8224 · Or on the Web at http://www.glyphs.com/moba · email: info@museumofbadart.com

moBa   museum of bad art

eaten. Devotees use them in decorations, dioramas, online slide shows, and sculptures. Some fans feel challenged to test their physical properties: On more than 200 Peeps Web sites, you can see fetishists skewering, microwaving, hammering, decapitating, and otherwise abusing the spongy confections.[19]

This fascination with a creepy little candy chick illustrates one of the fundamental premises of the modern field of consumer behavior: *People often buy products not for what they do but for what they mean.* This principle does not imply that a product's basic function is unimportant, but rather that the roles products play in our lives extend well beyond the tasks they perform. The deeper meanings of a product may help it to stand out from other similar goods and services. All things being equal, we choose the brand that has an image (or even a personality!) consistent with our underlying needs.

For example, although most people probably couldn't run faster or jump higher if they were wearing Nikes instead of Reeboks, many die-hard loyalists swear by their favorite brand. These archrivals are largely marketed in terms of their *images*—meanings that have been carefully crafted with the help of legions of rock stars, athletes, slickly produced commercials, and many millions of dollars. So, when you buy a Nike "swoosh," you are doing more than choosing shoes to wear to the mall: you also make a lifestyle statement about the type of person you are or wish you were. For a relatively simple item made of leather and laces, that's quite a feat!

Our allegiances to sneakers, musicians, and even soft drinks help us define our place in modern society, and these choices also help each of us to form bonds with others who share similar preferences. This comment by a participant in a focus group captures the curious bonding that can be caused by consumption choices: "I was at a Super Bowl party, and I picked up an obscure drink. Somebody else across the room went 'yo!' because he had the same thing. People feel a connection when you're drinking the same thing."[20]

The sociological perspective of **role theory** takes the view that much of consumer behavior resembles actions in a play.[21] As in a play, each consumer has the lines, props, and costumes necessary to put on a good performance. Because people act out many different roles, they sometimes alter their consumption decisions depending on the particular "play" they are in at the time. The criteria they use to evaluate products and services in one of their roles may be quite different from those they use in other roles. That's why it's important for marketers to provide each of us "actors" with the props we need to play all of our varied roles; these might include "up-and-coming executive," "geek," or "big man on campus."

As we have seen, one trademark of marketing strategies today is that many organizations try very hard to build relationships with customers. The nature of these relationships can vary, but these bonds help us to understand some of the possible meanings products have for us. Furthermore, researchers find that, like friendships and love affairs with other people, our relationships with brands evolve over time. Some resemble deep friendships, whereas others are more like exciting but short-lived flings.[22]

Here are some of the types of relationships a person might have with a product:

- **Self-concept attachment**—The product helps to establish the user's identity.
- **Nostalgic attachment**—The product serves as a link with a past self.
- **Interdependence**—The product is a part of the user's daily routine.
- **Love**—The product elicits emotional bonds of warmth, passion, or other strong emotion.[23]

The Global Consumer

The majority of people on Earth live in urban centers. Analysts predict that the number of *megacities,* defined as urban centers of 10 million or more, will grow to 26 by 2015.[24] Already, China boasts four shopping centers that are larger than the massive Mall of America in Minnesota, and very soon it will be home to seven of the world's largest malls.[25]

One by-product of sophisticated marketing strategies is the movement toward a **global consumer culture**, one that unites people around the world by their common

This ad for electronics products by Samsung focuses on pure desire—consuming as experience.
Source: Courtesy of Samsung Electronics America, Inc. Reprinted by permission.

devotion to brand-name consumer goods, movie stars, celebrities, and leisure activities.[26] Many multinational firms are household names, widely recognized (though not necessarily liked) by literally billions of people.

The rise of global marketing means that even small companies look to expand overseas—and this increases the pressure to understand how customers in other countries are the same or different from those in one's own country. In the restaurant industry, for example, Shakey's pizza restaurants are mushrooming in the Philippines, and food from the International House of Pancakes sells like hotcakes in Tokyo. But menu changes are sometimes called for to please local palates: Schlotzsky's in Malaysia offers Smokey Mountain Chicken Crunch with "half-virgin" chicken, and diners at Bob's Big Boy in Thailand snap up Tropical Shrimp, deep fried with "exotic breading."

The Digital Native: Living a Social [Media] Life

There's little doubt that the digital revolution is one of the most significant influences on consumer behavior, and the impact of the Web will continue to expand as more and more people around the world log in. Many of us are avid Web surfers, and it's hard to imagine a time when texting, Twittering, or Facebooking on our Androids and iPhones weren't an accepted part of daily life—not to mention those of us who compulsively check in on FourSquare at their local Starbucks 10 times a day!

Electronic marketing makes our lives a lot easier. You can shop 24/7 without leaving home, you can read today's newspaper without getting drenched picking up a hard copy in a rainstorm, and you don't have to wait for the 6:00 P.M. news to find out what the weather will be like tomorrow—whether at home or around the globe. With the increasing use of handheld devices and wireless communications, you can get that same information—from stock quotes to the weather—even when you're away from your computer.[27]

Also, it's not all about businesses selling to consumers (**B2C e-commerce**). The cyberspace explosion has created a revolution in consumer-to-consumer activity (**C2C e-commerce**): Welcome to the new world of *virtual brand communities*. Just as e-consumers are not limited to local retail outlets in their shopping, they are not limited to their local communities when they look for friends or fellow fans of wine, hip-hop, or skateboarding.

Picture a small group of local collectors who meet once a month at a local diner to discuss their shared interests over coffee. Now multiply that group by thousands, and include people from all over the world who are united by a shared passion for sports memorabilia, Barbie dolls, Harley-Davidson motorcycles, refrigerator magnets, or massively multiplayer online games (MMOGs) such as *World of Warcraft*. The Web also provides an easy way for consumers around the world to exchange information about their experiences with products, services, music, restaurants, and movies. The Hollywood Stock Exchange (hsx.com) offers a simulated entertainment stock market where traders predict the 4-week box office take for each film. Amazon.com encourages shoppers to write reviews of books, and (just as Gail did) you can even rate your professors at RateMyProfessors .com (don't tell your prof about this one; it'll be our secret). The popularity of chat rooms where consumers can go to discuss various topics with like-minded "Netizens" around the world grows every day, as do immersive virtual worlds such as Second Life, Habbo Hotel, and Kaneva. News reports tell us of the sometimes wonderful and sometimes horrific romances that have begun on the Internet as people check out potential mates on sites such as Match.com or OKCupid. In a recent month, one dating site (Plenty of Fish) alone had 122 million visits.[28]

If you're a typical student, you probably can't recall a time when the Internet was just a static, one-way platform that transmitted text and a few sketchy images. And, believe it or not, in the last century even *that* crude technique didn't exist. You may have read about this in a history class: People actually hand-wrote letters to each other and waited for printed magazines to arrive in their mailboxes to learn about current events! The term **digital native** originated in a 2001 article to explain a new type of student who was starting to turn up on campus. These consumers grew up "wired" in a highly networked, always-on world where digital technology had always existed.[29]

Fast-forward a decade: Today the Internet is the backbone of our society. Widespread access to devices like personal computers, digital video and audio recorders, webcams, and smart phones ensures that consumers of practically any age and who live in virtually any part of the world can create and share content. But information doesn't just flow from big companies or governments down to the people; today each of us can communicate with huge numbers of people by a click on a keypad, so information flows *across* people as well.

That's what we mean by a **horizontal revolution**. This horizontal revolution is characterized in part by the prevalence of social media. **Social media** are the online means of communication, conveyance, collaboration, and cultivation among interconnected and interdependent networks of people, communities, and organizations enhanced by technological capabilities and mobility.

Do you remember all those crazy Mentos/Diet Coke videos? At least 800 of them flooded YouTube after people discovered that when you drop the quarter-size candies into bottles of Diet Coke, you get a geyser that shoots 20 feet into the air. Needless to say, Mentos got a gusher of free publicity out of the deal, too.[30] Probably the biggest marketing phenomenon of this decade is **user-generated content**, whereby everyday people voice their opinions about products, brands, and companies on blogs, podcasts, and social networking sites such as Facebook and Twitter, and even film their own commercials that thousands view on sites such as YouTube. This important trend helps to define the era of **Web 2.0**: the rebirth of the Internet as a social, interactive medium from its original roots as a form of one-way transmission from producers to consumers.

The Internet and its related technologies that gave birth to Web 2.0 make what we know today as social media possible and prevalent. Every day the influence of social media expands as more people join online communities. Facebook, a social utility that offers **synchronous interactions** (those that occur in real time, like when you text back-and-forth with a friend) and **asynchronous interactions** (those that don't require all participants to respond immediately, like when you email a friend and get an answer the next day), photo-sharing, games, applications, groups, e-retailing, and more, has as of the time of this writing more than 600 million active users.[31] If Facebook were a country, it would be the third most populated in the world.

The explosion of online communications changes the media landscape as traditional media platforms try to adapt. This German newspaper ad says, "We sign our pets on Facebook. Are we ready for a new newspaper? *Welt Kompakt*. Concise. Different. Printed."
Source: Courtesy of WELT KOMPAKT.

People aren't just joining social communities. They are contributing too! YouTube users upload more than 35 hours of video every single minute of every day. That's roughly equivalent to 176,000 full-length movies uploaded weekly. In just 30 days on YouTube, more video is broadcast than in the past 60 years on CBS, NBC, and ABC broadcasting networks combined.[32] Consider these mind-boggling social media stats:[33]

- If you were paid $1 for every time an article was posted on Wikipedia, you would earn $156.23 per hour.
- It took radio 38 years to reach 50 million listeners. TV took 13 years to reach 50 million users. The Internet took 4 years to reach 50 million people. In less than 9 months, Facebook added 100 million users.
- About 70 percent of Facebook users are outside the United States.
- Social media activity has overtaken porn as the number-one online activity.
- One out of eight couples married last year met using a social media site.
- 80 percent of companies use LinkedIn as their primary recruiting tool.
- 25 percent of search results for the world's top 10 brands are to user-generated content.
- More than 1.5 billion pieces of content are shared on Facebook daily.
- 80 percent of Twitter usage is from mobile devices, and 17 percent have tweeted while in the toilet.

This is all exciting stuff, especially because social media platforms enable a **culture of participation**; a belief in democracy; the ability to freely interact with other people, companies and organization; open access to venues that allow users to share content from simple comments to reviews, ratings, photos, stories, and more; and the power to build on the content of others from your own unique point of view. Of course, just like democracy in the real world, we have to take the bitter with the sweet. There are plenty of unsavory things going on in cyberspace, and the hours people spend on Facebook, on online gambling sites, or in virtual worlds like Second Life have led to divorce, bankruptcy, or jail in the real world.

OBJECTIVE 5
Our beliefs and actions as consumers strongly connect to other issues in our lives.

Marketing Ethics and Public Policy

In business, conflicts often arise between the goal to succeed in the marketplace and the desire to maximize the well-being of consumers by providing them with safe and effective products and services. However, consumers may expect too much from companies and try to exploit these obligations. A case involving the Wendy's fast-food chain made national headlines when a woman claimed she had found a finger in her bowl of chili. The restaurants became the butt of jokes (some said they served nail clippers with their food instead of forks), and sales dropped dramatically at the company's franchises. This forced layoffs and reduced hours for many employees—until the woman was arrested for fraud.[34]

Business ethics are rules of conduct that guide actions in the marketplace; these are the standards against which most people in a culture judge what is right and what is wrong, good or bad. These universal values include honesty, trustworthiness, fairness, respect, justice, integrity, concern for others, accountability, and loyalty. Ethical business is good business. A Conference Board survey of U.S. consumers found that the most important criterion when forming opinions about corporations is social responsibility in such areas as labor practices, business ethics, and environmental issues.[35] Consumers think better of products made by firms that they feel behave ethically.[36]

Of course, notions of right and wrong differ among people, organizations, and cultures. Some businesses believe it is OK for salespeople to pull out all the stops to persuade customers to buy, even if it means giving them false information; other firms feel that anything less than total honesty with customers is terribly wrong. Because each culture has its own set of values, beliefs, and customs, companies around the world define ethical business behaviors quite differently. For example, one study found that because of differences in values, Mexican firms are less likely to have formal codes of ethics and they are more likely to bribe public officials than are U.S. or Canadian companies. However, because of different attitudes about work and interpersonal relationships, these companies also are more likely to treat lower-level employees better than do their northern neighbors.[37]

These cultural differences certainly influence whether business practices such as bribery are acceptable. Bribing foreigners to gain business has been against the law in the United States since 1977, under the Foreign Corrupt Practices Act. The Organization for Economic Cooperation and Development (OECD), to which most industrialized countries belong, also outlaws bribery. Still, these practices are common in many countries. In Japan, it's called *kuroi kiri* (black mist); in Germany, it's *schmiergeld* (grease money), whereas Mexicans refer to *la mordida* (the bite), the French say *pot-de-vin* (jug of wine), and Italians speak of the *bustarella* (little envelope). They're all talking about *baksheesh*, the Middle Eastern term for a "tip" to grease the wheels of a transaction. Giving "gifts" in exchange for getting business from suppliers or customers is common and acceptable in many countries, even though this may be frowned on elsewhere.

Regardless of whether they do it intentionally, some marketers do violate their bonds of trust with consumers. In some cases, these actions are actually illegal, as when a manufacturer deliberately mislabels the contents of a package. Or a retailer may adopt a "bait-and-switch" selling strategy that lures consumers into the store by offering inexpensive products with the sole intent of getting them to switch to higher-priced goods.

In other cases, marketing practices have detrimental effects on society even though they are not explicitly illegal. Some companies erect billboards for alcohol and tobacco products in low-income neighborhoods; others sponsor commercials depicting groups of people in an unfavorable light to get the attention of a target market. Civil rights groups, for example, charge that the marketing of menthol cigarettes by R. J. Reynolds to African Americans is illegal because menthol cigarettes are less safe than regular brands. A company spokeswoman responds, "This links to the bigger issue that minorities require some special protection. We find that offensive, paternalistic, and condescending."[38] Who is right?

Needs and Wants: Do Marketers Manipulate Consumers?

One of the most common and stinging criticisms of marketing is that companies convince consumers they "need" many material things and that they will be unhappy and inferior people if they do not have these "necessities." The issue is a complex one and is certainly worth considering: Do marketers give people what they want, or do they tell people what they *should* want?

Welcome to Consumerspace

Who controls the market, companies or consumers? This question is even more complicated as new ways of buying, having, and being are invented every day. It seems that the "good old days" of *marketerspace*—a time when companies called the shots and decided what they wanted their customers to know and do—are dead and gone. As we saw with Gail's surfing decisions, many people now feel empowered to choose how, when, or if they will interact with corporations as they construct their own **consumerspace**; in this new environment, individuals dictate to companies the types of products they want and how, when, and where (or even if) they want to learn about those products. In turn, companies need to develop and leverage brand equity in bold new ways to attract the loyalty of these consumer "nomads." People still "need" companies—but in new ways and on their own terms. Profound changes

The Tangled Web

One of the biggest ethical issues that faces many marketers today relates to how much they can—or should—know about their customers. Virtually anyone who surfs the Web or carries a cell phone (especially a smart phone with GPS capability) shares reams of personal information with all sorts of companies (whether they know it or not). Social network sites like Facebook and major companies like Apple have come under fire for their privacy policies. Still, it's unclear whether many digital natives are all that concerned about whether others know where they are or what they buy.

Indeed, one new application called Color is based on the premise that we *want* others to know what we're up to. The Color software creates a user network that combines location-based technology with social media so that users who are within range (50 feet) of the sender can see his or her images, videos, and texts from their other social networks. There is no password, no friending, and no way for users to limit private content to specific individuals. Color's founder observed, "there's no more electronic dog fence created by Facebook. It's all over. This is the post-PC world. It's a brand new way of sharing."[40] Still, other online data and tracking firms are a bit more concerned about what gets shared, and they want to preempt any consumer backlash that might prevent them from gathering valuable data. Several major firms are banding together to form an **Open Data Partnership**, which will allow consumers to edit the interests, demographics, and other profile information collected about them. It also will allow people to choose not to be tracked at all.[41]

in consumer behavior are influencing how people search for product information and evaluate alternative brands. In the brave new world of consumerspace, we have the potential to shape our own marketing destinies.[39]

Do Marketers Create Artificial Needs?

The marketing system has come under fire from both ends of the political spectrum. On the one hand, some members of the Religious Right believe that marketers contribute to the moral breakdown of society by presenting images of hedonistic pleasure and encouraging the pursuit of secular humanism at the expense of spirituality and the environment. A coalition of religious groups called the National Religious Partnership for the Environment claims that gas-guzzling cars and other factors that cause climate change are contrary to Christian moral teachings about protecting people and the earth.[42]

On the other hand, some leftists argue that the same deceitful promises of material pleasure function to buy off people who would otherwise be revolutionaries working to change the system.[43] According to this argument, the marketing system creates demand—demand that only its products can satisfy.

A Response. *A* **need** *is a basic biological motive; a* **want** *represents one way that society has taught to satisfy the need.* For example, thirst is biologically based; we are taught to want Coca-Cola to satisfy that thirst rather than, say, goat's milk. Thus, the need is already there; marketers simply recommend ways to satisfy it. A basic objective of marketing is to create awareness that needs exist, not to create needs.

Are Advertising and Marketing Necessary?

More than 50 years ago, the social critic Vance Packard wrote, "Large-scale efforts are being made, often with impressive success, to channel our unthinking habits, our purchasing decisions, and our thought processes by the use of insights gleaned from psychiatry and the social sciences."[44] The economist John Kenneth Galbraith charged that radio and television are important tools to accomplish this manipulation of the masses. Because consumers don't need to be literate to use these media, repetitive and compelling communications can reach almost everyone. This criticism may even be more relevant to online communications, where a simple click delivers a world of information to us.

Many feel that marketers arbitrarily link products to desirable social attributes, fostering a materialistic society in which we are measured by what we own. One influential critic even argued that the problem is that we are not materialistic enough—that is, we do not sufficiently value goods for the utilitarian functions they deliver but instead focus on the irrational value of goods for what they symbolize. According to this view, for example, "Beer would be enough for us, without the additional promise that in drinking it we show ourselves to be manly, young at heart, or neighborly. A washing machine would be a useful machine to wash clothes, rather than an indication that we are forward-looking or an object of envy to our neighbors."[45]

A Response. *Products are designed to meet existing needs, and advertising only helps to communicate their availability.*[46] According to the **economics of information** perspective, advertising is an important source of consumer information.[47] This view emphasizes the economic cost of the time spent searching for products. Accordingly, advertising is a service for which consumers are willing to pay because the information it provides reduces search time.

Do Marketers Promise Miracles?

Through advertising, consumers are led to believe that products have magical properties; that is, products will do special and mysterious things for consumers in a way that will transform their lives. We will be beautiful, have power over others' feelings, be successful, and be relieved of all ills. In this respect, advertising functions as mythology does in primitive societies: It provides simple, anxiety-reducing answers to complex problems.

A Response. *Advertisers simply do not know enough about people to manipulate them.* Consider that the failure rate for new products ranges from 40 to 80 percent. Although people think that advertisers have an endless source of magical tricks and scientific techniques to manipulate them, in reality the industry is successful when it tries to sell good products and unsuccessful when it sells poor ones.[48]

Public Policy and Consumerism

Concern for the welfare of consumers has been an issue since at least the beginning of the 20th century, and activists continue to voice concerns about a range of issues such as child labor, exploitative advertising, and genetically engineered food.[49] Recent deaths due to salmonella-infected peanut butter and contaminated toothpaste have added fuel to the fire.

Partly as a result of consumers' efforts in the United States, the U.S. government established many federal agencies to oversee consumer-related activities. These include the Department of Agriculture, the Federal Trade Commission, the Food and Drug Administration, the Securities and Exchange Commission, and the Environmental Protection Agency. After Upton Sinclair's 1906 book *The Jungle* exposed the awful conditions in the Chicago meatpacking industry, Congress was prompted to pass important pieces of legislation—the Pure Food and Drug Act in 1906 and the Federal Meat Inspection Act a year later—to protect consumers. A summary of some important consumer legislation enacted since that time appears in Table 1. You can find other information about consumer-related issues at consumerreports.org and cpsc.gov (the Consumer Product Safety Commission).

The Food and Drug Administration (FDA) polices advertising claims as well as the contents of edible products and pharmaceuticals, and its efforts have been more aggressive with the advent of the Obama administration. For example, as part of an FDA crackdown on consumer drug advertising, in 2009 Bayer HealthCare Pharmaceuticals launched a $20 million advertising campaign for Yaz, the most popular birth control pill

TABLE 1   Sample of Federal Legislation Intended to Enhance Consumers' Welfare

Year	Act	Purpose
1953	Flammable Fabrics Act	Prohibits the transportation of flammable fabrics across state lines.
1958	National Traffic and Safety Act	Creates safety standards for cars and tires.
1958	Automobile Information Disclosure Act	Requires automobile manufacturers to post suggested retail prices on new cars.
1966	Fair Packaging and Labeling Act	Regulates packaging and labeling of consumer products. (Manufacturers must provide information about package contents and origin.)
1966	Child Protection Act	Prohibits sale of dangerous toys and other items.
1967	Federal Cigarette Labeling and Advertising Act	Requires cigarette packages to carry a warning label from the Surgeon General.
1968	Truth-in-Lending Act	Requires lenders to divulge the true costs of a credit transaction.
1969	National Environmental Policy Act	Established a national environmental policy and created the Council on Environmental Quality to monitor the effects of products on the environment.
1972	Consumer Products Safety Act	Established the Consumer Product Safety Commission to identify unsafe products, establish safety standards, recall defective products, and ban dangerous products.
1975	Consumer Goods Pricing Act	Bans the use of price maintenance agreements among manufacturers and resellers.
1975	Magnuson-Moss Warranty-Improvement Act	Creates disclosure standards for consumer product warranties and allows the Federal Trade Commission to set policy regarding unfair or deceptive practices.
1990	The Nutrition Labeling and Education Act	Reaffirms the legal basis for the Food and Drug Administration's new rules on food labeling and establishes a timetable for the implementation of those rules. Regulations covering health claims became effective May 8, 1993. Those pertaining to nutrition labeling and nutrient content claims went into effect May 8, 1994.
1998	Internet Tax Freedom Act	Established a moratorium on special taxation of the Internet, including taxation of access fees paid to America Online and other Internet Service Providers.
2010	Dodd-Frank Wall Street Reform and Consumer Protection Act	Prompted by the recession that began in 2009, intends to promote the financial stability of the United States by improving accountability and transparency in the financial system, to end "too big to fail," to protect the American taxpayer by ending bailouts, and to protect consumers from abusive financial services practices.

in the United States. The twist is that the TV commercials, which ran during prime-time shows like *Grey's Anatomy* and on cable networks, warn that nobody should take Yaz hoping that it will also cure pimples or premenstrual syndrome. Bayer was required to run these ads to correct previous messages that regulators decided overstated the drug's ability to improve women's moods and clear up acne.[50]

Advertisers, retailers, and manufacturers typically try to police themselves to ensure that their messages and products are not harmful or inaccurate. In addition to good intentions, they have a very practical reason for doing so: They don't want governments to do it for them. Indeed, sometimes these efforts even seem to go a bit over the top. Consider, for example, a recent ruling by the National Advertising Division (NAD) of the Council of Better Business Bureaus, which is one of these industry watchdogs. Acting on a complaint by rival Kimberly-Clark, Procter & Gamble must add little flecks of cartoon toilet paper to the backsides of its Charmin cartoon bears in future ads for its toilet paper. Although P&G supported its claim that Charmin leaves "fewer pieces behind" than the Cottonelle brand (and showed the results of its test on the brand's Web site), the NAD decided that the test "did not accurately reflect the results consumers normally see and experience."[51]

However, many regulatory issues are a lot more important than flecks of toilet paper, and require active monitoring by policymakers. For example, a hot button right now is efforts to curb child obesity by encouraging advertisers to limit the messages they send to kids about foods that are high in sodium, saturated fat, and added sugars. The Obama administration issued a set of voluntary guidelines, and it's likely that most companies will comply with these suggestions, which will affect commercials on about 1,700 television programs. The guidelines stipulate that food products targeted to children ages 2 to 17 would have to provide a "meaningful contribution" to a healthy diet and would have to meet limits for harmful ingredients (e.g., no trans fats allowed).[52]

Consumer Activism: America™?

"Absolut Impotence." So reads a parody of a vodka ad created by Adbusters, a nonprofit organization that advocates for "the new social activist movement of the information age." The editor of the group's magazine argues that America is no longer a country, but rather a multitrillion-dollar brand subverted by corporate agendas. He claims that America™ is no different from McDonald's, Marlboro, or General Motors (well, let's at least hope our country's balance sheet starts to look a bit better than GM's).[53]

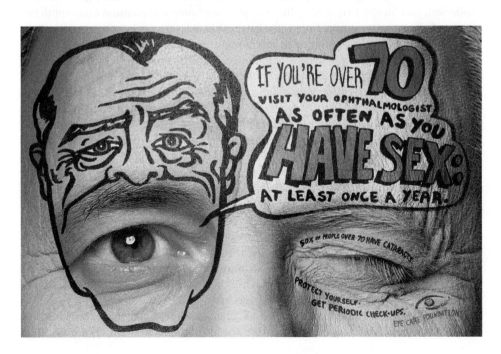

This Brazilian ad employs a novel message to encourage eye exams.
Source: Courtesy of Almap BBDO Communicacoes Ltda., photographer Alexandre Ermel.

BLACKSPOT SHOES   Indie Retail Network   Order Now

Hemp Uppers

Made in a Fair Trade Factory

Natural Rubber

Only sold in indie shops

Hand drawn sweet spot for kicking corporate ass

The independent alternative to Nike's Converse

V1: THE CLASSIC BLACKSPOT SNEAKER

To protest against what the organization claims are Nike's unfair labor practices, Adbusters sells its own Blackspot sneakers. They are made from hemp in a Portuguese factory where workers receive pay higher than the country's minimum wage and where many employees belong to a union.[56]

Source: Image courtesy of adbusters.org.

Adbusters sponsors numerous initiatives, including Buy Nothing Day and TV Turn-off Week, intended to discourage rampant commercialism. These efforts, along with biting ads and commercials that lampoon advertising messages, are examples of **culture jamming**, a strategy to disrupt efforts by the corporate world to dominate our cultural landscape. The movement believes that "culture jamming" will change the way information flows; the way institutions wield power; the way TV stations are run; and the way the food, fashion, automobile, sports, music, and culture industries set their agendas.[54] The *Culture Jammers Manifesto* proclaims opposition to the "mind-polluters": "On the rubble of the old culture, we will build a new one with non-commercial heart and soul."[55]

Although some in corporate America may dismiss these extreme sentiments as the ravings of a lunatic fringe, their proponents deserve to be taken seriously. The recent scandals involving such corporate icons as BP, AIG, Enron, Martha Stewart, Arthur Andersen, and Merrill Lynch have fueled a growing bonfire of mistrust and skepticism among the consuming public. Time will tell if these backlashes against companies will die down or continue to grow as new scandals continue to come to light. Clearly, we need to take dramatic steps to restore public confidence, as the business page of the newspaper starts to read like the crime blotter.

President John F. Kennedy ushered in the modern era of consumerism with his "Declaration of Consumer Rights" in 1962. These include the right to safety, the right to be informed, the right to redress, and the right to choice. The 1960s and 1970s were a time of consumer activism as consumers began to organize to demand better-quality products (and to boycott companies that did not provide them).

The publication of books such as Rachel Carson's *Silent Spring* in 1962, which attacked the irresponsible use of pesticides, and Ralph Nader's *Unsafe at Any Speed* in 1965, which exposed safety defects in General Motors' Corvair automobile, prompted these movements. Many consumers have a vigorous interest in consumer-related issues, ranging from environmental concerns such as global warming and climate change, toxic waste, and so on, to excessive violence and sex on television or in the lyrics of popular rock and rap songs. Recent controversies surrounding "shock jocks" such as Don Imus or Glenn Beck, who use the public airwaves to hurl insults about racial or religious groups, illustrate that people take these issues very seriously.

Indeed, some consumer researchers are themselves organizing, not only to study but also to rectify what they see as pressing social problems in the marketplace. This

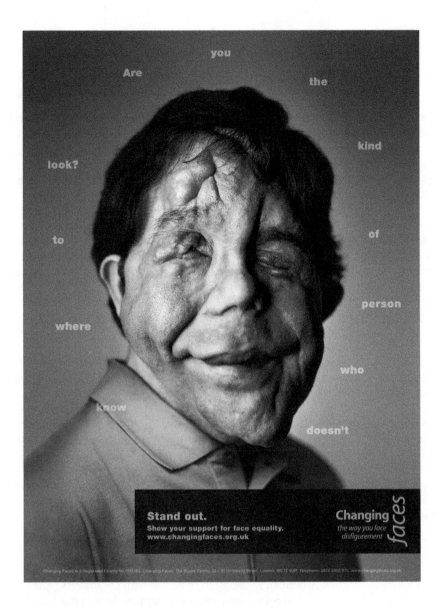

Are you the
look? kind
to of
where person
who
know doesn't

Stand out.
Show your support for face equality.
www.changingfaces.org.uk

Changing
*the way you face
disfigurement* faces

Changing Faces is a Registered Charity No 1011222. Changing Faces, The Square Centre, 03 – 33 University Street, London, WC1E 6JN. Telephone: 0845 4500 275. www.changingfaces.org.uk

This British social marketing campaign tries to change how people look at individuals with physical deformities.
Source: Courtesy of Changing Faces U.K. DDB, London; Photograph by Robert Wilson.

perspective is called *participatory action research (PAR)* or **Transformative Consumer Research (TCR)**. It promotes research projects that include the goal of helping people or bringing about social change. Consumers are not objects of research, but collaborators who work with the researchers to realize this change. Adherents of TCR work with at-risk populations, such as children, the disadvantaged, and the disabled, or on such topics as materialism, consumption of dangerous products, and compulsive consumption.[57]

Social Marketing

As the emerging TCR perspective shows, the field of consumer behavior can play an important role in improving our lives as consumers.[58] **Social marketing** strategies use the techniques that marketers normally employ to sell beer or detergent to encourage positive behaviors such as increased literacy and to discourage negative activities such as drunk driving.[59] Many researchers help to evaluate or create public policies to ensure that products are labeled accurately, to ensure that people can comprehend important information in advertising messages, or to prevent children from being exploited by program-length toy commercials that masquerade as television shows. For example,

CB AS I SEE IT

Professor Julie Ozanne, *Virginia Tech*

If you want to work to make the world a better place, then it is essential to understand consumers' behavior. Consumption lies at the heart of the most important problems facing the global community. In economically developed countries, we are drowning in a sea of things that are depleting our limited global resources at an alarming rate. We are overconsuming food and raising a generation of overweight and unhealthy children. We are engaging in risky consumption behaviors such as smoking, drinking, and gambling. Yet most of the people in the world face limited consumption opportunities and struggle to meet even basic nutritional needs.

Transformative Consumer Research is a new movement of consumer researchers who want to improve consumer well-being. Transformative consumer researchers engage in rigorous research to understand the nature of these pressing social problems. But then they seek to move outside the university to forge alliances with external stakeholders who can build programs of social change to improve the quality of life. Consumer researchers stand in a unique position because they understand and respect the interests of both consumers and businesses. Thus, they have the potential to act as honest brokers working with consumer interest groups, makers of public policy, and business leaders to foster positive social transformation.

This is an exciting time in which to create new models of business and new forms of consumption that are more sustainable and can strengthen our communities. Nobel Peace Prize winner Muhammad Yunis envisioned offering microcredit loans to poor consumers who wanted to start their own businesses, which is a new model of consumer financing that has literally pulled millions of people out of poverty. New models of consumption are also being created. Paris encourages bike-sharing by distributing bikes throughout the city, and does not charge for the first half-hour of rental, so that short trips are free. Similarly, carsharing, in which a fleet of cars is collectively owned and used, has spread to 600 cities worldwide.

My own research examines how the sharing of possessions can build and strengthen communities. For instance, toy-lending libraries operate similarly to book libraries by making toys available to children for a nominal fee. Networks of families form communities of sharing that become an important neighborhood resource for advice and support. Children get to enjoy a wide range of toys while learning important lessons, such as the pleasures of sharing and a respect for collective goods.

American Airlines and the American Association of People with Disabilities (AAPD) are joining forces to create television commercials that portray people with disabilities in a positive light.[60]

Green Marketing

Firms that adopt a **green marketing** philosophy choose to protect or enhance the natural environment as they go about their business activities. Some have focused their efforts on reducing wasteful packaging, as when Procter & Gamble introduced refillable containers for Downy fabric softener.[62]

NYC Condom Finder is an app that taps into your phone's GPS to identify the closest of the nearly 1,000 locations in New York City that distribute free condoms.[61]
Source: New York City Department of Health and Mental Hygiene.

Description

NYC Condom Finder by NYC Health helps you find FREE condoms no matter where you are in New York City. Find Condoms NYC uses your iPhone's GPS to locate and provide walking directions to the 5 nearest venues that distribute FREE NYC Condoms! With more than 3,000 locations throughout all 5 boroughs, no matter where you are, you'll

NYC Condom Finder by NYC Health Support ▸   ...More

What's New in Version 1.0.1

minor bug fixes

DEATH TO THE DEATH PENALTY AMNESTY INTERNATIONAL

139 COUNTRIES HAVE WIPED OUT THE DEATH PENALTY. ONLY 58 ARE LEFT TO CONVINCE. JOIN US AT WWW.AMNESTY. FR

Social marketing campaigns promote a wide range of causes. This appeal against the death penalty ran in France.
Source: Courtesy of TBWA\Paris.

OBJECTIVE 6
Many different types of specialists study consumer behavior.

Consumer Behavior as a Field of Study

By now it should be clear that the field of consumer behavior encompasses many things, from the simple purchase of a carton of milk to the selection of a complex networked computer system; from the decision to donate money to a charity to devious plans to rip off a company.

There's an awful lot to understand, and many ways to go about it. Although people have certainly been consumers for a long time, it is only recently that consumption per se has been the object of formal study. In fact, although many business schools now require that marketing majors take a consumer behavior course, most colleges did not even offer such a course until the 1970s.

Where Do We Find Consumer Researchers?

Where do we find consumer researchers? Just about anywhere we find consumers. Consumer researchers work for manufacturers, retailers, marketing research firms, governments and nonprofit organizations, and of course colleges and universities. You'll find them in laboratories, running sophisticated experiments that involve advanced neural

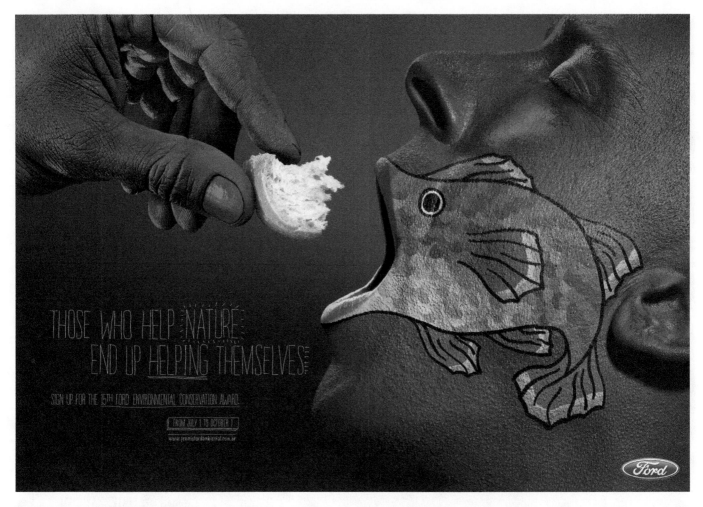

THOSE WHO HELP NATURE
END UP HELPING THEMSELVES.

SIGN UP FOR THE 15TH FORD ENVIRONMENTAL CONSERVATION AWARD.

FROM JULY 1 TO OCTOBER 1

A Ford ad in Brazil promotes conservation.
Source: Courtesy of J. Walter Thompson
Publicidade LTDA—Sao Paulo-Brazil.

imaging machinery, or in malls interviewing shoppers. They may conduct focus groups or run large-scale polling operations. For example, when the advertising agency began to work on a new campaign for retailer JCPenney, it sent staffers to hang out with more than 50 women for several days. They wanted to really understand the respondents' lives, so they helped them to clean their houses, carpool, cook dinner, and shop. As one of the account executives observed, "If you want to understand how a lion hunts, you don't go to the zoo—you go to the jungle."[63]

Researchers work on many types of topics, from everyday household products and high-tech installations to professional services, museum exhibits, and public policy issues such as the effect of advertising on children. Indeed, no consumer issue is too sacred for researchers: Some intrepid investigators bravely explore "delicate" categories like incontinence products and birth control devices. The marketing director for Trojan condoms noted that, "Unlike laundry, where you can actually sit and watch people do their laundry, we can't sit and watch them use our product." For this reason, Trojan relies on clinical psychologists, psychiatrists, and cultural anthropologists to understand how men relate to condoms.[64]

Interdisciplinary Influences on the Study of Consumer Behavior

Many different perspectives shape the young field of consumer behavior. Indeed, it is hard to think of a field that is more interdisciplinary. You can find people with training in a very wide range of disciplines—from psychophysiology to literature—doing consumer research.

Universities, manufacturers, museums, advertising agencies, and governments employ consumer researchers. Several professional groups, such as the Association for Consumer Research and the Society for Consumer Psychology, have been formed since the mid-1970s.

To gain an idea of the diversity of interests of people who do consumer research, consider the list of professional associations that sponsor the field's major journal, the *Journal of Consumer Research*: the American Association of Family and Consumer Sciences, the American Statistical Association, the Association for Consumer Research, the Society for Consumer Psychology, the International Communication Association, the American Sociological Association, the Institute of Management Sciences, the American Anthropological Association, the American Marketing Association, the Society for Personality and Social Psychology, the American Association for Public Opinion Research, and the American Economic Association. That's a pretty mixed bag.

So, with all of these researchers from diverse backgrounds interested in consumer behavior, which is the "correct" discipline to look into these issues? You might remember a children's story about the blind men and the elephant. The gist of the story is that each man touched a different part of the animal and, as a result, the descriptions each gave of the elephant were quite different. This analogy applies to consumer research as well. Depending on the training and interests of the researchers studying it, they will approach the same consumer phenomenon in different ways and at different levels. Table 2 illustrates how a "simple" topic such as magazine usage can be understood in many different ways.

Figure 2 provides a glimpse of some of the disciplines working in the field and the level at which each tackles research issues. We can roughly characterize them in terms of their focus on micro versus macro consumer behavior topics. The fields closer to the top of the pyramid concentrate on the individual consumer (micro issues), and those toward the base are more interested in the aggregate activities that occur among larger groups

| TABLE 2 | Interdisciplinary Research Issues in Consumer Behavior |

Disciplinary Focus	Magazine Usage Sample Research Issues
Experimental Psychology: product role in perception, learning, and memory processes	How specific aspects of magazines, such as their design or layout, are recognized and interpreted; which parts of a magazine people are most likely to read.
Clinical Psychology: product role in psychological adjustment	How magazines affect readers' body images (e.g., do thin models make the average woman feel overweight?)
Microeconomics/Human Ecology: product role in allocation of individual or family resources	Factors influencing the amount of money a household spends on magazines.
Social Psychology: product role in the behavior of individuals as members of social groups	Ways that ads in a magazine affect readers' attitudes toward the products depicted; how peer pressure influences a person's readership decisions
Sociology: product role in social institutions and group relationships	Pattern by which magazine preferences spread through a social group (e.g., a sorority)
Macroeconomics: product role in consumers' relations with the marketplace	Effects of the price of fashion magazines and expense of items advertised during periods of high unemployment
Semiotics/Literary Criticism: product role in the verbal and visual communication of meaning	Ways in which underlying messages communicated by models and ads in a magazine are interpreted
Demography: product role in the measurable characteristics of a population	Effects of age, income, and marital status of a magazine's readers
History: product role in societal changes over time	Ways in which our culture's depictions of "femininity" in magazines have changed over time
Cultural Anthropology: product role in a society's beliefs and practices	Ways in which fashions and models in a magazine affect readers' definitions of masculine versus feminine behavior (e.g., the role of working women, sexual taboos)

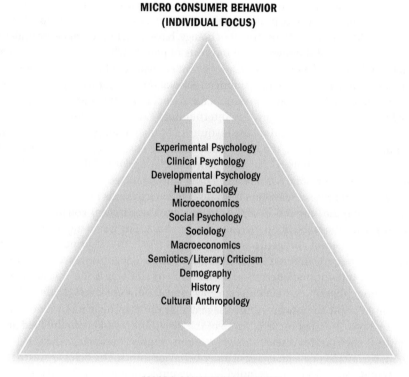

Figure 2 THE PYRAMID OF CONSUMER BEHAVIOR

MICRO CONSUMER BEHAVIOR
(INDIVIDUAL FOCUS)

Experimental Psychology
Clinical Psychology
Developmental Psychology
Human Ecology
Microeconomics
Social Psychology
Sociology
Macroeconomics
Semiotics/Literary Criticism
Demography
History
Cultural Anthropology

MACRO CONSUMER BEHAVIOR
(SOCIAL FOCUS)

of people, such as consumption patterns shared by members of a culture or subculture (macro issues).

Should Consumer Research Have an Academic or an Applied Focus?

Many researchers regard the field of consumer behavior as an applied social science. They argue that the value of the knowledge we generate should be judged in terms of its ability to improve the effectiveness of marketing practice. However, others argue that consumer behavior should not have a strategic focus at all; the field should not be a "handmaiden to business." It should instead focus on the understanding of consumption for its own sake rather than marketers applying this knowledge to making a profit.[65] Most consumer researchers do not hold this rather extreme view, but it has encouraged many to expand the scope of their work beyond the field's traditional focus on the purchase of consumer goods such as food, appliances, and cars to embrace social problems such as homelessness or preserving the environment. Certainly, it has led to some fiery debates among people working in the field!

OBJECTIVE 7
There are two major perspectives on consumer behavior.

Two Perspectives on Consumer Research

One general way in which we classify consumer research is in terms of the fundamental assumptions the researchers make about what they study and how to study it. We call a set of beliefs that guide our understanding of the world a **paradigm**. As in other fields of study, a paradigm dominates the discipline of consumer behavior, but some believe it is in the middle of a *paradigm shift*, which occurs when a competing paradigm challenges the dominant set of assumptions.

The basic set of assumptions underlying the dominant paradigm at this point in time is **positivism** (sometimes called *modernism*). This perspective has significantly influenced Western art and science since the late 16th century. It emphasizes that human reason is supreme and that there is a single, objective truth that science can discover. Positivism encourages us to stress the function of objects, to celebrate technology, and to regard the world as a rational, ordered place with a clearly defined past, present, and future.

The newer paradigm of **interpretivism** (or *postmodernism*) questions these assumptions.[66] Proponents of this perspective argue that our society emphasizes science and technology too much, and they feel that this ordered, rational view of behavior denies or ignores the complex social and cultural world in which we really live. Others feel that positivism puts too much emphasis on material well-being and that its logical outlook is directed by an ideology that stresses the homogenous views of a culture dominated by (dead) white males.

Interpretivists instead stress the importance of symbolic, subjective experience, and the idea that meaning is in the mind of the person—that is, we each construct our own meanings based on our unique and shared cultural experiences, so there are no right or wrong answers. In this view, the world in which we live is a **pastiche**, or mixture of images.[67] This perspective rejects the value we assign to products because they help us to create order; instead, it focuses on regarding consumption as offering a set of diverse experiences. Table 3 summarizes the major differences between these two perspectives on consumer research.

To understand how an interpretive framework helps us to understand marketing communications, let's refer to an analysis of one of the best-known and longest-running (1959–1978) advertising campaigns of all time: the work the advertising agency Doyle Dane Bernbach (DDB) did for the Volkswagen Beetle. This campaign, widely noted for its self-mocking wit, found many ways to turn the Beetle's homeliness, small size, and lack of power into positive attributes at a time when most car ads were emphasizing just the opposite.

An interpretative analysis of these messages used concepts from literature, psychology, and anthropology to ground the appeal of this approach within a broader cultural context. Analysts linked the image DDB created for the humble car to other examples of what scholars of comedy call the "Little Man" pattern. This is a type of comedic character who is related to a clown or a trickster, a social outcast who is able to poke holes in the stuffiness and rigidity of bureaucracy and conformity. Other examples of the "Little Man" character include Hawkeye in the TV sitcom *MASH*, the comedian Woody Allen, and

| TABLE 3 | Positivist versus Interpretivist Approaches to Consumer Behavior |

Assumptions	Positivist Approach	Interpretivist Approach
Nature of reality	Objective, tangible Single	Socially constructed Multiple
Goal	Prediction	Understanding
Knowledge generated	Time-free, context independent	Time-bound Context dependent
View of causality	Existence of real causes	Multiple, simultaneous shaping events
Research relationship	Separation between researcher and subject	Interactive, cooperative with researcher being part of phenomenon under study

Source: Adapted from Laurel A. Hudson and Julie L. Ozanne, "Alternative Ways of Seeking Knowledge in Consumer Research," *Journal of Consumer Research* 14 (March 1988): 508–21. Reprinted with the permission of the University of Chicago Press. Copyright © 1988 JCR, Inc.

Figure 3 THE WHEEL OF CONSUMER BEHAVIOR

Charlie Chaplin. When one looks at the cultural meaning of marketing messages this way, it is perhaps no coincidence that IBM chose the Charlie Chaplin character some years later to help it "soften" its stuffy, intimidating image as it tried to convince consumers that its new personal computer products were user-friendly.

CHAPTER SUMMARY

Now that you have finished reading this chapter, you should understand why:

1. **We use products to help them define our identities in different settings.**

   A consumer may purchase, use, and dispose of a product, but different people may perform these functions. In addition, we can think of consumers as role players who need different products to help them play their various parts.

2. **Consumer behavior is a process.**

   Consumer behavior is the study of the processes involved when individuals or groups select, purchase, use, or dispose of products, services, ideas, or experiences to satisfy needs and desires.

3. **Marketers need to understand the wants and needs of different consumer segments.**

Market segmentation is an important aspect of consumer behavior. Consumers can be segmented according to many dimensions, including product usage, demographics (the objective aspects of a population, such as age and sex), and psychographics (psychological and lifestyle characteristics). Emerging developments, such as the new emphasis on relationship marketing and the practice of database marketing, mean that marketers are much more attuned to the wants and needs of different consumer groups. This is especially important as people are empowered to construct their own consumerspace—accessing product information where and when they want it and initiating contact with companies on the Internet instead of passively receiving marketing communications.

4. **The Web is changing consumer behavior.**

The Web and social media are transforming the way consumers interact with companies and with each other. Online commerce allows us to locate obscure products from around the world, and consumption communities provide forums for people to share opinions and product recommendations. Potential problems accompany these benefits, including the loss of privacy and the deterioration of traditional social interactions as people log more time online.

5. **Our beliefs and actions as consumers strongly connect to other issues in our lives.**

Marketing activities exert an enormous impact on individuals. Consumer behavior is relevant to our understanding of both public policy issues (e.g., ethical marketing practices) and the dynamics of popular culture.

6. **Many different types of specialists study consumer behavior.**

The field of consumer behavior is interdisciplinary; it is composed of researchers from many different fields who share an interest in how people interact with the marketplace. These disciplines can be categorized by the degree to which their focus is micro (the individual consumer) or macro (the consumer as a member of groups or of the larger society).

7. **There are two major perspectives on consumer behavior.**

There are many perspectives on consumer behavior, but we can roughly divide research orientations into two approaches: The positivist perspective emphasizes the objectivity of science and the consumer as a rational decision maker. The interpretivist perspective, in contrast, stresses the subjective meaning of the consumer's individual experience and the idea that any behavior is subject to multiple interpretations rather than to one single explanation.

KEY TERMS

80/20 rule
alternate reality games (ARGs)
asynchronous interactions
B2C e-commerce
business ethics
C2C e-commerce
consumer
consumer behavior
consumerspace
consumption communities
culture jamming
culture of participation
database marketing
demographics

digital native
economics of information
exchange
global consumer culture
green marketing
guerrilla marketing
heavy users
horizontal revolution
interpretivism
market segmentation strategies
need
Open Data Partnership
paradigm
pastiche

popular culture
positivism
psychographics
relationship marketing
role theory
social marketing
social media
synchronous interactions
Transformative Consumer Research (TCR)
user-generated content
want
Web 2.0

REVIEW

1 Provide a definition of consumer behavior.
2 What are demographics? Give three examples of demographic characteristics.

3 What is market segmentation? Give three examples of market segments.
4 What is role theory, and how does it help us to understand consumer behavior?

5 What do we mean by an exchange?

6 Why is it important for businesses to learn about their heavy users?

7 What is database marketing?

8 What is popular culture, and how does this concept relate to marketing and consumer behavior?

9 What is the primary difference between Transformative Consumer Research and other kinds of consumer research?

10 This chapter states that "people often buy products not for what they do but for what they mean." Explain the meaning of this statement and provide an example.

11 What do we mean by the term *global consumer culture*?

12 What is the difference between C2C and B2C e-commerce?

13 The economics-of-information perspective argues that advertising is important. Why?

14 Give two examples of important legislation that relates to American consumers.

15 Define social marketing and give an example of this technique.

16 Name two different disciplines that study consumer behavior. How would their approaches to the same issue differ?

17 What are the major differences between the positivist and interpretivist paradigms in consumer research?

CONSUMER BEHAVIOR CHALLENGE

■ DISCUSS

1 This chapter states that people play different roles and that their consumption behaviors may differ depending on the particular role they are playing. State whether you agree or disagree with this statement, giving examples from your personal life. Try to construct a "stage set" for a role you play, specifying the props, costumes, and script that you use to play a role (e.g., job interviewee, conscientious student, party animal).

2 A company introduced a teddy bear for Valentine's Day called "Crazy for You." This toy aroused the ire of mental health advocates because a straitjacket restrains the cuddly bear's paws and the stuffed animal comes with institutional commitment papers. Supporters of the company's decision to keep selling the bear say opponents are too "politically correct."[68] What do you think?

3 Nonprofit organizations routinely rely on generous corporate donations, and it's common to name facilities after benefactors. The Nationwide Children's Hospital in Ohio is no exception; its name recognizes the insurance company's $50 million donation. Now the hospital is adding the Abercrombie & Fitch Emergency Department and Trauma Center and there is also the Limited Too & Justice Main Lobby. Abercrombie & Fitch is notorious for its use of alluring young people. The Campaign for a Commercial-Free Childhood opposes this partnership. The group's director commented that "Abercrombie & Fitch is really among the worst of corporate predators. A company with such cynical disregard for children's well-being shouldn't be able to claim the mantle of healing. . . . And, personally, I find it very concerning that they named their hospital after an insurance company."[69] What do you think? Is this over the line, or does it matter where the money comes from as long as the end result is beneficial?

4 From time to time advertisers use dark humor to get their messages across, as when a lonely calorie, repairman, or robot considers suicide. Or, an ad may imply that shoppers are "mentally ill" if they buy retail. Are these appeals a legitimate way to communicate a message, and if so under what circumstances?

5 Name some products or services that your social group uses a lot. State whether you agree or disagree with the notion that these products help to form group bonds. Support your argument with examples from your listing of products that your group uses.

6 List the three stages in the consumption process. Describe the issues that you considered in each of these stages when you made a recent important purchase.

7 What aspects of consumer behavior would interest a financial planner? A university administrator? A graphic arts designer? A social worker in a government agency? A nursing instructor?

8 Critics of targeted marketing strategies argue that this practice is discriminatory and unfair, especially if such a strategy encourages a group of people to buy a product that may be injurious to them or that they cannot afford. For example, community leaders in largely minority neighborhoods have staged protests against billboards promoting beer or cigarettes in these areas. However, the Association of National Advertisers argues that banning targeted marketing constitutes censorship and thus is a violation of the First Amendment. What are your views regarding this issue?

9 A 2007 book bemoans the new wave of consumer-generated content, labeling it "the cult of the amateur." It compares the social networking phenomenon to the old story about the monkeys: If you put an infinite number of monkeys in a room with an infinite number of typewriters, eventually they will (by hitting keys randomly) reproduce all the major works of literature. In other words, the large majority of user-generated content is at about the same level, and the future of professionally produced, quality work is in doubt.[70] Do you agree or disagree with this assertion?

10 A firm called Global Rainmakers Inc. (GRI) announced a partnership with Leon, a large city in Mexico, to deploy iris

scanning technology it developed to make Leon "the most secure city in the world." The city is creating a database of irises. It will automatically scan criminals' eyes when they are convicted, though other citizens will have the option to choose whether to have their data included. When residents catch a train or bus, or get money from an ATM, they will submit to an iris scan rather than swiping a card. They won't have to present identification at a bar or a liquor store. The police will monitor these actions, so (for example) a convicted shoplifter might not be allowed to enter a certain store. The company's CEO claims, "There's a lot of convenience to this—you'll have nothing to carry except your eyes. In ten years, you may just have one sensor that is literally able to identify hundreds of people in motion at a distance and determine their geo-location and their intent—you'll be able to see how many eyeballs looked at a billboard. . . . You can start to track from the point a person is browsing on Google and finds something they want to purchase, to the point they cross the threshold in a Target or Walmart and actually make the purchase. You start to see the entire life cycle of marketing." So, lots of convenience and enhanced security may be in our future. Is the tradeoff in terms of our privacy worth it, or is "Big Brother" knocking at the door?[71]

11 Will the Web bring people closer together or drive each of us into our own private virtual worlds? Wired Americans are spending less time with friends and family, less time shopping in stores, and more time working at home after hours. More than one-third of consumers who have access to the Internet report that they are online at least 5 hours a week. Also, 60 percent of Internet users say they have reduced their television viewing, and one-third say they spend less time reading newspapers (those that still remain, as many fold due to a lack of readership and advertising revenue).

However, a study by the Pew Internet and American Life Project reported that more than half of users the group surveyed feel that email actually strengthens family ties. Users reported far more off-line social contact than nonusers.[72] These results argue that people spend more time than ever with others. It's just that they form strong relationships over the Internet instead of in person. But the author of the first survey disagrees. As he observes, "If I go home at 6:30 in the evening and spend the whole night sending e-mail and wake up the next morning, I still haven't talked to my wife or kids or friends. When you spend your time on the Internet, you don't hear a human voice and you never get a hug."[73]

A follow-up study found that it works both ways: extroverts tend to make even more friends on the Web, whereas introverts feel even more cut off from the rest of the world. This has been termed the "rich get richer" model of Internet use.[74] What's your take on this issue? Is our wired world turning us into digital hermits, or does it help us to expand our boundaries by interacting with other people whom we might not otherwise meet? What are the good and bad consequences of this profound change in how we interact with other people?

APPLY

1 Will consumers trade lower prices for less privacy? Car owners now can let insurance companies monitor their driving, using a new technology, in exchange for lower rates. Customers who sign up for Progressive's TripSense program get a device the size of a Tic Tac box to plug into their cars. The device tracks speed and how many miles are driven at what times of day. Every few months, customers unplug the device from the car, plug it into a computer, download the data, and send the data to the company. Depending on results, discounts will range from 5 to 25 percent. In Great Britain, a major insurer is testing a program called Pay as You Drive. Volunteers will get a device the size of a Palm computer installed in their cars. The gadget will use global positioning satellite technology to track where the car goes, constantly sending information back to the insurance company. Cars that spend more time in safer areas will qualify for bigger discounts.[75] Of course, the potential downside to these efforts is that the insurance companies may be able to collect data on where you have driven, how long you stayed in one location, and so on.

Conduct a poll of 10 drivers of various ages in which you describe these programs and ask respondents if they would participate in order to receive a discount on their insurance premiums. What reasons do they give pro and con? Do you find any differences in attitudes based on demographic characteristics such as age or gender?

2 While you're talking to car owners, probe to see what (if any) relationships they have with their vehicles. Do these feelings correspond to the types of consumer/product attachments we discussed in this chapter? How are these relationships acted on? (Hint: See if any of the respondents have nicknames for their cars, or if they "decorate" them with personal items.)

3 Many college students "share" music by downloading clips from the Internet. Interview at least five people who have downloaded at least one song or movie without paying for it. Do they feel they are stealing? What explanations do they offer for this behavior? Try to identify any common themes as a result of these interviews. If you were devising an ad campaign to discourage free downloading, how might you use what you have learned to craft a convincing message?

MyMarketingLab Now that you have completed this chapter, return to www.mymktlab.com to apply concepts and explore the additional study materials.

Case Study

UNICEF WAGES GUERRILLA WARFARE

U.S. Fund for UNICEF

New Yorkers rush through Manhattan's Union Square on their way to work. As they move quickly through the crowds, they pass a water vending machine on the sidewalk, something very appealing on a hot day in the city. But there's a catch: This brightly colored vending machine dispenses water in flavors such as malaria, cholera, typhoid, dengue, hepatitis, dysentery, salmonella, and yellow fever! The machine is part of UNICEF's Dirty Water campaign. The organization wants Americans to realize that about 2 billion people worldwide lack access to clean water, and more than 4,000 children die daily due to waterborne disease. UNICEF also informs people, via a sign on the machine, that if they insert $1, they provide a child with clean water for 40 days.

UNICEF is a global humanitarian relief organization that provides children with health care and immunizations, clean water, nutrition, education, and emergency relief in more than 150 countries. This nonprofit has adopted so-called **guerrilla marketing** tactics: nontraditional methods to break through the clutter of competing messages in public areas (just as guerrillas use the element of surprise to overwhelm traditional armies with superior firepower). Being heard is an extra challenge for organizations like UNICEF; they have a more serious message

to deliver and it's tough to compete against the thousands of ads for glamorous clothes or cool cars with which we're confronted everyday.

Another major initiative for UNICEF is reducing the dangers of landmines throughout the world. These hidden explosives (usually left over from former wars) kill or injure 15,000 people a year, many of them children. UNICEF's street campaign for landmine awareness used another guerrilla tactic; this time it involved placing stickers on the streets of Zurich. The stickers, which matched the color of the sidewalk, were not easily noticed by pedestrians. A passerby would step on the sticker and it would stick to the bottom of his or her shoe. When the pedestrian turned a foot to see the sticker, he or she viewed a message from UNICEF that said, "In many other countries you would now be mutilated! Help the victims of landmines!"

Guerrilla marketing gets the attention of the jaded pedestrian, but it also has the potential to spread a message to many others as well with the help of social media. Wouldn't you tweet, post a video to YouTube, or upload a picture to your Facebook page if you saw something really cool and different, like malaria-flavored water or a landmine sticker on your way to class? Many of us learned as superstitious kids not to step on a crack in the sidewalk; maybe today other things we step on will result in good luck for worthy organizations like UNICEF.

DISCUSSION QUESTIONS

1. Do you think UNICEF's campaigns will be effective? Why or why not?
2. Guerrilla marketing tactics deliberately intend to "ambush" consumers in public places. Is this an effective marketing technique, or is it a violation of our right to go about our business undisturbed? Do these tactics intrude on our lives? In other words, is there a point where they cross a line?
3. What are other ways UNICEF could spread the word about its causes such as the dangers of dirty water?

Sources: Leon Kaye, "UNICEF's Dirty Water Vending Machines Raises Manhattan," www.triplepundit.com (July 19th, 2010), accessed June 24, 2011. "Unicef Landmine," www.yayeveryday.com, accessed June 24, 2011. www.unicef.com, accessed June 24, 2011.

NOTES

1. www.jewelmint.com, accessed May 9, 2011; www.oxygen.com, accessed May 9, 2011; www.ivillage.com, accessed May 9, 2011; www.hercampus.com, accessed May 9, 2011; www.ratemyprofessors.com, accessed May 9, 2011.

2. Michael R. Solomon and Elnora W. Stuart, *Marketing: Real People, Real Choices*, 2nd ed. (Upper Saddle River, NJ: Prentice Hall, 2000): 5–6.

3. www.sonystyle.com, accessed May 7, 2011; "Sony Walkman Series S, E and B Music Players Features and Suppring [sic] Formats" (May 29, 2009), http://techwizardz.blogspot.com/2009/05/sony-walkman-series-s-e-and-b-music.html, accessed June 27, 2009; Evan Ramstad, "Walkman's Plan for Reeling in the Ears of Wired Youths," *Wall Street Journal Interactive Edition* (May 18, 2000).

4. Anthony Bianco, "The Vanishing Mass Market," *BusinessWeek* (July 12, 2004): 61–67.

5. Tracy Tuten and Michael R. Solomon, *Social Media Marketing* (Upper Saddle River, NJ: Pearson, 2012); some material provided by Julie Channing, head planner at AKQA for The Lost Ring campaign.

6. Jack Neff, "Study: Package-Goods Brands' Consumer Bases Very Small, Yet Diverse," *Advertising Age* (December 8, 2008), www.adage.com, accessed December 8, 2008.

7. Jennifer Ordonez, "Cash Cows: Burger Joints Call Them 'Heavy Users'—But Not to Their Faces," *Wall Street Journal Interactive Edition* (January 12, 2000).

8. Steven Gray, "At Fast-Food Chains, Era of the Giant Burger (Plus Bacon) Is Here," *Wall Street Journal* (January 27, 2005), www.wsj.com, accessed January 27, 2005.

9. Allison Fass, "Kingdom Seeks Magic," *Forbes* (October 2006): 68–70.

10. Natalie Perkins, "Zeroing in on Consumer Values," *Advertising Age* (March 22, 1993): 23.

11. Hannah Karp, "Red Bull Aims at an Older Crowd," *Wall Street Journal* (June 7, 2004): B3.

12. Jack Neff, "Crest Spinoff Targets Women," *Advertising Age* (June 3, 2002): 1.

13. Charles M. Schaninger and William D. Danko, "A Conceptual and Empirical Comparison of Alternative Household Life Cycle Models," *Journal of Consumer Research* 19 (March 1993): 580–94; Robert E. Wilkes, "Household Life-Cycle Stages, Transitions, and Product Expenditures," *Journal of Consumer Research* 22 (June 1995): 27–42.

14. Richard P. Coleman, "The Continuing Significance of Social Class to Marketing," *Journal of Consumer Research* 10 (December 1983): 265–80.

15. Motoko Rich, "Region's Marketers Hop on the Bubba Bandwagon," *Wall Street Journal Interactive Edition* (May 19, 1999).

16. Sarah Ellison, "Prilosec OTC Blitz by P&G Represents New Drug Foray," *Wall Street Journal* (September 12, 2003), www.wsj.com, accessed September 12, 2003.

17. Constance L. Hayes, "What Wal-Mart Knows About Customers' Habits," *New York Times* (November 14, 2004), www.nytimes.com, accessed November 14, 2004.

18. Mylene Mangalindan, "Hollywood's 'Wedding Crashers' Inspires the Invitationless," *Wall Street Journal* (December 28, 2005): B1.

19. Thomas Vinciguerra, "Soft, Chewy and Taking over the World," *New York Times* (July 5, 2006): Sec. 4, p. 2.

20. Quoted in "Bringing Meaning to Brands," *American Demographics* (June 1997): 34.

21. Erving Goffman, *The Presentation of Self in Everyday Life* (Garden City, NY: Doubleday, 1959); George H. Mead, *Mind, Self, and Society* (Chicago: University of Chicago Press, 1934); Michael R. Solomon, "The Role of Products as Social Stimuli: A Symbolic Interactionism Perspective," *Journal of Consumer Research* 10 (December 1983): 319–29.

22. Jennifer Aaker, Susan Fournier, and S. Adam Brasel, "When Good Brands Do Bad," *Journal of Consumer Research* 31 (2004): 1–16.

23. Susan Fournier, "Consumers and Their Brands. Developing Relationship Theory in Consumer Research," *Journal of Consumer Research* 24 (March 1998): 343–73.

24. Brad Edmondson, "The Dawn of the Megacity," *Marketing Tools* (March 1999): 64.

25. David Barbosa, "China, New Land of Shoppers, Builds Malls on Gigantic Scale," *New York Times* (May 25, 2005), www.nytimes.com, accessed May 25, 2005.

26. For a discussion of this trend, see Russell W. Belk, "Hyperreality and Globalization: Culture in the Age of Ronald McDonald," *Journal of International Consumer Marketing* 8 (1995): 23–38.

27. Some material in this section was adapted from Michael R. Solomon and Elnora W. Stuart, *Welcome to Marketing.com: The Brave New World of E-Commerce* (Upper Saddle River, NJ: Prentice Hall, 2000).

28. Irina Slutsky, "Get Hooked up with the Big Business of Online Dating," *Advertising Age* (February 14, 2011), http://adage.com/article/ad-age-graphics/online-dating-a-a-1-3-billion-market/148845/, accessed May 7, 2011.

29. Marc Prensky, "Digital Natives, Digital Immigrants," *On the Horizon* 9(5) (October 2001): 1–6.

30. Steve Spangler, "Mentos Diet Coke Geyser," *SteveSpanglerScience.com*, http://www.stevespanglerscience.com/experiment/original-mentos-diet-coke-geyser, accessed May 7, 2011; Suzanne Vranica and Chad Terhune, "Mixing Diet Coke and Mentos Makes a Gusher of Publicity," *Wall Street Journal* (June 12, 2006): B1.

31. "Facebook Statistics," http://www.facebook.com/press/info.php?statistics, accessed November 15, 2010.

32. Chloe Albanesius, "YouTube Users Uploading 35 Hours of Video Every Minute," *PCMag.com* (November 11, 2010), http://www.pcmag.com/article2/0,2817,2372511,00.asp, accessed November 15, 2010.

33. Parts of this section are adapted from Tracy Tuten and Michael R. Solomon, *Social Media Marketing* (Upper Saddle River, NJ: Pearson Education, 2012).

34. "Woman in Wendy's Finger Case Is Arrested," *New York Times* (April 22, 2005), www.nytimes.com, accessed April 22, 2005.

35. Reported in *American Demographics* (December 1999): 18.

36. Valerie S. Folkes and Michael A. Kamins, "Effects of Information about Firms' Ethical and Unethical Actions on Consumers' Attitudes," *Journal of Consumer Psychology* 8 (1999): 243–59.

37. Jacqueline N. Hood and Jeanne M. Logsdon, "Business Ethics in the NAFTA Countries: A Cross-Cultural Comparison," *Journal of Business Research* 55 (2002): 883–90.

38. Quoted in Ira Teinowitz, "Lawsuit: Menthol Smokes Illegally Targeted to Blacks," *Advertising Age* (November 2, 1998): 16.

39. Michael R. Solomon, *Conquering Consumerspace: Marketing Strategies for a Branded World* (New York: AMACOM, 2003).

40. Diana Alison, "Color Labs Offers Location-Based Photo Sharing App," *Information Week* (March 24, 2011), http://www.informationweek.com/thebrainyard/news/social_networking_consumer/229400235/color-labs-offers-locationbased-photo-sharing-app, accessed April 30, 2011.

41. Emily Steel, "Some Data-Miners Ready to Reveal What They Know," *Wall Street Journal* (December 3, 2010), http://professional.wsj.com/article/SB10001424052748704377004575650802136721966.html?mod=WSJ_business_whatsNews&mg=reno-wsj, accessed April 30, 2011.

42. Jeffrey Ball, "Religious Leaders to Discuss SUVs with GM, Ford Officials," *Wall Street Journal Interactive Edition* (November 19, 2002); Danny Hakim, "The S.U.V. Is a Beast, and It's Hairy, Too," *New York Times* (February 2, 2005), www.nytimes.com, accessed February 2, 2005; www.nrpe.org/issues, accessed May 11, 2009.

43. William Leiss, Stephen Kline, and Sut Jhally, *Social Communication in Advertising: Persons, Products, and Images of Well-Being* (Toronto: Methuen, 1986); Jerry Mander, *Four Arguments for the Elimination of Television* (New York: William Morrow, 1977).

44. Packard (1957), quoted in Leiss et al., *Social Communication*, 11.

45. Raymond Williams, *Problems in Materialism and Culture: Selected Essays* (London: Verso, 1980).

46. Leiss et al., *Social Communication*.

47. George Stigler, "The Economics of Information," *Journal of Political Economy* (1961): 69.

48. Leiss et al., *Social Communication*, 11.

49. Robert V. Kozinets and Jay M. Handelman, "Adversaries of Consumption: Consumer Movements, Activism, and Ideology," *Journal of Consumer Research* 31 (December 2004): 691–704; cf. also Paul C. Henry (2010), "How Mainstream Consumers Think about Consumer Rights and Responsibilities," *Journal of Consumer Research* 37(4), 670–687.

50. Natasha Singer, "A Birth Control Pill That Promised Too Much," *New York Times* (February 10, 2009), www.nytimes.com, accessed February 10, 2009.

51. Jack Neff, "NAD to Charmin: No Bare Bear Bottoms: P&G Must Show Some Pieces of TP on Bruin's Bums," *Advertising Age* (August 12, 2010), http://adage.com/article/adages/advertising-p-g-show-pieces-charmin-bears/145379/, accessed April 29, 2011.

52. Janet Adamy, "Tough New Rules Proposed on Food Advertising for Kids," *Wall Street Journal* (April 29, 2011), http://professional.wsj.com/

article/NA_EP_PUB:SB10001424052748704330404576291091782255946
.html?lpe=WSJ_PRO&mg=com-wsj, accessed April 29, 2011.

53. "Adbusters," Adbusters Media Foundation, www.adbusters.org, accessed June 29, 2009.

54. Ibid.

55. www.nikesweatshop.net, accessed June 29, 2002.

56. Nat Ives, "Anti-Ad Group Tries Advertising," *New York Times* (September 21, 2004), www.nytimes.com, accessed September 21, 2004.

57. Julie L. Ozanne and Bige Saatcioglu, "Participatory Action Research," *Journal of Consumer Research* 35 (October 2008): 423–39.

58. For consumer research and discussions related to public policy issues, see Paul N. Bloom and Stephen A. Greyser, "The Maturing of Consumerism," *Harvard Business Review* (November–December 1981): 130–39; George S. Day, "Assessing the Effect of Information Disclosure Requirements," *Journal of Marketing* (April 1976): 42–52; Dennis E. Garrett, "The Effectiveness of Marketing Policy Boycotts: Environmental Opposition to Marketing," *Journal of Marketing* 51 (January 1987): 44–53; Michael Houston and Michael Rothschild, "Policy-Related Experiments on Information Provision: A Normative Model and Explication," *Journal of Marketing Research* 17 (November 1980): 432–49; Jacob Jacoby, Wayne D. Hoyer, and David A. Sheluga, *Misperception of Televised Communications* (New York: American Association of Advertising Agencies, 1980); Gene R. Laczniak and Patrick E. Murphy, *Marketing Ethics: Guidelines for Managers* (Lexington, MA: Lexington Books, 1985): 117–23; Lynn Phillips and Bobby Calder, "Evaluating Consumer Protection Laws: Promising Methods," *Journal of Consumer Affairs* 14 (Summer 1980): 9–36; Donald P. Robin and Eric Reidenbach, "Social Responsibility, Ethics, and Marketing Strategy: Closing the Gap Between Concept and Application," *Journal of Marketing* 51 (January 1987): 44–58; Howard Schutz and Marianne Casey, "Consumer Perceptions of Advertising as Misleading," *Journal of Consumer Affairs* 15 (Winter 1981): 340–57; Darlene Brannigan Smith and Paul N. Bloom, "Is Consumerism Dead or Alive? Some New Evidence," in Thomas C. Kinnear, ed., *Advances in Consumer Research* 11 (1984): 369–73.

59. Cf. Philip Kotler and Alan R. Andreasen, *Strategic Marketing for Nonprofit Organizations*, 4th ed. (Upper Saddle River, NJ: Prentice Hall, 1991); Jeff B. Murray and Julie L. Ozanne, "The Critical Imagination: Emancipatory Interests in Consumer Research," *Journal of Consumer Research* 18 (September 1991): 192–244; William D. Wells, "Discovery-Oriented Consumer Research," *Journal of Consumer Research* 19 (March 1993): 489–504.

60. Karl Greenberg, "American Airlines, AAPD to Create Positive Ads Featuring Disabled People," *Marketing Daily* (March 30, 2009), www.mediapost.com, accessed March 30, 2009.

61. Ben Parr, "Need Free Condoms? There's an App for That," *Mashable* (February 16, 2011), http://mashable.com/2011/02/16/condoms-nyc-app/?utm_source=feedburner&utm_medium=email&utm_campaign=Feed%3A+Mashable+%28Mashable%29, accessed April 30, 2011.

62. "Concerned Consumers Push for Environmentally Friendly Packaging," *Boxboard Containers* (April 1993): 4.

63. Suzanne Vranica, "Ad Houses Will Need to Be More Nimble, Clients Are Demanding More and Better Use of Consumer Data, Web," *Wall Street Journal* (January 2, 2008): B3.

64. Jack Neff, "Mucus to Maxi Pads: Marketing's Dirtiest Jobs, Frank Talk about Diapers and Condoms Lifts Taboos and Helps Make a Difference in Consumers' Lives, Say Those in the Trenches," *Advertising Age* (February 17, 2009), www.adage.com, accessed February 17, 2009.

65. Morris B. Holbrook, "The Consumer Researcher Visits Radio City: Dancing in the Dark," in Elizabeth C. Hirschman and Morris B. Holbrook, eds., *Advances in Consumer Research* 12 (Provo, UT: Association for Consumer Research, 1985): 28–31.

66. For an overview, see Eric J. Arnould and Craig J. Thompson, "Consumer Culture Theory (CCT): Twenty Years of Research," *Journal of Consumer Research* 31 (March 2005): 868–82.

67. Alladi Venkatesh, "Postmodernism, Poststructuralism and Marketing," paper presented at the American Marketing Association Winter Theory Conference, San Antonio, February 1992; see also Stella Proctor, Ioanna Papasolomou-Doukakis, and Tony Proctor, "What Are Television Advertisements Really Trying to Tell Us? A Postmodern Perspective," *Journal of Consumer Behavior* 1 (February 2002): 246–55; A. Fuat Firat and Alladi Venkatesh, "The Making of Postmodern Consumption," in Russell W. Belk and Nikhilesh Dholakia, eds., *Consumption and Marketing: Macro Dimensions* (Boston: PWS-Kent, 1993).

68. Pam Belluck, "Toy's Message of Affection Draws Anger and Publicity," *New York Times* (January 22, 2005), www.nytimes.com, accessed January 22, 2005.

69. Natalie Zmuda, "Children's Hospital in Hot Water over Corporate Sponsorships, Critics Dismayed by Association with Racy Retailer Abercrombie & Fitch," *Advertising Age* (March 12, 2008), www.adage.com, accessed March 12, 2008.

70. Andrew Keen, *The Cult of the Amateur: How Today's Internet Is Killing Our Culture* (New York: Currency 2007).

71. Quoted in Austin Carr, "Iris Scanners Create the Most Secure City in the World. Welcome, Big Brother," *Fast Company* (August 18, 2010), http://www.fastcompany.com/1683302/iris-scanners-create-the-most-secure-city-in-the-world-welcomes-big-brother?partner=homepage_newsletter, accessed April 30, 2011.

72. Rebecca Fairley Raney, "Study Finds Internet of Social Benefit to Users," *New York Times* (May 11, 2000), www.nytimes.com, accessed May 11, 2000.

73. John Markoff, "Portrait of a Newer, Lonelier Crowd Is Captured in an Internet Survey," *New York Times* (February 16, 2000), www.nytimes.com, accessed February 16, 2000.

74. Lisa Guernsey, "Professor Who Once Found Isolation Online Has a Change of Heart," *New York Times* (July 26, 2001), www.nytimes.com, accessed July 26, 2001.

75. Kevin Maney, "Drivers Let Big Brother in to Get a Break," *Ethics* (August 9, 2004): 1B.

NIELSEN NUGGET

For nearly a century, Nielsen has enabled organizations in various industries to make strategic decisions based on information it gathers through evolving research methodologies. Nielsen helps media companies better understand viewers, listeners, and the industry as a whole by providing insights for audience measurement, advertising effectiveness, and overall marketing performance and cross-platform strategies. Nielsen's broad range of consumer packaged goods (CPG) analytics and consulting services are specifically designed for, and with, top CPG manufacturers and retailers, to ensure that they have the most accurate view of the consumer and the marketplace. Spanning 80 countries across 5 continents, Nielsen maintains its leadership position by providing customized solutions based on local marketing research.

EXERCISE: Buying, Having, and Being

Scenario: Awesome Beans is a manufacturer with offerings across many categories. Although they have experienced flat sales in coffee over the past few years, the category has recently begun to show slight growth. Awesome Beans would like to capitalize on this trend, to make sure they are receiving at least their fair share of the category growth. The company recently conducted an attitudinal segmentation study. Survey research resulted in differentiating coffee consumers into four categories based on their common needs and buying motivation.

Challenge: Awesome Beans wants to identify which of the four segments offers the greatest opportunity for sales growth. In addition, the company hopes to better understand this attitudinal segment demographically, so it can determine how best to reach these coffee buyers in terms of placement and message.

After reviewing the data provided:

1 Determine which segment Awesome Beans should choose to target more aggressively.

2 Determine which of the household types identified would be the most appropriate demographically to target with promotions.

3 Which of the demographic dimensions discussed in this chapter should be considered as potential segment-defining variables?

Attitudinal Group	% Buyers	% Value	Index	$ Value (000s)
Coffee Bingers	29	25	86	$74,323
Café Callers	33	27	83	$80,295
Flavour Followers	13	12	96	$36,433
Premium People	24	35	145	$102,471

Attitudinal Groups were segmented based on their responses to survey questions. The data above show:
- The size of each group, in terms of share of coffee buyers (% Buyers)
- The percent of coffee dollar sales (% value)
- Dollar Index (% Value/% Buyers x 100). A score of 100 is average.
- $ Value—Total coffee $ spend by consumer segment

Buyer Index vs. All Shoppers	Coffee Bingers	Café Callers	Flavour Followers	Premium People
AWESOME BEANS	103	100	104	96
COMPETITOR 1	98	97	110	100
COMPETITOR 2	95	101	95	105
COMPETITOR 3	88	113	103	100

Buyer Index = % Buyers within each group/% Buyers of Total Respondents *100

Demographic	Coffee Bingers	Café Callers	Flavour Followers	Premium People
Young Families	20	12	16	24
Older Families	15	25	13	10
Older Singles and Couples	33	35	45	25
Adult Households	32	28	26	41

Column figures indicate the percentage each demographic represents within attitudinal segments.

Perception

Perception

When you finish reading this chapter you will understand why:

1. Perception is a three-stage process that translates raw stimuli into meaning.

2. The design of a product is now a key driver of its success or failure.

3. Products and commercial messages often appeal to our senses, but because of the profusion of these messages most of them won't influence us.

4. The concept of a sensory threshold is important for marketing communication.

5. Subliminal advertising is a controversial—but largely ineffective—way to talk to consumers.

6. We interpret the stimuli to which we do pay attention according to learned patterns and expectations.

7. The field of semiotics helps us to understand how marketers use symbols to create meaning.

MyMarketingLab
Visit **www.mymktlab.com** to find activities that help you learn and review in order to succeed in this chapter.

Source: LensKiss/Shutterstock.

The European vacation has been wonderful, and this stop in Lisbon is no exception. Still, after two weeks of eating his way through some of the continent's finest pastry shops and restaurants, Gary's getting a bit of a craving for his family's favorite snack—a good old American box of Oreos and an ice-cold carton of milk. Unbeknownst to his wife, Janeen, he had stashed away some cookies "just in case"—this was the time to break them out.

Now all he needs is the milk. On an impulse, Gary decides to surprise Janeen with a mid-afternoon treat. He sneaks out of the hotel room while she's napping and finds the nearest *grosa*. When he heads to the small refrigerated section, though, he's puzzled—no milk here. Undaunted, Gary asks the clerk, *"Leite, por favor?"* The clerk quickly smiles and points to a rack in the middle of the store piled with little white square boxes. No, that can't be right—Gary resolves to work on his Portuguese. He repeats the question, and again he gets the same answer.

Finally, he investigates and, sure enough, he sees that the boxes have labels saying they contain something called ultra heat treated (UHT) milk. Nasty! Who in the world would drink milk out of a little box that's been sitting on a warm shelf for who knows how long? Gary dejectedly returns to the hotel, his snack-time fantasies crumbling like so many stale cookies.

Sensory Systems

OBJECTIVE 1
Perception is a three-stage process that translates raw stimuli into meaning.

Gary would be surprised to learn that many people in the world drink milk out of a box every day. UHT is pasteurized milk that has been heated until the bacteria that cause it to spoil are destroyed, and it can last for 5 to 6 months without refrigeration if its aseptic container is unopened. The milk tastes slightly sweeter than fresh milk but otherwise it's basically the same stuff.

Shelf-stable milk is particularly popular in Europe, where refrigerator space in homes is smaller and stores tend to carry less inventory than in the United States. Seven out of ten Europeans drink it routinely. Manufacturers continue to try to crack the U.S. market as well, though analysts are dubious about their prospects. To begin with, milk consumption in the United States is declining steadily as teenagers choose soft drinks instead. Indeed, the Milk Industry Foundation pumped $44 million into an advertising campaign to promote milk drinking ("Got Milk?").

But it's even harder to entice Americans to drink milk out of a box. In focus groups, U.S. consumers say they have trouble believing the milk is not spoiled or unsafe. In addition, they consider the square, quart-sized boxes more suitable for dry food. Many schools and fast-food chains already buy UHT milk because of its long shelf life.[1] Still, although Americans may not think twice about drinking a McFlurry from McDonald's made with shelf-stable milk, it's going to be a long, uphill battle to change their perceptions about the proper partner for a bagful of Oreos.

Whether it's the taste of Oreos, the sight of an Obsession perfume ad, or the sound of the music group OutKast, we live in a world overflowing with sensations. Wherever we turn, a symphony of colors, sounds, and odors bombards us. Some of the "notes" in this symphony occur naturally, such as the loud barking of a dog, the shades of the evening sky, or the heady smell of a rose bush. Others come from people: The person who plops down next to you in class might wear swirling tattoos, bright pink pants, and enough nasty perfume to make your eyes water.

Marketers certainly contribute to this commotion. Consumers are never far from pop-up ads, product packages, radio and television commercials, and billboards—all clamoring for our attention. Sometimes we go out of our way to experience "unusual" sensations, whether they are thrills from bungee jumping; playing virtual reality games; or going to theme parks such as Universal Studios, which offers "Fear Factor Live" attractions that ask vacationers to swallow gross things or perform stomach-churning stunts.[2]

Only a select few try to cram down as many peanut butter and banana sandwiches, Moon Pies, or cheese steaks as (in)humanly possible in events sponsored by MLE/FOCE (Major League Eating/Federation of Competitive Eating). Others happily blast teeth-rattling 50 Cent cuts from booming car speakers. Each of us copes with the bombardment of sensations as we pay attention to some stimuli and tune out others. The messages to which we *do* choose to pay attention often wind up affecting us differently from what the sponsors intended; we each put our personal "spin" on things as we assign meanings consistent with our own unique experiences, biases, and desires. This chapter focuses on the process by which we absorb sensations and then use these to interpret the surrounding world.

Sensation refers to the immediate response of our sensory receptors (eyes, ears, nose, mouth, fingers, skin) to basic stimuli such as light, color, sound, odor, and texture. **Perception** is the process by which people select, organize, and interpret these sensations. The study of perception, then, focuses on what we *add* to these raw sensations in order to give them meaning.

Gary's encounter with milk in a box illustrates the perceptual process. He has learned to equate the cold temperature of refrigerated milk with freshness, so he experienced a negative physical reaction when confronted with a product that contradicted his expectations. Gary's evaluation was affected by factors such as the design of the package, the brand name, and even the section in the grocery store that displayed the milk. A consumer's cultural background largely determines these expectations by Europeans do not necessarily have the same perceptions of milk as Americans, and as a result their reactions to the product differ quite a bit from those of U.S. milk drinkers.

Like computers, we undergo stages of *information processing* in which we input and store stimuli. Unlike computers, though, we do *not* passively process whatever information happens to be present. In the first place, we notice only a very small number of the stimuli in our environment, simply because there are so many different ones out there vying for our attention. Of those we do notice, we attend to an even smaller number—and we might not process the stimuli that do enter consciousness objectively. Each individual interprets the meaning of a stimulus in a manner consistent with his or her own unique biases, needs, and experiences. As Figure 1 shows, these three stages of *exposure, attention,* and *interpretation* make up the process of perception. Before considering each of these stages, let's step back and look at the sensory systems that provide sensations to us in the first place.

Figure 1 AN OVERVIEW OF THE PERCEPTUAL PROCESS

Our brains receive external stimuli, or *sensory inputs,* on a number of channels. We may see a billboard, hear a jingle, feel the softness of a cashmere sweater, taste a new flavor of ice cream, or smell a leather jacket. The inputs our five senses detect are the raw data that begin the perceptual process. Sensory data emanating from the external environment (e.g., hearing a tune on the radio) can generate internal sensory experiences; a song might trigger a young man's memory of his first dance and bring to mind the smell of his date's perfume or the feel of her hair on his cheek. Marketers' messages are more effective when they speak to us via multiple sensory channels. For example, in a recent study participants who read ad copy for potato chips that emphasized the product's smell and texture in addition to its taste predicted that the chips would taste better than did those who just read copy that focused on taste alone.[4]

The unique sensory quality of a product helps it to stand out from the competition, especially if the brand creates a unique association with the sensation. The Owens-Corning Fiberglass Corporation was the first company to trademark a color when it used bright pink for its insulation material; it adopted the Pink Panther as its spokescharacter.[5] Harley-Davidson actually tried to trademark the distinctive sound a "hog" makes when it revs up. These responses are an important part of **hedonic consumption**: multisensory, fantasy, and emotional aspects of consumers' interactions with products.[6]

OBJECTIVE 2
The design of a product is now a key driver of its success or failure.

Hedonic Consumption and the Design Economy

In recent years, the sensory experiences we receive from products and services play an even bigger role when we choose among competing options. As manufacturing costs go down and the amount of "stuff" that people accumulate goes up, consumers increasingly want to buy things that will provide hedonic value in addition to simply doing what they're designed to do. A *Dilbert* comic strip poked fun at this trend when it featured a product designer who declared: "Quality is yesterday's news. Today we focus on the emotional impact of the product." Fun aside, the new focus on emotional experience is consistent with psychological research finding that people prefer additional experiences to additional possessions as their incomes rise.[7]

In this environment, form *is* function. Two young entrepreneurs named Adam Lowry and Eric Ryan discovered that basic truth when they quit their day jobs to develop a line of house-cleaning products they called Method. Cleaning products—what a yawn, right?

Think again: For years companies such as Procter & Gamble have plodded along, peddling boring boxes of soap powder to generations of housewives who suffered in silence, scrubbing and buffing, yearning for the daily respite of martini time. Lowry and Ryan gambled that they could offer an alternative: cleaners in exotic scents such as

MyMarketingLab
Visit **www.mymktlab.com** to test your understanding of chapter objectives.

cucumber, lavender, and ylang-ylang that come in aesthetically pleasing bottles. The bet paid off. Within 2 years, the partners were cleaning up, taking in more than $2 million in revenue. Shortly thereafter, they hit it big when Target contracted to sell Method products in its stores.[8]

There's a method to Target's madness. Design is no longer the province of upper-crust sophisticates who never got close enough to a cleaning product to be revolted by it. The store chain helped to make designers such as Karim Rashid, Michael Graves, Philippe Starck, Todd Oldham, and Isaac Mizrahi household names. In fact, recent research evidence suggests that our brains are wired to appreciate good design: Respondents who were hooked up to a brain apparatus called an fMRI (functional magnetic resonance imaging) scanner showed faster reaction times when they saw aesthetically pleasing packages even compared to well-known brands like Coca-Cola.[9] Mass-market consumers thirst for great design, and they reward those companies that give it to them with their enthusiastic patronage and loyalty. From razor blades such as the Gillette Sensor to the Apple iPad2 and even to the lowly trash can, design *is* substance. Form *is* function.

OBJECTIVE 3

Products and commercial messages often appeal to our senses, but because of the profusion of these messages most of them won't influence us.

Sensory Marketing

When guests at Omni luxury hotels visit the hotel chain's Web site to reserve a room, they hear the sound of soft chimes playing. The signature scent of lemongrass and green tea hits them as they enter the lobby. In their rooms, they will find eucalyptus bath salts and Sensation Bars, minibars stocked with items such as mojito-flavored jelly beans, and miniature Zen gardens.

Welcome to the new era of **sensory marketing**, where companies pay extra attention to the impact of sensations on our product experiences. From hotels to carmakers to brewers, they recognize that our senses help us decide which products appeal to us—and which ones stand out from a host of similar offerings in the marketplace. In this section, we'll take a closer look at how some smart marketers use our sensory systems to create a competitive advantage.

Sensory marketing emphasizes the link between our senses and product experiences.
Source: Courtesy of Coway USA.

CB AS I SEE IT

Professor Aradhna Krishna, *University of Michigan*

What is *sensory marketing*, what makes it important, and why is it so fascinating? I define it as "marketing that engages the consumers' senses and affects their behavior." The sensory characteristics of products such as the touch, smell, taste, sound, and look of products have a large impact on consumer behavior. These sensory inputs affect how we feel, how we think, what we remember, what we like, and even how we choose and use products. Specifically, by emphasizing the sensory characteristics of products and services, or even creating new sensations entirely, we can greatly enhance consumers' attitudes, perceptions, and satisfaction.

This concept of sensory marketing has received great attention from many top companies. Advertising within the food industry alone provides some illustrative examples, as companies try to incorporate more senses than just taste into their product experiences. A new brand of chewing gum that produces a seemingly one-dimensional sensory experience (taste) is named "5" for all five senses, and the tagline reiterates this approach ("stimulate your senses"). Other examples include ads for Magnum 5 Senses Ice Cream and Denny's breakfast ("taste it with all five senses"). Other products that provide a single sensory experience also try to stimulate the other senses. Axe Dark Temptation deodorant spray is advertised with an irresistible chocolate man that appeals to all the girls ("Become as irresistible as chocolate"). Even electronic products want to stimulate our senses, with names like BlackBerry, Chocolate, and Touch.

With this increasing attention to sensory marketing, products and businesses need to act quickly to establish a **sensory signature**. Managers need to ask themselves, "Is there something about my brand that leaves a sensory impression in people's mind?" What sensory characteristic of the product sticks with consumers, helping them to remember the product in a positively unique way? Do they emphasize a sensory experience with the product, or have they constructed a new one entirely? Do they own a sensory experience and thus establish a sensory signature? A terrific example of a company with a definitive sensory signature, and consequently one of the most commonly cited by consultants in this area, is Singapore Airlines. The airline focuses on creating a distinct visual signature, but perhaps more interesting and memorable is its signature aroma, Floridian Waters. This fragrance was developed specifically for use by Singapore Airlines, and is infused into their hot towels, dispersed throughout the planes, and even worn by flight attendants. The smell is not only invigorating; it also remains in passengers' minds, leading to positive responses upon future exposure to the aroma.

Sensory signatures are just one aspect of sensory marketing. Managers need to look at their offerings and ask themselves whether they can emphasize any sensory aspect of the product to make the product more appealing or create a new sensation completely. An example of the latter is Dippin' Dots: The company's Web site claims that *"After overcoming the sight of their ice cream beads 'pouring' into a cup there's the look of amazement that ice cream can be 'tingly and almost crunchy' [their words!]. When the smooth, creamy ice cream begins to melt in their mouth . . . a fan is born!"* Another example is the new fish spas that are opening all over the world, where tiny fish bite the dead skin off customers' feet and offer a different type of pedicure. There's more than one path to a distinctive sensory experience!

Vision

Sure, Apple's products usually work pretty well—but that's not why many people buy them. Sleek styling and simple, compact features telegraph an aura of modernity, sophistication, and just plain "cool." Marketers rely heavily on visual elements in advertising, store design, and packaging. They communicate meanings on the *visual channel* through a product's color, size, and styling.

Colors may even influence our emotions more directly. Evidence suggests that some colors (particularly red) create feelings of arousal and stimulate appetite, and others (such as blue) create more relaxing feelings. American Express launched its Blue card after its research found that people describe the color as "providing a sense of limitlessness and peace."[10] Advertisements of products presented against a backdrop of blue are better liked than the same ads shown against a red background, and cross-cultural research indicates a consistent preference for blue whether people live in Canada or Hong Kong.[11]

In Western culture the color black is often associated with sophistication while white connotes innocence.

Source: Used with permission of the San Francisco Ballet.

People who complete tasks when the words or images appear on red backgrounds perform better when they have to remember details, whereas they excel at tasks requiring an imaginative response when the words or images are displayed on blue backgrounds. Olympic athletes who wear red uniforms are more likely to defeat competitors in blue uniforms, and men rate women who wear red as more attractive than those who wear blue. In one study, interior designers created bars decorated primarily in red, yellow, or blue and invited people to choose one to hang out in. More people chose the yellow and red rooms, and these guests were more social and active—and ate more. But, partygoers in the blue room stayed longer.[12] Maybe the moral is: Get your prof to give you multiple-choice exams on red paper, essays on blue paper, and then celebrate afterward in a red room!

Some reactions to color come from learned associations. In Western countries, black is the color of mourning, whereas in some Eastern countries, notably Japan, white plays this role. In addition, we associate the color black with power. Teams in both the National Football League and the National Hockey League who wear black uniforms are among the most aggressive; they consistently rank near the top of their leagues in penalties during the season.[13]

Other reactions are a result of biological and cultural differences. Women are drawn toward brighter tones and they are more sensitive to subtle shadings and patterns. Some scientists attribute this to biology; females see color better than males do, and men are 16 times more likely to be color-blind. Age also influences our responsiveness to color. As we get older, our eyes mature and our vision takes on a yellow cast. Colors look duller to older people, so they prefer white and other bright tones. This helps to explain why mature consumers are much more likely to choose a white car; Lexus, which sells heavily in this market, makes 60 percent of its vehicles in white. The trend toward brighter and more complex colors also reflects the increasingly multicultural makeup of the United States. For example, Hispanics tend to prefer brighter colors as a reflection of the intense lighting conditions in Latin America; strong colors keep their character in strong sunlight.[14] That's why Procter & Gamble uses brighter colors in makeup it sells in Latin countries.[15]

Scientists and philosophers have talked about the meanings of colors since the time of Socrates in the 5th century B.C., but it took Sir Isaac Newton in the early 17th century to shine light through a prism and reveal the color spectrum. Even then, Newton's observations weren't totally scientific; he identified seven major colors to be consistent with the number of planets known at that time, as well as the seven notes of the diatonic scale.

We now know that perceptions of a color depend on both its physical wavelength and how the mind responds to that stimulus. Yellow is in the middle of wavelengths the human eye can detect, so it is the brightest and attracts attention. The *Yellow Pages* originally were colored yellow to heighten the attention level of bored telephone operators.[16] However, our culture and even our language affect the colors we see. For example, the Welsh language has no words that correspond to green, blue, gray, or brown in English, but it uses other colors that English speakers don't (including one that covers part of green, part of gray, and the whole of our blue). Hungarian has two words for what we call red; Navajo has a single word for blue and green, but two words for black.[17]

Because colors elicit such strong emotional reactions, obviously the choice of a *color palette* is a key issue in package design. These choices used to be made casually. For example, Campbell's Soup made its familiar can in red and white because a company executive liked the football uniforms at Cornell University!

Today, however, color choices are a serious business. These decisions help to "color" our expectations of what's inside the package. When it launched a white cheese as a "sister product" to an existing blue "Castello" cheese, a Danish company introduced it in a red package under the name of Castello Bianco. They chose this color to provide maximum visibility on store shelves. Although taste tests were very positive, sales were disappointing. A subsequent analysis of consumer interpretations showed that the red packaging and the name gave the consumers wrong associations with the product type and its degree of sweetness. Danish consumers had trouble associating the color red with the white cheese. Also, the name "Bianco" connoted a sweetness that was incompatible with the actual taste of the product. The company relaunched it in a white package and named it "White Castello." Almost immediately, sales more than doubled.[18]

Some color combinations come to be so strongly associated with a corporation that they become known as the company's **trade dress**, and the company may even be granted exclusive use of these colors. For example, Eastman Kodak has successfully protected its trade dress of yellow, black, and red in court. As a rule, however, judges grant trade dress protection only when consumers might be confused about what they buy because of similar coloration of a competitor's packages.[19]

Of course, fashion trends strongly influence our color preferences, so it's no surprise that we tend to encounter a "hot" color on clothing and in home designs in one season that something else replaces the next season (as when the *fashionistas* proclaim, "Brown is the new black!"). These styles do not happen by accident; most people don't know (but now *you* do) that a handful of firms produce *color forecasts* that manufacturers and retailers buy so they can be sure they stock up on the next hot hue. For example, Pantone, Inc. (one of these color arbiters), listed these colors as among its favorites for Fall 2011 women's fashions:[20]

- Bamboo: Like a filtered sunset on the waning days of fall, Bamboo is a standout yellow with a subtle green undertone.
- Honeysuckle: This playful, reddish pink works with any other color in the palette, especially fall staples like Coffee Liqueur and Nougat.
- Phlox: A magical, deep purple with a hint of mystery.

Dollars and Scents

Odors stir emotions or create a calming feeling. They invoke memories or relieve stress. Perhaps that explains why a French perfume company recently launched a Sex Pistols scent to commemorate the punk rocker band that created a cult following in the 1970s.[21] One study found that consumers who viewed ads for either flowers or chocolate and who also were exposed to flowery or chocolaty odors spent more time processing the product information and were more likely to try different alternatives within each product category.[22] Another reported that subjects showed higher recall of a test brand's attributes if it was embedded with a scent—and this effect persisted as long as two weeks after the experiment.[23]

Many consumers control the odors in their environments, and this growing interest has spawned a lot of new products since Glade marketed the first air freshener to suburban families in 1956. Today, younger people are at the forefront of scented air as they take advantage of plug-ins, fragrance fans, diffusers, and potpourri. Almost anything is fair game to be scented today; even the country of Lithuania created a perfume (appropriately called "Lithuania") that it will use in embassies, hotels, and other public buildings to convey the country's image. In addition to a blend of sandalwood, cedar, and musk, the designer noted that the fragrance carries the smell of wood fires that is intended to remind users of pagan rituals.[24] Then again, for awhile Burger King sold Flame, a body spray with "the scent of seduction" and a "hint of flame broiled meat."[25]

Some of our responses to scents result from early associations that call up good or bad feelings, and that explains why businesses explore connections among smell, memory, and mood.[26] Researchers for Folgers found that for many people the smell of coffee summons up childhood memories of their mothers cooking breakfast, so the aroma reminds them of home.

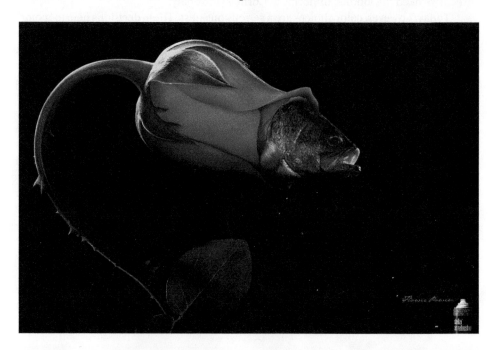

A Thai scent control product.
Source: Courtesy of McCann Worldgroup, Thailand.

The company turned this insight into a commercial in which a young man in an army uniform arrives home early one morning. He goes to the kitchen, opens a Folgers' package and the aroma wafts upstairs. His mother opens her eyes, smiles, and exclaims, "He's home!"[27]

Speaking of coffee, Starbucks recently reverted to its old policy that requires *baristas* to grind a batch of coffee beans each time they brew a new pot instead of just once each morning. The idea is to reclaim lost customers by intensifying the smell of the beans when they enter the store. As the chain grew and adopted more efficient techniques that automated the process, the chain's founder reversed course. He declared that a switch to preground coffee had taken the "romance and theatre" out of a trip to Starbucks: "We achieved fresh-roasted bagged coffee, but at what cost? The loss of aroma—perhaps the most powerful nonverbal signal we had in our stores."[28]

We process fragrance cues in the *limbic system,* the most primitive part of the brain and the place where we experience immediate emotions. One study even found that the scent of fresh cinnamon buns induced sexual arousal in a sample of male students![29] In another study, women sniffed T-shirts that men had worn for 2 days (wonder how much they paid them to do that?) and reported which they preferred. The women were most attracted to the odor of men who are genetically similar to themselves, though not *too* similar. The researchers claimed the findings were evidence that we are "wired" to select compatible mates, but not those so similar as to cause inbreeding problems.[30]

As scientists continue to discover the powerful effects of smell on behavior, marketers come up with ingenious ways to exploit these connections. Ad companies spend about $80 million per year on scent marketing; the Scent Marketing Institute estimates that number will reach more than $500 million by 2016.[31] This form of *sensory marketing* takes interesting turns as manufacturers find new ways to put scents into products, including men's suits, lingerie, detergents, and aircraft cabins.

The classic, contoured Coca-Cola bottle also attests to the power of touch. The bottle was designed approximately 90 years ago to satisfy the request of a U.S. bottler for a soft-drink container that people could identify even in the dark.
Source: © Rufus Stone/Alamy.

Sound

Coca-Cola chose an obscure Somalian musician named N-Kaan and made his song *Wavin' Flag* the centerpiece of its $300 million global advertising campaign linked to the 2010 World Cup. The company rerecorded the song in more than 20 regional flavors that included duets with local musicians (the U.S. version featured David Guetta and Will I Am). The tune became embedded with the world games as people around the world found themselves singing it. As a music industry executive explained, "Coke has used a technique we call **audio watermarking.** This is a popular and well-known trick that has been around for centuries and used by composers and producers to weave a sound/motif into a piece of music . . . [W]atermarking acts like an 'earworm,' which gets inside our brains and becomes so compulsive that we go around humming it as we walk down the street and not understanding why. We effectively become living, walking, singing commercials for Coke."[32]

Music and other sounds affect people's feelings and behaviors. Some marketers who come up with brand names pay attention to **sound symbolism**, the process by which the way a word sounds influences our assumptions about what it describes and attributes such as size. For example, consumers are more likely to recognize brand names that begin with a hard consonant like a K (Kellogg's) or P (Pepsi). We also tend to associate certain vowel and consonant sounds (or **phonemes**) with perceptions of large and small size. Mental rehearsal of prices containing numbers with small phonemes results in overestimation of price discounts, whereas mental rehearsal of prices containing numbers with large phonemes results in underestimation.[33]

Touch

Hint to retailers: Follow Apple's lead and encourage customers to handle your products in the store! One recent study demonstrated the potential power of touch: The researchers found that participants who simply touched an item (an inexpensive coffee mug) for 30 seconds or less created a greater level of attachment to the product; this connection in turn boosted what they were willing to pay for it.[34] Britain's Asda grocery chain removed the wrapping from several brands of toilet tissue in its stores so that shoppers could feel and compare textures. The result, the retailer says, was soaring sales for its own in-store brand, resulting in a 50-percent increase in shelf space for the line.[35]

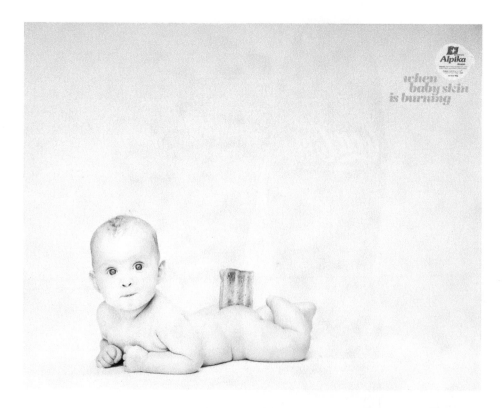

A Polish diaper rash cream.
Source: Courtesy of McCann Erickson Polska.

Sensations that reach the skin, whether from a luxurious massage or the bite of a winter wind, stimulate or relax us. Researchers even have shown that touch can influence sales interactions. In one study, diners whom wait staff touched gave bigger tips, and the same researchers reported that food demonstrators in a supermarket who lightly touched customers had better luck in getting shoppers to try a new snack product and to redeem coupons for the brand.[36] Another study showed that even the type of flooring in a store can influence how shoppers evaluate merchandise: soft carpeting creates a relaxed mood, whereas hard tile flooring causes fatigue that may result in harsher opinions.[37]

Some anthropologists view touch much like a primal language, one we learn well before writing and speech. Indeed, researchers are starting to identify the important role the **haptic** (touch) sense plays in consumer behavior. Haptic senses appear to moderate the relationship between product experience and judgment confidence. This confirms the commonsense notion that we're more sure about what we perceive when we can touch it (a major problem for those who sell products online). Individuals who score high on a "Need for Touch" (NFT) scale are especially influenced by the haptic dimension. Those with a high need for touch respond positively to such statements as:

- When walking through stores, I can't help touching all kinds of products.
- Touching products can be fun.
- I feel more comfortable purchasing a product after physically examining it.[38]

The Japanese take this idea a step farther with their practice of **Kinsei engineering**, a philosophy that translates customers' feelings into design elements. In one application, the designers of the Mazda Miata focused on young drivers who saw the car as an extension of their body, a sensation they call "horse and rider as one." After extensive research they discovered that making the stick shift exactly 9.5 centimeters long conveys the optimal feeling of sportiness and control.[39] Similar thinking went into the driver's seat of the Chrysler 300C, which is designed to make you feel a bit taller. In auto-industry speak, the car has a higher *H-point*, which refers to the location of the seated driver's hip. The change was prompted by the popularity of SUVs, pickups, and minivans that make drivers feel they are riding high on the highway. Ford calls its version "Command Seating" to reinforce the feeling of power it wants drivers to feel as they look down on all those little vehicles buzzing around below them.[40]

We have a tendency to want to touch objects, although typing or using a mouse are skills we have to learn. The proliferation of touchscreens on computers, ATM machines, digital cameras, GPS devices, and e-readers is an outgrowth of a philosophy of computer design known as **natural user interface**. This approach incorporates habitual human movements that we don't have to learn. Sony decided to offer touchscreens on its e-readers after its engineers repeatedly observed people in focus groups automatically swipe the screen of its older, nontouch models. Touchscreens also appear on exercise machines, in hospitals, at airport check-in terminals, and on Virgin America airplanes.[41]

Source: grafvision/shutterstock.com.

Taste

Our taste receptors obviously contribute to our experience of many products. So-called "flavor houses" develop new concoctions to please the changing palates of consumers. Scientists are right behind them as they build new devices to test these flavors. Alpha M.O.S. sells a sophisticated electronic tongue for tasting, and the company is working on what its executives call an electronic mouth, complete with artificial saliva, to chew food and to dissect its flavor. Coca-Cola and PepsiCo use the tongue to test the quality of corn syrups, whereas Bristol-Myers Squibb and Roche use the device to devise medicines that don't taste bitter.[42]

Cultural factors also determine the tastes we find desirable. A food item's image and the values we attach to it (such as how vegans regard beef menu items, which is not

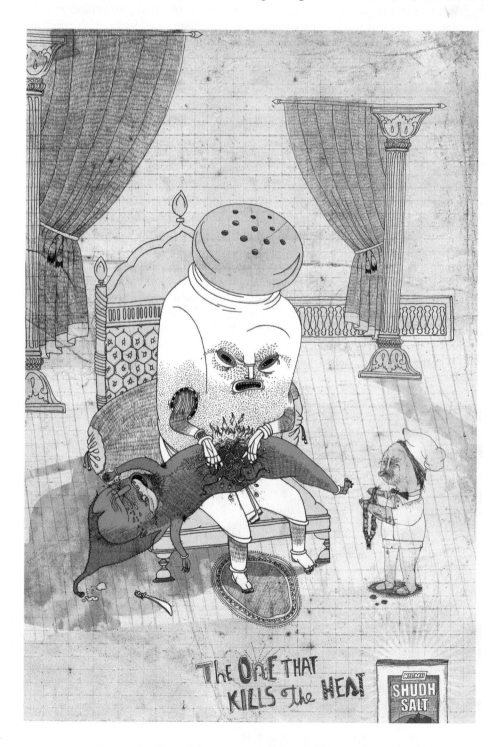

In India salt combats the sensory assault of spicy food.

Source: Courtesy of Taproot India. Contributors: Santosh Padhi, Agnello Dias, Pranan Bhide, and Chintan Ruparel.

kindly) influence how we experience the actual taste.[43] For example, consumers' greater appreciation of different ethnic dishes contributes to increased desires for spicy foods, so the quest for the ultimate pepper sauce continues. More than 50 stores in the United States supply fiery concoctions with names such as Sting and Linger, Hell in a Jar, and Religious Experience (comes in Original, Hot, and Wrath).[44]

Exposure

Exposure occurs when a stimulus comes within the range of someone's sensory receptors. Consumers concentrate on some stimuli, are unaware of others, and even go out of their way to ignore some messages. We notice stimuli that come within range for even a very short time—*if* we so choose. However, getting a message noticed in such a short time (or even in a longer one) is no mean feat. Before we consider what else people may choose not to perceive, let's consider what they are *capable* of perceiving.

OBJECTIVE 4

The concept of a sensory threshold is important for marketing communication.

Sensory Thresholds

If you have ever blown a dog whistle and watched your pooch respond to a sound you cannot hear, you won't be surprised to learn that there are some stimuli that people simply can't perceive. Some of us pick up sensory information that others whose sensory channels have diminished due to disability or age cannot. **Psychophysics** is the science that focuses on how the physical environment is integrated into our personal, subjective world.

The Absolute Threshold

When we define the lowest intensity of a stimulus our brains can register on a sensory channel, we speak of its *threshold.* It sounds like a great name for a rock band, but the **absolute threshold** refers to the minimum amount of stimulation a person can detect on a given sensory channel. The sound a dog whistle emits is at too high a frequency for human ears to pick up, so this stimulus is beyond our auditory absolute threshold. The absolute threshold is an important consideration when we design marketing stimuli. A highway billboard might have the most entertaining copy ever written, but this genius is wasted if the print is too small for passing motorists to see it.

The Differential Threshold

The **differential threshold** refers to the ability of a sensory system to detect changes in or differences between two stimuli. The minimum difference we can detect between two stimuli is the **j.n.d. (just noticeable difference).**

The issue of when and if consumers will notice a difference between two stimuli is relevant to many marketing situations. Sometimes a marketer may want to ensure that consumers notice a change, as when a retailer offers merchandise at a discount. In other situations, the marketer may want to downplay the fact that it has made a change, such as when a store raises a price or a manufacturer reduces the size of a package (see the "CB as I See It" box on reference prices).

A consumer's ability to detect a difference between two stimuli is relative. A whispered conversation that might be unintelligible on a noisy street can suddenly become public and embarrassingly loud in a quiet library. It is the *relative difference* between the decibel level of the conversation and its surroundings, rather than the absolute loudness of the conversation itself, that determines whether the stimulus will register.

In the 19th century, a psychophysicist named Ernst Weber found that the amount of change required for the perceiver to notice a change systematically relates to the intensity of the original stimulus. The stronger the initial stimulus, the greater a change must be for us to notice it. This relationship is known as **Weber's Law.**

Consider how Weber's Law works for a product when it goes on sale. If a retailer believes that a markdown should be at least 20 percent for the reduction to make an

Marketing Pitfall

As recession lingers and the cost of raw materials skyrockets due to shortages caused by natural disasters like the Tokyo earthquake and manmade ones like the conflict in the Middle East, some companies try to camouflage price increases by shrinking the size of packages instead of charging more. Sometimes marketers use code words to announce a change: they may label the smaller packages as greener because there is less plastic or cardboard in a smaller box, more "portable" when they squeeze products into little carry bags, or "healthier" because smaller amounts translate into fewer calories. For example, Kraft brought out "Fresh Stacks" packages for its Nabisco Premium saltines and Honey Maid graham crackers. Each holds about 15 percent fewer crackers than the standard boxes for the same price. But, Kraft notes that since the new packages include more sleeves of crackers, they are more portable—and the company notes that as an added benefit the smaller boxes supply crackers that will be fresher when you get around to eating them. A packaging expert noted that typically, when the economy recovers, companies respond with a new "jumbo" size product that is usually even more expensive per ounce. Then the process begins again: "It's a continuous cycle, where at some point the smallest package offered becomes so small that perhaps they're phased out and replaced by the medium-size package, which has been shrunk down."[52]

CB AS I SEE IT

Professor Larry Compeau, *Clarkson University*

Surveys consistently show that consumers consider price the most important factor when they buy, but marketers too often view price merely as an economic variable—that is, the amount of money the consumer must sacrifice to obtain the product. Years of recent research, however, show us that consumers regard price as more than simply the cost of a product.[45] To truly understand price, we need to think of it as an information stimulus, like color, aroma, and other more traditional stimuli we interpret. How consumers respond to and use price in their perceptual processes has been the focus of recent research. This research considers price as an information cue that is perceived and interpreted (attaching meaning to it). We call this area of research **behavioral pricing**.

One stream of behavioral pricing research looks at price as an information cue we use to judge a product.[46] You've certainly heard the old adage "You get what you pay for," which may or may not be true depending on the circumstances. Nonetheless, when consumers don't have other information on which they can rely, they often use price as an indicator of quality. In this sense, price is an important information source consumers use to help them decide among product options.

When we conceptualize price as an information cue or stimulus, then we must also accept the fact that price is subject to the same types of perceptual processes that lead to different judgments depending on the context. A common strategy sellers use in providing contextual information for consumers is to present a **reference price** along with the selling price.

This refers to a price against which buyers compare the actual selling price. Marketers usually present it in price advertisements, on price tickets, or even on store displays. When an item goes on sale and the old price and the new price are available to ascertain the savings, this price information is informative and helps the consumer. A reference price communicates the value of the deal to the buyer. But if a seller knows that consumers rely on semantic cues to assess the deal, the seller can alter the cue information to enhance the deal's attractiveness:

Which is the better deal on an LCD television?

- Product A: 47-inch, 1080p, high definition—regular price: $2,499; sale price: $1,499
- Product B: 47-inch, 1080p, high definition—regular price: $1,799; sale price: $1,499

Like most consumers, you probably picked product A. Why? To make your decision, you used the reference prices. Getting a $2,500 television for $1,500 is a better deal than getting a $1,800 television for $1,500—you save more, and you get a better television, right? What if the televisions are identical? Using higher reference prices, sellers can get consumers to increase their perceptions of the value of the deal, when in fact the deal is not better.[47] When this happens, consumers are more likely to purchase that item and less likely to shop around.[48]

Important public policy implications (i.e., government rules and regulations) arise from research on reference pricing.[49] We must consider how to protect consumers from deceptive practices, such as exaggerating reference prices, and this research plays a critical role in determining if deception occurs and what can be done about it.[50]

impact on shoppers, she should cut the price on a pair of socks that retails for $10 to $8 (a $2 discount) for shoppers to realize a difference. However, a sports coat that sells for $100 would not benefit from a $2 discount; the retailer would have to mark it down $20 to achieve the same impact.

Weber's Law, ironically, is a challenge to green marketers who try to reduce the sizes of packages when they produce concentrated (and more earth-friendly) versions of their products. Makers of laundry detergent brands have to convince their customers to pay the same price for about half the detergent. Also, because of pressure from powerful retailers such as Walmart that want to fit more bottles on their shelves, the size of detergent bottles is shrinking significantly. Procter & Gamble, Unilever, and Henkel all maintain that their new concentrated versions will allow people to wash the same number of loads with half the detergent. One perceptual trick they're using to try to convince consumers of this is the redesign of the bottle cap: Both P&G and Church & Dwight use a cap with a broader base and shorter sides to persuade consumers that they need a smaller amount.[51]

PEPSI 1898:

PEPSI 1905:

PEPSI 1906:

PEPSI 1940:

PEPSI 1950:

PEPSI 1962:

PEPSI 1974:

PEPSI 1987:

PEPSI 1991:

PEPSI 1998:

PEPSI 2003:

PEPSI 2006:

PEPSI 2009:

Figure 2 THE PEPSI LOGO OVER TIME
Source: PEPSI-COLA, PEPSI, PEPSI THROWBACK, the Pepsi Globe Design, the Pepsi Globe, Character Design are registered trademarks of PepsiCo, Inc. Used with permission.

Augmented Reality

Perceptual thresholds become even more interesting as we enter the new age of **augmented reality (AR).** This term refers to media that combine a physical layer with a digital layer to create a combined experience. If you've ever watched a 3D movie with those clunky glasses, you've experienced one form of augmented reality. Or, if you've seen that yellow line in an NFL game that shows the first down marker, you've also encountered AR in a simple form.

More likely, though, in the next few years you'll live in AR through your smartphone. New apps like Google Goggles (for Android phones) and Layar (for Android and Apple devices) impose a layer of words and pictures on whatever you see in your phone's viewer.

Augmented reality apps open new worlds of information (and marketing communications). Do you want to know the bio of the singer you see on a CD cover? Who painted that cool mural in your local bar? How much did that house you were looking at sell for last month? Just point your smartphone at each and the information will be superimposed on your screen.[53]

Web-Based AR

These techniques use your PC and webcam to offer an enhanced experience, often via a marker or image, or through motion capture. For example, the Fashionista dressing-room app you'll find in the online fashion boutique Tobi lets you "virtually" try on clothing items using your webcam and a marker on a printed piece of paper.

Kiosk-Based AR

This is similar to web-based AR, but you can often find more powerful applications that use 3D or facial tracking. At a toy store, shoppers can hold up a boxed Lego set to an in-store kiosk, and the kiosk will show an image of them holding the put-together Lego creation. At several shopping malls, Chevrolet showcases its key brands in kiosks that let shoppers use a virtual "professional air sprayer" and their fingers to paint the car, then move on to choose the rims, tires, decorative stripes, and other elements. When visitors finish building their cars, they are handed a 6-inch by 9-inch card with an augmented reality marker on the back. The person holds the card up to a camera mounted on a 65-inch TV screen that reads the marker and creates a computer-generated 3D model of a Camaro. By moving the card, the customers can "drive" the car as they hear the engine roar.[54]

Mobile AR

These applications use the viewfinder on a mobile phone to access enhanced digital information. The iButterfly app that the Dentsu advertising agency created in Japan lets you track and find digital butterflies using your iPhone GPS and camera. Hold your iPhone camera up at designated spots and when you look at your surroundings through the camera, you'll see animated butterflies flapping by. Each iButterfly contains coupons for nearby businesses.[55] eBay's Fashion app "See It On" allows the user to virtually try on sunglasses in real time. The app uses facial recognition to identify users and apply virtual sunglasses to their video images. Users are able to adjust the fit, and choose different styles, frames, lenses, and colors, to find their perfect look. Within the app they can then browse through eBay to find the perfect pair at the perfect price.[56]

OBJECTIVE 5
Subliminal advertising is a controversial—but largely ineffective—way to talk to consumers.

Subliminal Perception

Most marketers want to create messages *above* consumers' thresholds so people will notice them. Ironically, a good number of consumers instead believe that marketers design many advertising messages so they be perceived unconsciously, or *below* the threshold of recognition. Another word for threshold is *limen,* and we term stimuli that fall below the limen *subliminal*. **Subliminal perception** refers to a stimulus below the level of the consumer's awareness.

Subliminal perception is a topic that has captivated the public for more than 50 years, despite the fact that there is virtually no proof that this process has *any* effect on consumer behavior. A survey of American consumers found that almost two-thirds believe in the existence of subliminal advertising, and more than one-half are convinced that this technique can get them to buy things they do not really want.[57] ABC rejected a Kentucky Fried Chicken (KFC) commercial that invited viewers to slowly replay the ad to find a secret message, citing the network's long-standing policy against subliminal advertising. KFC argued that the ad wasn't subliminal at all because the company told viewers about the message and how to find it. The network wasn't convinced.[58]

Like this KFC ad, most examples of subliminal advertising that people "discover" are not subliminal at all—on the contrary, the images are quite apparent. Remember, if you can see it or hear it, it's not subliminal; the stimulus is above the level of conscious awareness. Nonetheless, the continuing controversy about subliminal persuasion has been important in shaping the public's beliefs about advertisers' and marketers' abilities to manipulate consumers against their will.

Subliminal Messaging Techniques

Marketers supposedly send subliminal messages on both visual and aural channels. **Embeds** are tiny figures they insert into magazine advertising via high-speed photography or airbrushing. These hidden figures, usually of a sexual nature, supposedly exert strong but unconscious influences on innocent readers. Some limited evidence hints at the possibility that embeds can alter the moods of men when they're exposed to sexually suggestive subliminal images, but the effect (if any) is very subtle—and may even work in the opposite direction if this creates negative feelings among viewers.[59] To date, the only real impact of this interest in hidden messages is to sell more copies of "exposés" written by a few authors and to make some consumers (and students taking a consumer behavior class) look a bit more closely at print ads, perhaps seeing whatever their imaginations lead them to see.

The possible effects of messages hidden on sound recordings also fascinate many consumers. We can see one attempt to capitalize on subliminal auditory perception techniques in the growing market for self-help audios. CDs and tapes, which typically feature the sounds of crashing waves or other natural sounds, supposedly contain subliminal messages to help listeners stop smoking, lose weight, gain confidence, and so on. Despite the rapid growth of this market, there is little evidence that subliminal stimuli transmitted on the auditory channel can bring about desired changes in behavior.[60]

Does Subliminal Perception Work?

Some research by clinical psychologists suggests that subliminal messages can influence people under very specific conditions, though it is doubtful that these techniques would be of much use in most marketing contexts. For this kind of message to have a prayer of working, an advertiser has to tailor it specifically to an individual rather than the mass messages suitable for the general public.[61] The stimulus should also be as close to the liminal threshold as possible. Here are other discouraging factors:

- There are wide individual differences in threshold levels. For a message to avoid conscious detection by consumers who have low thresholds, it would have to be so weak that it would not reach those who have high thresholds.
- Advertisers lack control over consumers' distance and position from a screen. In a movie theater, for example, only a small portion of the audience would be in exactly the right seats to be exposed to a subliminal message.
- The viewer must pay absolute attention to the stimulus. People who watch a television program or a movie typically shift their attention periodically, and they might not even notice when the stimulus appears.

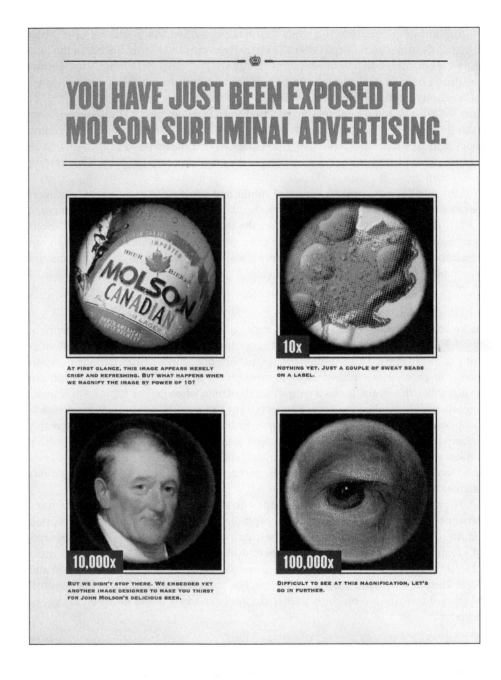

- Even if the advertiser induces the desired effect, it works only at a very general level. For example, a message might increase a person's thirst—but not necessarily for a specific drink. Because the stimulus just affects a basic drive, a marketer could find that after all the bother and expense of creating a subliminal message, demand for competitors' products increases as well!

Clearly, there are better ways to get our attention—let's see how.

Attention

As you sit in a lecture, you might find your mind wandering (yes, even you!). One minute you are concentrating on the professor's words, and the next you catch yourself day-dreaming about the upcoming weekend. Suddenly, you tune back in as you hear your

YOU MAY NOT BE AWARE OF IT, BUT RIGHT NOW YOUR SUBCONSCIOUS IS JONESING FOR A COLD, CRISP MOLSON. WHY? BECAUSE WE SLIPPED THROUGH THE BACK DOOR OF YOUR BRAIN AND PLANTED A FEW VISUAL CUES DEEP IN YOUR MIND. ANY OF THE IMAGES BELOW SEEM STRANGELY FAMILIAR?

100x

MAGNIFIED AT 100X HOWEVER, WE BEGIN TO SEE SOMETHING.

1,000x

AN IMAGE OF JOHN MOLSON PRINTED ON THE PAPER FIBER OF THE BEER LABEL. THOUGH MINUTE, YOUR BRAIN PICKED UP ON THIS SUBLIMINAL CUE TO A 219-YEAR HERITAGE OF BREWING GREAT-TASTING BEER.

1,000,000x

AH, THERE IT IS: AN IMAGE OF PEOPLE SOCIALIZING WITH AN ICE-COLD MOLSON.

10,000,000x

A MICROSCOPIC REMINDER THAT MOLSON HAS BEEN BRINGING FRIENDS TOGETHER SINCE 1786. SHOULD YOU SUDDENLY AWAKEN IN A CROWDED BAR ORDERING A ROUND OF MOLSON FOR EVERYONE, WE DID THAT. AND YOU'RE WELCOME.

name being spoken. Fortunately, it's a false alarm—the professor has called on another "victim" who has the same first name. But she's got your attention now.

Attention refers to the extent to which processing activity is devoted to a particular stimulus. As you know from sitting through both interesting and "less interesting" lectures, this allocation can vary depending on both the characteristics of the stimulus (i.e., the lecture itself) and the recipient (i.e., your mental state at the time).

Although we live in an "information society," we can have too much of a good thing. Consumers often are in a state of **sensory overload**, exposed to far more information than they can process. In our society, much of this bombardment comes from commercial sources, and the competition for our attention is steadily increasing. The average adult is exposed to about 3,500 pieces of advertising information every single day—up from about 560 per day 30 years ago.

This camera ad from Singapore reminds us that consumers tune out many stimuli that compete for their attention.
Source: Courtesy of Nikon/Euro RSCG/Singapore.

Marketing Pitfall

If you watch TV with a digital video recorder (DVR), you're 25 percent more likely to fast-forward past ads that don't interest you immediately. Another 25 percent of DVR users don't watch an entire commercial if it doesn't draw them in right away—no matter how entertaining it gets by the end. Ads that start out with a captivating story are more likely to hold an audience compared to those that get to the point more slowly. This finding may cast doubt on traditional ratings of advertisements where viewers in laboratory settings are forced to watch an entire commercial—in real life they may just zap through it.[62]

Multitasking and Attention

Getting the attention of young people in particular is a challenge—as your professor probably knows! As of 2010, more than half of teens report that they engage in **multitasking**, where they process information from more than one medium at a time as they attend to their cell phones, TVs, instant messages, and so on—and that's just during the time when they are doing homework![63] One study observed 400 people for a day and found that 96 percent of them were multitasking about a third of the time they used media.[64] Marketing researchers struggle to understand this new condition as they figure out how to reach people who do many things at once.

What impact does all this multitasking have on consumers' ability to absorb, retain, and understand information? One possible consequence: These bursts of stimulation provoke the body to secrete dopamine, which is addicting. When we go without these squirts, we feel bored. Some scientists warn that our cravings for more stimulation distract us from more prolonged thought processes and reduce our ability to concentrate (don't text and drive!). Studies find that heavy multitaskers have more trouble focusing, and they experience more stress. One study found that people interrupted by email reported significantly more stress than those who were allowed to focus on a task. The good news is that the brains of Internet users become more efficient at finding information, while some videogame players develop better eyesight. One team of researchers found that players of fast-paced video games can track the movement of a third more objects on a screen than nonplayers. They say the games can improve reaction and the ability to pick out details amid clutter. For better or worse, technology seems to be rewiring our brains to try to pay attention to more stimuli. Today we consume three times as much information each day as people did in 1960. We constantly shift attention: Computer users at work change windows or check email or other programs nearly 37 times an hour. Computer users visit an average of 40 Web sites a day.[65]

How Do Marketers Get Our Attention?

Marketers constantly search for ways to break through the clutter and grab people's attention. At times these efforts meet with mixed results:

- Networks try to engage viewers during commercial breaks when they wedge origi-nal content into the blocks of advertising time so that viewers will anticipate seeing something fun if they sit through a few ads. Fox Broadcasting televised a series of clips about an animated character named Oleg, a New York cab driver, who popped up in 8-second vignettes during commercial breaks in series such as *24*. In a Greek accent, Oleg urged viewers to visit Fox's Web site. In one clip, Oleg sang about himself to the Barry Manilow tune "Copacabana." In others, he drove celebrities such as Tom Cruise and Rosie O'Donnell. Although Oleg generated more than 100,000 Web-site hits on some nights, some viewers complained that he was an ethnic stereotype and others couldn't understand what he was saying—so Oleg is history. But it was a good idea in principle.[66]
- In the online world, advertisers are trying more tricks to get visitors to watch their messages. One of the most popular today is **rich media**—this technique uses move-ment to get viewers' attention. LowerMyBills.com is notorious for its endless loops of silhouetted dancers and surprised office workers, whereas other ads spring into action when you move the cursor over them. Other rich media are online versions of familiar TV commercials that sit frozen on the Web site until you click them. *Teaser ads*, much like those you see on TV that give you a taste of the story but make you return later for the rest, also turn up on Web sites.[67]
- Of course, a sure-fire way to grab our attention is to do something outrageous, or at least unusual, in a public place. To promote a new class at the New York Health and Racquet Club, six men and women stood outside the city's Grand Central Termi-nal flashing their underwear at strangers. The garments featured the club's logo and "Booty Call," the name of the class.

Because the brain's capacity to process information is limited, consumers are very selective about what they pay attention to. The process of **perceptual selection** means that people attend to only a small portion of the stimuli to which they are exposed. Con-sumers practice a form of "psychic economy," picking and choosing among stimuli to avoid being overwhelmed. How do they choose? Both personal and stimulus factors help to decide.

Personal Selection Factors

The actions of a Colorado judge illustrate how powerful our own tastes can be in deter-mining what we want to see and hear. He requires young people convicted of violating the city's noise ordinance to listen to music they don't like—including a heavy dose of such "favorites" as Wayne Newton, Dean Martin, and bagpipe recordings.[68] What, no Justin Bieber? **Experience,** which is the result of acquiring and processing stimulation over time, is one factor that determines how much exposure to a particular stimulus a person accepts. **Perceptual filters** based on our past experiences influence what we de-cide to process.

Perceptual vigilance is one such factor. Consumers are more likely to be aware of stimuli that relate to their current needs. A consumer who rarely notices car ads will be-come very much aware of them when she or he is in the market for a new car. A newspa-per ad for a fast-food restaurant that would otherwise go unnoticed becomes significant when one sneaks a glance at the paper in the middle of a five o'clock class.

Individual variations in perceptual processing may account for some differences. Indeed, one study reported that women are better than men in terms of their ability to identify visually incongruent products that are promoted among competing products. Females discriminate relational information among competing advertisements and use this information to identify incongruent products that would otherwise go unidentified.[69]

The flip side of perceptual vigilance is **perceptual defense**. This means that people see what they want to see—and don't see what they don't want to see. If a stimulus is threatening to us in some way, we may not process it, or we may distort its meaning so that it's more acceptable. For example, a heavy smoker may block out images of cancer-scarred lungs because these vivid reminders hit a bit too close to home.

Still another factor is **adaptation**, the degree to which consumers continue to notice a stimulus over time. The process of adaptation occurs when consumers no longer pay attention to a stimulus because it is so familiar. A consumer can "habituate" and require increasingly stronger "doses" of a stimulus to notice it. A commuter who is en route to work might read a billboard message when the board is first installed, but after a few days it simply becomes part of the passing scenery. Several factors can lead to adaptation:

- **Intensity**—Less-intense stimuli (e.g., soft sounds or dim colors) habituate because they have less sensory impact.
- **Duration**—Stimuli that require relatively lengthy exposure to be processed habituate because they require a long attention span.
- **Discrimination**—Simple stimuli habituate because they do not require attention to detail.
- **Exposure**—Frequently encountered stimuli habituate as the rate of exposure increases.
- **Relevance**—Stimuli that are irrelevant or unimportant habituate because they fail to attract attention.

Stimulus Selection Factors

In addition to the receiver's mindset, characteristics of the stimulus itself play an important role in determining what we notice and what we ignore. Marketers need to understand these factors so they can create messages and packages that will have a better chance of cutting through the clutter. For example, when researchers using infrared eye-tracking equipment measured what ads consumers look at, they found that visually complex ads are more likely to capture attention.[70]

In general, we are more likely to notice stimuli that differ from others around them (remember Weber's Law). A message creates **contrast** in several ways:

- **Size**—The size of the stimulus itself in contrast to the competition helps to determine if it will command attention. Readership of a magazine ad increases in proportion to the size of the ad.[71]
- **Color**—As we've seen, color is a powerful way to draw attention to a product or to give it a distinct identity. Black & Decker developed a line of tools it called DeWalt to target the residential construction industry. The company colored the new line yellow instead of black; this made the equipment stand out against other "dull" tools.[72]
- **Position**—Not surprisingly, we stand a better chance of noticing stimuli that are in places we're more likely to look. That's why the competition is so heated among suppliers to have their products displayed in stores at eye level. In magazines, ads that are placed toward the front of the issue, preferably on the right-hand side, also win out in the race for readers' attention. (Hint: The next time you read a magazine, notice which pages you're more likely to spend time looking at.)[73] A study that tracked consumers' eye movements as they scanned telephone directories also illustrates the importance of message position. Consumers scanned listings in alphabetical order, and they noticed 93 percent of quarter-page display ads but only 26 percent of plain listings. Their eyes were drawn to color ads first, and these were viewed longer than black-and-white ones. In addition, subjects spent 54 percent more time viewing ads for businesses they ended up choosing, which illustrates the influence of attention on subsequent product choice.[74]
- **Novelty**—Stimuli that appear in unexpected ways or places tend to grab our attention. One solution is to put ads in unconventional places, where there will be less competition for attention. These places include the backs of shopping carts, walls of tunnels, floors of sports stadiums, and yes, even public restrooms.[76] An outdoor advertising agency in London constructs huge ads in deserts and farm fields adjacent to

Figure 3 **GOLDEN TRIANGLE** Position is key in online advertising. Sophisticated eye-tracking studies clearly show that most search engine users find view only a very limited number of search results. When the typical shopper looks at a search page, her eye travels across the top of the search result, returns to the left of the screen, and then travels down to the last item shown on the screen without scrolling. Search engine marketers call this space on the screen where listings are virtually guaranteed to be viewed the **golden triangle**.[75]

Source: Enquiro Search Solutions, Inc. (Now Mediative Performance LP)

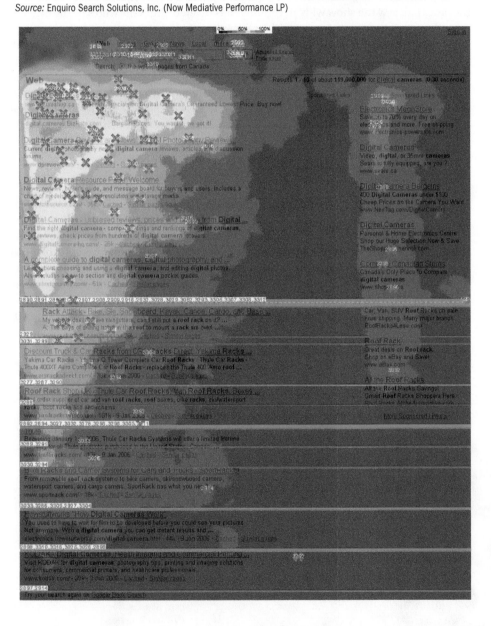

airports so that passengers who look out the window can't help but pay attention. It prints the digital ads on pieces of PVC mesh that sit on frames a few inches above the ground.[77] Other entrepreneurs equip billboards with tiny cameras that use software to determine that a person is standing in front of an outdoor ad. Then the program analyzes the viewer's facial features (like cheekbone height and the distance between the nose and the chin) to judge the person's gender and age. Once the software categorizes the passerby, it selects an advertisement tailored to this profile; for example, an Hispanic teenager sees a different message than the middle-aged Asian woman who walks behind him.[78]

Indeed, one study indicates that novelty in the form of interruptions actually *intensifies* our experiences; distraction increases our enjoyment of pleasant stimuli as it amplifies our dislike of unpleasant stimuli. In fact, the study reported that people actually enjoy TV shows *more* when commercials interrupt them. A group of undergraduates watched an episode of an old sitcom (*Taxi*) with which they were unfamiliar. Half viewed the original broadcast, which included ads for a jeweler, a lawyer, and other businesses; the other half saw the show with all commercials deleted. Students who saw the original actually gave it higher evaluations. The researchers found a similar pattern when they interrupted people who were getting a massage. In contrast, subjects reported that the irritating sound of a vacuum cleaner was even worse when they got a break from listening to it and then had to hear it resume! The researchers interpret these results as the outcome of adaptation: We experience events more intensely at first but then get used to them. When we experience an interruption and then start over, we revert to the original intensity level.[79]

OBJECTIVE 6
We interpret the stimuli to which we do pay attention according to learned patterns and expectations.

Interpretation

Interpretation refers to the meanings we assign to sensory stimuli. Just as people differ in terms of the stimuli that they perceive, the meanings we assign to these stimuli vary as well. Two people can see or hear the same event, but their interpretation of it can be as different as night and day, depending on what they had expected the stimulus to be. In one study, kids ages 3 to 5 who ate McDonald's French fries served in a McDonald's bag overwhelmingly thought they tasted better than those who ate the same fries out of a plain white bag. Even carrots tasted better when they came out of a McDonald's bag—more than half the kids preferred them to the same carrots served in a plain package! Ronald would be proud.[80]

A popular British retailer called French Connection relies on the priming process to evoke a response to its advertising by using an acronym that closely resembles another word.
Source: Used with permission TWBA London on behalf of French Connection.

CB AS I SEE IT

Prof. William E. Baker, *University of Akron*

Brand awareness and familiarity are important. Brands with high awareness are more likely to be in the consumers' consideration set. Brands that are familiar are more likely to be trusted. However, the first and most critical step in brand development may be **brand-name imprinting**.

A brand must own a niche in memory; a space that anchors it to a *specific* category (e.g., Porsche to sports car) or usage occasion (nighttime pain relief). Some researchers refer to this space as a "brand node." Weak imprinting occurs when the brand node is not clearly linked to a product category or usage occasion, *or* when it is linked to too broad a category (e.g., automobile) or usage situation (whenever you have pain).

Research has shown that if a new brand's name is imprinted by flashing it several times to consumers before they receive a presentation of the new brand's benefits, the information is better learned and linked to the brand than if the brand name is not imprinted prior to the presentation. Other research shows that if a brand node is ignited (i.e., cued) to memory by presenting the brand name/logo at the beginning of a video advertisement, the information that follows will be better linked to the brand than when the brand name is not revealed until the end of the advertisement.

The meaning we assign to a stimulus depends on the **schema**, or set of beliefs, to which we assign it. That helps to explain why Gary was so revolted at the thought of warm milk. In a process we call **priming**, certain properties of a stimulus evoke a schema. This in turn leads us to compare the stimulus to other similar ones we encountered in the past.

Identifying and evoking the correct schema is crucial to many marketing decisions, because this determines what criteria consumers will use to evaluate the product, package, or message. Extra Strength Maalox Whip Antacid flopped even though a spray can is a pretty effective way to deliver the product. To consumers, aerosol whips mean dessert toppings, not medication.[81] However, when a college cafeteria gave menu items descriptive labels (e.g., Red Beans with Rice versus Traditional Cajun Red Beans with Rice, Chocolate Pudding versus Satin Chocolate Pudding) so that diners had more information about each option and were able to better categorize them, sales increased by more than 25 percent.[82]

Even the location of a product's image on a package influences the way our brains make sense of it. For example, due to what we have learned about the law of gravity (heavy objects sink and light objects float), we assume that products that are lower down in a frame weigh more than products that appear higher in a frame. In addition, objects on the right of a frame appear heavier than products that appear on the left of a frame. This interpretation results from our intuition about levers: We know that the farther away an object is from a lever's fulcrum, the more difficult it is to raise the item. Because we read from left to right, the left naturally becomes the visual fulcrum and thus we perceive objects on the right as heavier. Manufacturers should bear these *package schematics* in mind, as they may influence our feelings about the contents in a package for better or worse. Think, for example, about a diet food marketer who wants shoppers to regard her menu items as lighter.[83]

Products often assume a "brand personality" because we tend to assign them common human traits such as sophistication or sexiness. In other words, we *anthropomorphize* objects when we think of them in human terms, and this thought process may encourage us to evaluate products using schemas we apply to classify other people. A recent study illustrates how this works: Subjects saw an advertisement with a picture of a car that had been modified to make it appear as though it was either "smiling" or "frowning." In some cases the text of the ad was written in the first person, to activate a human schema, while others saw the same ad written in the third person. When the human schema was active, those who saw the "smiling" car rated it more favorably than when they saw a "frowning" car.[84]

Stimulus Organization

One factor that determines how we will interpret a stimulus is the relationship we assume it has with other events, sensations, or images in memory. When RJR Nabisco introduced a version of Teddy Grahams (a children's product) for adults, it used understated packaging colors to reinforce the idea that the new product was for grown-ups. But sales were disappointing. Nabisco changed the box to bright yellow to convey the idea that this was a fun snack, and buyers' more positive association between a bright primary color and taste prompted adults to start buying the cookies.[85]

Our brains tend to relate incoming sensations to others already in memory, based on some fundamental organizational principles. These principles derive from *Gestalt psychology,* a school of thought which maintains that people interpret meaning from the *totality* of a set of stimuli rather than from any individual stimulus. The German word **Gestalt** roughly means *whole, pattern,* or *configuration,* and we summarize this term as "the whole is greater than the sum of its parts." A piecemeal perspective that analyzes each component of the stimulus separately can't capture the total effect. The *Gestalt* perspective provides several principles that relate to the way our brains organize stimuli:

- The **closure principle** states that people tend to perceive an incomplete picture as complete. That is, we tend to fill in the blanks based on our prior experience. This principle explains why most of us have no trouble reading a neon sign even if several of its letters are burned out. The principle of closure is also at work when we hear only part of a jingle or theme. Marketing strategies that use the closure principle encourage audience participation, which increases the chance that people will attend to the message.
- The **principle of similarity** tells us that consumers tend to group together objects that share similar physical characteristics. Green Giant relied on this principle when the company redesigned the packaging for its line of frozen vegetables. It created a "sea of green" look to unify all of its different offerings.

We recognize patterns of stimuli, such as familiar words. In this Austrian ad consumers will tend to see the word "kitchen" even though the letters are scrambled.
Source: Client: XXXLutz; Head of Marketing: Mag. Thomas Saliger; Agency: Demner, Merlicek & Bergmann; Account Supervisor: Andrea Kliment; Account Manager: Albin Lenzer; Creative Directors: Rosa Haider, Tolga Buyukdoganay; Art Directors: Tolga Buyukdoganay, Rene Pichler; Copywriter: Alistair Thompson.

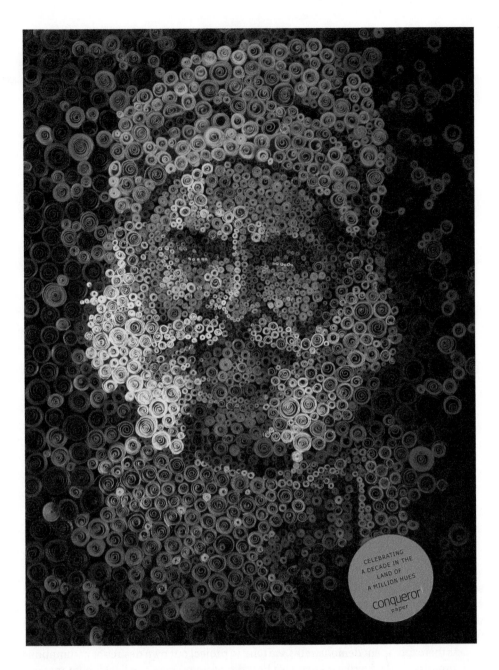

● The **figure-ground principle** states that one part of a stimulus will dominate (the *figure*), and other parts recede into the background (the *ground*). This concept is easy to understand if one thinks literally of a photograph with a clear and sharply focused object (the figure) in the center. The figure is dominant, and the eye goes straight to it. The parts of the configuration a person will perceive as figure or ground can vary depending on the individual consumer, as well as other factors. Similarly, marketing messages that use the figure-ground principle can make a stimulus the focal point of the message or merely the context that surrounds the focus.

The Eye of the Beholder: Interpretational Biases

The stimuli we perceive are often ambiguous. It's up to us to determine the meaning based on our past experiences, expectations, and needs. A classic experiment demonstrated the process of "seeing what you want to see": Princeton and Dartmouth students

The Australian postal service uses a unique application of the figure-ground principle.
Source: © M&C Saatchi, 2007.

If you really want to touch someone, send them a letter.

Part of every day

POST

separately viewed a movie of a particularly rough football game between the two rival schools. Although everyone was exposed to the same stimulus, the degree to which students saw infractions and the blame they assigned for those they did see depended on which college they attended.[86]

As this experiment demonstrates, we tend to project our own desires or assumptions onto products and advertisements. This interpretation process can backfire for marketers. Planters LifeSavers Company found this out when it introduced Planters Fresh Roast, a vacuum-packed peanuts package. The idea was to capitalize on consumers' growing love affair with fresh-roast coffee by emphasizing the freshness of the nuts in the same way. A great idea—until irate supermarket managers began calling to ask who was going to pay to clean the peanut gook out of their stores' coffee-grinding machines.[87]

Another experiment demonstrated how our assumptions influence our experiences; in this case, the study altered beer drinkers' taste preferences simply by telling them different stories about a specific brew's ingredients. The researcher offered bar patrons free beer if they would participate in a taste test (guess what: very few refused the offer). Participants tasted two beers each, one a regular draft of Budweiser or Samuel Adams and the other the same beer with a few drops of balsamic vinegar added. Although most beer *aficionados* would guess that vinegar makes the drink taste bad, in fact 60 percent of the respondents who did not know which beer contained the vinegar actually preferred the doctored version to the regular one! But when tasters knew in advance which beer had vinegar in it before they took a swig, only one-third preferred that version.[88]

OBJECTIVE 7

The field of semiotics helps us to understand how marketers use symbols to create meaning.

Semiotics: The Symbols around Us

As we've just seen, when we try to "make sense" of a marketing stimulus we interpret it in light of our prior associations. For this reason, much of the meaning we take away influences what we make of the symbolism we perceive. After all, on the surface many marketing images have virtually no literal connection to actual products. What does a cowboy have to do with a bit of tobacco rolled into a paper tube? How can a celebrity such as the basketball player LeBron James or the singer Rihanna enhance the image of a soft drink or a fast-food restaurant?

To help them understand how consumers interpret the meanings of symbols, some marketers turn to **semiotics**, a field that studies the correspondence between signs and symbols and their roles in how we assign meanings.[89] Semiotics is a key link to consumer behavior because consumers use products to express their social identities. Products carry learned meanings, and we rely on marketers to help us figure out what those meanings are. As one set of researchers put it, "Advertising serves as a kind of culture/consumption dictionary; its entries are products, and their definitions are cultural meanings."[90]

From a semiotic perspective, every marketing message has three basic components: an *object*, a *sign* (or symbol), and an *interpretant*. The **object** is the product that is the focus of the message (e.g., Marlboro cigarettes). The **sign** is the sensory image that represents the intended meanings of the object (e.g., the Marlboro cowboy). The **interpretant** is the meaning we derive from the sign (e.g., rugged, individualistic, American). Figure 4 diagrams this relationship.

According to semiotician Charles Sanders Peirce, signs relate to objects in one of three ways: They can resemble objects, connect to them, or tie to them conventionally. An **icon** is a sign that resembles the product in some way (e.g., the Ford Mustang has a galloping horse on the hood). An **index** is a sign that connects to a product because they share some property (e.g., the pine tree on some of Procter & Gamble's Spic and Span cleanser products conveys the shared property of fresh scent). A **symbol** is a sign that relates to a product by either conventional or agreed-on associations (e.g., the lion in Dreyfus Fund ads provides the conventional association with fearlessness and strength that it carries [or hopes to carry] over to the company's approach to investments).[91]

A lot of time, thought, and money go into creating brand names and logos that clearly communicate a product's image (even when a name like Exxon is generated by a computer!). In 2011, Starbucks removed the words Starbucks Coffee as it introduced a new

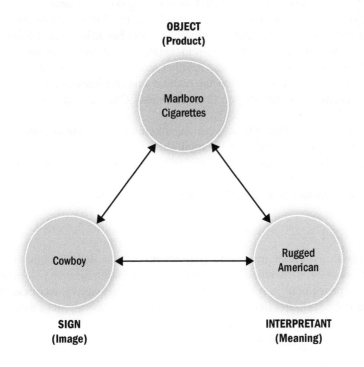

OBJECT
(Product)

Marlboro
Cigarettes

Cowboy

Rugged
American

SIGN
(Image)

INTERPRETANT
(Meaning)

Figure 4 SEMIOTIC RELATIONSHIPS

71

logo that features only the famous siren character. CEO Howard Schulz explained in an online video that this change means the company is thinking "beyond coffee."[92]

The choice of a logo is even more difficult when the brand has to travel across cultures. For example, as Chinese business becomes more global, companies refashion ancient Chinese pictograms into new corporate logos that resonate with both the East and the West. Chinese pictograms really are icons because the ancient symbols were once graphic depictions of the words they signify. For example, China Telecom's logo features two interlocking letter *C*s that together form the Chinese character for China but also represent the concept of "customer" and "competition," the firm's new focus. In addition, though, the symbol also resembles the horns of an ox, a hard-working animal. When the software company Oracle redesigned its logo for the Chinese market, it added three Chinese characters that signify the literal translation of the word *oracle:* "writing on a tortoise shell." The expression dates back to ancient China when mystics scrawled prophecies on bones. The California firm was enthusiastic about the translation because it conveyed Oracle's core competency—data storage.[93]

Hyperreality

One of the hallmarks of modern advertising is that it creates a condition of **hyperreality**. This refers to the process of making real what is initially simulation or "hype." Advertisers create new relationships between objects and interpretants when they invent new connections between products and benefits, such as when an ad equates Marlboro cigarettes with the American frontier spirit. In a hyperreal environment, over time it's no longer possible to discern the true relationship between the symbol and reality. The "artificial" associations between product symbols and the real world take on lives of their own. Here are some hyperreal sightings:

- A furniture designer launched a dining room set inspired by the TV series *Dexter*—the main character is a police blood splatter analyst who moonlights as a serial killer. The all-white table and chairs are festooned with big splotches of red.[95]
- "It's so easy even a caveman can do it." The "yuppie" cavemen from the insurance company GEICO's ad campaign became so popular that they actually spawned a (short-lived) TV sitcom.[96]

TV shows and movies incorporate real products on sets and in plotlines. **Reverse product placement** is a great example of hyperreality; in these cases fictional products that appear in shows become popular in the real world. The e-commerce site LastExitToNowhere.com sells T-shirts that bear the logos of companies featured in works of fiction. These include such made-up companies as Tyrell (the manufacturer of genetic replicants in the movie classic *Blade Runner*), Polymer Records (a music label in the cult movie *This Is Spinal Tap*), and the Weyland-Yutani Corporation (it made the spaceship freighter Nostromo in the *Alien* movies). Another online store—80sTees.com—proclaimed Duff beer, from *The Simpsons* TV show the number-one fake brand. Coming in second was Dunder Mifflin, the paper company on *The Office* series.[97] Other fake-to-real products include:

- Bertie Bott's Every Flavor Beans, which originated in the *Harry Potter* book series before the product moved to actual retail shelves.
- The movie *Forrest Gump* inspired the Bubba Gump Shrimp Company restaurant chain.
- Nestlé sells Wonka candy (from the *Willy Wonka* movie).[98]

Perceptual Positioning

So, we know that we often interpret a product stimulus in light of what we've learned about a product category and the characteristics of existing brands. Our perception of a brand comprises both its functional attributes (e.g., its features, its price, and so on) and its symbolic attributes (its image and what we think it says about us when we use it).

Last Exit to Nowhere sells T-shirts that bear the logos of companies featured in works of fiction.

Source: Images from LastExittoNowhere.com.

Our evaluation of a product typically is the result of what it means rather than what it does. This meaning—as consumers perceive it—constitutes the product's market position, and it may have more to do with our expectations of product performance as communicated by its color, packaging, or styling than with the product itself.

When a marketer understands how consumers think about a set of competing brands, it can use these insights to develop a **positioning strategy**, which is a fundamental component of a company's marketing efforts as it uses elements of the marketing mix (i.e., product design, price, distribution, and marketing communications) to influence the consumer's interpretation of its meaning in the marketplace relative to its competitors. For example, although consumers' preferences for the taste of one product over another are important, this functional attribute is only one component of product evaluation.

Marketers can use many dimensions to carve out a brand's position in the marketplace. These include:[99]

- **Lifestyle.** Grey Poupon mustard is a "higher-class" condiment.
- **Price leadership.** L'Oréal sells its Noisôme brand face cream in upscale beauty shops, whereas its Plenitude brand is available for one-sixth the price in discount stores—even though both are based on the same chemical formula.[100]

- **Attributes.** Bounty paper towels are "the quicker picker-upper."
- **Product class.** The Spyder Eclipse is a sporty convertible.
- **Competitors.** Northwestern Insurance is "the quiet company."
- **Occasions.** Wrigley's gum is an alternative at times when smoking is not permitted.
- **Users.** Levi's Dockers target men in their 20s to 40s.
- **Quality.** At Ford, "Quality is job 1."

CHAPTER SUMMARY

Now that you have finished reading this chapter, you should understand why:

1. Perception is a three-stage process that translates raw stimuli into meaning.

Perception is the process by which physical sensations, such as sights, sounds, and smells, are selected, organized, and interpreted. The eventual interpretation of a stimulus allows it to be assigned meaning. A perceptual map is a widely used marketing tool that evaluates the relative standing of competing brands along relevant dimensions.

2. The design of a product is now a key driver of its success or failure.

In recent years, the sensory experiences we receive from products and services have become a high priority when we choose among competing options. Consumers increasingly want to buy things that will give them hedonic value in addition to functional value. They often believe that most brands perform similarly, so they weigh a product's aesthetic qualities heavily when they select a brand.

3. Products and commercial messages often appeal to our senses, but because of the profusion of these messages most of them won't influence us.

Marketing stimuli have important sensory qualities. We rely on colors, odors, sounds, tastes, and even the "feel" of products when we evaluate them. Not all sensations successfully make their way through the perceptual process. Many stimuli compete for our attention, and we don't notice or accurately interpret the majority of them.

4. The concept of a sensory threshold is important for marketing communication.

People have different thresholds of perception. A stimulus must be presented at a certain level of intensity before our sensory detectors can detect it. In addition, a consumer's ability to detect whether two stimuli are different (the differential threshold) is an important issue in many marketing contexts, such as package design, the size of a product, or its price.

5. Subliminal advertising is a controversial—but largely ineffective—way to talk to consumers.

So-called subliminal persuasion and related techniques that expose people to visual and aural messages below the sensory threshold are controversial. Although evidence that subliminal persuasion is effective is virtually nonexistent, many consumers continue to believe that advertisers use this technique. Some of the factors that determine which stimuli (above the threshold level) do get perceived include the amount of exposure to the stimulus, how much attention it generates, and how it is interpreted. In an increasingly crowded stimulus environment, advertising clutter occurs when too many marketing-related messages compete for attention.

6. We interpret the stimuli to which we do pay attention according to learned patterns and expectations.

We don't attend to a stimulus in isolation. We classify and organize it according to principles of perceptual organization. A *Gestalt,* or overall pattern, guides these principles. Specific grouping principles include closure, similarity, and figure-ground relationships. The final step in the process of perception is interpretation. Symbols help us make sense of the world by providing us with an interpretation of a stimulus that others often share. The degree to which the symbolism is consistent with our previous experience affects the meaning we assign to related objects.

7. The field of semiotics helps us to understand how marketers use symbols to create meaning.

Marketers try to communicate with consumers by creating relationships between their products or services and desired attributes. A semiotic analysis involves the correspondence between stimuli and the meaning of signs. The intended meaning may be literal (e.g., an icon such as a street sign with a picture of children playing). Or it may be indexical if it relies on shared characteristics (e.g., the red in a stop sign means danger). Meaning also can be conveyed by a symbol in which an image is given meaning by convention or by agreement of members of a society (e.g., stop signs are octagonal, whereas yield signs are triangular). Marketer-created associations often take on lives of their own as consumers begin to believe that hype is, in fact, real. We call this condition hyperreality.

KEY TERMS

absolute threshold
adaptation
attention
audio watermarking
augmented reality (AR)
behavioral pricing
brand-name imprinting
closure principle
contrast
differential threshold
embeds
experience
exposure
figure-ground principle
golden triangle
Gestalt
haptic
hedonic consumption

hyperreality
icon
index
interpretant
interpretation
j.n.d. (just noticeable
    difference)
Kinsei engineering
multitasking
natural user interface
object
perception
perceptual defense
perceptual filters
perceptual selection
perceptual vigilance
phonemes
positioning strategy

priming
principle of similarity
psychophysics
reference price
reverse product placement
rich media
schema
semiotics
sensation
sensory marketing
sensory overload
sensory signature
sign
sound symbolism
subliminal perception
symbol
trade dress
Weber's Law

REVIEW

1 Define hedonic consumption and provide an example.
2 Does the size of a package influence how much of the contents we eat? Provide an example.
3 How does the sense of touch influence consumers' reactions to products?
4 Identify and describe the three stages of perception.
5 What is the difference between an absolute threshold and a differential threshold?
6 Does subliminal perception work? Why or why not?
7 "Consumers practice a form of "psychic economy." What does this mean?
8 Describe two factors that can lead to stimulus adaptation.

9 Define a "schema" and provide an example of how this concept is relevant to marketing.
10 "The whole is greater than the sum of its parts." Explain this statement.
11 List the three semiotic components of a marketing message, giving an example of each.
12 What do we mean by the concept of hyperreality? Give an example that is not discussed in the chapter. How does this concept differ from augmented reality?
13 What is a positioning strategy? What are some ways marketers can position their products?

CONSUMER BEHAVIOR CHALLENGE

■ DISCUSS

1 Many studies have shown that our sensory detection abilities decline as we grow older. Discuss the implications of the absolute threshold for marketers who want to appeal to the elderly.
2 Assuming that some forms of subliminal persuasion may have the desired effect of influencing consumers, do you think the use of these techniques is ethical? Explain your answer.
3 Do you believe that marketers have the right to use any or all public spaces to deliver product messages? Where would you draw the line in terms of places and products that should be off limits?

4 The slogan for the movie *Godzilla* was "Size does matter." Should this be the slogan for America as well? Many marketers seem to believe so. The average serving size for a fountain drink has gone from 12 ounces to 20 ounces. An industry consultant explains that the 32-ounce Big Gulp is so popular because "people like something large in their hands. The larger the better." Hardee's Monster Burger, complete with two beef patties and five pieces of bacon, weighs in at 63 grams of fat and more than 1,000 calories. The standard for TV sets used to be 19 inches; now it's 32 inches and growing. Hulking sport utility vehicles (SUVs) have replaced tiny sports cars as the status vehicle of the new

millennium. What's up with our fascination with bigness? Is this a uniquely American preference? Do you believe that "bigger is better"? Is this a sound marketing strategy?

5 Playmobil toys recreate real-life settings such as a police station or hospital. One offering the company calls Security Check Point features armed airport security officers, a metal detector, and an X-ray screening machine. Some parents protested; one wrote this comment on Amazon .com: "I applaud Playmobil for attempting to provide us with the tools we need to teach our children to unquestioningly obey the commands of the State Security Apparatus. But unfortunately, this product falls short of doing that. There's no brown figure for little Josh to profile, taser,

and detain." A Playmobil executive comments, "The whole premise behind Playmobil toys is to familiarize the child with the realities of life through play. If you're taking a child for a first flight to Florida from New Jersey to visit grandparents, you say, 'This is what the terminal looks like, and when we get here we have to take our shoes off and walk though security.'"[101] Where should toymakers draw the line between reality and play?

6 Augmented reality applications may reach the level of sophistication where we observe almost everything through the screen of our smartphones in order to receive an "enhanced" experience. Do you view this as a positive development or a problem?

■ APPLY

1 Interview three to five male and three to five female friends about their perceptions of both men's and women's fragrances. Construct a perceptual map for each set of products. Based on your map of perfumes, do you see any areas that are not adequately served by current offerings? What (if any) gender differences did you notice regarding both the relevant dimensions raters use and how they place specific brands along these dimensions?

2 Assume that you are a consultant for a marketer who wants to design a package for a new premium chocolate bar targeted to an affluent market. What recommendations would you provide in terms of such package elements as color, symbolism, and graphic design? Give the reasons for your suggestions.

3 Using magazines archived in the library, track the packaging of a specific brand over time. Find an example of gradual changes in package design that may have been below the j.n.d.

4 Visit a set of Web sites for one type of product (e.g., personal computers, perfumes, laundry detergents, or athletic shoes) and analyze the colors and other design principles they employ. Which sites "work" and which don't? Why? Look through a current magazine and select one ad that captures your attention over the others. Explain why this ad attracts you.

5 Find ads that use the techniques of contrast and novelty. Give your opinion of the effectiveness of each ad and whether the technique is likely to be appropriate for the consumers the ad targets.

MyMarketingLab Now that you have completed this chapter, return to **www.mymktlab.com** to apply concepts and explore the additional study materials.

Case Study

THE BRAVE NEW WORLD OF SUBWAY ADVERTISING

What do American Express, Target Stores, Coca-Cola, the Discovery Channel, Cadillac, Minute Maid, the Cartoon Network, Royal Caribbean, and Calvin Klein have in common? They all break through the clutter of traditional ad spaces to grab the attention of potential customers. And in the process, they dazzle them right out of the boredom of riding the subway.

Subway advertising has been around nearly as long as the subway itself. But advertising media pioneers Submedia and Sidetrack Technologies give the old venue a new twist. By employing an innovative technology similar to that of a childhood flip book, they illuminate dark subway tunnels and turn them into valuable showcases for major advertisers.

At the core of this new method is a series of lit panels that contain static images. The panels occupy 500 to 1,000 feet of space that normally holds only graffiti, grime, and the occasional rat. When you view one from a standstill, they appear as simple still images. But when a subway train passes by, they come to life for riders as a 15- to 30-second full-motion commercial.

Having just another place to air a commercial might not seem so appealing to advertisers. But in a media environment where consumers increasingly skip or fast-forward through ads, the placement of these messages in subway tunnels presents exceptional possibilities. Advertisers clamor for opportunities to break through the typical clutter. And these ads are really unique, so they're likely to grab the attention of even the most jaded commuter. "We think this will catch people so totally by surprise that when they see them, they can't help but watch them," said Dan Hanrahan, Royal Caribbean's senior vice president of marketing and sales.

But the uniqueness of this medium is only part of the formula that makes these ad agencies believe they're on to something. The rest is based on the nature of the subway audience: captive and bored. "Everybody overwhelmingly says it takes away from the boredom of the ride," said Joshua Spodek, founder of New York City–based Submedia. "It's not like it's taking away from a beautiful view, like a billboard as you're driving around a beautiful area in Vermont. A subway tunnel is a semi-industrial environment."

Whether it's because the ads give a bored audience something to do or because this new wave of out-of-home advertisements is truly cutting-edge, industry officials claim that the public reaction has been overwhelmingly positive. Submedia reports that 87 percent of riders look forward to seeing the next Submedia advertisement and 60 percent said the ad made their ride more enjoyable.

Comments like this make it easy to believe the claims of underground advertising agencies. One estimate asserts that more than 92 percent of consumers remember the advertised product, whereas only 13 percent have that same level of recall

for televisions ads. This means big ad revenues, and not just for the agencies. Mass transit organizations potentially can realize a big source of secondary income when they lease out this unused real estate.

Currently brightening the tunnels of numerous mass transit systems in North and South America, Asia, and Europe, these advertisements represent something every advertiser dreams of: an ad that people go out of their way to look at. In a world that is increasingly skeptical about too much advertising, this new platform is an express ride to success.

DISCUSSION QUESTIONS

1 Based on the principles of attention the chapter presents, explain why riders receive these new ads so positively.
2 Using the same principles, what should the ads' creators consider to avoid the potential burnout of this medium?

Sources: www.submediaworld.com/submediaworld/Tunnel_Advertising, accessed June 8, 2011; Katy Bachman, "Underground Film," *Mediaweek* 18, no. 15 (April 14, 2008): 24; Louis M. Brill, "Subway In-tunnel Advertising Gives Outdoor a New Direction," www.sub-media.com/press, accessed May 23, 2009.

NOTES

1. http://uhtmilk.net/, accessed May 9, 2011; http://wiki.answers.com/Q/What_is_the_difference_between_fresh_milk_and_uht_treated_milk_and_any_advantages_and_disadvantages, accessed March 28, 2011; Craig Baumrucker, "Why Does Organic Milk Last So Much Longer Than Regular Milk?," *Scientific American* (June 6, 2008), www.scientificamerican.com/article.cfm?id=experts-organic-milk-lasts-longer, accessed June 30, 2009.
2. http://www.universalorlando.com/Theme_Parks/Universal_Studios_Orlando/Attractions/fear_factor_live.aspx, accessed March 28, 2011; Nat Ives, "Putting Some Terror in Family Outings," *New York Times* (January 17, 2005), www.nytimes.com, accessed January 17, 2005.
3. Michelle Kung, "Gyrating at a Theater Near You: D-Box's Moving Movie Seats," *Wall Street Journal* (May 6, 2011), http://professional.wsj.com/article/SB10001424052748704810504576305363217225214.html?mg=reno-wsj, accessed May 6, 2011.
4. Ryan S. Elder and Aradhna Krishna (2010), "The Effects of Advertising Copy on Sensory Thoughts and Perceived Taste," *Journal of Consumer Research* 36, no. 5, 748–56.
5. Glenn Collins, "Owens-Corning's Blurred Identity," *New York Times* (August 19, 1994): D4.
6. Elizabeth C. Hirschman and Morris B. Holbrook, "Hedonic Consumption: Emerging Concepts, Methods, and Propositions," *Journal of Marketing* 46 (Summer 1982): 92–101.
7. Virginia Postrel, "The New Trend in Spending," *New York Times* (September 9, 2004), www.nytimes.com, accessed September 9, 2004.
8. Emily Cadei, "Cleaning Up: S. F. Duo Putting a Shine on Its Product Line," *San Francisco Business Times Online Edition* 17, no. 16 (December 6, 2002).
9. Martin Reimann, Judith Zaichkowsky, Carolin Neuhaus, Thomas Bender, and Bernd Weber, "Aesthetic Package Design: A Behavioral, Neural, and Psychological Investigation," *Journal of Consumer Psychology* 20 (2010): 431–41.
10. Adam Bryant, "Plastic Surgery at AmEx," *Newsweek* (October 4, 1999): 55.
11. Amitava Chattopadhyay, Gerald J. Gorn, and Peter R. Darke, *Roses Are Red and Violets Are Blue—Everywhere? Cultural Universals and Differences in Color Preference among Consumers and Marketing Managers* (unpublished manuscript, University of British Columbia, Fall 1999); Joseph Bellizzi and Robert E. Hite, "Environmental Color, Consumer Feelings, and Purchase Likelihood," *Psychology & Marketing* 9 (1992): 347–63; Ayn E. Crowley, "The Two-Dimensional Impact of Color on Shopping," *Marketing Letters* 4 (January 1993); Gerald J. Gorn, Amitava Chattopadhyay, and Tracey Yi, *Effects of Color as an Executional Cue in an Ad: It's in the Shade* (unpublished manuscript, University of British Columbia, 1994).
12. Pam Belluck, "Reinvent Wheel? Blue Room. Defusing a Bomb? Red Room," *New York Times* (February 5, 2009), www.nytimes.com, accessed February 5, 2009.
13. Mark G. Frank and Thomas Gilovich, "The Dark Side of Self and Social Perception: Black Uniforms and Aggression in Professional Sports," *Journal of Personality & Social Psychology* 54 (1988): 74–85.
14. Pamela Paul, "Color by Numbers," *American Demographics* (February 2002): 31–36.
15. Paulette Thomas, "Cosmetics Makers Offer World's Women an All-American Look with Local Twists," *Wall Street Journal* (May 8, 1995): B1.
16. Marc Gobé, *Emotional Branding: The New Paradigm for Connecting Brands to People* (New York: Allworth Press, 2001).
17. Dirk Olin, "Color Cognition," *New York Times* (November 30, 2003), www.nytimes.com, accessed November 30, 2003.
18. "Ny Emballage og Ny Navn Fordoblede Salget," *Markedsforing* 12 (1992): 24. Adapted from Michael R. Solomon, Gary Bamossy, and Soren Askegaard, *Consumer Behavior: A European Perspective*, 2nd ed. (London: Pearson Education, 2001).
19. Meg Rosen and Frank Alpert, "Protecting Your Business Image: The Supreme Court Rules on Trade Dress," *Journal of Consumer Marketing* 11 (1994): 50–55.
20. Excerpted from http://www.pantone.com/pages/MYP_mypantone/mypInfo.aspx?ca=75&pg=20875, accessed March 27, 2011.
21. Ana Teriz, "Smells like Celeb Spirit," *BrandChannel* (October 29, 2010), http://www.brandchannel.com/home/post/2010/10/29/Smells-like-Celeb-Spirit.aspx, accessed March 27, 2011.
22. Deborah J. Mitchell, Barbara E. Kahn, and Susan C. Knasko, "There's Something in the Air: Effects of Congruent or Incongruent Ambient Odor on Consumer Decision-Making," *Journal of Consumer Research* 22 (September 1995): 229–38; for a review of olfactory cues in store environments, see also Eric R. Spangenberg, Ayn E. Crowley, and Pamela W. Henderson, "Improving the Store Environment: Do Olfactory Cues Affect Evaluations and Behaviors?" *Journal of Marketing* 60 (April 1996): 67–80.
23. Krishna Aradhna, May O. Lwin and Maureen Morrin (2010), "Product Scent and Memory," *Journal of Consumer Research* 37, no. 1, 57–67.
24. "Lithuania Launches National Perfume," *Newstalk ZB/ONE News* (January 5, 2011), http://tvnz.co.nz/world-news/lithuania-launches-national-perfume-3992387, accessed March 27, 2011.

25. Emily Bryson York, "Make Your Man a Flamer, Mmmmmmm. Fresh Meat," *Advertising Age* (December 15, 2008), http://adage.com/adages/post?article_id=133264, accessed December 15, 2008.

26. Pam Scholder Ellen and Paula Fitzgerald Bone, "Does It Matter if It Smells? Olfactory Stimuli as Advertising Executional Cues," *Journal of Advertising* 27 (Winter 1998): 29–40.

27. Jack Hitt, "Does the Smell of Coffee Brewing Remind You of Your Mother?" *New York Times Magazine* (May 7, 2000): 73–77.

28. Quoted in Julie Jargon, "At Starbucks, It's Back to the Grind," *Wall Street Journal* (June 17, 2009), online at wsj.com/article/SB124517480498919731.html, accessed June 17, 2009.

29. Maxine Wilkie, "Scent of a Market," *American Demographics* (August 1995): 40–49.

30. Nicholas Wade, "Scent of a Man Is Linked to a Woman's Selection," *New York Times* (January 22, 2002), www.nytimes.com, accessed January 22, 2002.

31. Newman, Kara, "How to Sell with Smell," *Business 2.0* (April 2007): 36.

32. Quoted in Sheila Shayon, "World Cup Winner: Coca-Cola for Sonic Branding," *BrandChannel* (July 12, 2010), http://www.brandchannel.com/home/post/2010/07/12/Coca-Cola-World-Cup-Wavin-Flag.aspx, accessed March 28, 2011.

33. Bruce G. Vanden Bergh, Janay Collins, Myrna Schultz, and Keith Adler, "Sound Advice on Brand Names," *Journalism Quarterly* 61, no. 4 (1984): 835–40; Eric Yorkston and Geeta Menon, "A Sound Idea: Phonetic Effects of Brand Names on Consumer Judgments," *Journal of Consumer Research* 31 (June 2004): 43–51; Keith S. Coulter and Robin A. Coulter, "Small Sounds, Big Deals: Phonetic Symbolism Effects in Pricing," *Journal of Consumer Research* 37, no. 2 (2010): 315–28.

34. "You Can Look—But Don't Touch," *Science Daily* (January 20, 2009), www.sciencedaily.com, accessed January 30, 2009; Joann Peck and Suzanne B. Shu, "The Effect of Mere Touch on Perceived Ownership," *Journal of Consumer Research* 36, no. 3 (2009): 434–47.

35. Sarah Ellison and Erin White, "'Sensory' Marketers Say the Way to Reach Shoppers Is the Nose," *Advertising Age* (November 24, 2000): 1–3.

36. Jacob Hornik, "Tactile Stimulation and Consumer Response," *Journal of Consumer Research* 19 (December 1992): 449–58.

37. Joan Meyers-Levy, Rui (Juliet) Zhu, and Lan Jiang, "Context Effects from Bodily Sensations: Examining Bodily Sensations Induced by Flooring and the Moderating Role of Product Viewing Distance," *Journal of Consumer Research* 37, no. 1 (2010), 1–14.

38. J. Peck and T. L. Childers, "Individual Differences in Haptic Information Processing: The 'Need for Touch' Scale," *Journal of Consumer Research* 30, no. 3 (2003): 430–42.

39. Material adapted from a presentation by Glenn H. Mazur, QFD Institute, 2002.

40. Joseph B. White, "Taller in the Saddle: Higher Driver's Seats in Sedans Are Effort to Appeal to Fans of SUVs and Minivans," *Wall Street Journal* (August 23, 2004), www.wsj.com, accessed August 23, 2004.

41. Claire Cain Miller, "To Win over Users, Gadgets Have to Be Touchable," *New York Times* (September 1, 2010), http://www.nytimes.com/2010/09/01/technology/01touch.html?_r=1&emc=tnt&tntemail0=y, accessed March 27, 2011.

42. John Tagliabue, "Sniffing and Tasting with Metal and Wire," *New York Times* (February 17, 2002), www.nytimes.com, accessed February 17, 2002.

43. Michael W. Allen, Richa Gupta, and Arnaud Monnier, "The Interactive Effect of Cultural Symbols and Human Values on Taste Evaluation," *Journal of Consumer Research* 35 (August 2008): 294–308.

44. Becky Gaylord, "Bland Food Isn't So Bad—It Hurts Just to Think about This Stuff," *Wall Street Journal* (April 21, 1995): B1.

45. Dhruv Grewal and Larry D. Compeau, "Consumer Responses to Price and Its Contextual Information Cues: A Synthesis of Past Research, a Conceptual Framework, and Avenues for Further Research," *Review of Marketing Research* 3 (2007): 109–31; Kent B. Monroe, *Pricing: Making Profitable Decisions*, 3rd ed. (New York: McGraw-Hill, 2003); Dhruv Grewal, Kent B. Monroe, and R. Krishnan, "The Effects of Price Comparison Advertising on Buyers' Perceptions of Acquisition Value and Transaction Value," *Journal of Marketing* 62 (April 1998): 46–60.

46. William B. Dodds, Kent B. Monroe, and Dhruv Grewal, "Effects of Price, Brand, and Store Information on Buyers' Product Evaluations," *Journal of Marketing Research* 28 (August 1991): 307–19; Merrie Brucks, Valerie Zeithaml, and Gillian Naylor, "Price and Brand Name as Indicators of Quality Dimensions of Consumer Durables," *Journal of the Academy of Marketing Science* 28, no. 3 (2000): 359–74.

47. Larry D. Compeau and Dhruv Grewal, "Adding Value by Communicating Price Deals Effectively: Does It Matter How You Phrase It?," *Pricing Strategy and Practice: An International Journal* 2, no. 2 (1994): 28–36.

48. Joel E. Urbany, William O. Bearden, and Don C. Weilbaker, "The Effect of Plausible and Exaggerated Reference Prices on Consumer Perceptions and Price Search," *Journal of Consumer Research* 15 (1998): 95–110.

49. Larry D. Compeau and Dhruv Grewal, "Comparative Price Advertising: An Integrative Review," *Journal of Public Policy & Marketing* 17 (Fall 1998): 257–73; Dhruv Grewal and Larry D. Compeau, "Pricing and Public Policy: A Research Agenda and an Overview," *Journal of Public Policy & Marketing* 18 (Spring 1999): 3–10.

50. Larry D. Compeau, Dhruv Grewal, and Diana S. Grewal, "Adjudicating Claims of Deceptive Advertised Reference Prices: The Use of Empirical Evidence," *Journal of Public Policy & Marketing* 13 (Fall 1994): 312–18; Dhruv Grewal and Larry D. Compeau, *Journal of Public Policy and Marketing: Special Issue on Pricing and Public Policy* 18 (Spring 1999), Chicago, IL: American Marketing Association. Also see www.bbb.org/membership/codeofad.asp#Comparative%20Price and www.ftc.gov/bcp/guides/decptprc.htm for guidelines on use of reference prices.

51. Ellen Byron, "Selling Detergent Bottles' Big Shrink Suds Makers' Challenge: Convince Consumers Less Isn't Really Less," *Wall Street Journal* (May 21, 2007), www.wsj.com, accessed May 21, 2007.

52. Stephanie Clifford and Catherine Rampell, quoted in "Food Inflation Kept Hidden in Tinier Bags," *New York Times* (March 28, 2011), http://www.nytimes.com/2011/03/29/business/29shrink.html?pagewanted=all accessed March 29, 2011.

53. Bob Teheschi, "Seeing the World around You through Your Phone," *New York Times* (July 28, 2010), http://www.nytimes.com/2010/07/29/technology/personaltech/29smart.html?emc=tnt&tntemail0=y, accessed March 28, 2011.

54. Patricia Odell, "Chevy Puts a New Spin on an Old Model," *PROMO* (January 10, 2011), http://promomagazine.com/news/chevy-new-old-model-0110/, accessed March 28, 2011.

55. Matthew Szymczyk, "Digital Marketing Guide: Augmented Reality," *Advertising Age* (February 27, 2011), http://adage.com/article/special-report-digital-marketing-guide/digital-marketing-guide-augmented-reality/149109/, accessed March 28, 2011.

56. "Total Immersion and eBay Bring Virtual 'See It On' Feature to eBay's Fashion App," *Business Wire* (February 1, 2011), http://www.businesswire.com/news/home/20110201006053/en/Total-Immersion-eBay-Bring-Virtual-%E2%80%98See-On%E2%80%99, accessed March 28, 2011.

57. Michael Lev, "No Hidden Meaning Here: Survey Sees Subliminal Ads," *New York Times* (May 3, 1991): D7.

58. "ABC Rejects KFC Commercial, Citing Subliminal Advertising," *Wall Street Journal* (March 2, 2006), www.wsj.com, accessed March 2, 2006.

59. Andrew B. Aylesworth, Ronald C. Goodstein, and Ajay Kalra, "Effect of Archetypal Embeds on Feelings: An Indirect Route to Affecting Attitudes?," *Journal of Advertising* 28, no. 3 (Fall 1999): 73–81.

60. Philip M. Merikle, "Subliminal Auditory Messages: An Evaluation," *Psychology & Marketing* 5, no. 4 (1988): 355–72.

61. Joel Saegert, "Why Marketing Should Quit Giving Subliminal Advertising the Benefit of the Doubt," *Psychology & Marketing* 4 (Summer 1987): 107–20; see also Dennis L. Rosen and Surendra N. Singh, "An Investigation of Subliminal Embed Effect on Multiple Measures of Advertising Effectiveness," *Psychology & Marketing* 9 (March–April 1992): 157–73; for a more recent review, see Kathryn T. Theus, "Subliminal Advertising and the Psychology of Processing Unconscious Stimuli: A Review of Research," *Psychology & Marketing* (May–June 1994): 271–90.

62. Brian Steinberg, "How to Keep Ad Skippers from Fast-Forwarding Your Ad," *Advertising Age* (March 31, 2009), www.adage.com, accessed March 31, 2009.

63. Joseph Burris, "Plugged-in Generation Multi-Tasking Big Time," *Baltimore Sun* (February 17, 2010), http://articles.baltimoresun.com/2010-02-17/features/bal-md.pa.kids17feb17_1_cell-phones-multi-tasking-parental-controls, accessed May 5, 2011.

64. Sharon Waxman, "At an Industry Media Lab, Close Views of Multitasking," *New York Times* (May 15, 2006). http://www.nytimes.com/2006/05/15/technology/15research.html, accessed August 22, 2011.

65. Matt Richtel, "Attached to Technology and Paying a Price," *New York Times* (June 6, 2010), http://www.nytimes.com/2010/06/07/technology/07brain.html?pagewanted=1, accessed April 17, 2011.

66. Stuart Elliott, "Trying to Keep the Viewers When the Ads Come On," *New York Times* (May 14, 2007), www.nytimes.com, accessed May 14, 2007.

67. Lee Gomes, "As Web Ads Grow, Sites Get Trickier about Targeting You," *Wall Street Journal* (May 9, 2007): B1.

68. "Court Orders Bagpipes for Noise Violations," *Montgomery Advertiser* (March 6, 1999): 1A.

69. Theodore J. Noseworthy, June Cotte, and Seung Hwan (Mark) Lee, "The Effects of Ad Context and Gender on the Identification of Visually Incongruent Products," *Journal of Consumer Research* (August 2011, in press), published online January 24, 2011.

70. Rik Pieters, Michel Wedel, and Rajeev Batra, "The Stopping Power of Advertising: Measures and Effects of Visual Complexity," *Journal of Marketing* 74 (September 2010): 48–60.

71. Roger Barton, *Advertising Media* (New York: McGraw-Hill, 1964).

72. Suzanne Oliver, "New Personality," *Forbes* (August 15, 1994): 114.

73. Adam Finn, "Print Ad Recognition Readership Scores: An Information Processing Perspective," *Journal of Marketing Research* 25 (May 1988): 168–77.

74. Gerald L. Lohse, "Consumer Eye Movement Patterns on Yellow Pages Advertising," *Journal of Advertising* 26 (Spring 1997): 61–73.

75. Chris Sherman (March 8, 2005). A New F-Word for Google Search Results, *Search Engine Watch*, Available online: http://searchenginewatch.com/3488076, accessed June 29, 2010.

76. Michael R. Solomon and Basil G. Englis, "Reality Engineering: Blurring the Boundaries Between Marketing and Popular Culture," *Journal of Current Issues & Research in Advertising* 16, no. 2 (Fall 1994): 1–18; Michael McCarthy, "Ads Are Here, There, Everywhere: Agencies Seek Creative Ways to Expand Product Placement," *USA Today* (June 19, 2001): 1B.

77. Linda Stern, "Bigger Than at Times Square," March 24, 2008, www.newsweek.com.

78. Stephanie Clifford, "Billboards That Look Back," *New York Times* (May 31, 2008), www.nytimes.com, accessed May 31, 2008.

79. Benedict Carey, "Liked the Show? Maybe It Was the Commercials," *New York Times* (March 2, 2009), http://topics.nytimes.com/topics/reference/timestopics/people/c/benedict_carey/index.html, accessed March 3, 2009.

80. Nicholas Bakalar, "If It Says McDonald's, Then It Must Be Good," *New York Times* (August 14, 2007), www.nytimes.com, accessed August 14, 2007.

81. Robert M. McMath, "Image Counts," *American Demographics* (May 1998): 64.

82. Brian Wansink, James Painter, and Koert van Ittersum, "Descriptive Menu Labels' Effect on Sales," *Cornell Hotel & Restaurant Administration Quarterly* (December 2001): 68–72.

83. Xiaoyan Deng and Barbara E. Kahn, "Is Your Product on the Right Side? The 'Location Effect' on Perceived Product Heaviness and Package Evaluation," *Journal of Marketing Research* (December 2009). Vol. 46, No. 6, pp. 725–738.

84. Pankaj Aggarwal and Ann L. McGill, "Is That Car Smiling at Me? Schema Congruity as a Basis for Evaluating Anthropomorphized Products," *Journal of Consumer Behavior* 34 (December 2007): 468–79.

85. Anthony Ramirez, "Lessons in the Cracker Market: Nabisco Saved New Graham Snack," *New York Times* (July 5, 1990): D1.

86. Albert H. Hastorf and Hadley Cantril, "They Saw a Game: A Case Study," *Journal of Abnormal & Social Psychology* 49 (1954): 129–34; see also Roberto Friedmann and Mary R. Zimmer, "The Role of Psychological Meaning in Advertising," *Journal of Advertising* (1988): 31–40.

87. Robert M. McMath, "Chock Full of (Pea)nuts," *American Demographics* (April 1997): 60.

88. Benedict Carey, "Knowing the Ingredients Can Change the Taste," *New York Times* (December 12, 2006), www.nytimes.com, accessed December 12, 2006.

89. See David Mick, "Consumer Research and Semiotics: Exploring the Morphology of Signs, Symbols, and Significance," *Journal of Consumer Research* 13 (September 1986): 196–213.

90. Teresa J. Domzal and Jerome B. Kernan, "Reading Advertising: The What and How of Product Meaning," *Journal of Consumer Marketing* 9 (Summer 1992): 48–64.

91. Arthur Asa Berger, *Signs in Contemporary Culture: An Introduction to Semiotics* (New York: Longman, 1984); David Mick, "Consumer Research and Semiotics," 196–213; Charles Sanders Peirce, in Charles Hartshorne, Paul Weiss, and Arthur W. Burks, eds., *Collected Papers* (Cambridge, MA: Harvard University Press, 1931–1958); cf. also V. Larsen, D. Luna, and L. A. Peracchio, "Points of View and Pieces of Time: A Taxonomy of Image Attributes," *Journal of Consumer Research* 31, no. 1 (2004): 102–11.

92. Steven Heller, "A Makeover for the Starbucks Mermaid," *New York Times* (January 8, 2011), http://www.nytimes.com/2011/01/09/weekinreview/09heller.html?_r=1&scp=2&sq=starbucks&st=cse, accessed March 27, 2011.

93. Gabriel Kahn, "Chinese Characters Are Gaining New Meaning as Corporate Logos," *Wall Street Journal Interactive Edition* (July 18, 2002).

94. Stuart Elliot, "Gap Inc. Puts 'GAP' Back in Logo," *New York Times* (October 12, 2010), http://mediadecoder.blogs.nytimes.com/2010/10/12/gap-inc-puts-gap-back-in-logo/?scp=1&sq=gap%20logo&st=cse, accessed March 27, 2011.

95. Dexter Dining Room and Kitchen, *Metropolitan Home* (March 2009), www.metropolitanhome.com, accessed January 27, 2009.

96. Jeremy Mullman, "GEICO Cavemen Get a New Gig with ESPN, Will Act as Fantasy-Football Salesmen and Star in 'SportsCenter' Ads," *Advertising Age* (August 14, 2008), http://advertisingnews.wordpress.com/2008/08/15/geico-cavemen-get-a-new-gig-with-espn/ accessed August 22, 2011.

97. Rob Walker, "False Endorsement," *New York Times Magazine* (November 18, 2007), www.nytimes.com/2007/11/18/magazine/18wwln-consumed-t.html?_r=1&, accessed November 24, 2007; David Edery, "Reverse Product Placement in Virtual Worlds," *Harvard Business Review* (December 2006), http://hbr.org/2006/12/reverse-product-placement-in-virtual-worlds/ar/1, accessed August 22, 2011.

98. Walker, "False Endorsement."

99. Adapted from Michael R. Solomon and Elnora W. Stuart, *Marketing: Real People, Real Choices*, 2nd ed. (Upper Saddle River, NJ: Prentice Hall, 2000).

100. William Echikson, "Aiming at High and Low Markets," *Fortune* (March 22, 1993): 89.

101. Adam Newman, "Playmobil Finds Fun in the Police State," *New York Times* (February 15, 2009), www.nytimes.com, accessed February 15, 2009.

Learning and Memory

Learning and Memory

Chapter Objectives

When you finish reading this chapter you will understand why:

1. It is important to understand how consumers learn about products and services.

2. Conditioning results in learning.

3. Learned associations with brands generalize to other products, and why this is important to marketers.

4. There is a difference between classical and instrumental conditioning, and both processes help consumers to learn about products.

5. We learn about products by observing others' behavior.

6. Our brains process information about brands to retain them in memory.

7. The other products we associate with an individual product influence how we will remember it.

8. Products help us to retrieve memories from our past.

9. Marketers measure our memories about products and ads.

MyMarketingLab

Visit **www.mymktlab.com** to find activities that help you learn and review in order to succeed in this chapter.

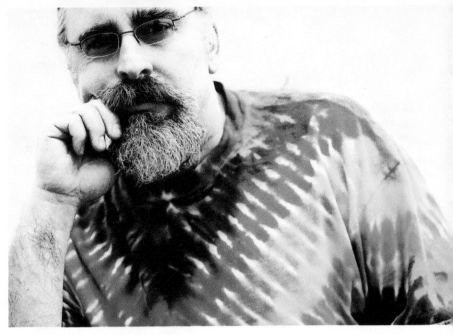

Source: Photos.com/Thinkstock.

Ah, Sunday morning! The sun is shining, the birds are singing, and Joe is feeling groovy! He puts on his vintage Levi's 501 jeans (circa 1968) and his Woodstock T-shirt (the "real" Woodstock, not that fake abomination they put on in 2009, thank you) and saunters down to the kitchen. Joe smiles in anticipation of his morning plans. He's just returned from his college reunion and now it's time to "process" all the people he's seen and the stories he heard about their old antics. Joe cranks up the Lava Lamp, throws a Jefferson Airplane record on the turntable (ah, the sublime joys of vinyl), and sits back on his Barcalounger as he clutches a huge bowl filled to the brim with his all-time favorite cereal, Cap'n Crunch. Let the memories begin!

OBJECTIVE 1

It is important to understand how consumers learn about products and services.

Learning

Joe journeys through time with the aid of many products that make him feel good because they remind him of earlier parts of his life. PepsiCo launched its "Throwback" campaign in 2011; now it sells Pepsi Throwback, Mountain Dew Throwback, and Doritos Taco Flavored chips in authentic packages from the past. Hostess brought back 1970s characters Twinkie the Kid, Captain CupCake, King Ding Dong, and Happy Ho Ho to adorn its snack cake packages. Disney is trying to revive its Tron franchise. As a PepsiCo marketing executive explained, "Retro is very cool with 20-somethings, because it ties in with their desire for simpler, cleaner, more authentic lives. Many of them are engaged in identity self-creation through their Facebook pages, Instagrams, Twitter and other social media, and they see nostalgia as a way to differentiate themselves."[1]

Marketers understand that long-standing, learned connections between products and memories like the ones Joe exhibits are a potent way to build and keep brand loyalty. In this chapter, we'll learn why learned associations among feelings, events, and products—and the memories they evoke—are an important aspect of consumer behavior.

Learning is a relatively permanent change in behavior caused by experience. The learner need not have the experience directly; we can also learn when we observe events that affect others.[2] We learn even when we don't try: We recognize many brand names and hum many product jingles, for example, even for products we don't personally use. We call this casual, unintentional acquisition of knowledge **incidental learning.**

Learning is an ongoing process. Our knowledge about the world constantly updates as we are exposed to new stimuli and as we receive ongoing feedback that allows us to modify our behavior when we find ourselves in similar situations at a later time. The concept of learning covers a lot of ground, ranging from a consumer's simple association between a stimulus such as a product logo (e.g., Coca-Cola) and a response (e.g., "refreshing soft drink") to a complex series of cognitive activities (e.g., writing an essay on learning for a consumer behavior exam).

A Brazilian company uses nostalgic imagery to promote a high-tech product—seminars on social media.
Source: Courtesy of MaxiMidia.

Psychologists who study learning advance several theories to explain the learning process. These theories range from those that focus on simple stimulus–response connections (*behavioral theories*) to perspectives that regard consumers as solvers of complex problems who learn abstract rules and concepts when they observe what others say and do (*cognitive theories*). It's important for marketers to understand these theories as well, because basic learning principles are at the heart of many consumer purchase decisions.

OBJECTIVE 2
Conditioning results in learning.

Behavioral Learning Theories

Behavioral learning theories assume that learning takes place as the result of responses to external events. Psychologists who subscribe to this viewpoint do not focus on internal thought processes. Instead, they approach the mind as a "black box" and emphasize the observable aspects of behavior. The observable aspects consist of things that go into the box (the stimuli or events perceived from the outside world) and things that come out of the box (the responses, or reactions to these stimuli).

Two major approaches to learning represent this view: *classical conditioning* and *instrumental conditioning*. According to the behavioral learning perspective, the feedback we receive as we go through life shapes our experiences. Similarly, we respond to brand names, scents, jingles, and other marketing stimuli because of the learned connections we form over time. People also learn that actions they take result in rewards and punishments; this feedback influences the way they will respond in similar situations in the future. Consumers who receive compliments on a product choice will be more likely to buy that brand again, while those who get food poisoning at a new restaurant are not likely to patronize that restaurant in the future.

Classical conditioning occurs when a stimulus that elicits a response is paired with another stimulus that initially does not elicit a response on its own. Over time, this second stimulus causes a similar response because we associate it with the first stimulus. Ivan Pavlov, a Russian physiologist who conducted research on digestion in animals, first demonstrated this phenomenon in dogs. Pavlov induced classically conditioned learning when he paired a neutral stimulus (a bell) with a stimulus known to cause a salivation response in dogs (he squirted dried meat powder into their mouths). The powder was an

unconditioned stimulus (UCS) because it was naturally capable of causing the response. Over time, the bell became a **conditioned stimulus (CS)**—it did not initially cause salivation, but the dogs learned to associate the bell with the meat powder and began to salivate at the sound of the bell only. The drooling of these canine consumers because of a sound, now linked to feeding time, was a **conditioned response (CR)**.

This basic form of classical conditioning that Pavlov demonstrated primarily applies to responses controlled by the autonomic (e.g., salivation) and nervous (e.g., eye blink) systems. That is, it focuses on visual and olfactory cues that induce hunger, thirst, sexual arousal, and other basic drives. When marketers consistently pair these cues with conditioned stimuli, such as brand names, consumers may learn to feel hungry, thirsty, or aroused when they encounter these brand cues at a later point.

Classical conditioning can have similar effects for more complex reactions, too. Even a credit card becomes a conditioned cue that triggers greater spending, especially because as a stimulus it's present only in situations where we spend money. People learn they can make larger purchases with credit cards, and they also leave larger tips than when they pay by cash.[3] Small wonder that American Express reminds us, "Don't leave home without it."

Repetition

Conditioning effects are more likely to occur after the conditioned (CS) and unconditioned (UCS) stimuli have been paired a number of times.[4] Repeated exposures—**repetition**—increase the strength of stimulus–response associations and prevent the decay of these associations in memory. Some research indicates that the intervals between exposures may influence the effectiveness of this strategy as well as the type of medium the marketer uses; the most effective repetition strategy is a combination of spaced exposures that alternate in terms of media that are more and less involving, such as television advertising complemented by print media.[5]

Many classic advertising campaigns consist of product slogans that companies repeat so often they are etched in consumers' minds. Conditioning will not occur or will take longer if the CS is only occasionally paired with the UCS. One result of this lack of association is **extinction,** which occurs when the effects of prior conditioning diminish and finally disappear. This can occur, for example, when a product is overexposed in the marketplace so that its original allure is lost. The Izod Lacoste polo shirt, with its distinctive crocodile crest, is a good example of this effect. When the once-exclusive crocodile started to appear on baby clothes and many other items, it lost its cachet. Other contenders, such as the Ralph Lauren polo player, successfully challenged it as a symbol of casual elegance. Now that Izod is being more careful about where its logo appears, the brand is starting to regain its "cool" in some circles.

Stimulus Generalization

Stimulus generalization refers to the tendency of stimuli similar to a CS to evoke similar, conditioned responses. For example, Pavlov noticed in subsequent studies that his dogs would sometimes salivate when they heard noises that only resembled a bell, such as keys jangling.

People also react to other, similar stimuli in much the same way they responded to the original stimulus; we call this generalization a **halo effect.** A drugstore's bottle of private-brand mouthwash that is deliberately packaged to resemble Listerine mouthwash may evoke a similar response among consumers, who assume that this "me-too" product shares other characteristics of the original. Indeed, consumers in one study on shampoo brands tended to rate those with similar packages as similar in quality and performance as well.[6] This "piggybacking" strategy can cut both ways: When the quality of the me-too product turns out to be lower than that of the original brand, consumers may exhibit even more positive feelings toward the original. However, if they perceive the quality of the two competitors to be about equal, consumers may conclude that the price premium they pay for the original is not worth it.[7]

Stimulus Discrimination

Stimulus discrimination occurs when a UCS does not follow a stimulus similar to a CS. When this happens, reactions weaken and will soon disappear. Part of the learning process involves making a response to some stimuli but not to other, similar stimuli. Manufacturers of well-established brands commonly urge consumers not to buy "cheap imitations" because the results will not be what they expect.

OBJECTIVE 3

Learned associations with brands generalize to other products, and why this is important to marketers.

Marketing Applications of Classical Conditioning Principles

Behavioral learning principles apply to many consumer phenomena, such as creating a distinctive brand image or linking a product to an underlying need. The transfer of meaning from an unconditioned stimulus to a conditioned stimulus explains why "made-up" brand names, such as Marlboro, Coca-Cola, or Reebok, exert such powerful effects on consumers. The association between the Marlboro man and the cigarette is so strong that in some cases the company no longer even bothers to include the brand name in its ads that feature the cowboy riding off into the sunset.

When researchers pair *nonsense syllables* (meaningless sets of letters) with such evaluative words as *beauty* or *success*, the meaning transfers to the fake words. This change in the symbolic significance of initially meaningless words shows that fairly simple associations can condition even complex meanings, and the learning that results can last a long time.[8] These associations are crucial to many marketing strategies that rely on the creation and perpetuation of **brand equity,** in which a brand has strong positive associations in a consumer's memory and commands a lot of loyalty as a result.[9]

Marketing Applications of Repetition

One advertising researcher argued that any more than three exposures to a marketing communication are wasted. The first exposure creates awareness of the product, the second demonstrates its relevance to the consumer, and the third reminds him or her of the product's benefits.[10] However, even this bare-bones approach implies that we need repetition to ensure that the consumer is actually exposed to (and processes) the message at least three times. This exposure is by no means guaranteed, because people tend to tune out or distort many marketing communications. Marketers that attempt to condition an association must ensure that the consumers they target will be exposed to the stimulus a sufficient number of times to make it "stick."

However, it is possible to have too much of a good thing. Consumers can become so used to hearing or seeing a marketing stimulus that they no longer pay attention to it. Varying the way in which the marketer presents the basic message can alleviate this problem of **advertising wear-out.** Toyota ran a commercial featuring a reworked version of The Fixx's 1983 hit "Saved by Zero" to promote its no-interest payment options so many times that close to 10,000 fed-up viewers organized a Facebook group to petition the company for mercy. As one worn-out group member posted, "There have been worse commercials, and there have been commercials that were played this often; but never before has a commercial this bad been aired so much."[11]

Marketing Applications of Conditioned Product Associations

Advertisements often pair a product with a positive stimulus to create a desirable association. Various aspects of a marketing message, such as music, humor, or imagery, can affect conditioning. In one study, for example, subjects who viewed a slide of pens paired with either pleasant or unpleasant music were more likely later to select the pen that appeared with the pleasant music.[13]

The order in which the conditioned stimulus and the unconditioned stimulus occur also can affect the likelihood that learning will occur. Generally speaking, a marketer should present the conditioned stimulus prior to the unconditioned stimulus. The opposite sequence of *backward conditioning*, such as when the company plays a jingle (the UCS) and then shows a soft drink (the CS), generally is not effective.[14] Because sequential presentation is desirable for conditioning to occur, classical conditioning is not as effective in static situations; for example, in magazine ads where (in contrast to TV or radio) the marketer cannot control the order in which the reader perceives the CS and the UCS.

Because of the danger of extinction, a classical conditioning strategy may not be as effective for products that consumers frequently encounter, because there is no guarantee that the CS will accompany them. A bottle of Pepsi paired with the refreshing sound of a carbonated beverage poured over ice may seem like a good application of conditioning. Unfortunately, people would also see the product in many other contexts in which this sound was absent, so this reduces the effectiveness of that conditioning strategy.

By the same reasoning, a marketer is better off if she chooses to pair a novel tune rather than a popular one with a product, because people will also hear the popular song in many situations where the product is absent.[15] Music videos in particular may serve as effective UCSs because they often have an emotional impact on viewers, and this effect may transfer to ads that accompany the video.[16]

Net Profit

How often should an advertiser repeat the ads it places on Web sites? Recent research indicates that the answer depends on whether the ad relates to the Web site's content, and whether or not competing ads are also present on the site. The study found support for the general idea that repetitive ad messages resulted in higher recall and interest in learning more about the advertised product (in this case, a laptop). However, repeating the same ad was primarily effective when competitors also showed ads on the site. Otherwise, it was better to vary the ad messages for the laptop (presumably because people tuned out the ad if it appeared repeatedly). These ads were also more effective when they appeared on a site where the content related to the advertised product.[12]

Marketing Applications of Stimulus Generalization

The process of stimulus generalization often is central to branding and packaging decisions that try to capitalize on consumers' positive associations with an existing brand or company name. We can clearly appreciate the value of this kind of linkage when we look at universities with winning sports teams: Loyal fans snap up merchandise, from clothing to bathroom accessories, emblazoned with the school's name. This business did not even exist 20 years ago when schools were reluctant to commercialize their images. Texas A&M was one of the first schools that even bothered to file for trademark protection, and that was only after someone put the Aggie logo on a line of handguns. Today it's a different story. Many college administrators crave the revenue they receive from sweatshirts, drink coasters, and even toilet seats emblazoned with school logos. Strategies that marketers base on stimulus generalization include:

- **Family branding**—Many products capitalize on the reputation of a company name. Companies such as Campbell's, Heinz, and General Electric rely on their positive corporate images to sell different product lines.
- **Product line extension**—Marketers add related products to an established brand. Dole, which we associate with fruit, introduced refrigerated juices and juice bars, whereas Sun Maid went from raisins to raisin bread. The gun manufacturer Smith & Wesson launched its own line of furniture and other home items. Starbucks Corp. and Jim Beam Brands teamed up to make Starbucks Coffee Liqueur. Meanwhile, Procter & Gamble cleans up with its Mr. Clean brand of liquid cleanser; it aggressively puts the name on new products such as Mr. Clean Magic Eraser, for removing crayon marks from walls and scuff marks from chair rails; and Mr. Clean Autodry, for leaving a freshly washed car spot-free without hand drying.[17]
- **Licensing**—Companies often "rent" well-known names, hoping that that the learned associations they have forged will "rub off" onto other kinds of products. Jamba Juice recently launched a clothing line.[19] Zippo Manufacturing Co., long known for its "windproof" cigarette lighters, is marketing a men's fragrance—and no, it doesn't smell like lighter fluid.[20]
- **Look-alike packaging**—Distinctive packaging designs create strong associations with a particular brand. Companies that make generic or private-label brands and want to communicate a quality image often exploit this linkage when they put their products in packages similar to those of popular brands.[21] How does this strategy affect consumers' perceptions of the original brand? One study found that a negative

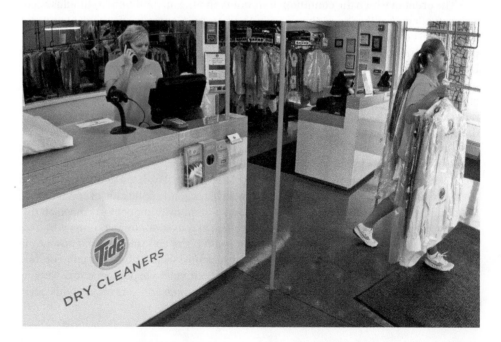

Procter & Gamble is opening a new line of Tide Dry Cleaners, named after its best-selling laundry detergent. P&G will rely on the more than 800,000 Facebook fans of Tide (what else do these people "like" on Facebook?) and other loyal detergent users to trust their clothes to the franchise stores. P&G plans to infuse the stores and its dry cleaning fluids with the familiar Tide scent just to underscore the connection.
Source: Courtesy of Boomburg via Getty Images

experience with an imitator brand actually *increased* consumers' evaluations of the original brand, whereas a positive experience with the imitator had the opposite effect of decreasing evaluations of the original brand.[22] Another study found that consumers tend to react positively to "copycat brands" as long as the imitator doesn't make grandiose claims that it can't fulfill.[23]

Of course, this strategy can make a lot of work for lawyers if the copycat brand gets *too* close to the original. Marketers of distinctive brands work hard to protect their designs and logos, and each year companies file numerous lawsuits in so-called *Lanham Act* cases that hinge on the issue of **consumer confusion**: How likely is it that one company's logo, product design, or package is so similar to another that the typical shopper would mistake one for the other? For example, Levi Strauss has sued almost 100 other apparel manufacturers that it claims have borrowed its trademark pocket design of a pentagon surrounding a drawing of a seagull in flight or its distinctive tab that it sews into its garments' vertical seams.[24]

Companies with a well-established brand image try to encourage stimulus discrimination when they promote the unique attributes of their brand—hence the constant reminders for American Express Travelers Cheques: "Ask for them by name." However, a brand name that a firm uses so widely that it is no longer distinctive becomes part of the public domain and competitors are free to borrow it: think of well-worn names such as aspirin, cellophane, yo-yo, escalator, and even google (which started as a noun and is now also a verb). This high degree of acceptance can be a tough barrier to jump when you're a competitor: Microsoft hopes that over time we will choose to "bing" rather than "google" when we want information.

OBJECTIVE 4

There is a difference between classical and instrumental conditioning, and both processes help consumers to learn about products.

Instrumental Conditioning

Instrumental conditioning (or *operant conditioning*) occurs when we learn to perform behaviors that produce positive outcomes and avoid those that yield negative outcomes. We most closely associate this learning process with the psychologist B. F. Skinner, who demonstrated the effects of instrumental conditioning by teaching pigeons and other animals to dance, play Ping-Pong, and perform other activities when he systematically rewarded them for desired behaviors.[25]

Whereas responses in classical conditioning are involuntary and fairly simple, we make those in instrumental conditioning deliberately to obtain a goal, and these may be more complex. We may learn the desired behavior over a period of time as a **shaping** process rewards our intermediate actions. For example, the owner of a new store may award prizes to shoppers who simply drop in; she hopes that over time they will continue to drop in and eventually even buy something.

Also, whereas classical conditioning involves the close pairing of two stimuli, instrumental learning occurs when a learner receives a reward *after* she performs the desired behavior. In these cases learning takes place over time, while the learner attempts and abandons other behaviors that don't get reinforced. A good way to remember the difference is to keep in mind that in instrumental learning the person makes a response because it is *instrumental* to gain a reward or avoid a punishment. Over time, consumers come to associate with people who reward them and to choose products that make them feel good or satisfy some need.

Instrumental conditioning occurs in one of three ways:

1 When the environment provides **positive reinforcement** in the form of a reward, this strengthens the response and we learn the appropriate behavior. For example, a woman who gets compliments after wearing Obsession perfume learns that using this product has the desired effect, and she will be more likely to keep buying the product.

2 **Negative reinforcement** also strengthens responses so that we learn the appropriate behavior. A perfume company might run an ad showing a woman sitting home alone

on a Saturday night because she did not wear its fragrance. The message this conveys is that she could have avoided this negative outcome if only she had used the perfume.

3. In contrast to situations where we learn to do certain things in order to avoid unpleasantness, **punishment** occurs when unpleasant events follow a response (such as when our friends ridicule us if we wear a nasty-smelling perfume). We learn the hard way not to repeat these behaviors.

To help you understand the differences among these mechanisms, keep in mind that reactions from a person's environment to his behavior can be either positive or negative, and that marketers can either apply or remove these outcomes (or anticipated outcomes). That is, under conditions of both positive reinforcement and punishment, the person receives a reaction when he does something. In contrast, negative reinforcement occurs when the person avoids a negative outcome—the removal of something negative is pleasurable and hence is rewarding.

Finally, when a person no longer receives a positive outcome, *extinction* is likely to occur, and the learned stimulus–response connection will not be maintained (as when a

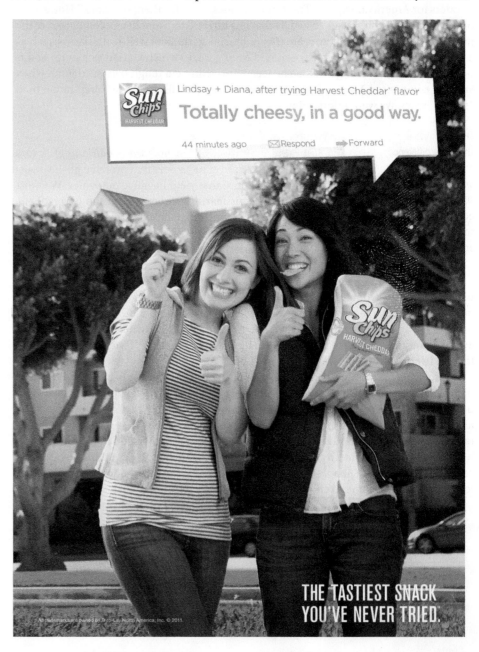

Positive reinforcement occurs after consumers try a new product and like it.
Source: Provided courtesy of Frito-Lay North America, Inc.

woman no longer receives compliments on her perfume). Thus, positive and negative reinforcement strengthen the future linkage between a response and an outcome because of the pleasant experience. This tie is weakened under conditions of both punishment and extinction because of the unpleasant experience. Figure 1 will help you to "reinforce" the relationships among these four conditions.

It's important for marketers to determine the most effective reinforcement schedule to use because this decision relates to the amount of effort and resources they must devote when they reward consumers who respond as they hope to their requests. Several schedules are possible:

- **Fixed-interval reinforcement**—After a specified time period has passed, the first response you make brings the reward. Under such conditions, people tend to respond slowly right after they get reinforced, but their responses get faster as the time for the next reinforcement approaches. For example, consumers may crowd into a store for the last day of its seasonal sale and not reappear until the next one.
- **Variable-interval reinforcement**—The time that must pass before you get reinforced varies based on some average. Because you don't know exactly when to expect the reinforcement, you have to respond at a consistent rate. This is the logic behind retailers' use of so-called *secret shoppers:* people who periodically test for service quality when they pose as customers at unannounced times. Because store employees never know exactly when to expect a visit, they must maintain high quality constantly "just in case."
- **Fixed-ratio reinforcement**—Reinforcement occurs only after a fixed number of responses. This schedule motivates you to continue performing the same behavior over and over. For example, you might keep buying groceries at the same store in order to earn a prize when you collect 50 register receipts.

Figure 1 TYPES OF REINFORCEMENT

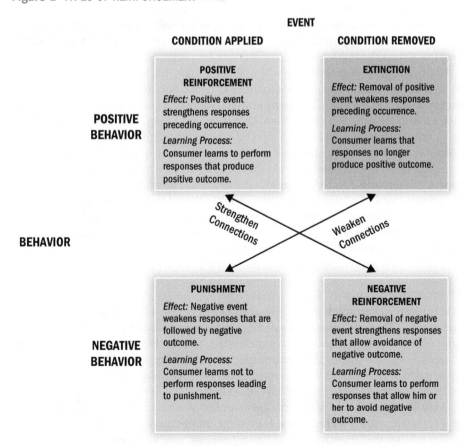

● **Variable-ratio reinforcement**—You get reinforced after a certain number of responses, but you don't know how many responses are required. People in such situations tend to respond at very high and steady rates, and this type of behavior is very difficult to extinguish. This reinforcement schedule is responsible for consumers' attractions to slot machines. They learn that if they keep throwing money into the machine, they will eventually win something (if they don't go broke first).

Marketing Applications of Instrumental Conditioning Principles

Principles of instrumental conditioning are at work when a marketer rewards or punishes a consumer for a purchase decision. Businesspeople shape behavior when they gradually reinforce the appropriate actions consumers take. A car dealer might encourage a reluctant buyer to simply sit in a floor model, then suggest a test drive, and then try to close the deal.

Marketers have many ways to reinforce consumers' behaviors, ranging from a simple "thank you" after a purchase to substantial rebates and follow-up phone calls. For example, a life insurance company obtained a much higher rate of policy renewal among a group of new customers who received a thank-you letter after each payment, compared to a control group that did not receive any reinforcement.[26]

Frequency marketing is a popular technique that rewards regular purchasers with prizes that get better as they spend more. The airline industry pioneered this instrumental learning strategy when it introduced "frequent flyer" programs in the early 1980s to reward loyal customers. The practice has spread to many other businesses as well, ranging from video stores to fast-food places.

Cognitive Learning Theory

In contrast to behavioral theories of learning, **cognitive learning theory** approaches stress the importance of internal mental processes. This perspective views people as problem solvers who actively use information from the world around them to master their environments. Supporters of this view also stress the role of creativity and insight during the learning process.

An Ocean Spray commercial for diet cranberry juice illustrates how marketers can harness their knowledge of cognitive theories to tweak marketing messages. The spot features two men, in the role of cranberry growers, who stand knee-deep in a bog. A group of women who are exercising joins them. Originally, the ad depicted the women having a party, but a cognitive scientist who worked on the campaign nixed that idea; she argued that the exercise class would send the diet message more quickly, whereas the party scene would confuse viewers who would spend too much time trying to figure out why the group was celebrating. This extra cognitive activity would distract from the ad's message. And, contrary to standard practice in advertising that the actors name the product as early as possible, she decided that the main characters should wait a few seconds before they mention the new diet product. She reasoned that viewers would need a second or so more time to process the images because of the additional action in the ad (the exercising). In a test of which ads got remembered best, this new version scored in the top 10 percent.[27]

Is Learning Conscious or Not?

A lot of controversy surrounds the issue of whether or when people are aware of their learning processes.[28] Whereas behavioral learning theorists emphasize the routine, automatic nature of conditioning, proponents of cognitive learning argue that even these simple effects are based on cognitive factors: They create expectations that a response will follow a stimulus (the formation of expectations requires mental activity). According to this school of thought, conditioning occurs because subjects develop conscious hypotheses and then act on them.

There is some evidence to support the existence of *nonconscious procedural knowledge*. People apparently do process at least some information in an automatic, passive way, a condition that researchers call "mindlessness" (we've all experienced that!).[29]

When we meet someone new or encounter a new product, for example, we have a tendency to respond to the stimulus in terms of existing categories we have learned, rather than taking the trouble to formulate new ones. In these cases a *trigger feature*—some stimulus that cues us toward a particular pattern—activates a reaction. For example, men in one study rated a car in an ad as superior on a variety of characteristics if a seductive woman (the trigger feature) was present, despite the fact that the men did not believe the woman's presence actually had an influence on their evaluations.[30]

Another study also illustrates this process. Undergraduates who were on their way to participate in a psychology experiment "accidentally" encountered a laboratory assistant who was laden with textbooks, a clipboard, papers, and a cup of hot or iced coffee—and asked for a hand with the cup. Guess what? The students who held a cup of iced coffee rated a hypothetical person they later read about as much colder, less social, and more selfish than did their fellow students who had helped out by holding a cup of hot coffee. Other researchers report similar findings: people tidy up more thoroughly when there's a faint tang of cleaning liquid in the air and they act more competitively if there's a briefcase in the room. In each case they change their behavior without being aware of doing so.[31] Indeed, a controversial best-selling book, *Blink: The Power of Thinking Without Thinking,* argues that we often make snap judgments that result in superior decisions compared to those we think about a lot, because we rely on our "adaptive unconscious" to guide us.[32] We'll talk more about the powerful (but often unnoticed) impact of our surroundings in later chapters.

Nonetheless, many modern theorists regard some instances of automatic conditioning as cognitive processes, especially when people form expectations about the linkages between stimuli and responses. Indeed, studies using *masking effects*, which make it difficult for subjects to learn CS/UCS associations, show substantial reductions in conditioning.[33] An adolescent girl may observe that women on television and in real life seem to be rewarded with compliments and attention when they smell nice and wear alluring clothing. She figures out that the probability of these rewards occurring is greater when she wears perfume, so she deliberately wears a popular scent to obtain the reward of social acceptance.

Observational Learning

OBJECTIVE 5

We learn about products by observing others' behavior.

Observational learning occurs when we watch the actions of others and note the reinforcements they receive for their behaviors. In these situations, learning occurs as a result of *vicarious* rather than direct experience. This type of learning is a complex process; people store these observations in memory as they accumulate knowledge and then they use this information at a later point to guide their own behavior. **Modeling** (not the runway kind) is the process of imitating the behavior of others. For example, a woman who shops for a new kind of perfume may remember the reactions her friend received when she wore a certain brand several months earlier, and she will mimic her friend's behavior in the hope that she will get the same feedback.

The modeling process is a powerful form of learning, and people's tendencies to imitate others' behaviors can have negative effects. Of particular concern is the potential of television shows and movies to teach violence to children. Children may be exposed to new methods of aggression by models (e.g., cartoon heroes) in the shows they watch. At some later point, when the child becomes angry, he may imitate these behaviors. A classic study demonstrates the effect of modeling on children's actions. Kids who watched an adult stomp on, knock down, and otherwise torture a large inflated "Bobo doll" repeated these behaviors when later left alone in a room with the doll; children who did not witness these acts did not.[34] Unfortunately, the relevance of this study to violent TV shows seems quite clear.

Figure 2 shows that for observational learning in the form of modeling to occur, the marketer must meet four conditions:[35]

1 The consumer's attention must be directed to the appropriate model, whom, for reasons of attractiveness, competence, status, or similarity, he must want to emulate.
2 The consumer must remember what the model says or does.
3 The consumer must convert this information into actions.
4 The consumer must be motivated to perform these actions.

Figure 2 THE OBSERVATIONAL LEARNING PROCESS

```
┌─────────────────┐   ┌─────────────────┐   ┌─────────────────┐   ┌─────────────────┐
│    ATTENTION    │   │    RETENTION    │   │   PRODUCTION    │   │   MOTIVATION    │
│  The consumer   │→  │  The consumer   │→  │    PROCESSES    │→  │ A situation     │
│  focuses on a   │   │  retains this   │   │  The consumer   │   │ arises          │
│    model's      │   │  behavior in    │   │  has the ability│   │ wherein the     │
│   behavior.     │   │    memory.      │   │  to perform the │   │ behavior        │
│                 │   │                 │   │    behavior.    │   │ is useful to the│
│                 │   │                 │   │                 │   │  consumer.      │
└─────────────────┘   └─────────────────┘   └─────────────────┘   └─────────────────┘
```

```
        ┌──────────────────────────────────┐
        │     OBSERVATIONAL LEARNING       │
        │  The consumer acquires and       │
        │  performs the behavior earlier   │
        │  demonstrated by a model.        │
        └──────────────────────────────────┘
```

Marketing Applications of Cognitive Learning Principles

Our ability to learn vicariously when we observe the outcomes of what others do makes the lives of marketers much easier. They don't necessarily have to directly reward or punish consumers when they make a purchase (think how expensive or even ethically questionable that might be!). Instead, they can show what happens to desirable models who use or do not use their products; they know that consumers often will imitate these actions at a later time. For example, a perfume commercial might depict a throng of admirers who compliment a glamorous woman when she wears a certain fragrance. Needless to say, this learning process is more practical than providing the same attention to each woman who actually buys the perfume (unless your brand's market share is really, really small!).

Consumers' evaluations of the people they model go beyond simple stimulus–response connections. For example, a celebrity's image elicits more than a simple reflexive response of good or bad.[36] It is a complex combination of many attributes. In general, the degree to which a person emulates someone else depends on that model's level of *social attractiveness*. Attractiveness comes from several components, including physical appearance, expertise, or similarity to the evaluator.

Memory

Memory is a process of acquiring information and storing it over time so that it will be available when we need it. Contemporary approaches to the study of memory employ an *information-processing approach*. They assume that the mind is in some ways like a computer: Data are input, processed, and output for later use in revised form. In the **encoding** stage, information enters in a way the system will recognize. In the **storage** stage, we integrate this knowledge with what is already in memory and "warehouse" it until it is needed. During **retrieval,** we access the desired information.[37] Figure 3 summarizes the memory process.

Many of our experiences are locked inside our heads, and they may surface years later if the right cues prompt them. Marketers rely on consumers to retain information

Figure 3 THE MEMORY PROCESS

```
┌──────────┐   ┌─────────────┐   ┌─────────────┐   ┌──────────────┐
│ EXTERNAL │→  │  ENCODING   │→  │   STORAGE   │→  │  RETRIEVAL   │
│  INPUTS  │   │Information is│  │Information is│  │Information    │
│          │   │ placed in   │   │ retained in │   │stored in     │
│          │   │  memory.    │   │   memory.   │   │memory is     │
│          │   │             │   │             │   │found as      │
│          │   │             │   │             │   │needed.       │
└──────────┘   └─────────────┘   └─────────────┘   └──────────────┘
```

they collect about products and services so they will apply it to future purchase decisions. During the *consumer decision-making process*, we combine this *internal memory* with *external memory*. This includes all the product details on packages and other marketing stimuli that permit us to identify and evaluate brand alternatives in the marketplace.[38]

The grocery shopping list is a good example of a powerful external memory aid. When consumers use shopping lists, they buy approximately 80 percent of the items on the list. The likelihood that a shopper will purchase a particular list item is higher if the person who wrote the list also participates in the shopping trip. This means that if marketers can induce a consumer to plan to purchase an item before she goes shopping, there is a high probability that she will buy it. One way to encourage this kind of advance planning is to provide peel-off stickers on packages so that, when the consumer notices the supply is low, she can simply peel off the label and place it directly on a shopping list.[39] Or, a retailer can support a phone app that generates a shopping list for the user (already more than 40 of these are available for the iPhone alone).[40]

How Our Brains Encode Information

The way we *encode*, or mentally program, information helps to determine how our brains will store this information. In general, it's more likely that we'll retain incoming data when we associate it with other things already in memory. For example, we tend to remember brand names that we link to physical characteristics of a product category (e.g., Coffee-Mate creamer or Sani-Flush toilet bowl cleaner) or that we can easily visualize (e.g., Tide detergent or Ford Mustang cars) compared to more abstract brand names.[41]

Types of Meaning

Sometimes we process a stimulus simply in terms of its *sensory meaning*, such as the literal color or shape of a package. We may experience a feeling of familiarity when, for example, we see an ad for a new snack food we have recently tasted. In many cases, though, we encode meanings at a more abstract level. *Semantic meaning* refers to symbolic associations, such as the idea that rich people drink champagne or that fashionable women have navel piercings. Let's take a closer look at how we encode these deeper meanings.

Marketing Opportunity

The choice of a great brand name is so important that companies often hire *naming consultants* to come up with a winner. These experts try to find *semantic associations* that click because they evoke some desirable connection. That strategy brought us names such as Qualcomm ("quality" and "communications"), Verizon (*veritas* is Latin for "truth," and "horizon" suggests forward-looking), and Intel ("intelligent" and "electronics"). The name Viagra rhymes with the famous waterfall Niagara. People associate water with both sexuality and life, and Niagara Falls is a honeymoon mecca. Philip Morris Companies renamed itself Altria Group to convey its expansion beyond cigarettes into packaged foods and brewing. This word means "high"; as one brand consultant commented, "I'm not sure 'high' is right for a company with many mood-altering products in its brand portfolio."[42]

These semantic combinations get harder to find, so some consultants appeal to our more basic instincts when they focus on linkages between the raw sounds of vowels and consonants (*phonemes*) and emotional responses. Studies on **sound symbolism** show that respondents who speak different languages associate the same sounds with such emotion-laden qualities as sad and insecure, alive and daring. To get at these associations, researchers usually give subjects pairs of nonsense names that differ in only a single phoneme—for example, *paressa* and *taressa*—and ask which sounds faster, more daring, nicer, and so on. They've found that sounds that come to a full stop (*p*, *b*, *t*, *d*) connote slowness, whereas the *f*, *v*, *s*, and *z* sounds seem faster. Prozac and Amazon convey a sense of speed (of recovery or of delivery).

When naming consultants got the assignment to label a new handheld personal digital assistant (PDA), they first thought of Strawberry because the little keyboard buttons resembled seeds. They liked the "berry" part of the name because they knew that people associated the letter *b* with reliability and a berry communicated smallness compared to other PDAs. But a linguist pointed out that "straw" is a slow syllable and the product needed to have a fast connotation. Voila! The BlackBerry PDA was born.[43]

This French ad for Pictionary requires the viewer to invest a fair amount of effort to understand it.
Source: Courtesy of Ogilvy & Mather, Paris.

Episodic memories relate to events that are personally relevant.[44] As a result, a person's motivation to retain these memories will likely be strong. Couples often have "their song," which reminds them of their first date or wedding. We call some especially vivid associations *flashbulb memories* (for example, where were you when you first heard that Osama bin Laden had been killed?). And recall of the past may affect future behavior. A college fund-raising campaign can raise more money when it evokes pleasant college memories than when it reminds alumni of unpleasant ones.

A **narrative,** or story is often an effective way to convey product information. Our memories store a lot of the social information we acquire in story form; it's a good idea to construct ads in the form of a narrative so they resonate with the audience. Narratives persuade people to construct mental representations of the information they see or hear. Pictures aid in this construction and allow us to develop more detailed mental representations.[45] Research supports the idea that we are more likely to positively evaluate and purchase brands when they connect with us like this.[46]

OBJECTIVE 6
Our brains process information about brands to retain them in memory.

Memory Systems

Researchers describe three distinct memory systems: *sensory memory*, *short-term memory (STM)*, and *long-term memory (LTM)*. Each plays a role in processing brand-related information. Figure 4 summarizes the interrelationships among these memory systems.

Sensory Memory

Sensory memory stores the information we receive from our senses. This storage is very temporary; it lasts a couple of seconds at most. For example, a man who walks past a donut shop gets a quick, enticing whiff of something baking inside. Although this sensation lasts only a few seconds, it is sufficient to allow him to consider whether he should investigate further. If he retains this information for further processing, it passes through an **attentional gate** and transfers to short-term memory.

Short-Term Memory

Short-term memory (STM) also stores information for a limited period of time, and it has limited capacity. Similar to a computer, this system is *working memory*; it holds the information we are currently processing. Our memories can store verbal input *acoustically* (in terms of how it sounds) or *semantically* (in terms of what it means).

We store this information by combining small pieces into larger ones in a process we call **chunking.** A *chunk* is a configuration that is familiar to the person and that he or

Figure 4 TYPES OF MEMORY

she can think about as a unit. For example, a brand name like Seven For All Mankind is a chunk that summarizes a great deal of detailed information about the product.

Initially, researchers believed that our STM was capable of processing between five and nine chunks of information at a time; they described this basic property as "the magical number 7+/−2." This is the reason our phone numbers today (at least in the United States) have seven digits.[48] It now appears that three to four chunks is the optimal size for efficient retrieval (we remember seven-digit phone numbers because we chunk the individual digits, so we may remember a three-digit exchange as one piece of information).[49] Phone calls aside, chunking is important to marketers because it helps determine how consumers keep prices in short-term memory when they comparison-shop.[50]

Long-Term Memory

Long-term memory (LTM) is the system that allows us to retain information for a long period of time. A cognitive process we call **elaborative rehearsal** allows information to move from short-term memory into long-term memory. This involves thinking about the meaning of a stimulus and relating it to other information already in memory. Marketers sometimes assist in the process when they devise catchy slogans or jingles that consumers repeat on their own.

How Our Memories Store Information

The relationship between short-term memory and long-term memory is a source of some controversy. The traditional *multiple-store* perspective assumes that STM and LTM are separate systems. More recent research has moved away from the distinction

An Australian ad for hair products evokes memories of an earlier time—that some of us might prefer to forget.
Source: Courtesy of Fudge Australia.

CB AS I SEE IT

Profs. Katherine and Michael LaTour, *The University of Nevada at Las Vegas*

In our view, consumer research is about "digging deeper" for insight into the mind of the market in a way that elicits useful knowledge for the marketing manager. Our research embraces this proposition by expanding knowledge about the complexities of consumer memory and framing that understanding in a way that enhances how practitioners approach their consumers.

A particular focus of our research is on consumer experience, particularly memory for experience. Experience is *noeic*, coming from Greek *nous* meaning intellect or understanding; knowledge as experienced directly with a feeling of certitude. Consumers genuinely believe that their experiences drive their decision making, and external

information like advertising has little impact. Our research has found otherwise. In early research, Kathy LaTour (formerly Braun) introduced the *theory of memory reconstruction* to marketing, and looked at how postexperience advertising could alter what consumers remembered about their direct tasting experience. In one experiment she had participants taste a sample of orange juice that had been doctored with vinegar, salt, and excess water. She found that when participants received advertising after that taste experience suggesting that the juice was fresh and flavorful, they "remembered" having tasted a better juice—in fact, identifying a better-quality juice as the one they had tasted earlier in the hour. In other research with Elizabeth Loftus (one of the most prominent cognitive psychologists studying human memory), we found that autobiographical advertising for Disneyland that included a false reference (to Bugs Bunny) led a significant portion of participants to "recall" that they had themselves met and shook Bugs Bunny's hand when they visited a Disney park as a child (an impossible event, as Bugs is a Warner Bros. character and so is not allowed to set foot on a Disney property).

Memory is paradoxical: Sometimes people remember great details about events, other times (as evidenced in our research mentioned earlier) people can be quite suggestible. Though the memory of Bugs Bunny was false in our experiments, the participants believed that they had had that experience, and in fact listed the overall

Disney vacation as one of their most significant childhood events. In our qualitative research, we have looked at how certain childhood experiences can extend their influence into adulthood, ranging from preference to car design to fast-food choice to cola choice to gambling style.

Our most recent research has looked at how marketers can teach consumers to better learn from their experiences. In that research we looked at wine aficionados, whom we define as drinking a lot of wine but having little conceptual knowledge about it. We found aficionados to be overconfident in their ability to judge a wine, acting more similarly to novices than expert sommeliers in blind taste tests. However, we found that providing these aficionados with a vocabulary (wine aroma wheel) led them to better retention of their taste experience, making them overall more accurate and less likely to be swayed by misleading marketing communication. Currently Kathy LaTour is training for her sommelier certification as a means both to understand the processes involved in obtaining expertise in wine and to learn important issues from a practitioner perspective that might guide future research projects (and Mike is enjoying the wine learning as well!). One of our goals is to develop research projects that can guide managers in their experience design in order to provide consumers experiences that are more memorable. The larger framework we work under is to develop innovative research projects and have fun in the process.[53]

between the two types of memory; it emphasizes the interdependence of the systems. According to this work, depending on the nature of the processing task, different levels of processing occur that activate some aspects of memory rather than others. We call these approaches **activation models of memory.**[52] The more effort it takes to process information (so-called deep processing), the more likely it is that information will transfer into LTM.

OBJECTIVE 7

The other products we associate with an individual product influence how we will remember it.

Associative Networks

According to activation models of memory, an incoming piece of information gets stored in an **associative network** that contains many bits of related information. We each have organized systems of concepts that relate to brands, manufacturers, and stores stored in our memories; the contents, of course, depend on our own unique experiences.

Think of these storage units, or *knowledge structures*, as complex spider webs filled with pieces of data. Incoming information gets put into nodes that connect to one another (if you haven't guessed, this is also why we call cyberspace the World Wide Web). When we view separate pieces of information as similar for some reason, we chunk them together under some more abstract category. Then, we interpret new, incoming information to be consistent with the structure we have created.[54] This helps explain why we are better able to remember brands or stores that we believe "go together"; for example, when Titleist rather than Chanel sponsors a golf tournament. Recent research indicates that people can recall brands that are not as obviously linked (for example, when an unlikely product sponsors an event), but in these cases marketers have to work harder to justify why the two things go together.[55]

In the associative network, links form between nodes. For example, a consumer might have a network for "perfumes." Each node represents a concept related to the category. This node can be an attribute, a specific brand, a celebrity the consumer identifies with a specific perfume brand, or even a related product. A network for perfumes might include concepts such as the brand names Britney Spears Curious for Women, Calvin Klein Eternity, and Elizabeth Arden Red Door, as well as attributes such as sexy and elegant.

When we ask the consumer to list perfumes, this consumer recalls only those brands that show up in the appropriate category. This group constitutes her **evoked set.** The task of a new entrant that wants to position itself as a category member (e.g., a new luxury perfume) is to provide cues that facilitate its placement in the appropriate category. Figure 5 shows a sample network for perfumes.

The Tangled Web

In the age of Google, Facebook, and Wikipedia, sometimes our problem is not remembering too little—it's remembering *too much*. The Internet records everything and forgets nothing, even when we wish it would. A survey Microsoft conducted found that 75 percent of U.S. recruiters do online research about job candidates, and many use social media sites like Facebook and photo-sharing sites to get the real 911 about prospective employees. Seventy percent have rejected candidates because of information they found online. It's hard to get away with anything when your behavior seems to get as much attention as the misdeeds of celebrities like Charlie Sheen! One 26-year-old woman told a reporter she dreaded being tagged in online photos because people would see the outfits she wears when she's out on the town. As she observed, "You have movie-star issues and you're just a person." This constant scrutiny means it's getting harder and harder to get a "mulligan" (a golf term for a replay)—in a wired world your former transgressions are never forgotten.[51]

- - - - - - - - - - - - - - -

Figure 5 AN ASSOCIATIVE NETWORK FOR PERFUMES

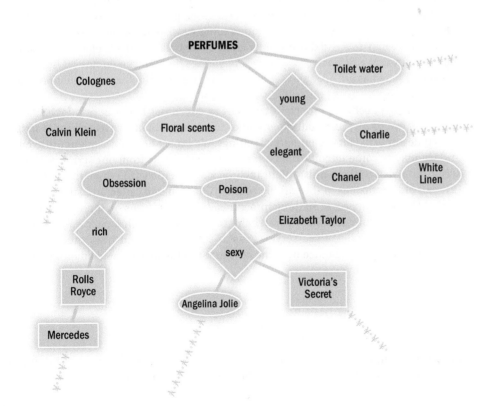

Spreading Activation

A marketing message may activate our memory of a brand directly (for example, when it shows us a picture of the package), or it may do so indirectly when it links to something else that's related to the brand in our knowledge structure. If it activates a node, it will also activate other linked nodes, much as tapping a spider's web in one spot sends movement reverberating across the web. Meaning thus spreads across the network, and we recall concepts, such as competing brands and relevant attributes, that we use to form attitudes toward the brand.

This process of **spreading activation** allows us to shift back and forth among levels of meaning. The way we store a piece of information in memory depends on the type of meaning we initially assign to it. This meaning type, in turn, will determine how and when something activates the meaning. For example, we could store the memory trace for an Axe men's fragrance ad in one or more of the following ways:

- **Brand-specific**—Memory is stored in terms of claims the brand makes ("it's macho").
- **Ad-specific**—Memory is stored in terms of the medium or content of the ad itself (a macho-looking guy uses the product).
- **Brand identification**—Memory is stored in terms of the brand name (e.g., "Axe").
- **Product category**—Memory is stored in terms of how the product works or where it should be used (a bottle of Axe sits in a guy's medicine cabinet).
- **Evaluative reactions**—Memory is stored as positive or negative emotions ("that looks cool").[56]

Levels of Knowledge

Within a knowledge structure, we code elements at different levels of abstraction and complexity. *Meaning* concepts (such as "macho") get stored as individual nodes. We may combine these concepts into a larger unit we call a *proposition* (or a *belief*). A proposition links two nodes together to form a more complex meaning, which can serve as a single chunk of information. For example, "Axe is cologne for macho men" is a proposition (though not necessarily a correct one!).

In turn, we integrate propositions to produce an even more complex unit called a *schema*. A schema is a cognitive framework we develop through experience. We encode information more readily when that information is consistent with an existing schema.[57] The ability to move up and down among levels of abstraction greatly increases processing flexibility and efficiency. For this reason, young children who do not yet have well-developed schemas are not able to make as efficient use of purchase information as are older children.[58]

One type of schema especially relevant to consumer behavior is a **script,** a sequence of events an individual expects to occur. As consumers we learn *service scripts* that guide our behavior in commercial settings. We expect a certain sequence of events, and we may become uncomfortable if the service departs from our script. A service script for a visit to the dentist might include such events as (1) drive to the dentist, (2) read old magazines in the waiting room, (3) hear name called and sit in dentist's chair, (4) dentist injects something into gums, (5) dentist turns on high-pitched drill, and so on. This desire to follow a script helps to explain why such service innovations as automatic bank machines, self-service gas stations, or "scan-your-own" grocery checkouts have met with resistance by some consumers who have trouble adapting to new sequences of events.[59]

How We Retrieve Memories When We Decide What to Buy

In one major study, only 23 percent of the respondents could recall a new product introduced in the past year.[60] Not an encouraging finding for marketers.

Retrieval is the process whereby we recover information from long-term memory. As evidenced by the popularity of the board game *Trivial Pursuit* or the TV show *Are You Smarter than a Fifth Grader?*, people have a vast quantity of information stored in their heads—a lot of which is not very useful unless you're playing the game! Although most of the information that enters long-term memory does not go away, it may be difficult or impossible to retrieve unless the appropriate cues are present. What factors influence the likelihood that we will remember the marketing messages that organizations work so hard to create?

Individual cognitive or physiological factors are responsible for some of the differences in retrieval ability among people.[61] Older adults consistently display inferior recall ability for current items, such as prescription drug instructions, although they may recall events that happened to them when they were younger with great clarity.[62] The recent popularity of puzzles, such as Sudoku, and centers that offer "mental gymnastics" attests to emerging evidence that we can keep our retrieval abilities sharp by exercising our minds, just as we keep our other muscles toned when we work out on a regular basis.

Situational factors also influence retrieval; these relate to the environment in which we encounter the message. Not surprisingly, recall is enhanced when we pay more attention to the message in the first place. Some evidence indicates that we can more easily retrieve information about a *pioneering brand* (the first brand to enter a market) from memory than we can for *follower brands,* because the first product's introduction is likely to be distinctive and, for the time being, no competitors divert our attention.[63] In addition, we are more likely to recall descriptive brand names than those that do not provide adequate cues as to what the product is.[64]

Not surprisingly, the way a marketer presents her message influences the likelihood that we'll be able to recall it later. The **spacing effect** describes the tendency for us to recall printed material more effectively when the advertiser repeats the target item periodically, rather than presenting it repeatedly in a short time period.[65] The viewing environment of a marketing message also affects recall. For example, commercials we see during baseball games yield the lowest recall scores among sports programs, because the activity is stop-and-go rather than continuous. Unlike football or basketball, the pacing of baseball gives many opportunities for attention to wander even during play. Similarly, General Electric found that its commercials fared better in television shows with continuous activity, such as stories or dramas, compared to variety shows or talk shows that are punctuated by a series of acts.[66] A large-scale analysis of TV commercials found that viewers recall commercials shown first in a series of ads better than those they see last.[67]

Finally, it goes without saying that the nature of the ad itself plays a big role in determining whether it's memorable. One study on print advertising reported that we are far more likely to remember spectacular magazine ads, including multipage spreads, three-dimensional pop-ups, scented ads, and ads with audio components. For example, a Pepsi Jazz two-page spread, which incorporated a three-dimensional pop-up of the opened bottle, a small audio chip that played jazz music from the bottle's opening, and a scratch-and-sniff tab that let readers smell its black cherry vanilla flavor, scored an amazing 100 percent in reader recall.[68] Unfortunately, that kind of multimedia treatment is very expensive; not every ad can mimic a Broadway production!

What Makes Us Forget?

Marketers obviously hope that consumers will not forget about their products. However, in a poll of more than 13,000 adults, more than half were unable to remember any specific ad they had seen, heard, or read in the past 30 days. How many can you remember right now? Clearly, forgetting by consumers is a big headache for marketers (not to mention a problem for students when they study for exams!).

Early memory theorists assumed that memories simply fade with the passage of time. In a process of **decay,** the structural changes that learning produces in the brain simply go away. Forgetting also occurs as a result of **interference;** as we learn additional information, it displaces the earlier information. Consumers may forget stimulus–response associations if they subsequently learn new responses to the same or similar stimuli; we call this process *retroactive interference.* Or, prior learning can interfere with new learning, a process we term *proactive interference.* Because we store pieces of information in memory as nodes that link to one another, we are more likely to retrieve a meaning concept that is connected by a larger number of links. But as we learn new responses, a stimulus loses its effectiveness in retrieving the old response.[69]

These interference effects help to explain problems in remembering brand information.[70] Consumers tend to organize attribute information by brand.[70] Additional attribute information regarding a brand or similar brands may limit the person's ability to recall old brand information. Recall may also be inhibited if the brand name is composed of frequently used words. These words cue competing associations and, as a result, we retain less brand information.[71]

In one study, brand evaluations deteriorated more rapidly when ads for the brand appeared with messages for 12 other brands in the same category than when researchers showed the ad along with ads for 12 dissimilar products.[72] Thus, when we increase the uniqueness of one brand, it impairs the recall of other brands.[73] However, when we call a competitor by name, this can result in poorer recall for our own brand.[74]

State-Dependent Retrieval

Is it true that you'll do better on an exam if you study for it in the classroom in which you'll take the test? Perhaps. The process we call **state-dependent retrieval** illustrates that we are better able to access information if our internal state is the same at the time of recall as when we learned the information. So, we are more likely to recall an ad if our mood or level of arousal at the time of exposure is similar to that in the purchase environment. When marketers re-create the cues that were present when they first presented the information, they can enhance recall. For example, on its box Life cereal uses a picture of "Mikey" from its commercial, which facilitates recall of brand claims and favorable brand evaluations.[75]

Familiarity and Recall

As a general rule, when we are already familiar with an item we're more likely to recall messages about it. Indeed, this is one of the basic goals of marketers who try to create and maintain awareness of their products. The more experience a consumer has with a product, the better use he or she makes of product information.[76] However, there is a possible fly in the ointment: As we noted earlier in this chapter, some evidence indicates that extreme familiarity can result in inferior learning and recall. When consumers are highly familiar with a brand or an advertisement, they may not pay much attention to a message for it, because they do not believe that any additional effort will increase their knowledge.[77] We call this process *automaticity.*[78] For example, when researchers expose consumers to a radio ad that repeats the audio track from a television ad they've already seen, they do very little critical, evaluative processing; they just mentally replay the video portion of the ad.[79]

We also tend to observe a **highlighting effect,** which occurs when the order in which consumers learn about brands determines the strength of association between these brands and their attributes. Consumers more strongly associate common attributes with early-learned brands and unique attributes with late-learned brands. More generally, we are more likely to recognize words, objects, and faces we learn early in life than similar items we learn later. This applies to brands as well; managers who introduce new entries into a market with well-established brand names need to work harder to create learning and memory linkages by exposing consumers to information about them more frequently.[80]

Salience and Recall

The **salience** of a brand refers to its prominence or level of activation in memory. Stimuli that stand out in contrast to their environments are more likely to command attention, which, in turn, increases the likelihood that we will recall them. Almost any technique that increases the novelty of a stimulus also improves recall (a result we call the **von Restorff effect**).[81] This explains why unusual advertising or distinctive packaging tends to facilitate brand recall.[82]

The tactic of introducing a surprise element in an ad can boost recall, even if the new information is not relevant to the remaining material.[83] In addition, *mystery ads*, in which the ad doesn't identify the brand until the end, are more effective if we want to build associations in memory between the product category and that brand—especially in the case of relatively unknown brands.[84]

Furthermore, the *intensity* and type of emotions we experience at the time also affect the way we recall the event later. We recall **mixed emotions** (e.g., those with positive and negative components) differently than **unipolar emotions** (e.g., those that are either wholly positive or wholly negative). The latter become even more polarized over time, so that we recall good things as even better than they really were and bad things as even worse (maybe the "good old days" weren't really so good after all!).[85]

The Viewing Context

Regardless of how awesome a commercial is, the show in which it appears influences its impact. Nielsen (the company that measures who watches which media) reports

CB AS I SEE IT

Professor Jennifer Aaker, *Stanford University*

Imagine you are at Disneyland about to board the Space Mountain ride. As you climb into your rocket, you feel joy and apprehension—a mixed feeling that persists even after the ride is over. You grip the safety bar, at once thrilled and frightened. You leave the Space Mountain ride dizzy with mixed emotions. How will you recall your experience a week later? Will you remember the mixed emotions you experienced on the ride? Or will the memory of those mixed emotions fade?

Questions regarding the memory of mixed emotions are important. Many of life's most important events are defined by mixtures of emotions where people find themselves feeling both positive and negative emotions—e.g., graduating from college ("I'm making

progress, but leaving my friends and family"), moving ("I'm starting a new life, but losing my old one"), or achieving major life goals ("I'm thrilled to have reached the destination, but I'm sad the journey is over").

To address these questions, we conducted a set of longitudinal experiments which show that the intensity of mixed emotions is underestimated at the time of recall—an effect that appears to increase over time and does not occur to the same degree with uniformly happy or sad emotions. Together, these results indicate that, as time passes, mixed emotions are increasingly difficult to recall, that memory for them fades, and that felt conflict underlies this recall bias.

The results of this work speak to several domains of research. For example, the results imply that individuals who are comfortable with inconsistency should recall mixed emotions more accurately. Similarly, if there is an increased desire to resolve the emotion of felt conflict, the effects documented here should be muted for individuals who are not disturbed by the ambiguity associated with mixed emotions. Also, the effects should

dissipate if the mixed emotions we experience consist of a dominant emotion (e.g., strong feelings of anger), thereby reducing the conflict we feel.

The results also speak to ongoing research in marketing, which suggests that emotional experiences can fundamentally affect purchase intent as well as foster brand loyalty. For example, the amount of warmth that emanates from a brand or the fun derived from a brand (e.g., iPhone) can fundamentally influence our relationship with it. However, in reality, most consumer–brand relationships are defined, at some point or another, by a transgression that gives rise to negative feelings among consumers, such as when something you buy breaks. Our research suggests that the degree to which a negative event is categorized as part of a mixed experience (as opposed a single negative event) affects the probability that the consumer will remember that experience and be influenced by it. If the transgression is mentally clumped together with positive interactions with the brand, the memory of the mixed emotional experience may indeed fade—which would not be the case if the transgression stood alone as an isolated negative event.

that viewers who enjoy a program are more likely to respond positively to a commercial and to say they want to buy the advertised product. Nielsen studied the responses of 10,000 people across 50 shows and 200 brands. Viewers are almost one-third more likely to remember brands whose products were placed in shows they enjoy. The impact of this factor varies across show format; it's weaker in sitcoms but much stronger in "lifestyle programs" such as *Extreme Makeover Home Edition*.[86]

It also helps when the marketer's message is consistent with the theme or events in the program—and it's even better when the advertised product actually makes a reference to the show. The Discovery Channel documented this effect during a broadcast of its program *Mythbusters*, which uses science to test the validity of urban legends. The network ran a brief ad for Guinness beer in which a character asked another whether it was a "myth that Guinness only has 125 calories." Viewers who saw this ad remembered the name of the Guinness brand 41 percent more often than they did when they saw a traditional ad for the beer. Other similar **hybrid ads** that include a program tie-in deliver similar results.[87]

Pictorial versus Verbal Cues: Is a Picture Worth a Thousand Words?

There is some evidence for the superiority of visual memory over verbal memory, but this advantage is unclear because it is more difficult to measure recall of pictures.[88] However, the available data indicate that we are more likely to recognize information we see in picture form at a later time.[89] Certainly, visual aspects of an ad are more likely to grab a consumer's attention. In fact, eye-movement studies indicate that about 90 percent of viewers look at the dominant picture in an ad before they bother to view the copy.[90]

Visual aspects of an ad grab a consumer's attention, especially when they are novel. That is certainly the case for this "pile of trash" that is actually an outdoor ad on a Dutch street for the MINI Cooper.

Source: Courtesy of UbachsWisbrun/JWT.

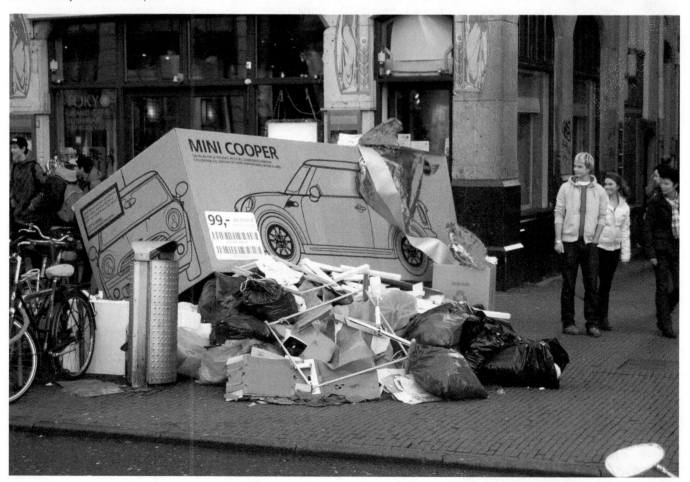

Although pictorial ads may enhance recall, they do not necessarily improve comprehension. One study found that television news items presented with illustrations (still pictures) as a backdrop result in improved recall for details of the news story, even though understanding of the story's content does not improve.[91] Another study confirmed that consumers typically recall ads with visual figures more often and they like them better.[92]

OBJECTIVE 8

Products help us to retrieve memories from our past.

Products as Memory Markers

The Disney theme parks' 2012 marketing campaign is called "Let the Memories Begin." It will focus on vacation memories; TV commercials, online ads, and brochures featuring photos and videos shot by park guests. Disney will project images of visitors on building facades each night.[93] The company understands just how powerful memories can be.

The pictures we take of ourselves using products and services (like when we pose with Mickey at Disney World) can themselves serve as powerful retrieval cues. Indeed, the three types of possessions consumers most value are furniture, visual art, and photos. These objects are likely to jog memories of the past.[94] Researchers find that valued possessions can evoke thoughts about prior events on several dimensions, including sensory experiences, friends and loved ones, and breaking away from parents or former partners.[95]

That helps to explain the popularity of photo-sharing sites like Flickr—this platform alone hosts more than 5 billion pictures and offers "Share This" tools for use on Facebook and Twitter.[96] A new app called Memolane goes a step farther: It lets you create a visual timeline from the posts on your social media accounts. You can compile these into a searchable, scrollable image that lets you remember the sequence of events from that memorable vacation or even (but let's hope not) that awesome first date.[97]

Even food can facilitate recall: One study looked at how favorite recipes stimulate memories of the past. When the researchers asked informants to list three of their favorite recipes and to talk about these choices, they found that people tended to link them with memories of past events, such as childhood memories, family holidays, milestone events (such as dishes they only make on special holidays, like corned beef and cabbage on St. Patrick's Day), heirlooms (recipes handed down across generations), and the passing of time (e.g., only eating blueberry cobbler in the summer).[98] Indeed, one of the most famous literary references is from the classic (3,000-page!) novel *Remembrance of Things Past* by Marcel Proust. The narrator dips a pastry (a "madeleine") into his tea, and this action unleashes a flood of memories that drive the rest of the book.

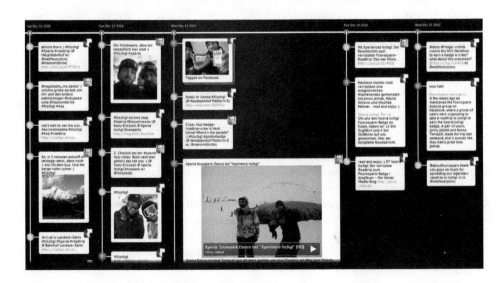

The Memolane app lets you create a timeline from the posts on your social media accounts.
Source: Courtesy of Memolane.

Products are particularly important as markers when our sense of the past is threatened, as, for example, when an event such as divorce, relocation, or graduation challenges a consumer's current identity.[99] Our cherished possessions often have *mnemonic* qualities that serve as a form of external memory when they prompt us to retrieve episodic memories. For example, family photography allows consumers to create their own retrieval cues; the 11 billion amateur photos we take annually form a kind of external memory bank for our culture. A stimulus is, at times, able to evoke a weakened response even years after we first perceived it. We call this effect **spontaneous recovery,** and this reestablished connection may explain consumers' powerful emotional reactions to songs or pictures they have not been exposed to in quite a long time.

OBJECTIVE 9
Marketers measure our memories about products and ads.

How We Measure Consumers' Recall of Marketing Messages

Because marketers pay so much money to place their messages in front of consumers, they hope that people will actually remember these ads later on. It seems that they have good reason to be concerned. In one study, fewer than 40 percent of television viewers made positive links between commercial messages and the corresponding products, only 65 percent noticed the brand name in a commercial, and only 38 percent recognized a connection to an important point.[100]

Even more sadly, only 7 percent of television viewers can recall the product or company featured in the most recent television commercial they watched. This figure represents less than half the recall rate recorded in 1965. We can explain this drop-off in terms of such factors as the increase of 30- and 15-second commercials and the practice of airing television commercials in clusters rather than in single-sponsor programs.[101]

Recognition versus Recall

One indicator of good advertising is, of course, the impression it makes on us. But how can we define and measure this impact? Two basic measures of impact are **recognition** and **recall.** In the typical *recognition test*, researchers show ads to subjects one at a time and ask if they have seen them before. In contrast, *free recall tests* ask consumers to independently think of what they have seen without being prompted for this information first; obviously, this task requires greater effort on their part.

Under some conditions, these two memory measures tend to yield the same results, especially when the researchers try to keep the viewers' interest in the ads constant (though, as we've already seen, that may be an overly artificial way to study true memory for ads).[102] Generally, though, recognition scores tend to be more reliable and do not decay over time the way recall scores do.[103] Recognition scores are almost always better than recall scores because recognition is a simpler process and the consumer has more retrieval cues available.

Both types of retrieval play important roles in purchase decisions, however. Recall tends to be more important in situations in which consumers do not have product data at their disposal, so they must rely on memory to generate this information.[104] However, recognition is more likely to be an important factor in a store, where retailers confront consumers with thousands of product options (i.e., external memory is abundantly available) and the task simply may be to recognize a familiar package. Unfortunately, package recognition and familiarity can have negative consequences; for example, consumers may ignore warning labels because they take those messages for granted and don't really notice them.[105]

Problems with Memory Measures

Although measuring an ad's memorability is important, analysts have questioned whether existing measures accurately assess these dimensions, for several reasons. First, the results we obtain from a measuring instrument are not necessarily based on what we measure, but rather on something else about the instrument or the respondent. This form of contamination is a **response bias.** For example, people tend to give "yes" responses to questions, regardless of what the item asks. In addition, experimental subjects often are eager to be "good subjects": They try to figure out what the experimenter is looking for and give the response they think they are supposed to give. This tendency is so strong that in some studies the rate at which subjects claim they recognize *bogus ads* (ads they have not seen before) is almost as high as their recognition rate for those they really have seen![106]

Memory Lapses

People are also prone to forget information or retain inaccurate memories (yes, even younger people). Typical problems include *omitting* (leaving facts out), *averaging* (the tendency to "normalize" memories by not reporting extreme cases), and *telescoping* (inaccurate recall of time).[107] These distortions are not just a problem in court cases that rely on eyewitness testimony; they also call into question the accuracy of product usage databases that rely on consumers to recall their purchase and consumption of food and household items. For example, one study asked people to describe what portion of various foods—small, medium, or large—they ate in a typical meal. However, the researchers used different definitions of "medium." Regardless of the definition they gave, about the same number of people claimed they typically ate "medium" portions.[108]

Another study documented the **illusion of truth effect,** where telling people (especially elderly subjects) that a consumer claim is false can make them misremember it as true. Respondents were repeatedly told that a claim was false; after a 3-day delay, they were likely to remember it as true. This is because the repetition of the claim increases familiarity with it, but respondents don't retain their memories of the context (where the claim was debunked). This effect has potentially important implications, especially for social marketing campaigns that try to educate people about false claims.[110]

Finally, although researchers continue to work on techniques that increase the accuracy of memory scores, these improvements do not address the more fundamental issue of whether recall is even necessary for advertising to have an effect. In particular, some critics argue that these measures do not adequately tap the impact of "feeling" ads whose objective is to arouse strong emotions rather than to convey concrete product benefits. Many ad campaigns, including those for Hallmark cards, Chevrolet, and Pepsi, use this approach.[111] In these cases, the marketers hope to create a long-term buildup of positive feelings rather than relying on a one-shot attempt to convince consumers to buy their products.

Also, it is not clear that recall translates into preference. We may recall the benefits touted in an ad but not believe them. Or the ad may be memorable because it is so

Marketing Pitfall

Can our financial problems decrease our ability to remember even the coolest commercials? The research firm Gallup & Robinson says yes. In 2009 the company studied 12 years' worth of surveys about recall and likability of Super Bowl ads. It reports a direct relationship between the confidence people have in the economy and the amount of attention they pay to these spots. When consumer confidence is weak, recall is 11 percent lower than average and 36 percent lower than in good times.[109] Perhaps people are worrying too much about where they will get money to pay attention to ads that tell them how to spend it.

Heinz and Pepsi are among numerous companies that recently issued "retro" versions of their packages.
Source: Courtesy of H. J. Heinz Company.

obnoxious and the product becomes one we "love to hate." The bottom line: Although recall is important, especially to create brand awareness, it is not necessarily sufficient to alter consumer preferences. To accomplish this, we need more sophisticated attitude-changing strategies.

Bittersweet Memories: The Marketing Power of Nostalgia

Marketers often resurrect popular characters and stories from days gone by; they hope that consumers' fond memories will motivate them to revisit the past. We had a 1950s revival in the 1970s, and consumers in the 1980s got a heavy dose of memories from the 1960s. Today, it seems that popular characters only need to be gone for a few years before someone tries to bring them back. Many companies have responded as they dig deep into their vaults to bring back old favorites. New commercials position Chevrolet as a classic American brand. Planters Peanuts recruited the actor Robert Downey, Jr., as the new voice of Mr. Peanut. "Retired" brand names, including Meister Brau beer, the brokerage firm Shearson, and Handi-Wrap plastic wrap, were recently auctioned off to companies that want to bring them back to life.[112] The biggest retro success story in recent years: the Old Spice Guy campaign that went viral and revived a men's deodorant brand that is more than 70 years old.

Nostalgia describes the bittersweet emotion that arises when we view the past with both sadness and longing.[113] References to "the good old days" are increasingly common, as advertisers call up memories of youth—and hope that these feelings will translate to what they're selling today.

A **retro brand** is an updated version of a brand from a prior historical period. These products trigger nostalgia, and researchers find that they often inspire consumers to

Fossil's product designs evoke memories of earlier, classic styles.

Source: Used with permission of Fossil Inc. Photography by Thom Jackson and Jon Kirk.

This ad from Chile uses a retro appeal.
Source: Courtesy of Volkswagen.

think back to an era when (at least in our memories) life was more stable, simple, or even utopian. Very simply, they let us "look backward through rose-colored glasses."[114]

Our prior experiences also help to determine what we like today. Consumer researchers created a *nostalgia index* that measures the critical ages during which our preferences are likely to form and endure over time. It turns out that a good predictor of whether a person will like a specific song is how old she was when that song was popular. On average, we are most likely to favor songs that were popular when we were 23.5 years old (so pay attention to the hot songs if you haven't turned 23 yet). Our preferences for fashion models peak at age 33, and we tend to like movie stars who were popular when we were 26 or 27 years old.[115]

CHAPTER SUMMARY

Now that you have finished reading this chapter you should understand why:

1. **It is important to understand how consumers learn about products and services.**

   Learning is a change in behavior that experience causes. Learning can occur through simple associations between a stimulus and a response or via a complex series of cognitive activities.

2. **Conditioning results in learning.**

   Behavioral learning theories assume that learning occurs as a result of responses to external events. Classical conditioning occurs when a stimulus that naturally elicits a response (an unconditioned stimulus) is paired with another stimulus that does not initially elicit this response. Over time, the second stimulus (the conditioned stimulus) elicits the response even in the absence of the first.

3. Learned associations with brands generalize to other products, and why this is important to marketers.

This response can also extend to other, similar stimuli in a process we call stimulus generalization. This process is the basis for such marketing strategies as licensing and family branding, where a consumer's positive associations with a product transfer to other contexts.

4. There is a difference between classical and instrumental conditioning, and both processes help consumers to learn about products.

Operant, or instrumental, conditioning occurs as the person learns to perform behaviors that produce positive outcomes and avoid those that result in negative outcomes. Whereas classical conditioning involves the pairing of two stimuli, instrumental learning occurs when reinforcement occurs following a response to a stimulus. Reinforcement is positive if a reward follows a response. It is negative if the person avoids a negative outcome by not performing a response. Punishment occurs when an unpleasant event follows a response. Extinction of the behavior will occur if reinforcement no longer occurs.

5. We learn about products by observing others' behavior.

Cognitive learning occurs as the result of mental processes. For example, observational learning occurs when the consumer performs a behavior as a result of seeing someone else performing it and being rewarded for it.

6. Our brains process information about brands to retain them in memory.

Memory is the storage of learned information. The way we encode information when we perceive it determines how we will store it in memory. The memory systems we call sensory memory, short-term memory, and long-term memory each play a role in retaining and processing information from the outside world.

7. The other products we associate with an individual product influence how we will remember it.

We don't store information in isolation; we incorporate it into a knowledge structure where our brains associate it with other related data. The location of product information in associative networks, and the level of abstraction at which it is coded, help to determine when and how we will activate this information at a later time. Some factors that influence the likelihood of retrieval include the level of familiarity with an item, its salience (or prominence) in memory, and whether the information was presented in pictorial or written form.

8. Products help us to retrieve memories from our past.

Products also play a role as memory markers; consumers use them to retrieve memories about past experiences (autobiographical memories), and we often value them because they are able to do this. This function also encourages the use of nostalgia in marketing strategies.

9. Marketers measure our memories about products and ads.

We can use either recognition or recall techniques to measure memory for product information. Consumers are more likely to recognize an advertisement if it is presented to them than they are to recall one without being given any cues. However, neither recognition nor recall automatically or reliably translates into product preferences or purchases.

KEY TERMS

activation models of memory	encoding	interference
advertising wear-out	episodic memories	learning
associative network	evoked set	licensing
attentional gate	extinction	long-term memory (LTM)
behavioral learning theories	family branding	look-alike packaging
brand equity	fixed-interval reinforcement	memory
chunking	fixed-ratio reinforcement	mixed emotions
classical conditioning	frequency marketing	modeling
cognitive learning theory	halo effect	narrative
conditioned response (CR)	highlighting effect	negative reinforcement
conditioned stimulus (CS)	hybrid ads	nostalgia
consumer confusion	illusion of truth effect	observational learning
decay	incidental learning	positive reinforcement
elaborative rehearsal	instrumental conditioning	product line extension

punishment	sensory memory	stimulus generalization
recall	shaping	storage
recognition	short-term memory (STM)	unconditioned stimulus (UCS)
repetition	sound symbolism	unipolar emotions
response bias	spacing effect	variable-interval reinforcement
retrieval	spontaneous recovery	variable-ratio reinforcement
retro brand	spreading activation	von Restorff effect
salience	state-dependent retrieval	
script	stimulus discrimination	

REVIEW

1 What is the difference between an unconditioned stimulus and a conditioned stimulus?

2 Give an example of a halo effect in marketing.

3 How can marketers use repetition to increase the likelihood that consumers will learn about their brand?

4 Why is it not necessarily a good idea to advertise a product in a commercial where a really popular song plays in the background?

5 What is the difference between classical conditioning and instrumental conditioning?

6 How do different types of reinforcement enhance learning? How does the strategy of frequency marketing relate to conditioning?

7 What is the major difference between behavioral and cognitive theories of learning?

8 Name the three stages of information processing.

9 What is external memory and why is it important to marketers?

10 Give an example of an episodic memory.

11 Why do phone numbers have seven digits?

12 List the three types of memory, and explain how they work together.

13 How is associative memory like a spider web?

14 How does the likelihood that a person wants to use an ATM machine relate to a schema?

15 Why does a pioneering brand have a memory advantage over follower brands?

16 If a consumer is familiar with a product, advertising for it can work by either enhancing or diminishing recall. Why?

17 How does learning new information make it more likely that we'll forget things we've already learned?

18 Define *nostalgia,* and explain why it's such a widely used advertising strategy.

19 Name the two basic measures of memory and describe how they differ from one another.

20 List three problems with measures of memory for advertising.

CONSUMER BEHAVIOR CHALLENGE

■ DISCUSS

1. In his book, *Blink: The Power of Thinking Without Thinking,* author Malcolm Gladwell argues that hallowed marketing research techniques such as focus groups aren't effective because we usually react to products quickly and without much conscious thought; thus, it's better simply to solicit consumers' first impressions rather than getting them to think at length about why they buy. What's your position on this issue?

2. Some die-hard fans were not pleased when the Rolling Stones sold the tune "Start Me Up" for about $4 million to Microsoft, which wanted the classic song to promote its Windows 95 launch. The Beach Boys sold "Good Vibrations" to Cadbury Schweppes for its Sunkist soft drink, Steppenwolf offered his "Born to Be Wild" to plug the Mercury Cougar, and even Bob Dylan sold "The Times They Are A-Changin'" to Coopers & Lybrand (now called Price-WaterhouseCoopers).[116] Other rock legends have refused to play the commercial game, including Bruce Springsteen, the Grateful Dead, Led Zeppelin, Fleetwood Mac, R.E.M., and U2. According to U2's manager, "Rock'n roll is the last vestige of independence. It is undignified to put that creative effort and hard work to the disposal of a soft drink or beer or car."[117] Singer Neil Young is especially adamant about not selling out; in his song "This Note's for You," he croons, "Ain't singing for Pepsi, ain't singing for Coke, I don't sing for nobody, makes me look like a joke." What's your take on this issue? How do you react when one of your favorite songs turns up in a commercial? Is this use of nostalgia an effective way to market a product? Why or why not?

■ APPLY

1 Devise a product jingle memory test. Compile a list of brands that are or have been associated with memorable jingles, such as Chiquita Banana or Alka-Seltzer. Read this list to friends, and see how many jingles they remember. You may be surprised at their level of recall.

2 A physician borrowed a page from product marketers when she asked for their advice to help persuade people in the developing world to wash their hands habitually with soap. Diseases and disorders caused by dirty hands—like diarrhea—kill a child somewhere in the world about every 15 seconds, and about half those deaths could be prevented with the regular use of soap. The project adapted techniques that major marketers use to encourage habitual product usage of items such as skin moisturizers, disinfecting wipes, air fresheners, water purifiers, toothpaste, and vitamins. For example, beer commercials often depict a group of guys together, because research shows that being with a group of friends tends to trigger habitual drinking! The researchers found that when people in Ghana experienced a feeling of disgust, this was a cue to wash their hands. However, as in many developing countries, toilets are actually a symbol of cleanliness because they have replaced pit latrines. So, an advertising campaign included messages that reminded people of the germs they could still pick up even in modern bathrooms: mothers and children walked out of restrooms with a glowing purple pigment on their hands that contaminated everything they touched. These images in turn triggered the habit of handwashing, and the project resulted in a significant increase in the number of consumers who washed their hands with soap.[118] How can other organizations that work to improve public health, the environment, or other social issues harness our knowledge about consumer learning and habitual behavior to create or reenergize positive habits?

3 Identify some important characteristics of a product with a well-known brand name. Based on these attributes, generate a list of possible brand extension or licensing opportunities, as well as some others that consumers would not be likely to accept.

4 Collect some pictures of "classic" products that have high nostalgia value. Show these pictures to others, and allow them to free-associate. Analyze the types of memories that these products evoke, and think about how a marketer might employ these associations in a product's promotional strategy.

MyMarketingLab Now that you have completed this chapter, return to **www.mymktlab.com** to apply concepts and explore the additional study materials.

Case Study

DO AVATARS DREAM ABOUT VIRTUAL SHOPPING?

When he ventures online, he's a muscular, bronzed, 23-year-old surfer. But, after a few hours chilling in the virtual world of Second Life, it's time for this shy, 110-pound student to get back to work. Sound weird? It's not. He is one of the 38,000 "residents" who is logged into Second Life at any given time. Welcome to the world of avatars! Marketers are just beginning to understand how the time people spend in virtual worlds influences the way they learn about brands.

Second Life, which Linden Labs first launched in 2002, is one of the largest virtual worlds. In Second Life, and other sites, users create an avatar to represent themselves online. Some people create avatars that look a lot like them in the real world, but many residents choose avatars that represent the person they would like to be, fantasy creatures, or even individuals of the opposite gender. With these alternate personalities they go out and explore virtual worlds. So what does this mean to marketers? A lot more than some pixels on a computer screen. Avatars interact with real brands in these virtual worlds. They can purchase products such as jeans for their avatars, and they can attend events such as concerts or lectures.

But it's not just virtual worlds like Second Life that want to understand how to make money from the legions of avatars out there. Web site designers and developers also realize the importance of avatars that interact with visitors on corporate Web sites. Several companies offer software applications that design avatars to greet and guide visitors (for one example, check out Sitepal.com). Some of these avatars take the form of famous people, including rock stars, actors, and historical figures. Research suggests that these avatars might increase users' satisfaction with the Web sites and affect purchases.

Organizations and educators are just beginning to realize the impact of avatars and virtual worlds. Many companies now host their business meetings online; they encourage employees to develop their own avatars when they attend the meetings. Several university presidents hold online forums with students and create avatars to discuss current issues of concern with their students. The world of avatars and virtual worlds will continue to challenge marketers in the years to come.

DISCUSSION QUESTIONS

1 How might classical conditioning operate for a consumer who visits a new tutoring Web site and is greeted by the Web site's avatar who resembles Albert Einstein?

2 How might a consumer who purchases a new outfit for his avatar on a virtual world be influenced by instrumental conditioning?

3 Do consumers build associative networks from their avatar's experience? Do you think this network is part of the consumer's overall associative network for that brand, or is it a separate network?

Sources: Natalie Wood, Michael R. Solomon, and Basil G. Englis, "Personalization of the Web Interface: The Impact of Web Avatars on Users' Responses to E-commerce Sites," _Journal of Website Promotion_ 2, no. 1/2 (2006): 53–69; Natalie T. Wood and Michael R. Solomon, "Virtual Worlds, Real Impact: Advertising in Immersive Digital Environments," in Matthew S. Eastin, Terry Daugherty, and Neal M. Burns, eds., _Handbook of Research on Digital Media and Advertising: User Generated Content Consumption_ (IGI Global, 2011): 521–534.

NOTES

1. Jenna Goudreau, "These Old Brands Are Poised for a 2011 Comeback: Nostalgia Will Help Sell to Consumers Who Aren't Happy with the Present," _Forbes_ (December 31, 2010), http://today.msnbc.msn.com/id/40856091/ns/today-entertainment, accessed April 4, 2011.

2. Robert A. Baron, _Psychology: The Essential Science_ (Boston: Allyn & Bacon, 1989).

3. Richard A. Feinberg, "Credit Cards as Spending Facilitating Stimuli: A Conditioning Interpretation," _Journal of Consumer Research_ 13 (December 1986): 348–56.

4. R. A. Rescorla, "Pavlovian Conditioning: It's Not What You Think It Is," _American Psychologist_ 43 (1988): 151–60; Elnora W. Stuart, Terence A. Shimp, and Randall W. Engle, "Classical Conditioning of Consumer Attitudes: Four Experiments in an Advertising Context," _Journal of Consumer Research_ 14 (December 1987): 334–39.

5. C. Janiszewski, H. Noel, and A. G. Sawyer, "A Meta-analysis of the Spacing Effect in Verbal Learning: Implications for Research on Advertising Repetition and Consumer Memory," _Journal of Consumer Research_ 30, no. 1 (2003): 138–49.

6. James Ward, Barbara Loken, Ivan Ross, and Tedi Hasapopoulous, "The Influence of Physical Similarity of Affect and Attribute Perceptions from National Brands to Private Label Brands," in Terence A. Shimp et al., eds., _American Marketing Educators' Conference_ (Chicago: American Marketing Association, 1986): 51–56.

7. Judith Lynne Zaichkowsky and Richard Neil Simpson, "The Effect of Experience with a Brand Imitator on the Original Brand," _Marketing Letters_ 7, no. 1 (1996): 31–39.

8. Randi Priluck Grossman and Brian D. Till, "The Persistence of Classically Conditioned Brand Attitudes," _Journal of Advertising_ 21, no. 1 (1998): 23–31; Chris T. Allen and Thomas J. Madden, "A Closer Look at Classical Conditioning," _Journal of Consumer Research_ 12 (December 1985): 301–15; Chester A. Insko and William F. Oakes, "Awareness and the Conditioning of Attitudes," _Journal of Personality & Social Psychology_ 4 (November 1966): 487–96; Carolyn K. Staats and Arthur W. Staats, "Meaning Established by Classical Conditioning," _Journal of Experimental Psychology_ 54 (July 1957): 74–80.

9. Kevin Lane Keller, "Conceptualizing, Measuring, and Managing Customer-Based Brand Equity," _Journal of Marketing_ 57 (January 1993): 1–22.

10. Herbert Krugman, "Low Recall and High Recognition of Advertising," _Journal of Advertising Research_ (February–March 1986): 79–80.

11. Brian Steinberg, "Ad Nauseam: Repetition of TV Spots Risks Driving Consumers Away, Fragmenting Media, Smaller Budgets Make for More of the Same Ads," _Crain's Detroit Business_ (December 1, 2008), www.Crainsdetroit.Com/Article/20081201/Email01/812010278/1092, accessed December 1, 2008.

12. Yaveroglu Donthu and Naveen Donthu, "Advertising Repetition and Placement Issues in On-Line Environments," _Journal of Advertising_ 37 (Summer 2008): 31–43.

13. Gerald J. Gorn, "The Effects of Music in Advertising on Choice Behavior: A Classical Conditioning Approach," _Journal of Marketing_ 46 (Winter 1982): 94–101.

14. Noreen Klein, Virginia Tech, personal communication (April 2000); Calvin Bierley, Frances K. McSweeney, and Renee Vannieuwkerk, "Classical Conditioning of Preferences for Stimuli," _Journal of Consumer Research_ 12 (December 1985): 316–23; James J. Kellaris and Anthony D. Cox, "The Effects of Background Music in Advertising: A Reassessment," _Journal of Consumer Research_ 16 (June 1989): 113–18.

15. Frances K. McSweeney and Calvin Bierley, "Recent Developments in Classical Conditioning," _Journal of Consumer Research_ 11 (September 1984): 619–31.

16. Basil G. Englis, "The Reinforcement Properties of Music Videos: 'I Want My . . . I Want My . . . I Want My . . . MTV,'" paper presented at the meetings of the Association for Consumer Research, New Orleans (1989).

17. Andrew Martin, "Smelling an Opportunity," _New York Times_ (December 8, 2010), http://www.nytimes.com/2010/12/09/business/09tide.html?_r=1&ref=business, accessed May 7, 2011; Anand Natarajan, "Branding: Interiors by Smith & Wesson," _BusinessWeek_ (November 10, 2003): 16; James B. Arndorfer, "Starbucks Wakes Up to Liquor Possibilities," _Advertising Age_ (November 22, 2004): 4; Claudia Deutsch, "Will Real Men Buy Mr. Clean?," _New York Times_ (September 24, 2003), www.nytimes.com, accessed September 24, 2003.

18. http://www.edhardywines.com/, accessed April 6, 2011; quoted in Dan Neil, "Ed Hardy Wines? Christian Audigier's Branding Machine Grinds On," _Los Angeles Times_ (April 28, 2009), www.latimes.com/business, accessed April 28, 2009.

19. Dan Macsai, "Jamba Juice Launches Clothing Line," _Fast Company_ (July 1, 2010), http://www.fastcompany.com/magazine/147/unwanted-wear-your-smoothie.html?partner=homepage_newsletter, accessed April 6, 2011.

20. James R. Hagerty, "Zippo Preps for a Post-Smoker World," _Wall Street Journal_ (March 8, 2011), http://online.wsj.com/article/SB10001424052748704076804576180411173921454.html?mod=dist_smartbrief&mod=WALL STREET JOURNAL_hp_MIDDLENextto WhatsNewsThird, accessed April 6, 2011.

21. "Look-Alikes Mimic Familiar Packages," _New York Times_ (August 9, 1986): D1.

22. Zaichkowsky and Simpson, "The Effect of Experience with a Brand Imitator on the Original Brand," 31–39.

23. Luk Warlop and Joseph W. Alba, "Sincere Flattery: Trade-Dress Imitation and Consumer Choice," _Journal of Consumer Psychology_ 14, nos. 1 & 2 (2004): 21–27.

24. Michael Barbaro and Julie Creswell, "Levi's Turns to Suing Its Rivals," _New York Times_ (January 29, 2007), www.nytimes.com/2007/01/29/business/29jeans.html, accessed June 30, 2009.

25. For a comprehensive approach to consumer behavior–based operant conditioning principles, see Gordon R. Foxall, "Behavior Analysis and Consumer Psychology," _Journal of Economic Psychology_ 15 (March 1994): 5–91.

26. J. Blaise Bergiel and Christine Trosclair, "Instrumental Learning: Its Application to Customer Satisfaction," _Journal of Consumer Marketing_ 2 (Fall 1985): 23–28.

27. Suzanne Vranica, "Agencies Don Lab Coats to Reach Consumers, Firms Deploy Scientists Within Creative Groups to Make Messages Stick," _Wall Street Journal_ (June 4, 2007): B8.

28. Cf., for example, E. M. Eisenstein and J. W. Hutchinson, "Action-Based Learning: Goals and Attention in the Acquisition of Market Knowledge," _Journal of Marketing Research_ 43, no. 2 (2006): 244–58.

29. Ellen J. Langer, _The Psychology of Control_ (Beverly Hills, CA: Sage, 1983).

30. Robert B. Cialdini, _Influence: Science and Practice_, 2nd ed. (New York: William Morrow, 1984); Y. Rottenstreich, S. Sood, and L. Brenner, "Feeling and Thinking in Memory-Based versus Stimulus-Based Choices," _Journal of Consumer Research_ 33, no. 4 (2007): 461–69.

31. Benedict Carey, "Who's Minding the Mind?" _New York Times Online_ (July 31, 2007). http://www.nytimes.com/2007/07/31/health/psychology/31subl.html

32. Malcolm Gladwell, *Blink: The Power of Thinking Without Thinking* (New York: Little, Brown, 2005).

33. Chris T. Allen and Thomas J. Madden, "A Closer Look at Classical Conditioning," *Journal of Consumer Research* 12 (December 1985): 301–15; see also Terence A. Shimp, Elnora W. Stuart, and Randall W. Engle, "A Program of Classical Conditioning Experiments Testing Variations in the Conditioned Stimulus and Context," *Journal of Consumer Research* 18 (June 1991): 1–12.

34. Terence A. Shimp, "Neo-Pavlovian Conditioning and Its Implications for Consumer Theory and Research," in Thomas S. Robertson and Harold H. Kassarjian, eds., *Handbook of Consumer Behavior* (Upper Saddle River, NJ: Prentice Hall, 1991).

35. Albert Bandura, *Social Foundations of Thought and Action: A Social Cognitive View* (Upper Saddle River, NJ: Prentice Hall, 1986).

36. *Ibid.*

37. R. C. Atkinson and I. M. Shiffrin, "Human Memory: A Proposed System and Its Control Processes," in K. W. Spence and J. T. Spence, eds., *The Psychology of Learning and Motivation: Advances in Research and Theory*, vol. 2 (New York: Academic Press, 1968): 89–195.

38. James R. Bettman, "Memory Factors in Consumer Choice: A Review," *Journal of Marketing* (Spring 1979): 37–53. For a study that explores the relative impact of internal versus external memory on brand choice, see Joseph W. Alba, Howard Marmorstein, and Amitava Chattopadhyay, "Transitions in Preference over Time: The Effects of Memory on Message Persuasiveness," *Journal of Marketing Research* 29 (1992): 406–16.

39. Lauren G. Block and Vicki G. Morwitz, "Shopping Lists as an External Memory Aid for Grocery Shopping: Influences on List Writing and List Fulfillment," *Journal of Consumer Psychology* 8, no. 4 (1999): 343–75.

40. Rob Griffiths, "Shop Shop Shopping List Review," macworld.com, http://www.macworld.com/appguide/app.html?id=71541&expand=false, accessed May 7, 2011.

41. Kim Robertson, "Recall and Recognition Effects of Brand Name Imagery," *Psychology & Marketing* 4 (Spring 1987): 3–15.

42. Stuart Elliott, "If Philip Morris becomes Altria, its corporate image may lose some of the odor of stale smoke," *New York Times* (November 19, 2001). http://www.nytimes.com/2001/11/19/business/media-business-advertising-if-philip-morris-becomes-altria-its-corporate-image.html, accessed August 24, 2011.

43. Sharon Begley, "StrawBerry Is No BlackBerry: Building Brands Using Sound," *Wall Street Journal* (August 26, 2002), www.wsj.com, accessed August 26, 2002.

44. Endel Tulving, "Remembering and Knowing the Past," *American Scientist* 77 (July–August 1989): 361.

45. Rashmi Adaval and Robert S. Wyer, Jr., "The Role of Narratives in Consumer Information Processing," *Journal of Consumer Psychology* 7, no. 3 (1998): 207–46; cf. also R. F. Baumeister and L. S. Newman, "How Stories Make Sense of Personal Experiences: Motives that Shape Autobiographical Narratives," *Personality & Social Psychology Bulletin* 20, no. 6 (1994): 676–90; J. Bruner, *Actual Minds, Possible Worlds* (Cambridge, MA: Harvard University Press, 1986).

46. Jennifer Edson Escalas, "Narrative Processing: Building Consumer Connections to Brands," *Journal of Consumer Psychology* 14, nos. 1 & 2 (2004): 168–80.

47. Beth Snyder Bulik, "What's in a (Good) Product Name? Sales Cellphone Study Finds 'Cognitive' Monikers Work; Numerics Flop," February 2, 2009, www.namedevelopment.com/Articles/Good-Cellphone-Names.html, accessed February 27, 2009.

48. George A. Miller, "The Magical Number Seven, Plus or Minus Two: Some Limits on Our Capacity for Processing Information," *Psychological Review* 63 (1956): 81–97.

49. James N. MacGregor, "Short-Term Memory Capacity: Limitation or Optimization?" *Psychological Review* 94 (1987): 107–8.

50. M. Vanhuele, G. Laurent, and X. Dréze, "Consumers' Immediate Memory for Prices," *Journal of Consumer Research* 33, no. 2 (2006): 163–72.

51. Jeffrey Rosen, "The Web Means the End of Forgetting," *New York Times* (July 21, 2010), http://www.nytimes.com/2010/07/25/magazine/25privacy-t2.html?ref=magazine, accessed April 4, 2011.

52. See Catherine A. Cole and Michael J. Houston, "Encoding and Media Effects on Consumer Learning Deficiencies in the Elderly," *Journal of Marketing Research* 24 (February 1987): 55–64; A. M. Collins and E. F. Loftus, "A Spreading Activation Theory of Semantic Processing," *Psychological Review* 82 (1975): 407–28; Fergus I. M. Craik and Robert S. Lockhart, "Levels of Processing: A Framework for Memory Research," *Journal of Verbal Learning & Verbal Behavior* 11 (1972): 671–84.

53. Kathryn A. Braun, "Post-Experience Advertising Effects on Consumer Memory," *Journal of Consumer Research* 25 (March 1999), 319–34; Kathryn A. Braun-LaTour, Michael S. LaTour, Jacqueline Pickrell, and Elizabeth F. Loftus, "How (and When) Advertising Can Influence Memory for Consumer Experience," *Journal of Advertising* 33, no. 4 (2004): 7–26; Kathryn A. Braun-LaTour, Michael S. LaTour, and George M. Zinkhan, "Using Childhood Memories to Gain Insight into Brand Meaning," *Journal of Marketing* 71 (April 2007): 45–60.

54. Walter A. Henry, "The Effect of Information-Processing Ability on Processing Accuracy," *Journal of Consumer Research* 7 (June 1980): 42–48.

55. T. B. Cornwell, M. S. Humphreys, A. M. Maguire, C. S. Weeks, and C. L. Tellegen, "Sponsorship-Linked Marketing: The Role of Articulation in Memory," *Journal of Consumer Research* 33, no. 3 (2006): 312–21.

56. Kevin Lane Keller, "Memory Factors in Advertising: The Effect of Advertising Retrieval Cues on Brand Evaluations," *Journal of Consumer Research* 14 (December 1987): 316–33. For a discussion of processing operations that occur during brand choice, see Gabriel Biehal and Dipankar Chakravarti, "Consumers' Use of Memory and External Information in Choice: Macro and Micro Perspectives," *Journal of Consumer Research* 12 (March 1986): 382–405.

57. Susan T. Fiske and Shelley E. Taylor, *Social Cognition* (Reading, MA: Addison-Wesley, 1984).

58. Deborah Roedder John and John C. Whitney Jr., "The Development of Consumer Knowledge in Children: A Cognitive Structure Approach," *Journal of Consumer Research* 12 (March 1986): 406–17.

59. Michael R. Solomon, Carol Surprenant, John A. Czepiel, and Evelyn G. Gutman, "A Role Theory Perspective on Dyadic Interactions: The Service Encounter," *Journal of Marketing* 49 (Winter 1985): 99–111.

60. Aaron Baar, "New Product Messages Aren't Making Intended Impressions," *Marketing Daily* (March 6, 2008), http://publications.mediapost.com/Index.Cfm?Fuseaction=Articles.Showarticle&Art_Aid=779, accessed March 6, 2008.

61. S. Danziger, S. Moran, and V. Rafaely, "The Influence of Ease of Retrieval on Judgment as a Function of Attention to Subjective Experience," *Journal of Consumer Psychology* 16, no. 2 (2006): 191–95.

62. Roger W. Morrell, Denise C. Park, and Leonard W. Poon, "Quality of Instructions on Prescription Drug Labels: Effects on Memory and Comprehension in Young and Old Adults," *The Gerontologist* 29 (1989): 345–54.

63. Frank R. Kardes, Gurumurthy Kalyanaram, Murali Chandrashekaran, and Ronald J. Dornoff, "Brand Retrieval, Consideration Set Composition, Consumer Choice, and the Pioneering Advantage" (unpublished manuscript, The University of Cincinnati, Ohio, 1992).

64. Judith Lynne Zaichkowsky and Padma Vipat, "Inferences from Brand Names," paper presented at the European meeting of the Association for Consumer Research, Amsterdam (June 1992).

65. H. Noel, "The Spacing Effect: Enhancing Memory for Repeated Marketing Stimuli," *Journal of Consumer Psychology* 16, no. 3 (2006): 306–20; for an alternative explanation, see S. L. Appleton-Knapp, R. A. Bjork, and T. D. Wickens, "Examining the Spacing Effect in Advertising: Encoding Variability, Retrieval Processes, and Their Interaction," *Journal of Consumer Research* 32, no. 2 (2005): 266–76.

66. Herbert E. Krugman, "Low Recall and High Recognition of Advertising," *Journal of Advertising Research* (February–March 1986): 79–86.

67. Rik G. M. Pieters and Tammo H. A. Bijmolt, "Consumer Memory for Television Advertising: A Field Study of Duration, Serial Position, and Competition Effects," *Journal of Consumer Research* 23 (March 1997): 362–72.

68. Erik Sass, "Study Finds Spectacular Print Ads Get Spectacular Recall," *Marketing Daily* (February 23, 2007), www.mediapost.com, accessed February 23, 2007.

69. Raymond R. Burke and Thomas K. Srull, "Competitive Interference and Consumer Memory for Advertising," *Journal of Consumer Research* 15 (June 1988): 55–68.

70. Eric J. Johnson and J. Edward Russo, "Product Familiarity and Learning New Information," *Journal of Consumer Research* 11 (June 1984): 542–50.

71. Joan Meyers-Levy, "The Influence of Brand Name's Association Set Size and Word Frequency on Brand Memory," *Journal of Consumer Research* 16 (September 1989): 197–208.

72. Michael H. Baumgardner, Michael R. Leippe, David L. Ronis, and Anthony G. Greenwald, "In Search of Reliable Persuasion Effects: II. Associative Interference and Persistence of Persuasion in a Message-Dense Environment," *Journal of Personality & Social Psychology* 45 (September 1983): 524–37.

73. Joseph W. Alba and Amitava Chattopadhyay, "Salience Effects in Brand Recall," *Journal of Marketing Research* 23 (November 1986): 363–70.

74. Margaret Henderson Blair, Allan R. Kuse, David H. Furse, and David W. Stewart, "Advertising in a New and Competitive Environment: Persuading Consumers to Buy," *Business Horizons* 30 (November–December 1987): 20.

75. Kevin Lane Keller, "Memory Factors in Advertising: The Effect of Advertising Retrieval Cues on Brand Evaluations," *Journal of Consumer Research* 14 (December 1987): 316–33.

76. Eric J. Johnson and J. Edward Russo, "Product Familiarity and Learning New Information," *Journal of Consumer Research* 11 (June 1984): 542–50.

77. Eric J. Johnson and J. Edward Russo, "Product Familiarity and Learning New Information," in Kent Monroe, ed., *Advances in Consumer Research 8* (Ann Arbor, MI: Association for Consumer Research, 1981): 151–55; John G. Lynch and Thomas K. Srull, "Memory and Attentional Factors in Consumer Choice: Concepts and Research Methods," *Journal of Consumer Research* 9 (June 1982): 18–37.

78. Joseph W. Alba and J. Wesley Hutchinson, "Dimensions of Consumer Expertise," *Journal of Consumer Research* 13 (March 1988): 411–54; Julie A. Edell and Kevin Lane Keller, "The Information Processing of Coordinated Media Campaigns," *Journal of Marketing Research* 26 (May 1989): 149–64; cf. also Jeff Galak, Joseph P. Redden, and Justin Kruger, "Variety Amnesia: Recalling Past Variety Can Accelerate Recovery from Satiation," *Journal of Consumer Research* 36, no. 4 (2009): 575–84.

79. Marcus Cunha, Jr., and Juliano Laran, "Asymmetries in the Sequential Learning of Brand Associations: Implications for the Early Entrant Advantage," *Journal of Consumer Research* 35, no. 5 (2009): 788–99; Julie A. Edell and Kevin Lane Keller, "The Information Processing of Coordinated Media Campaigns," *Journal of Marketing Research* 26 (May 1989): 149–64; cf. also Galak, Redden, and Kruger, "Variety Amnesia: Recalling Past Variety Can Accelerate Recovery from Satiation."

80. Cunha, Jr., and Laran, "Asymmetries in the Sequential Learning of Brand Associations: Implications for the Early Entrant Advantage"; Andrew W. Ellis, Selina J. Holmes, and Richard L. Wright, "Age of Acquisition and the Recognition of Brand Names: On the Importance of Being Early," *Journal of Consumer Psychology* 20, no. 1 (2010): 43–52.

81. John G. Lynch and Thomas K. Srull, "Memory and Attentional Factors in Consumer Choice: Concepts and Research Methods," *Journal of Consumer Research* 9 (June 1982): 18–37.

82. Joseph W. Alba and Amitava Chattopadhyay, "Salience Effects in Brand Recall," *Journal of Marketing Research* 23 (November 1986): 363–70; Elizabeth C. Hirschman and Michael R. Solomon, "Utilitarian, Aesthetic, and Familiarity Responses to Verbal versus Visual Advertisements," in Thomas C. Kinnear, ed., *Advances in Consumer Research 11* (Provo, UT: Association for Consumer Research, 1984): 426–31.

83. Susan E. Heckler and Terry L. Childers, "The Role of Expectancy and Relevancy in Memory for Verbal and Visual Information: What Is Incongruency?" *Journal of Consumer Research* 18 (March 1992): 475–92.

84. Russell H. Fazio, Paul M. Herr, and Martha C. Powell, "On the Development and Strength of Category-Brand Associations in Memory: The Case of Mystery Ads," *Journal of Consumer Psychology* 1, no. 1 (1992): 1–13.

85. Jennifer Aaker, Aimee Drolet, and Dale Griffin, "Recalling Mixed Emotions," *Journal of Consumer Research* 35 (August 2008): 268–78.

86. Alex Mindlin, "Commercials Bask in a Show's Glow," *New York Times Online* (December 17, 2007), www.nytimes.com, accessed December 17, 2008.

87. Suzanne Vranica, "New Ads Take on Tivo, Tie-Ins to TV Shows Aim to Prevent Fast-Forwarding," *Wall Street Journal* (October 5, 2007): B4.

88. Hirschman and Solomon, "Utilitarian, Aesthetic, and Familiarity Responses to Verbal versus Visual Advertisements."

89. Terry Childers and Michael Houston, "Conditions for a Picture-Superiority Effect on Consumer Memory," *Journal of Consumer Research* 11 (September 1984): 643–54; Terry Childers, Susan Heckler, and Michael Houston, "Memory for the Visual and Verbal Components of Print Advertisements," *Psychology & Marketing* 3 (Fall 1986): 147–50.

90. Werner Krober-Riel, "Effects of Emotional Pictorial Elements in Ads Analyzed by Means of Eye Movement Monitoring," in Thomas C. Kinnear, ed., *Advances in Consumer Research 11* (Provo, UT: Association for Consumer Research, 1984): 591–96.

91. Hans-Bernd Brosius, "Influence of Presentation Features and News Context on Learning from Television News," *Journal of Broadcasting & Electronic Media* 33 (Winter 1989): 1–14.

92. Edward F. McQuarrie and David Glen Mick, "Visual and Verbal Rhetorical Figures under Directed Processing versus Incidental Exposure to Advertising," *Journal of Consumer Research* 29 (March 2003): 579–87; cf. also Ann E. Schlosser, "Learning through Virtual Product Experience: The Role of Imagery on True Versus False Memories," *Journal of Consumer Research* 33, no. 3 (2006): 377–83.

93. Hugo Martin, "Disney's 2011 Marketing Campaign Centers on Family Memories," *Los Angeles Times* (September 23, 2010), http://latimesblogs.latimes.com/money_co/201009/disney-to-market-on-memories.html, accessed April 4, 2011.

94. Russell W. Belk, "Possessions and the Extended Self," *Journal of Consumer Research* 15 (September 1988): 139–68.

95. Morris B. Holbrook and Robert M. Schindler, "Nostalgic Bonding: Exploring the Role of Nostalgia in the Consumption Experience," *Journal of Consumer Behavior* 3, no. 2 (December 2003): 107–27.

96. Alexia Tsotsis, "Flickr Dips Its Toes into Social with Twitter and Facebook 'Share This' Features," *TechCrunch* (March 30, 2011), http://techcrunch.com/2011/03/30/flickr-dips-its-toes-into-social-with-twitter-and-facebook-share-this-features/, accessed April 6, 2011.

97. Sarah Kessler, "Memolane Creates an Automatic Scrapbook of Your Social Media Activity," *Mashable* (March 11, 2011), http://mashable.com/2011/03/11/memolane/, accessed April 4, 2011.

98. Stacy Menzel Baker, Holli C. Karrer, and Ann Veeck, "My Favorite Recipes: Recreating Emotions and Memories through Cooking," *Advances in Consumer Research* 32, no. 1 (2005): 304–5.

99. Russell W. Belk, "The Role of Possessions in Constructing and Maintaining a Sense of Past," in Marvin E. Goldberg, Gerald Gorn, and Richard W. Pollay, eds., *Advances in Consumer Research* 16 (Provo, UT: Association for Consumer Research, 1989): 669–78.

100. "Only 38% of T.V. Audience Links Brands with Ads," *Marketing News* (January 6, 1984): 10.

101. "Terminal Television," *American Demographics* (January 1987): 15.

102. Richard P. Bagozzi and Alvin J. Silk, "Recall, Recognition, and the Measurement of Memory for Print Advertisements," *Marketing Science* 2 (1983): 95–134.

103. Adam Finn, "Print Ad Recognition Readership Scores: An Information Processing Perspective," *Journal of Marketing Research* 25 (May 1988): 168–77.

104. James R. Bettman, "Memory Factors in Consumer Choice: A Review," *Journal of Marketing* (Spring 1979): 37–53.

105. Mark A. Deturck and Gerald M. Goldhaber, "Effectiveness of Product Warning Labels: Effects of Consumers' Information Processing Objectives," *Journal of Consumer Affairs* 23, no. 1 (1989): 111–25.

106. Surendra N. Singh and Gilbert A. Churchill, Jr., "Response-Bias-Free Recognition Tests to Measure Advertising Effects," *Journal of Advertising Research* (June–July 1987): 23–36.

107. William A. Cook, "Telescoping and Memory's Other Tricks," *Journal of Advertising Research* 27 (February–March 1987): 5–8.

108. "On a Diet? Don't Trust Your Memory," *Psychology Today* (October 1989): 12.

109. Brian Steinberg, "Bad Times Affect Ad Recall for Bowl Spots, Gallup: Weak Consumer Confidence Can Mean Less Attention," *Advertising Age* (January 20, 2009), www.adage.com, accessed January 20, 2009.

110. I. Skurnik, C. Yoon, D. C. Park, and N. Schwarz, "How Warnings about False Claims Become Recommendations," *Journal of Consumer Research* 31, no. 4 (2005): 713–24.

111. Hubert A. Zielske and Walter A. Henry, "Remembering and Forgetting Television Ads," *Journal of Advertising Research* 20 (April 1980): 7–13; Cara Greenberg, "Future Worth: Before It's Hot, Grab It," *New York Times* (1992): C1; S. K. List, "More Than Fun and Games," *American Demographics* (August 1992): 44.

112. Stuart Elliot, "From Retired Brands, Dollars and Memories," *New York Times* (December 8, 2010), http://www.nytimes.com/2010/12/09/business/media/09adco.html?_r=1&adxnnl=1&ref=media&adxnnlx=1301951891-EMjJs87oEc62npAZxAn7Gw, accessed April 4, 2011; Goudreau, "These Old Brands Are Poised for a 2011 Comeback."

113. Susan L. Holak and William J. Havlena, "Feelings, Fantasies, and Memories: An Examination of the Emotional Components of Nostalgia," *Journal of Business Research* 42 (1998): 217–26.

114. Stephen Brown, Robert V. Kozinets, and John F. Sherry, "Teaching Old Brands New Tricks: Retro Branding and the Revival of Brand Meaning," *Journal of Marketing* 67 (July 2003): 19–33.

115. Robert M. Schindler and Morris B. Holbrook, "Nostalgia for Early Experience as a Determinant of Consumer Preferences," *Psychology & Marketing* 20, no. 4 (April 2003): 275–302; Morris B. Holbrook and Robert M. Schindler, "Some Exploratory Findings on the Development of Musical Tastes," *Journal of Consumer Research* 16 (June 1989): 119–24; Morris B. Holbrook and Robert M. Schindler, "Market Segmentation Based on Age and Attitude Toward the Past: Concepts, Methods, and Findings Concerning Nostalgic Influences on Consumer Tastes," *Journal of Business Research* 37 (September 1996): 27–40.

116. Thomas F. Jones, "Our Musical Heritage Is Being Raided," *San Francisco Examiner* (May 23, 1997).

117. Kevin Goldman, "A Few Rockers Refuse to Turn Tunes into Ads," *New York Times* (August 25, 1995): B1.

118. Charles Duhigg, "Warning: Habits May Be Good for You," *New York Times Magazine* (July 17, 2008), www.ntyimes.com/2008/07/13/Business/13habit.html, accessed July 17, 2008.

Motivation and Global Values

Motivation and Global Values

Chapter Objectives

When you finish reading this chapter you will understand why:

1. It is important for marketers to recognize that products can satisfy a range of consumer needs.

2. The way we evaluate and choose a product depends on our degree of involvement with the product, the marketing message, and/or the purchase situation.

3. Our deeply held cultural values dictate the types of products and services we seek out or avoid.

4. Consumers vary in the importance they attach to worldly possessions, and this orientation in turn influences their priorities and behaviors.

5. Products that succeed in one culture may fail in another if marketers fail to understand the differences among consumers in each place.

6. Western (and particularly American) culture have a huge impact around the world, although people in other countries don't necessarily ascribe the same meanings to products as we do.

MyMarketingLab
Visit **www.mymktlab.com** to find activities that help you learn and review in order to succeed in this chapter.

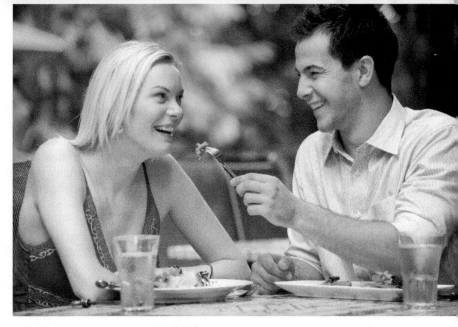

As Basil scans the menu at the trendy health-food restaurant Paula has dragged him to, he reflects on what a man will give up for love. Now that Paula has become a die-hard vegan, she's slowly but surely working on him to forsake those juicy steaks and burgers for healthier fare. He can't even hide from tofu and other delights at school; the dining facility in his dorm just started to offer "veggie" alternatives to its usual assortment of greasy "mystery meats" and other delicacies he loves.

Paula is totally into it; she claims that eating this way not only cuts out unwanted fat but also is good for the environment. Just his luck to fall head-over-heels for a "tree-hugger." As Basil gamely tries to decide between the stuffed artichokes with red pepper vinaigrette and the grilled marinated zucchini, fantasies of a sizzling 14-ounce T-bone dance before his eyes.

OBJECTIVE 1

It is important for marketers to recognize that products can satisfy a range of consumer needs.

The Motivation Process: Why Ask Why?

Paula certainly is not alone in her belief that eating green is good for the body, the soul, and the planet. About 7 percent of the general population is vegetarian, and women and younger people are even more likely to adopt a meatless diet. An additional 10 to 20 percent of consumers explore vegetarian options in addition to their normal dead-animal fare. More and more people are taking the next step, too, as they adopt a vegan lifestyle. *Vegetarianism* refers only to a diet that excludes meat (some animal products that do not involve the death of an animal, such as milk, cheese, and butter, may be included). *Veganism,* in contrast, links to a set of ethical beliefs about use of and cruelty to animals. In addition to objecting to hunting or fishing, adherents protest cruel animal training; object to the degrading use of animals in circuses, zoos, rodeos, and races; and also oppose the testing of drugs and cosmetics on animals.[1]

Although the proportion of vegetarian or vegan consumers is quite small compared to those of us who still like to pound down a Quarter Pounder, big companies are taking notice of this growing interest in vegetarian and cruelty-free products. Colgate purchased a controlling interest in Tom's of Maine, and Dean Foods (America's largest processor of dairy foods) bought Silk and its parent company White Wave. PETA (People for the Ethical Treatment of Animals) offers resources to promote an animal-friendly lifestyle, including an Online Vegetarian Starter Kit for kids.[2] The beef industry fights back with a high-profile advertising campaign: "Beef. It's What's for Dinner" and a Web site to promote meat consumption (beefitswhatsfordinner.com).[3] It's obvious that our menu choices have deep and far-reaching consequences.

The forces that drive people to buy and use products are generally straightforward—for example, when a person chooses what to have for lunch. As hard-core vegetarians demonstrate, however, even the basic food products we consume also relate to wide-ranging beliefs regarding what we think is appropriate or desirable. In some cases, these emotional responses create a deep commitment to the product. Sometimes people are not even fully aware of the forces that drive them toward some products and away from others.

To understand motivation is to understand why consumers do what they do. Why do some people choose to bungee-jump off a bridge or compete on reality shows, whereas others spend their leisure time playing chess or gardening? Whether it is to quench a thirst, kill boredom, or attain some deep spiritual experience, we do everything for a reason, even if we can't articulate what that reason is. We teach marketing students from Day 1 that the goal of marketing is to satisfy consumers' needs. However, this insight is useless unless we can discover what those needs are and why they exist. A beer commercial once asked, "Why ask why?" In this chapter, we'll find out.

Motivation refers to the processes that lead people to behave as they do. It occurs when a need is aroused that the consumer wishes to satisfy. The need creates a state of tension that drives the consumer to attempt to reduce or eliminate it. This need may be *utilitarian* (i.e., a desire to achieve some functional or practical benefit, as when a person loads up on green vegetables for nutritional reasons) or it may be *hedonic* (i.e., an experiential need, involving emotional responses or fantasies, as when Basil longs for a juicy steak). The desired end state is the consumer's **goal.** Marketers try to create products and services to provide the desired benefits and help the consumer to reduce this tension.

Whether the need is utilitarian or hedonic, the magnitude of the tension it creates determines the urgency the consumer feels to reduce it. We call this degree of arousal a **drive.** We can satisfy a basic need in any number of ways, and the specific path a person chooses is influenced both by her unique set of experiences and by the values her culture instills.

These personal and cultural factors combine to create a **want**, which is one manifestation of a need. For example, hunger is a basic need that all of us must satisfy; the lack of food creates a tension state that we reduce when we eat cheeseburgers, double-fudge Oreo cookies, raw fish, or bean sprouts. The specific route to drive reduction is culturally and individually determined. When a person attains the goal, this reduces the tension and the motivation recedes (for the time being). We describe motivation in terms of its *strength*, or the pull it exerts on the consumer; and its *direction*, or the particular way the consumer attempts to reduce it.

This ad from the United Arab Emirates appeals to our basic drive to reduce hunger.
Source: Designed & released by Publinet Advertising & Publicity LLC, Dubai, UAE.

Motivational Strength

The degree to which a person will expend energy to reach one goal as opposed to another reflects his or her motivation to attain that goal. Psychologists have advanced many theories to explain why people behave the way they do. Most share the basic idea that people have some finite amount of energy that we direct toward our goals.

Early work on motivation ascribed behavior to *instinct*, the innate patterns of behavior that are universal in a species. This view is now largely discredited. For one thing, the existence of an instinct is difficult to prove or disprove because we infer the instinct from the behavior it is supposed to explain (we call this type of circular explanation a *tautology*).[4] It is like saying that a consumer buys products that are status symbols because he is motivated to attain status—hardly a satisfying explanation.

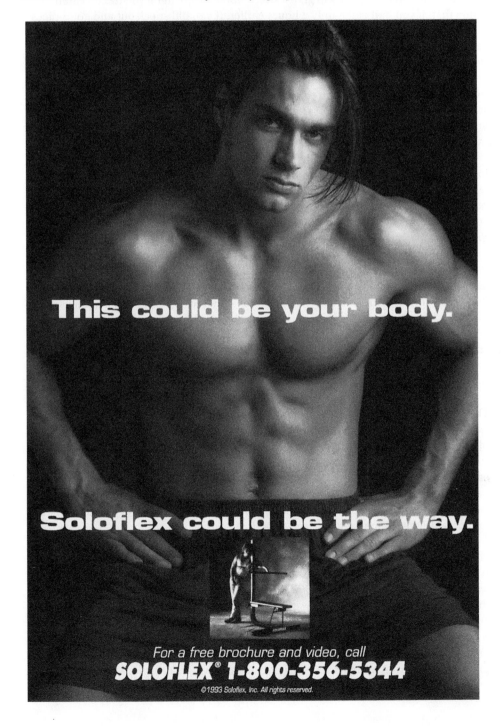

This ad for exercise equipment shows an ideal body (as dictated by contemporary Western culture), and suggests a solution (purchase of the equipment) to attain it.
Source: Used with permission of Soloflex.

Biological versus Learned Needs

Drive theory focuses on biological needs that produce unpleasant states of arousal (e.g., your stomach grumbles during a morning class). The arousal this tension causes motivates us to reduce it. Some researchers believe that this need to reduce arousal is a basic mechanism that governs much of our behavior.

In a marketing context, *tension* refers to the unpleasant state that exists if a person's consumption needs are not fulfilled. A person may be grumpy if he hasn't eaten, or he may be dejected or angry if he cannot afford that new car he wants. This state activates goal-oriented behavior, which attempts to reduce or eliminate this unpleasant state and return to a balanced one that we call **homeostasis**.

If a behavior reduces the drive, we'll naturally tend to repeat that behavior. Your motivation to leave class early to grab a snack would be greater if you hadn't eaten in 24 hours than if you had eaten only 2 hours earlier. If you did sneak out and got indigestion afterward, say, from wolfing down a package of Twinkies, you would be less likely to repeat this behavior the next time you want a snack. One's degree of motivation, then, depends on the distance between one's present state and the goal.

Drive theory runs into difficulties when it tries to explain some facets of human behavior that run counter to its predictions. People often do things that increase a drive state rather than decrease it. For example, people may *delay gratification*. If you know you are going out for a lavish dinner, you might decide to forego a snack earlier in the day even though you are hungry at that time.

Most current explanations of motivation focus on cognitive factors rather than biological ones to understand what motivates behavior. **Expectancy theory** suggests that expectations of achieving desirable outcomes—positive incentives—rather than being pushed from within motivate our behavior. We choose one product over another because we expect this choice to have more positive consequences for us. Thus, we use the term *drive* here loosely to refer to both physical and cognitive processes.

Motives have direction as well as strength. They are goal-oriented in that they drive us to satisfy a specific need. We can reach most goals by a number of routes, and the objective of a company is to convince consumers that the alternative it offers provides the best chance to attain the goal. For example, a consumer who decides that she needs a pair of jeans to help her reach her goal of being admired by others can choose among Levi's, Wranglers, True Religion, Diesel, Seven for All Mankind, and many other alternatives, each of which promises to deliver certain benefits.

Needs versus Wants

The specific way we choose to satisfy a need depends on our unique history, learning experiences, and cultural environment. Two classmates may feel their stomachs rumble during a lunchtime lecture. If neither person has eaten since the night before, the strength of their respective needs (hunger) would be about the same. However, the ways each person goes about satisfying this need might be quite different. The first person may be a vegetarian like Paula, who fantasizes about gulping down a big handful of trail mix, whereas the second person may be a meat hound like Basil who gets turned on by the prospect of a greasy cheeseburger and fries.

What Do We Need?

We are born with a need for certain elements necessary to maintain life, such as food, water, air, and shelter. These are *biogenic needs*. We have many other needs, however, that are not innate. We acquire *psychogenic needs* as we become members of a specific culture. These include the needs for status, power, and affiliation. Psychogenic needs reflect the priorities of a culture, and their effect on behavior will vary from environment to environment. For example, a U.S. consumer devotes a good chunk of his income to products that permit him to display his individuality, whereas his Japanese counterpart may work equally hard to ensure that he does not stand out from his group.

One utilitarian need is very simple—we need to replenish products when we run out of them.
Source: Shalmor Avnon Amichay/Y&R.

We can also be motivated to satisfy either utilitarian or hedonic needs. When we focus on a *utilitarian need,* we emphasize the objective, tangible attributes of products, such as miles per gallon in a car; the amount of fat, calories, and protein in a cheeseburger; or the durability of a pair of blue jeans. *Hedonic needs* are subjective and experiential; here we might look to a product to meet our needs for excitement, self-confidence, or fantasy—perhaps to escape the mundane or routine aspects of life.[5] Many items satisfy our hedonic needs (there's even a popular resort called Hedonism). Luxury brands in particular thrive when they offer the promise of pleasure to the user—how badly do you "need" that Armani suit or Tiffany brooch?[6]

Of course, we can also be motivated to purchase a product because it provides *both* types of benefits. For example, a woman (perhaps a politically incorrect one) might buy a mink coat because of the luxurious image it portrays and because it also happens to keep her warm through the long, cold winter. Indeed, recent research on novel consumption experiences indicates that even when we choose to do unusual things (like eating bacon ice cream or staying in a freezing ice hotel), we may do so because we have what the authors term a **productivity orientation.** This refers to a continual striving to use time constructively: Trying new things is a way to check them off our "bucket list" of experiences we want to achieve before moving on to others.

Motivation and Emotion

Motivation is largely driven by raw emotions, or what social scientists call **affect**. At the most basic level, we are driven to heighten positive emotion, or mood, and to reduce negative feelings. Our emotional reactions in turn influence the likelihood that we will engage in an activity next time—they positively or negatively reinforce us. That explains why so many marketing activities and messages focus on altering mood and linking products or services to affect.[7]

A television commercial by the paint company Valspar is a good example: The spot never shows an interior, or people painting a wall. It opens with a couple walking on white sand toward a white wall, which resembles a drive-in movie screen, as a voiceover begins, "To some, a wall is just a wall—a divider between here and there." The couple interacts with the wall to bring up a series of spectacular landscapes, and the wall assumes the color of the backdrops, from the incandescent green of flora near a waterfall to the warm tan of a hayfield to the reddish brown of a mountain setting. As one of the advertising agency executives explained, "What you see in almost every paint commercial is couples [sic] in blue jeans and flannel shirts holding rollers and going up and down on the wall and whistling while they work, and Valspar didn't need to go there. We don't show people painting walls, or interiors, or any of the kind of mundane aspects of the chore. It's more about the mind-space of the consumer—we're talking to their imagination and emotions."[8]

This appeal to emotions also explains the popularity of soap operas, as well as reality TV shows like *The Bachelor* and *Extreme Makeover (Home Edition)*: They encourage

Some advertising messages appeal to our motivation to avoid negative outcomes like bad breath. This Indian ad for a mint certainly does.

Source: McCann Erickson India.

viewers to engage emotionally with the participants and to develop a "relationship" with them (just witness the outrage when hard-core soaps addicts learned that the venerable *Days of Our Lives* was being cancelled after airing for more than 40 years). So, in a sense, marketers/producers harness consumers' emotions and convert them into capital, as this affect is what they use to build loyalty to the product.[9]

How Social Media Tap into Our Emotions

Social media platforms also strongly relate to our moods. Arby's offers an app to allow users to match their moods to illustrated characters and items on the chain's Value Menu, and view the moods of others across the Web.[10] We may share particularly good or bad feelings on Facebook or Twitter, or even resort to corny emoticons like :) in texts or emails to convey how we feel. To push sales of its Jell-O brand, Kraft unveiled a "Mood Monitor" on Twitter, in which it will randomly send coupons to users it finds who type in a :(emoticon. Kraft will monitor the Twittersphere and the company will launch coupons whenever the national average of smiley faces dips below 51%[11]. LOL!

In fact, it's so common for people to express their moods and also their emotional reactions to products that these posts can be a treasure trove for marketers who want to learn more about how their offerings make people feel. A technique called **sentiment analysis** does this; this refers to a process (sometimes also called *opinion mining*) that scours the social media universe to collect and analyze the words people use when they describe a specific product or company. When people feel a particular way, they are likely

Reality shows like *The Bachelor* encourage viewers to engage emotionally with contestants.
Source: © Craig Sjodin/American Broadcasting Companies, Inc.

to choose certain words that tend to relate to the emotion. From these words, the researcher creates a **word-phrase dictionary** (sometimes called a *library*) to code the data. The program scans the text to identify whether the words in the dictionary appear.

Consider this example based on Canon's PowerShot A540. A review on *Epinions*, a product review site, included this statement, "The Canon PowerShot A540 had good aperture and excellent resolution." A sentiment analysis would extract the entities of interest from the sentence, identifying the product as the Canon PowerShot A540 and the relevant dimensions as aperture and resolution. The sentiment would then be extracted for each dimension: the sentiment for aperture is *good* while that for resolution is *excellent*. Text-mining software would collect these reactions and combine them with others to paint a picture of how people are talking about the product. There are several sentiment analysis programs that do similar things; a new one called ToneCheck even reports on the emotions it detects in people's emails.[12]

Motivational Conflicts

A goal has *valence*, which means that it can be positive or negative. We direct our behavior toward goals we value positively; we are motivated to *approach* the goal and to seek out products that will help us to reach it. However, sometimes we're also motivated to *avoid* a negative outcome

The new Moodagent app generates a music playlist based on the user's mood.
Source: Copyright Syntonetic Media Solutions A/S, 2011.

rather than achieve a positive outcome. We structure purchases or consumption activities to reduce the chances that we will experience a nasty result. For example, many consumers work hard to avoid rejection by their peers (a negative goal). They stay away from products that they associate with social disapproval. Products such as deodorants and mouthwash frequently rely on consumers' negative motivation when ads depict the onerous social consequences of underarm odor or bad breath.

Because a purchase decision can involve more than one source of motivation, consumers often find themselves in situations in which different motives, both positive and negative, conflict with one another.[13] Marketers attempt to satisfy consumers' needs by providing possible solutions to these dilemmas. As Figure 1 shows, there are three general types of conflicts we should understand. Let's review each kind.

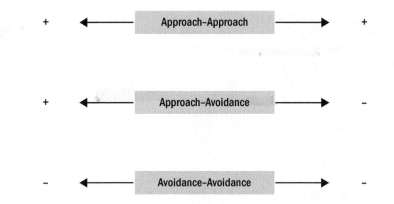

Figure 1 TYPES OF MOTIVATIONAL CONFLICTS

Approach–Approach Conflict

A person has an **approach–approach conflict** when she must choose between two desirable alternatives. A student might be torn between going home for the holidays and going on a skiing trip with friends. Or, she might have to choose between two CDs to download (assuming that she's going to pay for one of them!). The **theory of cognitive dissonance** is based on the premise that people have a need for order and consistency in their lives and that a state of *dissonance* (tension) exists when beliefs or behaviors conflict with one another. We resolve the conflict that arises when we choose between two alternatives through a process of *cognitive dissonance reduction*, where we look for a way to reduce this inconsistency (or dissonance) and thus eliminate unpleasant tension.

Dissonance occurs when a consumer must choose between two products, both of which possess good and bad qualities. When he chooses one product and not the other, the person gets the bad qualities of the product he buys and loses out on the good qualities of the one he didn't buy. This loss creates an unpleasant, dissonant state that he wants to reduce. We tend to convince ourselves, after the fact, that the choice we made was the smart one as we find additional reasons to support the alternative we did choose—perhaps when we discover flaws with the option we did not choose (sometimes we call this *rationalization*). A marketer can bundle several benefits together to resolve an approach–approach conflict. For example, Miller Lite's claim that it is "less filling" *and* "tastes great" allows the drinker to "have his beer and drink it too."

Many of the products and services we desire have negative consequences attached to them as well. We may feel guilty or ostentatious when we buy a luxury product like a fur coat (especially when others around us lose their jobs), or we might feel like gluttons when we crave a tempting package of Twinkies. An **approach–avoidance conflict** occurs when we desire a goal but wish to avoid it at the same time.

Some solutions to these conflicts include the proliferation of fake furs, which eliminate guilt about harming animals to make a fashion statement, and the success of diet programs like Weight Watchers that promise good food without the calories.[14] Many marketers try to help consumers overcome guilt by convincing them that they deserve these luxuries. As the model for L'Oréal cosmetics exclaims, "Because I'm worth it!"

Sometimes we find ourselves caught "between a rock and a hard place." We may face a choice with two undesirable alternatives: for instance, the option of either spending more money on an old car or buying a new one. Don't you hate when that happens? Marketers frequently address an **avoidance–avoidance conflict** with messages that stress the unforeseen benefits of choosing one option (e.g., when they emphasize special credit plans to ease the pain of car payments).

How We Classify Consumer Needs

Some analysts set out to define a universal inventory of needs they could trace systematically to explain virtually all behavior. One such inventory that the psychologist Henry

Murray developed delineates a set of 20 *psychogenic needs* that (sometimes in combination) result in specific behaviors. These needs include such dimensions as *autonomy* (being independent), *defendance* (defending the self against criticism), and even *play* (engaging in pleasurable activities).[15]

Murray's framework is the basis for a number of personality tests that modern-day psychologists use, such as the Thematic Apperception Test (TAT). In the TAT, the analyst shows test subjects four to six ambiguous pictures and asks them to write answers to four direct questions about the pictures:

1 What is happening?
2 What led up to this situation?
3 What is being thought?
4 What will happen?

McDonald's promises its coffee will satisfy a physiological need—to wake up.
Source: Courtesy of McDonald's.

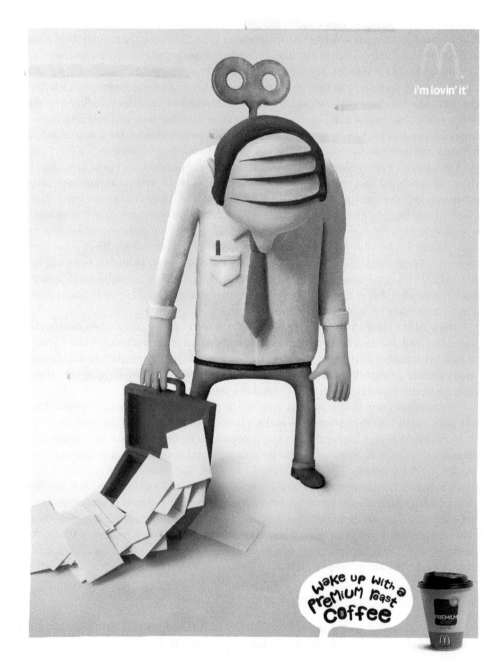

The researcher then analyzes each answer for references to certain needs. The theory behind the test is that people will freely project their own subconscious needs onto the neutral stimulus. By getting responses to the pictures, the analyst really gets at the person's true needs for achievement or affiliation or whatever other need may be dominant. Murray believed that everyone has the same basic set of needs but that individuals differ in their priority rankings of these needs.[16]

Other motivational approaches focus on specific needs and their ramifications for behavior. For example, individuals with a high *need for achievement* strongly value personal accomplishment.[17] They place a premium on products and services that signify success because these consumption items provide feedback about the realization of their goals. These consumers are good prospects for products that provide evidence of their achievement. One study of working women found that those who were high in achievement motivation were more likely to choose clothing they considered businesslike and less likely to be interested in apparel that accentuated their femininity.[18] Some other important needs that are relevant to consumer behavior include:

- **Need for affiliation**—(to be in the company of other people).[19] The need for affiliation is relevant to products and services for people in groups, such as participating in team sports, frequenting bars, and hanging out at shopping malls.
- **Need for power**—(to control one's environment).[20] Many products and services allow us to feel that we have mastery over our surroundings (to quote the famous line from *Seinfeld*, we are "masters of our domain")! These products range from "hopped-up" muscle cars and loud boom boxes (large portable radios that impose one's musical tastes on others) to luxury resorts that promise to respond to every whim of their pampered guests.
- **Need for uniqueness**—(to assert one's individual identity).[21] Products satisfy the need for uniqueness when they pledge to bring out our distinctive qualities. For example, Cachet perfume claims to be "as individual as you are."

Maslow's Hierarchy of Needs

Psychologist Abraham Maslow originally developed his influential **hierarchy of needs** to understand personal growth and how people attain spiritual "peak experiences." Marketers later adapted his work to understand consumer motivations.[22] Maslow proposed a hierarchy of biogenic and psychogenic needs that specifies certain levels of motives. This *hierarchical* structure implies that the order of development is fixed—that is, we must attain a certain level before we activate a need for the next, higher one. Marketers embraced this perspective because it (indirectly) specifies certain types of product benefits people might look for, depending on their stage of mental or spiritual development or on their economic situation.[23]

Figure 2 summarizes this model. At each level, the person seeks different kinds of product benefits. Ideally, an individual progresses up the hierarchy until his or her dominant motivation is a focus on "ultimate" goals, such as justice and beauty. Unfortunately, this state is difficult to achieve (at least on a regular basis); most of us have to be satisfied with occasional glimpses, or *peak experiences*. One study of men aged 49 to 60 found that these respondents engaged in three types of activities to attain self-fulfillment: (1) *sport and physical activity*, (2) *community and charity*, and (3) *building and renovating*. Regardless of whether these activities were related to their professional work, these so-called *magnetic points* gradually took the place of those that were not as fulfilling.[24]

The Hierarchy and Product Benefits

The basic lesson of Maslow's hierarchy is that we must first satisfy basic needs before we progress up the ladder (a starving man is not interested in status symbols, friendship, or self-fulfillment). This implies that consumers value different product attributes depending on what is currently available to them. For example, consumers in the former Eastern bloc are now bombarded with images of luxury goods, yet may still have trouble obtaining

Figure 2 MASLOW'S HIERARCHY OF NEEDS

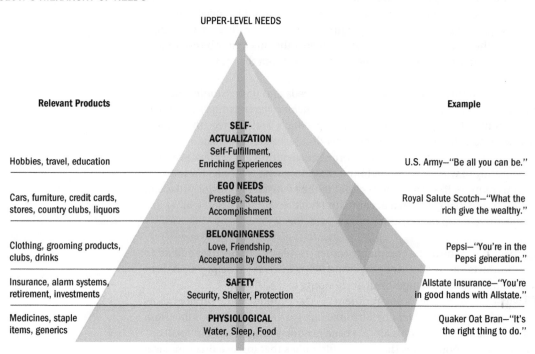

UPPER-LEVEL NEEDS

Relevant Products

Example

SELF-ACTUALIZATION
Self-Fulfillment,
Enriching Experiences

Hobbies, travel, education

U.S. Army—"Be all you can be."

EGO NEEDS
Prestige, Status,
Accomplishment

Cars, furniture, credit cards,
stores, country clubs, liquors

Royal Salute Scotch—"What the
rich give the wealthy."

BELONGINGNESS
Love, Friendship,
Acceptance by Others

Clothing, grooming products,
clubs, drinks

Pepsi—"You're in the
Pepsi generation."

SAFETY
Security, Shelter, Protection

Insurance, alarm systems,
retirement, investments

Allstate Insurance—"You're
in good hands with Allstate."

PHYSIOLOGICAL
Water, Sleep, Food

Medicines, staple
items, generics

Quaker Oat Bran—"It's
the right thing to do."

LOWER-LEVEL NEEDS

basic necessities. In one study, Romanian students named the products they hoped to acquire. Their wish lists included not only the expected items, such as sports cars and the latest-model televisions, but also staples such as water, soap, furniture, and food.[25] In today's economic environment, the hierarchy helps to explain why many consumers take a closer look at the price and reliability of a product rather than whether it will impress their friends.

This Italian ad reinforces the need for safety in Maslow's Hierarchy of Needs.
Source: Courtesy of Subaru Italy.

Issues with Applying the Hierarchy of Needs

Marketers' application of this hierarchy has been somewhat simplistic, especially as the same product or activity can gratify different needs. For example, one study found that gardening could satisfy needs at every level of the hierarchy:[27]

- **Physiological**—"I like to work in the soil."
- **Safety**—"I feel safe in the garden."
- **Social**—"I can share my produce with others."
- **Esteem**—"I can create something of beauty."
- **Self-actualization**—"My garden gives me a sense of peace."

Another problem with taking Maslow's Hierarchy of Needs too literally is that it is culture-bound; its assumptions may apply only to Western culture. People in other cultures (or, for that matter, even some in Western cultures as well) may question the order of the levels it specifies. A religious person who has taken a vow of celibacy would not necessarily agree that physiological needs must be satisfied before self-fulfillment can occur.

Similarly, many Asian cultures value the welfare of the group (belongingness needs) more highly than needs of the individual (esteem needs). The point is that this hierarchy, although marketers widely apply it, is helpful primarily because it reminds us that consumers may have different need priorities in different consumption situations and at different stages in their lives—not because it *exactly* specifies a consumer's progression up the ladder of needs.

OBJECTIVE 2
The way we evaluate and choose a product depends on our degree of involvement with the product, the marketing message, and/or the purchase situation.

Consumer Involvement

Do consumers form strong relationships with products and services? If you don't believe so, consider these events:

- A consumer in Brighton, England, loves a local restaurant called the All in One so much that he had its name and phone number tattooed on his forehead. The owner remarked, "Whenever he comes in, he'll go straight to the front of the queue."[28]
- *Lucky* is a magazine devoted to shopping for shoes and other fashion accessories. The centerfold of the first issue featured rows of makeup sponges. The editor observed, "It's the same way that you might look at a golf magazine and see a spread of nine irons. *Lucky* is addressing one interest in women's lives, in a really obsessive, specific way."[29]
- After his girlfriend jilted him, a Tennessee man tried to marry his car. His plan was thwarted, however, when he listed his fiancée's birthplace as Detroit, her father as Henry Ford, and her blood type as 10W40. Under Tennessee law, only a man and a woman can legally wed.[30] So much for that exciting honeymoon at the carwash.

Clearly, we can get pretty attached to products. Our motivation to attain a goal increases our desire to acquire the products or services that we believe will satisfy it. However, not everyone is motivated to the same extent: One person might be convinced he can't live without the latest Apple iPhone, whereas another is perfectly happy with his 3-year-old LG.

Involvement is "a person's perceived relevance of the object based on their inherent needs, values, and interests."[31] We use the word *object* in the generic sense to refer to a product (or a brand), an advertisement, or a purchase situation. Consumers can find involvement in all these *objects*. Figure 3 shows that different factors may create it. These factors can be something about the person, something about the object, or something about the situation.

MyMarketingLab

Visit **www.mymktlab.com** to test your understanding of chapter objectives.

Figure 3 CONCEPTUALIZING INVOLVEMENT

INVOLVEMENT = f (Person, Situation, Object)

The level of involvement may be influenced by one or more of these three factors. Interactions among persons, situation, and object factors are likely to occur.

Involvement reflects our level of motivation to process information.[32] To the degree that you feel knowing more about a product will help you to achieve some goal, you'll be motivated to pay attention to information about it. As our involvement with a product increases, we devote more attention to ads related to the product, we exert more cognitive effort to understand these ads, and we focus more attention on the product-related information in the ads.[33]

Levels of Involvement: From Inertia to Passion

The type of information processing that occurs depends on the consumer's level of involvement. It can range from *simple processing*, where she considers only the basic features of a message, all the way to *elaboration*, where she links this information to her preexisting knowledge system.[34]

Inertia

Think of a person's degree of involvement as a continuum that ranges from absolute lack of interest in a marketing stimulus at one end to obsession at the other. **Inertia** describes consumption at the low end of involvement, where we make decisions out of habit because we lack the motivation to consider alternatives. At the high end of involvement, we find the devotion we reserve for people and objects that carry great meaning for us. For example, the passion of some consumers for famous people (those living, such as Oprah Winfrey, or—supposedly—dead, such as Elvis Presley) demonstrates the high end of the involvement continuum.

When consumers are truly involved with a product, an ad, or a Web site, they enter a **flow state**. This experience is the Holy Grail of Web designers, who want to create sites that are so entrancing the surfer loses all track of time as he becomes engrossed in the

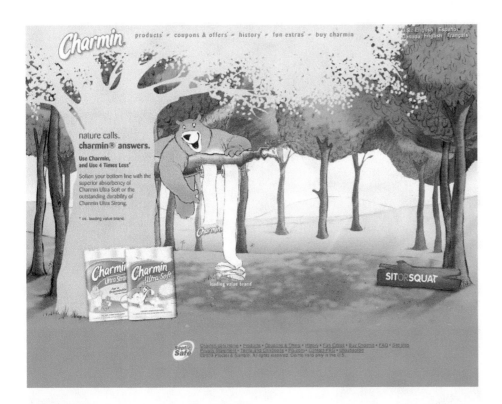

site's contents (and hopefully buys stuff in the process!). Flow is an optimal experience with these qualities:

- A sense of playfulness
- A feeling of being in control
- Concentration and highly focused attention
- Mental enjoyment of the activity for its own sake
- A distorted sense of time
- A match between the challenge at hand and one's skills.[35]

Cult Products

When Apple put its first iPhone on sale, thousands of adoring iCultists around the country (including the mayor of Philadelphia) waited in front of Apple stores for days to be one of the first to buy the device—even though they could order the phone online and have it delivered in 3 days. Somehow that was too long to wait for a cell phone with a touch-screen. As one loyal consumer admitted, "If Apple made sliced bread, yeah, I'd buy it."[36]

OK, a useful product like a smartphone is one thing—but a cookie? When Kellogg surrendered to the all-powerful Oreo and took its Hydrox cookies off the market, hard-core fans were bereft. As one wrote on a Web site devoted to the product, "This is a dark time in cookie history. And for those of you who say, 'Get over it, it's only a cookie,' you have not lived until you have tasted a Hydrox."[37] **Cult products** like Hydrox, Apple, Harley-Davidson, Jones Soda, Manolo Blahnik designer shoes (think Carrie on *Sex and the City*), and the Boston Red Sox command fierce consumer loyalty, devotion, and maybe even worship by consumers.[38]

The Many Faces of Involvement

A freelance software programmer who calls himself Winter is on a mission to visit every Starbucks in the world. To date he's been to more than 10,000 outlets in numerous countries. When he learned that a Starbucks store in British Columbia was scheduled to close

This German ad hopes to ramp up involvement with potatoes, a low involvement product. The ad for ready-to-serve potato dishes declares, "Good stuff from potatoes."
Source: Courtesy of Unilever/Germany.

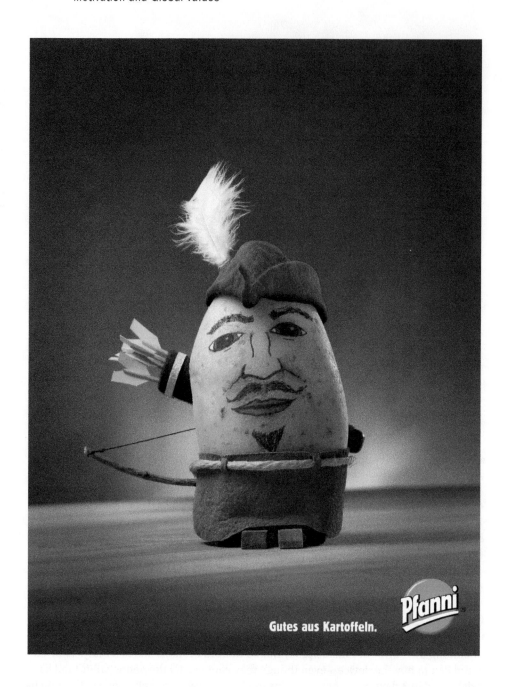

the next day, he spent $1,400 to fly there immediately just to order a cup of coffee in the nick of time. He chronicles his odyssey on his Web site, starbuckseverywhere.net.[39]

OK, maybe Winter needs to get a life. Still, his passion demonstrates that involvement takes many forms. It can be cognitive, as when a "gearhead" is motivated to learn all she can about the latest specs of a new multimedia personal computer (PC), or emotional, as when the thought of a new Armani suit gives a clotheshorse goose bumps.[40] What's more, the very act of *buying* the Armani may be highly involving for people who are passionately devoted to shopping.

To further complicate matters, advertisements such as those Nike or Adidas produce may themselves be involving for some reason (e.g., because they make us laugh or cry, or inspire us to exercise harder). So, it seems that involvement is a fuzzy concept, because it overlaps with other things and means different things to different people. Indeed, the consensus is that there are actually several broad types of involvement we can relate to the product, the message, or the perceiver.[41]

Product Involvement

Product involvement refers to a consumer's level of interest in a particular product. Many sales promotions aim to increase this type of involvement. Consider the woman who won Roto-Rooter's "Pimped-Out John" contest (winning out over 318,000 other entries). Her prizes to maximize her bathroom experience included these goodies:[42]

- An Avanti 4.3-cubic-foot compact refrigerator with a beer tap
- A Gateway eMachines Notebook
- A dual-sided magnification mirror
- A Microsoft Xbox 360 core system
- A Philips progressive-scan DVD player
- A TiVo Series2 digital video recorder
- A Philips 20-inch LCD flat-panel TV
- A personal cooling fan
- An Apple iPod
- An iCarta stereo dock for iPod with bath tissue holder
- A Baseline resistive pedal exerciser
- A Roto-Rooter Service button
- A megaphone so anyone in the house can hear her from up to 300 feet away

Talk about satisfying utilitarian and hedonic needs at the same time!

The more closely marketers can tie a brand to an individual, the higher the involvement they will create. This process is especially powerful when the producer allows the customer to *participate* in creating the product. That's why Coca-Cola launched a program that gave the band Maroon 5 24 hours to come up with a new song—with the help of its fans. The project, which streamed live from London, used interactive technology to allow listeners to weigh in on lyrics, riffs, and rhythms that would go into the new single. Coke promoted the program from its Facebook page, which has more than 20 million fans.[43]

That kind of product involvement is great, but how can a company accomplish the same thing for thousands or even millions of customers? **Mass customization** is the personalization of products and services for individual customers at a mass-production price.[44] This strategy applies to a wide range of products and services, from newspaper Web sites that allow readers to choose which sections of the paper they want to see, to Dell computers that you can configure, to Levi's blue jeans that have a right leg one inch shorter than a left leg to fit an asymmetrical body (this is more common than you think). Mars Snackfood USA introduced M&M's Faces to encourage consumers to bond with its chocolates: At mymms.com, you can upload a photo and order a batch of M&Ms with a face and personal message printed on the candy shell.[45]

Measuring involvement is important for many marketing applications. For example, research evidence indicates that a viewer who is more involved with a television show will respond more positively to commercials he sees during that show and that these spots will have a greater chance to influence his purchase intentions.[46] Table 1 shows one of the most widely used scales for assessing level of involvement.

Message–Response Involvement

Media platforms possess different qualities that influence how motivated we are to pay attention to what they tell us. Television is a *low-involvement medium* because it requires a passive viewer who exerts relatively little control (remote-control "zipping" notwithstanding) over content. In contrast, print is a *high-involvement medium*. The reader actively processes the information and is able to pause and reflect on what he or she has read before moving on.[47] In fact, some messages (including really well-made advertisements) are so involving that they trigger a stage of **narrative transportation**, where people become immersed in the storyline (much like the flow state we described earlier). One recent study showed that people who are feeling lucky engage in this process when they look at an advertisement for a lottery; once immersed it is hard to distract them from the message.[48] No a great thing for compulsive gamblers, but a powerful effect nonetheless.

TABLE 1	A Scale to Measure Involvement

To Me [Object to Be Judged] Is

1. important	_:_:_:_:_:_:_	unimportant*
2. boring	_:_:_:_:_:_:_	interesting
3. relevant	_:_:_:_:_:_:_	irrelevant*
4. exciting	_:_:_:_:_:_:_	unexciting*
5. means nothing	_:_:_:_:_:_:_	means a lot to me
6. appealing	_:_:_:_:_:_:_	unappealing*
7. fascinating	_:_:_:_:_:_:_	mundane*
8. worthless	_:_:_:_:_:_:_	valuable
9. involving	_:_:_:_:_:_:_	uninvolving*
10. not needed	_:_:_:_:_:_:_	needed

A recent campaign to promote hip hop mogul Jay-Z's autobiography *Decoded* illustrates the power of message-response involvement. It took the form of a scavenger hunt, where all 320 pages of the book were reprinted in unusual places in 13 cities, sites included a rooftop in New Orleans, a pool bottom in Miami, cheeseburger wrappers in New York City, and on a basketball backboard in the star's old neighborhood. Fans who found all of the hidden pages won two tickets to any Jay-Z concert anywhere, for life.[49]

Although consumers differ in their levels of involvement with respect to a product message, marketers do not have to simply sit back and hope for the best. By being aware of some basic factors that increase or decrease attention, they can take steps to increase the likelihood that product information will get through. A marketer can boost a person's motivation to process relevant information via one or more of the following techniques:[50]

- **Appeal to the consumers' hedonic needs**—Ads that use sensory appeals like those generate higher levels of attention.[51]
- **Use novel stimuli, such as unusual cinematography, sudden silences, or unexpected movements, in commercials**—When a British firm called Egg Banking introduced a credit card to the French market, its ad agency created unusual commercials to make people question their assumptions. One ad stated, "Cats always land on their paws," and then two researchers in white lab coats dropped a kitten off a rooftop—never to see it again (animal rights activists were not amused).[52]
- **Use prominent stimuli, such as loud music and fast action, to capture attention in commercials**—In print formats, larger ads increase attention. Also, viewers look longer at colored pictures than at black-and-white ones.
- **Include celebrity endorsers to generate higher interest in commercials**—People process more information when it comes from someone they admire (or maybe even Charlie Sheen).
- **Provide value that customers appreciate**—Charmin bathroom tissue set up public toilets in Times Square that hordes of grateful visitors used. Thousands more people (evidently with time on their hands) visited the brand's Web site to view the display.[53]
- **Let customers make the messages**—*Consumer-generated content,* where freelancers and fans film their own commercials for favorite products, is one of the hottest trends in marketing right now. This practice creates a high degree of *message-response involvement* (also called *advertising involvement*), which refers to the consumer's interest in processing marketing communications.[54] At the least, give customers a say if you're contemplating a change: Gap found this out the hard way when it rolled out an

CB AS I SEE IT

Professor Laurie Meamber, *George Mason University*

Have you ever attended a live performance and been bombarded by sensorial content: the sights and sounds of the performers, their costumes, and the staging that surrounds them? Have you ever visited a place, such as a theme park or a historical site, and been amazed at the way it has been designed to engage your senses? Have you ever bought a car and enjoyed its looks and feel both inside and out? These are all instances of aesthetic consumption. *Aesthetics* is a term that derives from the Greek word *aesthesis* and means perceiving the world with the senses. Aesthetic experiences are sensorial in nature and include everyday consumption of places, products, and events, including art and performance. Consumers are ensconced in aesthetic experiences as they go about their daily lives and often make choices based on aesthetic factors. Aesthetic value has become important in the late 20th and early 21st centuries. Some writers assert that the aesthetic age

was reborn during this period with the increasing attention to design of everyday objects and experiences by companies such as Apple, Disney, and even General Motors, which marketed the iconic Hummer brand vehicles from the late 1990s until the retirement of the brand in 2010. Objects and experiences contain aesthetic value when they offer unique aesthetic identities that appeal to the consumer's senses. Aesthetic value does not replace other values, such as performance value, symbolic value, and monetary value or other consumption-specific or product-specific values. Instead, aesthetic value supplements these other forms of value. My own research with several collaborators examines various instances of aesthetic consumption in the realm of the arts, experiences, and consumer products. In the realm of the arts, we are witnessing an explosion of immersive and interactive artistic experiences, whether it is an installation that engages consumers' senses through a multimedia experience or a live performance that uses computer-generated projections to alter scale, time, location, commingling with live performers, connecting with remote performers, and audiences, such as those developed by Cyburbia Productions.

Involving consumers in sensorial experiences is nothing new in the arts, but sophisticated immersive offerings have increased as new media

technology has become readily accessible. Themed environments, likewise, are creating a particular experience of the world for their visitors using a range of aesthetic experiences to delight consumer sensibilities. For example, at many historic homes open to the public, interactive exhibits—such as those that allow visitors to animate the milling process at a gristmill or films shown in theaters replete with seats that shake to replicate the jolt from cannon fire—allow consumers to get a sense of what life was like for those living this history. Also, consumer products are ripe with sensorial content. As mentioned previously, Hummer-brand vehicles, which were based on the look of the Humvee military vehicle, are noted for their unique design, inside and out. Consumers in our study conducted on the Hummer brand indicated that these vehicles had a rugged interior and the looks of a body builder. Even mundane consumer products contain sensorial qualities that offer aesthetic value. For example, consumers we interviewed discussed how objects such as coffee makers inspired emotional reactions because of their beautiful appearance. This research suggests that consumers do not always separate art products from craft products when making consumption choices, and experience similar emotional reactions to both original pieces and mass-produced products.

updated version of its logo on its Web site without warning fans first. Almost instantly, more than 2,000 customers posted complaints on Facebook. The company first tried to stand by its decision, but eventually it folded and returned to the tried-and-true. The president of Gap Brand North America admitted that the company "did not go about this in the right way" and missed the "opportunity to engage with the online community."[55]

What are some other tactics to increase message involvement? One is to invent new media platforms to grab our attention. Procter & Gamble printed trivia questions and answers on its Pringles snack chips with ink made of blue or red food coloring, and a company called Speaking Roses International patented a technology to laser-print words,

Dairy Queen helped to create the DQ Tycoon videogame, which boosts involvement as it lets players run their own fast-food franchise. They have to race against the clock to complete mundane tasks such as preparing Peanut Buster Parfaits, taking orders, restocking the refrigerator, and dipping cones.
Source: Courtesy of American Dairy Queen Corporation.

images, or logos on flower petals.[56] An Australian firm creates hand stamps that night-clubs use to identify paying customers; the stamps include logos or ad messages so par-tiers' hands become an advertising platform.[57]

Another tactic is to create **spectacles** or *performances*, where the message is itself a form of entertainment. In the early days of radio and television, ads literally were performances—show hosts integrated marketing messages into the episodes. Today live advertising is making a comeback as marketers try harder and harder to captivate jaded consumers:[58]

- Axe body products sponsored a posh Hamptons (New York) nightclub for the whole season, where it became The Axe Lounge sporting branding on the DJ booth and menu and Axe products in the restrooms.
- A British show broadcast a group of skydivers who performed a dangerous jump to create a human formation in the air that spelled out the letters *H, O, N, D,* and *A.*
- Honda built a musical road in Lancaster, PA; grooves in the cement create a series of pitches that play the William Tell Overture when a car drives over them.
- A New York campaign for Jameson Irish Whiskey projects an ad onto a wall—an op-erator scans the street for pedestrians who fit the brand's profile and inserts live text messages directed at them into the display.
- To promote the 25th anniversary of the Michael Jackson album *Thriller*, which fea-tured zombies dancing in a music video, Sony BMG staged such a performance on the London Underground. A group of "passengers" suddenly burst into a zombie-like dance before they disappeared into the crowd—and this videotaped scene was posted online. The video inspired similar performances in other countries, and within a week more than a million people had downloaded these films.
- In a similar stunt for T-Mobile, several hundred commuters at the Liverpool rail sta-tion broke into a dance; more than 15 million people watched the performance on YouTube in the following weeks. These (not so) spontaneous **flashmobs** have be-come increasingly common—which probably means they will wane in popularity as the spectacle of hundreds of people suddenly exploding into dance or song becomes almost a ho-hum experience. Oh well, on to the next thing.

Purchase Situation Involvement

Purchase situation involvement refers to differences in motivation during the process of interacting with a store or Web sit. One way to increase this kind of involvement is to personalize the messages shoppers receive at the time of purchase. For example, a few marketers tailor the recommendations they give shoppers in a store based on what they picked up from a shelf—and in the near future based on their appearance. At a few Dunkin' Donuts locations, a person who orders a morning coffee sees an ad at the cash register that pushes hash browns or breakfast sandwiches. At a German store, Procter & Gamble places RFID (radio-frequency identification) tags on products; when a shopper lifts a package off a shelf, this action changes the message on a digital screen in front of him or her. For example, if you pull out shampoo for thick hair, the screen recommends the best conditioner or other hair products. Emerging applications make use of facial-recognition technology; this actually classifies shoppers into groups based on their approximate age and their likely gender (some hairstyles and facial piercings will make this challenge interesting). The technology analyzes features like the size and shape of the nose, eyes, cheekbones, and jaw line and compares these to databases to make a guess as to which category the person should belong in.[59]

Many of us experience heightened purchase situation involvement when we log in to our favorite social media sites. Some of the most successful new applications involve some form of **social game**: a multiplayer, competitive, goal-oriented activity with defined rules of engagement and online connectivity among a community of players. Most social games include a few key elements:

Leaderboards—a listing of the leaders in the game competition

Achievement badges—symbols awarded to show game levels achieved, shared with the community

Friend (buddy) lists with chat—a list of contacts with whom one plays and the ability to communicate within the game.

Brands can utilize social games for marketing in several ways—and they should! When the Microsoft search engine Bing ran an ad that offered players the chance to earn *FarmVille* cash for becoming a fan of Bing on Facebook, the brand won 425,000 new fans in the first day.[61]

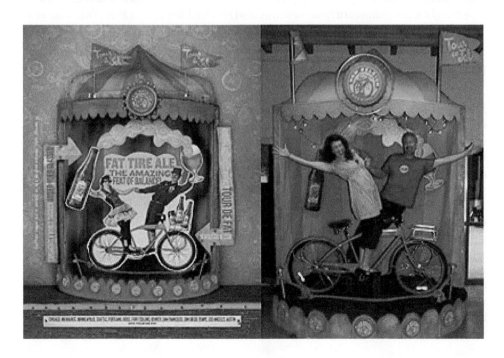

Visitors who tour the New Belgium brewery are invited to pose within a life-size, 3-D recreation of its' Fat Tire Ale print ad. All props are solidly welded together to insure visitors' safety even after they have sampled the beers.[60]

Source: Courtesy of New Belgium Brewing Company.

A study about clubbing (or "raves") illustrates how a social activity is co-created by producers and consumers. These experiences started in the UK as spontaneous gatherings in empty warehouses. Although these events are banned in many places, the consumer researchers showed how the promoters and the clubbers cooperate with local authorities to make possible this "contained illegality": for example, by regulating the drugs (particularly Ecstasy) that are consumed and instituting safeguards to prevent violence.[65]
Source: dwphotos/istockphoto.

One specific tactic we will see more of in the booming world of social games is **transactional advertising**, which rewards players if they respond to a request.[62] The offers can be for *virtual goods* (which players can use in the game or offer as gifts to friends), *currency* (used to advance in the game), or *codes* (used to unlock prizes and limited-access player experiences). Players are rewarded with the virtual goods, currencies, or codes if they make a purchase, "friend" the brand, watch a commercial, or perhaps answer a survey. ProFlowers used transactional advertising as part of a Valentine's Day promotion in Playfish's *Pet Society* game. Players who sent real flowers from within the game were rewarded with Playfish Cash.[63] The hugely popular *FarmVille* social game teamed with the also hugely popular Lady Gaga in 2011 to launch a special version of the game called *GagaVille*; an entire area inside the game with Gaga-themed items like unicorns. Fans who bought a $25 game card from Best Buy also received her album *Born This Way* as a free download.[64]

Values

A religious official in Saudi Arabia decreed that children there should not be allowed to watch Mickey Mouse, because the cartoon character is a "soldier of Satan."[66] This observation may surprise most of us, but then again we don't live in this deeply conservative Islamic culture. A **value** is a belief that some condition is preferable to its opposite. For example, it's safe to assume that most people prefer freedom to slavery. Others avidly pursue products and services that will make them look younger rather than older. A person's set of values plays a very important role in consumption activities. Consumers purchase many products and services because they believe these products will help to attain a value-related goal.

Two people can believe in and exhibit the same behaviors (e.g., vegetarianism), but their underlying *belief systems* may be quite different (e.g., animal activism versus health concerns). The extent to which people share a belief system is a function of individual, social, and cultural forces. Advocates of a belief system often seek out others with similar beliefs so that social networks overlap; as a result, believers tend to be exposed to information that supports their beliefs (e.g., tree-huggers rarely hang out with loggers).[67]

Core Values

The actress Kim Kardashian wasn't pleased when her picture ran on the April 2011 cover of *Cosmopolitan Turkey*, especially when it was released on the same date that some countries commemorate the alleged Armenian genocide in the last days of the Ottoman Empire. Because the magazine is published in 64 different countries, it is difficult to be sure readers everywhere experience the content the same way. In addition to political differences, marketers have to be sensitive to cultural values: In some countries, because of local norms about modesty, some female readers have to hide the magazine from their husbands! Different cultures emphasize varying belief systems that define what it means to be female, feminine, or appealing—and what people consider appropriate to see in print on these matters. Publishers of the Chinese version aren't even permitted to mention sex at all, so they replace articles about uplifting cleavage with uplifting stories about youthful dedication. Ironically, there isn't much down-and-dirty material in the Swedish edition either—but for the opposite reason: The culture is so open about this topic that it doesn't grab readers' attention the way it would in the United States.[68]

Values regarding issues such as sexuality are important in the United States as well:

- In a controversial commercial for Trojan condoms, women in a bar sit next to pigs. One magically turns into a handsome suitor after it buys a condom from a vending machine. The tag line reads, "Evolve. Use a condom every time." The CBS and FOX networks rejected the ad, and some local NBC affiliates refused to run it.[69]
- In an ad Kraft Foods ran for its Athenos yogurt brand, a Greek grandmother berates her granddaughter for dressing "like a prostitute." In another spot, Grandma warns the girl that she's "going to hell" for living with a guy to whom she's not married.[70]
- Fashion retailer Forever 21, which caters to a fairly young clientele, debuted a collection of maternity wear it called Love 21. The clothing was distributed to locations in Arizona, Alaska, California, Utah, and Texas, which also happen to be the U.S. states with the highest rates of teen pregnancy. A store executive responded to criticism by claiming, "Forever 21 did not create, design or distribute Love 21 Maternity to target, or appeal specifically to pregnant teens. Any relationship between teen pregnancy rates and the locations of our stores is unintentional."[71]

Or, take the core value of cleanliness: Everyone wants to be clean, but some societies are more fastidious than others and won't accept products and services that they think cut corners. Italian women on average spend 21 hours a week on household chores other than cooking—compared with only 4 hours for Americans, according to Procter & Gamble's research. The Italian women wash kitchen and bathroom floors at least four times a week, Americans only once. Italian women typically iron nearly all their wash, even socks and sheets, and they buy more cleaning supplies than women elsewhere do.

So they should be ideal customers for cleaning products, right? That's what Unilever thought when it launched its all-purpose Cif spray cleaner there, but it flopped. Similarly, P&G's best-selling Swiffer wet mop bombed big time. Both companies underestimated this market's desire for products that are tough cleaners, not timesavers. Only about 30 percent of Italian households have dishwashers, because many women don't trust machines to get dishes as clean as they can get them by hand, manufacturers say. Many of those who do use machines tend to thoroughly rinse the dishes before they load them into the dishwasher The explanation for this value: After World War II, Italy remained a poor country until well into the 1960s, so labor-saving devices, such as washing machines, which had become popular in wealthy countries, arrived late. Italian women joined the workforce later than many other European women and in smaller numbers. Young Italian women increasingly work outside the home, but they still spend nearly as much time as their mothers did on housework.

When Unilever did research to determine why Italians didn't take to Cif, they found that these women weren't convinced that a mere spray would do the job on tough kitchen grease or that one product would adequately clean different surfaces (it turns out that 72 percent of Italians own more than eight different cleaning products). The company reformulated the product and reintroduced it with different varieties instead of as an all-in-one. It also made the bottles 50 percent bigger, because Italians clean so frequently, and changed its advertising to emphasize the products' cleaning strength rather than convenience. P&G also reintroduced its Swiffer, this time adding beeswax and a Swiffer duster that is now a bestseller. It sold 5 million boxes in the first 8 months, twice the company's forecasts.[72]

In many cases, of course, values are universal. Who does not desire health, wisdom, or world peace? What sets cultures apart is the *relative importance*, or ranking, of these universal values. This set of rankings constitutes a culture's **value system**.[73] For example, one study found that North Americans have more favorable attitudes toward advertising messages that focus on self-reliance, self-improvement, and the achievement of personal goals as opposed to themes stressing family integrity, collective goals, and the feeling of harmony with others. Korean consumers exhibited the reverse pattern.[74]

We characterize every culture in terms of its members' endorsement of a value system. Not every individual will endorse these values equally, and in some cases, values may even seem to contradict one another (e.g., Americans appear to value both conformity and individuality, and try to find some accommodation between the two). Nonetheless, it is usually possible to identify a general set of **core values** that uniquely define a culture. Core values such as freedom, youthfulness, achievement, materialism, and activity characterize American culture.

In contrast, most Japanese are happy to trade off a bit of independence for security and a feeling of safety—especially when it comes to their children. It's common for communities to post guards along school routes and for parents to place global positioning system (GPS) devices and safety buzzers in their kids' backpacks. Numerous indoor parks in Japan are highly secure environments designed to ease parents' minds. At a typical one called the Fantasy Kids Resort, there are uniformed monitors, security cameras, and antibacterial sand. Visitors spray their stroller wheels with antiseptic soap, and guards require identification from visitors before they admit them.[75] Despite living under enormous stress and deprivation after the 2011 earthquake and tsunami, thousands of Japanese who were marooned in public shelters still found ways to maintain order and hygiene to the greatest extent possible.[76]

How do we determine what a culture values? We term the process of learning the beliefs and behaviors endorsed by one's own culture **enculturation**. In contrast, we call the process of learning the value system and behaviors of another culture (often a priority for those who wish to understand consumers and markets in foreign countries) **acculturation**. *Socialization agents*, including parents, friends, and teachers, impart these beliefs to us.

Another important type of agent is the media; we learn a lot about a culture's priorities when we look at the values that advertising communicates. For example, sales strategies differ significantly between the United States and China. U.S. commercials are more likely to present facts about products and suggestions from credible authorities, whereas Chinese advertisers tend to focus more on emotional appeals without bothering too much about substantiating their claims. U.S. ads tend to be youth-oriented, whereas Chinese ads are more likely to stress the wisdom of older people.[77]

How Do Values Link to Consumer Behavior?

Despite their importance, values haven't helped us to understand consumer behavior as much as we might expect. One reason is that broad-based concepts such as freedom, security, or inner harmony are more likely to affect general purchasing patterns than to differentiate between brands within a product category. This is why some researchers distinguish among broad-based *cultural values* such as security or happiness, *consumption-specific values* such as convenient shopping or prompt service, and *product-specific values* such as ease of use or durability, which affect the relative importance people in different cultures place on possessions.[78] One way to clearly see the impact of shifting cultural values on consumption is to look at the increasing emphasis on the importance of health and wellness. In 2010, top-performing new food/beverage products featured items with natural or organic ingredients, such as Chobani yogurt and Nature's Pride bread.[79]

A study of product-specific values looked in depth at Australians who engage in extreme sports such as surfing, snowboarding, and skateboarding. The researchers identified four dominant values that drove brand choice: freedom, belongingness, excellence, and connection. For example, one female surfer they studied embraced the value of belongingness. She expressed this value when she wore popular brands of surfing apparel even when these major brands had lost their local roots by going mainstream. In contrast, another surfer in the study valued connection: he expressed this as he selected only locally made brands and supported local surfing events.[80]

Some aspects of brand image, such as sophistication, tend to be common across cultures, but others are more likely to be relevant in specific places. The Japanese tend to value peacefulness, whereas Spaniards emphasize passion, and the value of ruggedness appeals to Americans.[81] Because values drive much of consumer behavior (at least in a very general sense), we might say that virtually *all* consumer research ultimately relates to identifying and measuring values. In this section we'll describe some specific attempts by researchers to measure cultural values and apply this knowledge to marketing strategy.

Hofstede's Cultural Dimensions

One of the most widely used measures of cross-cultural values is an instrument developed by Geert Hofstede, a Dutch researcher.[82] This measure scores a country in terms of its standing on five dimensions so that users can compare and contrast values:[83]

- **Power Distance**—The extent to which the less powerful members of organizations and institutions (like the family) accept and expect that power is distributed unequally.
- **Individualism**—The degree to which individuals are integrated into groups.
- **Masculinity**—The distribution of roles between the genders.
- **Uncertainty Avoidance**—A society's tolerance for uncertainty and ambiguity.
- **Long-Term Orientation**—Values associated with Long-Term Orientation are thrift and perseverance; values associated with Short-Term Orientation are respect for tradition, fulfilling social obligations, and protecting one's "face."

The Rokeach Value Survey

The psychologist Milton Rokeach identified a set of **terminal values**, or desired end states, that apply to many different cultures. The *Rokeach Value Survey* also includes a set of **instrumental values**, or actions we need to take to achieve these terminal values.[84] Table 2 lists these two sets of values.

Some evidence indicates that differences in these global values do translate into product-specific preferences and differences in media usage. Nonetheless, marketing researchers have not widely used the Rokeach Value Survey.[85] One reason is that our society is evolving into smaller and smaller sets of *consumption microcultures* within a larger culture, each with its own set of core values. For example, in the United States, a sizable number of people are strong believers in natural health practices and alternative medicine. This focus on wellness instead of mainstream medical approaches to sickness influences many of their behaviors, from food choices to the use of alternative medical practitioners, as well as their opinions on political and social issues.[86]

The List of Values (LOV)

The **List of Values (LOV) Scale** isolates values with more direct marketing applications. This instrument identifies nine consumer segments based on the values members endorse and relates each value to differences in consumption behaviors. These segments

TABLE 2	Terminal and Instrumental Values
Instrumental Values	**Terminal Values**
Ambitious	A comfortable life
Broad-minded	An exciting life
Capable	A sense of accomplishment
Cheerful	A world of peace
Clean	A world of beauty
Courageous	Equality
Forgiving	Family security
Helpful	Freedom
Honest	Happiness
Imaginative	Inner harmony
Independent	Mature love
Intellectual	National security
Logical	Pleasure
Loving	Salvation
Obedient	Self-respect
Polite	Social recognition
Responsible	True friendship
Self-controlled	Wisdom

Source: Richard W. Pollay, "Measuring the Cultural Values Manifest in Advertising," *Current Issues and Research in Advertising* (1983): 71–92. Reprinted by permission, CtC Press. All rights reserved.

include consumers who place priorities on such values as a sense of belonging, excitement, warm relationships with others, and security. For example, people who endorse the sense-of-belonging value are older, are more likely to read *Reader's Digest* and *TV Guide*, drink and entertain more, and prefer group activities more than people who do not endorse this value as highly. In contrast, those who endorse the value of excitement are younger and prefer *Rolling Stone* magazine.[87]

The Means–End Chain Model

Another research approach that incorporates values is the **means–end chain model**. This approach assumes that people link very specific product attributes (indirectly) to terminal values: We choose among alternative means to attain some end state that we value (such as freedom or safety). Thus, we value products to the extent that they provide the means to some end we desire. A technique researchers call **laddering** uncovers consumers' associations between specific attributes and these general consequences. Using this approach, they help consumers climb up the "ladder" of abstraction that connects functional product attributes with desired end states.[88] Based on consumer feedback, they then create *hierarchical value maps* that show how specific product attributes get linked to end states.

Figure 4 shows three different hierarchical value maps from a study of consumers' perceptions of cooking oils in three European countries.[89] The laddering technique illustrates stark differences among product/values links across cultures. For Danish people, health is the most important end state. The British also focus on health, but saving money and avoiding waste are more important for them than for people elsewhere. And, unlike the other two countries, French people link olive oil to their cultural identity.

Figure 4 HIERARCHICAL VALUE MAPS FOR VEGETABLE OIL IN THREE COUNTRIES

(a) DENMARK

(b) ENGLAND

(c) FRANCE

Source: N. A. Nielsen, T. Bech-Larsen, and K. G. Grunert, "Consumer Purchase Motives and Product Perceptions: A Laddering Study on Vegetable Oil in Three Countries," *Food Quality and Preference* 9(6) (1998): 455–66. © 1998 Elsevier. Used with permission.

Syndicated Surveys

A number of companies track changes in values through large-scale surveys. They sell the results of these studies to marketers, who receive regular updates on changes and trends. This approach originated in the mid-1960s, when Playtex was concerned about sagging girdle sales (pun intended). The company commissioned the market research firm of Yankelovich, Skelly & White to see why sales had dropped. Their research linked the decline to a shift in values regarding appearance and naturalness. Playtex went on to design lighter, less restrictive garments, while Yankelovich went on to track the impact of these types of changes in a range of industries.

Gradually, the firm developed the idea of one big study to track U.S. attitudes. In 1970, it introduced the Yankelovich *Monitor*™, which is based on 2-hour interviews with 4,000 respondents.[90] This survey attempts to pick up changes in values; for example, it reported a movement among American consumers toward simplification and away from hype as people try to streamline their hectic lives and reduce their concerns about gaining the approval of others through their purchases. **Voluntary simplifiers** believe that once we satisfy our basic material needs, additional income does not add to happiness. Instead of adding yet another SUV to the collection in the garage, simplifiers are into community building, public service, and spiritual pursuits (think about the self-actualization level we saw in Maslow's Hierarchy earlier in the chapter).[91] Members range from senior citizens who downsize their homes to young, mobile professionals who don't want to be tied down to or by their possessions.

Today, many other syndicated surveys also track changes in values. Advertising agencies perform some of these so that they can stay on top of important cultural trends and help shape the messages they craft for clients. These services include VALS2™, GlobalScan (operated by the advertising agency Backer Spielvogel Bates), New Wave (the Ogilvy & Mather advertising agency), and the Lifestyles Study conducted by the DDB World Communications Group.

Conscientious Consumerism: A New American Core Value?

Are U.S. consumers finally going green—for real? In one survey, 8 in 10 consumers said they believe it's important to buy green brands and products from green companies, and that they'll pay more to do so. The U.S. consumer's focus on personal health is merging with a growing interest in global health. Some analysts call this new value **conscientious consumerism**.[92]

However, it's important to note that attitudes don't always predict behavior—especially for pocketbook issues. When people have less money to spend, they may not purchase environmentally friendly or healthy products if they have to pay a premium for them. As the old saying goes, "The road to hell is paved with good intentions."

Cultural Creatives

Still, it's clear that at least a sizable number of Americans' values are shifting. In particular, marketers point to a segment of consumers they call *LOHAS*—an acronym for "lifestyles of health and sustainability." This label refers to people who worry about the environment, want products to be produced in a sustainable way, and spend money to advance what they see as their personal development and potential. These so-called "Lohasians" (others refer to this segment as *cultural creatives*) represent a great market for products such as organic foods, energy-efficient appliances, and hybrid cars, as well as alternative medicine, yoga tapes, and ecotourism. One organization that tracks this group estimates that they make up about 16 percent of the adults in the United States, or 35 million people; it values the market for socially conscious products at more than $200 billion.[93]

Numerous companies respond to these desires as they develop new "green" formulations or partner with other organizations to promote environmentally friendly behavior. Clorox teamed up with the Sierra Club to promote a new line of ecofriendly Clorox

A WHOLE NEW SECTION OF VEGETARIAN DOG FOOD

SM STORE
PITAMPURA

A growing concern with health also extends to our pets. This Indian store features vegetarian pet food.

Source: Agency—Out of the Box/Creative Directors—Viral Pandya, Sabu Paul, Guneet Pandya/Art Directors—Viral Pandya, Guneet Pandya/Writers—Sabu Paul, Viral Pandya, Guneet Pandya/Tyopgrapher—Ajay Yadav/Digital Artist—Sunil Singh.

products in exchange for a share of the profit. The cleaners are made from natural ingredients such as coconuts and lemon oil, contain no phosphorus or bleach, are biodegradable, and are not animal-tested. Their packaging bottles are recyclable and bear the Sierra Club's name and logo—a giant sequoia tree framed by mountain peaks.[94]

Ethical behavior aside for a moment, is there a financial reward waiting for those companies that pay closer attention to what goes into their products and who makes them? One study that examined this question suggests that the answer is yes. The researchers gave subjects a description of a coffee company that either used or did not use Fair Trade principles to buy its beans. They found that participants were willing to pay an additional $1.40 for a pound of the coffee if it was ethically sourced and were very negative about the company if it did not adhere to these principles. The study obtained similar results for shirts that were made with organic cotton.[95]

147

As of 2010, Burt's Bees and Whole Foods topped the list of U.S. brands people perceive to be the greenest, followed by Tom's of Maine, Trader Joe's, Google, Aveeno, S.C. Johnson, Publix, Microsoft, and IKEA. Ironically, the *2010 ImagePower Green Brands Survey* that polled consumers worldwide also found that Americans are more concerned about the economy than the environment, whereas in developing countries, such as Brazil and India, the situation is reversed![96]

Greenwashing

Despite the impact of the recession, many consumers still express concern about the environmental impact of what they buy. Whether they will pay a premium for green products is still open to debate. One problem for marketers is somewhat self-inflicted: Consumers simply don't believe most of the green claims companies make about their brands. Almost one-fourth of American consumers say they have "no way of knowing" if a product is green or actually does what it claims. Their skepticism is probably justified: According to one report, more than 95 percent of consumer products marketed as "green," including all toys surveyed, make misleading or inaccurate claims. Another survey found that the number of products claiming to be green has increased by 73 percent since 2009—but of the products investigated, almost one-third had fake labels, and 70 made green claims without offering any proof to back them up.[97]

All of this hype results in so-called **greenwashing**, and causes consumers not to believe the claims marketers make and in some cases actually avoid brands that promise they are green. One survey reported that 71 percent of respondents say they will stop buying a product if they feel they've been misled about its environmental impact, and 37 percent are so angry about greenwashing that they believe this justifies a complete boycott of everything the company makes.[98]

OBJECTIVE 4

Consumers vary in the importance they attach to worldly possessions, and this orientation in turn influences their priorities and behaviors.

Materialism: "He Who Dies with the Most Toys Wins"

Our possessions play a central role in our lives, and our desire to accumulate them shapes our value systems. **Materialism** refers to the importance people attach to worldly possessions.[99] We sometimes take the bounty of products and services for granted, until we remember how recent this abundance is. For example, in 1950, two of five American homes did not have a telephone, and in 1940, half of all households still did not possess complete indoor plumbing.

During World War II, members of "cargo cults" in the South Pacific literally worshiped cargo salvaged from crashed aircraft or washed ashore from ships. They believed that their ancestors piloted the ships and planes passing near their islands, so they tried to attract them to their villages. They went so far as to construct fake planes from straw to lure the real ones![100]

We may not worship products to that extent, but many of us certainly work hard to attain our vision of the good life, which abounds in material comforts. Most young people can't imagine a life without cell phones, MP3 players, and other creature comforts. In fact, we can think of marketing as a system that provides certain standards of living to consumers. To some extent, then, the standards of living we expect and desire influence our lifestyles, either by personal experience or as a result of the affluent characters we see on TV and in movies.[101]

Materialists

Materialistic values tend to emphasize the well-being of the individual versus the group, which may conflict with family or religious values. That conflict may help to explain why people with highly material values tend to be less happy.[102] Furthermore, materialism is highest among early adolescents (12 to 13 years old) in comparison to children or late adolescents—perhaps it's no coincidence that this is the age group that also has the lowest level of self-esteem.[103]

Materialists are more likely to value possessions for their status and appearance-related meanings, whereas those who do not emphasize this value tend to prize products that connect them to other people or that provide them with pleasure when they use them.[104] As a result, high materialists prefer expensive products that they publicly consume. A study that compared specific items that low versus high materialists value found that people low on the materialism value cherished items such as a mother's wedding gown, picture albums, a rocking chair from childhood, or a garden, whereas those who scored high preferred things such as jewelry, china, or a vacation home.[105] Materialistic people appear to link more of their self-identity to products. One study found that when people who score high on this value fear the prospect of dying, they form even stronger connections to brands.[106] Another study reported that consumers who are "love-smitten" with their possessions tend to use these relationships to compensate for loneliness and a lack of affiliation with social networks.[107]

Materialism and Economic Conditions

One byproduct of the Great Recession has been to force many consumers to reconsider the value of their possessions. As one woman observed, "The idea that you need to go bigger to be happy is false. I really believe that the acquisition of material goods doesn't bring about happiness." This doesn't necessarily mean that people will stop buying—but perhaps, at least for a while, they will do so more carefully. In the words of one industry analyst, "We're moving from a conspicuous consumption—which is 'buy without regard'—to a calculated consumption." In 2010, American consumers on average saved more than 6 percent of their incomes—before the recession the rate was 1 to 2 percent.

Ironically, bad economic conditions may make at least some people happier. Research on the relationship between consumption and happiness tends to show that people are happier when they spend money on experiences instead of material objects, when they relish what they plan to buy long before they buy it, and when they stop trying to outdo their neighbors. One study reported that the only consumption category that was positively related to happiness involved leisure: vacations, entertainment, sports and equipment like golf clubs and fishing poles. This finding is consistent with changes in buying patterns, which show that consumers have tended to choose experiences over objects during the last couple of years. For example, they may choose to entertain themselves at home rather than going out, or even to forgo a trip to Disney World for a "stay-cation" in the backyard.

Another factor is just how much of a "buzz" we get from the stuff we buy. The research evidence points to the idea that consumers get more "bang for their buck" when they buy a bunch of smaller things over time, rather than blowing it all on one big purchase. This is due to what psychologists call **hedonic adaptation**; it basically means that to maintain a fairly stable level of happiness, we tend to become used to changes, big or small, wonderful or terrible. That means that over time the rush from a major purchase will dissipate and we're back to where we started (emotionally speaking). So, the next time you get a bonus or find an envelope stuffed with cash on the street, take a series of long weekends instead of splurging on that three-week trip to Maui.[108]

Cross-Cultural Values

Innovations know no geographic boundaries; in modern times they travel across oceans and deserts with blinding speed. Just as Marco Polo brought noodles from China and colonial settlers introduced Europeans to the "joys" of tobacco, today multinational firms conquer new markets when they convince legions of foreign consumers to desire what they make.

As if understanding the dynamics of one's own culture weren't hard enough, these issues get even more complicated when we consider what drives consumers in other cultures. The consequences of ignoring cultural sensitivities can be costly. Think about problems a prominent multinational company such as McDonald's encounters as it

Net Profit

A value that's related to materialism is **cosmopolitanism**. Researchers define a *cosmopolitan* as someone who tries to be open to the world and who strives for diverse experiences. This is a quality that used to be linked to the wealthy, but now—with improved access to media and of course the Internet—it's no longer necessary to be rich to express an interest in a range of culturally diverse products. Cosmopolitans respond well to brands that have a "worldly" (i.e., international or global) image. They think it's important to own consumer electronics products and are more likely to engage in electronic media activities such as email, Web surfing, and buying DVDs.[109] A scale to identify these consumers includes measures such as these:

- I enjoy exchanging ideas with people from other cultures or countries.
- I am interested in learning more about people who live in other countries.
- I find people from other cultures stimulating.

CB AS I SEE IT

Professor Lon Chaplin, *Villanova University*

Today's children are arguably the most materialistic generation ever. At age 2, toddlers are already showing clear signs of developing into savvy consumers with strong preferences for products and brands across a variety of product categories. When we look at adults, we know that although they believe that material possessions will make them happy, those who are more materialistic tend to be less happy. Is this true for children as well? What individual traits are associated with materialistic tendencies in children? What causes children to be materialistic? What socialization factors influence children's materialism (e.g., parents, peers, media, and marketing)?

My research examines how materialism develops throughout childhood and adolescence. *Materialism* is the importance a person places on the acquisition of material possessions at the expense of self-transcendent and/or prosocial pursuits, such as helping others in the community, volunteering, and donating, to achieve happiness. Although some research on youth materialism exists, most of the studies focus on adolescents. Only a handful of studies including younger children are beginning to emerge. Studies with a wide age range (e.g., 6- to 18-year-olds) would be ideal, as they would help parents and educators to understand how developmental changes in children's cognitive abilities and social awareness affect the degree to which they focus on acquiring material goods to achieve happiness.

To have confidence in the results, materialism researchers must use reliable and valid measures that are appropriate for younger populations who have less sophisticated verbal and reading skills. Thus, one of my research interests involves developing creative measurement tools that are more amenable to measuring materialism in a children's population. My collaborator, Professor Deborah Roedder John, and I have found that projective techniques such as collages work well to study children's materialism. We essentially ask children to create a "Happiness" collage made of people, pets, material things, achievements, sports, and achievements that make them happy. When they describe what makes them happy, kids who place more importance on material things as opposed to less materialistic sentiments are considered to be more materialistic. Not only is the collage a familiar and engaging task that allows for more thoughtful responses, but it also masks the fact that we are studying a value that society deems to be negative.

Understanding children's materialism will continue to be an important topic for many reasons. No other consumer segment has grown as much in purchasing power and influence in the last decade as the children and adolescent segment. Additionally, materialism is a topic in consumer research that holds considerable interest from a public policy perspective, especially given recent concerns over children's well-being and the role that marketers play in convincing children that they *need* certain products or brands to be "cool." I look forward to the challenges that lie ahead, as the benefits to having happier, less materialistic children are substantial.

---

expands globally—even as today the iconic American chain's worldwide operations are far bigger than its U.S. domestic business:

- During the 1994 soccer World Cup, the fast-food giant reprinted the Saudi Arabian flag, which includes sacred words from the Koran, on disposable packaging it used in promotions. Muslims around the world protested this borrowing of sacred imagery, and the company had to scramble to correct its mistake.
- In 2002, McDonald's agreed to donate $10 million to Hindu and other groups as partial settlement of litigation involving its mislabeling of French fries and hash browns as vegetarian (it cooked them in oil tainted with meat residue).
- Also in 2002, the company abruptly cancelled its plans to introduce its new McAfrika sandwich in its Norwegian restaurants. The CEO of McDonald's in Norway acknowledged on national television that introducing this menu item at a time of growing famine in Africa was "coincidental and unfortunate."
- In India, the company doesn't sell any of its famous beef hamburgers. Instead, it offers customized entrees such as a Pizza McPuff, McAloo Tikki (a spiced-potato burger), Paneer Salsa McWrap, and even a Crispy Chinese burger, to capitalize on the great popularity of Chinese food in India. It makes its mayonnaise without eggs, and all stores

maintain separate kitchen sections for vegetarian and nonvegetarian dishes. Workers from the nonvegetarian section must shower before they cross over to the other area.

- In 2005, McDonald's introduced the spicy Prosperity Burger in nine countries, from South Korea to Indonesia, in recognition of the Lunar New Year.
- Today the chain's Big Tasty burger is an 840-calorie behemoth that consists of a 5.5-ounce beef patty slathered in smoky barbecue sauce and topped with three slices of cheese. The menu entrée was first introduced in Sweden, and it's now available in other parts of Europe as well as in Latin America and Australia.[110]
- Although the Japanese are well-known for their healthy diets, McDonald's numerous customers there are clamoring for high-calorie sandwiches—even as the company's American consumers welcome new diet-friendly entrees like the Fruit 'n Walnut salad. As part of its new Big America 2 campaign, McD's in Japan offer the 713-calorie Idaho burger (topped with melted cheese, a deep-fried hash brown, strips of bacon, onions, and pepper-and-mustard sauce) and several other U.S.-themed items.[111] It seems there's more than one way to translate "Big America."
- A McDonald's ad in France created some *sangfroid* because it features the French hero, Asterix, and his merry band of warriors eating in the restaurant. The character has been the topic of numerous movies and an Asterix theme park is very popular. The spot deliberately does not show the characters cramming burgers or fries, but some French bloggers are not amused.[112]

In this section, we'll consider some of the issues that confront marketers who want to understand the cultural dynamics of other countries. We'll also consider the consequences of the "Americanization" of global culture. As U.S. (and to some extent, Western European) marketers continue to export Western popular culture to a globe full of increasingly affluent consumers, many customers eagerly replace their traditional products with the likes of McDonald's, Levi's, and MTV. But, as we'll also see, there are plenty of obstacles to success for multinational firms—especially Yankee ones.

Rather than ignore the global characteristics of their brands, firms have to manage them strategically. That's critical, because future growth for most companies will come from foreign markets. In 2002, developed countries in North America, Europe, and East Asia accounted for 15 percent of the world's population of 6.3 billion. By 2030, according to the World Bank, the planet's population will rise to 9 billion—and 90 percent of these people will live in developing countries.

As corporations compete in many markets around the world, the debate intensifies: Should an organization develop separate marketing plans for each culture, or should it craft a single plan to implement everywhere? Let's briefly consider each viewpoint.

Adopt a Standardized Strategy

As Procter & Gamble strategizes about the best way to speak to consumers around the world, the company finds large segments in many countries that share the same outlooks, style preferences, and aspirations. These include teenagers, working women who try to juggle careers and families, and baby boomers. As the head of P&G's Global Health and Feminine Care division explained, "We're seeing global tribes forming around the world that are more and more interconnected through technology. If you focus on the similarities instead of the differences [in these tribes], key business opportunities emerge." For example, brand managers find that teenage girls everywhere have the same concerns and questions about puberty, so the company makes the same content available in 40 countries.[114]

Proponents of a standardized marketing strategy argue that many cultures, especially those of industrialized countries, are now so homogenized that the same approach will work throughout the world. If it develops one approach for multiple markets, a company can benefit from economies of scale, because it does not have to incur the substantial time and expense to develop a separate strategy for each culture.[115] This viewpoint represents an **etic perspective**, which focuses on commonalities across cultures. An etic approach to a culture is objective and analytical; it reflects impressions of a culture as outsiders view it.

The Tangled Web

A Japanese food and soy sauce brand launched a Facebook app that allows people to "Asianate" themselves. To give yourself an "Urban Asian look," you upload your photo and software merges your features with those of a Japanese sumo wrestler. The app was created by the company's branch in the Netherlands, which bills its Web site as "Your portal to what's happening in Asia's city life today." Well, maybe not so much . . .![113]

Ford is introducing a worldwide line of compact cars, under the Ford Focus name, that will include hybrid, plug-in hybrid, and electric models. The company calls the 2012 Focus its first truly global product because it was "purposely designed to share as many parts as possible wherever it is built or sold." Television and print ads to promote the Focus will look similar around the world; they will stress technological features like assisted parking and Wi-Fi hot-spot capability.[116]

Source: Ford Images.

Adopt a Localized Strategy

Unlike Disney World in Orlando, visitors to the Walt Disney Studios theme park at Disneyland Paris don't hear the voices of American movie stars narrating their guided tours. Instead, European actors such as Jeremy Irons, Isabella Rossellini, and Nastassja Kinski provide commentary in their native tongues.

Disney learned the hard way about the importance of being sensitive to local cultures after it opened its Euro Disney Park in 1992. The company got slammed because its new location didn't cater to local customs (such as serving wine with meals). Visitors to Euro Disney from many countries took offense, even at what seem to be small slights. For example, initially the park only sold a French sausage, which drew complaints from Germans, Italians, and others who believed their own local versions to be superior. Euro Disney's CEO explained, "When we first launched there was the belief that it was enough to be Disney. Now we realize that our guests need to be welcomed on the basis of their own culture and travel habits."[117]

Disney applied the lessons it learned in cultural sensitivity to its newer Hong Kong Disneyland. Executives shifted the angle of the front gate by 12 degrees after they consulted a *feng shui* specialist, who said the change would ensure prosperity for the park. Disney also put a bend in the walkway from the train station to the gate to make sure the flow of positive energy, or *chi*, did not slip past the entrance and out to the China Sea. Cash registers are close to corners or along walls to increase prosperity. The company burned incense as it finished each building, and it picked a lucky day (September 12) for the opening. One of the park's main ballrooms measures 888 square meters, because eight is a lucky number in Chinese culture. And because the Chinese consider the number four bad luck, you won't find any fourth-floor buttons in hotel elevators. Disney also recognizes that Chinese family dynamics are different, so it revamped its advertising: Print ads showed a grandmother, mother, and daughter who wear tiaras at the park. In China, bonding between parents and children is difficult because of the culture's hierarchical nature, so an executive explained, "We want to say it's OK to let your hair down." Camping out with stopwatches, the company's designers discovered that Chinese people take an average of 10 minutes longer to eat than Americans, so they added 700 extra seats to dining areas. Now, Disney is building another theme park and resort in Shanghai—but it's making more big changes to please Chinese visitors. The Chinese government insisted that the new venue not resemble Disneyland, which is a symbol of American culture. This one will be the only Disney park without classic American features like a Main Street.[118]

Disney's experience supports the view of marketers who endorse an **emic perspective** that stresses variations across cultures. They feel that each culture is unique, with its own value system, conventions, and regulations. This perspective argues that each country has a *national character*; a distinctive set of behavior and personality characteristics.[119] A marketer must therefore tailor its strategy to the sensibilities of each specific culture. An emic approach to a culture is subjective and experiential: It attempts to explain a culture as insiders experience it.

Sometimes this strategy means that a manufacturer has to modify what it makes or a retailer has to change the way it displays the product so that it's acceptable to local tastes. When Walmart started to open stores abroad in the early 1990s, it offered a little piece of America to foreign consumers—and that was the problem. It promoted golf clubs in soccer-mad Brazil and pushed ice skates in Mexico. It trained its German clerks to smile at customers—who thought they were flirting. Now Walmart tries to adapt to local preferences. Its Chinese stores sell live turtles and snakes and lure shoppers who come on foot or bicycle with free shuttle buses and home delivery for refrigerators and other large items.[120]

In some cases, consumers in one place simply do not like some products that are popular elsewhere, or their different lifestyles require companies to rethink their designs. IKEA finally realized that Americans use a lot of ice in their drinks and so didn't buy the smaller European glasses the stores stocked. The Swedish furniture chain also figured out that compared to Europeans, Americans sleep in bigger beds, need bigger bookshelves, and like to curl up on sofas rather than sit on them.[121] Snapple failed in Japan because the drink's cloudy appearance and the floating pulp in the bottles were a turnoff. Similarly, Frito-Lay stopped selling Ruffles potato chips (too salty) and Cheetos (the Japanese didn't appreciate orange fingers after they ate a handful).[122] The company still makes Cheetos in China, but the local version doesn't contain any cheese, which is not a staple of the Chinese diet. Instead, local flavors come in varieties such as Savory American Cream and Japanese Steak.[123]

China recently overtook Japan as the world's second-largest economy, and some multinational marketers are creating new brands specifically for Chinese consumers. Levi Strauss & Co. launched a more accessible global brand, Denizen™, in China and three other Asian countries last fall. Following the successful launch in Asia, the company continues introducing the brand in other global markets, including Mexico and the U.S.A. The Hermès luxury brand offers its new Shang Xia line (which means "Up Down" in Mandarin), while PepsiCo taps the Chinese taste for green tea with Spritea, which it only sells in mainland China.
Source: Courtesy of Levi Strauss & Co.

Cross-Cultural Differences Relevant to Marketers

So, which perspective is correct, the emic or the etic? As you might guess, the best bet probably is a combination of both.[124] Some researchers argue that the relevant dimension to consider is **consumer style**, a pattern of behaviors, attitudes, and opinions that influences all of a person's consumption activities—including attitudes toward advertising, preferred channels of information and purchase, brand loyalty, and price consciousness. These researchers identified four major clusters of consumer styles when they looked at data from the United States, the United Kingdom, France, and Germany:[125]

- Price-sensitive consumers
- Variety seekers
- Brand-loyal consumers
- Information seekers

Given the sizable variations in tastes within the United States alone, it is hardly surprising that people around the world develop their own unique preferences. Panasonic touted the fact that its rice cooker kept the food from getting too crisp—until the company learned that consumers in the Middle East *like* to eat their rice this way. Unlike Americans, Europeans favor dark chocolate over milk chocolate, which they think of as a children's food. Sara Lee sells its pound cake with chocolate chips in the United States, raisins in Australia, and coconuts in Hong Kong. Crocodile handbags are popular in Asia and Europe but not in the United States.[126]

OBJECTIVE 5
Products that succeed in one culture may fail in another if marketers fail to understand the differences among consumers in each place.

Does Global Marketing Work?

So, what's the verdict? Does global marketing work or not? Perhaps the more appropriate question is, "*When* does it work?" Although the argument for a homogenous world culture is appealing in principle, in practice it hasn't worked out too well. One reason is that consumers in different countries have varying conventions and customs, so they simply do not use products the same way. Kellogg, for example, discovered that in Brazil people don't typically eat a big breakfast—they're more likely to eat cereal as a dry snack.

In fact, significant cultural differences even show up within the same country. We certainly feel that we've traveled to a different place as we move around the United States. Advertisers in Canada know that when they target consumers in French-speaking Quebec, their messages must be much different from those addressed to residents of English-speaking regions. Ads in Montreal tend to be a lot racier than those in Toronto, reflecting differences in attitudes toward sexuality between consumers with French versus British roots.[129]

Some large corporations, such as Coca-Cola, have successfully crafted a single, international image. Still, even the soft-drink giant must make minor modifications to the way it presents itself in each culture. Although Coke commercials are largely standardized, the company permits local agencies to edit them so they highlight close-ups of local faces.[130] To maximize the chances of success for these multicultural efforts, marketers must locate consumers in different countries who nonetheless share a common *worldview*. This is more likely to be the case among people whose frame of reference is relatively more international or cosmopolitan, or who receive much of their information about the world from sources that incorporate a worldwide perspective.

Who is likely to fall into this category? Two consumer segments are particularly good candidates: (1) affluent people who are "global citizens" and who come into contact with ideas from around the world through their travels, business contacts, and media experiences; and (2) young people whose tastes in music and fashion are strongly influenced by MTV and other media that broadcast many of the same images to multiple countries. For example, viewers of MTV Europe in Rome or Zurich can check out the same "buzz clips" as their counterparts in London or Luxembourg.[131]

A large-scale study of consumers in 41 countries identified the characteristics that people associate with global brands, and it also measured the relative importance of those dimensions when consumers buy products.[132] The researchers grouped consumers who evaluate global brands in the same way. They identified four major segments:

- **Global citizens**—The largest segment (55 percent of consumers) uses the global success of a company as a signal of quality and innovation. At the same time, they are concerned about whether companies behave responsibly on issues such as consumer health, the environment, and worker rights.
- **Global dreamers**—The second-largest segment, at 23 percent, consists of consumers who see global brands as quality products and readily buy into the myths they author. They aren't nearly as concerned with social responsibility as are the global citizens.
- **Antiglobals**—Thirteen percent of consumers are skeptical that transnational companies deliver higher-quality goods. They dislike brands that preach American values, and they don't trust global companies to behave responsibly. They try to avoid doing business with transnational firms.
- **Global agnostics**—The remaining 9 percent of consumers don't base purchase decisions on a brand's global attributes. Instead, they evaluate a global product by the same criteria they use to judge local brands and don't regard its global nature as meriting special consideration.

OBJECTIVE 6

Western (and particularly American) culture have a huge impact around the world, although people in other countries don't necessarily ascribe the same meanings to products as we do.

The Diffusion of Consumer Culture

Coca-Cola is the drink of choice among young people in Asian countries, and McDonald's is their favorite restaurant.[133] The National Basketball Association sells $500 million of licensed merchandise every year *outside* of the United States.[134] Patrons of the Starlite Urban Drive-In in London sit in rows of cars as they watch American "classics" like *Grease* and *Dirty Dancing* while they chow down on burgers, meatloaf, and sweet potato pie, followed by ice cream sundaes or chocolate brownies and cream.[135]

Walk the streets of Lisbon or Buenos Aires, and the sight of Nike hats, Gap T-shirts, and Levi's jeans will accost you at every turn. The allure of American consumer culture spreads throughout the world—but with a lot of pushback in many places. Critics in other countries deplore the creeping Americanization of their cultures because of what they view as excessive materialism. One French critic summarized this resistance to the diffusion of American culture: he described the Euro Disney theme park as "a horror made of cardboard, plastic, and appalling colors—a construction of hardened chewing gum and idiotic folklore taken straight out of a comic book written for obese Americans."[136]

A survey in Beijing found that nearly half of all children under 12 think McDonald's is a domestic Chinese brand![137] The West (and especially the United States) is a net exporter of popular culture. Many consumers equate Western lifestyles in general and the English language in particular with modernization and sophistication, and numerous American brands slowly but surely insinuate themselves into local cultures. Indeed, some global brands are so widespread that many are only vaguely aware of their countries of origin. In surveys, consumers routinely guess that Heineken is German (it's really Dutch) and that Nokia is Japanese (it's Finnish).[138]

American television inspires knockoffs around the world. But to be fair, many U.S. viewers don't realize that American reality show hits such as *Big Brother* and *American Idol* started out as European concepts that U.S. producers imported. In fact, the U.K. version of *Big Brother* briefly went off the air after a fight broke out and housemates threatened to kill each other. The German version attracted accusations of "shameless voyeurism" after a female contestant had her nipple pierced on live TV—without anesthetic.[139] In contrast, a Malaysian show that borrows the *American Idol* format is called *Imam Muda* (Young Leader). Contestants debate religious topics and recite passages from the Koran. The winner doesn't get a recording contract. Instead, he receives a job as an imam, or religious leader, a scholarship to study in Saudi Arabia, and an all-expenses-paid pilgrimage to Mecca, Islam's holiest city.[140]

Emerging Consumer Cultures in Transitional Economies

In the early 1980s, the Romanian Communist government broadcast the American TV show *Dallas* to point out the decadence of Western capitalism. This strategy backfired: The devious (but rich!) J. R. Ewing became a revered icon in parts of Eastern Europe and the Middle East. A popular tourist attraction outside of Bucharest includes a big white log gate that announces (in English) the name, "South Fork Ranch."[141] Western "decadence" appears to be infectious.[142]

More than 60 countries have a gross national product of less than $10 billion, and there are at least 135 transnational companies with revenues greater than that. The dominance of these marketing powerhouses creates a **globalized consumption ethic**. Tempting images of luxury cars, glam rock stars on MTV, and modern appliances that make life easier surround us wherever we turn. People the world over begin to share the ideal of a material lifestyle and value well-known brands that symbolize prosperity. Shopping evolves from a wearying, task-oriented struggle to locate even basic necessities to a leisure activity. Possessing these coveted items becomes a mechanism to display one's status—often at great personal sacrifice.

After the downfall of communism, Eastern Europeans emerged from a long winter of deprivation into a springtime of abundance. The picture is not all rosy, however. It's not easy for many people who live in **transitional economies** to attain consumer goods. This term describes countries such as China, Portugal, and Romania that struggle as they adapt from a controlled, centralized economy to a free-market system. In these situations, rapid changes occur in social, political, and economic dimensions as the populace suddenly is exposed to global communications and external market pressures.[143]

Some of the consequences of the transition to capitalism include a loss of confidence and pride in the local culture, as well as alienation, frustration, and increased stress as citizens sacrifice their leisure time to work ever harder to buy consumer goods. The yearning for the trappings of Western material culture is perhaps most evident in parts of Eastern Europe, where citizens who threw off the shackles of communism now have direct access to coveted consumer goods from the United States and Western Europe—if they can afford them. One analyst observed, "As former subjects of the Soviet empire dream it, the American dream has very little to do with liberty and justice for all and a great deal to do with soap operas and the Sears Catalogue."[144]

One study, conducted in 2009, looked at how Chinese consumers think about Western brands. The researchers found that their interpretations depended on their unique perspective about the history of relations between China and the West. The researchers in fact identified four different *narratives* (themes) in their sample: West as liberator, as oppressor, as subjugated, and as partner. Depending on which view they endorsed, respondents viewed Western brands as instruments of democratization, domination, a symbol of Asian ascendancy as Chinese domestic brands start to gain traction, or as instruments of economic progress that will help China to grow its economy in partnership with the United States and Western Europe.[145]

As the global consumption ethic spreads, rituals and product preferences in different cultures become homogenized. For example, some urbanites in Muslim Turkey now celebrate Christmas even though gift-giving is not customary in many parts of the country—even on birthdays. In China, Christmas fever grips China's newly rising urban middle class as an excuse to shop, eat, and party. People there snap up Christmas trees, ornaments, and Christian religious objects (even though the street vendors who peddle images of Jesus and Mary can't always identify who they are). Chinese consumers embrace Christmas because to them the holiday is international and modern, not because it's a traditional Christian celebration. The government encourages this practice because it stimulates consumer spending. To make the holiday even merrier, China exports about $1 billion worth of Christmas products every year, and its factories churn out $7.5 billion of the toys people worldwide put under their trees.[146]

Does this homogenization mean that in time consumers who live in Nairobi, New Guinea, or the Netherlands will all be indistinguishable from those in New York or Nashville? Probably not, because the meanings of consumer goods mutate to blend with local customs and values. For example, in Turkey some urban women use their ovens to dry clothes and their dishwashers to wash muddy spinach. A person in Papua New Guinea may combine a traditional clothing style such as a *bilum* with Western items such as Mickey Mouse shirts or baseball caps.[147] These processes make it unlikely that global homogenization will overwhelm local cultures, but it is likely that there will be multiple consumer cultures, each of which blends global icons such as Nike's pervasive "swoosh" with indigenous products and meanings. In Vietnam, for example, local fast-food chains dominate the market as they duplicate a McDonald's approach but add a local flavor. The country's hugely successful Kinh Do red and yellow outlets sell specialties like dried squid buns. In the Philippines, the Jollibee Foods Corp. burger chain also copies the McDonald's look—and it outsells McDonald's there.[148]

Creolization occurs when foreign influences integrate with local meanings. Modern Christianity adapted the pagan "Christmas" tree into its own rituals. In India, handicapped beggars sell bottles of Coke from tricycles, and Indipop, a popular music hybrid, mixes traditional styles with rock, rap, and reggae.[149] Young Hispanic Americans bounce between hip-hop and *Rock en Español*, blend Mexican rice with spaghetti sauce, and spread peanut butter and jelly on tortillas.[150] In Argentina, Coca-Cola launched Nativa, a soft drink flavored with the country's traditional *yerba mate* herbal tea, as part of a strategy to broaden its portfolio with products it makes from indigenous ingredients.[151]

The creolization process sometimes results in bizarre permutations of products and services when locals modify them to be compatible with their customs. Consider these creolized adaptations, for example:[152]

- In Peru, Indian boys carry rocks painted to look like transistor radios.
- In highland Papua New Guinea, tribespeople put Chivas Regal wrappers on their drums and wear Pentel pens instead of nosebones.
- Bana tribespeople in the remote highlands of Kako, Ethiopia, pay to watch *Pluto the Circus Dog* on a View-Master.
- When an African Swazi princess marries a Zulu king, she wears a traditional costume of red touraco wing feathers around her forehead and a cape of windowbird feathers and oxtails. But guests record the ceremony on a Kodak movie camera while the band plays "The Sound of Music."
- The Japanese use Western words as a shorthand for anything new and exciting, even if they do not understand what the words mean. They give cars names such as Fairlady, Gloria, and Bongo Wagon. Consumers buy *deodoranto* (deodorant) and *appuru pai* (apple pie). Ads urge shoppers to *stoppu rukku* (stop and look), and products claim to be *yuniku* (unique).[153] Coca-Cola cans say, "I feel Coke & sound special," and a company called Cream Soda sells products with the slogan, "Too old to die, too young to happy."[154] Other Japanese products with English names include Mouth Pet (breath freshener), Pocari Sweat ("refreshment water"), Armpit (electric razor), Brown Gross Foam (hair-coloring mousse), Virgin Pink Special (skin cream), Cow Brand (beauty soap), and Mymorning Water (canned water).[155]

CHAPTER SUMMARY

Now that you have finished reading this chapter you should understand why:

1. It's important for marketers to recognize that products can satisfy a range of consumer needs.

Marketers try to satisfy consumer needs, but the reasons people purchase any product can vary widely. The identification of consumer motives is an important step to ensure that a product will satisfy appropriate needs. Traditional approaches to consumer behavior focus on the abilities of products to satisfy rational needs (utilitarian motives), but hedonic motives (e.g., the need for exploration or for fun) also play a key role in many purchase decisions.

As Maslow's hierarchy of needs demonstrates, the same product can satisfy different needs, depending on the consumer's state at the time. In addition to this objective situation (e.g., have basic physiological needs already been satisfied?), we must also consider the consumer's degree of involvement with the product.

2. The way we evaluate and choose a product depends on our degree of involvement with the product, the marketing message, and/or the purchase situation.

Product involvement can range from very low, where purchase decisions are made via inertia, to very high, where consumers form very strong bonds with what they buy. In addition to considering the degree to which consumers are involved with a product, marketing strategists also need to assess consumers' extent of involvement with marketing messages and with the purchase situation.

3. Our deeply held cultural values dictate the types of products and services we seek out or avoid.

Underlying values often drive consumer motivations. Products thus take on meaning because a person thinks they will help him or her to achieve some goal that is linked to a value, such as individuality or freedom. A set of core values characterizes each culture, to which many of its members adhere.

4. Consumers vary in the importance they attach to worldly possessions, and this orientation in turn influences their priorities and behaviors.

Materialism refers to the importance people attach to worldly possessions. Although we describe many Americans as materialists, there are indications of a value shift within a sizable portion of the population—and this accompanies much greater interest in environmentally sustainable products and services.

5. Products that succeed in one culture may fail in another if marketers fail to understand the differences among consumers in each place.

Because a consumer's culture exerts such a big influence on his or her lifestyle choices, marketers must learn as much as possible about differences in cultural norms and preferences when they do business in more than one country. One important issue is the extent to which we need to tailor our marketing strategies to each culture. Followers of an etic perspective believe that people in many cultures appreciate the same universal messages. Believers in an emic perspective argue that individual cultures are too unique to permit such standardization; marketers must instead adapt their approaches to local values and practices. Attempts at global marketing have met with mixed success. In many cases this approach is more likely to work if the messages appeal to basic values or if the target markets consist of consumers who are internationally rather than locally oriented.

6. Western (and particularly American) culture have a huge impact around the world, although people in other countries don't necessarily ascribe the same meanings to products as we do.

The United States is a net exporter of popular culture. Consumers around the world eagerly adopt American products, especially entertainment vehicles and items they link to an American lifestyle (e.g., Marlboro cigarettes, Levi's jeans). Despite the continuing "Americanization" of world culture, some people resist globalization because they fear it will dilute their own local cultures. In other cases, they practice creolization as they integrate these products with existing cultural practices.

KEY TERMS

acculturation	consumer style	drive theory
affect	core values	emic perspective
approach–approach conflict	cosmopolitanism	enculturation
approach–avoidance conflict	creolization	etic perspective
avoidance–avoidance conflict	cult products	expectancy theory
conscientious consumerism	drive	flashmobs

flow state	List of Values (LOV) Scale	social game
goal	LOHAS	spectacles
globalized consumption ethic	long-term orientation	terminal values
greenwashing	masculinity	theory of cognitive dissonance
hedonic adaptation	mass customization	transactional advertising
Hierarchy of Needs (Maslow's)	materialism	transitional economies
homeostasis	means–end chain model	uncertainty avoidance
individualism	motivation	value
inertia	narrative transportation	value system
instrumental values	power distance	voluntary simplifiers
involvement	productivity orientation	want
laddering	sentiment analysis	word-phrase dictionary

REVIEW

1 What is motivation, and how is this idea relevant to consumer behavior?

2 Describe three types of motivational conflicts, citing an example of each from current marketing campaigns.

3 Explain the difference between a need and a want.

4 What is cognitive dissonance?

5 Name the levels in Maslow's hierarchy of needs, and give an example of a marketing appeal that is focused at each level.

6 What is consumer involvement? How does this concept relate to motivation?

7 Why would marketers want their customers to enter into a flow state when shopping for their products?

8 List three types of consumer involvement, giving an example of each type.

9 What are some strategies marketers can use to increase consumers' involvement with their products?

10 What are values, and why should marketers care?

11 What is the difference between enculturation and acculturation?

12 What is LOHAS, and why are people who follow this lifestyle important?

13 Describe at least two alternative techniques marketing researchers have used to measure values.

14 What is materialism, and why is it relevant to marketing?

15 What is the difference between an emic and an etic perspective on globalization?

16 Why is the United States a net exporter of popular culture?

17 What country provides an example of a transitional economy?

18 Define creolization and provide an example.

CONSUMER BEHAVIOR CHALLENGE

■ DISCUSS

1 "College students' concerns about the environment and vegetarianism are simply a passing fad; a way to look 'cool.'" Do you agree?

2 Marketers continue to push the envelope as they challenge society's norms regarding what topics are appropriate to discuss in public. Products that people only used to whisper about now pop up in ads and billboards; these include feminine hygiene products, condoms, lubricants, grooming aids, and pregnancy tests. A commercial for a digital home-pregnancy test kit even broke a taboo when it showed urination on TV. As a stream of liquid flows onto the device, a voiceover says, "Introducing the most sophisticated piece of technology . . . you will ever pee on." Ads for feminine hygiene products used to barely hint at their function (typically they depicted a smiling woman who wore white to subtly signal how well the item worked). Today, Procter & Gamble's Always line of menstrual pads advertises with the cheerful theme, "Have a happy period."[156] Where do we cross the line in what we show in advertising?

3 Some market analysts see a shift in values among young people. They claim that this generation has not had a lot of stability in their lives. They are fed up with superficial relationships and yearn for a return to tradition. What's your take on this? Are young people indeed returning to the values of their parents (or even their grandparents)? How have these changes influenced your perspective on marriage and family?

4 Core values evolve over time. What do you think are the three to five core values that best describe Americans today?

5 Which of the needs in Maslow's Hierarchy do you satisfy when you participate in social networks like Facebook and Foursquare? How could these sites add new features to help you satisfy these needs?

6 The chapter mentions new facial recognition technology that marketers will soon use to classify shoppers in terms of their appearance so they can serve up ads that appeal to people in certain demographic categories. This makes advertising more useful because it reduces the amount of irrelevant information we will see. However, is there a downside to this technique? Do you see any potential for negative applications that use (for example) racial profiling to decide what information consumers should receive? Do the potential benefits outweigh these negative applications?

7 Because of higher competition and market saturation, marketers in industrialized countries try to develop Third World markets. Asian consumers alone spend $90 billion a year on cigarettes, and U.S. tobacco manufacturers push relentlessly into these markets. We find cigarette advertising, which often depicts glamorous Western models and settings, just about everywhere—on billboards, buses, storefronts, and clothing—and tobacco companies sponsor many major sports and cultural events. Some companies even hand out cigarettes and gifts in amusement areas, often to preteens. Should governments allow these practices, even if the products may be harmful to their citizens or divert money that poor people should spend on essentials? If you were a trade or health official in a Third World country, what guidelines, if any, might you suggest to regulate the import of luxury goods from advanced economies?

■ APPLY

1 Devise separate promotional strategies for an article of clothing, each of which stresses one of the levels of Maslow's Hierarchy of Needs.

2 Collect a sample of ads that appeals to consumers' values. What value is being communicated in each ad, and how is this done? Is this an effective approach to designing a marketing communication?

3 Describe how a man's level of involvement with his car would affect how different marketing stimuli influence him. How might you design a strategy for a line of car batteries for a segment of low-involvement consumers, and how would this strategy differ from your attempts to reach a segment of men who are very involved in working on their cars?

4 Interview members of a celebrity fan club. Describe their level of involvement with the "product," and devise some marketing strategies to reach this group.

5 A group of psychologists recently argued that we need to revise Maslow's Hierarchy. They claim we should delete "self-actualization" from the pinnacle and replace it with "parenting." Right below this peak, they added "mate retention" and "mate acquisition. They claim that too many people see Maslow's triangle as "aspirational"—a description of what fulfilled individuals "should" do—rather than as an explanation of how human motivation actually works. Their perspective is evolutionary; if the only purpose of art, music, and literature is self-fulfillment, how does that contribute to the survival of the species? One of the proponents of this view observes, "If you are a good poet or a good musician, there is a reproductive payoff: women are attracted to men with these abilities. What a man is saying when he is playing his guitar up there is 'look at my good genes.'" What do you think—do our motivations to buy, have, and be ultimately come down to survival of our gene pool?[157]

MyMarketingLab Now that you have completed this chapter, return to **www.mymktlab.com** to apply concepts and explore the additional study materials.

Case Study

IS BEAUTY MORE THAN SKIN DEEP?

They are thin, possess flawless skin, and have beautiful hair. They are the models and celebrities we see in television, print, and billboard ads that tout the latest shampoos, antiaging creams, and skin cleansers. The message is clear. Buy our product and you too can look like this.

Beginning in 2004, Dove, a division of Unilever, started to send out a radically different message when the brand launched its "Campaign for Real Beauty." The first step in Dove's campaign, a tactic to support its skin-firming cream, introduced the nation to billboards that showed unretouched photographs of "normal" women of various sizes in just their underwear.

Dove sent the message that women do not need to conform to the standards of beauty the fashion industry determines. Every woman, regardless of her age or body size, is beautiful. The campaign continued to build strongly over the next couple of years, and gained more steam with the viral release of the video "Evolution." The ad featured an average-looking woman who enters a film studio. The video then speeds through a series of hair, makeup, and shocking computer-enhancement techniques. In 60 seconds she emerges as a gorgeous model on a billboard. Immediately after the final shot of the billboard, the video blacks out to the statement, "No wonder our perception of beauty is distorted." This viral video was followed with "Onslaught," an equally powerful ad, which shows the intensity of personal care, diet, and exercise advertising as viewed through the eyes of a young girl. The ad ends with another powerful message, "Talk to your daughter before the beauty industry does."

An important part of the Campaign for Real Beauty is the Dove Self-Esteem Fund. With young girls reporting alarmingly low levels of self-worth, this arm of the campaign works to provide confidence-building tools and workshops for young girls. Dove partners with the Girl Scouts, the Boys and Girls Clubs of America, and girls.inc to educate girls on the importance of self-esteem.

Dove reaped a lot of public relations benefits from the campaign, but it is not without its critics. Some charge that Unilever, which owns Dove, is as guilty as the rest of the industry in promoting false ideals of beauty. Ads for the company's Axe brand often are cited as flagrant examples of messages that objectify women. In addition, the antiaging and firming creams Unilever sells thrive on women's insecurities about their looks. If she is supposed to be satisfied with her natural beauty, then why does a woman need these products? In addition, there was controversy concerning the airbrush techniques Dove used to photograph these "normal" women. An article in the *New Yorker* cited a prominent photo editor who claimed that he had done a large amount of retouching and mentioned what a challenge it was to make the women look attractive. Unilever's response was that it did not digitally alter the photos but retouched them only to correct color and remove dust. Still, this was a damaging accusation against Dove and its ad agency Ogilvy & Mather, especially since the "Evolution" campaign criticizes retouching tricks.

Finally, there is the question of whether such an emotionally charged campaign actually boosts sales. It certainly helps to break through the clutter and bring recognition to the brand, but does it resonate with the consumer over the long term? Dove reported a doubling of its sales in the first five years after the campaign launched. Will this unconventional beauty theme continue to strike a chord—while it sells beauty products at the same time?

DISCUSSION QUESTIONS

1 Describe the level of consumer involvement with personal care products in general. How might the Dove brand be different?

2 What terminal values relate to the Campaign for Real Beauty? Do they tie into the consumer's needs for this product?

Sources: www.dove.us, accessed June 8, 2011; Neol Bussey, "Dove Abandons Its Soapbox to Focus on the Soap," *Campaign* (August 28, 2008); Molly Prior, "Reality Check: Would You Buy Beauty Products from These Women?," *WWD* (April 20, 2007); Jack Neff, "Retouching Ruckus Leaves Dove Flailing," *Advertising Age* (May 12, 2008).

NOTES

1. "Vegetarianism in America," *Vegetarian Times*, http://www.vegetarian-times.com/features/archive_of_editorial/667, accessed May 9, 2011.
2. www.petakids.com, accessed May 9, 2011.
3. http://beefitswhatsfordinner.com, accessed May 9, 2011.
4. Robert A. Baron, *Psychology: The Essential Science* (Boston: Allyn & Bacon, 1989).
5. Russell W. Belk, Guliz Ger, and Søren Askegaard, "The Fire of Desire: A Multisited Inquiry into Consumer Passion," *Journal of Consumer Research* 30 (2003): 326–51; cf. also Yu Chen, "Possession and Access: Consumer Desires and Value Perceptions Regarding Contemporary Art Collection and Exhibit Visits," *Journal of Consumer Research* 35 (April 2009): 925–40.
6. Henrik Hagtvedt and Vanessa M. Patrick, "The Broad Embrace of Luxury: Hedonic Potential as a Driver of Brand Extendibility," *Journal of Consumer Psychology* 19, no. 4 (2009): 608–18.
7. For a study that looks at cross-cultural differences in expression of emotion, cf. Ana Valenzuela, Barbara Mellers, and Judi Strebel (2010), "Pleasurable Surprises: A Cross-Cultural Study of Consumer Responses to Unexpected Incentives," *Journal of Consumer Research* 36, no. 5 (2010): 792–805.
8. Quoted in Andrew Adam Newman, "Using Appeals to Emotions to Sell Paint," *New York Times* (June 7, 2010), http://www.nytimes.com/2010/06/08/business/media/08adco.html?_r=1&adxnnl=1&emc=eta1&adxnnlx=1304103633-mStFlnofYaYKKni2WfWtLA, accessed April 29, 2011.
9. Samuel K. Bonsu, Aron Darmody, and Marie-Agnes Parmentier, (2010), "Arrested Emotions in Reality Television," *Consumption Markets & Culture* 13, no. 1 (2010): 91–107.
10. "Arby's App Ties User Moods to Value Menu Items," *Marketing Daily* (October 25, 2010), http://www.mediapost.com/publications/?fa=Articles.showArticle&art_aid=138232&nid=120043, accessed April 29, 2011.
11. E. J. Schultz, "Turning the Frown Upside Down: Kraft's Jell-O Plans Twitter Mood Monitor," *Advertising Age* (May 8, 2011), http://adage.com/article/news/kraft-s-jell-o-plans-twitter-mood-monitor/227439/, accessed May 10, 2011.
12. Tracy Tuten and Michael R. Solomon, *Social Media Marketing* (Upper Saddle River, NJ: Pearson Education, 2012); Jennifer Van Grove, "How a Sentiment Analysis Startup Profits by Checking Emotion in E-mail, *Mashable* (January 20, 2011), http://mashable.com/2011/01/20/lymbix/?utm_source=feedburner&utm_medium=email&utm_campaign=Feed%3A+Mashable+%28Mashable%29, accessed April 29, 2011.
13. Thomas Kramer and Song-Oh Yoon, "Approach-Avoidance Motivation and the Use of Affect as Information," *Journal of Consumer Psychology* 17, no. 2 (2007): 128–38.
14. www.weightwatchers.com/index.aspx, accessed June 30, 2009.
15. See Paul T. Costa and Robert R. McCrae, "From Catalog to Classification: Murray's Needs and the Five-Factor Model," *Journal of Personality & Social Psychology* 55 (1988): 258–65; Calvin S. Hall and Gardner Lindzey, *Theories of Personality*, 2nd ed. (New York: Wiley, 1970); James U. McNeal and Stephen W. McDaniel, "An Analysis of Need-Appeals in Television Advertising," *Journal of the Academy of Marketing Science* 12 (Spring 1984): 176–90.
16. Michael R. Solomon, Judith L. Zaichkowsky, and Rosemary Polegato, *Consumer Behaviour: Buying, Having, and Being—Canadian Edition* (Scarborough, Ontario: Prentice Hall Canada, 1999).
17. See David C. McClelland, *Studies in Motivation* (New York: Appleton-Century-Crofts, 1955).
18. Mary Kay Ericksen and M. Joseph Sirgy, "Achievement Motivation and Clothing Preferences of White-Collar Working Women," in Michael R. Solomon, ed., *The Psychology of Fashion* (Lexington, MA: Lexington Books, 1985): 357–69.
19. See Stanley Schachter, *The Psychology of Affiliation* (Stanford, CA: Stanford University Press, 1959).
20. Eugene M. Fodor and Terry Smith, "The Power Motive as an Influence on Group Decision Making," *Journal of Personality & Social Psychology* 42 (1982): 178–85.
21. C. R. Snyder and Howard L. Fromkin, *Uniqueness: The Human Pursuit of Difference* (New York: Plenum, 1980).
22. Abraham H. Maslow, *Motivation and Personality*, 2nd ed. (New York: Harper & Row, 1970).
23. An integrative view of consumer goal structures and goal-determination processes proposes six discrete levels of goals wherein higher-level (versus lower-level) goals are more abstract, more inclusive, and less mutable. In descending order of abstraction, these goal levels are life themes and values, life projects, current concerns, consumption intentions, benefits sought, and feature preferences. See Cynthia Huffman, S. Ratneshwar, and David Glen Mick, "Consumer Goal Structures and Goal-Determination Processes: An Integrative Framework," in S. Ratneshwar, David Glen Mick, and Cynthia Huffman, eds., *The Why of Consumption* (London: Routledge, 2000): 9–35.
24. Paul Henry, "Magnetic Points for Lifestyle Shaping: The Contribution of Self-Fulfillment, Aspirations and Capabilities," *Qualitative Market Research* 9 no. 2 (2006): 170.

25. Russell W. Belk, "Romanian Consumer Desires and Feelings of Deservingness," in Lavinia Stan, ed., *Romania in Transition* (Hanover, NH: Dartmouth Press, 1997): 191–208, 193.

26. Adapted in part from Jack Loechner, "Emotional Business Bonding on Social Networks," *Research Brief*, Center for Media Research (December 27, 2007), http://blogs.mediapost.com/research_brief/ ?p=1603, accessed December 27, 2007.

27. Study conducted in the Horticulture Department at Kansas State University, cited in "Survey Tells Why Gardening's Good," *Vancouver Sun* (April 12, 1997): B12; see also Paul Hewer and Douglas Brownlie, "Constructing 'Hortiporn': On the Aesthetics of Stylized Exteriors," *Advances in Consumer Research* 33, no. 1 (2006).

28. "Forehead Advertisement Pays Off," *Montgomery Advertiser* (May 4, 2000): 7A.

29. Alex Kuczynski, "A New Magazine Celebrates the Rites of Shopping," *New York Times Online* (May 8, 2000). http://www.nytimes.com/2000/05/08/business/media-a-new-magazine-celebrates-the-rites-of-shopping.html?scp=1&sq=A%20New%20Magazine%20Celebrates%20the%20Rites%20of%20Shopping&st=cse, accessed August 24, 2011.

30. "Man Wants to Marry His Car," *Montgomery Advertiser* (March 7, 1999): 11A.

31. Judith Lynne Zaichkowsky, "Measuring the Involvement Construct in Marketing," *Journal of Consumer Research* 12 (December 1985): 341–52.

32. Andrew Mitchell, "Involvement: A Potentially Important Mediator of Consumer Behavior," in William L. Wilkie, ed., *Advances in Consumer Research* 6 (Provo, UT: Association for Consumer Research, 1979): 191–96.

33. Richard L. Celsi and Jerry C. Olson, "The Role of Involvement in Attention and Comprehension Processes," *Journal of Consumer Research* 15 (September 1988): 210–24.

34. Anthony G. Greenwald and Clark Leavitt, "Audience Involvement in Advertising: Four Levels," *Journal of Consumer Research* 11 (June 1984): 581–92.

35. Mihaly Csikszentmihalyi, *Flow: The Psychology of Optimal Experience* (New York: HarperCollins, 1991); Donna L. Hoffman and Thomas P. Novak, "Marketing in Hypermedia Computer-Mediated Environments: Conceptual Foundations," *Journal of Marketing* (July 1996): 50–68.

36. Jeremy W. Peters, "Gave up Sleep and Maybe a First-Born, but at Least I Have an iPhone," *New York Times Online* (June 30, 2007). http://www.nytimes.com/2007/06/30/technology/30phone.html?scp=1&sq=Gave%20up%20Sleep%20and%20Maybe%20a%20First-Born,%20but%20at%20Least%20I%20Have%20an%20iPhone&st=Search, accessed August 24, 2011.

37. Christopher Rhoads, "The Hydrox Cookie Is Dead, and Fans Won't Get Over It," *Wall Street Journal* (January 19, 2008): A1.

38. Robert W. Pimentel and Kristy E. Reynolds, "A Model for Consumer Devotion: Affective Commitment with Proactive Sustaining Behaviors," *Academy of Marketing Science Review*, no. 5 (2004), www.amsreview.org/articles/pimentel05-2004.pdf

39. starbuckseverywhere.net, accessed May 10, 2011; Julie Jargon, "A Fan Hits a Roadblock on Drive to See Every Starbucks," *Wall Street Journal* (May 23, 2009), http://online.wsj.com/article/SB124301100481847767.html, accessed May 25, 2009.

40. Judith Lynne Zaichkowsky, "The Emotional Side of Product Involvement," in Paul Anderson and Melanie Wallendorf, eds., *Advances in Consumer Research* 14 (Provo, UT: Association for Consumer Research): 32–35.

41. For a discussion of interrelationships between situational and enduring involvement, see Marsha L. Richins, Peter H. Bloch, and Edward F. McQuarrie, "How Enduring and Situational Involvement Combine to Create Involvement Responses," *Journal of Consumer Psychology* 1, no. 2 (1992): 143–53. For more information on the involvement construct, see "Special Issue on Involvement," *Psychology & Marketing* 10, no. 4 (July–August 1993).

42. "A Woman Wins Roto-Rooter's Tricked Out Toilet," *PROMO* (April 3, 2007), www.promomagazine.com/news/woman_winsroto_rooters_toilet_043007/index.html; www.designnews.com/blog/1080000108/post/650006865.html, accessed June 27, 2007.

43. Todd Wasserman, "Coca-Cola to Help Maroon 5 Crowdsource a New Song," *Mashable* (March 1, 2011), http://mashable.com/2011/03/01/coca-cola-maroon-5/, accessed April 30, 2011; Page C. Moreau and Kelly B. Herd, "To Each His Own? How Comparisons with Others Influence Consumers' Evaluations of Their Self-Designed Products," *Journal of Consumer Research* 36, no. 5 (2010): 806–19; Wendy Liu and David Gal, "Bringing Us Together or Driving Us Apart: The Effect of Soliciting Consumer Input on Consumers' Propensity to Transact with an Organization," *Journal of Consumer Research* 38 (August 2011, in press).

44. Joseph B. Pine, II, and James H. Gilmore, *Markets of One: Creating Customer-Unique Value through Mass Customization* (Boston: Harvard Business School Press, 2000); www.managingchange.com/masscust/overview.htm, accessed May 30, 2005.

45. Neeraj Arora, Xavier Dréze, Anindya Ghose, James D. Hess, Reghuram Iyengar, Bing Jing, Yogesh Joshi, V. Kumar, Nicholas Lurie, Scott Neslin, S. Sajeesh, Meng Su, Niladri Syam, Jacquelyn Thomas, and Z. John Zhang, "Putting One-to-One Marketing to Work: Personalization, Customization, and Choice," *Marketing Letters* (2008): 305–21; Mike Beirne, "Mars Gives M&M's a Face," *Brandweek* (May 22, 2008), www.Brandweek.Com/Bw/News/Recent_Display.Jsp?Vnu_Content_Id=1003807134, accessed May 22, 2008.

46. Kevin J. Clancy, "CPMs Must Bow to 'Involvement' Measurement," *Advertising Age* (January 20, 1992): 26.

47. Herbert E. Krugman, "The Impact of Television Advertising: Learning Without Involvement," *Public Opinion Quarterly* 29 (Fall 1965): 349–56.

48. Brent McFerran, Darren W. Dahl, Gerald J. Gorn, and Heather Honea, "Motivational Determinants of Transportation into Marketing Narratives," *Journal of Consumer Psychology* 20, no. 3 (2010): 306–16.

49. Tyler Gray, "Jay-Z "Decoded': 32 Pages Revealed," *Fast Company* (November 19, 2010), http://www.fastcompany.com/pics/jay-z-decoded-32-pages-revealed#6, accessed August 25, 2011.

50. David W. Stewart and David H. Furse, "Analysis of the Impact of Executional Factors in Advertising Performance," *Journal of Advertising Research* 24 (1984): 23–26; Deborah J. MacInnis, Christine Moorman, and Bernard J. Jaworski, "Enhancing and Measuring Consumers' Motivation, Opportunity, and Ability to Process Brand Information from Ads," *Journal of Marketing* 55 (October 1991): 332–53.

51. Morris B. Holbrook and Elizabeth C. Hirschman, "The Experiential Aspects of Consumption: Consumer Fantasies, Feelings, and Fun," *Journal of Consumer Research* 9 (September 1982): 132–40.

52. Elaine Sciolino, "Disproving Notions, Raising a Fury," *New York Times* (January 21, 2003), www.nytimes.com, accessed January 21, 2003.

53. Louise Story, "Times Sq. Ads Spread via Tourists' Cameras," *New York Times* (December 11, 2006), www.nytimes.com, accessed December 11, 2006.

54. Rajeev Batra and Michael L. Ray, "Operationalizing Involvement as Depth and Quality of Cognitive Responses," in Alice Tybout and Richard Bagozzi, eds., *Advances in Consumer Research* 10 (Ann Arbor, MI: Association for Consumer Research, 1983): 309–13.

55. Quoted in "Gap Scraps New Logo after Online Outcry," *Reuters* (October 12, 2010), http://www.reuters.com/article/2010/10/12/us-gap-idUSTRE69B05Z20101012?utm_source=feedburner&utm_medium=feed&utm_campaign=Feed%3A+Reuters%2FInternetNews+%28News+%2F+US+%2F+Internet+News%29, accessed April 30, 2011.

56. "Read My Chips? Pringles Has Plans to Print Jokes, Trivia on Its Potatoes," *Wall Street Journal* (May 20, 2004): C13; David Serchuk, "A Rose with Another Name," *Forbes* (December 27, 2004): 52.

57. "Ads That Stay with You," *Newsweek* (November 19, 2007), www.newsweek.com/Id/68904, accessed November 19, 2007.

58. Stephanie Clifford, "Axe Body Products Puts Its Brand on the Hamptons Club Scene," *New York Times* (May 22, 2009): B6; Alana Semuels, "Honda Finds a Groovy New Way to Pitch Products: The Musical Road," *Los Angeles Times* (October 13, 2008), www.latimes.com/Business/La-Fi-Roads13-2008oct13,0,4147014.Story; accessed October 13, 2008; Eric Pfanner, "A Live Promotion, At 14,000 Feet," *New York Times* (June 6, 2008), www.nytimes.com, accessed June 6, 2008; Les Luchter, "Jameson Whiskey Texts Targets on N.Y. Streets," *Marketing Daily* (August 8, 2008), www.mediapost.com, accessed August 8, 2008; Doreen Carvajal, "Dancers in the Crowd Bring Back 'Thriller,'" *New York Times* (March 10, 2008), www.nytimes.com, accessed March 10, 2008; Eric Pfanner, "When Consumers Help, Ads Are Free," *New York Times* (June 21, 2009), www.nytimes.com, accessed June 22, 2009.

59. "Billboards with Face Recognition Collect Demographic Data in Japan" (July 19, 2010), http://adverlab.blogspot.com/2010/07/billboards-with-face-recognition.html, accessed May 12, 2011; Emily Steel, "The Ad Changes with the Shopper in Front of It," *Wall Street Journal* (August 21, 2008): B7.

60. Karlene Lukovitz, "New Belgium Fat Tire Ale 'Inserts' Fans In Print Ad, *Marketing Daily* (June 2, 2010), http://www.mediapost.com/publications/?fa=Articles.showArticle&art_aid=129339, accessed April 10, 2011.

61. Drew Elliott, "Opportunities for Brands in Social Games," *Ogilvy PR Blog* (May 2010), http://blog.ogilvypr.com/2010/05/opportunities-for-brands-in-social-games/, accessed July 12, 2010.

62. Andiara Petterle, "Reaching Latinos through Virtual Goods," *Media Post* (June 10, 2010), http://www.mediapost.com/publications/?fa=Articles.showArticle&art_aid=129857, accessed July 13, 2010.

63. Adapted from Tracy Tuten and Michael R. Solomon, *Social Media Marketing* (Upper Saddle River, NJ: Pearson Education, 2012).

64. "Gagaville," http://gagaville.org/, accessed May 12, 2011.

65. Christina Goulding, Avi Shankar, Richard Elliott, and Robin Canniford, "The Marketplace Management of Illicit Pleasure," *Journal of Consumer Research* 35 (February 2009): 759–71.

66. Robert F. Worth, "Arab TV Tests Societies' Limits with Depictions of Sex and Equality," *New York Times* (September 26, 2008), www.nytimes.com/2008/09/27/World/Middleast/27beirut.Html?_R=1&Scp=1&Sq=N..., accessed September 26, 2008.

67. Ajay K. Sirsi, James C. Ward, and Peter H. Reingen, "Microcultural Analysis of Variation in Sharing of Causal Reasoning about Behavior," *Journal of Consumer Research* 22 (March 1996): 345–72.

68. Vercihan Ziflioğlu, "TV Celebrity Kardashian Lashes Out at Turkish Cosmo Cover," *Hürriyet Daily News* (April 12, 2011), http://www.hurriyetdailynews

.com/n.php?n=american-tv-personality-angry-for-her-ghotos-on-turkish-magazine-2011-04-12, accessed May 10, 2011; David Carr, "Romance in *Cosmo*'s World Is Translated in Many Ways," *New York Times* (May 26, 2002), www.nytimes.com, accessed May 26, 2002.

69. Quoted in Andrew Adam Newman, "With Condoms in Particular, Local Stations Can Say No," *New York Times* (July 16, 2007), www.nytimes.com, accessed July 16, 2007.

70. Bruce Horovitz, "Kraft Ads with Criticizing Grandma Get Criticized," *USA Today*, http://www.usatoday.com/money/advertising/2011-02-28-pro-fanegranny28_ST_N.htm, accessed April 10, 2011.

71. Sheila Shay, "Forever 21 CEO: We Don't Have Designs on Pregnant Teens," *BrandChannel* (July 27, 2010), http://www.brandchannel.com/home/post/2010/07/27/Forever-21-Maternity-Controversy.aspx, accessed April 10, 2011.

72. Deborah Ball, "Women in Italy Like to Clean but Shun the Quick and Easy: Convenience Doesn't Sell When Bathrooms Average Four Scrubbings a Week," *Wall Street Journal* (April 25, 2006): A1.

73. Milton Rokeach, *The Nature of Human Values* (New York: Free Press, 1973).

74. Sang-Pil Han and Sharon Shavitt, "Persuasion and Culture: Advertising Appeals in Individualistic and Collectivistic Societies," *Journal of Experimental Social Psychology* 30 (1994): 326–50.

75. Chisaki Watanabe, "Japanese Parents Embrace Ultra-Secure Children's Park," *Philadelphia Inquirer* (September 4, 2006): A2.

76. Jay Alabaster and Ryan Nakashima, "Japanese Comforted or Cramped in Evacuee Shelters," *MSNBC.com* (April 19, 2011), http://www.msnbc.msn.com/id/42672467/ns/world_news-asia-pacific/t/japanese-comforted-or-cramped-evacuee-shelters/, accessed May 10, 2011.

77. Carolyn A. Lin, "Cultural Values Reflected in Chinese and American Television Advertising," *Journal of Advertising* 30 (Winter 2001): 83–94.

78. Donald E. Vinson, Jerome E. Scott, and Lawrence R. Lamont, "The Role of Personal Values in Marketing and Consumer Behavior," *Journal of Marketing* 41 (April 1977): 44–50; John Watson, Steven Lysonski, Tamara Gillan, and Leslie Raymore, "Cultural Values and Important Possessions: A Cross-Cultural Analysis," *Journal of Business Research* 55 (2002): 923–31.

79. Karlene Lukovitz, "New-Product Hits Tap In-Home, Health Trends," *Marketing Daily* (April 1, 2011), http://www.mediapost.com/publications/?fa=Articles.showArticle&art_aid=147857&nid=125349, accessed April 10, 2011.

80. Pascale Quester, Michael Beverland, and Francis Farrelly, "Brand-Personal Values Fit and Brand Meanings: Exploring the Role Individual Values Play in Ongoing Brand Loyalty in Extreme Sports Subcultures," *Advances in Consumer Research* 33, no. 1 (2006): 21–28.

81. Jennifer Aaker, Veronica Benet-Martinez, and Jordi Garolera, "Consumption Symbols as Carriers of Culture: A Study of Japanese and Spanish Brand Personality Constructs," *Journal of Personality & Social Psychology* (2001). 81 (3), 492-508.

82. Geert Hofstede, *Culture's Consequences: Comparing Values, Behaviors, Institutions, and Organizations across Nations* (Thousand Oaks, CA: Sage, 2001). For a recent critique of this instrument, cf. Aron M. Levin, Irwin P. Levin, and Michael P. Cook, "Measuring and Accounting for Cross-Country Response Biases in Marketing Food and Drink Products," *International Journal of Consumer Marketing*, in press.

83. Adapted from "What Are Hofstede's Five Cultural Dimensions?," www.geert-hofstede.com, accessed May 22, 2009.

84. Milton Rokeach, *Understanding Human Values* (New York: Free Press, 1979); see also J. Michael Munson and Edward McQuarrie, "Shortening the Rokeach Value Survey for Use in Consumer Research," in Michael J. Houston, ed., *Advances in Consumer Research 15* (Provo, UT: Association for Consumer Research, 1988): 381–86.

85. B. W. Becker and P. E. Conner, "Personal Values of the Heavy User of Mass Media," *Journal of Advertising Research* 21 (1981): 37–43; Vinson, Scott, and Lamont, "The Role of Personal Values in Marketing and Consumer Behavior."

86. Craig J. Thompson and Maura Troester, "Consumer Value Systems in the Age of Postmodern Fragmentation: The Case of the Natural Health Microculture," *Journal of Consumer Research* 28 (March 2002): 550–71.

87. Sharon E. Beatty, Lynn R. Kahle, Pamela Homer, and Shekhar Misra, "Alternative Measurement Approaches to Consumer Values: The List of Values and the Rokeach Value Survey," *Psychology & Marketing* 2 (1985): 181–200; Lynn R. Kahle and Patricia Kennedy, "Using the List of Values (LOV) to Understand Consumers," *Journal of Consumer Marketing* 2 (Fall 1988): 49–56; Lynn Kahle, Basil Poulos, and Ajay Sukhdial, "Changes in Social Values in the United States During the Past Decade," *Journal of Advertising Research* 28 (February–March 1988): 35–41; see also Wagner A. Kamakura and Jose Alfonso Mazzon, "Value Segmentation: A Model for the Measurement of Values and Value Systems," *Journal of Consumer Research* 18 (September 1991): 28; Jagdish N. Sheth, Bruce I. Newman, and Barbara L. Gross, *Consumption Values and Market Choices: Theory and Applications* (Cincinnati, OH: South-Western, 1991).

88. Thomas J. Reynolds and Jonathan Gutman, "Laddering Theory, Method, Analysis, and Interpretation," *Journal of Advertising Research*

(February–March 1988): 11–34; Beth Walker, Richard Celsi, and Jerry Olson, "Exploring the Structural Characteristics of Consumers' Knowledge," in Melanie Wallendorf and Paul Anderson, eds., *Advances in Consumer Research 14* (Provo, UT: Association for Consumer Research, 1986): 17–21; Tania Modesto Veludo-de-Oliveira, Ana Akemi Ikeda, and Marcos Cortez Camporar, "Laddering in the Practice of Marketing Research: Barriers and Solutions," *Qualitative Market Research: An International Journal* 9, no. 3 (2006): 297–306. For a recent critique of this technique, cf. Elin Brandi Sørenson and Søren Askegaard, "Laddering: How (Not) to Do Things with Words," *Qualitative Market Research: An International Journal* 10, no. 1 (2007): 63–77.

89. This example was adapted from Michael R. Solomon, Gary Bamossy, and Søren Askegaard, *Consumer Behaviour: A European Perspective*, 2nd ed. (London: Pearson Education Limited, 2002).

90. "25 Years of Attitude," *Marketing Tools* (November–December 1995): 38–39.

91. Amitai Etzioni, "The Good Society: Goals Beyond Money," *The Futurist* 35, no. 4 (2001): 68–69; D. Elgin, *Voluntary Simplicity: Toward a Way of Life That Is Outwardly Simple, Inwardly Rich* (New York: Quill, 1993); "PNA Trend in Consumer Behavior Called 'Voluntary Simplicity' Poses Challenges for Marketers," *Ascribe Higher Education News Service* (December 6, 2001); Caroline Bekin, Marylyn Carrigan, and Isabelle Szmigin, "Defying Market Sovereignty: Voluntary Simplicity at New Consumption Communities," *Qualitative Market Research* 8, no. 4 (2005): 413.

92. Emily Burg, "Whole Foods Is Consumers' Favorite Green Brand," *Marketing Daily*, www.mediapost.com, accessed May 10, 2007.

93. www.lohas.com/about.htm, accessed May 12, 2011.

94. "Deal with Clorox Spurs Sierra Club Feud," *Los Angeles Times* (July 17, 2008), www.latimes.com/Business/La-Fi-Clorox17-2008jul17,0,1163469. Story?Track=Rss, accessed July 17, 2008.

95. Remi Trudel and June Cotte, "Does It Pay to Be Good?," *MIT Sloan Management Review* 61 (Winter 2009): 61–68.

96. Karen Egolf, "Burt's Bees, Whole Foods Top U.S. Green Brands," *Ad Age Blogs* (June 9, 2010), http://adage.com/article/goodworks/burt-s-bees-foods-top-u-s-green-brands/144341/, accessed April 10, 2011.

97. Wendy Koch, "'Green' Product Claims Are Often Misleading," *USA Today* (October 26, 2010), http://content.usatoday.com/communities/greenhouse/post/2010/10/green-product-claims/1?csp=34money&utm_source=feedburner&utm_medium=feed&utm_campaign=Feed%3A+UsatodaycomMoney-TopStories+%28Money+-+Top+Stories%29, accessed April 10, 2011.

98. Mark Dolliver, "Thumbs Down on Corporate Green Efforts," *Adweek* (August 31, 2010), http://www.adweek.com/aw/content_display/news/client/e3i84260d4301c885f91b2cd8a712f323cf, accessed April 10, 2011; Sarah Mahoney, "Americans Hate Faux Green Marketers," *Marketing Daily* (March 25, 2011), http://www.mediapost.com/publications/?fa=Articles.showArticle&art_aid=147413&nid=125122, accessed April 10, 2011.

99. Susan Schultz Kleine and Stacy Menzel Baker, "An Integrative Review of Material Possession Attachment," *Academy of Marketing Science Review*, no. 1 (2004).

100. Russell W. Belk, "Possessions and the Extended Self," *Journal of Consumer Research* 15 (September 1988): 139–68; Melanie Wallendorf and Eric J. Arnould, "'My Favorite Things': A Cross-Cultural Inquiry into Object Attachment, Possessiveness, and Social Linkage," *Journal of Consumer Research* 14 (March 1988): 531–47.

101. L. J. Shrum, Jaehoon Lee, James E. Burroughs, and Aric Rindfleisch, "Online Process Model of Second-Order Cultivation Effects: How Television Cultivates Materialism and Its Consequences of Life Satisfaction," *Human Communication Research* 37 (January 2011): 34–57; L. J. Shrum, James E. Burroughs, and Aric Rindfleisch, "Television's Cultivation of Material Values," *Journal of Consumer Research* 32, no. 3 (2005): 473–79.

102. James E. Burroughs and Aric Rindfleisch, "Materialism and Well-Being: A Conflicting Values Perspective," *Journal of Consumer Research* 29 (December 2002): 348–70.

103. Lan Nguyen Chaplin and Deborah Roedder John, "Growing Up in a Material World: Age Differences in Materialism in Children and Adolescents," *Journal of Consumer Research* 34 (December 2007): 480–93.

104. Marsha L. Richins, "Special Possessions and the Expression of Material Values," *Journal of Consumer Research* 21 (December 1994): 522–33.

105. *Ibid.*

106. Aric Rindfleisch, James E. Burroughs, and Nancy Wong. "The Safety of Objects: Materialism, Existential Insecurity, and Brand Connection," *Journal of Consumer Research* 36 (June 2009): 1–16.

107. John L. Lastovicka and Nancy J. Sirianni, "Truly, Madly, Deeply: Consumers in the Throes of Material Possession Love," *Journal of Consumer Research* (in press).

108. Stephanie Rosenbloom, "But Will It Make You Happy?," *New York Times* (August 7, 2010), http://www.nytimes.com/2010/08/08/business/08consume.html?pagewanted=1&_r=2&ref=business, accessed April 10, 2011.

109. Mark Cleveland, Michel Laroche, and Nicolas Papadopoulos, "Cosmopolitanism, Consumer Ethnocentrism, and Materialism: An Eight-Country

Study of Antecedents and Outcomes," *Journal of International Marketing* 17, no. 1 (2009): 116–46.

110. Peter Gumbel, "Big Mac's Local Flavor," *CNNmoney.com* (May 2, 2008), http://money.cnn.com/2008/04/29/news/companies/big_macs_local. fortune/index.htm, accessed May 2, 2008; Geoffrey A. Fowler, "For Prosperity Burger, McDonald's Tailors Ads to Asian Tastes," *Wall Street Journal* (January 24, 2005), www.wsj.com, accessed January 24, 2005; Saritha Rai, "Tastes of India in U.S. Wrappers," *New York Times* (April 29, 2003), www.nytimes.com, accessed April 29, 2003; Gerard O'Dwyer, "McD's Cancels McAfrika Rollout," *Advertising Age* (September 9, 2002): 14; "McDonald's to Give $10 Million to Settle Vegetarian Lawsuit," *Wall Street Journal* (June 4, 2002), www.wsj.com, accessed June 4, 2002; "Packaging Draws Protest," *Marketing News* (July 4, 1994): 1.

111. Mariko Sanchanta and Yoree Koh, "Beefing Up McDonald's," *Wall Street Journal* (January 12, 2011), http://online.wsj.com/article/SB10001424052 7487037919045760754506092538030.html, accessed April 10, 2011.

112. Charles Onians, "By Toutatis! Asterix McDonald's Ad Irks French" (August 19, 2010), http://www.google.com/hostednews/afp/article/ ALeqM5hmwaTJFdWfl0_J3N6qe2YA6Vximw, accessed April 28, 2011.

113. Abe Sauer, "'Asianate Yourself' with Amoy. Actually, Please Don't," *Brandchannel* (March 9, 2011), http://www.brandchannel.com/home/ post/2011/03/09/Asianate-Yourself-With-Amoy.aspx, accessed April 30, 2011; http://www.amoy.nl/web/#/home, accessed May 11, 2011.

114. www.beinggirl.com/en_US/home.jsp, accessed June 25, 2009; Carol Hymowitz, "Marketers Focus More on Global 'Tribes' than on Nationalities," *Wall Street Journal* (December 10, 2007): B1.

115. Theodore Levitt, *The Marketing Imagination* (New York: Free Press, 1983).

116. Stuart Elliott, "Ford Tries a Global Campaign for Its Global Car," *New York Times* (February 24, 2011), http://www.nytimes.com/2011/02/25/business/media/25adco.html?_r=2&ref=business, accessed April 30, 2011.

117. Geoffrey A. Fowler, "Main Street, H.K.: Disney Localizes Mickey to Boost Its Hong Kong Theme Park," *Wall Street Journal* (January 23, 2008): B1; Merissa Marr, "Small World: Disney Rewrites Script to Win Fans in India; China, Latin America Are Also in Turnaround," *Wall Street Journal* (June 11, 2007): A1; Laura M. Holson, "The Feng Shui Kingdom," *New York Times* (April 25, 2005), www.nytimes.com, accessed April 25, 2005; Keith Bradsher, "Disneyland for Chinese Offers a Soup and Lands in a Stew," *New York Times* (June 17, 2005): A1; Paulo Prada and Bruce Orwall, "Disney's New French Theme Park Serves Wine—and Better Sausage," *Wall Street Journal* (March 12, 2002), www.wsj.com, accessed March 12, 2002.

118. David Barboza and Brooks Barnes, "Disney Plans Lavish Park in Shanghai," *New York Times* (April 7, 2011), http://www.nytimes.com/2011/04/08/business/media/08disney.html?pagewanted=1&_r=1&ref=business, accessed April 10, 2011.

119. Terry Clark, "International Marketing and National Character: A Review and Proposal for an Integrative Theory," *Journal of Marketing* 54 (October 1990): 66–79.

120. Geraldo Samor, Cecilie Rohwedder, and Ann Zimmerman, "Innocents Abroad? Walmart's Global Sales Rise as It Learns from Mistakes; No More Ice Skates in Mexico," *Wall Street Journal* (May 16, 2006): B1.

121. Marc Gobé, *Emotional Branding: The New Paradigm for Connecting Brands to People* (New York: Allworth Press, 2001).

122. Norihiko Shirouzu, "Snapple in Japan: How a Splash Dried Up," *Wall Street Journal* (April 15, 1996): B1.

123. Glenn Collins, "Chinese to Get a Taste of Cheese-Less Cheetos," *New York Times* (September 2, 1994): D4.

124. For a case study that explores how the Guinness brand does this, cf. John Amis and Michael L. Silk, "Transnational Organization and Symbolic Production: Creating and Managing a Global Brand," *Consumption Markets & Culture* 13, no. 2 (2010): 159–79.

125. Martin McCarty, Martin I. Horn, Mary Kate Szenasy, and Jocelyn Feintuch, "An Exploratory Study of Consumer Style: Country Differences and International Segments," *Journal of Consumer Behaviour* 6, no. 1 (2007): 48.

126. Julie Skur Hill and Joseph M. Winski, "Goodbye Global Ads: Global Village Is Fantasy Land for Marketers," *Advertising Age* (November 16, 1987): 22.

127. Shelly Reese, "Culture Shock," *Marketing Tools* (May 1998): 44–49; Steve Rivkin, "The Name Game Heats Up," *Marketing News* (April 22, 1996): 8; David A. Ricks, "Products That Crashed into the Language Barrier," *Business & Society Review* (Spring 1983): 46–50.

128. Mark Lasswell, "Lost in Translation," *Business* (August 2004): 68–70.

129. Clyde H. Farnsworth, "Yoked in Twin Solitudes: Canada's Two Cultures," *New York Times* (September 18, 1994): E4.

130. Hill and Winski, "Goodbye Global Ads."

131. MTV Europe, personal communication, 1994; see also Teresa J. Domzal and Jerome B. Kernan, "Mirror, Mirror: Some Postmodern Reflections on Global Advertising," *Journal of Advertising* 22 (December 1993): 1–20; Douglas P. Holt, "Consumers' Cultural Differences as Local Systems of Tastes: A Critique of the Personality-Values Approach and an Alternative Framework," *Asia Pacific Advances in Consumer Research* 1 (1994): 1–7.

132. Douglas B. Holt, John A. Quelch, and Earl L. Taylor, "How Global Brands Compete," *Harvard Business Review* (September 2004): 68–75.

133. Normandy Madden, "New GenerAsians Survey Gets Personal with Asia-Pacific Kids," *Advertising Age International* (July 13, 1998): 2.

134. Adam Thompson and Shai Oster, "NBA in China Gets Milk to Sell Hoops," *Wall Street Journal* (January 22, 2007): B1; "They All Want to Be Like Mike," *Fortune* (July 21, 1997): 51–53.

135. Emma Hall, "Volvo Parks Brits at the Drive-in Movie: 'Starlite' Promo Allows Locals to Soak up American Car Culture," *Ad Age Global* (July 7, 2010), http://adage.com/article/global-news/marketing-volvo-parks-brits-drive-movie/144824/, accessed April 28, 2011.

136. Alan Riding, "Only the French Elite Scorn Mickey's Debut," *New York Times* (April 13, 1992): A1.

137. Elisabeth Rosenthal, "Buicks, Starbucks and Fried Chicken, Still China?" *New York Times* (February 25, 2002), www.nytimes.com, accessed February 25, 2002.

138. Special Report, "Brands in an Age of Anti-Americanism," *BusinessWeek* (August 4, 2003): 69–76.

139. Suzanne Kapner, "U.S. TV Shows Losing Potency around World," *New York Times* (January 2, 2003), www.nytimes.com, accessed January 2, 2003; "Big Brother Nipple Sparks Outrage," *BBCNews* (September 10, 2004), www.bbcnews.com, accessed September 10, 2004.

140. Liz Gooch, "A Reality Show Where Islam Is the Biggest Star," *New York Times* (July 28, 2010), http://www.nytimes.com/2010/07/29/world/ asia/29imam.html?scp=1&sq=islamic%20reality%20show&st=cse, accessed April 10, 2011.

141. Professor Russell Belk, University of Utah, personal communication, July 25, 1997.

142. Material in this section adapted from Güliz Ger and Russell W. Belk, "I'd Like to Buy the World a Coke: Consumptionscapes of the 'Less Affluent World,'" *Journal of Consumer Policy* 19, no. 3 (1996): 271–304; Russell W. Belk, "Romanian Consumer Desires and Feelings of Deservingness," in Lavinia Stan, ed., *Romania in Transition* (Hanover, NH: Dartmouth Press, 1997): 191–208; see also Güliz Ger, "Human Development and Humane Consumption: Well Being Beyond the Good Life," *Journal of Public Policy & Marketing* 16 (1997): 110–25.

143. Professor Güliz Ger, Bilkent University, Turkey, personal communication, July 25, 1997.

144. Erazim Kohák, "Ashes, Ashes . . . Central Europe after Forty Years," *Daedalus* 121 (Spring 1992): 197–215; Belk, "Romanian Consumer Desires and Feelings of Deservingness."

145. Lily Dong and Kelly Tian, "The Use of Western Brands in Asserting Chinese National Identity," *Journal of Consumer Research* 36 (October 2009).

146. David Murphy, "Christmas's Commercial Side Makes Yuletide a Hit in China," *Wall Street Journal* (December 24, 2002), www.wsj.com, accessed December 24, 2002.

147. This example courtesy of Professor Russell Belk, University of Utah, personal communication, July 25, 1997.

148. James Hookway, "In Vietnam, Fast Food Acts Global, Tastes Local," *Wall Street Journal* (March 12, 2008), http://online.wsj.com/ article/Sb120528509133029135.html?mod=mm_hs_marketing_strat, accessed March 12, 2008.

149. Miriam Jordan, "India Decides to Put Its Own Spin on Popular Rock, Rap and Reggae," *Wall Street Journal* (January 5, 2000), www.wsj.com, accessed January 5, 2000; Rasul Bailay, "Coca-Cola Recruits Paraplegics for 'Cola War' in India," *Wall Street Journal* (June 10, 1997).

150. Rick Wartzman, "When You Translate 'Got Milk' for Latinos, What Do You Get?" *Wall Street Journal* (June 3, 1999).

151. Charles Newbery, "Coke Goes Native with New Soft Drink," *Advertising Age* (December 1, 2003): 34.

152. Eric J. Arnould and Richard R. Wilk, "Why Do the Natives Wear Adidas: Anthropological Approaches to Consumer Research," *Advances in Consumer Research* 12 (Provo, UT: Association for Consumer Research, 1985): 748–52.

153. John F. Sherry, Jr., and Eduardo G. Camargo, "May Your Life Be Marvelous: English Language Labelling and the Semiotics of Japanese Promotion," *Journal of Consumer Research* 14 (1987): 174–88.

154. Bill Bryson, "A Taste for Scrambled English," *New York Times* (July 22, 1990): 10; Rose A. Horowitz, "California Beach Culture Rides Wave of Popularity in Japan," *Journal of Commerce* (August 3, 1989): 17; Elaine Lafferty, "American Casual Seizes Japan: Teen-agers Go for N.F.L. Hats, Batman and the California Look," *Time* (November 13, 1989): 106.

155. Lucy Howard and Gregory Cerio, "Goofy Goods," *Newsweek* (August 15, 1994): 8.

156. Nina M. Lentini, "Products No Longer So Personal," *Marketing Daily* (February 9, 2007), www.mediapost.com, accessed February 9, 2007; Karin Bittar, "'Pee Ship' Enterprise for Clearblue Pregnancy Test," *Marketing Daily* (December 20, 2006), www.mediapost.com, accessed December 20, 2006.

157. Lisa Belkin, "Living to Be a Parent," *New York Times* (September 10, 2010), http://www.nytimes.com/2010/09/12/magazine/12fob-wwln-t.html?_ r=1&ref=magazine, accessed April 10, 2011.

NIELSEN NUGGET

EXERCISE: Motivation and Global Values

Scenario: Xtr Clean Inc. is a large global producer of home cleaning products. With the economy struggling, both manufacturers and retailers are resorting to new and creative promotions, discounts, and price wars in the battle to win consumers. Xtr Clean is interested in strengthening its position through a better understanding of point-of-sale (POS) trade promotion efforts and their effectiveness in catching consumers' attention in the store aisle.

Challenge: To determine strategies to increase promotional effectiveness of POS efforts for home cleaning products. The company believes that a better understanding of the relative effectiveness of in-store promotions will be of key importance in developing effective strategies. Xtr Clean is also interested in understanding why consumers choose *not* to buy home cleaning products.

After reviewing the data provided:

1. Develop recommendations for reducing the number of nonbuyers of home cleaning products.
2. Develop recommendations concerning which in-store promotions should be emphasized.
3. Describe the purchase situation involvement level likely in this case. How could it be affecting consumer choices?

POS Promotions Stimulating Purchases	Effectiveness Rate
Two or more identical products with discount	46%
Two or more different products with discount	31%
One identical additional product free	5%
Cash discount over the total purchase	5%
Second product at half price	5%
Credit card discount	3%
Didn't know/answer	5%

Reasons for Not Buying	Rate (Multiple choices allowed)
Product out of stock at time of purchase	34%
Remembered already having one at home	23%
Just comparing prices and variants	13%
Was not exactly what wanted	4%
Was not sure what product was needed	3%
Product consumed at a very rapid rate	1%
High price	33%
Other	3%

The Self

The Self

When you finish reading this chapter you will understand why:

1. The self-concept strongly influences consumer behavior.

2. Products often play a key role in defining the self-concept.

3. Society's expectations of masculinity and femininity help to determine the products we buy to meet these expectations.

4. The way we think about our bodies (and the way our culture tells us we should think) is a key component of self-esteem.

5. Our desire to live up to cultural expectations of appearance can be harmful.

6. Every culture dictates certain types of body decoration or mutilation.

MyMarketingLab

Visit **www.mymktlab.com** to find activities that help you learn and review in order to succeed in this chapter.

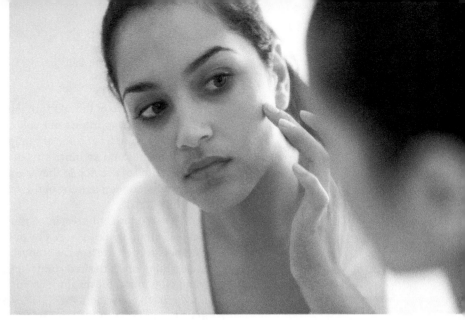

Lisa is trying to concentrate on the report her client expects by 5:00 P.M. She has worked hard to maintain this important account for the firm, but today she is distracted thinking about her date with Eric last night. Although things seemed to go OK, she couldn't shake the feeling that Eric regards her more as a friend than as a potential romantic partner.

As she leafs through *Glamour* and *Cosmopolitan* during her lunch hour, Lisa is struck by all the articles about ways to become more attractive by dieting, exercising, and wearing sexy clothes. She begins to feel depressed as she looks at the svelte models in the many advertisements for perfumes, apparel, and makeup. Each woman is more glamorous and beautiful than the last. Surely they've had "adjustments"—women simply don't look that way in real life. Then again, it's unlikely that Eric could ever be mistaken for Brad Pitt on the street.

In her down mood, Lisa actually thinks that maybe she should look into cosmetic surgery. Even though she's never considered herself unattractive, maybe if she got a new nose or removed that mole on her cheek she'd feel better about herself. Who knows, she might look so good she'll get up the nerve to submit a photo to that Web site hotornot.com that everyone's talking about. But wait: On second thought, is Eric even worth it?

OBJECTIVE 1
The self-concept strongly influences consumer behavior.

What Is the Self?

Lisa isn't the only person who feels that her physical appearance and possessions affect her "value" as a person. Consumers' insecurities about their appearance are rampant. We buy many products, from cars to cologne, because we want to highlight or hide some aspect of the self. In this chapter, we'll focus on how consumers' feelings about themselves shape their consumption practices, particularly as they strive to fulfill their society's expectations about how a male or female should look and act.

Does the Self Exist?

Most of us can't boast of coming close to Lady Gaga's 10 million followers on Twitter, but many of us do have hundreds of followers in addition to legions of Facebook friends.[1] The explosion of these and other social networking services enables everyone to focus on himself or herself and share mundane or scintillating details about their lives with anyone who's interested (*why* they are interested is another story!).

Today it seems natural to think of ourselves as potential celebs waiting for our 15 minutes of fame (as the pop icon Andy Warhol once predicted). However, the idea that each single human life is unique rather than a part of a group only developed in late medieval times (between the 11th and 15th centuries). Furthermore, the emphasis on the unique nature of the self is much greater in Western societies.[2] Many Eastern cultures stress the importance of a *collective self,* where a person derives his or her identity in large measure from a social group. Both Eastern and Western cultures believe that the self divides into an inner, private self and an outer, public self. Where cultures differ is in terms of which part they see as the "real you"; the West tends to subscribe to an independent understanding of the self, which emphasizes the inherent separateness of each individual.

Non-Western cultures, in contrast, tend to focus on an interdependent self where we define our identities largely by our relationships with others.[3] For example, a Confucian perspective stresses the importance of "face": others' perceptions of the self and maintaining one's desired status in their eyes. One dimension of face is *mien-tzu,* the reputation one achieves through success and ostentation. Some Asian cultures developed explicit rules about the specific garments and even colors that certain social classes and occupations were allowed to display. These traditions live on today in Japanese style manuals that set out very detailed instructions for dressing and how to address people of differing status.[4]

That orientation is a bit at odds with such Western conventions as "casual Friday," which encourages employees to express their unique selves through dress (at least short of muscle shirts and flip-flops). To further illustrate these cross-cultural differences, a Roper Starch Worldwide survey compared consumers in 30 countries to see which were the most and least vain. Women who live in Venezuela were the chart toppers: 65 percent said they thought about their appearance all the time.[5] Other high-scoring countries included Russia and Mexico. The lowest scorers lived in the Philippines and in Saudi Arabia, where only 28 percent of consumers surveyed agreed with this statement.

Self-Concept

The **self-concept** summarizes the beliefs a person holds about his own attributes and how he evaluates the self on these qualities. Although your overall self-concept may be positive, there certainly are parts of it you evaluate more positively than others. For example, Lisa feels better about her professional identity than she does about her feminine identity.

The self-concept is a very complex structure. We describe attributes of self-concept along such dimensions as *content* (e.g., facial attractiveness versus mental aptitude), *positivity* (i.e., self-esteem), *intensity and stability* over time, and *accuracy* (i.e., the degree to which one's self-assessment corresponds to reality).[6] As we'll see later in this chapter, consumers' self-assessments can be quite distorted, especially with regard to their physical appearance.

However, most people feel reasonably positive about themselves, and we are drawn to others whom we feel are similar in personality or appearance. One study demonstrated just how powerful this attraction can be: Researchers used "morphing" software to manipulate photos of political candidates from the 2008 presidential primaries and other elections. This technique combines the facial features of the study participant with the candidate so that the resulting photo actually is a mixture of the two. Subjects who saw the morphed photos of the candidates liked the candidates better than those who saw the undoctored photos—even though they were unaware that the images included their own features![7]

Self-Esteem

Self-esteem refers to the positivity of a person's self-concept. People with low self-esteem expect that they will not perform very well, and they will try to avoid embarrassment, failure, or rejection. When it developed a new line of snack cakes, for example, Sara Lee found that consumers low in self-esteem preferred portion-controlled snack items because they felt they lacked self-control.[8] In contrast, a more recent study found that individuals who are made to feel powerful spend more money on themselves ("because I'm worth it!"), whereas those who experience a feeling of powerlessness spend more on others than on themselves.[9]

Subject

Hillary Clinton

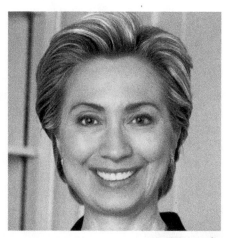

Morph
(35% Subject, 65% Clinton)

Study participants tend to prefer photos of political candidates whose features have been combined with their own.
Source: Photos courtesy of Prof. Jeremy Bailenson, Stanford University.

Alberto-Culver uses a self-esteem appeal to promote a product that reflects our changing society: Soft & Beautiful Just for Me Texture Softener, an alternative to hair pressing or relaxing. It's targeted to white mothers who don't know how to care for the hair of their multiracial children who have "hair texture" issues. The self-esteem portion of the campaign, dubbed "Love Yourself. Love Your Hair," includes a Web site, texturesoftener.com, that offers "conversation starters" to help parents find ways to talk to their daughters about self-image.[10]

How do marketers influence self-esteem? Exposure to ads such as the ones Lisa checked out can trigger a process of **social comparison**, in which the person tries to evaluate her appearance by comparing it to the people depicted in these artificial images.[11] This is a basic human tendency, and many marketers tap into our need for benchmarks when they supply idealized images of happy, attractive people who just happen to use their products. An ad campaign for Clearasil is a good example. In one typical ad, two teenage boys enter a kitchen where a 40-ish mother is mixing something in a bowl. When her son leaves the room, his friend hits on Mom. The ad's tagline: "Clearasil may cause confidence."

In a study that illustrates the social comparison process, female college students who were exposed to beautiful women in advertisements afterward expressed lowered satisfaction with their own appearance, as compared to other participants who did not view ads with attractive models.[12] Another study reported that young women alter their perceptions of their own body shapes and sizes after they watch as little as 30 minutes of TV programming.[13] Researchers report similar findings for men.[14] This process even operates when we decide how much to eat: A study found that people who were served food by a server who was either fat or thin choose different portion sizes.[15]

Many consumers try to bolster their self-esteem as they accumulate evidence of their achievements. In a results-oriented and competitive society, we continue to find ways to trumpet our successes. We display these **badges** by way of car bumper stickers ("My son is an honor student") or even grownup equivalents of the merit badges that the Boy Scouts award. Adults can buy their own Nerd Merit Badges recognizing geeky achievements, including "Open Source" (contribution to an open-source project), "Family Tech Support," or "I Have an Actual Human Skeleton in My Office." When they go online to **geospatial platforms** that use their smartphones to identify their physical locations, consumers earn pins people on Gowalla to certify that they've eaten in certain restaurants, or badges on FourSquare that testify to personal qualities such as "Photogenic," "Gossip Girl," or even "Crunked" (for hitting more than four bars in a single night).[16]

Real and Ideal Selves

When a consumer compares some aspect of himself to an ideal, this judgment influences his self-esteem. He might ask, "Am I as good-looking as I would like to be?" or "Do I make

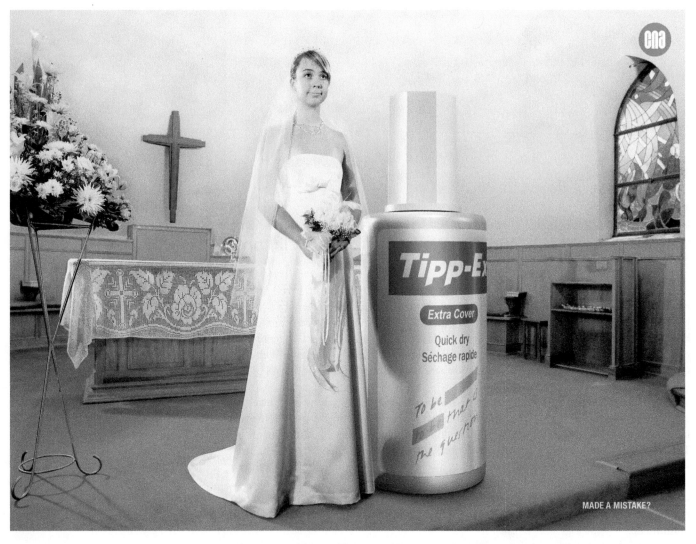

A South African ad conveys a feeling of insecurity.
Source: Courtesy of Tipp-Ex/Jupiter Drawing Room, South Africa.

as much money as I should?" The **ideal self** is a person's conception of how he would like to be, whereas the **actual self** refers to our more realistic appraisal of the qualities we do and don't have. We choose some products because we think they are consistent with our actual self, while we buy others to help us reach an ideal standard. We also often engage in a process of **impression management** in which we work hard to "manage" what others think of us; we strategically choose clothing and other products that will show us off to others in a good light.[17]

This process applies to all sorts of behaviors, from professional contexts and dating to markers of religious observance. For example, an increasing number of Islamic men in Egypt have a *zebibah* (Arabic for "raisin")—a dark circle of callused skin or a bump—between the hairline and the eyebrows. It marks the spot where the worshipper repeatedly presses his forehead into the ground during his daily prayers (observant Muslims pray five times a day). Some add prayers so that the bump will become even more pronounced; the owner of the mark thus broadcasts his degree of piousness on his head. As an Egyptian newspaper editor explains, "there is a kind of statement in it. Sometimes as a personal statement to announce that he is a conservative Muslim and sometimes as a way of outbidding others by showing them that he is more religious or to say that they should be like him."[18]

This impression management process is very apparent when people exaggerate their positive qualities on their Facebook pages or on dating sites (yes, a little hype has been known to occur). One Web site called Cloud Girlfriend lets you create a fantasy character and set up Chat Dates with others who also are role playing—although the site uses Facebook Connect to verify the gender of users as a safety precaution. The founder explains, "We allow people to define their ideal self, find their perfect girlfriend or boyfriend and connect and interact as if that person existed. It can help in learning how to manage a real relationship, and they then take it into the real world."[19]

Fantasy: Bridging the Gap Between the Selves

Most people experience a discrepancy between their real and ideal selves, but for some consumers this gap is especially large. These people are especially good targets for marketing communications that employ *fantasy appeals*.[20] A **fantasy** or daydream is a self-induced shift in consciousness, which is sometimes a way to compensate for a lack of external stimulation or to escape from problems in the real world.[21] Many products and services succeed because they appeal to our fantasies. An ad may transport us to an unfamiliar, exciting situation; things we purchase may permit us to "try on" interesting or provocative roles. And, with today's technology, such as the *virtual makeovers* that several Web sites offer, consumers can experiment with different looks before they actually take the plunge in the real world.[22] Several major retailers are testing a "virtual mirror" that simulates what makeup and hair dye would look like on shoppers. With the EZFace system, a person stands in front of the screen and an internal camera takes a picture. Then the person scans the bar codes of various cosmetics—such as mascara, foundation, eye shadow, blush, and lip gloss—and each

A German shampoo helps users to fantasize.
Source: Courtesy of JWT/Frankfurt.

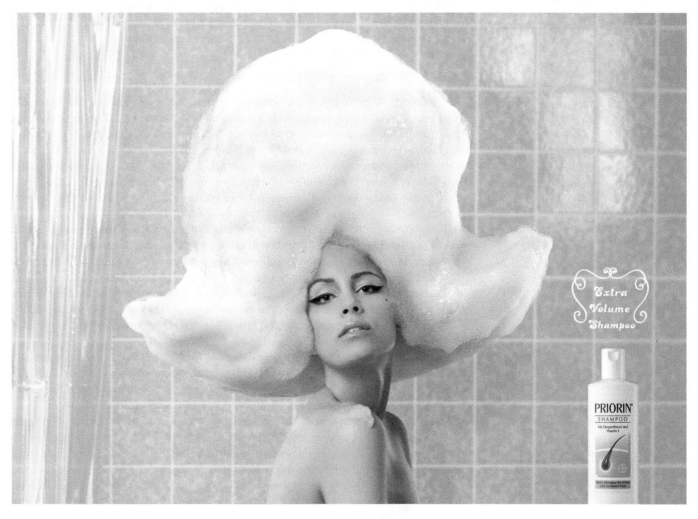

automatically appears on the appropriate part of the face. The customer can print out the image, send it by email, or post it on Facebook.

Multiple Selves

In a way, each of us really is a number of different people—your mother probably would not recognize the "you" that emerges at a party at 2:00 in the morning! We have as many selves as we do different social roles. Depending on the situation, we act differently, use different products and services, and even vary in terms of how much we *like* the aspect of ourselves we put on display. A person may require a different set of products to play each of her roles: She may choose a sedate, understated perfume when she plays her professional self, but splash on something more provocative on Saturday night as she transitions to her *femme fatale* self.

The dramaturgical perspective on consumer behavior views people as actors who play different roles. We each play many roles, and each has its own script, props, and costumes.[24] The self has different components, or *role identities,* and only some of these are active at any given time. Some identities (e.g., husband, boss, student) are more central to the self than others, but other identities (e.g., dancer, gearhead, or advocate for the homeless) may dominate in specific situations.[25] Indeed, some roles may conflict with one another. For example, one study of Iranian young people who live in the UK described what the authors termed the **torn self**, where respondents struggle with retaining an authentic culture while still enjoying Western freedom (and dealing with assumptions of others who believe they might be terrorists).[26]

Strategically, this means a marketer may want to ensure that the appropriate role identity is active before she pitches products that customers need to play a particular role. One obvious way to do this is to place advertising messages in contexts in which people are likely to be well aware of that role identity; for example, when fortified drink and energy bar product companies hand out free product samples to runners at a marathon.

Virtual Identity

In the influential cyberpunk novel *Snow Crash,* author Neal Stephenson envisioned a virtual world he called the *Metaverse* as a successor to the Internet. In the Metaverse, everyday people take on glamorous identities in a 3-D immersive digital world. The book's main character delivers pizza in real life (RL), but in the Metaverse, he's a warrior prince and champion sword fighter.[27] The hugely popular *Matrix* movie trilogy paints a similar (though more sinister) picture of a world that blurs the lines between physical and digital reality, as did *Avatar* when the hero transformed from a disabled soldier to a 10-foot-tall blue warrior.

Today these fictional depictions come to life as we witness the tremendous growth of real-time, interactive virtual worlds that allow people to assume **virtual identities** in cyberspace. More than 11 million people worldwide belong to the virtual world of *Second Life,* more than 8 million play the online game *World of Warcraft,* and the majority of Korean adults belong to *CyWorld.* Add to that the millions more who play *The Sims Online* or who visit other **computer-mediated environments (CMEs)** such as *Webkinz, Habbo Hotel,* MTV's *Virtual Laguna Beach,* and more than 200 other virtual worlds, and you're looking at a lot of serious role-playing.[28]

On these sites people assume visual identities, or **avatars**, that range from realistic versions of themselves to tricked-out versions with exaggerated physical characteristics or winged dragons or superheroes. Researchers are just starting to investigate how these online selves will influence consumer behavior and how the identities we choose in CMEs relate to our RL (or "meat-world") identities. Already we know that when people take on avatar forms, they tend to interact with other avatars much as their "meat-world" selves interact with other RL people. For example, just as in the RL, males in *Second Life* leave more space between them when they talk to other males versus females, and they are less likely to maintain eye contact than females are. When avatars get very close to one another, they tend to look away from each other—the norms of the RL steadily creep into

The Tangled Web

A word to the wise: Corporate recruiters often complain about students who show up for job interviews in sloppy or revealing clothing—these applicants failed to "read the program" about which role they're expected to play in professional settings! Those who post photos of their actual selves in unflattering situations (that must have been a pretty wild party . . .) may come to regret their actions as potential employers start to check out their pages before they look at the would-be candidates' résumés. Some even turn to services such as Reputation.com that scour the Internet to remove embarrassing postings before the boss (or Mom) sees them.[23] What can visitors learn about *you* when they visit your profile?

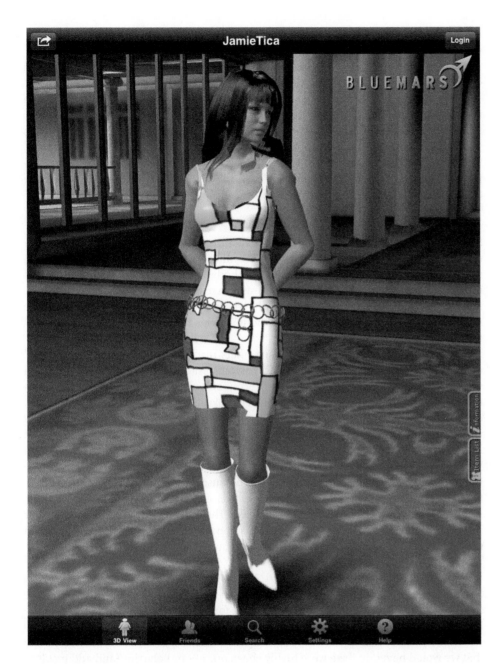

The Hot or Not web site was an early web sensation when it debuted in 2000, letting you rate how attractive women or men were with a simple voting system. Now Avatar Reality, the maker of the Blue Mars virtual world, lets iPhone users vote on how hot, or not, your avatar is.

Source: Courtesy of Avatar Reality, Inc.

the virtual world.[29] With new platforms like Microsoft's Kinect that eliminate the need for hand controllers, our online and offline selves will continue to fuse. Already, scientists have been able to transmit the minds of volunteers from their physical bodies to their avatars for the first time; in one project volunteers wore skullcaps that contained electrodes to monitor brain activity while they also wore a set of goggles that showed them a different body in a different world. Researchers found that the subjects started to react as if their avatars were their real bodies.[30]

Symbolic Interactionism

If each person potentially has many social selves, how does each develop? How do we decide which self to "activate" at any point in time? The sociological tradition of **symbolic interactionism** stresses that relationships with other people play a large part in forming the self.[31] According to this perspective, we exist in a symbolic environment. We assign meaning to any situation or object when we interpret the symbols in this environment. As members of society, individuals learn to agree on shared meanings. Thus, we "know" that a red light means stop, the "golden arches" mean fast food, and "blondes have more fun." That's important in understanding consumer behavior because it implies that our possessions play a key role as we evaluate ourselves and decide "who we are."[32]

Each of us, then, interprets our identity, and this assessment continually evolves as we encounter new situations and people. In symbolic interactionist terms, we *negotiate* these meanings over time. Essentially, each of us poses the question: "Who am I in this situation?" Those around us greatly influence how we answer this query, and we ask, "Who do *other people* think I am?" We tend to pattern our behavior on the perceived expectations of others, as a form of *self-fulfilling prophecy*. When we act the way we assume others expect us to act, we often confirm these perceptions.

The Looking-Glass Self

Some clothing stores are testing an interactive mirror that doubles as a high-resolution digital screen. When you choose a garment, the mirror superimposes it on your reflection so that you can see how it would look on your body. A camera relays live images of you modeling your virtual outfit to an Internet site where your friends can log in to instant message (IM) you to tell you what they think; their comments pop up on the side of the mirror for you to read. They can also select virtual items for you to try on that the "magic" mirror will reflect.[33]

Sociologists call the process of imagining others' reactions "taking the role of the other," or the **looking-glass self**.[34] According to this view, our desire to define ourselves operates as a sort of psychological sonar: We take readings of our own identity when we "bounce" signals off others and try to project their impression of us. Like the distorted mirrors in a funhouse, our appraisal of who we are varies depending on whose perspective we consider and how accurately we predict their evaluations of us. A confident career woman like Lisa may sit morosely at a nightclub, imagining that others see her as a dowdy, unattractive woman with little sex appeal (regardless of whether these perceptions are true). A *self-fulfilling prophecy* like the one we described comes into play here because these "signals" influence Lisa's actual behavior. If she doesn't believe she's attractive, she may choose frumpy, unflattering clothing that actually does make her less attractive. The next morning at work, however, her self-confidence at the office may cause her to assume that others hold her "executive self" in even higher regard than they actually do (we all know people like that)!

Self-Consciousness

If you have ever walked into a class in the middle of a lecture and been convinced that all eyes were on you as you awkwardly searched for a seat, you can understand the feeling of *self-consciousness*. In contrast, sometimes we behave with shockingly little self-consciousness. For example, we may do things in a stadium, a riot, or at a fraternity party that we would never do if we were highly conscious of our behavior (and add insult to injury when we post these escapades to our Facebook page!).[35]

Some people seem to be more sensitive in general to the image they communicate to others. However, we all know people who act as if they're oblivious to the impression they are making. A heightened concern about the nature of one's public "image" also results in more concern about the social appropriateness of products and consumption activities.

Consumers who score high on a scale of *public self-consciousness* express more interest in clothing and use more cosmetics than others who score lower.[36] In one study, highly self-conscious subjects expressed greater willingness to buy personal products, such as a douche or a gas-prevention remedy, that are somewhat embarrassing to buy but may avoid awkward public incidents later.[37]

Similarly, high *self-monitors* are more attuned to how they present themselves in their social environments, and their estimates of how others will perceive their product choices influence what they choose to buy.[38] A scale to measure self-monitoring asks consumers how much they agree with statements such as "I guess I put on a show to impress or entertain others" or "I would probably make a good actor." Perhaps not surprisingly, publicly visible types such as college football players and fashion models tend to score higher on these dimensions.[39]

To promote its Double Down chicken filet sandwich, KFC recruited female college students to serve as human billboards. The brand ambassadors wore sweatpants bearing a branded message for the bun-less sandwich on their backsides.[41]

Source: Photo Courtesy KFC Corporation.

Consumption and Self-Concept

Identity marketing is a promotional strategy whereby consumers alter some aspects of their selves to advertise for a branded product:[40]

- A British marketing firm paid five people to legally change their names for one year to "Turok," the hero of a video game series about a time-traveling Native American who slays bionically enhanced dinosaurs.
- The Internet Underground Music Archive (IUMA) paid a Kansas couple $5,000 to name their baby boy Iuma.
- Air New Zealand created "cranial billboards" in exchange for a round-trip ticket to New Zealand—30 Los Angeles participants shaved their heads and walked around with an ad for the airline on their skulls. The Casa Sanchez restaurant in San Francisco gives free lunches for life to anyone who gets its logo tattooed on his or her body. The Daytona Cubs baseball team awards free season tickets for life to anyone who will tattoo the Cubs logo on his or her body. According to the International Trademark Association, the Harley tattoo is still the most widespread corporate logo tattoo in North America, but other contenders include Nike, Adidas, Budweiser, Corona, Apple computers, Ford, Chevy, and Volkswagen.

OBJECTIVE 2

Products often play a key role in defining the self-concept.

Are You What You Consume?

Remember that the reflected self helps shape self-concept, which implies that people see themselves as they imagine others see them. Because what others see includes a person's clothing, jewelry, furniture, car, and so on, it stands to reason that these products also help to create the perceived self. A consumer's possessions place her into a social role, which helps to answer the question, "Who am I now?"

People use an individual's consumption behaviors to identify that person's social identity. In addition to checking out a person's clothes and grooming habits, we make inferences about personality based on her choice of leisure activities (e.g., squash versus bowling), food preferences (e.g., tofu and beans versus steak and potatoes), cars, and home decorating choices. When researchers show people pictures of someone's living room, for example, study participants make surprisingly accurate guesses about the occupant's personality.[42] In the same way that a consumer's use of products influences others' perceptions, the same products can help to determine his own self-concept and social identity.[43]

We are *attached* to an object to the extent we rely on it to maintain our self-concept.[44] Objects act as a security blanket when they reinforce our identities, especially in unfamiliar situations. For example, students who decorate their dorm rooms with personal items are less likely to drop out of college. This coping process may protect the self from being diluted in a strange environment.[45] When a pair of researchers asked children of various ages to create "who am I?" collages, for which they chose pictures that represented their selves, older kids between middle childhood and early adolescence inserted more photos of branded merchandise. Also, as they aged, their feelings about these objects evolved from concrete relationships (e.g., "I own it") to more sophisticated, abstract relationships (e.g., "It is like me").[46]

Our use of consumption information to define the self is especially important when we have yet to completely form a social identity, such as when we have to play a new role in life. Think, for example, of the insecurity many of us felt when we first started college or reentered the dating market after leaving a long-term relationship. **Symbolic self-completion theory** suggests that people who have an incomplete self-definition tend to complete this identity when they acquire and display symbols they associate with that role.[47]

Adolescent boys, for example, may use "macho" products such as cars and cigarettes to bolster their developing masculinity; these items act as a "social crutch" during a period of uncertainty about their new identity as adult males. As we mature into a role, we actually rely less on the products people associate with it: For example, when kids start to skateboard, they often invest in pro skateboard "decks" with graphics and branding that cost between $40 and $70 even without the "trucks" (wheels and axles). But—to the chagrin of the skateboard industry—as they get more serious about boarding, many think it's just fine to buy blank decks, the plain wood boards that cost only $15 to $30.[48]

The contribution of possessions to self-identity is perhaps most apparent when we lose these treasured objects. One of the first acts of institutions that want to repress individuality and encourage group identity, such as prisons or the military, is to confiscate personal possessions.[49] Victims of burglaries and natural disasters commonly report feelings of alienation, depression, or of being "violated." One consumer's comment after she was robbed is typical: "It's the next worse thing to being bereaved; it's like being raped."[50] Burglary victims exhibit a diminished sense of community, lowered feelings of privacy, and less pride in their houses' appearance than do their neighbors.[51]

A study of postdisaster conditions, where consumers may have lost literally everything but the clothes on their backs following a fire, hurricane, flood, or earthquake, highlights the dramatic impact of product loss. Some people are reluctant to undergo the process of re-creating their identities by acquiring new possessions. Interviews with disaster victims reveal that some hesitate to invest the self in new possessions and so become more detached about what they buy. This comment from a woman in her 50s is representative of this attitude: "I had so much love tied up in my things. I can't go through that kind of loss again. What I'm buying now won't be as important to me."[52]

The Extended Self

As we noted earlier, many of the props and settings consumers use to define their social roles become parts of their selves. Those external objects that we consider a part of us constitute the **extended self**. In some cultures, people literally incorporate objects into the self: they lick new possessions, take the names of conquered enemies (or in some cases eat them), or bury the dead with their possessions.[66]

We don't usually go that far, but some people do cherish possessions as if they were a part of them. In fact, some of us willingly (and perhaps eagerly) label ourselves as *fanatics* about a cherished product.[67] Consider shoes, for example: You don't have to be Carrie of *Sex and the City* fame to acknowledge that many people feel a strong bond to their footwear. One study found that people commonly view their shoes as magical emblems of self, Cinderella-like vehicles for self-transformation. Based on data collected from consumers, the researcher concluded that (like their sister Carrie) women tend to be more attuned to the symbolic implications of shoes than men. A common theme that emerged was that a pair of shoes obtained when younger—whether a first pair of leather shoes, a first pair of high heels, or a first pair of cowboy boots—had a big impact even later in life. These experiences were similar to those that occur in such well-known fairy tales and stories as Dorothy's red shoes in *The Wizard of Oz* (1939), Karen's magical red shoes in Hans Christian Anderson's *The Red Shoes* (1845), and Cinderella's glass slippers.[68]

In addition to shoes, of course, many material objects—ranging from personal possessions and pets to national monuments or landmarks—help to form a consumer's identity. Just about everyone can name a valued possession that has a lot of the self "wrapped up" in it, whether it is a beloved photograph, a trophy, an old shirt, a car, or a cat. Indeed, usually we can construct a pretty accurate "biography" of someone when we simply catalog the items he displays in his bedroom or office. A recent study illustrates that the product/self doesn't even have to be that strong to influence a consumer's self-concept. In

Adzookie, a mobile ad network, has received numerous responses to its offer to pay the mortgage for homeowners who let it brand the exterior of their homes.

Source: Courtesy of Adzookie.com.

one experiment, researchers approached women in a shopping mall and gave them one of two shopping bags to walk around with for an hour. Women who received a bag from Victoria's Secret later reported to the researchers that they felt more sensual and glamorous. In another experiment, M.B.A. students were asked to take notes for six weeks using a pen embossed with the MIT logo; they reported feeling smarter at the end of the term.[69]

We describe four levels of the extended self, ranging from very personal objects to places and things that allow people to feel as though they are rooted in their larger social environments:[71]

1 **Individual level**—Consumers include many of their personal possessions in self-definition. These products can include jewelry, cars, clothing, and so on. The saying "You are what you wear" reflects the belief that one's things are a part of one's identity.

FRANCESCO**BIASIA**
HANDBAGS

This Italian ad demonstrates that our favorite products are part of the extended self.
Source: Used with permission of Francesco Biasia and D'Adda, Lorenzini, Vigorelli BBDO.

181

2 **Family level**—This part of the extended self includes a consumer's residence and the furnishings in it. We can think of the house as a symbolic body for the family, and the place where we live often is a central aspect of who we are.

3 **Community level**—It is common for consumers to describe themselves in terms of the neighborhood or town from which they come. For farm families or other residents with close ties to a community, this sense of belonging is particularly important.

4 **Group level**—We regard our attachments to certain social groups as a part of the self; we'll consider some of these consumer *subcultures* in later chapters. A consumer also may feel that landmarks, monuments, or sports teams are a part of the extended self.

OBJECTIVE 3
Society's expectations of masculinity and femininity help to determine the products we buy to meet these expectations.

Sex Roles

The Indian government banned a TV spot for Axe men's deodorant: The spot shows a man who turns into a walking chocolate figurine after he sprays himself with the brand's Dark Temptation deodorant. As he walks through the city, women throw themselves at him as they lick him and bite off various parts of his body. Although the same ad played in Argentina and Europe without any problem, traditional Indian culture doesn't approve of such blatant imagery. The government yanked another ad for Amul Macho underwear, in which a young woman comes to a river to do her husband's laundry, pulls out a pair of boxer shorts and begins to wash them by hand as she gives sultry looks to the camera and throws her head back in a suggestive manner, as a voiceover says, "Amul Macho. Crafted for fantasies." Members of a Hindu organization called The Army of Ram (a Hindu god) attacked a group of female college students in a bar because they were drinking and dancing with men.[72] Clearly, sex roles are not set in stone around the world.

Sexual identity is a very important component of a consumer's self-concept. People often conform to their culture's expectations about how those of their gender should act, dress, or speak; we refer to these sets of expectations as **sex roles**. Of course, these guidelines change over time, and they differ radically across societies. In India and elsewhere, a society communicates its assumptions about the proper roles of men and women as it defines ideal behaviors for each gender.

It's not clear to what extent gender differences are innate rather than culturally shaped, but they're certainly evident in many consumption situations. Consider the gender differences market researchers observe when they compare the food preferences of men to those of women. Women eat more fruit; men are more likely to eat meat. As one food writer put it, "Boy food doesn't grow. It is hunted or killed."[73] The sexes also differ sharply in the quantities of food they eat: When researchers at Hershey discovered that women eat smaller amounts of candy, they created a white chocolate confection called Hugs, one of the most successful food introductions of all time. In contrast, a man in a Burger King Whopper ad ditches his date at a fancy restaurant, complaining that he is "too hungry to settle for chick food." Pumped up on Whoppers, a swelling mob of men shake their fists, punch one another, toss a van off a bridge, and sing, "I will eat this meat until my innie turns into an outie," and "I am hungry. I am incorrigible. I am man."[74]

Gender Differences in Socialization

Can the smell of burning rubber and gasoline light the fires of love? Harlequin, a major publisher of romance novels with a predominantly female readership, partnered with male-dominated NASCAR to turn out racing-themed stories. In one, the heroine is an ex-kindergarten teacher who falls in love with a real NASCAR driver named Lance Cooper after he hits her with his car (subtle, right?); she winds up driving his racing team's motor coach from race to race. In a typical passage, the novel describes a kiss: "It wasn't gentle, it wasn't passive, it was a kiss that instantly proved the two of them were like high-octane

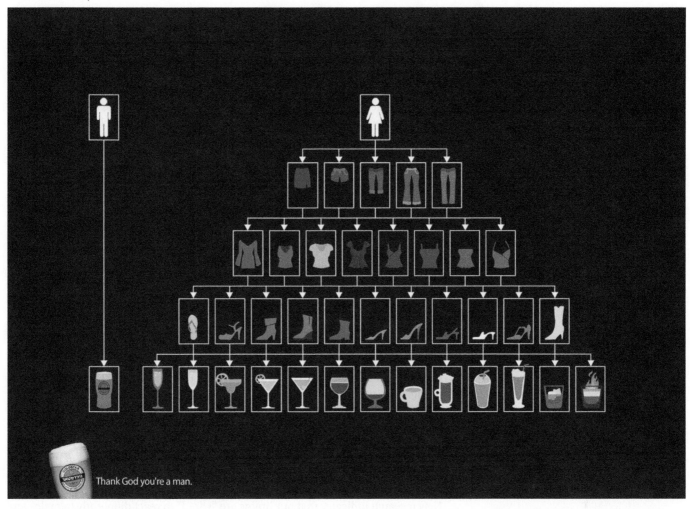

Thank God you're a man.

This Israeli poster that appeared in men's restrooms illustrates cultural assumptions about sex role differences.
Source: Courtesy of Goldstar.

fuel, their flesh sparking off each other . . . ."[75] Yet another case of boy meets girl, boy runs over girl.

Many commercial sources, in addition to parents and friends, provide lessons in *gender socialization* for both girls and boys:

- Mattel partnered with Bonne Bell to market a line of cosmetics to young girls aged 6 to 9. The popular Bratz doll line already licenses its name to a cosmetics line that also targets this age group. ESPN Zone in Chicago is a male preserve that lets boys be boys and men be . . . boys. Customers perceive the venue as a safe haven where buddies can watch men's sports and establish camaraderie with other men.[76] Sony created a TV ad for its Bravia line of liquid-crystal-display (LCD) televisions that offers different endings to each gender. The spot shows a man and a woman gazing through a storefront window at a Bravia LCD. Unaware of each other, the two simultaneously whisper: "Nice picture." Suddenly, two buttons appear on the screen that read: "Ending for Men" and "Ending for Women." The male ending is either a funny clip from a sports show or a cartoon spoof of a martial-arts movie. Women see either a 1950s-era musical centered on shoes or a tear-jerker about a female doctor who saves the life of an orphan.[77]

As these examples illustrate, manufacturers and retailers tend to reinforce a society's expectations regarding the "correct" way for boys and girls, men and women, to look and act. Even countries that are physically close to each other may send very different messages. In comparing Malaysian and Singaporean commercials, for example, researchers found that Malaysian males tend to dominate ads for technical products, whereas females dominate the Singaporean ones, which suggests that in Singapore people accept women's assumption of professional roles to a greater degree. To support this argument, they also found that ads in Malaysia portray men more often in high-level business or professional roles, whereas those in Singapore portray both genders equally.[78]

Many societies expect males to pursue **agentic goals**, which stress self-assertion and mastery. However, they teach females to value **communal goals**, such as affiliation and the fostering of harmonious relations.[79] One study even found that people perceived a male voice emanating from a computer to be more accurate and authoritative than a female voice reading the very same words. Participants also valued computer-generated words of praise to a greater extent when the voice was male![80] Similarly, an analysis of TV commercials aimed at children in the United States and Australia found that they depict boys as more knowledgeable, active, aggressive, and instrumental.[81]

These differences in orientation show up early in our development. When Mattel decided to develop Ello, a building toy for girls, its designers carefully observed the play patterns of 5- to 10-year-olds. The toy features interconnecting plastic squares, balls, triangles, squiggles, flowers, and sticks, in pastel colors and with rounded corners, that let users snap pieces together to create houses, people, jewelry, and picture frames. As one of the developers observed, "Boys enjoy stacking blocks and working towards a goal, such as finishing a building. Their play is more physically active, and they like to create conflict between characters. Girls don't like repetitive stacking. They prefer to create relationships between characters, building communities and decorative spaces."[82]

Not surprisingly, we observe the same gender difference in social media: Women are just more enthusiastic about connecting with others. Although there are more men online on the global Internet, women spend about 8 percent more time online, averaging 25 hours per month on the Web. Women the world over spend 20 percent more time on retail sites overall than men. In a typical month, about 76 percent of all women globally interact with a social networking site, as compared to only 70 percent of men. Also, women spend significantly more time on social networking sites than men, with women averaging 5.5 hours per month compared to 4 hours for men.[83]

New research indicates that our brains are "wired" to react differently to males and females—and it may help to explain why men tend to objectify women. A study that used brain-scanning technology showed photos of women wearing bikinis to a group of heterosexual male college students and tracked which areas of their brains lit up. The activated areas were the same as those that get aroused when males handle tools. In a follow-up study, men tended to associate bikini-clad women with first-person action verbs such as I "push," "handle" and "grab" instead of the third-person forms such as she "pushes," "handles" and "grabs." In contrast, when they saw photos of fully clothed women, they reverted to the third-person forms, which implied that they perceived these women as being in control of their own actions. Female subjects who responded to both sets of pictures did not display this difference.[84]

Gender versus Sexual Identity

Gender-role identity is a state of mind as well as body. A person's biological gender (i.e., male or female) does not totally determine whether he or she will exhibit **sex-typed traits**, characteristics we stereotypically associate with one gender or the other. A consumer's subjective feelings about his or her sexuality are crucial as well.[85]

Unlike maleness and femaleness, masculinity and femininity are *not* biological characteristics. A behavior that one culture considers to be masculine might get a different response in another. For example, the norm in the United States is that male friends avoid touching each other (except in "safe" situations such as on the football field). In some Latin and European cultures, however, it is common for men to hug and kiss one another as a form of greeting. Note that even this norm continues to evolve, as American teenagers of both sexes adopt the new fad of hugging as a standard form of greeting (sometimes accompanied by the high-five or the fist-bump) and male friends (encouraged by the MTV show of the same name) feel free to talk about having a **bromance** (affection between straight male friends).[86]

Sex-Typed Products

A popular book once proclaimed, *Real Men Don't Eat Quiche.* Many products (in addition to quiche) also are sex-typed. They take on masculine or feminine attributes, and consumers associate them with one gender or another.[87] Marketers often encourage the sex typing of products such as Princess telephones, boys' and girls' bicycles, or Luvs color-coded diapers. A vodka brand called Thor's Hammer illustrates this stereotyping. The booze comes in a short, squat bottle, and the company's vice president of marketing describes it as "bold and broad and solid. This is a man's kind of vodka . . . it's not your frosted . . . girly-man vodka." Thor was the Norse god of thunder, and the company claims the name has no connection to the slang phrase "getting hammered," which can happen if you drink too much of the stuff.[88] In contrast, Dell recently launched *Della,* a female-targeted microsite to attract women who want to buy netbooks. The home page featured three women whose clothes matched their laptops, along with "Tech Tips" that included advice on how to count calories and share recipes online. Many people didn't appreciate this treatment: A Twitter comment sums up the reaction: "Della, new website 4 women who r 2 stupid 2 go 2 dell.com."[89]

Female Sex Roles

In the 1949 movie *Adam's Rib,* Katherine Hepburn played a stylish and competent lawyer. This film was one of the first to show that a woman can have a successful career and still be happily married. Today, the evolution of a new managerial class of women has forced marketers to change their traditional assumptions about women as they target this growing market. For example, Suzuki appeals to the growing number of women in India who achieve financial independence and buy their own cars. Its Zen Estilo (*estilo* means "style" in Spanish) model comes in eight colors, including "purple fusion," "virgin blue," and "sparkling olive."[102]

Still, it's premature to proclaim the death of traditional sex-role stereotypes. This is certainly true in traditional Islamic countries that require women to be completely covered in public and that prohibit them from working as salespeople in stores open to the public (even if the store sells female intimate apparel).[103] In Iraq, a mosque offers free scarves to women who agree to "keep their promise to God" and not wear clothes that will inflame men's imaginations. It promotes the belief that, due to the influx of satellite TV and DVD images from the non-Muslim world, men will turn into lustful beasts if they look at women who wear revealing Western dress, and the women who wear these items will burn in hell for eternity. As one local man acknowledged, "Yes, I do look at women when I see them dressed up with tight jeans. That is one of the problems. It means the devil is doing a good job."[104]

To further complicate matters, sex roles constantly evolve. In a complex society like ours, we often encounter contradictory messages about "appropriate" behavior, and we may find ourselves putting on a very different face as we jump from situation to situation. A recent exploration of what the authors labeled **contemporary young mainstream female achievers (CYMFA)** identified different roles these women play in different contexts. For example, as a mother or partner they enact a highly feminine role; as a tough, pitiless businessperson, they play a masculine role; and with a friend they might evoke both roles at once.[105]

As anyone who understands the logic of market segmentation understands, it's often not realistic to paint a huge group of consumers with the same brush; we often need to subdivide them into segments that share important characteristics. This logic certainly applies to women, and smart marketers know they can't assume that all female consumers have been socialized the same way. For example, a research company called Cohorts identifies nine segments of single women alone. Cohorts describes the three most promising segments:[107]

1 **Megan**—A stylish, tech-savvy student with a median income of $16,000. She reads *Self, Rolling Stone, InStyle,* and *Us Weekly.* She is likely to channel-surf when ads come on

Women consume many products intended to alter their appearance to be in line with cultural expectations.

Source: Agency: Downtown Partners Chicago. Writer: Sean Austin. Art Directors: Joe Stuart and Tom Kim.

TV, and she wouldn't watch TV at all without cable. Her favorite channels are Oxygen, Nick at Nite, Disney Channel, MTV, VH1, E!, and TBS. She's turned on by what's cool or the latest thing, she's liberal, seizes opportunities, and she spends on a whim.

2 **Allison**—An educated working woman with a median income of $52,000. She reads *Elle, Shape, Cosmopolitan,* and *Entertainment Weekly.* Her favorite channels are Lifetime, Bravo, Cartoon Network, E!, FX, TBS, and TLC. She's into travel and her career, and she prides herself on her sophisticated tastes.

3 **Elizabeth**—An affluent career woman with a median income of $174,000. She reads *Vogue, Harper's Bazaar, People,* and *Martha Stewart Living.* When she takes time to watch TV, she tunes in to networks such as Lifetime, WE, Comedy Central, MTV, CNBC, E!, HBO, A&E, Bravo, and AMC. She values foreign travel, fitness, and her career, and she's savvy and spontaneous.

Male Sex Roles

A European ad for designer Dolce & Gabbana depicts a group of sweaty men in tight jeans who surround a woman wearing spike heels who is pinned to the ground. Other ads for long-time household products spokescharacter Mr. Clean claim that only a strong man is powerful enough to tackle dirt.[108] To promote the new Dr Pepper Ten drink, the company is sending a mobile "Man Cave" to U.S. cities. The trailer will park in "testosterone zones" such as ball fields or car shows and give men a place to watch TV and play video games. The accompanying advertising campaign features a muscled commando type who totes a space-age weapon. "Hey ladies, enjoying the film?" he asks. "'Course not. Because this is our movie, and Dr Pepper Ten is our soda."[109]

Our culture's stereotype of the ideal male is a tough, aggressive, muscular man who enjoys "manly" sports (and MavTV—"TV created by men for men").[110] When global entrepreneur and CEO of Virgin Airlines Richard Branson lost a racing bet to the owner of AirAsia, his "sentence" was to dress as a female flight attendant for the winner's airline. The winner gloated, "I'm looking forward to him sucking up to me as a stewardess!"[111]

Just as for women, however, the true story is more complicated than being "a man's man." Indeed, scholars of **masculinism** study the male image and the complex cultural meanings of masculinity.[112] Like women, men receive mixed messages about how they are supposed to behave and feel. In a new Procter & Gamble campaign, the maker of products like Pampers and Ivory soap created a Web site for family men, ManoftheHouse .com, that offers husbands and fathers advice about outdoor grilling, cleaning toilets, and "conquering sex problems." As it promotes Gillette razors, Head & Shoulders shampoo, and other products, the site promises, "We'll make men out of you yet."[113] Chevrolet's "Guy's Night Out" commercial depicts a new dad's night out with friends where they wind up watching his toddler's sing-a-long CD. Sprint aired a commercial about a boy who is dumped by his girlfriend via text message.[114]

One study examined how American men pursue masculine identities through their everyday consumption. The researchers suggest that men are trying to make sense out of three different models of masculinity that they call *breadwinner, rebel,* and *man-of-action hero,* as they figure out just who they are supposed to be. On the one hand, the breadwinner model draws from the American myth of success and celebrates respectability, civic

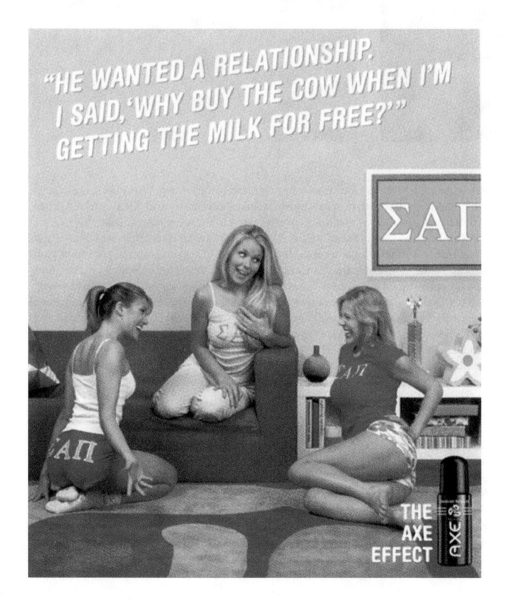

The Axe line of male personal care products puts a twist on an old stereotype by depicting men as sex objects.
Source: Courtesy of Bartle Bogle Hegarty New York aka BBH.

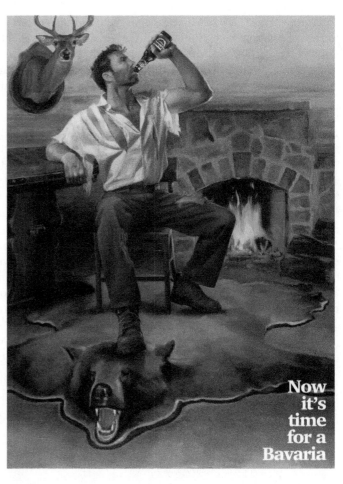

This Dutch beer ad communicates expectations about the male sex role.

Source: KesselsKramer, Amsterdam.
KesselsKramer, Sabine Gilhuijs, Lauriergracht 39, 1016 RG Amsterdam. The Netherlands.

virtues, pursuit of material success, and organized achievement. The rebel model, on the other hand, emphasizes rebellion, independence, adventure, and potency. The man-of-action hero is a synthesis that draws from the best of the other two models.[115]

One consequence of the continual evolution of sex roles is that men are concerned as never before with their appearance. Men spend $7.7 billion on grooming products globally each year. A wave of male cleansers, moisturizers, sunscreens, depilatories, and body sprays washes up on U.S. shores, largely from European marketers. L'Oréal Paris reports that men's skincare products are now its fastest-growing sector. In Europe, 24 percent of men younger than age 30 use skincare products—and 80 percent of young Korean men do. In the United States, Norelco reported a 24 percent rise in sale of facial hair grooming products in 2008. Mintel reports big growth, especially in products with antiaging and exfoliating ingredients. Even some cosmetics products, like foundation and eyeliner, are catching on in some segments, though men aren't comfortable owning up to using them. In fact, a British makeup product looks like a ballpoint pen so men can apply it secretly at the office.[116]

Androgyny

Androgyny refers to the possession of both masculine and feminine traits.[90] Researchers make a distinction between *sex-typed people,* who are stereotypically masculine or feminine, and *androgynous people,* whose orientation isn't as clearly defined. People who don't neatly fit into one gender category or another may create uncertainty among others who aren't sure how to relate to them. A study demonstrated that sex-role assumptions travel into cyberspace as well. The researchers asked each volunteer to interact with another respondent via a chat room. They showed subjects an avatar to represent the other person, with images ranging from "an obviously female" blonde to one with no clear gender to a strong-jawed male. The subjects rated their partners as less "credible" when they saw an androgynous avatar than when they saw one with sex-typed facial characteristics.[91]

Of course, the "normality" of sex-typed behaviors varies across cultures. For example, although acceptance of homosexuality varies in Asian cultures, it doesn't occur to most Asians to assume that a man with some feminine qualities is gay. A recent survey of Korean consumers found that more than 66 percent of men and 57 percent of women younger than age 40 were living self-described "androgynous" lifestyles—with men having more traditionally female traits and women having more traditionally male ones than they might have years ago. But the respondents didn't link that with sexual orientation. Although Koreans nickname males with feminine interests "flower men," they don't consider this to be a derogatory term.[92] In Japan, men that people call *gyaru-o* ("male gals") are common on city streets. Tanned and meticulously dressed (and usually heterosexual), these fops cruise Tokyo's stylish boutiques.[93]

Differences in sex-role orientation can influence how we respond to marketing stimuli, at least under some circumstances.[94] For example, females are more likely to undergo more elaborate processing of message content, so they tend to be more sensitive to specific pieces of information when they form a judgment, whereas males are more influenced by overall themes.[95] In addition, women with relatively strong masculine components in their sex-role identity prefer ad portrayals that include nontraditional women.[96] Some research indicates that sex-typed people are more sensitive to the sex-role depictions of characters in advertising, although women appear to be more sensitive generally to gender-role relationships than are men.

In one study, subjects read two versions of a beer advertisement couched in either masculine or feminine terms. The masculine version contained phrases such as

This ad for Bijan illustrates how sex role identities are culturally bound by contrasting the expectations of how women should appear in two different countries.
Source: Courtesy of Bijan Fragrances c/o Fashion World.

MANBAGS?
NOT ON MY WATCH.

Call them what you will,
a handbag is a handbag
in anyone's language.
Especially in ours.

This is hard country
and we want to keep it
that way. Nothing soft
gets in. No manbags,
no tofu, no hair gels
or male fragrances,
no designer sunglasses,
no small yappy dogs and
definitely no soft vehicles.
City people don't know
what they're facing out
here. We're only protecting
them from themselves.
You really need a tough
gutsy vehicle in the bush,
nothing else will survive.
Quality, durability and
reliability. That's why
we only drive Toyota
4WDs: LC200, LC70, Prado
and HiLux. And they're as
smart as they are strong.

Some of the features
we rely on – KDSS*
suspension control keeps
the car steady on the
shakiest of surfaces,
CRAWL* system maintains
an even speed for
stable off-road driving,
constant 4WD† impressive
torque and power, double
wishbone front suspension,
Anti-skid Braking System*
(ABS), Dual SRS airbags
and impressive towing
power for pulling soft
vehicles out of ditches.
We're the front line
between the country
and the city, it's our
sworn duty to keep out
unwanted items like pastel
coloured polo shirts.

NOTHING SOFT GETS IN

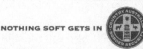

Features listed are not available on all Toyota 4WD models.
See a Toyota dealer or toyota.com.au for details of model applicability.

**Toyota in Australia makes a strong
statement about the masculinity
of 4WD vehicles.**

Source: Courtesy of Toyota Motor Corporation
Australia.

"X beer has the strong aggressive flavor that really asserts itself with good food and good company," and the feminine version made claims such as "Brewed with tender care, X beer is a full-bodied beer that goes down smooth and gentle." People who rated themselves as highly masculine or highly feminine preferred the version that was described in (respectively) very masculine or very feminine terms.[97] Sex-typed people in general are more concerned with ensuring that their behavior is consistent with their culture's definition of gender appropriateness.

Researchers developed a scale to identify "nontraditional males" (NTMs) who exhibit stereotypically female tendencies. The scale included statements such as these:

- I enjoy looking through fashion magazines.
- In our family, I take care of the checkbook and pay the bills.
- I am concerned about getting enough calcium in my diet. I am good at fixing mechanical things.
- I would do better than average in a fistfight.

Not too surprisingly, strong differences emerged between men who rated the statements along traditional sex-role lines and those who had nontraditional orientations.

When asked how they would like others to see them, NTMs were more likely than traditional males (TMs) to say that they would like to be considered stylish, sophisticated, up to date, and trendsetting. They were also more likely to say that they would like to be seen as sensitive, spiritual, affectionate, organized, and thrifty, but less likely to say they would like to be seen as "outdoorsy."[98]

The **Goth subculture**, inspired by vampire myths and gothic traditions, illustrates an androgynous approach to gender identity. Participants express different forms of sexuality regardless of their biological membership; they use costume to express hyper-masculinity, hyperfemininity, or androgyny (such as skeletons). The vampire narrative also is androgynous, as both males and females can dominate or search for beauty.[99]

Gender-Bending Products

Smart marketers try to think about new markets for their products. Some companies that sell exclusively to one gender therefore may decide to test the waters with the other sex when they promote **gender-bending products**—a traditionally sex-typed item adapted to the opposite gender. Here are some recent gender benders:[100]

- Febreze is now the "Official Air Freshener of the N.F.L." A television commercial features a woman in a football jersey spraying her living room with Febreze. "Earlier today your living room was game day central—a place for friends, family and your husband's trademark victory dance," says an announcer. "Now the crowd is gone and all that remains is the stink. But you're ready, because Febreze Air Effects cleans away tough game-day odors in the air—sweat socks, chicken wings, garlic dip—and leaves a light, fresh scent." It turns out that about one-third of N.F.L. viewers are female. More women watch the Super Bowl than the combined number of men and women who watch the Academy Awards.[101]

- Taking a page from a classic *Seinfeld* TV episode, Japanese lingerie retailer Wish Room discovered that some men secretly would like to wear a bra. It sold hundreds of "mansierres." Rubbermaid introduced a line of grooming tools specifically for men, including tweezers and clippers. As a manager explained, "Most men don't want to go to what we call the 'pink aisle' of the store to get tweezers and clippers that are made for women. They want products that look masculine and are made for their specific grooming needs." The tools fit better in men's hands and are stronger, to address issues such as thicker toenails and hair that grows in different places. In addition to drug stores, men can buy the products at Home Depot. The company that designed the line is now trying to launch a women's product it calls "Siren": a condom designed to fit in a lipstick-like tube.

- Frito-Lay's salty snacks traditionally appeal to men, but the company is working hard to change that with baked versions of chips and 100-calorie packages of snacks. After conducting extensive research (including asking several hundred women to keep detailed journals of their daily activities), the company's marketers concluded that the typical woman looks for a reminder that she's eating something healthy. As one result of this work, the bag for Baked Lay's will change from shiny yellow to a matte beige that displays pictures of ingredients like spices or ranch dressing.

- Harley-Davidson backed a Guinness World Record attempt for the number of women motorcycle riders trained in one weekend. Its dealerships host women-only Garage Parties.

- In Aurora, Colorado, Best Buy opened an electronics store designed for women that displays flat-screen TVs and appliances in home-like settings. The company enlisted local women to provide ideas; the design includes a private room for new moms complete with free diapers and a rocking chair.

- As fewer men take up the sport of hunting, the industry is going after women—and former Alaska Governor Sarah Palin (who apparently knows how to shoot and field-dress a moose) probably helped to publicize the sport during the 2008 presidential election. As one female hunter observed, companies first tried simply to "pink it and shrink it," but now they're taking more sophisticated steps. They manufacture lighter crossbows and produce TV shows that star women shooters, such as *American Huntress* and *Family Traditions with Haley Heath*. Apparel makers, including SHE Safari and Foxy Huntress, sell women's camouflage clothing.

Marketing Pitfall

A wave in one direction may set off a ripple in another. We can clearly see this in the messages girls have been getting from the media for the last several years: It's cool to be slutty. Role models like Paris Hilton, Lindsay Lohan, Britney Spears, and even Bratz dolls convey standards about how far preteens and teens should go when they broadcast their sexuality. Now, as these messages seem to go over the top (at least in the eyes of some concerned parents), we start to see early signs of a backlash, as some advocate a return to styles that leave almost everything to the imagination. At the *PureFashion* Web site, girls get style tips recommending skirts and dresses that fall no more than four fingers above the knee and no tank tops without a sweater or jacket over them; the *ModestApparel* site proclaims, "because a modest woman is a beautiful woman."[106] Is our culture moving from a celebration of "girls gone wild" to "girls gone mild?" Stay tuned.

Gay, Lesbian, Bisexual, and Transgender (GLBT) Consumers

Kurt, the gay character on the hit show *Glee* (played by actor Chris Colfer) is but the latest celebrity to publicize the issues that GLBT consumers face. To promote better understanding of these problems, Google Chrome created a supportive video for GLBT teens as part of the "It Gets Better" campaign that aired during a 2011 episode; actors included Adam Lambert, Lady Gaga, Kathy Griffin, and even Woody from *Toy Story*. Among other celebrities who are participating in this effort, President Obama uploaded a video on the campaign's YouTube channel to let GLBT teens know that "there are people out there who love you and care about you just the way you are."[117] The gay market is going mainstream.

The proportion of the population that is gay or lesbian is difficult to determine, and efforts to measure this group have been controversial.[118] Estimates among academics and marketing experts range widely from about 4 percent to 8 percent of the total U.S. population, or between 11 million and 23 million people. The 2000 Census reported 1.2 million same-sex "unmarried" partners in the United States, and this number excludes single gays and lesbians (the 2010 Census specifically counted same-sex married couples).[119] The respected research company Yankelovich Partners Inc., which has tracked consumer values and attitudes since 1971 in its annual *Monitor*™ survey, now includes a question about sexual identity in its instrument and reports that about 6 percent of respondents identify themselves as gay/homosexual/lesbian. This study was virtually the first to use a sample that reflects the population as a whole instead of polling only smaller or biased groups (such as readers of gay publications) whose responses may not be as representative of all consumers.

To put things in perspective, the GLBT market is at least as large, if not larger, than the Asian American population (currently at about 12 million people). These consumers spend in the range of $250 billion to $350 billion a year. A Simmons study of readers of gay publications found that these readers are almost 12 times more likely to hold professional jobs, twice as likely to own a vacation home, and eight times more likely to own a notebook computer compared to heterosexuals.[120]

The Asterix Group conducted a large-scale segmentation study of the gay market. This survey reminds us of the perils of assuming that everyone in a large market is the same. It identified five distinct segments:

1 "Super Gays" (26 percent of respondents) are highly educated, earn high incomes, and describe themselves as sophisticated, activist, complex, intellectual, mature, risk-taking, and extroverted. Nearly 90 percent report that they are "completely out," and about the same percentage report that they consider being gay to be a big part of who they are. About three-quarters of them live in big cities. They are the segment most likely to connect to a company that "actively speaks on behalf of LGBT causes."
2 "Habitaters" (25 percent) are older and most likely to be in a stable, living-together relationship. They describe themselves as serious, down-to-earth, emotional, simple, traditional, responsible, and mature. They are the most likely to live in suburban areas, and watch the most TV of any segment. Habitaters are most likely to connect with a company that offers domestic partner benefits to employees.
3 "Gay Mainstream" (23 percent) tend to be conservative. Fewer than half are "completely out," but more than half are in stable relationships. They are most likely to say that they prefer to watch TV programs in which being gay is part of the story.
4 "Party People" (14 percent) are young and the least-educated; most live in big cities. They describe themselves as youthful, down-to-earth, simple, cutting-edge, extroverted, rebellious, and risk-taking. They are far more likely than other segments to agree that "being gay is a choice." Three-quarters say they visit GLBT bars/clubs frequently, and they spend more time and money in restaurants.

Marketing Opportunity

Since 2004, when Massachusetts became the first state to allow it, there have been an estimated 40,000 legal same-sex marriages in the United States, and approximately 84,000 couples live in civil unions or domestic partnerships. As the movement grows in other states to legalize same-sex marriage, businesses are searching for ways to meet the needs of this new, potentially very lucrative market. Already the online magazine EquallyWed offers tips on wedding planning and OutVite.com sells "custom printed gay and lesbian stationery." Other targeted Web sites include QueerlyWed, SoYou'reEGAYged, GayWeddings.com, and RainbowWeddingNetwork.com. After it received pressure from gay rights groups, the "Today" show on NBC invited same-sex couples to compete in its annual wedding contest. *Brides* magazine ran its first feature about a wedding between one of the magazine's photo editors and her longtime girlfriend. A year earlier, *Martha Stewart Weddings* published a pictorial of two gay grooms stomping on a glass and sharing a kiss.[122]

CB AS I SEE IT

Professor Susan Dobscha, *Bentley University*

Imagine the excitement a young couple feels when they find out they are pregnant with their first child. They may learn this from a doctor's visit or from a pregnancy test they purchased at the drugstore. Once the pregnancy is confirmed and friends and relatives receive the good news, the couple must now begin the extensive planning process that gets them ready for the new addition to their family. Not surprisingly, a large portion of this process requires the planning and purchasing of goods and services. There are thousands of books on how to be a new parent, most of them geared toward the mother. Although there are several books that give advice on how to be a new father, the book market reflects the still widely accepted cultural norms that mothers are the primary caretakers of children, while fathers largely play a secondary role. A recent study found that although both new mothers and new fathers believed that responsibilities of parenting should be shared equally, the majority of those same mothers and

fathers did not feel that responsibility was equally shared in their household. Sex roles remain fairly stable over time, even if expectations about them change dramatically.

The VOICE Group, an international research team currently undertaking a global study of motherhood, asked new mothers about their husbands' role in the planning process as a run up to the new baby arriving. Despite the fact that most of our participants claimed that their husbands were "excited" and "involved," the reality for most women was that their partner's level of involvement was lower than their own. Our study focused on mothers' perceptions of fathers' attitudes toward consumption decisions related to the introduction of the first child in the family. The data revealed that men, according to their wives' perceptions, used consumption as a virtual umbilical cord, although levels of consumption involvement varied from co-involvement for most purchases, to limited involvement, and/or involvement for big-ticket items, particularly travel systems and technical products. This research also revealed that men partook in highly masculinized forms of "nesting," and in general shunned pregnancy book reading, though some did engage in "research" activities such as searching the Internet for product safety information. We concluded from this study that the transition into parenthood can be difficult

for men due to their lack of a physical connection to the pregnancy, a perception that the baby industry is not designed for them, the continuance of male stereotypes in the media, and also the time available to men to become involved in consumption activities immediately prior to a baby's birth.

An interesting question for consumer researchers is: How do sex roles change over time, and to what extent does the marketplace reflect or in some cases hinder that change? In this study, we found that the books geared toward new dads typically displayed a tongue-in-cheek tone; they implied that new dads are incapable of taking a serious look at their new role as caretaker of a young child. The baby stores are also somewhat intimidating to men (although the women felt just as intimidated by the large box baby stores) because of men's general lack of experience with caring for infants and lack of information on or awareness of what that infant's needs would be once he or she arrived.

If men have an expectation about themselves that they will be co-parents, equally responsible in the caretaking of their child, does the lack of marketplace offerings directed at new dads hinder those dads from enacting those new roles? Are there opportunities here for enterprising marketers who can develop products to better meet these needs?

---

5 The "Closeted" segment (12 percent) is older, and just 4 percent are "completely out." They describe themselves as serious, sideliners, traditional, introverted, mature, and cautious. Nearly half live in rural areas, and they're the most likely to connect to a company that "reaches out to gays and lesbians in traditional media."[121]

American Express, Stolichnaya vodka, Atlantic Records, and Naya bottled water are among those corporations that run ads in lesbian publications (an ad for American Express Travelers Cheques for Two shows two women's signatures on a check). Acting on research showing that lesbians are four times as likely as the average consumer to own one of their cars, Subaru of America decided to target this market in a big way. In one of the first mainstream pitches to directly address the controversy over gay marriage, Grand Marnier, a French cognac, launched print ads that read: "Your sister is finally getting remarried. Her fiancée's name is Jill."[123]

OBJECTIVE 4
The way we think about our bodies (and the way our culture tells us we should think) is a key component of self-esteem.

Body Image

For many women, trying on jeans is a painful exercise. Levi Strauss recently launched an online fitting service called the Curve ID System to make the process a little more comfortable. The digital offering is available in 20 languages and 50 countries; it is based on 60,000 women's figures worldwide and its goal is to provide a more customized experience to ease the frustration many women feel as they search for the perfect pair of jeans.[124] Now for some Spanx shapewear for some "tummy-taming," "butt boosting," or "thigh trimming" before you wear your new pants in public. . . . [125]

A person's physical appearance is a large part of his self-concept. **Body image** refers to a consumer's subjective evaluation of his physical self. As with a person's overall self-concept, this image is not necessarily accurate. A man may think of himself as being more muscular than he really is, or a woman may feel she appears fatter than is actually the case. Some marketers exploit consumers' tendencies to distort their body images when they prey on our insecurities about appearance. They try to create a gap between the real and the ideal physical selves and consequently motivate a person to purchase products and services he thinks will narrow that gap.

Body cathexis refers to a person's feelings about his body. The word *cathexis* refers to the emotional significance of some object or idea; we know that some parts of the body are more central to self-concept than are others. One study of young adults' feelings about their bodies found that the respondents were the most satisfied with their hair and eyes and that they had the least positive feelings about their waists. These feelings also linked to grooming products the respondents said they used. Consumers who were more satisfied with their bodies were more frequent users of such "preening" products as hair conditioner, blow dryers, cologne, facial bronzer, tooth polish, and pumice soap.[126]

Ideals of Beauty

Our satisfaction with the physical image we present to others depends on how closely we think the image corresponds to the ideal our culture values. An **ideal of beauty** is a particular model, or *exemplar,* of appearance. Ideals of beauty for both men and women may include physical features (e.g., big breasts or small, bulging muscles or not) as well as clothing styles, cosmetics, hairstyles, skin tone (pale versus tan), and body type (petite, athletic, voluptuous, etc). Our desires to match up to these ideals—for better or worse—drive a lot of our purchase decisions. What's more, the pressure to exhibit these traits starts earlier and earlier: The retailer Abercrombie & Fitch first came under fire a few years ago for selling thongs to preteens. More recently, critics blasted the chain because it offers padded bikini tops to the same age group.[127]

Is Beauty Universal?

It's no secret that, despite the popular saying "You can't judge a book by its cover," people can and do. Fairly or not, we assume that more attractive people are smarter, more interesting, and more competent. Researchers call this the *"what is beautiful is good"* stereotype.[128] Indeed, recent research evidence indicates that there is some truth to this assumption: beautiful people are generally happier than average- or below-average-looking people, and economists calculate that about half of that boost stems from the fact that they make more money![129] By the way, this bias affects both men and women.

Men with above-average looks earn about 5 percent more than those of average appearance, and those who are below average in appearance make an average of 9 percent less than the norm. Hitting close to home, in one study researchers collected teaching evaluations for 463 courses taught by 94 faculty members at the University of Texas at Austin, along with some characteristics of the instructors, such as sex and race and whether they were on tenure track. They asked a panel of undergrads to rate photos of the professors in terms of their physical attractiveness. Guess what? Good-looking professors got significantly higher scores—and this effect was even more pronounced for male professors than for females. Fortunately, your consumer behavior professor is no doubt near the top of the scale.[130]

Virtually every culture displays this beauty bias, even though the standards by which people judge what is hot and what is not may differ. Communist China once banned

Your beauty. Up in smoke.

Tobacco will destroy your face cell by cell, from the inside out. That's the ugly truth.

WORLD NO TOBACCO DAY
McCANN HEALTHCARE WORLDWIDE

This Japanese anti-smoking ad appeals to women's concerns about appearance to drive home a message.
Source: Courtesy of McCann Worldgroup Holdings Japan.

beauty contests as "spiritual pollution," but then again China recently hosted the "Miss World" pageant. The Chinese consider appearance so important that they view plastic surgery as a commercial investment, and it's common for people to take out loans to fund procedures.[131]

Research published in 2004 indicates that preferences for some physical features rather than others are "wired in" genetically, and that these preferences tend to be the same among peoples around the world. When researchers show babies as young as 5 hours old pictures of faces that adults rate as beautiful and not so beautiful, they report that the infants spend more time looking at the attractive faces. Specifically, people appear to favor features we associate with good health and youth, attributes we link to reproductive ability and strength. These characteristics include large eyes, high cheekbones, and a narrow jaw. Another cue that people across ethnic and racial groups use to signal sexual desirability is whether the person's features are balanced. People with symmetrical features on average start having sex 3 to 4 years earlier than those with unbalanced features.[132]

Men also are more likely to use a woman's body shape as a sexual cue; an evolutionary explanation is that feminine curves provide evidence of reproductive potential. During puberty, a typical female gains almost 35 pounds of "reproductive fat" around the hips and thighs that supply the approximately 80,000 extra calories she will need to support a pregnancy. Most fertile women have waist–hip ratios of 0.6 to 0.8, an hourglass shape that also happens to be the one men rank highest. Even though preferences for overall weight change over time, waist–hip ratios tend to stay in this range. Even the superthin model Twiggy (who pioneered the "waif look" decades before Kate Moss) had a ratio of 0.73.[133]

Women, however, favor men with heavy lower faces (an indication of a high concentration of androgens that impart strength), those who are slightly above average in height, and those with prominent brows. A recent study provided evidence that women judge potential mates by how masculine their features are. Respondents viewed a series of male headshots that had been digitally altered to exaggerate or minimize masculine traits. They saw men with square jaws and well-defined brow ridges as good short-term partners, whereas they preferred those with feminine traits, such as rounder faces and fuller lips, for long-term mates.

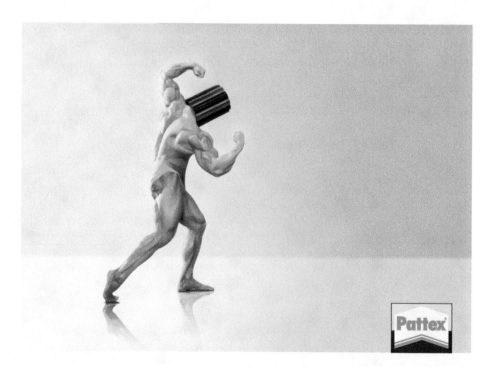

This German ad evokes a masculine ideal of beauty to highlight the strength of a glue product.
Source: Courtesy of DDB Tribal Hamburg.

Overwhelmingly, participants said those with more masculine features were likely to be risky and competitive and also more apt to fight, challenge bosses, cheat on spouses, and put less effort into parenting. They assume that men with more feminine faces would be good parents and husbands, hard workers, and emotionally supportive mates.[134]

There is increasingly tantalizing evidence that these preferences are triggered physiologically; women's behaviors and preferences in men link to hormonal changes. In one study, researchers tested female university students who came to their lab when they were ovulating and when they were not. They photographed each woman twice—once in her fertile phase and once in her least-fertile phase. Then the researchers asked a separate panel of men and women to look at these pairs of photos (with the faces blacked out) and choose the one in which the person tries to look more attractive. These judges were more likely to select the photo of each woman when she was ovulating, and in these pictures the women tended to wear flashier clothing and jewelry; the researchers compared this behavior to animals that commonly signal when they are fertile via scents or changes in skin color. In another study, researchers showed women in Japan and Scotland a series of computer-generated photos of male faces that were systematically altered in terms of such dimensions as the size of the jaw and the prominence of the eyebrow ridge.[135] Women in the study preferred the heavier masculine features when they were ovulating, but these choices shifted during other parts of their monthly cycles. Most recently, researchers reported that women who are at peak fertility choose sexy rather than conservative clothing, apparently as a way to lure males away from other women.[136]

Jaw size aside, the way we "package" our bodies still varies enormously, and that's where marketers come in: Advertising and other forms of mass media play a significant role in determining which forms of beauty we consider desirable at any point in time. An ideal of beauty functions as a sort of cultural yardstick. Consumers compare themselves to some standard (often one the fashion media advocate at that time), and they are dissatisfied with their appearance to the extent that they don't match up to it. This may lower their own self-esteem or, in some cases, possibly diminish the effectiveness of an ad because of negative feelings aroused by a highly attractive model.[137]

Our language provides phrases to sum up these cultural ideals. We may talk about a "bimbo," a "girl-next-door," or an "ice queen," or we may refer to specific women who have come to embody an ideal, such as J-Lo, Gwyneth Paltrow, or the late Princess Diana.[138] Similar descriptions for men include "jock," "pretty boy," and "bookworm," or a "Brad Pitt type," a "Wesley Snipes type," and so on.

The Western Ideal of Beauty

Beauty is about more than aesthetics. We use cues such as skin color and eye shape to make inferences about a person's status, sophistication, and social desirability. People in less powerful cultures tend to adopt the standards of beauty prevalent in dominant cultures. For example, an ad on Malaysian television showed an attractive college student who can't get a second glance from a boy at the next desk. "She's pretty," he says to himself, "but. . . . " Then she applies Pond's Skin Lightening Moisturizer by Unilever PLC, and she reappears looking several shades paler. Now the boy wonders, "Why didn't I notice her before?" In many Asian cultures, people historically equate light skin with wealth and status, and they associate dark skin with the laboring class that toils in the fields. This stereotype persists today: In a survey, 74 percent of men in Malaysia, 68 percent in Hong Kong, and 55 percent in Taiwan said they are more attracted to women with fair complexions. About a third of the female respondents in each country said they use skin-whitening products. Olay has a product it calls White Radiance, and L'Oréal sells a White Perfect line.[139]

As media images of glamorous American (Caucasian) celebrities proliferate around the globe, women who buy into the Western ideal of beauty—big round eyes, tiny waists, large breasts, blond hair, and blue eyes—literally go under the knife to achieve these attributes:

- A model, who was the local spokeswoman for Lux soap and Omega watches, became the first blue-eyed Miss Thailand. She's one of a generation of racially mixed Thais who now dominate the local fashion and entertainment industries as the public abandons the round face, arched eyebrows, and small mouth of the classical Thai look in favor of a Western ideal. Many buy blue contact lenses to enhance their looks. In a poll to name the sexiest men and the sexiest women in Thailand, seven out of the nine top scorers were of mixed blood.[140] The Thai language reflects the stigma of darker skin. One common insult is *tua dam,* or "black body," and another is *dam tap pet,* or "black like a duck's liver."[141]

- Year after year, winners of the Most Beautiful Girl in Nigeria performed very poorly in the Miss World competition. Local organizers had about given up on the idea that an African woman could win a contest that Western beauties dominated. Then a Nigerian woman went on to win the Miss World title. She was the first African winner in the contest's 51-year history. However, pride mixed with puzzlement: The new Miss World didn't possess the voluptuous figure African culture prized. In West and Central Africa, people revere big women; many beauty contestants weigh more than 200 pounds. In Niger, women even eat livestock feed or special vitamins to bulk up. The Calabari in southeastern Nigeria send prospective brides to fattening farms, where they are fed huge amounts of food and massaged into rounder shapes. After weeks of this regimen, the bigger brides proudly parade in the village square.[142] As one African explained, "Plumpness means prosperity. Thin represents everything you don't want: poverty, AIDS, and other diseases, misery and hunger." In contrast, the contest winner is 6 feet tall and skinny. Older Nigerians did not find the winner especially attractive at all, and some bitingly described her as a white girl in black skin. But younger people feel different. For them, thin is in. In Lagos, fashionable thin girls are called *lepa* and there is even a popular song with this title. A movie called *Lepa Shandi* celebrates the more svelte look—the title means a girl as slim as a 20-naira bill.[143]

- Japanese retailers are scrambling to stock larger dress sizes to keep up with a new look the fashion industry calls *bonkyu-bon.* This means "big-small-big" and it stands for a change in that culture's body ideal: Japanese women are getting curvier. Today, the average Japanese woman's hips, at 35 inches, are about an inch wider than those of women a generation older. Women in their 20s wear bras at least two sizes larger than those of their mothers, whereas waist sizes have gotten smaller. The government reports that the average 20-year-old is also nearly 3 inches taller than she was in 1950. These changes are the result of a diet that is becoming more Westernized; the traditional meal of fish, vegetables, and tofu is now more likely to have been replaced by a meal of red meat, dairy, and decadent desserts such as Krispy Kreme doughnuts and Cold Stone Creamery ice cream. Juicy Couture, known for its figure-hugging terrycloth tracksuits, opened one of its biggest stores in Tokyo, and other department stores feature larger sizes from other American designers. Wacoal Corp., Japan's largest lingerie company, was once known for its super-padded brassieres. Now the company has a new bestseller: the "Love Bra," a cleavage-boosting creation with less padding, aimed at curvier women in their 20s.[144]

Ideals of Beauty over Time

Although beauty may be only skin deep, throughout history women have worked very hard to attain it. They have starved themselves; painfully bound their feet; inserted plates into their lips; spent countless hours under hair dryers, in front of mirrors, and beneath tanning lights; and opted for breast reduction or enlargement operations to alter their appearance and meet their society's expectations of what a beautiful woman should look like.

We often characterize periods of history by a specific "look," or ideal of beauty. Often these relate to broader cultural happenings, such as today's emphasis on fitness and toned bodies. A look at U.S. history reveals a succession of dominant ideals. For example, in sharp contrast to today's emphasis on health and vigor, in the early 1800s it was fashionable to appear delicate to the point of looking ill. The poet John Keats described the ideal woman of that time as "a milk white lamb that bleats for man's protection." Other past looks include the voluptuous, lusty woman that Lillian Russell made popular; the athletic Gibson Girl of the 1890s; and the small, boyish flapper of the 1920s exemplified by the silent movie actress Clara Bow.[145]

In much of the 19th century, the desirable waistline for U.S. women was 18 inches, a circumference that required the use of corsets pulled so tight that they routinely caused headaches, fainting spells, and possibly even the uterine and spinal disorders common among women of the time. Although modern women are not quite as "straight-laced," many still endure such indignities as high heels, body waxing, eyelifts, and liposuction. In addition to the millions women spend on cosmetics, clothing, health clubs, and fashion magazines, these practices remind us that—rightly or wrongly—the desire to conform to current standards of beauty is alive and well.

Our culture communicates these standards—subtly and not so subtly—virtually everywhere we turn: on magazine covers, in department store windows, on TV shows.

College student Galia Slayen created a "life-size" Barbie (39″ bust, 18″ waist and 33″ hips) for an eating disorders awareness event at her college. When she was interviewed on NBC's Today Show about the impact the doll had on her as she was growing up, she commented, "I'm not blaming Barbie [for her own eating disorder] . . . . "I'm blond and blue-eyed and I figured that was what I was supposed to look like. She was my idol. It impacted the way I looked at myself."

Source: Courtesy of Galia Slayen.

Feminists argue that fashion dolls, such as the ubiquitous Barbie, reinforce an unnatural ideal of thinness. When we extrapolate the dimensions of these dolls to average female body sizes, indeed they are unnaturally long and thin.[146] If the traditional Barbie doll were a real woman, her dimensions would be 38-18-34! Mattel conducted "plastic surgery" on Barbie to give her a less pronounced bust and slimmer hips, but she is still not exactly dumpy.[147] The company now sells an even more realistic Barbie featuring wider hips and a smaller bust (and for the first time Barbie has a belly button).[148]

As we've seen, the ideal body type of Western women changes over time—check out portraits of models from several hundred years ago by Botticelli and others to appreciate by just how much. These changes periodically cause us to redefine *sexual dimorphic markers*—those aspects of the body that distinguish between the sexes. The first part of the 1990s saw the emergence of the controversial "waif" look in which successful models (most notably Kate Moss) were likely to have bodies that resembled those of young boys. Using heights and weights from winners of the Miss America pageant, nutrition experts concluded that many beauty queens were in the undernourished range. In the 1920s, contestants had a body mass index in the range now considered normal (20 to 25). Since then, an increasing number of winners have had indexes under 18.5, which is the World Health Organization's standard for undernutrition.[149]

Similarly, a study of almost 50 years of *Playboy* centerfolds shows that the women have become less shapely and more androgynous since Marilyn Monroe graced the first edition with a voluptuous hourglass figure of 37-23-36. However, a magazine spokesman comments, "As time has gone on and women have become more athletic, more in the business world and more inclined to put themselves through fitness regimes, their bodies have changed, and we reflect that as well. But I would think that no one with eyes to see would consider playmates to be androgynous."[150] Fair enough. Indeed, a recent reexamination of centerfold data for the years 1979 to 1999 shows that the trend toward increasing thinness seems to have stabilized and may actually have begun to reverse. Still, although the women shown in the magazine became somewhat heavier over the 21-year period the researchers reviewed, the Playmates remain markedly below weights medical experts consider normal for their age group.[151]

Is the Ideal Getting Real?

Fed up because you don't get mistaken for a svelte supermodel on the street? Dove's well-known Campaign for Real Beauty that features women with imperfect bodies in their underwear may help. One ad reads, "Let's face it, firming the thighs of a size 8 supermodel wouldn't have been much of a challenge." Unilever initiated the campaign after its research showed that many women didn't believe its products worked because the women shown using them were so unrealistic.[152] When the company asked 3,200 women around the world to describe their looks, most summed themselves up as "average" or "natural." Only 2 percent called themselves "beautiful."

Marketers of its Dove brand sensed an opportunity, and they set out to reassure women about their insecurities by showing them as they are—wrinkles, freckles, pregnant bellies, and all. Taglines ask "Oversized or Outstanding?" or "Wrinkled or Wonderful?" The brand also sponsored a survey of 1,800 American women to assess how they felt about their looks. Overall, they found that women were satisfied with who they are, and these positive feelings were even stronger in subgroups such as African American and Hispanic women, younger women, and wealthier women. Fifty-two percent of women between the ages of 18 and 39 said that "looking beautiful" describes them very well, whereas 37 percent of women aged 40 and older felt the same. Furthermore, 75 percent of the women agreed that beauty does not come from a woman's looks but from her spirit and love of life. Only 26 percent felt that our society uses reasonable standards to evaluate women's beauty.[153]

However, Unilever's experience with Chinese women reminds us again that appearance norms are strongly rooted in culture. Dove's Campaign for Real Beauty flopped in China; after the fact Unilever's research showed that many Chinese women *do* believe they can attain the kind of airbrushed beauty they see in advertising. As a result the company scrapped the campaign there and instead launched a Chinese version of *Ugly Betty*—a

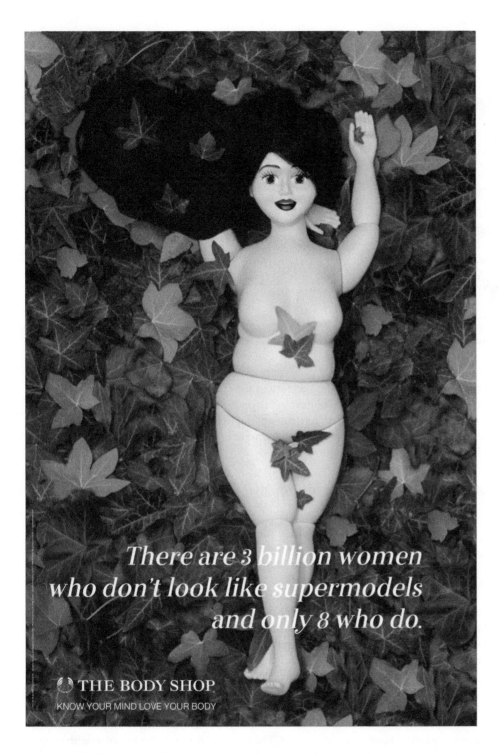

The Body Shop taps into the growing sentiment against unrealistic ideals of beauty.

Source: Reproduced with the kind permission of The Body Shop International, plc.

successful American sitcom, which was in turn adapted from a Colombian telenovela. The show, *Ugly Wudi*, focuses on fictional ad agency employee Lin Wudi, who strives to unveil her own beauty, aided by the numerous Dove products that appear in the show. As you might expect, it helps that the actress who played Wudi has perfect skin and actually is quite attractive once you strip away the oversized glasses and the fake braces.[154]

Male Ideals of Beauty

We also distinguish among ideals of beauty for men in terms of facial features, musculature, and facial hair—who could confuse Justin Bieber with Johnny Depp? In fact, one national survey that asked both men and women to comment on male aspects of

Advertising often reflects a dominant standard of beauty for men.
Source: Courtesy of Simplot Australia.

appearance found that the dominant standard of beauty for men is a strongly masculine, muscled body—though women tend to prefer men with less muscle mass than men themselves strive to attain.[155] Advertisers appear to have the males' ideal in mind; a study of men who appear in advertisements found that most sport the strong and muscular physique of the male stereotype.[156]

OBJECTIVE 5

Our desire to live up to cultural expectations of appearance can be harmful.

Working on the Body

The Japanese company Wacoal recently launched a men's girdle to flatten big stomachs. Levi Strauss introduced Levi's Ultimate Lift 544, a new figure-enhancing jean for women. The new style creates a cup shape in each seat panel to mold the wearer's derriere.[157] No doubt, there's a lot of shaping going on out there.

Because many consumers experience a gap between their real and ideal physical selves, they often go to great lengths to change aspects of their appearance. From girdles to bras, cosmetics to plastic surgery, tanning salons to diet drinks, a multitude of products and services promise to alter aspects of the physical self. It is difficult to overstate the importance of the physical self-concept (and consumers' desires to improve their appearances) to many marketing activities.

Fattism

As the expression "You can never be too thin or too rich" reminds us, it's no secret that our society has an obsession with weight. The media continually bombard us with images of thin, happy people. In one survey, more than twice as many female respondents said they were concerned about their weight than about cancer, heart disease, or diabetes. Only 40 percent said they were satisfied with their physical appearance.[158]

Fattism is deeply ingrained in our culture: As early as nursery school age, children prefer drawings of peers in wheelchairs, on crutches, or with facial disfigurements to those of fat children. One survey of girls aged 12 to 19 reported that 55 percent said they see ads "all the time" that make them want to go on a diet.[159] One advertising controversy from 2011 testifies to our thinness mania: It was bad enough when Pepsi unveiled its new "skinny" diet soda can. When the company paired the launch with Fashion Week—the huge promotion for an industry that celebrates skinny models (some of whom have died from anorexia)—the National Eating Disorders Association protested and Pepsi had to apologize. The organization also persuaded Apple to shut down its first iPod ad campaign because it was built around the message, "You can never be too thin or too powerful."[160]

Although Americans' obsession with weight is legendary worldwide, a cultural priority on thinness is spreading—even as obesity rates around the globe skyrocket:

- In traditional Fijian culture the body ideal for females is, to put it delicately, robust. When a woman started to lose weight in Fiji, this was cause for concern and a sign of probable illness. Then, a few years ago the island finally got satellite TV feeds that exposed Fijians for the first time to American TV shows, such as *Melrose Place* and *Beverly Hills 90210,* that feature casts of skinny stars. Now the tables have turned, as teenage girls in Fiji exhibit eating disorders. A study found that teens who watched TV three or more nights per week were 50 percent more likely to feel too fat than were other girls. Participants cited actresses such as Heather Locklear as inspiration to change their bodies.[161] As in Fiji, Egyptians traditionally preferred somewhat plumper women—and the belly dancing tradition encouraged this. Now, though, weight-loss diets are fashionable.

- The head of Egyptian television announced that overweight female newscasters had 3 months to shed those extra pounds (10 to 20 pounds in most cases) or he would fire them. A popular television exercise show encourages weight loss—but in deference to Islamic sensibilities, the female exercisers wear only loose-fitting clothes even though they do aerobic exercises, and the women aren't allowed to breathe too heavily.[162]

- Japan now requires companies and local governments to measure the waistlines of citizens between the ages of 40 and 74 as part of their annual checkups. Persons who exceed government limits—33.5 inches for men and 35.4 inches for women—are provided with medical education. Eventually the government plans to impose financial penalties on organizations that fail to meet weight targets.[163]

- Jump over to Europe, where the diet brand Slim-Fast tackled a common stereotype: British women are the plump ones on the beaches of Europe. The United Kingdom has the highest obesity rate in Europe; nearly one in five of all 15-year-olds are overweight. The company ran ads that rally British women to lose weight or lose face to their sexier Continental counterparts in France, Spain, and Sweden. In one Slim-Fast ad, a French model says, "I love British women. They make me look great." In another spot, a shapely Spanish woman scolds, "Face it, British women, it's not last year's bikini getting smaller."[164]

Cosmetic Surgery

Consumers increasingly choose to have cosmetic surgery to change a poor body image or simply to enhance appearance.[167] In Venezuela, billboards advertise bank loans to obtain breast augmentations; a political candidate even tried to finance his campaign by raffling off a breast lift.[168] As the middle class booms in China, cosmetic surgery is now the fourth most popular way to spend discretionary income—only houses, cars, and travel rank higher. The most popular surgeries make eyes appear larger by adding a crease in the eyelid to form what doctors call a double eyelid. The second most popular operation raises the bridge of the nose to make it more prominent (the opposite of the typical nose job in the West). Young people often request these procedures as a high school graduation present to enhance their prospects in the competitive job market.[169]

According to the American Academy of Cosmetic Surgery, doctors in the U.S.A. perform nearly 860,000 cosmetic-surgery procedures each year—and men make up more than 150,000 of the patients. As cosmetic surgery becomes increasingly acceptable (even expected in some circles), consumers and the medical profession expand the scope of body parts they want to alter. Perhaps spurred by fashions such as low-rise jeans and spandex workout gear that call attention to the derrière, for example, buttock augmentation surgery is gaining in popularity. The operation typically costs about $20,000, so clearly it's not intended for the bottom of the market.[170]

The craze for "modifications" even extends to younger consumers who (one would think) don't need it—at least not yet. The American Society of Plastic Surgeons reports that about 12,000 Botox injections are given to U.S. teens aged 13 to 19 annually. Although

Marketing Opportunity

The size and shape of the "average" U.S. consumer today is dramatically different from what it was 60 years ago. The U.S. government estimates that two-thirds of American adults are overweight or obese. Nevertheless, apparel companies still develop clothing lines based on a 1941 military study that set sizing standards based on a small sample of mostly white, young (and presumably physically fit) female soldiers.

Those standards are finally starting to change, because the typical woman's body is no longer as "petite" as it used to be. The most commonly purchased dress today is a size 14; it was a size 8 in 1985! Slowly but surely, standards change as many women reject the unrealistic body ideal of the waif and subscribe to the battle cry: "Big is beautiful!" The popularity of "full-figured" women, such as Oprah, Queen Latifah, and Rosie O'Donnell, and plus-size spokesmodels, such as Emme, also has helped to improve the self-esteem of larger women. In reality, plus-size clothes have been available for more than 90 years, ever since a Lithuanian immigrant, Lena Bryant (her name was later misspelled as "Lane" on a business form), transformed a maternity-wear business into a line for stout women in the 1920s. Today, mass-market stores like Forever 21 and Target and expensive designers like Elie Tahari have turned their attention to the larger woman, and with good reason: In a recent 12-month period, the plus-size market increased 1.4 percent while the market for overall women's apparel declined 0.8 percent.

In addition, standards based on this outdated snapshot of U.S. women need to recognize the diversity of today's ethnic population: According to current criteria, 78 percent of African American women and 72 percent of Hispanic women are overweight, compared with 58 percent of white women. Non-Caucasian body shapes differ as well: for example, Hispanic Americans and Asian Americans tend to be shorter than their Caucasian counterparts.

The clothing industry can't take the market potential of this segment lightly. Women spend about $47 billion on plus-size garments each year, which accounts for 20 percent of the total apparel market. Now, the apparel industry sponsors Size USA, an ambitious project to revamp the way we think about body size and shape. This survey uses sophisticated 3-D body scanners to

there are some sound medical reasons for this, such as abnormal twitching of the eyelid or involuntary contractions of neck muscles, apparently most young patients elect the treatment to address perceived imperfections such as a too-gummy smile and a too-square jaw. Some teenagers mistakenly think that Botox can prevent wrinkles.[171]

Virtually any body part is fair game for surgical alteration. Bellybutton reconstruction is a popular form of cosmetic surgery in Japan. The navel is an important part of Japanese culture, and mothers often save a baby's umbilical cord in a wooden box. In Japanese, a "bent navel" is a grouch, and a phrase meaning "give me a break" translates as "yeah, and I brew tea in my bellybutton." A popular insult among children is "Your mother has an outie."[172] Interest in the United States tends to center elsewhere. Popular operations for men include the implantation of silicon pectoral muscles (for the chest) and even calf implants to fill out "chicken legs."[173]

Traveling upward, our culture tends to equate breast size with sex appeal. Consumer research that an underwear company performed demonstrates the impact of breast size on self-concept. While she conducted focus groups on bras, an analyst noted that small-chested women typically reacted with hostility when they discussed the subject. The participants would unconsciously cover their chests with their arms as they spoke and complained that the fashion industry ignored them. To meet this overlooked need, the company introduced a line of A-cup bras it called "A-OK"—and gave birth to a new market segment.

Some women elect to have breast augmentation procedures because they feel that larger breasts will increase their allure.[174] Although some of these procedures have generated controversy as a result of negative side effects, it is unclear whether potential medical problems will deter large numbers of women from choosing surgical options to enhance their (perceived) femininity. And, as Lisa discovered, many companies promote nonsurgical alterations by pushing push-up bras that merely create the illusion of larger cleavage. These products offer "cleavage enhancement" that uses a combination of wires and internal pads (the industry calls them "cookies") to create the desired effect.

OBJECTIVE 6	Body Decoration and Mutilation

OBJECTIVE 6

Every culture dictates certain types of body decoration or mutilation.

Body Decoration and Mutilation

People in every culture adorn or alter their bodies in some way. Decorating the self serves a number of purposes:[175]

- **To separate group members from nonmembers**—The Chinook, Native Americans of North America, pressed the head of a newborn between two boards for a year, which permanently altered its shape. In our society, teens go out of their way to adopt distinctive hair and clothing styles that will separate them from adults.
- **To place the individual in the social organization**—Many cultures engage in puberty rites during which a boy symbolically becomes a man. Some young men in part of Ghana paint their bodies with white stripes to resemble skeletons to symbolize the death of their child status. In Western cultures, this rite may involve some form of mild self-mutilation or engaging in dangerous activities.
- **To place the person in a gender category**—The Tchikrin, Native Americans of South America, insert a string of beads in a boy's lip to enlarge it. Western women wear lipstick to enhance femininity. At the turn of the 20th century, small lips were fashionable because they represented women's submissive role at that time.[176] Today, big, red lips are provocative and indicate an aggressive sexuality. Some women, including a number of famous actresses and models, receive collagen injections or lip inserts to create large, pouting lips (insiders in the modeling industry call them "liver lips").[177]
- **To enhance sex-role identification**—We can compare the modern use of high heels, which podiatrists agree are a prime cause of knee and hip problems, backaches, and fatigue, with the traditional Asian practice of foot binding to enhance femininity. As one doctor observed, "When [women] get home, they can't get their high-heeled shoes off fast enough. But every doctor in the world could yell from now until Doomsday, and women would still wear them."[178]

- **To indicate desired social conduct**—The Suya of South America wear ear ornaments to emphasize the importance placed on listening and obedience in their culture. In Western society, some gay men may wear an earring in the left or right ear to signal what role (submissive or dominant) they prefer in a relationship.
- **To indicate high status or rank**—The Hidates, Native Americans of North America, wear feather ornaments that indicate how many people they have killed. In our society, some people wear glasses with clear lenses, even though they do not have eye problems, to enhance their perceived status.
- **To provide a sense of security**—Consumers often wear lucky charms, amulets, and rabbits' feet to protect them from the "evil eye." Some modern women wear a "mugger whistle" around their necks for a similar reason.

Tattoos

Mattel Inc. recently released Totally Stylin' Tattoos Barbie, which comes with tiny tattoos her young owners can put on her body. The doll also comes with wash-off tats kids can use to ink themselves.[179] The singer Beyoncé also introduced a line of temporary tattoos at Sephora that include a photo of her in a blond updo draped over a motorcycle.[180]

Tattoos—both temporary and permanent—today are a popular form of body adornment.[181] Although consumers young and old (okay, mostly young) sport body art to make statements about the self, these skin designs actually serve some of the same functions that other kinds of body painting do in primitive cultures. Tattoos (from the Tahitian *ta-tu*) have deep roots in folk art. Until recently, the images were crude and were primarily death symbols (e.g., a skull), animals (especially panthers, eagles, and snakes), pinup women, or military designs. More current influences include science fiction themes, Japanese symbolism, and tribal designs.

Historically, people associated tattoos with social outcasts. For example, authorities in sixth-century Japan tattooed the faces and arms of criminals to identify them, and these markings served the same purpose in 19th-century prisons and 20th-century concentration camps. Marginal groups, such as bikers or Japanese *yakuze* (gang members), often use these emblems to express group identity and solidarity.

Today, a tattoo is a fairly risk-free way to express an adventurous side of the self. A Harris Poll reported that one-third of Americans aged 25 to 29 and one-fourth of those between 30 and 39 have tattoos. Consistent with our previous discussion, when we compare respondents who sport a tattoo to those who don't, the latter are more likely to think that people who have one are deviant and rebellious. In contrast, one-third of those who do have a tattoo say it makes them feel sexier.[182]

As more people jump on the tattoo bandwagon (the FDA estimates that 17 million Americans have gotten inked), it's inevitable that some of them will regret this decision later (perhaps when they wake up in the morning?). Tattoo removal centers with names such as Dr. Tattoff, Tat2BeGone, and Tattoo MD meet the need to deal with so-called "tattoo regret." One industry member estimates that as many as 100,000 Americans undergo tattoo removal each year. Unfortunately—at least for now—it's a lot more complicated to remove a tattoo than to put one on you. A design that cost several hundred dollars could require several thousand dollars and many laser sessions to remove. A special laser device shatters tattoo pigment into particles that the body's lymphatic system clears. Full removal takes an average of eight treatments, spaced at least a month apart, using different lasers for different colored inks.[183] The moral: Before you get a significant other's name etched onto your body, be pretty sure you plan to stay together.

Body Piercing

Decorating the body with various kinds of metallic inserts also has evolved from a practice associated with fringe groups to a popular fashion statement. Historians credit the initial impetus for the mainstreaming of what had been an underground West Coast fad to Aerosmith's 1993 video "Cryin'," in which Alicia Silverstone gets both a navel ring and a tattoo.[184] Piercings can range from a hoop protruding from a navel to scalp implants;

measure the complete physical dimensions of 10,000 people who represent the entire U.S. population. If and when these new standards make their way into designers' lines, today's size 14 might become tomorrow's size 8.

Furthermore, while many companies such as NutriSystem, Jenny Craig, and Weight Watchers address the need to lose weight, other companies see a chance to earn their weight in gold. One of these is the Casual Male Retail Group, which owns Casual Male XL, the nation's largest chain of men's plus-size clothing and apparel stores. The company targets the largely untapped market for specialty products that make life easier for the growing population of obese men and women. In its LivingXL catalog, you can buy a lawn chair that supports up to 800 pounds, or a "Big John" toilet seat with a 1,200-pound capacity.[165]

Still, the plus-size market can be a tough sell. As the woman who founded "Full-Figured Fashion Week" observed, "I've been told several times that no one fantasizes about being a plus-size woman, and that's probably true, but the fact remains that you have to work with what you have." Larger women have some shopping issues their smaller counterparts don't worry about. Some don't like to try on clothes in the same fitting rooms as smaller women. Plus-size stocks take up valuable storage space, and not everyone is big in the same way, meaning stores cannot count on, say, a size 16 dress fitting most 180-pound women—one might have a larger torso, another bigger thighs and another wider hips. Big opportunities wait for companies to address the needs of larger women: women's plus-size clothing still makes up only 17 percent of the women's apparel market today, even though many of us get bigger each year.[166]

• • • • • • • • • • • • •

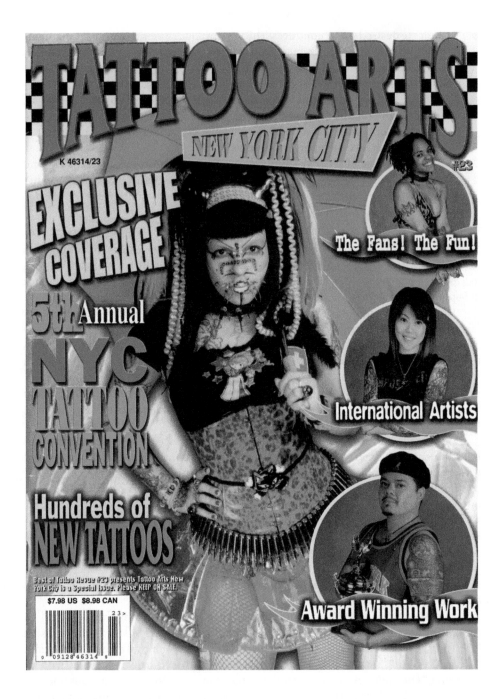

where metal posts are inserted in the skull (do not try this at home!). Publications such as *Piercing Fans International Quarterly* see their circulations soar, and Web sites attract numerous followers.

Body Image Distortions

In less than two months, four young Brazilian women died in widely publicized cases of anorexia, which sparked an international debate about body image and eating disorders. The first to die was a 21-year-old model who stood 5 feet, 8 inches tall but weighed slightly more than 80 pounds when she collapsed at a fashion shoot in Japan. In Spain, the government imposed a controversial ban on extremely thin models as measured by their body mass index, or BMI (a formula that takes into account both height and weight). It requires a BMI greater than 17.4 for female models younger than 18 years old, or 18.5 for models older than 18 years old. For a 5-foot, 9-inch model older than 18, that translates to a weight requirement of 126 pounds. Unilever, in turn, banned the use of so-called "size 0" models in its ads for products ranging from Lux shower gel and Sunsilk shampoo to Slim-Fast diet drinks.[185]

Some people exaggerate the connection between self-esteem and appearance to such an extent that they sacrifice their health to attain what they consider to be a desirable body image. Women in particular tend to pick up messages from the media that the quality of their bodies reflects their self-worth, so it is not surprising that most (though certainly not all) major distortions of body image occur among females.

Men do not tend to differ in ratings of their current figure, their ideal figure, and the figure they think is most attractive to women. In contrast, women rate both the figure they think is most attractive to men and their ideal figure as much thinner than their actual figure.[186] In one survey, two-thirds of college women admitted that they resort to unhealthy behavior to control weight. Advertising messages that convey an image of slimness help to reinforce these activities when they arouse insecurities about weight.[187]

Researchers link a distorted body image to eating disorders, which are particularly prevalent among young women. People with *anorexia* perceive themselves as too fat, and they virtually starve themselves in the quest for thinness. This condition often results in *bulimia*, which involves two stages. First, binge eating occurs (usually in private), in which a person may consume more than 5,000 calories at one time. The binge is followed by induced vomiting, abuse of laxatives, fasting, or overly strenuous exercise—a "purging" process that reasserts the woman's sense of control.

Most eating disorders occur among white, upper-middle-class teens and college-age women. Victims often have brothers or fathers who are hypercritical of their weight, and these disorders are also associated with a history of sexual abuse.[188] In addition, one's peers can encourage binge eating; groups such as athletic teams, cheerleading squads, and sororities may reinforce this practice. In one study of a college sorority, members' popularity within the group increased the more they binged.[189]

Although about 90 percent of the teens whom doctors treat for eating disorders are female, body image disturbances in men may be more widespread than most of us believe. Psychiatrists report increasing cases of **body dysmorphic disorder** (an obsession with perceived flaws in appearance) among young males (the average age of onset is 15). Symptoms of this disorder include excessive checking of mirrors and attempts to camouflage imagined deformities. Eating disorders in males are especially common among jockeys, boxers, and other athletes who must conform to weight requirements.[191]

As with women, media images and products encourage men to attain an unrealistic physique; as we've seen recently in the steroid scandals plaguing major league sports, professional athletes certainly are not immune to this pressure. Consider, for example, that if the dimensions of the original GI Joe action figure were projected onto a real 5-foot 10-inch man, he would have a 32-inch waist, a 44-inch chest, and 12-inch biceps. Or how about the same exercise for the Batman action figure: If this superhero came to life, he would boast a 30-inch waist, 57-inch chest, and 27-inch biceps.[192] Holy steroids, Robin!

The Tangled Web

At least 400 Web sites attract young people with "ana" and "mia," nicknames for anorexia and bulimia. These "communities" offer tips on crash dieting, bingeing, vomiting, and hiding weight loss from concerned parents. Group dieting is a growing problem as consumers patronize blog rings devoted to excessive weight loss—especially when they challenge female college students to lose as much weight as possible before events such as spring break. In one typical post, a woman confessed to eating "one cracker, one strawberry and a little bit of soup" in a 24-hour period, whereas another recounted a lunch of a slice of mango and a stick of gum. These sites, often adorned with photos of ultrathin celebrities and slogans such as "Diet Coke Is Life" appeal to followers of an underground movement called *pro-ana* (pro-anorexia) who sometimes identify themselves in public when they wear red bracelets. As one blog proclaims, "Welcome to the Pro-Ana Webring! Our Mission: To assist all who walk Ana's Path in connecting with like-minded individuals who also Live with AN, EDNOS-restrictive subtype, and/or are practitioners of Volitional Anorexia."[190]

CHAPTER SUMMARY

Now that you have finished reading this chapter you should understand why:

1. The self-concept strongly influences consumer behavior.

Consumers' self-concepts are reflections of their attitudes toward themselves. Whether these attitudes are positive or negative, they will help to guide many purchase decisions; we can use products to bolster self-esteem or to "reward" the self.

2. Products often play a pivotal role in defining the self-concept.

We choose many products because we think that they are similar to our personalities. The symbolic interactionist perspective of the self implies that each of us actually has many selves, and we require a different set of products as props to play each role. We view many things other than the body as part of who we are. People use valued objects, cars, homes, and even attachments to sports teams or national monuments to define the self, when they incorporate these into the extended self.

3. Society's expectations of masculinity and femininity help to determine the products we buy to meet these expectations.

A person's sex-role identity is a major component of self-definition. Conceptions about masculinity and femininity, largely shaped by society, guide the acquisition of "sex-typed" products and services.

The media play a key role in teaching us how to behave as "proper" males and females. Advertising and other media play an important role because they socialize consumers to be male and female. Although traditional women's roles have often been perpetuated in advertising depictions, this situation is changing somewhat. The media do not always portray men accurately either.

4. The way we think about our bodies (and the way our culture tells us we should think) is a key component of self-esteem.

A person's conception of his or her body also provides feedback to self-image. A culture communicates specific ideals of beauty, and consumers go to great lengths to attain these. Many consumer activities involve manipulating the body, whether through dieting, cosmetic surgery, piercing, or tattooing.

5. Our desire to live up to cultural expectations of appearance can be harmful.

Sometimes these activities are carried to an extreme, as people try too hard to live up to cultural ideals. One common manifestation is eating disorders, diseases in which women in particular become obsessed with thinness.

6. Every culture dictates certain types of body decoration or mutilation.

Body decoration or mutilation may serve such functions as separating group members from nonmembers, marking the individual's status or rank within a social organization or within a gender category (e.g., homosexual), or even providing a sense of security or good luck.

KEY TERMS

actual self
agentic goals
androgyny
avatars
badges
body cathexis
body dysmorphic disorder
body image
bromance
communal goals
computer-mediated environments (CMEs)
contemporary young mainstream female achievers (CYMFA)

extended self
fantasy
fattism
gender-bending products
geospatial platforms
Goth subculture
ideal of beauty
ideal self
identity marketing
impression management
looking-glass self
masculinism

metrosexual
self-concept
self-esteem
self-image congruence models
sex roles
sexting
sex-typed traits
social comparison
symbolic interactionism
symbolic self-completion theory
torn self
virtual identities

REVIEW

1 How do Eastern and Western cultures differ in terms of how people think about the self?

2 List three dimensions that describe the self-concept.

3 Compare and contrast the real versus the ideal self. List three products for which a person is likely to use each type of self as a reference point when he or she considers a purchase.

4 What does "the looking-glass self" mean?

5 How do feelings about the self influence the specific brands people buy?

6 Define the extended self and provide three examples.

7 What is the difference between agentic and communal goals?

8 Is masculinity/femininity a biological distinction? Why or why not?

9 Give two examples of sex-typed products.

10 What is body cathexis?

11 Have ideals of beauty in the United States changed during the past 50 years? If so, how?

12 What is fattism?

13 How did tattoos originate?

CONSUMER BEHAVIOR CHALLENGE

■ DISCUSS

1 Shopping for back-to-school "basics" used to mean T-shirts, jeans, socks, and some notebooks. Now, many parents have a new item to add to the list: tattoos. About 45 percent of parents polled say that hair highlights, teeth whitening, even tattoos are among the items they will buy their kids to go back to school.[193] What (if any) age is appropriate for kids to get these grownup additions?

2 Should potential employers have the right to look at your personal Facebook page before they extend a job offer?

3 No doubt one of the biggest marketing buzzwords over the past decade is **metrosexual**: a straight, urban male who is keenly interested in fashion, home design, gourmet cooking, and personal care. A gay writer named Mark Simpson actually coined the term way back in a 1994 article when he "outed" British (and now American) soccer star and pop icon David Beckham as a metrosexual. Simpson noted that Beckham is "almost as famous for wearing sarongs and pink nail polish and panties belonging to his wife, Victoria (aka Posh from the Spice Girls), as he is for his impressive ball skills."[194] Hype aside, how widespread is the metrosexual phenomenon? Do you see men in your age group changing their ideas about acceptable interests for males (e.g., home design, cooking, etc.)?

4 How prevalent is the Western ideal of beauty among your peers? How do you see this ideal evolving now (if at all)?

5 Some historians and social critics say our obsession with thinness is based less on science than on morality. They equate our society's stigmatizing of obese people (treating them as "sick," disabled, or weak) with the Salem witch trials or McCarthyism (the paranoid anticommunism movement of the 1950s). These critics argue that the definition of obesity has often arbitrarily shifted throughout history. Indeed, being slightly overweight was once associated with good health (as we've seen, in some parts of the world, it still is) in a time when many of the most troubling illnesses were wasting diseases such as tuberculosis. Plumpness used to be associated with affluence and the aristocracy (King Louis XIV of France padded his body to look more imposing), whereas today it is associated with the poor and their supposedly bad eating habits.[195]

6 Some authorities are so concerned about the practice of sexting that they are trying to prosecute young people who do this for distributing child pornography. How does sexting reflect on a consumer's self-concept? Should it be a matter for concern?

7 Should fast-food restaurants be liable if customers sue them for contributing to the customers' obesity?

8 How might the creation of a self-conscious state be related to consumers who are trying on clothing in dressing rooms? Does the act of preening in front of a mirror change the dynamics by which people evaluate their product choices? Why?

9 Is it ethical for marketers to encourage infatuation with the self?

10 To date, the bulk of advertising targeted to gay consumers has been placed in exclusively gay media. If it were your decision to make, would you consider using mainstream media as well to reach gays, who constitute a significant proportion of the general population? Or, remembering that members of some targeted segments have serious objections to this practice, especially when the product (e.g., liquor, cigarettes) may be viewed as harmful in some way, should marketers single out gays at all?

11 Some consumer advocates have protested the use of super-thin models in advertising, claiming that these women encourage others to starve themselves to attain the "waif" look. Other critics respond that the media's power to shape behavior has been overestimated, and that it is insulting to people to assume that they are unable to separate fantasy from reality. What do you think?

12 Does sex sell? There's certainly enough of it around, whether in print ads, television commercials, or on Web sites. When Victoria's Secret broadcast a provocative fashion show of skimpy lingerie live on the Web (after advertising the show on the Super Bowl), 1.5 million visitors checked out the site before it crashed as a result of an excessive number of hits. Of course, the retailer was taking a risk because, by its own estimate, 90 percent of its sales are to women. Some of them did not like this display of skin. One customer said she did not feel comfortable watching the Super Bowl ad with her boyfriend: "It's not that I'm offended by it; it just makes me feel inferior." Perhaps the appropriate question is not does sex sell, but *should* sex sell? What are your feelings about the blatant use of sex to sell products? Do you think this tactic works better when selling to men than to women? Does exposure to unbelievably attractive men and women models only make the rest of us "normal" folks unhappy and insecure? Under what conditions (if any) should sex be used as a marketing strategy?

13 Some activists object to Axe's male-focused marketing; they claim that its commercials demean women. In contrast, Dove's campaign has been applauded because it promotes a healthy body image for girls. Guess what? Both Axe and Dove are owned by Unilever. Is it hypocritical for a big company to sponsor positive messages about women in one of its divisions while it sends a different message in another?[196]

14 Millions of people have posted photos at Hot or Not, a popular Web site two engineers founded where visitors rate each picture on a scale from 1 to 10. One of the site's creators remembers, "Basically, we were sitting around drinking beers in the middle of the afternoon when a comment Jim made about a woman he had seen at a party made us think, wouldn't it be cool if there was a Web site where you could tell if a girl was a perfect 10?" The phenomenal

success of the site spawned hundreds of copycats, many of them not exactly the PG-rated environment this site offers. Some of the photos people send in aren't what you would call flattering (especially the ones submitted as jokes on unsuspecting friends); one possible explanation is the psychological concept of self-handicapping, where we set ourselves up for failure so that in case ratings are low we can blame the picture rather than ourselves. Another is that the world is crowded with people so hungry for attention that they will submit to any number of indignities to have others look at them. What do you think—is this practice hot or not?[197]

APPLY

1 Watch a set of ads on TV that feature men and women. Try to imagine the characters with reversed roles (i.e., the male parts played by women and vice versa). Can you see any differences in assumptions about sex-typed behavior?

2 Construct a "consumption biography" of a friend or family member. Make a list of or photograph his or her favorite possessions, and see if you or others can describe this person's personality just from the information provided by this catalog.

3 Interview victims of burglaries, or people who have lost personal property in floods, hurricanes, or other natural disasters. How did they go about reconstructing their possessions, and what effect did the loss appear to have on them? Similarly, poll your class: If their house or apartment was on fire and they could only take one possession with them as they evacuate, what would it be?

4 Locate additional examples of self-esteem advertising. Evaluate the probable effectiveness of these appeals. Is it true that "Flattery gets you everywhere?"

MyMarketingLab Now that you have completed this chapter, return to www.mymktlab.com to apply concepts and explore the additional study materials.

Case Study

RIDING THE PLUS-SIZE WAVE

For years, Hollywood and the advertising media perpetuated a stereotypical image of women. As a result, many consumers have the unrealistic expectation that many women are (or should be) poreless, hipless, silken-haired, high-cheekboned, size 0, 20-year-old goddesses. But is this beauty myth finally changing? Companies like Charming Shoppes, Inc., parent to plus-size retailer Lane Bryant, are doing their darnedest to see that it does.

Lane Bryant was founded in 1900 in New York as the first women's apparel retailer devoted exclusively to plus sizes. Acquired by Charming Shoppes, Inc., in 2001 from Limited Brands Inc., Lane Bryant is part of the retail holding company's strategic plan to pull itself back from the brink of bankruptcy. Now, 74 percent of Charming Shoppes' revenue comes from sales of plus-size apparel.

The future looks even brighter. The apparel industry defines plus-size as 14 and up—today that includes 62 percent of American women. According to Mintel, the plus-size-clothing sector rang up $34 billion in sales in 2008. Although this shift in demographics bodes well for Lane Bryant, the increase in the plus-size market does not directly translate into heftier sales. Plus-size customers tend to spend less as a percentage of their disposable income on apparel compared with women who are junior and misses sizes. Most analysts attribute this gap to the fact that retailers have not done a good job of making fashionable clothing available to larger women. According to one executive, "People are more accepting of their bodies today, and I think there has been a positive influence with role models. Years ago, manufacturers were only interested in making low-end plus-size merchandise because they thought customers were always in transition. Now no longer."

Lane Bryant is fighting this tide. With new product lines and promotional campaigns, the company sends the message that it's not only OK to be a plus-size, but that women in this category can be as stylish as anyone. Lane Bryant focuses on *en vogue* styles previously available only to more modestly sized shoppers. Its strategy includes offering larger sizes in the upscale Seven Jean Collection. It also includes an expansion into the lingerie category with its new Cacique brand. In addition to selling lingerie in Lane Bryant stores, Charming Shoppes is positioning itself as a Victoria's Secret competitor by opening dozens of stand-alone Cacique stores.

Other retailers are noticing this market and beginning to make a move. Will Lane Bryant's efforts change how society perceives the "typical" woman? Charming Shoppes' recent financial performance seems to indicate that this may be the case. Revenue for 2008 was at just over $3 billion. In addition, the company claims to rank number two in women's plus-size sales overall behind Walmart.

Other retailers are also getting in the game. Hot Topic, Gap/Old Navy, Target, Lands' End, Saks Fifth Avenue, and Macy's are among national retailers offering or expanding their assortments of plus apparel sizes and increasing promotional efforts for this category. With these industry changes, who knows what images of women the media of the future will celebrate?

DISCUSSION QUESTIONS

1 Explain the success that Lane Bryant is currently experiencing in relation to self-concept, self-esteem, and self-consciousness. How can the plus-size industry leverage what we know about consumer behavior to address self-esteem issues?

2 Discuss the real-world changes that appear to be occurring with respect to media images of women. What are the reasons for this?

3 How do you reconcile the greater degree of acceptance of plus-size women with the parallel emphasis our society continues to place on thinness (as evidenced by the billions we spend on diet products, exercise, and so on)? Given the health problems associated with obesity (heart disease, diabetes, etc.) should the industry continue to encourage this acceptance?

Sources: http://cacique.lanebryant.com, accessed June 13, 2011; www.spoke.com, accessed May 23, 2009; "Plus Size Teens and Women—US—November 2008," *Mintel Oxygen*, accessed May 23, 2009; Leigh Gragan, "Looking Good: Plus-Size Styles Are All about the Fashion," *McClatchy Tribune Business News* (March 26, 2008); Keiko Morris, "Finding Both Fashion and Fit: Plus-Size Retailing Is Becoming Hot as Demand Grows for Trendy Clothing in Size 14 and Up," *Knight Ridder Tribune Business News* (May 28, 2007): 1.

NOTES

1. http://wiki.answers.com/Q/Who_has_the_most_Twitter_followers, accessed May 28, 2011.
2. Harry C. Triandis, "The Self and Social Behavior in Differing Cultural Contexts," *Psychological Review* 96, no. 3 (1989): 506–20; H. Markus and S. Kitayama, "Culture and the Self: Implications for Cognition, Emotion, and Motivation," *Psychological Review* 98 (1991): 224–53.
3. Markus and Kitayama, "Culture and the Self."
4. Nancy Wong and Aaron Ahuvia, "A Cross-Cultural Approach to Materialism and the Self," in Dominique Bouchet, ed., *Cultural Dimensions of International Marketing* (Denmark: Odense University, 1995): 68–89.
5. Lisa M. Keefe, "You're So Vain," *Marketing News* (February 28, 2000): 8.
6. Morris Rosenberg, *Conceiving the Self* (New York: Basic Books, 1979); M. Joseph Sirgy, "Self-Concept in Consumer Behavior: A Critical Review," *Journal of Consumer Research* 9 (December 1982): 287–300; www.mediapost.com, accessed February 15, 2007; Roy F. Baumeister, Dianne M. Tice, and Debra G. Hutton, "Self-Presentational Motivations and Personality Differences in Self-Esteem," *Journal of Personality* 57 (September 1989): 547–75; Ronald J. Faber, "Are Self-Esteem Appeals Appealing?" in Leonard N. Reid, ed., *Proceedings of the 1992 Conference of the American Academy of Advertising* (1992): 230–35.
7. Jeremy N. Bailenson, Shanto Iyengar, Nick Yee, and Nathan A. Collins, "Facial Similarity Between Candidates Causes Influence," *Public Opinion Quarterly* 72, no. 5 (2008): 935–61.
8. Emily Yoffe, "You Are What You Buy," *Newsweek* (June 4, 1990): 59.
9. Derek D. Rucker, David Dubois, and Adam D. Galinsky, "Generous Paupers and Stingy Princes: Power Drives Consumer Spending on Self versus Others," *Journal of Consumer Research* 37, no. 6 (April 2011): 1015-1029.
10. Christine Bittar, "Alberto-Culver Ties Hair Relaxer to Self-Esteem," www.mediapost.com, accessed February 15, 2007; www.texturesoftener.com, accessed May 29, 2009.
11. Michael Hafner, "How Dissimilar Others May Still Resemble the Self: Assimilation and Contrast after Social Comparison," *Journal of Consumer Psychology* 14, nos. 1 & 2 (2004): 187–96.
12. Marsha L. Richins, "Social Comparison and the Idealized Images of Advertising," *Journal of Consumer Research* 18 (June 1991): 71–83; Mary C. Martin and Patricia F. Kennedy, "Advertising and Social Comparison: Consequences for Female Preadolescents and Adolescents," *Psychology & Marketing* 10 (November–December 1993): 513–30.
13. Philip N. Myers, Jr., and Frank A. Biocca, "The Elastic Body Image: The Effect of Television Advertising and Programming on Body Image Distortions in Young Women," *Journal of Communication* 42 (Summer 1992): 108–33.
14. Charles S. Gulas and Kim McKeage, "Extending Social Comparison: An Examination of the Unintended Consequences of Idealized Advertising Imagery," *Journal of Advertising* 29 (Summer 2000): 17–28.
15. Brent McFerran, Darren W. Dahl, Gavan J. Fitzsimons, and Andrea C. Morales, "Might an Overweight Waitress Make You Eat More? How the Body Type of Others Is Sufficient to Alter Our Food Consumption," *Journal of Consumer Psychology* 20, no. 2 (2010), 146–51; cf. also Michael Häfner and Debra Trampe, "When Thinking Is Beneficial and When It Is Not: The Effects of Thin and Round Advertising Models," *Journal of Consumer Psychology* 19, no. 4 (2009): 619–28.
16. https://foursquare.com/user/2509238/badges/foursquare, accessed May 28, 2011; Rob Walker, "Lifelong Earning," *New York Times* (June 11, 2010), http://www.nytimes.com/2010/06/13/magazine/13fobconsumed-t.html?emc=eta1, accessed April 10, 2011.
17. For the seminal treatment of this process, cf. Erving Goffman, *The Presentation of Self in Everyday Life* (New York: Doubleday, 1959).
18. Quoted in Michael Slackman, "Fashion and Faith Meet, on Foreheads of the Pious," *New York Times* (December 18, 2007), www.nytimes.com, accessed December 18, 2007.
19. Quoted in Alexia Tsotsis, "Cloud Girlfriend Launches as a Dating Site, NOT a Virtual Girlfriend Service," *Tech Crunch* (April 26, 2011), http://techcrunch.com/2011/04/26/cloud-girlfriend-launches-as-a-dating-site-not-a-virtual-girlfriend-service/, accessed May 28, 2011.
20. Harrison G. Gough, Mario Fioravanti, and Renato Lazzari, "Some Implications of Self versus Ideal-Self Congruence on the Revised Adjective Check List," *Journal of Personality & Social Psychology* 44, no. 6 (1983): 1214–20.
21. Steven Jay Lynn and Judith W. Rhue, "Daydream Believers," *Psychology Today* (September 1985): 14.
22. www.taaz.com, accessed May 29, 2009; www.dailymakeover.com, accessed May 29, 2009.
23. http://www.reputation.com/, accessed May 29, 2011.
24. Erving Goffman, *The Presentation of Self in Everyday Life* (Garden City, NY: Doubleday, 1959); Michael R. Solomon, "The Role of Products as Social Stimuli: A Symbolic Interactionism Perspective," *Journal of Consumer Research* 10 (December 1983): 319–29.
25. A. Reed, "Activating the Self-Importance of Consumer Selves: Exploring Identity Salience Effects on Judgments," *Journal of Consumer Research* 31, no. 2 (2004): 286–95.
26. Aliakbar Jafari and Christina Goulding, "'We Are Not Terrorists!' UK-Based Iranians, Consumption Practices and the 'Torn Self,'" *Consumption Markets & Culture* 11 (June 2008): 73–91.
27. Neal Stephenson, *Snow Crash* (New York: Bantam Books, 1992).
28. "Virtual World Reaches 50,000 Virtual Worlds," *San Francisco Chronicle* (March 31, 2011), http://www.sfgate.com/cgi-bin/article.cgi?f=/g/a/2011/03/31/prweb8256005.DTL, accessed May 28, 2011.
29. Natalie Wood and Michael R. Solomon, eds., *Virtual Social Identity* (Newport Beach, CA: Sage, 2010); Peter Svensson, "Study: Virtual Men Are Standoffish Too," *MyFox 21* (February 2007), http://matei.org/ithink/2007/02/22/study-virtual-men-are-standoffish-too-yahoo-news/, accessed February 22, 2007.
30. "Virtual Reality Avatars Created," *The Drum* (February 17, 2011), http://www.thedrum.co.uk/news/2011/02/17/18810-virtual-reality-avatars-created/, accessed April 10, 2011.
31. George H. Mead, *Mind, Self and Society* (Chicago: University of Chicago Press, 1934).
32. Debra A. Laverie, Robert E. Kleine, and Susan Schultz Kleine, "Reexamination and Extension of Kleine, Kleine, and Kernan's Social Identity

Model of Mundane Consumption: The Mediating Role of the Appraisal Process," *Journal of Consumer Research* 28 (March 2002): 659–69.

33. Natasha Singer, "If the Mirror Could Talk (It Can)," *New York Times* (March 18, 2007), www.nytimes.com, accessed March 18, 2007.

34. Charles H. Cooley, *Human Nature and the Social Order* (New York: Scribner's, 1902).

35. J. G. Hull and A. S. Levy, "The Organizational Functions of the Self: An Alternative to the Duval and Wicklund Model of Self-Awareness," *Journal of Personality & Social Psychology* 37 (1979): 756–68; Jay G. Hull, Ronald R. Van Treuren, Susan J. Ashford, Pamela Propsom, and Bruce W. Andrus, "Self-Consciousness and the Processing of Self-Relevant Information," *Journal of Personality & Social Psychology* 54, no. 3 (1988): 452–65.

36. Arnold W. Buss, *Self-Consciousness and Social Anxiety* (San Francisco: Freeman, 1980); Lynn Carol Miller and Cathryn Leigh Cox, "Public Self-Consciousness and Makeup Use," *Personality & Social Psychology Bulletin* 8, no. 4 (1982): 748–51; Michael R. Solomon and John Schopler, "Self-Consciousness and Clothing," *Personality & Social Psychology Bulletin* 8, no. 3 (1982): 508–14.

37. Loraine Lau-Gesk and Aimee Drolet, "The Publicly Self-Conscious Consumer: Prepare to Be Embarrassed," *Journal of Consumer Psychology* 18 (April 2008): 127–36.

38. Morris B. Holbrook, Michael R. Solomon, and Stephen Bell, "A Re-Examination of Self-Monitoring and Judgments of Furniture Designs," *Home Economics Research Journal* 19 (September 1990): 6–16; Mark Snyder, "Self-Monitoring Processes," in Leonard Berkowitz, ed., *Advances in Experimental Social Psychology* (New York: Academic Press, 1979): 85–128.

39. Mark Snyder and Steve Gangestad, "On the Nature of Self-Monitoring: Matters of Assessment, Matters of Validity," *Journal of Personality & Social Psychology* 51 (1986): 125–39; Timothy R. Graeff, "Image Congruence Effects on Product Evaluations: The Role of Self-Monitoring and Public/Private Consumption," *Psychology & Marketing* 13 (August 1996): 481–99; Richard G. Netemeyer, Scot Burton, and Donald R. Lichtenstein, "Trait Aspects of Vanity: Measurement and Relevance to Consumer Behavior," *Journal of Consumer Research* 21 (March 1995): 612–26.

40. "Video Game Company Tries Human Branding," *New York Times* (August 12, 2002), www.nytimes.com, accessed August 12, 2002; Angela Orend-Cunningham, "Corporate Logo Tattoos: Literal Corporate Branding?," *Consumers, Commodities & Consumption* 5, no. 1 (December 2003); www.airnewzealand.com/aboutus/mediacentre/cranial-billboards-campaign.htm, accessed May 29, 2009.

41. "KFC Deploys Human Billboards," *Marketing Daily* (September 22, 2010), http://www.mediapost.com/publications/?fa=Articles.showArticle&art_aid=136160&nid=118926, accessed April 10, 2011.

42. Jack L. Nasar, "Symbolic Meanings of House Styles," *Environment & Behavior* 21 (May 1989): 235–57; E. K. Sadalla, B. Verschure, and J. Burroughs, "Identity Symbolism in Housing," *Environment & Behavior* 19 (1987): 579–87.

43. Solomon, "The Role of Products as Social Stimuli"; Robert E. Kleine III, Susan Schultz-Kleine, and Jerome B. Kernan, "Mundane Consumption and the Self: A Social-Identity Perspective," *Journal of Consumer Psychology* 2, no. 3 (1993): 209–35; Newell D. Wright, C. B. Claiborne, and M. Joseph Sirgy, "The Effects of Product Symbolism on Consumer Self-Concept," in John F. Sherry Jr. and Brian Sternthal, eds., *Advances in Consumer Research 19* (Provo, UT: Association for Consumer Research, 1992): 311–18; Susan Fournier, "A Person-Based Relationship Framework for Strategic Brand Management" (doctoral dissertation, University of Florida, 1994).

44. A. Dwayne Ball and Lori H. Tasaki, "The Role and Measurement of Attachment in Consumer Behavior," *Journal of Consumer Psychology* 1, no. 2 (1992): 155–72.

45. William B. Hansen and Irwin Altman, "Decorating Personal Places: A Descriptive Analysis," *Environment & Behavior* 8 (December 1976): 491–504.

46. Lan Nguyen Chaplin and Deborah Roedder John, "The Development of Self-Brand Connections in Children and Adolescents," *Journal of Consumer Research* 32 (June 2005): 119–29.

47. R. A. Wicklund and P. M. Gollwitzer, *Symbolic Self-Completion* (Hillsdale, NJ: Erlbaum, 1982).

48. Paul Glader, "Avid Boarders Bypass Branded Gear;" *Wall Street Journal* (July 27, 2007): B1.

49. Erving Goffman, *Asylums* (New York: Doubleday, 1961).

50. Floyd Rudmin, "Property Crime Victimization Impact on Self, on Attachment, and on Territorial Dominance," *CPA Highlights, Victims of Crime Supplement* 9, no. 2 (1987): 4–7.

51. Barbara B. Brown, "House and Block as Territory," paper presented at the Conference of the Association for Consumer Research, San Francisco, 1982.

52. Shay Sayre and David Horne, "I Shop, Therefore I Am: The Role of Possessions for Self-Definition," in Shay Sayre and David Horne, eds., *Earth, Wind, and Fire and Water: Perspectives on Natural Disaster* (Pasadena, CA: Open Door Publishers, 1996), 353–70; cf. also Jill G. Klein and Laura

Huang, "After All Is Lost: Meeting the Material Needs of Adolescent Disaster Survivors," *Journal of Public Policy & Marketing* 26, no. 1 (Spring 2007): 1–12.

53. Quoted in Fred Meier, "Girls Named Zoe Lose Suit against Renault for Naming Electric Car Zoe," *DriveOn* (November 10, 2010), http://content.usatoday.com/communities/driveon/post/2010/11/girls-lose-renault-zoe-electric-car-lawsuit-over-name/1, accessed April 10, 2011.

54. Deborah A. Prentice, "Psychological Correspondence of Possessions, Attitudes, and Values," *Journal of Personality & Social Psychology* 53, no. 6 (1987): 993–1002.

55. Jennifer L. Aaker, "The Malleable Self: The Role of Self-Expression in Persuasion," *Journal of Marketing Research* 36 (February 1999): 45–57; Sak Onkvisit and John Shaw, "Self-Concept and Image Congruence: Some Research and Managerial Implications," *Journal of Consumer Marketing* 4 (Winter 1987): 13–24. For a related treatment of congruence between advertising appeals and self-concept, see George M. Zinkhan and Jae W. Hong, "Self-Concept and Advertising Effectiveness: A Conceptual Model of Congruency, Conspicuousness, and Response Mode," in Rebecca H. Holman and Michael R. Solomon, eds., *Advances in Consumer Research 18* (Provo, UT: Association for Consumer Research, 1991): 348–54.

56. C. B. Claiborne and M. Joseph Sirgy, "Self-Image Congruence as a Model of Consumer Attitude Formation and Behavior: A Conceptual Review and Guide for Further Research," paper presented at the Academy of Marketing Science Conference, New Orleans, 1990.

57. Susan Fournier, and Julie L. Yao, "Reviving Brand Loyalty: A Reconceptualization within the Framework of Consumer-Brand Relationships," *International Journal of Research in Marketing* 14, no. 5 (December 1997): 451–72; Caryl E. Rusbult, "A Longitudinal Test of the Investment Model: The Development (and Deterioration) of Satisfaction and Commitment in Heterosexual Involvements," *Journal of Personality & Social Psychology* 45, no. 1 (1983): 101–17.

58. Allison R. Johnson, Maggie Matear, and Matthew Thomson, "A Coal in the Heart: Self-Relevance as a Post-Exit Predictor of Consumer Anti-Brand Actions," *Journal of Consumer Research* 38, no. 1 (June 2011): 108–125.

59. Özlem Sandikci and Güliz Ger, "Aesthetics, Ethics and Politics of the Turkish Headscarf," in Susanne Küchler and Daniel Miller, eds., *Clothing as Material Culture* (Oxford, UK: Berg, 2005): Chapter 4.

60. Marc Lacey, "Where Showing Skin Doesn't Sell, a New Style is a Hit," *New York Times* (March 20, 2006), www.nytimes.com.

61. Jennifer L. Aaker, "The Malleable Self: The Role of Self-Expression in Persuasion," *Journal of Marketing Research* 36 (February 1999): 45–57.

62. A. L. E. Birdwell, "A Study of Influence of Image Congruence on Consumer Choice," *Journal of Business* 41 (January 1964): 76–88; Edward L. Grubb and Gregg Hupp, "Perception of Self, Generalized Stereotypes, and Brand Selection," *Journal of Marketing Research* 5 (February 1986): 58–63.

63. Benedict Carey, "With That Saucy Swagger, She Must Drive a Porsche," *New York Times* (June 13, 2006), www.nytimes.com, accessed June 13, 2006.

64. Ira J. Dolich, "Congruence Relationship between Self-Image and Product Brands," *Journal of Marketing Research* 6 (February 1969): 80–84; Danny N. Bellenger, Earle Steinberg, and Wilbur W. Stanton, "The Congruence of Store Image and Self Image as It Relates to Store Loyalty," *Journal of Retailing* 52, no. 1 (1976): 17–32; Ronald J. Dornoff and Ronald L. Tatham, "Congruence between Personal Image and Store Image," *Journal of the Market Research Society* 14, no. 1 (1972): 45–52.

65. Naresh K. Malhotra, "A Scale to Measure Self-Concepts, Person Concepts, and Product Concepts," *Journal of Marketing Research* 18 (November 1981): 456–64.

66. Ernest Beaglehole, *Property: A Study in Social Psychology* (New York: Macmillan, 1932).

67. Scott Smith, Dan Fisher, and S. Jason Cole, "The Lived Meanings of Fanaticism: Understanding the Complex Role of Labels and Categories in Defining the Self in Consumer Culture," *Consumption, Markets & Culture* 10 (June 2007): 77–94.

68. Russell W. Belk, "Shoes and Self," *Advances in Consumer Research* (2003): 27–33.

69. Park Ji Kyung and Deborah Roedder John, "Got to Get You into My Life: Do Brand Personalities Rub Off on Consumers?" *Journal of Consumer Research* 37, no. 4 (2010), 655–69.

70. Sean D. Hamill, "Students Sue Prosecutor in Cellphone Photos Case," *New York Times* (March 25, 2009), www.nytimes.com/2009/03/26/us/26sextext.html, accessed March 26, 2009.

71. Russell W. Belk, "Possessions and the Extended Self," *Journal of Consumer Research* 15 (September 1988): 139–68.

72. Somini Sengupta, "Attack on Women at an Indian Bar Intensifies a Clash of Cultures," *New York Times* (February 8, 2009), www.nytimes.com, accessed February 8, 2009; Niraj Sheth and Tariq Engineer, "As the Selling Gets Hot, India Tries to Keep Cool, New-Age Dilemma: Too Sexy? Just Fun? The Chocolate Man," *Wall Street Journal* (September 9, 2008), www.wsj.com, accessed September 9, 2008.

73. Diane Goldner, "What Men and Women Really Want . . . to Eat," *New York Times* (March 2, 1994): C1(2).

74. Nina M. Lentini, "McDonald's Tests 'Angus Third Pounder' in California," *Marketing Daily* (March 27, 2007), www.mediapost.com, accessed March 27, 2007.

75. Charles McGrath, "In Harlequin-NASCAR Romance, Hearts Race," *New York Times* (February 19, 2007), www.nytimes.com, accessed February 19, 2007.

76. John F. Sherry, Jr., Robert V. Kozinets, Adam Duhachek, Benet DeBerry-Spence, Krittinee Nuttavuthisit, and Diana Storm, "Gendered Behavior in a Male Preserve: Role Playing at ESPN Zone Chicago," *Journal of Consumer Psychology* 14, nos. 1 & 2 (2004): 151–58.

77. Suzanne Vranica, "Sony Tries to Lure DVR Ad-Skippers," *Wall Street Journal* (September 20, 2006): A20.

78. Thomas Tsu Wee Tan, Lee Boon Ling, and Eleanor Phua Cheay Theng, "Gender-Role Portrayals in Malaysian and Singaporean Television Commercials: An International Advertising Perspective," *Journal of Business Research* 55 (2002): 853–61.

79. Joan Meyers-Levy, "The Influence of Sex Roles on Judgment," *Journal of Consumer Research* 14 (March 1988): 522–30.

80. Anne Eisenberg, "Mars and Venus, on the Net: Gender Stereotypes Prevail," *New York Times* (October 12, 2000), www.nytimes.com, accessed October 12, 2000.

81. Beverly A. Browne, "Gender Stereotypes in Advertising on Children's Television in the 1990s: A Cross-National Analysis," *Journal of Advertising* 27 (Spring 1998): 83–97.

82. Lisa Bannon, "Mattel Sees Untapped Market for Blocks: Little Girls," *Wall Street Journal* (June 6, 2002): B1.

83. Gavin O'Malley, "Study: Men Are from Hulu, Women Are from Facebook," *Online Media Daily* (July 28, 2010), http://www.mediapost.com/publications/?fa=Articles.showArticle&art_aid=132841&nid=117095, accessed April 10, 2011.

84. Elizabeth Landau, "Men See Bikini-Clad Women as Objects, Psychologists Say," *CNN* (February 19, 2009), www.cnnhealth.com, accessed February 19, 2009.

85. Eileen Fischer and Stephen J. Arnold, "Sex, Gender Identity, Gender Role Attitudes, and Consumer Behavior," *Psychology & Marketing* 11 (March–April 1994): 163–82.

86. Sarah Kershaw, "For Teenagers, Hello Means 'How about a Hug?'" *New York Times* (May 27, 2009), www.nytimes.com, accessed May 28, 2009.

87. Clifford Nass, Youngme Moon, and Nancy Green, "Are Machines Gender Neutral? Gender-Stereotypic Responses to Computers with Voices," *Journal of Applied Social Psychology* 27, no. 10 (1997): 864–76; Kathleen Debevec and Easwar Iyer, "Sex Roles and Consumer Perceptions of Promotions, Products, and Self: What Do We Know and Where Should We Be Headed," in Richard J. Lutz, ed., *Advances in Consumer Research 13* (Provo, UT: Association for Consumer Research, 1986): 210–14; Joseph A. Bellizzi and Laura Milner, "Gender Positioning of a Traditionally Male-Dominant Product," *Journal of Advertising Research* (June–July 1991): 72–79.

88. Hillary Chura, "Barton's New High-End Vodka Exudes a 'Macho Personality,'" *Advertising Age* (May 1, 2000): 8; www.thorshammervodka.com, accessed May 29, 2009.

89. Teressa Iezzi, "Dell's Della Debacle an Example of Wrong Way to Target Women," *Advertising Age* (May 25, 2009), www.adage.com, accessed May 25, 2009.

90. Sandra L. Bem, "The Measurement of Psychological Androgyny," *Journal of Consulting & Clinical Psychology* 42 (1974): 155–62; Deborah E. S. Frable, "Sex Typing and Gender Ideology: Two Facets of the Individual's Gender Psychology That Go Together," *Journal of Personality & Social Psychology* 56, no. 1 (1989): 95–108.

91. "Gender-Bending Avatars Suffer Lack of Trust," *SAWF News* (July 11, 2007), http://news.sawf.org/Lifestyle/39848.aspx, accessed July 11, 2007.

92. Geoffrey A. Fowler, "Asia's Lipstick Lads," *Wall Street Journal* (May 27, 2005), www.wsj.com, accessed May 27, 2005.

93. Matt Alt and Hiroko Yoda, "Big Primpin' in Tokyo," *Wired* (May 2007): 46.

94. See D. Bruce Carter and Gary D. Levy, "Cognitive Aspects of Early Sex-Role Development: The Influence of Gender Schemas on Preschoolers' Memories and Preferences for Sex-Typed Toys and Activities," *Child Development* 59 (1988): 782–92; Bernd H. Schmitt, France Le Clerc, and Laurette Dube-Rioux, "Sex Typing and Consumer Behavior: A Test of Gender Schema Theory," *Journal of Consumer Research* 15 (June 1988): 122–27.

95. Carol Gilligan, *In a Different Voice: Psychological Theory and Women's Development* (Cambridge, MA: Harvard University Press, 1982); Joan Meyers-Levy and Durairaj Maheswaran, "Exploring Differences in Males' and Females' Processing Strategies," *Journal of Consumer Research* 18 (June 1991): 63–70.

96. Lynn J. Jaffe and Paul D. Berger, "Impact on Purchase Intent of Sex-Role Identity and Product Positioning," *Psychology & Marketing* (Fall 1988): 259–71; Lynn J. Jaffe, "The Unique Predictive Ability of Sex-Role Identity

97. in Explaining Women's Response to Advertising," *Psychology & Marketing* 11 (September–October 1994): 467–82.

97. Leila T. Worth, Jeanne Smith, and Diane M. Mackie, "Gender Schematicity and Preference for Gender-Typed Products," *Psychology & Marketing* 9 (January 1992): 17–30.

98. Qimei Chen, Shelly Rodgers, and William D. Wells, "Better Than Sex: Identifying Within-Gender Differences Creates More Targeted Segmentation," *Marketing Research* (Winter 2004): 17–22.

99. Christina Goulding and Michael Saren, "Performing Identity: An Analysis of Gender Expressions at the Whitby Goth Festival," *Consumption, Markets & Culture* 12 (March 2009): 27–46; Ayalla Ruvio and Russell Belk, "Conflicting Selves and the Role of Possessions: Exploring Transgenders' Self-Identity Conflict," in Darren W. Dahl, Gita V. Johar, and Stijn M. J. van Osselaer, eds., *Advances in Consumer Research 38* (Duluth, MN: Association for Consumer Research, 2010).

100. Rupal Parekh, "Gender-Bending Brands an Easy Way to Increase Product Reach," *Advertising Age* (March 2, 2009), www.adage.com, accessed March 2, 2009; Sarah Mahoney, "Best Buy Opens Store Designed for Women," *Marketing Daily* (October 6, 2008), www.mediapost.com, accessed October 6, 2008; Kevin Helliker, "The Solution to Hunting's Woes? Setting Sights on Women," *Wall Street Journal* (October 1, 2008), http://online.wsj.com/Article/Sb122281550760292225.Html?Mod=Dist_Smartbrief, accessed October 2, 2008; Stephanie Clifford, "Frito-Lay Tries to Enter the Minds (and Lunch Bags) of Women," *New York Times* (February 24, 2009), www.nytimes.com, accessed February 24, 2009; Karl Greenberg, "Harley Says Guys Ride Back Seat in May," *Marketing Daily* (February 3, 2009), www.mediapost.com, accessed February 3, 2009.

101. Andres Adam Newman, "N.F.L.'s Official Air Freshener Aims at Female Fans, and the Cleanup," *New York Times*, (September 2, 2010), http://www.nytimes.com/2010/09/03/business/media/03adco.html?_r=2&ref=business, accessed April 10, 2011.

102. Eric Bellman, "Suzuki's Stylish Compacts Captivate India's Women," *Wall Street Journal* (May 11, 2007): B1.

103. Craig S. Smith, "Underneath, Saudi Women Keep Their Secrets," *New York Times* (December 3, 2002), www.nytimes.com, accessed December 3, 2002.

104. Quoted in John Leland and Duraid Adnan, "Mannequins Wear a Message for Iraq's Women," *New York Times* (February 8, 2011), http://www.nytimes.com/2011/02/09/world/middleeast/09baghdad.html?_r=1&scp=1&sq=mannequin&st=cse, accessed April 10, 2011.

105. Marylouise Caldwell, Ingeborg Astrid Kelppe, and Paul Henry, "Prosuming Multiple Gender Role Identities: A Multi-Country Written and Audio-Visual Exploration of Contemporary Young Mainstream Female Achievers," *Consumption, Markets & Culture* 10 (June 2007): 95–115.

106. Jennie Yabroff, "Girls Going Mild(er): A New 'Modesty Movement' Aims to Teach Young Women They Don't Have to Be Bad, or Semiclad," *Newsweek* (July 23, 2007), http://boards.youthnoise.com/eve/forums/a/tpc/f/573295355/m/38310644, accessed July 18, 2007; www.purefashion.com, accessed May 28, 2011; www.modestapparelusa.com, accessed May 31, 2011.

107. Adapted from www.cohorts.com/meet_the_cohorts.html, accessed June 1, 2007.

108. Doreen Carvajal, "Europe Takes Aim at Sexual Stereotyping in Ads," *New York Times* (September 9, 2008), www.nytimes.com/2008/09/10/Business/Media/10adco.Html?_R=1&Ei=5070&Emc=Et . . . , accessed September 10, 2008.

109. Quoted in Natalie Zmuda, "Can Dr Pepper's Mid-Cal Soda Score a 10 with Men?," *Advertising Age* (February 21, 2011), http://adage.com/article/news/dr-pepper-10-avoid-marketing-missteps-pepsi-coke/148983/, accessed April 10, 2011.

110. www.mavtv.com, accessed May 28, 2011.

111. Quoted in Barry Silverstein, "Ever the Publicity Hound, Branson Readies to Be an Airline Hostess," *BrandChannel* (November 18, 2010), http://www.brandchannel.com/home/post/2010/11/18/Richard-Branson-Loses-Bet.aspx, accessed April 10, 2011.

112. Barbara B. Stern, "Masculinism(s) and the Male Image: What Does It Mean to Be a Man?," in Tom Reichert and Jacqueline Lambiase, eds., *Sex in Advertising: Multi-Disciplinary Perspectives on the Erotic Appeal* (Mahwah, NJ: Erlbaum, 2003): 215–228.

113. Andrew Martin, "As the Web Turns," *New York Times* (January 12, 2011), http://www.nytimes.com/2011/01/13/business/13advice.html?_r=2&ref=media, accessed April 10, 2011; www.manofthehouse.com, accessed May 28, 2011.

114. "NBCU Brand Index: Women Love Gender Bender Ads," *Media Daily News* (February 28, 2011), http://www.mediapost.com/publications/?fa=Articles.showArticle&art_aid=145748, accessed April 10, 2011.

115. Douglas B. Holt and Craig J. Thompson, "Man-of-Action Heroes: The Pursuit of Heroic Masculinity in Everyday Consumption," *Journal of Consumer Research* 31 (September): 425–40.

116. Vivian Manning-Schaffel, "Metrosexuals: A Well-Groomed Market?," *Brand Channel* (May 22, 2006), www.brandchannel.com, accessed May 22, 2006; Jack Neff, "A Lipstick Index for Men? Philips' Norelco Posits that Guys Are Growing Beards to Protest Recession," *Advertising Age* (April 2, 2009), www.adage.com, accessed April 2, 2009; Aaron Baar, "Move Over, Ladies; Men Are Walking Down Beauty Aisles," *Marketing Daily* (December 22, 2008), www.mediapost.com, accessed December 22, 2008.

117. Ben Parr, "Google Chrome Commercial Lets Gay Teens Know 'It Gets Better,'" Mashable.com, http://mashable.com/2011/05/04/google-chrome-it-gets-better/, accessed May 28, 2011.

118. Projections of the incidence of homosexuality in the general population often are influenced by assumptions of the researchers, as well as the methodology they employ (e.g., self-report, behavioral measures, fantasy measures). For a discussion of these factors, see Edward O. Laumann, John H. Gagnon, Robert T. Michael, and Stuart Michaels, *The Social Organization of Homosexuality* (Chicago: University of Chicago Press, 1994).

119. Lisa Leff, "2010 Census Will Count Same-Sex Couples in Reversal of Bush Policy," June 19, 2009, *Huffington Post*, http://www.huffingtonpost.com/2009/06/20/210-census-will-count-sam_n_218489.html, accessed May 28, 2011; Lee Condon, "By the Numbers (Census 2000)," *The Advocate: The National Gay & Lesbian Newsmagazine* (September 25, 2001): 37.

120. For a recent academic study of this subculture, cf. Steven M. Kates, "The Dynamics of Brand Legitimacy: An Interpretive Study in the Gay Men's Community," *Journal of Consumer Research* 31 (September 2004): 455–64.

121. Karlene Lukovitz, "Consumer Preferences Vary among Gay/Lesbian Segments," *Marketing Daily* (October 24, 2007), www.mediapost.com/ publications/?fa=Articles.showArticle&art_aid=69729; accessed October 24, 2007.

122. Kevin Sack, "When the Bride Takes a Bride, Businesses Respond," *New York Times* (July 15, 2010), http://www.nytimes.com/2010/07/16/us/16marriage.html?emc=eta1, accessed April 10, 2011; http://equally-wed.com/, accessed May 28, 2011; http://www.outvite.com/?Cobrand=OutVite&Site=OutVite&vk=1777211146, accessed May 28, 2011.

123. Ellen Byron, "Cognac and a Splash of Controversy," *Wall Street Journal* (April 29, 2004): B5.

124. Sheila Shayon, "Levi's for Women: Shape, Not Size, Matters," *Brand-Channel* (September 17, 2010), http://www.brandchannel.com/home/post/2010/09/17/Levis-Women-Curve-ID-Digital.aspx, accessed April 10, 2011; http://us.levi.com/shop/index.jsp?categoryId=3146849&AB=CMS_Home_CurveID_081010, accessed May 28, 2011.

125. http://www.spanx.com/category/index.jsp?categoryId=2992553&clickid=topnav_shapers_txt, accessed May 28, 2011.

126. Dennis W. Rook, "Body Cathexis and Market Segmentation," in Michael R. Solomon, ed., *The Psychology of Fashion* (Lexington, MA: Lexington Books, 1985): 233–41; for research that examines how body image influences the likelihood of using virtual models, cf. Ellen C. Garbarino and José Antonio Rosa, "Body Esteem, Body Image Discrepancy and Body Boundary Aberration as Influencers of the Perceived Accuracy of Virtual Models," working paper, Weatherhead School of Management, Case Western Reserve University (2006).

127. Nina Mandell, "Padded Swimsuits for All? Abercrombie and Fitch Marketing Padded Tops to Young Girls," *New York Daily News* (March 27, 2011), http://www.nydailynews.com/lifestyle/fashion/2011/03/27/2011-03-27_padded_swimsuits_for_all_abercrombie_and_fitch_marketing_padded_tops_to_young_gi.html, accessed April 10, 2011.

128. Karen K. Dion, "What Is Beautiful Is Good," *Journal of Personality & Social Psychology* 24 (December 1972): 285–90.

129. Sharon Jayson, "Study: Beautiful People Cash in on Their Looks," *USA Today* (March 31, 2011), http://www.usatoday.com/money/perfi/basics/2011-03-30-beauty30_ST_N.htm, accessed April 10, 2011.

130. Hal R. Varian, "The Hunk Differential," *New York Times* (August 28, 2003), www.nytimes.com, accessed August 28, 2003.

131. "Saving Face," *The Economist* (July 10, 2004): 55.

132. Emily Flynn, "Beauty: Babes Spot Babes," *Newsweek* (September 20, 2004): 10.

133. For some results that provide exceptions to this overall phenomenon, cf. Elizabeth Cashdan, "Waist-to-Hip Ratio across Cultures: Trade-Offs between Androgen- and Estrogen-Dependent Traits," *Current Anthropology* 49, no. 6 (2008): 1099–1107.

134. Abigail W. Leonard, "How Women Pick Mates vs. Flings," *LiveScience* (January 2, 2007), www.livescience.com/health/070102_facial_features.html, accessed January 3, 2007.

135. Corky Siemaszko, "Depends on the Day: Women's Sex Drive a Very Cyclical Thing," *New York Daily News* (June 24, 1999): 3.

136. http://science.netscape.com/story/2006/10/10/fertile-women-dress-to-impress, accessed February 1, 2007; Kristina M. Durante, Vladas Griskevicius, Sarah E. Hill, Carin Perilloux, and Norman P. Li, "Ovulation, Female Competition, and Product Choice: Hormonal Influences on Consumer Behavior," *Journal of Consumer Research* 37 (April 2011): 921–34.

137. Amanda B. Bower, "Highly Attractive Models in Advertising and the Women Who Loathe Them: The Implications of Negative Affect for Spokesperson Effectiveness," *Journal of Advertising* 30 (Fall 2001): 51–63.

138. Basil G. Englis, Michael R. Solomon, and Richard D. Ashmore, "Beauty before the Eyes of Beholders: The Cultural Encoding of Beauty Types in Magazine Advertising and Music Television," *Journal of Advertising* 23 (June 1994): 49–64; Michael R. Solomon, Richard Ashmore, and Laura Longo, "The Beauty Match-Up Hypothesis: Congruence between Types of Beauty and Product Images in Advertising," *Journal of Advertising* 21 (December 1992): 23–34.

139. Thomas Fuller, "A Vision of Pale Beauty Carries Risks for Asia's Women," *International Herald Tribune Online* (May 14, 2006), accessed May 16, 2006.

140. Seth Mydans, "Oh Blue-Eyed Thais, Flaunt Your Western Genes!" *New York Times* (August 29, 2002), www.nytimes.com, accessed August 29, 2002.

141. Fuller, "A Vision of Pale Beauty Carries Risks for Asia's Women."

142. Norimitsu Onishi, "Globalization of Beauty Makes Slimness Trendy," *New York Times* (October 3, 2002), www.nytimes.com, accessed October 3, 2002.

143. Ellen Knickermeyer, "Full-Figured Females Favored," *Opelika-Auburn News* (August 7, 2001).

144. Amy Chozick, "; "The 'Love Bra' Catches Fire," *Wall Street Journal* (May 7, 2007): A1.

145. Lois W. Banner, *American Beauty* (Chicago: University of Chicago Press, 1980); for a philosophical perspective, see Barry Vacker and Wayne R. Key, "Beauty and the Beholder: The Pursuit of Beauty through Commodities," *Psychology & Marketing* 10 (November–December 1993): 471–94.

146. Elaine L. Pedersen and Nancy L. Markee, "Fashion Dolls: Communicators of Ideals of Beauty and Fashion," paper presented at the International Conference on Marketing Meaning, Indianapolis, IN, 1989; Dalma Heyn, "Body Hate," *Ms.* (August 1989): 34; Mary C. Martin and James W. Gentry, "Assessing the Internalization of Physical Attractiveness Norms," *Proceedings of the American Marketing Association Summer Educators' Conference* (Summer 1994): 59–65.

147. Lisa Bannon, "Barbie Is Getting Body Work, and Mattel Says She'll Be 'Rad,'" *Wall Street Journal Interactive Edition* (November 17, 1997).

148. Lisa Bannon, "Will New Clothes, Bellybutton Create 'Turn Around' Barbie," *Wall Street Journal Interactive Edition* (February 17, 2000). ditto

149. "Report Delivers Skinny on Miss America," *Montgomery Advertiser* (March 22, 2000): 5A.

150. "Study: Playboy Models Losing Hourglass Figures," CNN.com (December 20, 2002), www.CNN.com.

151. Anthony H. Ahrensa, Sarah F. Etua, James J. Graya, James E. Mosimanna, Mia Foley Sypecka, and Claire V. Wisemanb, "Cultural Representations of Thinness in Women, Redux: *Playboy* Magazine's Depiction of Beauty from 1979 to 1999," *Body Image* (September 2006): 229–35.

152. Erin White, "Dove 'Firms' with Zaftig Models: Unilever Brand Launches European Ads Employing Non-Supermodel Bodies," *Wall Street Journal* (April 21, 2004): B3.

153. "The Dove Report: Challenging Beauty," *Unilever* 2004, www.dove.com/real_beauty/article.asp? id=430, accessed June 15, 2005.

154. Geoffrey A. Fowler, "Unilever Gives 'Ugly Betty' a Product-Plug Makeover in China," *Wall Street Journal* (December 29, 2008), www.wsj.com, accessed December 29, 2008.

155. Jill Neimark, "The Beefcaking of America," *Psychology Today* (November–December 1994): 32.

156. Richard H. Kolbe and Paul J. Albanese, "Man to Man: A Content Analysis of Sole-Male Images in Male-Audience Magazines," *Journal of Advertising* 25 (Winter 1996): 1–20.

157. Nina Lentini, "Levi's Launches 'Ultimate Lift' for Female Derriere," *Marketing Daily* (November 17, 2008), www.mediapost.com/Publications/?Fa=Articles.Showarticle&Art_Aid=94943, accessed November 23, 2008; Miho Inada, "Is a Girdle Just for Men a Stretch? Japanese Company Calls Product 'Exercise Wear,' Says It Tones Muscles," *Wall Street Journal* (December 28, 2007): B3.

158. Jack Loechner, "Appearance and Weight Trumps Disease in Women's Concerns," Center for Media Research (May 26, 2008), http://blogs.mediapost.com/Research_Brief/?P=1714, accessed May 26, 2008.

159. David Goetzl, "Teen Girls Pan Ad Images of Women," *Advertising Age* (September 13, 1999): 32; Carey Goldberg, "Citing Intolerance, Obese People Take Steps to Press Cause," *New York Times* (November 5, 2000). http://www.nytimes.com/2000/11/05/us/fat-people-say-an-intolerant-world-condemns-them-on-first-sight.html, accessed September 1, 2011.

160. Shirley S. Wang, "Diet Pepsi's 'Skinny Can' Campaign Riles Eating Disorders Group," *Wall Street Journal* (February 15, 2011), http://blogs.WallStreetJournal.com/health/2011/02/15/diet-pepsis-skinny-can-campaign-riles-eating-disorders-group/, accessed April 10, 2011.

161. "Fat-Phobia in the Fijis: TV-Thin Is In," *Newsweek* (May 31, 1999): 70.

162. Amy Dockser Marcus, "With an Etiquette of Overeating, It's Not Easy Being Lean in Egypt," *Wall Street Journal Interactive Edition* (March 4, 1998).

163. Norimitsu Onishi, "Japan, Seeking Trim Waists, Measures Millions," *New York Times* (June 13, 2008), www.nytimes.com, accessed June 13, 2008.

164. Erin White and Deborah Ball, "Slim-Fast Pounds Home Tough Talk Ads Aimed at U.K. Women," *Wall Street Journal* (May 28, 2004): B3.

165. www.livingxl.com/store/en_US/index.jsp, accessed May 29, 2009; "Retailer Has Big Plans for Big Customers: LivingXL Sells Lifestyle Products for an Increasingly Obese America," www.MSNBC.com, accessed May 30, 2007; Rebecca Gardyn, "The Shape of Things to Come," *American Demographics* (July/August 2003): 25–49.

166. Stephanie Clifford, "Plus-Size Revelation: Bigger Women Have Cash, Too," *New York Times* (June 18, 2010), http://www.nytimes.com/2010/06/19/business/19plus.html?emc=eta1, accessed April 10, 2011.

167. John W. Schouten, "Selves in Transition: Symbolic Consumption in Personal Rites of Passage and Identity Reconstruction," *Journal of Consumer Research* 17 (March 1991): 412–25; Janet Whitman, "Extreme Makeovers Blur Line between Medicine and Cosmetics," *Wall Street Journal* (January 7, 2004), www.wsj.com, accessed January 7, 2004.

168. Simon Romero, "Chávez Tries to Rally Venezuela against a New Enemy: Breast Lifts," *New York Times* (March 14, 2011), http://www.nytimes.com/2011/03/15/world/americas/15venezuela.html?scp=1&sq=breast&st=cse, accessed April 10, 2011.

169. Sharon Lafranierek, "For Many Chinese, New Wealth and a Fresh Face," *New York Times* (April 23, 2011), http://www.nytimes.com/2011/04/24/world/asia/24beijing.html?_r=1&ref=todayspaper, accessed April 29, 2011.

170. Natasha Singer, "How to Stuff a Wild Bikini Bottom," *New York Times* (March 2, 2006), www.nytimes.com, accessed March 2, 2006.

171. Catherine Saint Louis, "This Teenage Girl Uses Botox. No, She's Not Alone," *New York Times* (August 11, 2010), http://www.nytimes.com/2010/08/12/fashion/12SKIN.html?_r=1&scp=2&sq=botox&st=cse, accessed April 10, 2011.

172. Jane E. Brody, "Notions of Beauty Transcend Culture, New Study Suggests," *New York Times* (March 21, 1994): A14; Norihiko Shirouzu, "Reconstruction Boom in Tokyo: Perfecting Imperfect Belly-Buttons," *Wall Street Journal* (October 4, 1995): B1.

173. Emily Yoffe, "Valley of the Silicon Dolls," *Newsweek* (November 26, 1990): 72.

174. Jerry Adler, "New Bodies for Sale," *Newsweek* (May 27, 1985): 64.

175. Ruth P. Rubinstein, "Color, Circumcision, Tattoos, and Scars," in Michael R. Solomon, ed., *The Psychology of Fashion* (Lexington, MA: Lexington Books, 1985): 243–54; Peter H. Bloch and Marsha L. Richins, "You Look 'Mahvelous': The Pursuit of Beauty and Marketing Concept," *Psychology & Marketing* 9 (January 1992): 3–16.

176. Sondra Farganis, "Lip Service: The Evolution of Pouting, Pursing, and Painting Lips Red," *Health* (November 1988): 48–51.

177. Michael Gross, "Those Lips, Those Eyebrows; New Face of 1989 (New Look of Fashion Models)," *New York Times Magazine* (February 13, 1989): 24.

178. "High Heels: Ecstasy's Worth the Agony," *New York Post* (December 31, 1981).

179. Tiffany Hsu and Don Lee, "At 50 Years Old, Barbie Gets Tattoos—And a Megastore in China," *Los Angeles Times* (March 6, 2009), http://articles.latimes.com/2009/mar/06/business/fi-tattoobarbie6, accessed March 6, 2009.

180. "Beyoncé Unveils Temporary Tats at Sephora," *Marketing Daily* (September 26, 2010), http://www.mediapost.com/publications/?fa=Articles.showArticle&art_aid=136408&nid=119045, accessed April 10, 2011.

181. Dannie Kjeldgaard and Anders Bengtsson, "Consuming the Fashion Tattoo," in Geeta Menon and Akshay R. Rao, eds., *Advances in Consumer Research 32* (Duluth, MN: Association for Consumer Research, 2005): 172–77.

182. "Three in Ten Americans with a Tattoo Say Having One Makes Them Feel Sexier," (February 12, 2008), www.harrisinteractive.com/harris_poll/index.asp?PID=868, accessed May 29, 2009.

183. Natasha Singer, "Erasing Tattoos, Out of Regret or for a New Canvas," *New York Times* (June 17, 2007), www.nytimes.com, accessed June 17, 2007.

184. www.pathfinder.com:80/altculture/aentries/p/piercing.html, accessed August 22, 1997.

185. Caroline Muspratt, "Unilever Bans 'Size Zero' Models in Ads," *London Telegraph* (May 9, 2007), www.telegraph.co.uk, accessed May 9, 2007; Larry Rohter, "Burst of High-Profile Anorexia Deaths Unsettles Brazil," *New York Times* (December 30, 2006), www.nytimes.com, accessed December 30, 2006; Eric Wilson, "Doctors Fault Designers' Stance over Thin Models," *New York Times* (January 9, 2007), www.nytimes.com, accessed January 9, 2007.

186. Debra A. Zellner, Debra F. Harner, and Robbie I. Adler, "Effects of Eating Abnormalities and Gender on Perceptions of Desirable Body Shape," *Journal of Abnormal Psychology* 98 (February 1989): 93–96.

187. Robin T. Peterson, "Bulimia and Anorexia in an Advertising Context," *Journal of Business Ethics* 6 (1987): 495–504.

188. Jane E. Brody, "Personal Health," *New York Times* (February 22, 1990): B9.

189. Christian S. Crandall, "Social Contagion of Binge Eating," *Journal of Personality & Social Psychology* 55 (1988): 588–98.

190. http://proanatips.net/, accessed May 29, 2011; quoted in http://hub.webring.org/hub/proana, accessed May 29, 2011; Doreen Carvajal, "French Bill Takes Chic Out of Being Too Thin," *New York Times* (April 16, 2008), www.nytimes.com, accessed April 16, 2008; Alex Williams, "Before Spring Break, the Anorexic Challenge," *New York Times* (April 2, 2006), www.nytimes.com, accessed April 2, 2006.

191. Judy Folkenberg, "Bulimia: Not for Women Only," *Psychology Today* (March 1984): 10.

192. Stephen S. Hall, "The Bully in the Mirror," *New York Times Magazine* (August 22, 1999), www.nytimes.com, accessed August 22, 1999; Natalie Angier, "Drugs, Sports, Body Image and G.I. Joe," *New York Times* (December 22, 1998): D1.

193. Parija Kavilanz, "Back-to-School Checklist: Whiter Teeth & Tattoos," *CNNMoney.com* (September 2, 2010), http://money.cnn.com/2010/09/02/news/economy/americanexpress_backtoschool_spending_trends/index.htm, accessed April 10, 2011.

194. "Defining Metro Sexuality," *Metrosource* (September/October/November 2003).

195. Dinitia Smith, "Demonizing Fat in the War on Weight," *New York Times* (May 1, 2004), www.nytimes.com, accessed May 1, 2004.

196. Stephanie Clifford, "Axe Body Products Puts Its Brand on the Hamptons Club Scene," *New York Times* (May 22, 2009): B6.

197. Gary Rivlin, "Facing the World with Egos Exposed," *New York Times* (June 3, 2004), www.nytimes.com, accessed June 3, 2004.

Personality
and Psychographics

From Chapter 6 of *Consumer Behavior: Buying, Having, and Being*, Tenth Edition. Michael R. Solomon. Copyright © 2013 by Pearson Education, Inc. All rights reserved.

Personality
and Psychographics

Chapter Objectives

When you finish reading this chapter you will understand why:

1. A consumer's personality influences the way he responds to marketing stimuli, but efforts to use this information in marketing contexts meet with mixed results.

2. Psychographics go beyond simple demographics to help marketers understand and reach different consumer segments.

3. Consumer activities can be harmful to individuals and to society.

J ackie and Hank, executives in a high-powered Los Angeles advertising agency, are exchanging ideas about how they are going to spend the big bonus everyone in the firm is getting for landing a new account—quite a feat when most agencies are laying off people instead of adding new business! They can't help but snicker at their friend Rose in accounting, who avidly surfs the Internet for information about a state-of-the-art home theater system she plans to install in her condo. What a couch potato! Hank, who fancies himself a bit of a daredevil, plans to blow his bonus on a thrill-seeking trip to Colorado, where a week of outrageous bungee jumping awaits him (assuming he lives to tell about it, but that uncertainty is half the fun). Jackie replies, "Been there, done that . . . Believe it or not, I'm staying put right here—heading over to Santa Monica to catch some waves." Seems that the surfing bug has bitten her since she stumbled onto Jetty Girl, an online resource for women who surf.[1]

Jackie and Hank marvel at how different they are from Rose, who's content to spend her downtime watching sappy old movies or actually reading books. All three make about the same salary, and Jackie and Rose were sorority sisters at USC. How can their tastes be so different? Oh well, they figure, that's why they make chocolate and vanilla.

Personality

OBJECTIVE 1
A consumer's personality influences the way he responds to marketing stimuli, but efforts to use this information in marketing contexts meet with mixed results.

Jackie and Hank are typical of many people who search for new (and even risky) ways to spend their leisure time. This desire translates into big business for the "adventure travel" industry, which provides white-knuckle experiences.[2] In the old days, the California beach culture relegated women to the status of landlocked "Gidgets" who sat on shore while their boyfriends rode the surf. Now (spurred by the female surfers in the movie *Blue Crush*), women fuel the sport's resurgence in popularity. Roxy rides the wave with its collections of women's surf apparel; it even includes a feature on its Web site that lets users design their own bikinis.[3]

Just what does make Jackie and Hank so different from their more sedate friend Rose? One answer may lie in the concept of **personality**, which refers to a person's unique psychological makeup and how it consistently influences the way a person responds to her environment. Do all people *have* personalities? Certainly we can wonder about some we meet! Actually, even though the answer seems like a no-brainer, some psychologists argue that the concept of personality may not be valid. Many studies find that people do not seem to exhibit stable personalities. Because people don't necessarily behave the same way in all situations, they argue that this is merely a convenient way to categorize people.

Intuitively, this argument is a bit hard to accept, because we tend to see others in a limited range of situations, and so they *do* appear to act consistently. However, we each

CB AS I SEE IT

Professor Donna L. Hoffman, *University of California, Riverside*

How and why do consumers use social media? As social media applications continue to proliferate and the dynamics of online social interaction continue to evolve, consumer behavior researchers are calling for a deeper understanding of consumers' use of social media so that theoretically consistent models linking consumer motivations, social media goals, and perceptions of well-being can be constructed. The need for such models is increasingly acute as consumer participation in new forms of social media increases and marketers seek to incorporate into their content applications those social components that best satisfy consumers' basic needs and lead to the most positive outcomes.

My colleague Professor Tom Novak and I have proposed that the fundamental interactivity of social media allows for four higher-order goals: connect, create, consume, and control. These "4Cs" capabilities of social media undoubtedly explain in part why so many people spend so much of their time using social media and why social media are so popular. Although there has been a surge of research lately examining social media usage, few studies are based or focused on

a conceptual framework that can help explain what drives use and how usage goals relate subjective well-being.

To address this gap, we designed two large-scale studies to evaluate how consumer motivations may differentially drive social media goal pursuit and investigate how those goals and subjective well-being are associated. Individuals for whom social media satisfies needs should experience a positive impact on well-being. This line of reasoning is closely related to the idea of optimal online experience we pursued in our previous research, where we found that individuals who experience flow during their online navigational experiences are more likely to achieve positive outcomes compared to individuals who cannot attain these compelling online experiences. For both studies, we used our 4Cs of connecting, creating, consuming, and controlling social media experiences to organize consumers' social media goals.

In the first study, we examined social media goal pursuit in the context of the core social motive of the need to relate, the additional fundamental needs for autonomy and competence, individuals' orientation toward intrinsic and external locus of causality, and two aspects of self-esteem in the context of social identity. Results suggested that connect goals ("social" goals) are associated with relatedness needs, an external locus of control, intrinsic motivation to connect with others, and positive evaluations of the social media groups to which consumers belong (private collective self-esteem). Consumers' pursuit to create goals is associated with autonomy, competence, and relatedness

needs; an external locus of control; higher social media involvement; and contribution to sense of self (identity self-esteem). Consume goals ("nonsocial" goals) appear to be intrinsically motivated and negatively associated with autonomy and competence. Control goals satisfy autonomy and competence needs, and are associated with an external locus of causality and social media knowledge.

In the second study, we evaluated whether individuals with different primary 4Cs social media goals differed in terms of their perceptions of well-being. We found a clear link between differential social media goal pursuit and subjective well-being (connectors and creators are happiest), with clear differences in terms of the higher-order focus of the online interaction (connectors are happiest pursuing person-interaction while creators are happiest pursuing content-interaction).

Our findings that different social media goals are supported by different needs and motivations and do not relate equally to perceptions of well-being have important implications for research and marketing practice. The results may help researchers understand whether and how increased participation in social media will enhance well-being. Marketing managers believe that social media offer the potential for the "killer app," and one recurring question is how marketers can develop applications that are more "social." Marketers can use the results to help focus strategic efforts as they examine the relationship between social media goals and consumer response to marketing efforts in interactive media environments.

know that we ourselves are not all *that* consistent; we may be wild and crazy at times and serious and responsible at others. Although certainly not all psychologists have abandoned the idea of personality, many now recognize that a person's underlying characteristics are but one part of the puzzle, and situational factors often play a very large role in determining behavior.[4] Still, marketing strategies often include some aspects of personality.

Consumer Behavior on the Couch: Freudian Theory

Sigmund Freud proposed the idea that much of one's adult personality stems from a fundamental conflict between a person's desire to gratify her physical needs and the necessity to function as a responsible member of society. This struggle is carried out in the mind among three systems. (Note: These systems do *not* refer to physical parts of the brain.) Let's quickly review each.

Freudian Systems

The **id** is about immediate gratification—it is the "party animal" of the mind. It operates according to the **pleasure principle**; that is, our basic desire to maximize pleasure and avoid pain guides our behavior. The id is selfish and illogical. It directs a person's psychic energy toward pleasurable acts without any regard for consequences.

The **superego** is the counterweight to the id. This system is essentially the person's conscience. It internalizes society's rules (especially as parents teach them to us) and tries to prevent the id from seeking selfish gratification. Finally, the **ego** is the system that

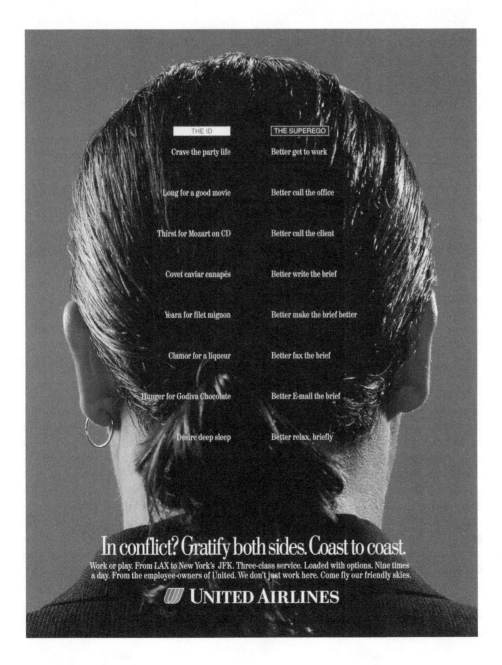

This ad focuses on the conflict between the desire for hedonic gratification (represented by the id) versus the need to engage in rational, task-oriented activities (represented by the superego).
Source: Used with permission of United Airlines.

221

mediates between the id and the superego. It's basically a referee in the fight between temptation and virtue. The ego tries to balance these opposing forces according to the **reality principle**, which means it finds ways to gratify the id that the outside world will find acceptable. (Hint: This is where Freudian theory applies to marketing.) These conflicts occur on an unconscious level, so the person is not necessarily aware of the underlying reasons for his or her behavior.

Consumer researchers have adapted some of Freud's ideas. In particular, his work highlights the potential importance of unconscious motives that guide our purchases. The implication is that consumers cannot necessarily tell us their true motivation when they choose products, even if we can devise a sensitive way to ask them directly. The Freudian perspective also raises the possibility that the ego relies on the symbolism in products to compromise between the demands of the id and the prohibitions of the superego. The person channels her unacceptable desire into acceptable outlets when she uses products that signify these underlying desires. This is the connection between product symbolism and motivation: The product stands for, or represents, a consumer's true goal, which is socially unacceptable or unattainable. By acquiring the product, the person vicariously experiences the forbidden fruit.

Sometimes a Cigar Is Just a Cigar

Most Freudian applications in marketing relate to a product's supposed sexual symbolism. For example, some analysts speculate that owning a sports car is a substitute for sexual gratification (especially for men going through a "midlife crisis"). Indeed, some people do seem inordinately attached to their cars, and may spend many hours lovingly washing and polishing them. An Infiniti ad reinforces the belief that cars symbolically satisfy consumers' sexual needs in addition to their functional ones when it describes one model as "what happens when you cross sheet metal and desire." Other approaches focus on male-oriented symbolism—so-called *phallic symbols*—that appeals to women. Although Freud joked that "sometimes a cigar is just a cigar," many popular applications of Freud's ideas revolve around the use of objects that resemble sex organs (e.g., cigars, trees, or swords for male sex organs; tunnels for female sex organs). This focus stems from Freud's analysis of dreams, which he believed communicate repressed desires in the form of symbolically rich stories.

Motivational Research

In the 1950s, **motivational research** borrowed Freudian ideas to understand the deeper meanings of products and advertisements. This approach adapted psychoanalytical (Freudian) interpretations with a heavy emphasis on unconscious motives. It basically assumed that we channel socially unacceptable needs into acceptable outlets—including product substitutes.

This perspective relies on *depth interviews* with individual consumers. Instead of asking many consumers a few general questions about product usage and combining these responses with those of many other consumers in a representative statistical sample, a motivational researcher talks to only a few people, but probes deeply into each respondent's purchase motivations. A depth interview might take several hours, and it's based on the assumption that the respondent cannot immediately articulate his *latent* or underlying motives. A carefully trained interviewer can derive these only after extensive questioning and interpretation.

Ernest Dichter, a psychoanalyst who trained with Freud's disciples in Vienna in the early part of the 20th century, pioneered this work. Dichter conducted in-depth interview studies on more than 230 different products, and actual marketing campaigns incorporated many of his findings.[5] For example, Esso (now Exxon in the United States) for many years reminded consumers to "Put a Tiger in Your Tank" after Dichter found that people responded well to this powerful animal symbolism containing vaguely sexual undertones. Table 1 provides a summary of major consumption motivations he identified.

Some critics reacted to the motivational studies that ad agencies conducted in much the same way they did to subliminal perception studies. They charged that this approach gave advertisers the power to manipulate consumers.[6] However,

TABLE 1	A Motivational Researcher Identifies Consumption Motives

Motive	Associated Products
Power-masculinity-virility	Power: Sugary products and large breakfasts (to charge oneself up), bowling, electric trains, hot rods, power tools Masculinity-virility: Coffee, red meat, heavy shoes, toy guns, buying fur coats for women, shaving with a razor
Security	Ice cream (to feel like a loved child again), full drawer of neatly ironed shirts, real plaster walls (to feel sheltered), home baking, hospital care
Eroticism	Sweets (to lick), gloves (to be removed by woman as a form of undressing), a man lighting a woman's cigarette (to create a tension-filled moment culminating in pressure, then relaxation)
Moral purity-cleanliness	White bread, cotton fabrics (to connote chastity), harsh household cleaning chemicals (to make housewives feel moral after using), bathing (to be equated with Pontius Pilate, who washed blood from his hands), oatmeal (sacrifice, virtue)
Social acceptance	Companionship: Ice cream (to share fun), coffee, Love and affection: Toys (to express love for children), sugar and honey (to express terms of affection) Acceptance: Soap, beauty products
Individuality	Gourmet foods, foreign cars, cigarette holders, vodka, perfume, fountain pens
Status	Scotch: ulcers, heart attacks, indigestion (to show one has a high-stress, important job!), carpets (to show one does not live on bare earth like peasants)
Femininity	Cakes and cookies, dolls, silk, tea, household curios
Reward	Cigarettes, candy, alcohol, ice cream, cookies
Mastery over environment	Kitchen appliances, boats, sporting goods, cigarette lighters
Disalienation (a desire to feel connectedness to things)	Home decorating, skiing, morning radio broadcasts (to feel "in touch" with the world)
Magic-mystery	Soups (having healing powers), paints (change the mood of a room), carbonated drinks (magical effervescent property), vodka (romantic history), unwrapping of gifts

Source: Adapted from Jeffrey F. Durgee, "Interpreting Dichter's Interpretations: An Analysis of Consumption Symbolism," in *The Handbook of Consumer Motivation, Marketing and Semiotics: Selected Papers from the Copenhagen Symposium*, eds. Hanne Hartvig-Larsen, David Glen Mick, and Christian Alstead (Copenhagen, 1991).

many consumer researchers felt the research lacked sufficient rigor and validity because the interpretations are so subjective.[7] Because the analyst bases his conclusions on his own judgment after he interviews a small number of people, critics were dubious about whether the findings would generalize to a larger market. In addition, because the original motivational researchers were heavily influenced by orthodox Freudian theory, their interpretations usually involved sexual themes. This emphasis tends to overlook other plausible causes for behavior. Still, motivational research had great appeal to at least some marketers for several reasons, including these:

- Motivational research is less expensive to conduct than large-scale, quantitative survey data collection because interviewing and data-processing costs are relatively minimal.
- The knowledge a company derives from motivational research may help it develop marketing communications that appeal to deep-seated needs and thus provide a more powerful hook to reel in consumers. Even if they are not necessarily valid for all consumers in a target market, these insights can still be valuable to an advertiser who wants to create copy that will resonate with customers.
- Some of the findings seem intuitively plausible after the fact. For example, motivational studies concluded that we associate coffee with companionship, that we avoid prunes because they remind us of old age, and that men fondly equate the first car they owned as an adolescent with the onset of their sexual freedom.

Other interpretations were hard for some researchers to swallow; such as the observation that women equate the act of baking a cake with birth, or that men are reluctant to give blood because they feel it drains their vital fluids. However, we do sometimes say a pregnant woman has "a bun in the oven," and Pillsbury claims that "nothing says lovin' like something from the oven." When the Red Cross hired motivational researcher Dichter to boost blood donation rates, he did report that men (but not women) tend to drastically overestimate the amount of blood they give. As a result, the Red Cross counteracted men's fear of losing their virility when the organization symbolically equated the act of giving blood with fertilizing a female egg: "Give the gift of life." Despite its drawbacks, some ad agencies today still use some forms of motivational research. The approach is most useful, however, when we use it as an exploratory technique to provide insights that inform more rigorous research approaches.

Neo-Freudian Theories

Freud's work had a huge influence on subsequent theories of personality. Although he opened the door to the realization that explanations for behavior may lurk beneath the surface, many of his colleagues and students felt that an individual's personality is more influenced by how he handles relationships with others than by how he resolves sexual conflicts. We call these theorists *neo-Freudian* (meaning following from or being influenced by Freud).

Karen Horney

One of the most prominent neo-Freudians was Karen Horney. This pioneering psychotherapist described people as moving toward others (*compliant*), away from others (*detached*), or against others (*aggressive*).[8] Indeed, one early study found that compliant people are more likely to gravitate toward name-brand products, detached types are more likely to be tea drinkers, and males the researchers classified as aggressive preferred brands with a strong masculine orientation (e.g., Old Spice deodorant).[9] Other well-known neo-Freudians include Alfred Adler, who proposed that a prime motivation is to overcome feelings of inferiority relative to others; and Harry Stack Sullivan, who focused on how personality evolves to reduce anxiety in social relationships.[10]

Carl Jung

Carl Jung was also a disciple of Freud (who was being groomed as Freud's successor). However, Jung was unable to accept Freud's emphasis on sexual aspects of personality, and this was a contributing factor in the eventual dissolution of their relationship. Jung went on to develop his own method of psychotherapy, which he called *analytical psychology*.

Jung believed that the cumulative experiences of past generations shape who we are today. He proposed that we each share a *collective unconscious,* a storehouse of memories we inherit from our ancestors. For example, Jung would argue that many people are afraid of the dark because their distant ancestors had good reason to fear it. These shared memories create **archetypes**, or universally recognized ideas and behavior patterns. Archetypes involve themes, such as birth, death, or the devil, that appear frequently in myths, stories, and dreams.

Jung's ideas may seem a bit far-fetched, but advertising messages in fact do often include archetypes. For example, some of the archetypes Jung and his followers identified include the "old wise man" and the "earth mother."[11] These images appear frequently in marketing messages that use characters such as wizards, revered teachers, or even Mother Nature. Our culture's current infatuation with stories such as *Harry Potter* and *The Lord of the Rings* speaks to the power of these images—to say nothing of the "wizard" who helps you repair your laptop.

Young & Rubicam (Y&R), a major advertising agency, uses the archetype approach in its BrandAsset® Archetypes model depicted in Figure 1. The model proposes healthy relationships among Archetypes as well as unhealthy ones. A healthy personality is one in which the Archetypes overwhelm their corresponding Shadows; a sick personality results when one or more Shadows prevail. When a brand's Shadows dominate, this cues the agency to take action to guide the brand to a healthier personality, much as one would try

Figure 1 BRANDASSET VALUATOR ® ARCHETYPES

Characteristics

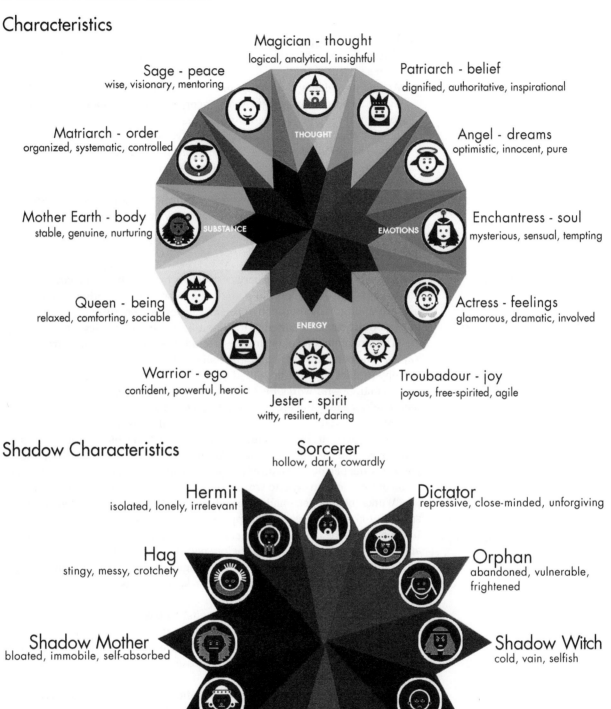

Magician - thought
logical, analytical, insightful

Sage - peace
wise, visionary, mentoring

Patriarch - belief
dignified, authoritative, inspirational

Matriarch - order
organized, systematic, controlled

Angel - dreams
optimistic, innocent, pure

Mother Earth - body
stable, genuine, nurturing

Enchantress - soul
mysterious, sensual, tempting

Queen - being
relaxed, comforting, sociable

Actress - feelings
glamorous, dramatic, involved

Warrior - ego
confident, powerful, heroic

Troubadour - joy
joyous, free-spirited, agile

Jester - spirit
witty, resilient, daring

THOUGHT · SUBSTANCE · EMOTIONS · ENERGY

Shadow Characteristics

Sorcerer
hollow, dark, cowardly

Hermit
isolated, lonely, irrelevant

Dictator
repressive, close-minded, unforgiving

Hag
stingy, messy, crotchety

Orphan
abandoned, vulnerable, frightened

Shadow Mother
bloated, immobile, self-absorbed

Shadow Witch
cold, vain, selfish

Slave
oppressed, tormented, despondent

Addict
wounded, jealous, tragic

Destroyer
angry, aggressive, destructive

Idiot
silly, dimwitted, goofy

Trickster
tricky, phony, scheming

Source: BrandAsset® Consulting: A Young & Rubican Brands Company.

to counsel a psychologically ill person. The agency feels that this approach has numerous advantages:

- Because Archetypes are grounded in the human psyche across all cultures and points in time, it is easy to understand a brand's personality—often multinationally—using such a structure.
- Archetypes telegraph instantly to those responsible for brand communication; indeed, the best of this group already incorporate these notions into how they think of the brand. The model helps the rest of them "catch up."
- Linking measures of BrandAsset® Archetypes to more objective brand perception measures provides strong evidence to assure marketing decision makers that the changes Y&R recommends will achieve concrete business objectives.
- Measuring the health of a brand's personality can act as an "early warning" signal that a brand is in trouble, sometimes years in advance of marketplace indicators. This alerts marketing managers in enough time to tweak the brand as appropriate.[12]

Trait Theory

Popular online matchmaking services such as match.com and eharmony.com offer to create your "personality profile" and then hook you up with other members whose profiles are similar. This approach to personality focuses on the quantitative measurement of **personality traits,** defined as the identifiable characteristics that define a person.

The technique that eLoyalty uses exemplifies the application of trait theory to marketing. This company, which builds tools and services for call centers, compiles personality profiles of each individual caller and matches them with a customer service representative who works best with that personality type. The system is based on a methodology called the Process Communication Model, which NASA used to weed out astronaut candidates and Bill Clinton used to tailor his speeches. The system's creator divided people into six main personality types, each of which has a different communication style and each of which has different stress triggers. It's based on the idea that if you know the personality type of the person you're speaking with, you can modify your own communication style to work more effectively with that person. One such type is the "Workaholic," a personality type who is very task-oriented. If a customer service rep starts chit-chatting to establish rapport with a Workaholic, this approach will backfire. In contrast, a type called the "Reactor" is relationship-oriented, so a rep who does *not* acknowledge the caller's feelings before getting down to business is doomed to failure. The automated system analyzes callers' language patterns to identify their personality type so that each time the customer calls back, he or she is directed to a rep who is a good match for that caller's type.[13]

What are some crucial personality traits? One is that we tend to describe people in terms of whether they are socially outgoing (the trait of *extroversion*); in our opening story Rose is an *introvert* (quiet and reserved), whereas her coworker Jackie is an *extrovert*.[14] Some research evidence suggests that ad messages that match how a person thinks about himself are more persuasive.[15]

According to research firm Mindset Media, personality traits are better predictors of the type of media consumers choose than are demographic variables such as age, gender, and income. The company also claims that the TV shows you watch offer marketers insights into your personality and the types of brands you're likely to prefer, based upon your dominant personality traits and the (perceived) matchup with a brand's image. To find out which personalities are attracted to which TV shows, it recently analyzed self-reported data from about 25,000 TV viewers across more than 70 TV shows. These are some of the media/trait/brand linkages the company generated in its analysis:[16]

- Viewers of *Mad Men* are emotionally sensitive and intellectually curious types who often tend to be dreamers rather than realists. Good brand matches are Apple and the Audi A6.

Products like these from a German company appeal to people who like to be well-organized.
Source: Photo provided courtesy of The Container Store.

- Viewers of *Family Guy* are rebels who don't like authority, rules, or structure they deem unfair, and usually won't hesitate to make their feelings known with anger or sarcasm. Good brand matches are DiGiorno and the Ford F150.
- Viewers of *Glee* are open people who believe that imagination and intellectual pursuits contribute to a good life, and go out in search of unique and varied experiences. They are in touch with their own feelings and may even feel happiness or sadness more intensely than others. Good brand matches are Evian and the Volkswagen Jetta.
- Viewers of *Dancing with the Stars* are traditionalists: who prefer stability and the tried-and-true. They respect authority and generally have their feet firmly grounded. Good brand matches are Kraft and the Chrysler Town and Country.
- Viewers of *The Office* consider themselves superior to others and like to brag about their accomplishments. They also like to be in charge. Good brand matches are Starbucks and the BMW Series 3.

Some specific traits relevant to consumer behavior include *innovativeness* (the degree to which a person likes to try new things), *materialism* (the amount of emphasis a person places on acquiring and owning products), *self-consciousness* (the degree to which a person deliberately monitors and controls the image of the self that he or she projects to others), and *need*

227

for cognition (the degree to which a person likes to think about things and, by extension, expends the necessary effort to process brand information).[17]

Frugality

Another trait relevant to consumer behavior is *frugality*. Frugal people deny short-term purchasing whims; they choose instead to resourcefully use what they already own. For example, this personality type tends to favor cost-saving measures such as timing showers and bringing leftovers from home to have for lunch at work.[18] Obviously, during tough economic times many people reveal their "inner frugalista" as they search for ways to save money. Indeed, in 2008, as the Great Recession invaded, Google searches for the term *frugality* increased by roughly 2,500 percent. As of April 2009, the savings rate—or percentage of income consumers sock away rather than spend—climbed to almost 6 percent, which is a 14-year high. Whereas many of us splurged on expensive cars or Jimmy Choo shoes (or both) in the past, many analysts predict that more of us will be frugal down the road, even if/when the economy improves. They expect to see us buy smaller houses and (gasp!) live within our means as we forsake heavy credit card debt. How accurate is this prediction? Maybe the answer depends on how many of us truly have frugal personality traits versus those who are merely "taking a break" until the economy improves.

Problems with Trait Theory in Consumer Research

Because consumer researchers categorize large numbers of consumers according to whether they exhibit various traits, we can apply this approach to segment markets. If a car manufacturer, for example, determines that drivers who fit a given trait profile prefer a car with certain features, it can use this information to great advantage. The notion that consumers buy products that are extensions of their personalities makes intuitive sense. As we'll see shortly, many marketing managers endorse this idea as they try to create *brand personalities* to appeal to different types of consumers.

Unfortunately, the use of standard personality trait measurements to predict product choices has met with mixed success at best. In general, marketing researchers simply have not been able to predict consumers' behaviors on the basis of measured personality traits. The following are some logical explanations for these less-than-stellar results:[19]

- Many of the scales are not sufficiently valid or reliable; they do not adequately measure what they are supposed to measure, and their results may not be stable over time.
- Psychologists typically develop personality tests for specific populations (e.g., people who are mentally ill); marketers then "borrow" them to apply to a more general population where they have questionable relevance.
- Often marketers don't administer the tests under the appropriate conditions; people who are not properly trained may give them in a classroom or at a kitchen table.
- The researchers often make changes in the instruments to adapt them to their own situations and needs; in the process they may add or delete items and rename variables. These *ad hoc* changes dilute the validity of the measures and also reduce researchers' ability to compare results across consumer samples.
- Many trait scales measure gross, overall tendencies (e.g., emotional stability or introversion); marketers then use these results to make predictions about purchases of specific brands.
- In many cases, marketers ask consumers to respond to a large number of scales with no advance thought about how they will relate these measures to consumer behavior. The researchers then use a "shotgun approach," as they follow up on anything that happens to look interesting. As any statistician will tell you, this approach capitalizes on chance and can produce distorted results that may not be reproducible (or surface at all) in other studies.

Although marketing researchers largely abandoned the use of personality measures after many studies failed to yield meaningful results, some researchers have not given up on the early promise of this line of work. More recent efforts (mainly in Europe) try to learn from past mistakes. Researchers use more specific measures of personality traits that they have reason to believe are relevant to economic behavior. They try to increase the validity of these measures, primarily by including multiple measures of behavior rather than just a single personality scale. In addition, these researchers tone down their expectations of what personality traits can tell them about consumers. They now recognize that traits are only part of the solution; they have to incorporate personality data with information about people's social and economic conditions for it to be useful.[20] As a result, some more recent research has had better success at relating personality traits to such consumer behaviors as alcohol consumption among young men or shoppers' willingness to try new, healthier food products.[21]

Brand Personality

Are Apple users better than the rest of us? Many of us know an "Apple-holic" who likes to turn up his or her nose at the uneducated masses that have to get by with their primitive PCs or Android phones. In fact, a survey of 20,000 people claims that iPad users are unkind and have little empathy; it labels them a "selfish elite." It also described them as "six times more likely to be wealthy, well-educated, power-hungry, over-achieving, sophisticated, unkind and non-altruistic 30- to 50-year-olds. They are self-centered workaholics with an overwhelming interest in business and finance who cherish 'power and achievement' and will not cross the street to help others."[22] Ouch! That's a pretty harsh way to describe people who happen to gravitate toward a successful brand. Do products have personalities, or influence their owners' traits? Let's step back to explore this intriguing question.

In 1886, a momentous event occurred in marketing history: the Quaker Oats man first appeared on boxes of hot cereal. Quakers had a reputation in 19th-century America for being shrewd but fair, and peddlers sometimes dressed as members of this religious group to cash in on their credibility. When the cereal company decided to "borrow" this imagery for its packaging, it hoped that its customers might make the same association.[23]

Today thousands of brands also borrow personality traits of individuals or groups to convey an image they want customers to form of them. A **brand personality** is the set of traits people attribute to a product as if it were a person. An advertising agency wrote the following memo to help it figure out how to portray one of its clients. Based on this description of the "client," can you guess who he is? "He is creative . . . unpredictable . . . an imp. . . . He not only walks and talks, but has the ability to sing, blush, wink, and work with little devices like pointers. . . . He can also play musical instruments. . . . His walking motion is characterized as a 'swagger.' . . . He is made of dough and has mass."[24] Of course, we all know today that packaging and other physical cues create a "personality" for a product (in this case, the Pillsbury Doughboy).

Many of the most recognizable figures in popular culture are spokescharacters for long-standing brands, such as the Jolly Green Giant, the Keebler Elves, Mr. Peanut, or Charlie the Tuna.[25] These personalities periodically get a makeover to keep their meanings current. For example, Bayer recently recast Speedy Alka-Seltzer: In the 1950s and later, he was an all-around good guy who was ready to help with any sort of indigestion. Today he appears as a "wing man" for men in their 20s and 30s who tend to "overindulge" on food and drink. (Do you know anyone who fits this description?) The creative director on the campaign explained that the goal is to introduce Speedy as "the good-times enabler who shows up whenever guys are being guys."[26]

Like people, brand personalities do change over time—whether marketers like Alka-Seltzer want them to or not. To give you an idea of how much things change, Americans ranked these brands as the most stylish in 1993:

1 Levi's
2 Nike
3 Bugle Boy
4 Guess
5 L.A. Gear

A recent study found that consumers infer strong differences in a wine's "personality" based on the bottle's label design.

Source: Reprinted with permission from *Journal of Marketing*, published by the American Marketing Association, Ulrich R. Orth & Keven Malkewitz, May 2008, Vol. 72, p. 73.

Personality Traits		Low	High
Sincerity	Down-to-earth Honest Wholesome Cheerful		
Excitement	Daring Spirited Imaginative Up-to-date		
Competence	Reliable Intelligent Successful		
Sophistication	Upper class Charming		
Ruggedness	Outdoorsy Tough		

By 2008, these were the top five:

1 Victoria's Secret
2 Ralph Lauren
3 Nine West
4 Calvin Klein
5 Coach[27]

Forging a successful brand personality often is key to building brand loyalty, but it's not as easy to accomplish as it might appear. One reason is that many consumers (particularly younger ones) have a very sensitive "BS detector" that alerts them when a brand doesn't live up to its claims or is somehow inauthentic. When this happens, the strategy may backfire as consumers rebel. They may create Web sites to attack the brand or post parodies that make fun of it on YouTube. One set of researchers terms this phenomenon a **Doppelgänger brand image** (one that looks like the original but is in fact a critique of it). For example, many consumers were immensely loyal to the Snapple brand until Quaker purchased it. These loyalists felt that Quaker had stripped the brand of its offbeat, grassroots sensibility; one shock jock renamed it "Crapple" on his radio show.[28]

Our feelings about a brand's personality are part of *brand equity*, which refers to the extent to which a consumer holds strong, favorable, and unique associations with a brand in memory—and the extent to which she or he is willing to pay more for the branded version of a product than for a nonbranded (generic) version.[29] Building strong brands is good business. If you don't believe it, consider that, in a study of 760 *Fortune* 1,000 companies after the stock market took a nosedive in October 1997, the 20 strongest corporate brands (e.g., Microsoft, GE) actually gained in market value, whereas the 20 weakest lost an average of $1 billion each.[30]

So, how do people think about brands? Advertisers are keenly interested in this question, and ad agencies often conduct extensive consumer research to help them understand how consumers will relate to a brand before they roll out campaigns. DDB Worldwide does a global study called "Brand Capital" of 14,000 consumers; Leo Burnett's "Brand Stock" project involves 28,000 interviews. WPP Group has "BrandZ" and Young & Rubicam uses its BrandAsset Valuator®. DDB's worldwide brand planning director observes, "We're not marketing just to isolated individuals. We're marketing to society. How I feel about a brand is directly related to and affected by how others feel about that brand."[31] Some researchers argue that, just as they use the two basic dimensions of warmth and competence to judge people, consumers employ the same labels when they form perceptions of firms; one study found that people perceive nonprofits as being warmer than for-profits but also as being less competent.[32] Table 2 shows some of the things a marketer can do to influence consumers' perceptions of a brand's personality.

We use some personality dimensions to compare and contrast the perceived characteristics of brands in various product categories, including these:[33]

- Old-fashioned, wholesome, traditional
- Surprising, lively, "with it"
- Serious, intelligent, efficient
- Glamorous, romantic, sexy
- Rugged, outdoorsy, tough, athletic

Indeed, consumers appear to have little trouble assigning personality qualities to all sorts of inanimate products, from personal care products to more mundane, functional ones—even kitchen appliances. Whirlpool's research showed that people saw its products as more feminine than they saw competing brands. When respondents were asked to imagine the appliance as a person, many of them pictured a modern, family-oriented woman living in the suburbs—attractive but not flashy. In contrast, they envisioned the

TABLE 2   Brand Behaviors and Possible Personality Trait Inferences

Brand Action	Trait Inference
Brand is repositioned several times or changes its slogan repeatedly	Flighty, schizophrenic
Brand uses continuing character in its advertising	Familiar, comfortable
Brand charges a high price and uses exclusive distribution	Snobbish, sophisticated
Brand frequently available on deal	Cheap, uncultured
Brand offers many line extensions	Versatile, adaptable
Brand sponsors show on PBS or uses recycled materials	Helpful, supportive
Brand features easy-to-use packaging or speaks at consumer's level in advertising	Warm, approachable
Brand offers seasonal clearance sale	Planful, practical
Brand offers five-year warranty or free customer hotline	Reliable, dependable

Source: Based on Susan Fournier, "A Consumer-Brand Relationship Framework for Strategic Brand Management," unpublished doctoral dissertation, University of Florida, 1994, Table 2.2, p. 24.

company's Kitchen Aid brand as a modern professional woman who was glamorous, wealthy, and enjoyed classical music and the theater.[34]

A product that creates and communicates a distinctive brand personality stands out from its competition and inspires years of loyalty. However, personality analysis helps marketers identify a brand's weaknesses that have little to do with its functional qualities: Adidas asked kids in focus groups to imagine that the brand came to life and was at a party, and to tell what they would expect the brand to be doing there. The kids responded that Adidas would be hanging around the keg with its pals, talking about girls. Unfortunately, they also said Nike would *be with* the girls![35] The results reminded Adidas' brand managers that they had some work to do. We compare this process to **animism**, the common cultural practice whereby people attribute to inanimate objects qualities that make them somehow alive.[36]

We tend to *anthropomorphize* objects, which happens when we attribute human characteristics to them. We may think about a cartoon character or mythical creation as

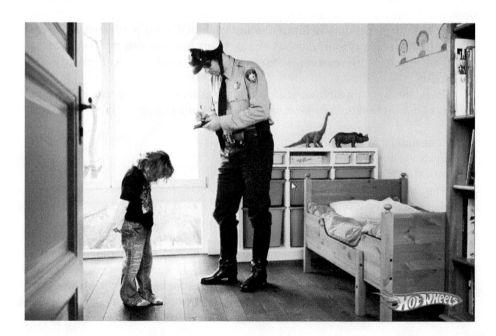

Advertisers often rely on vivid images to communicate part of a brand's personality.
Source: Courtesy of Mattel.

if it were a person and even assume that it has human feelings. Again, think about familiar spokescharacters such as Charlie the Tuna, the Keebler Elves, or the Michelin Man—or consider the frustration some people feel when they come to believe their computer is smarter than they are or even that it's "conspiring" to make them crazy! In research for its client Sprint Business Services, Grey Advertising found that when customers imagined long-distance carriers as animals, they envisioned AT&T as a lion, MCI as a snake, and Sprint as a puma. Grey used these results to position Sprint as a company that could "help you do more business" rather than taking the more aggressive approach of its competitors.[38]

In a sense, a brand personality is a statement about the brand's market position. Understanding this is crucial to marketing strategy, especially if consumers don't see the brand the way its makers intend them to and they must attempt to *reposition* the product (i.e., give it a personality makeover). That's the problem Volvo now faces: Its cars are renowned for safety, but drivers don't exactly see them as exciting or sexy. A safe and solid brand personality makes it hard to sell a racy convertible like the C70 model, so a British ad tried to change that perception with the tagline, "Lust, envy, jealousy. The dangers of a Volvo." Just as with people, however, you can only go so far to convince others that your personality has changed. Volvo has been trying to jazz up its image for years, but for the most part consumers aren't buying it. In an earlier attempt in the United Kingdom, the company paired action images like a Volvo pulling a helicopter off a cliff with the headline "Safe Sex"—but market research showed that people didn't believe the new image. As one brand consultant observed, "You get the sort of feeling you get when you see your grandparents trying to dance the latest dance. Slightly amused and embarrassed."[39] Still, Volvo keeps trying to morph into a sexy brand. It calls its new S60 model the Naughty S60, and to launch to the car in Europe the company hosted underground parties in London, Paris, Milan, Berlin, and Madrid. What the partygoers didn't know was that at each event Volvo created—and filmed—a series of experiments, "carefully designed to measure guests' naughtiness, conformity, daring, confidence, curiosity and desire." More than 3,000 partygoers were secretly filmed (check out the videos on Volvo's Subject360 YouTube channel) to see which city's residents were most likely to break the rules. Spoiler alert: Paris is officially the "Naughty Capital of Europe."[40]

OBJECTIVE 2

Psychographics go beyond simple demographics to help marketers understand and reach different consumer segments.

Psychographics

When Cadillac introduced its Escalade sport utility vehicle, critics scoffed at the bizarre pairing of this old-line luxury brand with a truck. However, consumers quickly associated the vehicle with the hip-hop lifestyle. Artists such as Jennifer Lopez, Outkast, and Jay-Z referred to it in songs, and Jermaine Dupri proclaimed, "Gotta have me an Escalade." Three years later, Cadillac went even further when it rolled out its 18-foot Escalade EXT pickup with a sticker price of $50,000.

The Escalade brand manager describes the target customer for luxury pickups as a slightly earthier version of the SUV buyer. She says that although the two drivers may own $2 million homes next door to each other, the typical luxury SUV driver is about 50, has an MBA from Harvard, belongs to a golf club, maintains connections with his college friends, and works hard at keeping up with the Joneses. In contrast, the luxury pickup driver is roughly 5 years younger. He might have inherited his father's construction business, and he's been working since he was 18 years old. He may or may not have attended college, and unlike the SUV driver, he is absolutely still connected to his high school friends.[41]

As this example shows, marketers often find it useful to develop products that appeal to different lifestyle groups; simply knowing a person's income doesn't predict whether he or she will drive a Cadillac Escalade SUV, pickup, or a Cadillac El Dorado sedan. As

Marketing Pitfall

Yes, colleges have brand personalities too—though, as with other products, these images aren't always an accurate (or desirable) reflection of the place. ESPN had to pull the plug on an advertising campaign for its collegiate basketball coverage after managers learned that Anomaly, the advertising agency ESPN had retained for the campaign, intended to recruit actors who would play the stereotypical students at numerous schools. The idea was to have the students stationed at a call center; they would phone consumers to convince them to watch their school play on TV. Here are just a few of the "brand personalities" a leaked memo described:

- U. Tennessee: "a slutty girl who would hang out at the cowgirl hall of fame."
- Duke: "a smart, with it, young white male. He's handsome. He's from money. He is, in short, the kind of guy everyone can't stand. He is the kind of guy everyone wants to be."
- Oklahoma: "is awesome and he thinks everything is awesome. He's very enthusiastic about all things call center and all things life and he wants to share this contagious enthusiasm with everyone he meets. Wide-eyed, as naive as they come."
- Purdue: "child prodigy. 14-year-old. Or open to an 18-year-old who looks 14. Aeronautical engineering. Wiz kid. Think McLovin from *Superbad*."
- Kansas: "straight off the farm. However, he takes great pains to point out that Kansas is very cosmopolitan, as witnessed by their record, their burgeoning tech industry, and their hybrid corns (bonus: modified by fish genes!)."
- Villanova: "the poor man's Duke—he's not quite as handsome, he's not quite as rich, he's not quite as dapper. After 2 or 3 beers though, who cares? . . . he's friendly enough."
- Pittsburgh: "a tomboy. She obviously grew up in the neighborhood and isn't going to take any guff from anyone and she'll wallop you in the eye with a crowbar if you suggest different. So don't. Think Tina Fey type."
- Georgetown: "a 4.36 GPA who's lived in 9 world-class cities, but all the time in her sister's shadow (her GPA is 4.37). She's sort of the female Duke, except most people like her. Think Reese Witherspoon."[37]

As this Spanish ad implies, psychographic analyses allow marketers to match up consumers with products and styles that reflect their identities.
Source: Ad Agency: SCPF, Photographer: Biel Capllonch, Model: Mamen Bayer.

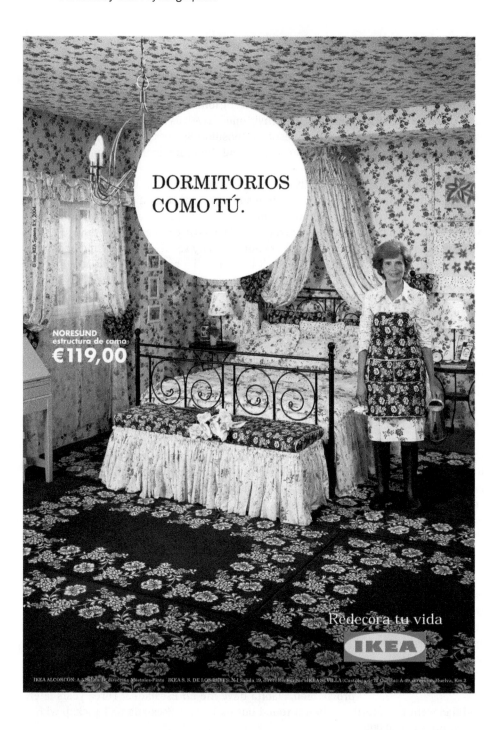

DORMITORIOS COMO TÚ.

NORESUND
estructura de cama
€119,00

Redecora tu vida

IKEA

IKEA ALCORCÓN: A-5 Salida 17, dirección Móstoles-Pinto IKEA S. S. DE LOS REYES: N-1 Salida 19, dirección Burgos IKEA SEVILLA (Castilleja de la Cuesta): A-49, dirección Huelva, Km.2

Jackie's, Hank's, and Rose's choices demonstrated, consumers can share the same demographic characteristics and still be very different people. For this reason, marketers need a way to "breathe life" into demographic data to really identify, understand, and target consumer segments that will share a set of preferences for their products and services.

Earlier in this chapter we discussed some of the differences in consumers' personalities that may influence their product choices. When marketers combine personality variables with knowledge of lifestyle preferences, they have a powerful lens they can focus on consumer segments. Adidas, for example, describes different types of shoe buyers in terms of lifestyles so that it can address the needs of segments such as *Gearheads* (hard-core, older runners who want high-performance shoes), *Popgirls* (teeny-boppers who hang out at the mall and wear Skechers), and *Fastidious Eclectus* (bohemian, cutting-edge types who want hip, distinctive products).[42] It's fairly common for companies to divide up their customers along lifestyle dimensions and label them to quickly communicate to their creative and strategy people just how to talk to different groups. The makers of the popular Sigg water bottle, which is available in many different designs, actually choose from about 3,000 different concepts each year with specific customers in mind. These include the *Whole Foods Woman,* who lives in a city, practices yoga, and buys organic produce; and the *Geek Chic Guy,* who listens to Radiohead and wears vintage Converse sneakers.[43]

We call this approach **psychographics,** which involves the "use of psychological, sociological, and anthropological factors . . . to determine how the market is segmented by the propensity of groups within the market—and their reasons—to make a particular decision about a product, person, ideology, or otherwise hold an attitude or use a medium."[44]

The Roots of Psychographics

Marketers first developed psychographic research methodologies in the 1960s and 1970s to address the shortcomings of two other types of consumer research: motivational research and quantitative survey research. Recall that motivational research, which involves intensive, one-to-one interviews and projective tests, yields a lot of information about a few people. As we've seen, though, this information is often idiosyncratic and therefore it may not be very reliable. At the other extreme, quantitative survey research, or large-scale demographic surveys, yields only a little information about a lot of people. As some researchers observed, "The marketing manager who wanted to know why people ate the competitor's cornflakes was told '32 percent of the respondents said taste, 21 percent said flavor, 15 percent said texture, 10 percent said price, and 22 percent said don't know or no answer.'"[45]

Sigg water bottles are designed with specific types of users in mind.

Source: Bill Hogan/Chicago Tribune/Newscom.

235

Marketers use many psychographic variables to segment consumers, but all of these dimensions go beyond surface characteristics to investigate consumers' motivations for purchasing and using products. Demographics allows us to describe *who* buys, but psychographics tells us *why* they do. A classic example involves a very popular Canadian advertising campaign for Molson Export beer that included insights from psychographic findings. The company's research showed that Molson's target customers tend to be like boys who never grew up, who were uncertain about the future, and who were intimidated by women's newfound freedoms. Accordingly, the ads featured a group of men, "Fred and the boys," whose get-togethers emphasized male companionship, protection against change, and the reassuring message that the beer "keeps on tasting great."[46]

How Do We Perform a Psychographic Analysis?

Some early attempts at lifestyle segmentation "borrowed" standard psychological scales (that psychologists use to measure pathology or personality disturbances) and related test scores to product usage. As we saw earlier in the chapter, such efforts were largely disappointing. These tests were never intended to be related to everyday consumption activities, so they didn't do much to explain people's purchases. The technique is more effective when the marketers include variables that are more closely related to actual consumer behaviors. If you want to understand purchases of household cleaning products, you are better off asking people about their attitudes toward household cleanliness than testing for personality disorders!

Psychographic studies take several different forms:

- **A lifestyle profile** looks for items that differentiate between users and nonusers of a product.
- **A product-specific profile** identifies a target group and then profiles these consumers on product-relevant dimensions.
- **A general lifestyle segmentation** places a large sample of respondents into homogenous groups based on similarities of their overall preferences.
- **A product-specific segmentation study** tailors questions to a product category. For example, if a researcher wants to conduct research for a stomach medicine, she might rephrase the item, "I worry too much" as, "I get stomach problems if I worry too much." This allows her to more finely discriminate among users of competing brands.[47]

In this British ad, Honda targets eco-conscious consumers.

Source: Courtesy of Honda/Wieden & Kennedy, London.

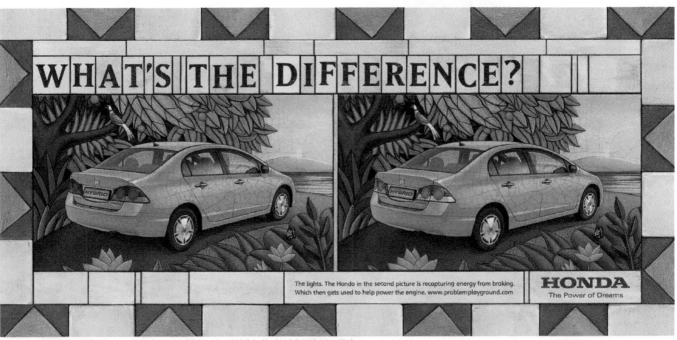

WHAT'S THE DIFFERENCE?

The lights. The Honda in the second picture is recapturing energy from braking. Which then gets used to help power the engine. www.problemplayground.com

HONDA
The Power of Dreams

Model shown is Honda Civic Hybrid I.4 IMA in mpg (L/100km): Urban 54.3 (5.2), Extra Urban 65.7 (4.3), Combined 61.4 (4.6), CO2 Emissions 109 g/km.

TABLE 3	Lifestyle Dimensions		
Activities	**Interests**	**Opinions**	**Demographics**
Work	Family	Themselves	Age
Hobbies	Home	Social issues	Education
Social events	Job	Politics	Income
Vacation	Community	Business	Occupation
Entertainment	Recreation	Economics	Family size
Club membership	Fashion	Education	Dwelling
Community	Food	Products	Geography
Shopping	Media	Future	City size
Sports	Achievements	Culture	Stage in life cycle

Source: William D. Wells and Douglas J. Tigert, "Activities, Interests, and Opinions," *Journal of Advertising Research* 11 (August 1971): 27–35. © 1971 by The Advertising Research Foundation. Used with permission.

AIOs

Most contemporary psychographic research attempts to group consumers according to some combination of three categories of variables: activities, interests, and opinions, which we call **AIOs**. Using data from large samples, marketers create profiles of customers who resemble each other in terms of their activities and patterns of product usage.[48] Table 3 lists commonly used AIO dimensions.

To group consumers into AIO categories, researchers give respondents a long list of statements and ask them to indicate how much they agree with each one. Thus, we can "boil down" a person's lifestyle by discovering how he spends his time, what he finds interesting and important, and how he views himself and the world around him.

Typically, the first step in conducting a psychographic analysis is to determine which lifestyle segments yield the bulk of customers for a particular product. According to a very general rule of thumb that marketers call the **80/20 rule**—only 20 percent of a product's users account for 80 percent of the volume of product a company sells—researchers attempt to determine who uses the brand and try to isolate heavy, moderate, and light users. They also look for patterns of usage and attitudes toward the product. In many cases, only a few lifestyle segments account for the majority of brand users.[49] Marketers primarily target these heavy users, even though they may constitute a relatively small number of total users.

After marketers identify and understand their heavy users, they consider more specifically how these customers relate to the brand. Heavy users may have quite different reasons for using the product; often we can further subdivide them in terms of the *benefits* they derive from using the product or service. For instance, marketers at the beginning of the walking-shoe craze assumed that all purchasers were basically burned-out joggers. Subsequent psychographic research showed that there were actually several different groups of "walkers," ranging from those who walk to get to work to those who walk for fun. This realization resulted in shoes that manufacturers aimed at different segments, from Footjoy Joy-Walkers to Nike Healthwalkers.

How Do We Use Psychographic Data?

Marketers use the results of these studies in several ways:

- **To define the target market**—This information allows the marketer to go beyond simple demographic or product usage descriptions (e.g., middle-aged men or frequent users).

- **To create a new view of the market**—Sometimes marketers create their strategies with a "typical" customer in mind. This stereotype may not be correct, because the actual customer may not match these assumptions. For example, marketers of a face cream for women were surprised to find that older, widowed women were their heavy users rather than the younger, sociable women to whom they were pitching their appeals.
- **To position the product**—Psychographic information can allow the marketer to emphasize features of the product that fit in with a person's lifestyle. A company that wants to target people whose lifestyle profiles show a high need to be around other people might focus on its product's ability to help meet this social need.
- **To better communicate product attributes**—Psychographic information can offer very useful input to advertising creatives who must communicate something about the product. The artist or copywriter obtains a much richer mental image of the target consumer than she can simply by looking at dry statistics. For example, research that the Schlitz beer company conducted found that heavy beer drinkers tended to feel that life's pleasures were few and far between. In response, the brewer developed commercials with the tagline, "You only go around once, so reach for all the gusto you can."[50]
- **To develop product strategy**—Understanding how a product fits, or does not fit, into consumers' lifestyles allows the marketer to identify new product opportunities, chart media strategies, and create environments most consistent and harmonious with these consumption patterns.
- **To market social and political issues**—Psychographic segmentation can be an important tool in political campaigns, and policy makers can also employ the technique to find commonalities among consumers who engage in destructive behaviors, such as drug use or excessive gambling. A psychographic study of men aged 18 to 24 who drink and drive highlights the potential for this perspective to help in the eradication of harmful behaviors. Researchers divided this segment into four groups: "good timers," "well adjusted," "nerds," and "problem kids." They found that one group in particular—"good timers"—was more likely to believe that it is fun to be drunk, that the chances of having an accident while driving drunk are low, and that drinking increases one's appeal to the opposite sex. Because the study showed that this group is also the most likely to drink at rock concerts and parties, is most likely to watch MTV, and tends to listen to album-oriented rock radio stations, reaching "good timers" with a prevention campaign became easier.[51]

Psychographic Segmentation Typologies

Marketers constantly search for new insights so they can identify and reach groups of consumers united by common lifestyles. To meet this need, many research companies and advertising agencies develop their own *segmentation typologies*. Respondents answer a battery of questions that allow the researchers to cluster them into a set of distinct lifestyle groups. The questions usually include a mixture of AIOs plus other items relating to feelings about specific brands, favorite celebrities, and media preferences. Companies that want to learn more about their customers and potential customers then buy one or more of these systems for their own use.

At least at a superficial level, many of these typologies are fairly similar to one another; they usually divide the population into roughly five to eight segments. Researchers give each cluster a descriptive name, and clients receive a profile of "typical" members. Unfortunately, it is often difficult to compare or evaluate different typologies because the methods and data that analysts use to devise these systems frequently are *proprietary;* that is, the company owns the information and does not share its findings with outsiders. Let's review a few typical approaches to classifying consumers in terms of lifestyles.

Perhaps the best-known segmentation system is *The Values and Lifestyles System* (*VALS2*™) that SBI International developed. SBI built the original VALS™ system on consumers' extent of agreement with various social issues such as abortion rights. After about 10 years, SBI discovered that the social issues it used to categorize consumers were not as predictive of consumer behavior as they once had been. SBI searched for a more powerful way to segment consumers, and the company discovered that certain lifestyle indicators such as "I like a lot of excitement in my life" were better predictors of purchase behavior than the degree to which a person agreed or disagreed with a social value.

The current VALS2™ system uses a battery of 39 items (35 psychological and 4 demographic) to divide U.S. adults into groups, each with distinctive characteristics. As Figure 2 shows, the typology arranges groups vertically by their resources (including such factors as income, education, energy levels, and eagerness to buy) and horizontally by self-orientation.

Three self-orientations constitute the horizontal dimension. Consumers with an *Ideals* orientation rely on a belief system to make purchase decisions, and they are not concerned with the views of others. People with an *Achievement* orientation are more competitive; they take into account what their peers will think about their decisions and how these choices will reflect on them. Finally, those with a *Self-Expression* orientation are more concerned with the emotional aspects of purchases and the satisfaction they will personally receive from products and services.

- **Innovators**—the top VALS2™ group, are successful consumers with many resources. This group is concerned with social issues and is open to change.

The next three groups also have sufficient resources, but differ in their outlooks on life:[52]

- **Thinkers**—are satisfied, reflective, and comfortable.
- **Achievers**—are career oriented and prefer predictability to risk or self-discovery.
- **Experiencers**—are impulsive, young, and enjoy offbeat or risky experiences.

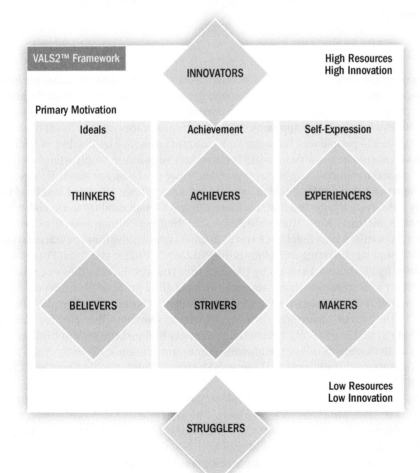

Figure 2 VALS2™
Source: SRI International, Menlo Park, CA.

The next four groups have fewer resources:

- **Believers**—have strong principles and favor proven brands.
- **Strivers**—are similar to Achievers but have fewer resources. They are very concerned about the approval of others.
- **Makers**—are action oriented and tend to focus their energies on self-sufficiency. They will often be found working on their cars, canning their own vegetables, or building their own houses.
- **Strugglers**—are at the bottom of the economic ladder. They are most concerned with meeting the needs of the moment and have limited ability to acquire anything beyond the basic goods needed for survival.

The VALS2™ system is a useful way to understand people like Jackie and Hank. SBI estimates that 12 percent of American adults are thrill seekers, who tend to fall into the system's Experiencer category and are likely to agree with statements such as, "I like a lot of excitement in my life" and "I like to try new things." Experiencers like to break the rules, and extreme sports such as sky surfing or bungee-jumping attract them. Not too surprisingly, one-third of consumers aged 18 to 34 belong in this category, so it has attracted the interest of many marketers who are trying to appeal to younger people. For example, VALS2™ helped Isuzu market its Rodeo sport utility vehicle by focusing on Experiencers, many of whom believe it is fun to break rules in ways that do not endanger others. Isuzu positioned the Rodeo as a vehicle that lets a driver do just that. It created advertising to support this idea by showing kids jumping in mud puddles, running with scissors, and coloring outside the lines.[53] Isuzu sales increased significantly after this campaign. If you want to see what VALS2™ type you are, go to www.strategicbusinessinsights.com/vals/presurvey.shtml.

Geodemography

Geodemography refers to analytical techniques that combine data on consumer expenditures and other socioeconomic factors with geographic information about the areas in which people live, in order to identify consumers who share common consumption patterns. Researchers base this approach on the common assumption that "birds of a feather flock together"—people who have similar needs and tastes also tend to live near one another, so it should be possible to locate "pockets" of like-minded people whom marketers can reach more economically by direct mail and other methods. For example, a marketer who wants to reach white, single consumers who are college educated and tend to be fiscally conservative may find that it is more efficient to mail catalogs to zip codes 20770 (Greenbelt, MD) and 90277 (Redondo Beach, CA) than to adjoining areas in either Maryland or California, where there are fewer consumers who exhibit these characteristics.

One popular clustering technique is the **PRIZM NE** (PRIZM stands for Potential Rating Index by Zip Market) system by Claritas, Inc. This system classifies every U.S. Zip Code into 1 of 66 categories, ranging from the most affluent "Blue-Blood Estates" to the least well-off "Public Assistance."[54] It terms a resident of Southern California "Money & Brains" if she lives in Encino (Zip Code 91316), whereas someone living in Sherman Oaks (Zip Code 91423) is a "Young Influential."[55] Claritas updated the system from its original set of 40 clusters to reflect the growing ethnic and economic diversity of the United States; some new clusters include "American Dreams," "Kids & Cul-de-Sacs," and "Young Literati."[56]

Residents of different clusters display marked differences in their consumption of products, from annuities to Ziploc bags. The system also ranks these groupings by income, home value, and occupation (i.e., a rough index of social class) on a ZQ (Zip Quality) scale. Table 4 provides an idea of how dramatically different the consumption patterns of two clusters can be. This table compares consumption data for "Furs & Station Wagons," the third-highest-ranking cluster, with "Tobacco Roads," the third-lowest. You can check out your own Zip Code at MyBestSegments.com.[57]

TABLE 4	A Comparison of Two PRIZM Clusters

Furs & Station Wagons (ZQ3)		Tobacco Roads (ZQ38)	
New money, parents in 40s and 50s		Racially mixed farm towns in the South	
Newly built subdivisions with tennis courts, swimming pools, gardens		Small downtowns with thrift shops, diners, and laundromats; shanty-type homes without indoor plumbing	
Sample neighborhoods:		Sample neighborhoods:	
Plano, TX (75075)		Belzoni, MI (39038)	
Dunwoody, GA (30338)		Warrenton, NC (27589)	
Needham, MA (02192)		Gates, VA (27937)	
High Usage	**Low Usage**	**High Usage**	**Low Usage**
Country clubs	Motorcycles	Travel by bus	Knitting
Wine by the case	Laxatives	Asthma relief remedies	Live theater
Lawn furniture	Nonfilter cigarettes	Malt liquors	Smoke detectors
Gourmet magazine	Chewing tobacco	*Grit* magazine	*Ms.* magazine
BMW 5 Series	*Hunting* magazine	Pregnancy tests	Ferraris
Rye bread	Chevrolet Chevettes	Pontiac Bonnevilles	Whole-wheat bread
Natural cold cereal	Canned stews	Shortening	Mexican foods

Note: Usage rates as indexed to average consumption across all 40 clusters.
Source: "A Comparison of Two Prizm Clusters" from *The Clustering of America* by Michael J. Weiss. Copyright © 1988 by Michael J. Weiss. Reprinted by permission of the Sagalyn Literary Agency.

Although consumers in two very different clusters may purchase a product at an equivalent rate, these similarities end when we take their other purchases into account. These differences highlight the importance of going beyond simple product-category purchase data and demographics to really understand a market (remember the earlier discussion of product complementarity). For example, people in "Urban Gold Coast," "Money & Brains," and "Blue-Blood Estates" communities buy a lot of high-quality binoculars, but so do those in the "Grain Belt," "New Homesteaders," and "Agri-Business" clusters. The difference is that the former groups use the binoculars to watch birds and other wildlife, whereas the latter use them to help line up the animals in their gun sights. Furthermore, whereas the bird watchers do a lot of foreign travel, listen to classical music, and host cocktail parties, the bird hunters travel by bus, like country music, and belong to veterans' clubs.

Behavioral Targeting

The latest and hottest extension of lifestyle marketing is **behavioral targeting**, where e-commerce marketers serve up customized ads on Web sites or cable TV stations based on a customer's prior activity.[58] A long-term study conducted by Comcast reported that people who lived in households that received targeted ads were about one-third less likely to change the channel than those who were shown traditional ads.[59] Customized messaging continues to entice advertisers; CBS Mobile recently announced a partnership with the social networking service Loopt to track participating families on their cell phones. The idea is to tailor promotions to consumers so specifically that they can receive special offers as they walk by specific stores and restaurants.[60]

As the technology to track where we go online continues to improve, so too does marketers' ability to send very specific messages to us based upon the other places we've surfed. Increasingly we will see ads for categories of products we have shown interest in before, whether these are tennis rackets or bank loans. The advertising industry refers to this technique as **personalized retargeting**. This is a form of behavioral targeting, but unlike other techniques that just serve up messages based on general interests (e.g., if you visit an NFL team's site you might get an ad for Under Armour workout clothing), retargeting provides messages that refer to the exact product you checked out. It's almost starting to feel as if companies are sitting right behind us as we move from Web site to Web site. What's really happening is that when you visit an e-commerce site like Zappos and check out a pair of Steve Madden shoes, a cookie gets inserted in your browser that links to that item. When you use your computer again, the advertising system creates an ad for that same item. Google introduced this technique in 2009, and now the company makes it available to all advertisers who use its AdWords network.[61]

MyMarketingLab

The Tangled Web

As online tracking methods proliferate, your surfing choices become part of a broad network of data that specialized companies buy and sell. These operations embed a code called a **beacon** in people's hard drives that captures what they type on Web sites, such as their comments on music, clothes, or even their interest in getting pregnant or buying a treatment for erectile dysfunction. They package that data into anonymous profiles, then sell these profiles to companies that want to reach just those kinds of people. For example, a typical deal for a buyer that wants to locate movie lovers is about $1.00 per thousand names.

How widespread is this practice? A *Wall Street Journal* study found that the nation's 50 top Web sites, on average, installed 64 pieces of tracking technology onto the computers of visitors, usually with no warning. Profiles are bought and sold on stock-market-like exchanges. For example, a company called BlueKai sells 50 million pieces of information like this about specific individuals' browsing habits, for as little as a tenth of a cent apiece. The auctions can happen instantly, as a Web site is visited.

When the researchers at the newspaper used their company computer as a guinea pig, they found that major Web sites such as MSN.com and Yahoo's ad network placed numerous tracking files filled with data that enabled the programmers to predict a user's age, Zip Code, gender, income, marital status, presence of children, and home ownership, as well as lifestyle interests such as concerns about weight loss.[62]

OBJECTIVE 3
Consumer activities can be harmful to individuals and to society.

The Dark Side of Consumer Behavior

In late 2008, a crowd assembled for a big holiday sale at a Wal-Mart store in New York. When the doors opened, the crowd trampled a temporary worker to death as people rushed to grab discounted merchandise off the store shelves. A lawsuit filed on behalf of the man's survivors claimed that in addition to providing inadequate security, the retailer "engaged in specific marketing and advertising techniques to specifically attract a large crowd and create an environment of frenzy and mayhem."[63] Just how far will people go to secure a bargain?

Despite the best efforts of researchers, government regulators, and concerned industry people, sometimes consumers' worst enemies are themselves. We think of individuals as rational decision makers, calmly doing their best to obtain products and services that will maximize the health and well-being of themselves, their families, and their society. In reality, however, consumers' desires, choices, and actions often result in negative consequences to individuals and the society in which they live.

Some of these actions are relatively harmless, but others have more onerous consequences. Some harmful consumer behaviors, such as excessive drinking or cigarette smoking, stem from social pressures, and the cultural value many of us place on money encourages activities such as shoplifting and insurance fraud. Exposure to unattainable ideals of beauty and success can create dissatisfaction with ourselves. Let's review some dimensions of the "dark side" of consumer behavior.

Consumer Terrorism

The terrorist attacks of 2001 were a wake-up call to the free-enterprise system. They revealed the vulnerability of nonmilitary targets and reminded us that disruptions of our financial, electronic, and supply networks can potentially be more damaging to our way of life than the fallout from a conventional battlefield. These incursions may be deliberate or not—economic shockwaves from "mad cow" disease in Europe are still reverberating in the beef industry.[64] Assessments by the Rand Corporation and other analysts point to the susceptibility of the nation's food supply as a potential target of **bioterrorism**.[65]

Even before the anthrax scares of 2001, toxic substances placed in products threatened to hold the marketplace hostage. This tactic first drew public attention in the United States in 1982, when seven people died after taking Tylenol pills that had been laced with cyanide. A decade later, Pepsi weathered its own crisis when more than 50 reports of syringes found in Diet Pepsi cans surfaced in 23 states. In that case, Pepsi pulled off a PR *coup de grace* by convincing the public that the syringes could not have been introduced during the manufacturing process. The company even showed an in-store surveillance video that caught a customer slipping a syringe into a Diet Pepsi can while the cashier's head was turned.[66] Pepsi's aggressive actions underscore the importance of responding to such a crisis head-on and quickly.

More recently, a publicity campaign for a late-night cartoon show backfired when it aroused fears of a terrorist attack and temporarily shut down the city of Boston. The "guerrilla marketing" effort consisted of 1-foot-tall blinking electronic signs with hanging wires and batteries that marketers used to promote the Cartoon Network TV show *Aqua Teen Hunger Force* (a surreal series about a talking milkshake, a box of fries, and a meatball). The signs were placed on bridges and in other high-profile spots in several U.S. cities. Most depicted a boxy, cartoon character giving passersby the finger. The bomb squads and other police personnel required to investigate the mysterious boxes cost the city of Boston more than $500,000—and a lot of frayed nerves.[67]

Addictive Consumption

Although most people equate addiction with drugs, consumers can use virtually any product or service to relieve (at least temporarily) some problem or satisfy some need to the point that reliance on it becomes extreme. Though addictions of course include alcoholism, drug addiction, and nicotine addiction, it seems we can become dependent on almost anything—there is even a Chapstick Addicts support group with 250 active members![68] **Consumer addiction** is a physiological or psychological dependency on products or services. Many companies profit from selling addictive products or from selling solutions for kicking a bad habit.

This ad from Singapore discourages young people from using ketamine, an animal tranquilizer.
Source: Used with permission of Saatchi & Saatchi of Singapore.

Addiction to Technology

Even technology can be addicting, as anyone with a BlackBerry can attest: Some people call this little device by the nickname of "CrackBerry" because it's so hard to stop checking it constantly. Some psychologists compare social media addiction to chemical dependency, to the point of inducing symptoms of withdrawal when users are deprived of their fix. As one noted, "Everyone is a potential addict—they're just waiting for their drug of choice to come along, whether heroin, running, junk food or social media."[69] The country with the largest number of social media addicts today? According to a Nielsen survey, it's Italy, which has the highest per capita use of Facebook of any nation. Psychologists there report that addicts are ignoring the real world as they choose to stay connected to their virtual worlds day and night. The country's 16 million Facebook users spend an average of 6 hours and 27 minutes on the site per month.[70] The problem continues to grow as more of us "drink the Kool-Aid"; you may have spent that much time on your Facebook page before you came to class today!

Internet addiction has been a big headache for several years already in South Korea, where 90 percent of homes connect to cheap, high-speed broadband. Many young Koreans' social lives revolve around the "PC *bang*," dim Internet parlors that sit on practically every street corner. A government study estimates that up to 30 percent of South Koreans under 18 are at risk of Internet addiction. Many already exhibit signs of actual addiction, including an inability to stop themselves from using computers, rising levels of tolerance that drive them to seek ever-longer sessions online, and withdrawal symptoms such as anger and craving when they can't log on. Some users have literally dropped dead from exhaustion after playing online games for days on end.[71]

Other problems arise when people become overly involved in playing online games. Consider these two tragic cases:

- In the UK, a 33-year-old widowed mother let her two dogs starve to death and neglected her three kids after becoming hooked on the online game *Small World*. A judge banned her from going on the Internet. The woman slept only two hours a night as she played the virtual reality game (in which dwarves and giants battle to conquer the world) almost nonstop for six months. Her children—aged 9, 10, and 13—had no hot food and "drank" cold baked beans from tins because there were no spoons. When the family's two dogs died from neglect, she left their bodies rotting in the dining room for two months.[72]
- An American woman pled guilty to a charge of second-degree murder in the death of her three-month-old son. The 22-year-old mother lost her temper when her child began crying while she was playing *FarmVille* on Facebook; she shook the baby until it died.

Compulsive Consumption

Some consumers take the expression "born to shop" quite literally. They shop because they are compelled to do so rather than because shopping is a pleasurable or functional task. **Compulsive consumption** refers to repetitive and often excessive shopping performed as an antidote to tension, anxiety, depression, or boredom.[73] "Shopaholics" turn to shopping much the way addicted people turn to drugs or alcohol.[74] One man diagnosed with *compulsive shopping disorder* (*CSD*) bought more than 2,000 wrenches and never used any of them. Therapists report that women clinically diagnosed with CSD outnumber men by four to one. They speculate that women are attracted to items such as clothes and cosmetics to enhance their interpersonal relationships, whereas men tend to focus on gadgetry, tools, and guns to achieve a sense of power.

One out of twenty U.S. adults is unable to control the buying of goods that he or she does not really want or need. Some researchers say compulsive shopping may be related to low self-esteem. It affects an estimated 2 to 16 percent of the adult U.S. population.[75] In some cases, like a drug addict the consumer has little or no control over his or her consumption. Whether it is alcohol, cigarettes, chocolate, diet colas, or even Chapstick, the products control the consumer. Even the act of shopping itself is an addicting experience for some people. Three common elements characterize many negative or destructive consumer behaviors:[76]

1 The behavior is not done by choice.
2 The gratification derived from the behavior is short-lived.
3 The person experiences strong feelings of regret or guilt afterward.

Gambling is an example of a consumption addiction that touches every segment of consumer society. Whether it takes the form of casino gambling, playing the "slots," betting on sports events with friends or through a bookie, or even buying lottery tickets, excessive gambling can be quite destructive. Taken to extremes, gambling can result in lowered self-esteem, debt, divorce, and neglected children. According to one psychologist, gamblers exhibit a classic addictive cycle: They experience a "high" while in action and depression when they stop gambling, which leads them back to the thrill of the action. Unlike drug addicts, however, money is the substance that hard-core gamblers abuse.

Consumed Consumers

Consumed consumers are people who are used or exploited, willingly or not, for commercial gain in the marketplace. The situations in which consumers become commodities can range from traveling road shows that feature dwarfs and midgets to the selling of body parts and babies. Check out these consumed consumers:

- Prostitutes—Expenditures on prostitution in the United States alone are estimated at $20 billion annually. These revenues are equivalent to those in the domestic shoe industry.[78]
- Organ, blood, and hair donors—By one estimate, you could make about $46 million if you donated every reusable part of your body (do not try this at home).[79] In the United States, millions of people sell their blood. A lively market also exists for organs (e.g., kidneys), and some women sell their hair to be made into wigs. Bidding for a human kidney on eBay went to more than $5.7 million before the company ended the auction (it's illegal to sell human organs online . . . at least so far). The seller wrote, "You can choose either kidney. . . . Of course only one for sale, as I need the other one to live. Serious bids only."[80]

IN 2066, BIN LADEN WILL BE CAUGHT.

LIVE TO SEE IT. QUIT SMOKING NOW

ADESF

This Brazilian ad is part of a campaign to combat cigarette addiction. It looks like we're actually ahead of schedule!
Source: Courtesy of ADESF Association for Smoker Awareness; Neoqama/BBH.

● **Babies for sale**—Several thousand surrogate mothers have been paid to be medically impregnated and carry babies to term for infertile couples. A fertile woman between the ages of 18 and 25 can "donate" one egg every 3 months and rake in $7,000 each time. Over 8 years, that's 32 eggs for a total of $224,000.[81] In one case in Germany, police arrested a couple when they tried to auction their 8-month-old son on eBay. The parents claimed that the offer, which read "Baby—collection only. Offer my nearly new baby for sale because it cries too much. Male, 70 cm long" was just a joke.[82]

Illegal Activities

In addition to being self-destructive or socially damaging, many consumer behaviors are illegal as well. Analysts estimate the cost of crimes that consumers commit against business at more than $40 billion per year. A survey the McCann-Erickson advertising agency conducted revealed the following tidbits:[83]

● Ninety-one percent of people say they lie regularly. One in three fibs about his or her weight, one in four about income, and 21 percent lie about their age. Nine percent even lie about their natural hair color.
● Four out of ten Americans have tried to pad an insurance bill to cover the deductible.
● Nineteen percent say they've snuck into a theater to avoid paying admission.
● More than three out of five people say they've taken credit for making something from scratch when they have done no such thing. According to Pillsbury's CEO, this "behavior is so prevalent that we've named a category after it—speed scratch."

Consumer Theft and Fraud

Who among us has never received an email offering us fabulous riches if we help to recover a lost fortune from a Nigerian bank account? Of course, the only money changing hands will be yours if you fall for the pitch from a so-called *advance-fee fraud artist*. These con men have successfully scammed many victims out of hundreds of millions of dollars. However, a small but intrepid group of "counterscammers" sometimes give these crooks a taste of their own medicine by pretending to fall for a scam and humiliating the perpetrator. One common strategy is to trick the con artist into posing for pictures holding a self-mocking sign and then posting these photos on Internet sites. Both online and off-line, fraud is rampant.

Stealing from stores is the most common. Someone commits a retail theft every 5 seconds. **Shrinkage** is the industry term for inventory and cash losses from shoplifting and employee theft (it does not refer to the condition George experienced in a famous episode of *Seinfeld*). This is a massive problem for businesses that gets passed on to consumers in the form of higher prices (about 40 percent of the losses can be attributed to employees rather than shoppers). Shopping malls spend $6 million annually on security, and a family of four spends about $300 extra per year because of markups to cover shrinkage.[84]

Indeed, shoplifting is America's fastest-growing crime. A comprehensive retail study found that shoplifting is a year-round problem that costs U.S. retailers $9 billion annually. The most frequently stolen products are tobacco products, athletic shoes, logo and brand-name apparel, designer jeans, and undergarments. The average theft amount per incident is $58.43, up from $20.36 in a 1995 survey.[85] The problem is equally worrisome in Europe; retailers there catch well over 1 million shoplifters every year. The United Kingdom has the highest rate of shrinkage (as a percent of annual sales), followed by Norway, Greece, and France. Switzerland and Austria have the lowest rates.[86]

The large majority of shoplifting is not done by professional thieves or by people who genuinely need the stolen items.[87] About 2 million Americans are charged with shoplifting each year, but analysts estimate that for every arrest, 18 unreported incidents occur.[88] About three-quarters of those caught are middle- or high-income people who shoplift for the thrill of it or as a substitute for affection. Shoplifting is also common among adolescents. Research evidence indicates that teen shoplifting is influenced by factors such as having friends who also shoplift. It is also more likely to occur if the adolescent does not believe that this behavior is morally wrong.[89]

And what about shoppers who commit fraud when they abuse stores' exchange and return policies? Some big companies, such as Guess, Staples, and Sports Authority, use new software that lets them track a shopper's track record of bringing items back. They are trying to crack down on **serial wardrobers** "who buy an outfit, wear it once, and return it"; customers who change price tags on items, then return one item for the higher amount; and shoppers who use fake or old receipts when they return a product. The retail industry loses approximately $16 billion a year to these and other forms of fraudulent behavior. Retail analysts estimate that about 9 percent of all returns are fraudulent.[90]

Anticonsumption

Some types of destructive consumer behavior are **anticonsumption**, events in which people deliberately deface or mutilate products and services. Some of these actions are relatively harmless, as when a person goes online at dogdoo.com to send a bag of dog manure to a lucky recipient. This site even lets customers calibrate the size of the "gift" by choosing among three "Poo Poo Packages": Econo-Poop (20-pound dog), Poo Poo Special (50-pound dog), and the ultimate in payback, the Poo Poo Grande (110-pound dog).[91] The moral: Smell your packages before opening.

Anticonsumption ranges from relatively mild acts like spray-painting graffiti on buildings and subways to serious incidences of product tampering or even the release of computer viruses that can bring large corporations to their knees. It can also take the form of political protest in which activists alter or destroy billboards and other advertisements that promote what they feel to be unhealthy or unethical acts. For example, some members of the clergy in areas heavily populated by minorities have organized rallies to protest the proliferation of cigarette and alcohol advertising in their neighborhoods; these protests sometimes include the defacement of billboards promoting alcohol or cigarettes.

CHAPTER SUMMARY

Now that you have finished reading this chapter you should understand why:

1. **A consumer's personality influences the way he responds to marketing stimuli, but efforts to use this information in marketing contexts meet with mixed results.**

   The concept of *personality* refers to a person's unique psychological makeup and how it consistently influences the way that person responds to her environment. Marketing strategies based on personality differences have met with mixed success, partly because of the way researchers have measured and applied these differences in *personality traits* to consumption contexts. Some analysts try to understand underlying differences in small samples of consumers by employing techniques based on Freudian psychology and variations of this perspective, whereas others have tried to assess these dimensions more objectively in large samples using sophisticated, quantitative techniques.

2. **Psychographics go beyond simple demographics to help marketers understand and reach different consumer segments.**

   Psychographic techniques classify consumers in terms of psychological, subjective variables in addition to observable characteristics (demographics). Marketers have developed systems to identify consumer "types" and to differentiate them in terms of their brand or product preferences, media usage, leisure time activities, and attitudes toward broad issues such as politics and religion.

3. **Consumer activities can be harmful to individuals and to society.**

   Although textbooks often paint a picture of the consumer as a rational, informed decision maker, in reality many consumer activities are harmful to individuals or to society. The "dark side" of consumer behavior includes terrorism, addiction, the use of people as products (consumed consumers), and theft or vandalism (anticonsumption).

KEY TERMS

80/20 rule
AIOs
animism
anticonsumption
archetypes
beacon
behavioral targeting
bioterrorism
brand personality
compulsive consumption

consumed consumers
consumer addiction
Doppelgänger brand image
ego
geodemography
id
motivational research
personality
personality traits
personalized retargeting

pleasure principle
PRIZM NE
psychographics
reality principle
serial wardrobers
shrinkage
superego
The Values and Lifestyles System
    (VALS2™)

REVIEW

1 Describe the id, ego, and superego and tell how they work together according to Freudian theory.
2 What is motivational research? Give an example of a marketing study that used this approach.
3 Describe three personality traits relevant to marketers.
4 List three problems that arise when we apply trait theory to marketing contexts.
5 Define a brand personality and give two examples.
6 Define psychographics, and describe three ways marketers can use it.

7 What are three specific kinds of AIOs?
8 What is VALS2™, and how do marketers use it?
9 Alcohol drinkers vary sharply in terms of the number of drinks they may consume, from those who occasionally have one at a cocktail party to regular imbibers. Explain how the 80/20 rule applies to this product category.
10 Define consumer addiction and give two examples of it.
11 What is an example of a consumed consumer?
12 What is shrinkage, and why is it a problem?
13 Define anticonsumption, and provide two examples of it.

CONSUMER BEHAVIOR CHALLENGE

■ DISCUSS

1 The Chinese culture has a unique way of dealing with shoplifters: When a merchant catches one, he demands a stiff fee as a penalty. Some storekeepers post a traditional slogan: "Steal one, fine 10." Some Chinese shopkeepers have adopted this practice, though it's not clear that this deterrent would be legal in the United States. For example, in a Chinese grocery store in New York City, suspected shoplifters caught by the store's security guards or staff members have their identification seized. Then, they are photographed holding up the items they are accused of trying to steal. Finally, workers at the store threaten to display the photographs to embarrass them, and to call the police—unless the accused thieves hand over money. Some store owners share their photographs with other stores, or post them in other store branches they own.[92] Is this an effective and ethical response, and is it likely to deter shoplifting?

2 Geodemographic techniques assume that people who live in the same neighborhood have other things in common as well. Why do they make this assumption, and how accurate is it?

3 Behavioral targeting techniques give marketers access to a wide range of information about a consumer when they tell them what Web sites he visits. Do you believe this "knowledge power" presents any ethical problems with regard to consumers' privacy? Should the government regulate access to such information? Should consumers have the right to limit access to these data?

4 Should organizations or individuals be allowed to create Web sites that advocate potentially harmful practices? Should hate groups such as al-Qaeda be allowed to recruit members online? Why or why not?

5 An entrepreneur made international news when he set up a Web site to auction the egg cells of fashion models to the highest bidder (minimum bid: $15,000). The site was targeted to people who wanted to have very attractive babies because they believed this would maximize their offsprings' chances of succeeding in our society. Is the buying and selling of humans just another example of consumer behavior at work? Do you agree that this service is simply a more efficient way to maximize the chance of having happy, successful children? Should this kind of marketing activity be allowed? Would you sell your eggs or sperm on a Web site?

■ APPLY

1 Construct a brand personality inventory for three different brands within a product category. Ask a small number of consumers to rate each brand on about 10 different personality dimensions. What differences can you identify? Do these "personalities" relate to the advertising and packaging strategies used to differentiate these products?

2 Compile a set of recent ads that attempt to link consumption of a product with a specific lifestyle. How does a marketer usually accomplish this goal?

3 Political campaigns may use psychographic analyses. Conduct research on the marketing strategies a candidate used in a recent, major election. How did the campaign segment voters in terms of values? Can you find evidence that the campaign's communications strategies used this information?

4 Construct separate advertising executions for a cosmetics product that targets the Believer, Achiever, Experiencer, and Maker VALS2™ types. How would the basic appeal differ for each group?

MyMarketingLab Now that you have completed this chapter, return to **www.mymktlab.com** to apply concepts and explore the additional study materials.

Case Study

ZIPCAR CREATES A RENTAL CAR CULTURE

U.S. travelers have been able to rent cars since 1946, when Avis offered three cars for hire at a small Michigan airport. Today the rental car industry is a mature business that is fiercely competitive in terms of price and service levels. But, about a decade ago a new company shook up the market with a brand-new business model. Zipcar was a Cambridge, Massachusetts, start-up with a radical concept: Rent cars by the hour. Along with the motto, "Wheels when you need them," Zipcar eliminated trips to car rental centers, extended contracts, and confusing insurance options. It was a godsend to people in urban areas or on large college campuses who just needed a set of wheels to run errands or go out for an evening.

Mention Zipcar to any driver in the 50 cities or 100 college campuses where the company operates, and odds are they know the name. Beyond simple awareness, though, they most likely have a sense of the brand's unique personality. That's because Zipcar works hard to establish its service as simple and fun. A customer can get a car in minutes by reserving online or through a mobile app, or simply by walking to the nearest Zipcar lot. *Fast Company* describes the company's Web site as "fun, conversational and clever." Instead of a boring corporate video on how a business works, when you visit the site you watch a retro geeky guy talking about Zipcar in what feels like a homemade video.

Zipcar works hard to build a culture around the brand and its loyal users. It doesn't call its customers renters; they are *Zipsters*. The company defines a Zipster as:

> One who uses Zipcar. A gender neutral term for a person (or people: Zipsters) who believe in cost-effective transportation solutions that are good for the planet and easy on the wallet.

Zipcar's goal is not only to rent cars, but also to transform urban life by making it more rewarding, sustainable, and affordable for individuals. As of April 2011, it seems that investors also believe in Zipcar: The upstart had an IPO (initial public offering) of $174 million and a stock price that jumped 66 percent right after the IPO. With plans to expand internationally, watch for Zipcar and Zipsters to pop up around the globe.

DISCUSSION QUESTIONS

1 Compare the brand personality of Zipcar to that of Avis or Hertz.

2 How would you describe the psychographic profile of a typical Zipster?

Sources: Jeff Cram, "Web Sites with Personality: What Marketers Can Learn from *Zipcar.com*," *Fastcompany.com* (August 3, 2010), accessed June 22, 2011; Kathy Marquardt, "5 Keys to Zipcar's Success," *U.S. News and World Report.com* (June 5, 2008), accessed June 22, 2011; "Zipcar IPO Soars 66% Out of the Gate," *www.wsj.com* (April 14, 2011), accessed June 22, 2011; *www.zipcar.com*, accessed June 22, 2011.

NOTES

1. www.jettygirl.com, accessed May 29, 2011.
2. For an interesting ethnographic account of skydiving as a voluntary high-risk consumption activity, see Richard L. Celsi, Randall L. Rose, and Thomas W. Leigh, "An Exploration of High-Risk Leisure Consumption Through Skydiving," *Journal of Consumer Research* 20 (June 1993): 1–23.

3. www.roxy.com/home/index.jsp, accessed May 29, 2011.
4. See J. Aronoff and J. P. Wilson, *Personality in the Social Process* (Hillsdale, NJ: Erlbaum, 1985); Walter Mischel, *Personality and Assessment* (New York: Wiley, 1968).

5. Ernest Dichter, *A Strategy of Desire* (Garden City, NY: Doubleday, 1960); Ernest Dichter, *The Handbook of Consumer Motivations* (New York: McGraw-Hill, 1964); Jeffrey J. Durgee, "Interpreting Dichter's Interpretations: An Analysis of Consumption Symbolism," in *The Handbook of Consumer Motivations* (unpublished manuscript, Rensselaer Polytechnic Institute, Troy, New York, 1989); Pierre Martineau, *Motivation in Advertising* (New York: McGraw-Hill, 1957).

6. Vance Packard, *The Hidden Persuaders* (New York: D. McKay, 1957).

7. Harold Kassarjian, "Personality and Consumer Behavior: A Review," *Journal of Marketing Research* 8 (November 1971): 409–18.

8. Karen Horney, *Neurosis and Human Growth* (New York: Norton, 1950).

9. Joel B. Cohen, "An Interpersonal Orientation to the Study of Consumer Behavior," *Journal of Marketing Research* 6 (August 1967): 270–78; Pradeep K. Tyagi, "Validation of the CAD Instrument: A Replication," in Richard P. Bagozzi and Alice M. Tybout, eds., *Advances in Consumer Research 10* (Ann Arbor, MI: Association for Consumer Research, 1983): 112–14.

10. For a comprehensive review of classic perspectives on personality theory, see Calvin S. Hall and Gardner Lindzey, *Theories of Personality*, 2nd ed. (New York: Wiley, 1970).

11. See Carl G. Jung, "The Archetypes and the Collective Unconscious," in H. Read, M. Fordham, and G. Adler, eds., *Collected Works*, vol. 9, part 1 (Princeton, NJ: Princeton University Press, 1959).

12. This material was contributed by Rebecca H. Holman, senior vice president and director, Consumer Knowledge Structures, The Knowledge Group, Young & Rubicam Brands, July 2005.

13. E. B. Boyd, "How a Personality Test Designed to Pick Astronauts Is Taking the Pain out of Customer Support," *Fast Company* (December 1, 2010), http://www.fastcompany.com/1706766/how-a-system-designed-to-weed-out-nasa-astronauts-is-taking-the-pain-out-of-customer-support-call?partner=homepage_newsletter, accessed April 13, 2011.

14. For an application of trait theory, cf. Adam Duhachek and Dawn Iacobucci, "Consumer Personality and Coping: Testing Rival Theories of Process," *Journal of Consumer Psychology* 15, no. 1 (2005): 52–63.

15. S. Christian Wheeler, Richard E. Petty, and George Y. Bizer, "Self-Schema Matching and Attitude Change: Situational and Dispositional Determinants of Message Elaboration," *Journal of Consumer Research* 31 (March, 2005): 787–97.

16. Adapted from information presented in Beth Snyder Bulik, "You Are What You Watch: Market Data Suggest Research Links Personality Traits to Consumers' Viewing Habits, Helps Marketers Match Brands with Audiences," *Advertising Age* (November 1, 2010), http://adage.com/article/news/research-links-personality-traits-tv-viewing-habits/146779/, accessed April 13, 2011.

17. Linda L. Price and Nancy Ridgway, "Development of a Scale to Measure Innovativeness," in Richard P. Bagozzi and Alice M. Tybout, eds., *Advances in Consumer Research 10* (Ann Arbor, MI: Association for Consumer Research, 1983): 679–84; Russell W. Belk, "Three Scales to Measure Constructs Related to Materialism: Reliability, Validity, and Relationships to Measures of Happiness," in Thomas C. Kinnear, ed., *Advances in Consumer Research 11* (Ann Arbor, MI: Association for Consumer Research, 1984): 291; Mark Snyder, "Self-Monitoring Processes," in Leonard Berkowitz, ed., *Advances in Experimental Social Psychology* (New York: Academic Press, 1979), 85–128; Gordon R. Foxall and Ronald E. Goldsmith, "Personality and Consumer Research: Another Look," *Journal of the Market Research Society* 30, no. 2 (1988): 111–25; Ronald E. Goldsmith and Charles F. Hofacker, "Measuring Consumer Innovativeness," *Journal of the Academy of Marketing Science* 19, no. 3 (1991): 209–21; Curtis P. Haugtvedt, Richard E. Petty, and John T. Cacioppo, "Need for Cognition and Advertising: Understanding the Role of Personality Variables in Consumer Behavior," *Journal of Consumer Psychology* 1, no. 3 (1992): 239–60.

18. John L. Lastovicka, Lance A. Bettencourt, Renee Shaw Hughner, and Ronald J. Kuntze, "Lifestyle of the Tight and Frugal: Theory and Measurement," *Journal of Consumer Research* 26 (June 1999): 85–98; The Hartman Group, "The Continuing Economic Maelstrom & the US Consumer: Implications for CPG, Restaurant and Retail January 2009," 9 http://www.hartman-group.com/publications/white-papers/the-continuing-economic-maelstrom-the-us-consumer, accessed September 3, 2011; Joseph Lazzaro, "US Savings Rate Soars to 14-Year High," *Daily Finance* (June 1, 2009), www.dailyfinance.com/2009/06/01/us-savings-rate-soars-to-14-year-high, accessed June 1, 2009; Andrea K. Walker, "Economy Breeds a Frugal Consumer," *Baltimore Sun* (April 20, 2009), www.baltimoresun.com/business/bal-te.bz.shoppinghabits19apr20,0,1577826.story, accessed June 1, 2009.

19. Jacob Jacoby, "Personality and Consumer Behavior: How Not to Find Relationships," in *Purdue Papers in Consumer Psychology*, no. 102 (Lafayette, IN: Purdue University, 1969); Harold H. Kassarjian and Mary Jane Sheffet, "Personality and Consumer Behavior: An Update," in Harold H. Kassarjian and Thomas S. Robertson, eds., *Perspectives in Consumer Behavior*, 4th ed. (Glenview, IL: Scott Foresman, 1991): 291–353; John Lastovicka and

Erich Joachimsthaler, "Improving the Detection of Personality Behavior Relationships in Consumer Research," *Journal of Consumer Research* 14 (March 1988): 583–87. For an approach that ties the notion of personality more directly to marketing issues, see Jennifer L. Aaker, "Dimensions of Brand Personality," *Journal of Marketing Research* 34 (August 1997): 347–57.

20. See Girish N. Punj and David W. Stewart, "An Interaction Framework of Consumer Decision-Making," *Journal of Consumer Research* 10 (September 1983): 181–96.

21. J. F. Allsopp, "The Distribution of On-Licence Beer and Cider Consumption and Its Personality Determinants Among Young Men," *European Journal of Marketing* 20, no. 3 (1986): 44–62; Gordon R. Foxall and Ronald E. Goldsmith, "Personality and Consumer Research: Another Look," *Journal of the Market Research Society* 30, no. 2 (April 1988): 111–25.

22. Quoted in Stuart O'Brien, "iPad Owners are 'Self-Centered Workaholics,'" *Mobile Entertainment* (July 30, 2010), http://www.mobile-ent.biz/news/read/ipad-owners-are-self-centered-workaholics, accessed April 13, 2011.

23. Thomas Hine, "Why We Buy: The Silent Persuasion of Boxes, Bottles, Cans, and Tubes," *Worth* (May 1995): 78–83.

24. Bradley Johnson, "They All Have Half-Baked Ideas," *Advertising Age* (May 12, 1997): 8.

25. Yongjun Sung and Spencer F. Tinkham, "Brand Personality Structures in the United States and Korea: Common and Culture-Specific Factors," *Journal of Consumer Psychology* 15, no. 4 (2005): 334–50; Beverly T. Venable, Gregory M. Rose, Victoria D. Bush, and Faye W. Gilbert, "The Role of Brand Personality in Charitable Giving: An Assessment and Validation," *Journal of the Academy of Marketing Science* 33 (July 2005): 295–312.

26. Quoted in Stuart Elliott, "A 1950s Brand Mascot Fights 21st-Century Indigestion," *New York Times* (March 5, 2008), www.nytimes.com, accessed March 5, 2008.

27. Susan Nelson, "Our Changing View of Style," *Marketing Daily* (February 17, 2009), www.mediapost.com, accessed February 17, 2009.

28. Craig J. Thompson, Aric Rindfleisch, and Zeynep Arsel, "Emotional Branding and the Strategic Value of the Doppelganger Brand Image," *Journal of Marketing* 70, no. 1 (2006): 50.

29. Kevin L. Keller, "Conceptualization, Measuring, and Managing Customer-Based Brand Equity," *Journal of Marketing* 57 (January 1993): 1–22.

30. Linda Keslar, "What's in a Name?," *Individual Investor* (April 1999): 101–2.

31. Kathryn Kranhold, "Agencies Beef up Brand Research to Identify Consumer Preferences," *Wall Street Journal Interactive Edition* (March 9, 2000), accessed March 9, 2000.

32. Jennifer Aaker, Kathleen D. Vohs, and Cassie Mogilner (2010), "Nonprofits Are Seen as Warm and For-Profits as Competent: Firm Stereotypes Matter," *Journal of Consumer Research* 37, no. 2 (2010): 224–37.

33. Jennifer L. Aaker, "Dimensions of Brand Personality," *Journal of Marketing Research* 34 (August 1997): 347–57.

34. Tim Triplett, "Brand Personality Must Be Managed or It Will Assume a Life of Its Own," *Marketing News* (May 9, 1994): 9.

35. Seth Stevenson, "How to Beat Nike," *New York Times* (January 5, 2003), www.nytimes.com, accessed January 5, 2003.

36. Susan Fournier, "Consumers and Their Brands: Developing Relationship Theory in Consumer Research," *Journal of Consumer Research* 24, no. 4 (March 1998): 343–73.

37. Michael Hiestand, "ESPN Drops Ad Campaign That Was to Portray College Stereotypes," *USA Today* (November 14, 2008), www.usatoday.com/money/advertising/2008-11-13-espn-ad-campaign-killed_N.html, accessed November 14, 2008.

38. Rebecca Piirto Heath, "The Frontiers of Psychographics," *American Demographics* (July 1996): 38–43.

39. Quoted in Erin White, "Volvo Sheds Safe Image for New, Dangerous Ads," *Wall Street Journal* (June 14, 2002), www.wsj.com, accessed June 14, 2002; Viknesh Vijayenthiran, "Volvo's Upmarket Plans Hindered by Brand Image, Poor CO_2 Emissions," *Motor Authority* (November 24, 2008), www.motorauthority.com/volvo-continuing-with-plans-to-move-upmarket.html, accessed June 1, 2009.

40. Shirley Brady, "Volvo's Naughty S60 Experiment," *BrandChannel* (July 28, 2010), http://www.brandchannel.com/home/post/2010/07/28/Volvo-Naughty-S60-Experiment.aspx, accessed April 13, 2011.

41. Danny Hakim, "Cadillac, Too, Shifting Focus to Trucks," *New York Times* (December 21, 2001) http://www.nytimes.com/2001/12/21/business/cadillac-too-shifting-focus-to-trucks.html, accessed September 3, 2011.

42. Stevenson, "How to Beat Nike."

43. Helen Coster, "The $25 Water Bottle," *Forbes* (March 19, 2009), www.forbes.com, accessed March 19, 2009; www.mysigg.com, accessed June 3, 2009.

44. See Lewis Alpert and Ronald Gatty, "Product Positioning by Behavioral Life Styles," *Journal of Marketing* 33 (April 1969): 65–69; Emanuel H. Demby, "Psychographics Revisited: The Birth of a Technique," *Marketing*

News (January 2, 1989): 21; William D. Wells, "Backward Segmentation," in Johan Arndt, ed., *Insights into Consumer Behavior* (Boston: Allyn & Bacon, 1968): 85–100.

45. William D. Wells and Douglas J. Tigert, "Activities, Interests, and Opinions," *Journal of Advertising Research* 11 (August 1971): 27.

46. Ian Pearson, "Social Studies: Psychographics in Advertising," *Canadian Business* (December 1985): 67.

47. Rebecca Piirto Heath, "Psychographics: Qu'est-Ce Que C'est?," *Marketing Tools* (November–December 1995).

48. Alfred S. Boote, "Psychographics: Mind over Matter," *American Demographics* (April 1980): 26–29; William D. Wells, "Psychographics: A Critical Review," *Journal of Marketing Research* 12 (May 1975): 196–213.

49. Joseph T. Plummer, "The Concept and Application of Life Style Segmentation," *Journal of Marketing* 38 (January 1974): 33–37.

50. Berkeley Rice, "The Selling of Lifestyles," *Psychology Today* (March 1988): 46.

51. John L. Lastovicka, John P. Murry, Erich A. Joachimsthaler, Gurav Bhalla, and Jim Scheurich, "A Lifestyle Typology to Model Young Male Drinking and Driving," *Journal of Consumer Research* 14 (September 1987): 257–63.

52. Martha Farnsworth Riche, "VALS 2," *American Demographics* (July 1989): 25. Additional information provided by William D. Guns, Director, Business Intelligence Center, SBI Consulting, Inc., personal communication, May 1997.

53. Rebecca Piirto Heath, "You Can Buy a Thrill: Chasing the Ultimate Rush," *American Demographics* (June 1997): 47–51.

54. Michael J. Weiss, *The Clustering of America* (New York: Harper & Row, 1988).

55. Bob Minzesheimer, "You Are What You Zip," *Los Angeles Times* (November 1984): 175.

56. Christina Del Valle, "They Know Where You Live and How You Buy," *BusinessWeek* (February 7, 1994): 89; www.claritas.com, accessed June 3, 2005.

57. www.claritas.com/MyBestSegments/Default.jsp, accessed June 3, 2009.

58. Stephanie Kang and Vishesh Kumar, "TV Learning Importance of Targeting," *Wall Street Journal* (April 4, 2008): B7.

59. Laura M. Holson, "In CBS Test, Mobile Ads Find Users," *New York Times* (February 6, 2008), www.nytimes.com, accessed February 6, 2008.

60. Emily Steel and Vishesh Kumar, "Targeted Ads Raise Privacy Concerns, Pressure Could Imperil Online Strategy Shared by Phone and Cable-TV Firms," *Wall Street Journal* (July 8, 2008): B1.

61. Miguel Helft and Tanzina Vega, "Retargeting Ads Follow Surfers to Other Sites," *New York Times* (August 29, 2010), http://www.nytimes.com/2010/08/30/technology/30adstalk.html?_r=1&ref=media, accessed April 13, 2011.

62. Julia Angwin, "The Web's New Gold Mine: Your Secrets," *Wall Street Journal* (July 30, 2010), http://professional.wsj.com/article/SB10001424052748703940904575395073512989404.html?mod=dist_smartbrief&mg=reno-wsj, accessed April 13, 2011.

63. Jack Neff, "Lawsuit: Marketing Blamed in Wal-Mart Trampling Death," *Advertising Age* (December 4, 2008), www.adage.com, accessed December 4, 2008; www.Freerepublic.Com/Focus/F-News/ 2142920/Posts, accessed December 4, 2008.

64. "Japan Calls for Tighter Food Security Against Mad Cow Disease," *Xinhua News Agency* (May 20, 2002), www.xinhuanet.com/English, accessed June 29, 2002.

65. Kenneth E. Nusbaum, James C. Wright, and Michael R. Solomon, "Attitudes of Food Animal Veterinarians to Continuing Education in Agriterrorism," paper presented at the 53rd Annual Meeting of the Animal Disease Research Workers in Southern States, University of Florida (February 2001).

66. Betty Mohr, "The Pepsi Challenge: Managing a Crisis," *Prepared Foods* (March 1994): 13.

67. "Boston Officials Livid over Ad Stunt," *New York Times* (February 1, 2007), www.nytimes.com, accessed February 1, 2007.

68. http://www.experienceproject.com/groups/Am-Addicted-To-Chapstick/34083, accessed May 29, 2011.

69. Erik Sass, "Woman Kills Baby for Interrupting FarmVille," *Social Media & Marketing Daily* (October 28, 2010), http://www.mediapost.com/publications/?fa=Articles.showArticle&art_aid=138502&nid=120184, accessed April 30, 2011.

70. "Psychiatrists Drafted in to Treat Italian Facebook Addicts," *The Drum* (November 19, 2010), http://www.thedrum.co.uk/news/2010/11/19/16713-psychiatrists-drafted-in-to-treat-italian-facebook-addicts/, accessed February 23, 2011.

71. Martin Fackler, "In Korea, A Boot Camp Cure for Web Obsession," *New York Times* (November 18, 2007), www.nytimes.com/2007/11/18/Technology/18rehab.Html, accessed November 19, 2007.

72. Chris Pollard, "A Cruel World," *The Sun (U.K.)* (September 13, 2010), http://www.diigo.com/cached?url=http%3A%2F%2Fwww.thesun.co.uk%2Fsol%2Fhomepage%2Fnews%2F3135278%2FMum-addicted-to-Small-World-neglected-kids-and-let-dogs-starve-to-death.html, accessed February 23, 2011.

73. Derek N. Hassay and Malcolm C. Smith, "Compulsive Buying: An Examination of the Consumption Motive," *Psychology & Marketing* 13 (December 1996): 741–52.

74. Nancy M. Ridgway, Monika Kukar-Kinney, and Kent B. Monroe, "An Expanded Conceptualization and a New Measure of Compulsive Buying," *Journal of Consumer Research* 35, no. 4 (2008): 622–39; Thomas C. O'Guinn and Ronald J. Faber, "Compulsive Buying: A Phenomenological Explanation," *Journal of Consumer Research* 16 (September 1989): 154.

75. Curtis L. Taylor, "Guys Who Buy, Buy, Buy," *Newsday* (October 6, 2006); Jim Thornton, "Buy Now, Pay Later," *Men's Health* (December, 2004): 109–12.

76. Georgia Witkin, "The Shopping Fix," *Health* (May 1988): 73; see also Arch G. Woodside and Randolph J. Trappey III, "Compulsive Consumption of a Consumer Service: An Exploratory Study of Chronic Horse Race Track Gambling Behavior," working paper #90-MKTG-04, A. B. Freeman School of Business, Tulane University (1990); Rajan Nataraajan and Brent G. Goff, "Manifestations of Compulsiveness in the Consumer-Marketplace Domain," *Psychology & Marketing* 9 (January 1992): 31–44; Joann Ellison Rodgers, "Addiction: A Whole New View," *Psychology Today* (September–October 1994): 32.

77. Matthew Creamer, "Pepsi Opens a Vein of Controversy with New Suicide-Themed Ads; Prints Ad Depict a Cartoonish Calorie Offing Itself," *Advertising Age* (December 2, 2008), http://adage.com/ Globalideanetwork/Post?Article_Id=132952, accessed December 3, 2008.

78. Helen Reynolds, *The Economics of Prostitution* (Springfield, IL: Thomas, 1986).

79. Patrick Di Justo, "How to Sell Your Body for $46 Million," *Wired* (August 2003): 47.

80. Amy Harmon, "Illegal Kidney Auction Pops up on eBay's Site," *New York Times* (September 3, 1999), www.nytimes.com, accessed September 3, 1999.

81. Di Justo, "How to Sell Your Body for $46 Million."

82. Reuters, "German Parents Offer Baby on eBay," *New York Times* (May 25, 2008), www.nytimes.com/2008/05/25/world/europe/ 25ebayby.html?_r=1&scp=1&sq=baby..., accessed May 25, 2008.

83. "Advertisers Face up to the New Morality: Making the Pitch," *Bloomberg* (July 8, 1997).

84. "Shoplifting: Bess Myerson's Arrest Highlights a Multibillion-Dollar Problem That Many Stores Won't Talk About," *Life* (August 1988): 32.

85. "New Survey Shows Shoplifting Is a Year-Round Problem," *Business Wire* (April 12, 1998).

86. "Customer Not King, But Thief," *Marketing News* (December 9, 2002): 4.

87. Catherine A. Cole, "Deterrence and Consumer Fraud," *Journal of Retailing* 65 (Spring 1989): 107–20; Stephen J. Grove, Scott J. Vitell, and David Strutton, "Non-Normative Consumer Behavior and the Techniques of Neutralization," in Terry Childers et al., eds., *Marketing Theory and Practice*, 1989 AMA Winter Educators' Conference (Chicago: American Marketing Association, 1989): 131–35.

88. Mark Curnutte, "The Scope of the Shoplifting Problems," *Gannett News Service* (November 29, 1997).

89. Anthony D. Cox, Dena Cox, Ronald D. Anderson, and George P. Moschis, "Social Influences on Adolescent Shoplifting—Theory, Evidence, and Implications for the Retail Industry," *Journal of Retailing* 69 (Summer 1993): 234–46.

90. Stephanie Kang, "New Return Policy: Retailers Say 'No' to Serial Exchangers," *Wall Street Journal* (November 29, 2004): B1.

91. www.dogdoo.com, accessed May 29, 2011.

92. Corey Kilgannon and Jeffrey E. Singer, "Stores' Treatment of Shoplifters Tests Rights," *New York Times* (June 21, 2010), http://www.nytimes.com/2010/06/22/nyregion/22shoplift.html?emc=eta1, accessed April 13, 2011.

Attitudes and Persuasion

Attitudes and Persuasion

When you finish reading this chapter you will understand why:

1. It is important for consumer researchers to understand the nature and power of attitudes.

2. Attitudes are more complex than they first appear.

3. We form attitudes in several ways.

4. A need to maintain consistency among all of our attitudinal components often motivates us to alter one or more of them.

5. We use attitude models to identify specific components and combine them to predict a consumer's overall attitude toward a product or brand.

6. The communications model identifies several important components for marketers when they try to change consumers' attitudes toward products and services.

7. The consumer who processes a message is not necessarily the passive receiver of information marketers once believed him or her to be.

8. Several factors influence the effectiveness of a message source.

9. The way a marketer structures his or her message determines how persuasive it will be.

10. Audience characteristics help to determine whether the nature of the source or the message itself will be relatively more effective.

MyMarketingLab

Visit **www.mymktlab.com** to find activities that help you learn and review in order to succeed in this chapter.

Source: Lucky Business/Shutterstock.

atalie is sorting through today's mail: bill, ad, bill, fund-raising letter from political candidate, offer for another credit card.

Aha! Here it is—the envelope she's been waiting for: an invitation to a posh cocktail party at her friend Evelyn's ad agency. This will be her chance to see and be seen, to mingle, network, and maybe even land a job offer. But, what to wear? Somehow her industrial grunge clothes don't seem appropriate for the new life she imagines as an account executive. Natalie needs help, so she does what comes naturally. First, she Tweets her friends to let them know about the event; then she fires up her computer to check out what the *fashionistas* who roam the blogosphere recommend this season. She browses Polyvore to see what looks celebrities are posting, and she's immediately grabbed by a sheer royal-blue tunic that actress Blake Lively is wearing—though the set that features a Nanette Lepore jazz band dress isn't bad either. But wait: She might make a real entrance if she turns up in the Rachel Pally Aphrodite Fame Dress that Kim Kardashian wears, an off-the-shoulder Grecian-inspired dress "for the modern goddess." Hey, if it works for Kim, it works for her![1] Natalie quickly copies some snapshots from the site and posts them on her Facebook page to get their votes. It's fun to get a reality check from her "peeps" in addition to fashion industry snobs.

The Power of Attitudes

OBJECTIVE 1

It is important for consumer researchers to understand the nature and power of attitudes.

People use the term *attitude* in many contexts. A friend might ask you, "What is your attitude toward abortion?" A parent might scold, "Young man, I don't like your attitude." Some bars even euphemistically refer to happy hour as "an attitude adjustment period." For our purposes, though, an **attitude** is a lasting, general evaluation of people (including oneself), objects, advertisements, or issues.[2] We call anything toward which one has an attitude an **attitude object (A_o).**

An attitude is lasting because it tends to endure over time. It is general because it applies to more than a momentary event, such as hearing a loud noise, though you might, over time, develop a negative attitude toward all loud noises. Consumers have attitudes toward a wide range of attitude objects, from very product-specific behaviors (e.g., you use Crest toothpaste rather than Colgate) to more general, consumption-related behaviors (e.g., how often you should brush your teeth). Attitudes help to determine whom you choose to date, what music you listen to, whether you will recycle aluminum cans, or whether you choose to become a consumer researcher for a living. In this chapter we'll consider the contents of an attitude, how we form attitudes, and how we measure them. We will also review some of the surprisingly complex relationships between attitudes and behavior and then take a closer look at how marketers can change these attitudes.

Psychologist Daniel Katz developed the **functional theory of attitudes** to explain how attitudes facilitate social behavior.[3] According to this pragmatic approach, attitudes exist *because* they serve some function for the person. Consumers who expect that they will need to deal with similar situations at a future time will be more likely to start to form an attitude in anticipation.[4] Two people can each have an attitude toward some object for very different reasons. As a result, it's helpful for a marketer to know *why* an attitude is held before she tries to change it. These are different attitude functions:

- **Utilitarian function**—The **utilitarian function** relates to the basic principles of reward and punishment. We develop some attitudes toward products simply because they provide pleasure or pain. If a person likes the taste of a cheeseburger, that person will develop a positive attitude toward cheeseburgers. Ads that stress straightforward product benefits (e.g., you should drink Diet Coke "just for the taste of it") appeal to the utilitarian function.
- **Value-expressive function**—Attitudes that perform a **value-expressive function** relate to the consumer's central values or self-concept. A person forms a product attitude in this case because of what the product says about him as a person (e.g., "What sort of man reads *Playboy*?"). Value-expressive attitudes also are highly relevant to the psychographic analyses, which consider how consumers cultivate a cluster of activities, interests, and opinions to express a particular social identity.
- **Ego-defensive function**—Attitudes we form to protect ourselves either from external threats or internal feelings perform an **ego-defensive function**. An early marketing study showed that housewives in the 1950s resisted the use of instant coffee because it threatened their conception of themselves as capable homemakers (this doesn't seem to be a very big issue for most anymore!).[5] Products that promise to help a man project a "macho" image (e.g., Marlboro cigarettes) appeal to his insecurities about his masculinity. Another example is deodorant campaigns that stress the dire, embarrassing consequences when you're caught with underarm odor in public.
- **Knowledge function**—We form some attitudes because we need order, structure, or meaning. A **knowledge function** applies when a person is in an ambiguous situation ("it's OK to wear casual pants to work, but only on Friday") or she confronts a new product (e.g., "Bayer wants you to know about pain relievers").

OBJECTIVE 2
Attitudes are more complex than they first appear.

The ABC Model of Attitudes

When Subaru of America began work on a new marketing strategy, the automaker discovered that even though most auto buyers had heard of the brand, very few had strong emotional connections to it. However, Subaru owners expressed strong passion and even love for the brand. To ramp up this emotional connection for nonowners, the new campaign targets people who are in three different stages of buying a car—what Subaru calls the *heart*, the *head*, and the *wallet*. The *heart* stage focuses on the love owners show for their cars; commercials share personal stories of their attachment. The *head*-stage ads, in contrast, present the rational side of specific models as they emphasize how the cars benefit their owners in terms of reliability, economy, and so on. Then, the *wallet* ads deal with the financial details of actually buying a Subaru; these include special offers from local dealers.[6]

Like the Subaru campaign, an attitude has three components: affect, behavior, and cognition. **Affect** describes how a consumer *feels* about an attitude object. **Behavior** refers to his intentions to *take action* about it (but, as we will discuss at a later point, an intention does not always result in an actual behavior). **Cognition** is what he *believes* to be true about the attitude object. You can remember these three components of an attitude as the **ABC model of attitudes**.

The ABC model emphasizes the interrelationships among knowing, feeling, and doing. We can't determine consumers' attitudes toward a product if we just identify their cognitions (beliefs) about it. For example, a researcher may find that shoppers "know" a particular camcorder has an 8:1 power zoom lens, auto focus, and a flying erase head, but simply knowing this doesn't indicate whether they feel these attributes are good, bad, or irrelevant, or whether they would actually buy the camcorder.

Hierarchies of Effects

Which comes first: knowing, feeling, or doing? It turns out that each element may lead things off, depending on the situation. Attitude researchers developed the concept of a **hierarchy of effects** to explain the relative impact of the three components. Each hierarchy specifies that a fixed sequence of steps occurs en route to an attitude. Figure 1 summarizes these three different hierarchies.

The Standard Learning Hierarchy

Think → Feel → Do: The **standard learning hierarchy** assumes that a person approaches a product decision as a problem-solving process. First, she forms beliefs about a product as she accumulates knowledge (*beliefs*) regarding relevant attributes. Next, she evaluates these beliefs and forms a feeling about the product (*affect*).[7] Then she engages in a relevant behavior, such as when she buys a product that offers the attributes she feels good about. This hierarchy assumes that a consumer is highly involved when she makes a purchase decision.[8] She's motivated to seek out a lot of information, carefully weigh alternatives, and come to a thoughtful decision.

The Low-Involvement Hierarchy

Do → Feel → Think: The **low-involvement hierarchy of effects** assumes that the consumer initially doesn't have a strong preference for one brand over another; instead, she acts on the basis of limited knowledge and forms an evaluation only *after* she has bought the product.[9] The attitude is likely to come about through behavioral learning, as good or bad experiences reinforce her initial choice.

The possibility that consumers simply don't care enough about many decisions to carefully assemble a set of product beliefs and then evaluate them is important. This implies that all of our concern about influencing beliefs and carefully communicating information about product attributes may often be wasted. Consumers aren't necessarily going to pay attention anyway; they are more likely to respond to simple stimulus-response connections when they make purchase decisions. For example, a consumer who chooses among paper towels might remember that "Bounty is the quicker picker-upper" rather than systematically comparing all the brands on the shelf. Get a life!

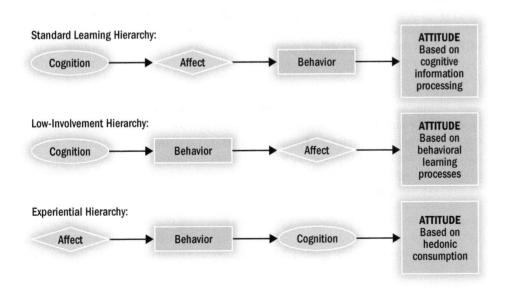

Figure 1 HIERARCHIES OF EFFECTS

This ad for New York's famous Smith & Wollensky restaurant emphasizes that marketers and others associated with a product or service are often more involved with it than are their customers.
Source: Courtesy of Smith & Wollensky Steak House.

Steak is our life. All we ask is that you make it your lunch.

Smith & Wollensky.
The quintessential New York City steakhouse.
49th St. & 3rd Ave. (212) 753-1530.

Winner of The *Wine Spectator's* 1987 Grand Award.

The notion of consumers' low involvement is a bitter pill for some marketers to swallow. Who wants to admit that what they market is not very important to the people who buy it? A brand manager for, say, a brand of bubble gum or cat food may find it hard to believe that consumers don't put that much thought into purchasing her product, because she herself spends many of her waking (and perhaps sleeping) hours thinking about it.

For marketers, the ironic silver lining to this low-involvement cloud is that under these conditions, consumers are not motivated to process a lot of complex, brand-related information. Instead, they will be swayed by principles of behavioral learning, such as the simple responses that conditioned brand names or point-of-purchase displays elicit.

The Experiential Hierarchy

Feel → Think → Do: According to the **experiential hierarchy of effects**, we act on the basis of our emotional reactions. The experiential perspective highlights the idea that intangible product attributes, such as package design, advertising, brand names, and the nature of the setting in which the experience occurs, can help shape our attitudes toward a brand. We may base these reactions on hedonic motivations, such as whether using the product is exciting (like the Nintendo Wii).

Even the emotions the communicator expresses have an impact. A smile is infectious; in a process we term *emotional contagion*, messages that happy people deliver enhance our attitude toward the product.[10] Numerous studies demonstrate that the mood a person is in when she sees or hears a marketing message influences how she will process the ad, the likelihood that she will remember the information she sees, and how she will feel about the advertised item and related products in the future.[11]

OBJECTIVE 3
We form attitudes in several ways.

How Do We Form Attitudes?

We all have lots of attitudes, and we don't usually question how we got them. Certainly, you're not born with the heartfelt conviction that, say, Pepsi is better than Coke, or that alternative music liberates the soul. From where do these attitudes come?

We form an attitude in several different ways, depending on the particular hierarchy of effects that operates. We may form an attitude toward a brand due to classical conditioning: A marketer repeatedly pairs an attitude object such as the Pepsi name with a catchy jingle ("You're in the Pepsi Generation"). Or we can form an attitude due to instrumental conditioning: The marketer reinforces us when we consume the attitude object (e.g., you take a swig of Pepsi and it quenches your thirst). Or this learning can result from a very complex cognitive process. For example, a teenager may model the behavior of friends and media endorsers, such as Beyoncé, who drink Pepsi because they believe that this will allow them to fit in with the desirable lifestyle that Pepsi commercials portray.

All Attitudes Are Not Created Equal

It's important to distinguish among types of attitudes, because not all are formed in the same way.[12] One consumer may be highly brand-loyal; she has an enduring, deeply held positive attitude toward an attitude object, and it would be difficult to weaken this involvement. However, another woman may be a more fickle consumer: She may have a mildly positive attitude toward a product but be quite willing to abandon it when something better comes along. In this section, we'll consider the differences between strongly and weakly held attitudes and briefly review some of the major theoretical perspectives researchers use to explain how attitudes form and relate to our other attitudes.

Consumers vary in their *commitment* to an attitude; the degree of commitment relates to their level of involvement with the attitude object.[13] Let's look at three (increasing) levels of commitment:

1 **Compliance**—At the lowest level of involvement, **compliance**, we form an attitude because it helps us to gain rewards or avoid punishment. This attitude is very superficial; it is likely to change when others no longer monitor our behavior or when another option becomes available. You may drink Pepsi because the cafeteria sells it, and it is too much trouble to go elsewhere for a Coca-Cola.

2 **Identification**—**Identification** occurs when we form an attitude to conform to another person's or group's expectations. Advertising that depicts the dire social consequences when we choose some products over others relies on the tendency of consumers to imitate the behavior of desirable models.

3 **Internalization**—At a high level of involvement called **internalization**, deep-seated attitudes become part of our value system. These attitudes are very difficult to change because they are so important to us. The infamous Coke debacle of the 1980s (still a standard in marketing textbooks today) illustrates what can happen when a marketer messes with strongly held attitudes. In this case Coca-Cola decided to change its flavor formula to meet the needs of younger consumers who often preferred a sweeter taste (more characteristic of Pepsi). The company conducted rigorous blind *taste tests* that showed people who didn't know what brands they were drinking preferred the flavor of the new formula. Much to its surprise, when New Coke hit the shelves, the company faced a consumer revolt as die-hard Coke fans protested. This allegiance to Coke was obviously more than a minor taste preference for these people; the brand had become intertwined with their social identities and took on intense patriotic and nostalgic properties.

The Consistency Principle

OBJECTIVE 4

A need to maintain consistency among all of our attitudinal components often motivates us to alter one or more of them.

Have you ever heard someone say, "Pepsi is my favorite soft drink. It tastes terrible," or "I love my boyfriend. He's the biggest idiot I've ever met"? Probably not (at least until the couple gets married!), because these beliefs or evaluations don't go together. According to the **principle of cognitive consistency**, we value harmony among our thoughts, feelings, and behaviors, and a need to maintain uniformity among these elements motivates us. This desire means that, if necessary, we change our thoughts, feelings, or behaviors to make them consistent with other experiences. That boyfriend may slip up and act like a noob occasionally, but his girlfriend (eventually) will find a way to forgive him—or dump him. The consistency principle is an important reminder that we don't form our attitudes in a vacuum: A big factor is how well they fit with other, related attitudes we already hold.

The **theory of cognitive dissonance** states that when a person is confronted with inconsistencies among attitudes or behaviors, he will take some action to resolve this

Advertisers often need to resort to creative imagery to capture consumers' attention and build awareness for their clients.
Source: Courtesy of Energy BBDO.

"dissonance"; perhaps he will change his attitude or modify his behavior to restore consistency. The theory has important ramifications for consumer behavior. We often confront situations in which there is some conflict between our attitudes toward a product or service and what we actually do or buy.[14]

According to the theory, our motivation to reduce the negative feelings of dissonance makes us find a way for our beliefs and feelings to fit together. The theory focuses on situations in which two cognitive elements clash. A *cognitive element* can be something a person believes about himself, a behavior he performs, or an observation about his surroundings. For example, the two cognitive elements "I know smoking cigarettes causes cancer" and "I smoke cigarettes" are *dissonant* with one another. This psychological inconsistency creates a feeling of discomfort that the smoker tries to reduce. The magnitude of dissonance depends on both the importance and number of dissonant elements.[15] In other words, we're more likely to observe dissonance in high-involvement situations where there is more pressure to reduce inconsistencies.

We reduce dissonance when we eliminate, add, or change elements. For example, a person can stop smoking (*eliminating*), or remember Great-Aunt Sophie who smoked until the day she died at age 90 (*adding*). Alternatively, he might question the research that links cancer and smoking (*changing*), perhaps by believing industry-sponsored studies that try to refute this connection.

Dissonance theory can help to explain why evaluations of a product tend to increase *after* we buy the product. The cognitive element, "I made a stupid decision," is dissonant with the element, "I am not a stupid person," so we tend to find even more reasons to like something after it becomes ours. A classic study at a horse race demonstrated this *post-purchase dissonance*. Bettors evaluated their chosen horse more highly and were more confident of its success *after* they placed a bet than before. Because the bettor financially commits to the choice, she reduces dissonance as she increases the attractiveness of the chosen alternative relative to the unchosen ones.[16] One implication of this phenomenon is that consumers actively seek support for their decisions so they can justify them; therefore, marketers should supply their customers with additional reinforcement after they purchase to bolster these decisions.

Self-Perception Theory

Do we always change our attitudes to be in line with our behavior because we're motivated to reduce cognitive dissonance? **Self-perception theory** provides an alternative explanation of dissonance effects.[17] It assumes that we observe our own behavior to determine just what our attitudes are, much as we assume that we know what another person's attitude is when we watch what he does. The theory states that we maintain consistency as we infer that we must have a positive attitude toward an object if we have bought or consumed it (assuming that we freely made this choice). Thus, you might say to yourself, "I guess I must be into Facebook pretty big time. I seem to spend half my life on it."

Self-perception theory helps to explain the effectiveness of a strategy salespeople call the **foot-in-the-door technique**: They know that a consumer is more likely to comply with a big request if he agrees to a smaller one.[18] The name for this technique comes from the practice of door-to-door selling; salespeople learn to plant their foot in a door so the prospect (they hope) doesn't slam it on them. A good salesperson knows that she is more likely to get an order if she can persuade the customer to open the door and talk. By agreeing to do so, the customer signals that he's willing to listen to the salesperson's pitch. Placing an order is consistent with the self-perception that "I'm the kind of person who is willing to buy something from a salesperson who knocks on my door."[19] Recent research also points to the possibility that when salespeople ask consumers to make a series of choices, these decisions are cognitively demanding and deplete the resources the person has available to monitor his behavior. As a result, the target will opt for easier decisions down the road; in some cases it may be easier just to comply with the request than to search for reasons why you shouldn't.[20]

Social Judgment Theory

Social judgment theory also assumes that people assimilate new information about attitude objects in light of what they already know or feel.[21] The initial attitude acts as a frame of reference, and we categorize new information in terms of this existing standard. Just as our decision that a box is heavy depends in part on the weight of other boxes we lift, we develop a subjective standard when we judge attitude objects.

One important aspect of the theory is that people differ in terms of the information they will find acceptable or unacceptable. They form **latitudes of acceptance and rejection** around an attitude standard. They will consider and evaluate ideas falling within the latitude favorably, but they are more likely to reject out of hand those that fall outside of this zone. People tend to perceive messages within their latitude of acceptance as more consistent with their position than those messages actually are. We call this exaggeration an *assimilation effect*.

However, we tend to see messages that fall in our latitude of rejection as even more unacceptable than they actually are—this results in an exaggeration we call a *contrast effect*.[22] As a person becomes more involved with an attitude object, her latitude of acceptance gets smaller. In other words, the consumer accepts fewer ideas farther from her own position and she tends to oppose even mildly divergent positions. Discriminating buyers have a smaller latitude of acceptance (e.g., "choosy mothers choose Jif peanut butter"). However, relatively uninvolved consumers consider a wider range of alternatives. They are less likely to be brand loyal and are more likely to switch brands.

Balance Theory

Have you ever heard the expression, "Any friend of Joe's is a friend of mine?" How about "My enemy's enemy is my friend?" **Balance theory** considers how a person perceives relations among different attitude objects, and how he alters his attitudes so that these remain consistent (or "balanced").[23] This perspective involves relations (always from the perceiver's subjective point of view) among three elements, so we call the resulting attitude structures *triads*. Each triad contains (1) a person and his perceptions of (2) an attitude object and (3) some other person or object. The theory specifies that we want relations among elements in a triad to be harmonious. If they are unbalanced, this creates tension that we are motivated to reduce by changing our perceptions in order to restore balance.

We link elements together in one of two ways: They can have either a *unit relation,* where we think that a person is somehow connected to an attitude object (something like a belief); or they can have a *sentiment relation,* where a person expresses liking or disliking for an attitude object. You might perceive that a dating couple has a positive sentiment relation. On getting married, they will have a positive unit relation. If they get divorced, they sever the unit relation.

To see how balance theory might work, consider the following scenario:

● Alex would like to date Elliott, who is in her consumer behavior class. In balance theory terms, Alex has a positive sentiment relation with Elliott.
● One day, Elliott shows up in class wearing an earring. Elliott has a positive unit relation with the earring.
● Alex is turned off by men who wear earrings. She has a negative sentiment relation with men's earrings.

According to balance theory, Alex faces an unbalanced triad. As Figure 2 shows, she will experience pressure to restore balance by altering some aspect of the triad. How can she do this? She could decide that she does not like Elliott after all. Or her liking for Elliott could prompt her to decide that earrings on men are really pretty cool. She might even try to negate the unit relation between Elliott and the earring by deciding that he must wear it as part of a fraternity initiation (this reduces the free-choice element). Finally,

Figure 2 BALANCE THEORY

she could choose to "leave the field" by accepting a date with Elliott's roommate Byron who doesn't wear an earring (but who has an awesome tattoo). Note that although the theory does not specify which of these routes Alex will choose, it does predict that she will change one or more of her perceptions to achieve balance. Although this example is an oversimplified representation of most attitude processes, it helps to explain a number of consumer behavior phenomena.

Balance theory reminds us that when we have balanced perceptions, our attitudes also are likely to be stable. However, when we experience inconsistencies, we also are more likely to change our attitudes. Balance theory helps explain why consumers like to be linked to positively valued objects. Forming a unit relation with a popular product (e.g., buying and wearing fashionable clothing, driving a flashy car, or even being part of a rap singer's posse) may improve the chances that other people will include you as a positive sentiment relation in their triads.

This "balancing act" is at the heart of celebrity endorsements, in which marketers hope that the star's popularity will transfer to the product or when a nonprofit organization recruits a celebrity to discourage harmful behaviors.[24] We will consider this strategy at length later in this chapter. For now, it pays to remember that creating a unit relation between a product and a star can backfire if the public's opinion of the celebrity endorser shifts from positive to negative. For example, Pepsi pulled an ad that featured Madonna after she released a controversial music video involving religion and sex; it also happened when celebrity bad girl Paris Hilton got busted. The strategy can also cause trouble if people question the star–product unit relation: This occurred when the late singer Michael Jackson, who also did promotions for Pepsi, subsequently confessed that he didn't even drink soda.

Marketing Opportunity

Consumers often like to publicize their connections with successful people or organizations (no matter how shaky the connection) to enhance their own standing. Researchers call this tactic **basking in reflected glory**. A series of studies at Arizona State University (ASU) showed how students' desires to identify with a winning image—in this case, ASU's football team—influenced their consumption behaviors. After the team played a game each weekend, observers recorded the incidence of school-related items, such as ASU T-shirts and caps, that students walking around campus wore. The researchers correlated the frequency of these behaviors to the team's performance. If the team won on Saturday, students were more likely to show off their school affiliation (basking in reflected glory) the following Monday than if the team lost. And the bigger the point spread, the more likely they were to observe students who wore clothes with the ASU logo.[25]

At the college level, many schools in addition to ASU reap huge revenues when they license their school's name and logo. Universities with strong athletic programs, such as Michigan, Penn State, and Auburn, clean up when they sell millions of dollars worth of merchandise (everything from T-shirts to toilet seats). Yale was a relative latecomer to this game, but the director of licensing explained the decision to profit from the use of the school's name and the likeness of bulldog mascot Handsome Dan: "We recognize that our name means a lot—even to people who didn't go here. Plus, this way we can crack down on the Naked Coed Lacrosse shirts out there with Yale on them."[26]

. . . .

OBJECTIVE 5

We use attitude models to identify specific components and combine them to predict a consumer's overall attitude toward a product or brand.

Attitude Models

When market researchers want to assess consumers' attitudes toward beer brands, they might simply go to a bar and ask a bunch of guys, "How do you feel about Budweiser?" However, as we saw earlier, attitudes can be a lot more complex than that. One problem is that many attributes or qualities may link to a product or service and, depending on the individual, some of these will be more or less important ("Less filling!" "Tastes great!"). Another problem is that when a person decides to take action toward an attitude object, other factors influence his behavior, such as whether he feels that his family or friends would approve. *Attitude models* specify the different elements that might work together to influence people's evaluations of attitude objects.

Multiattribute Attitude Models

A simple response does not always tell us everything we need to know, either about *why* the consumer feels a certain way toward a product or about what marketers can do to change her attitude. Our beliefs (accurate or not) about a product often are key to how we evaluate it. Warner-Lambert discovered this when it conducted research for its Fresh Burst Listerine mouthwash. A research firm paid 37 families to allow it to set up cameras in their bathrooms and watch their daily routines (maybe they should have just checked out YouTube). Participants who bought both Fresh Burst and rival Scope said they used mouthwash to make their breath smell good. But Scope users swished around the liquid and then spit it out, whereas Listerine users kept the product in their mouths for a long time (one respondent held the stuff in until he got in the car and finally spit it out in a sewer a block away!). These findings told Listerine that the brand still hadn't shaken its medicine-like image.[27]

Because attitudes are so complex, marketing researchers may use **multiattribute attitude models** to understand them. This type of model assumes that a consumer's attitude toward an attitude object (A_o) depends on the beliefs she has about several of its attributes. When we use a multiattribute model, we assume that we can identify these specific beliefs and combine them to derive a measure of the consumer's overall attitude. We'll describe how these models work with the example of a consumer who evaluates a complex attitude object that should be very familiar to you: a college.

Basic multiattribute models contain three specific elements:[28]

- *Attributes* are characteristics of the A_o. A researcher tries to identify the attributes that most consumers use when they evaluate the A_o. For example, one of a college's attributes is its scholarly reputation.
- *Beliefs* are cognitions about the specific A_o (usually relative to others like it). A belief measure assesses the extent to which the consumer perceives that a brand possesses a particular attribute. For example, a student might believe that the University of North Carolina is strong academically (or maybe this is consistency theory at work, since your humble author got his PhD there!).
- *Importance weights* reflect the relative priority of an attribute to the consumer. Although people might consider an A_o on a number of attributes, some attributes are likely to be more important than others (i.e., consumers will give them greater weight). Furthermore, these weights are likely to differ across consumers. In the case of colleges and universities, for example, one student might stress research opportunities, whereas another might assign greater weight to athletic programs.

The Fishbein Model. The most influential multiattribute model is called the *Fishbein model*, named after its primary developer.[29] The model measures three components of attitude:

- *Salient beliefs* people have about an A_o (i.e., those beliefs about the object a person considers during evaluation).

- *Object-attribute linkages,* or the probability that a particular object has an important attribute.
- *Evaluation* of each of the important attributes.

When we combine these three elements, we compute a consumer's overall attitude toward an object (we'll see later how researchers modify this equation to increase its accuracy). The basic formula is:

$$A_{jk} = \Sigma \beta_{ijk} I_{ik}$$

where

i = attribute
j = brand
k = consumer
I = the importance weight given attribute i by consumer k
β = consumer k's belief regarding the extent to which brand j possesses attribute i
A = a particular consumer's (k's) attitude score for brand j

We obtain the overall attitude score (A) when we multiply a consumer's rating of each attribute for all the brands she considered by the importance rating for that attribute.

To see how this basic multiattribute model works, let's suppose we want to predict which college a high school senior is likely to attend. After months of waiting anxiously, Saundra gets accepted to four schools. Because she must now decide among these, we would first like to know which attributes Saundra will consider when she forms an attitude toward each school. We can then ask Saundra to assign a rating regarding how well each school performs on each attribute and also determine the relative importance of the attributes to her.

By summing scores on each attribute (after we weight each by its relative importance), we compute an overall attitude score for each school. Table 1 shows these hypothetical ratings. Based on this analysis, it seems that Saundra has the most favorable attitude toward Smith. She is clearly someone who would like to attend a college for women with a solid academic reputation rather than a school that offers a strong athletic program or a party atmosphere.

TABLE 1 The Basic Multiattribute Model: Saundra's College Decision

Attribute (*I*)	Importance (*I*)	Beliefs (*B*)			
		Smith	Princeton	Rutgers	Northland
Academic reputation	6	8	9	6	3
All women	7	9	3	3	3
Cost	4	2	2	6	9
Proximity to home	3	2	2	6	9
Athletics	1	1	2	5	1
Party atmosphere	2	1	3	7	9
Library facilities	5	7	9	7	2
Attitude score		163	142	153	131

Marketing Applications of the Multiattribute Model

Suppose you were the director of marketing for Northland College, another school Saundra considered. How might you use the data from this analysis to improve your image?

Capitalize on Relative Advantage. If prospective students view one brand as superior on a particular attribute, a marketer needs to convince consumers like Saundra that this particular attribute is important. For example, although Saundra rates Northland's social atmosphere highly, she does not believe this attribute is a valued aspect for a college. As Northland's marketing director, you might emphasize the importance of an active social life, varied experiences, or even the development of future business contacts that a student forges when she makes strong college friendships.

Strengthen Perceived Product/Attribute Linkages. A marketer may discover that consumers do not equate his brand with a certain attribute. Advertising campaigns often address this problem when they stress a specific quality to consumers (e.g., "new and improved"). Saundra apparently does not think much of Northland's academic quality, athletic programs, or library facilities. You might develop an informational campaign to improve these perceptions (e.g., "little-known facts about Northland").

Add a New Attribute. Product marketers frequently try to distinguish themselves from their competitors when they add a product feature. Northland College might try to emphasize some unique aspect, such as a hands-on internship program for business majors that takes advantage of ties to the local community.

Influence Competitors' Ratings. Finally, you can decrease your competitors' higher ratings with a *comparative advertising* strategy. In this case, you might publish an ad that lists the tuition rates of a number of area schools with which Northland compares favorably and emphasize the value for the money its students get.

Do Attitudes Predict Behavior?

Consumer researchers have used multiattribute models for many years, but a major problem plagues them: In many cases, a person's attitude doesn't predict her behavior. In a classic demonstration of "do as I say, not as I do," many studies report a very low correlation between a person's reported attitude toward something and her actual behavior toward it. Some researchers are so discouraged that they question whether attitudes are of any use at all when we try to understand behavior.

This questionable linkage between attitudes and behavior is a big headache for advertisers: Consumers can love a commercial, yet still not buy the product. For example, one of the most popular TV commercials in recent years featured basketball player Shaquille O'Neal for Pepsi. Although the company spent $67 million on this spot and other similar ones in a single year, sales of Pepsi-Cola fell by close to 2 percent, even as sales of archrival Coca-Cola increased by 8 percent during the same period.[30]

The Extended Fishbein Model

In response, researchers tinkered with the Fishbein model to improve its predictive ability. They call the newer version the **theory of reasoned action**.[31] This model contains several important additions to the original, and although the model is still not perfect, it does a better job of prediction.[32] Let's look at some of the modifications to this model.

Intentions versus Behavior

Attitudes have both direction and strength. A person may like or dislike an attitude object with varying degrees of confidence or conviction. It is helpful to distinguish between firmly held attitudes and those that are more superficial, especially because a person who holds an attitude with greater conviction is more likely to act on it. One study on environmental issues and marketing activities found, for example, that people who express greater conviction in their feelings regarding environmentally responsible behaviors such as recycling show greater consistency between attitudes and behavioral intentions.[33]

However, as the old expression goes, "the road to hell is paved with good intentions." Many factors might interfere with performing the intended behavior. Say you save up to buy a new Apple iPhone. Although you have every intention to get it, stuff happens: You might lose your job, get mugged on the way to the Apple store, or arrive at the store only to find they've run out of the item. It is not surprising, then, that in some instances researchers find that instead of knowing our intentions, our past purchase behavior does a better job of predicting our future behavior (this is one of the foundations of direct marketing techniques that identify likely customers based on their purchase histories). The theory of reasoned action aims to measure *behavioral intentions*—it recognizes that certain uncontrollable factors (such as that mugger) limit our ability to predict the future with 100 percent accuracy.

Social Pressure

Perhaps most importantly, the theory acknowledges the power of other people to influence what we do. Much as we may hate to admit it, what we think others would *like* us to do may override our own preferences. Some research approaches assess the extent to which people's "public" attitudes and purchase decisions might differ from what they do in private. For example, one firm uses a technique it calls "engineered theatre." Researchers go to the actual site where people use a product, such as a bar. They arrange for the bartender to "mistakenly" serve the wrong drink and then observe the consumer's "naked response" to the new brand and her reaction to consuming the brand in a social context.[35]

This Vietnamese ad employs social pressure (the subjective norm) to address people's attitudes toward wearing helmets.
Source: Courtesy of Ogilvy & Mather/Asia Injury Prevention Foundation; Photo by Pro-I Studio.

Marketing Opportunity

Social pressure can play a useful role in motivating consumers to engage in socially responsible behaviors. One study assessed this possibility when it compared the effectiveness of different ways a hotel might encourage guests to reuse their towels. When researchers used a social appeal ("the majority of guests reuse their towels"), this worked better than a functional appeal ("help save the environment"). They also found that compliance was boosted when they phrased the requests in terms of directly relevant others ("the majority of guests in this room reuse their towels") compared to more general group appeals (such as the "majority of men and women reuse their towels").[36]

• • • • • • • • • • • • • • • • • •

Returning to Saundra's college choice, you can see in Table 1 that she was very positive about going to a predominantly female school. However, if she felt that this choice would be unpopular (perhaps her friends would think she was crazy), she might ignore or downgrade this preference when she made her decision. Researchers added a new element, the **subjective norm (SN)**, to account for the effects of what we believe other people think we should do. They use two factors to measure SN: (1) the intensity of a *normative belief (NB)* that others believe we should take or not take some action and (2) the *motivation to comply (MC)* with that belief (i.e., the degree to which the consumer takes others' anticipated reactions into account when she evaluates a purchase).

Attitude Toward Buying

The newer model also measures **attitude toward the act of buying (A_{act})**, rather than only the attitude toward the product itself. In other words, it focuses on the perceived consequences of a purchase. Knowing how someone feels about buying or using an object turns out to be more valid than merely knowing the consumer's evaluation of the object itself.[37]

To understand this distinction, consider a marketing researcher who wants to measure college students' attitudes toward safe sex and wearing condoms. Although many college students she interviews would probably report a positive attitude toward condom use, can she conclude from these responses that these respondents will actually buy and use them? She might get more accurate results if she simply asks the same students how likely they are to *buy* condoms. A person might have a positive A_o toward condoms, but A_{act} (attitude toward the act of obtaining the attitude object) might be negative because of the embarrassment or the hassle involved.

Obstacles to Predicting Behavior in the Theory of Reasoned Action

Despite improvements to the Fishbein model, problems arise when researchers misapply it. Sometimes researchers use a model in ways it was not intended or where certain assumptions about human behavior may not be warranted.[38] Here are some other obstacles to predicting behavior:

- The model tries to predict actual behavior (e.g., taking a diet pill), not the *outcomes* of behavior that some studies assess (e.g., losing weight).
- Some outcomes are beyond our control, such as when the purchase requires the cooperation of other people. For instance, a woman might *want* to get a mortgage, but this intention will be worthless if she cannot find a banker to give her one.
- The basic assumption that behavior is intentional may be invalid in a variety of cases, including impulsive acts, sudden changes in situation, novelty seeking, or even simple repeat buying. One study found that such unexpected events as having guests, changes in the weather, or reading articles about the healthfulness of certain foods significantly affected actual behaviors.[39]
- Measures of attitude often do not really correspond to the behavior they are supposed to predict, either in terms of the A_o or when the act will occur. One common problem is a difference in the level of abstraction researchers employ. For example, knowing a person's attitude toward sports cars may not predict whether she will purchase a BMW Z4. It is very important to match the level of specificity between the attitude and the behavioral intention.
- A similar problem relates to the *time frame* of the attitude measure. In general, the longer the time between the attitude measurement and the behavior it is supposed to assess, the weaker the relationship will be. For example, predictability improves greatly if we ask a consumer the likelihood that she will buy a house in the next week as opposed to within the next five years.
- We form stronger and more predictive attitudes through direct, personal experience with an A_o than those we form indirectly through advertising.[40] According to

the *attitude accessibility perspective,* behavior is a function of the person's immediate perceptions of the A_o, in the context of the situation in which she encounters it. An attitude will guide the evaluation of the object but *only* if a person's memory activates it when she encounters the object. These findings underscore the importance of strategies that induce trials (e.g., by widespread product sampling to encourage the consumer to try the product at home, by taste tests, test drives, etc.) as well as those that maximize exposure to marketing communications.

In addition, most researchers apply the theory of reasoned action in Western settings. Certain assumptions inherent in the model may not necessarily apply to consumers from other cultures. Several cultural roadblocks diminish the universality of the theory of reasoned action:[41]

- The model predicts the performance of a voluntary act. Across cultures, however, many activities, ranging from taking exams and entering military service to receiving an inoculation or even choosing a marriage partner, are not necessarily voluntary.
- The relative impact of subjective norms may vary across cultures. For example, Asian cultures tend to value conformity and "face saving," so it is possible that subjective norms involving the anticipated reactions of others to the choice will have an even greater impact on behavior for many Asian consumers. Indeed, a study conducted during an election in Singapore successfully predicted how people would vote as it assessed their voting intentions beforehand. These intentions were in turn influenced by such factors as voters' attitudes toward the candidate, attitudes toward the political party, and subjective norms—which in Singapore includes an emphasis on harmonious and close ties among members of the society.
- The model measures behavioral intentions and thus presupposes that consumers are actively thinking ahead and planning future behaviors. The intention concept assumes that consumers have a linear time sense; they think in terms of past, present, and future. Not all cultures subscribe to this perspective on time.
- A consumer who forms an intention implicitly claims that he is in control of his actions. Some cultures (e.g., Muslim peoples) tend to be fatalistic and do not necessarily believe in the concept of free will. Indeed, one study that compared students from the United States, Jordan, and Thailand found evidence for cultural differences in assumptions about fatalism and control over the future.

Trying to Consume

Other theorists propose different perspectives on the attitude–behavior connection. For example, a model its authors call the **multiple pathway anchoring and adjustment (MPAA) model** emphasizes multiple pathways to attitude formation, including outside-in (object-centered) and inside-out (person-centered) pathways.[42]

Another perspective tries to address some of these problems as it focuses instead on consumers' goals and what they believe they have to do to attain them. The **theory of trying** states that we should replace the criterion of behavior in the reasoned action model with *trying* to reach a goal. As Figure 3 shows, this perspective recognizes that additional factors might intervene between intent and performance—both personal and environmental barriers might prevent the individual from attaining the goal. For example, a person who intends to lose weight may have to deal with numerous issues: He may not believe he is capable of slimming down, he may have a roommate who loves to cook and who leaves tempting goodies lying around the apartment, his friends may be jealous of his attempts to diet and encourage him to pig out, or he may be genetically predisposed to obesity and cutting down on calories simply will not produce the desired results.[43]

Figure 3 THEORY OF TRYING

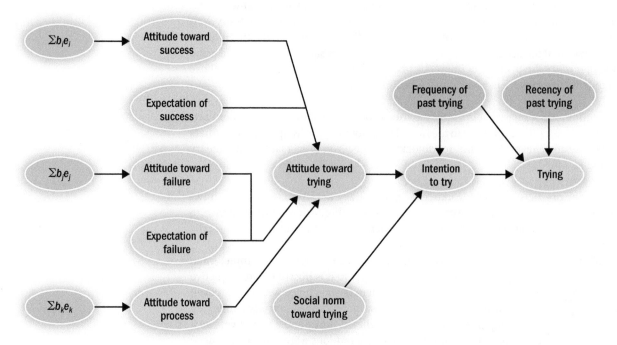

How Do Marketers Change Attitudes?

BUY NOW! Advertisers constantly bombard us with messages imploring us to change our attitudes—and of course buy their products. These persuasion attempts can range from logical arguments to graphic pictures, from peers who try to intimidate us to celebrities who try to charm us. Now we'll review some of the factors that help gauge the effectiveness of marketing communications. Our focus will be on some basic aspects of communication that specifically help to determine how and if consumers will form new attitudes or modify existing ones.

Persuasion involves an active attempt to change attitudes. This is of course Job #1 for many marketing communications. Later we'll learn more about how marketers try to accomplish this, but for now we'll set the stage by listing some basic psychological principles that influence people to change their minds or comply with a request:[44]

- **Reciprocity**—We are more likely to give if first we receive. That's why including money in a mail survey questionnaire increases the response rate by an average of 65 percent over surveys that come without financial incentives in the envelope.
- **Scarcity**—Like people, items are more attractive when they aren't available. In one study, researchers asked people to rate the quality of chocolate chip cookies. Participants who only got one cookie liked them better than did those who evaluated more of the same kind of cookie. That helps explain why we tend to value "limited-edition" items.
- **Authority**—We believe an authoritative source much more readily than one that is less authoritative. That explains why the American public's opinion on an issue can shift by as much as 2 percent when the *New York Times* (but not the *National Enquirer*) runs an article about it.
- **Consistency**—As we saw earlier in this chapter, people try not to contradict themselves in terms of what they say and do about an issue. In one study, students at an Israeli university who solicited donations to help disabled people doubled the amount they normally collected in a neighborhood if they first asked the residents to sign a petition supporting this cause two weeks before they actually asked for the donations.

- **Liking**—We agree with those we like or admire. In one study, good-looking fundraisers raised almost twice as much as other volunteers who were not as attractive.
- **Consensus**—We consider what others do before we decide what to do. People are more likely to donate to a charity if they first see a list of the names of their neighbors who have already done so.

Decisions, Decisions: Tactical Communications Options

Suppose Audi wants to create an advertising campaign for a new ragtop it targets to young drivers. As it plans this campaign, the automaker must develop a message that will arouse desire for the car. To craft persuasive messages that might persuade someone to buy this car instead of the many others available, we must answer several questions:

- Who will drive the car in the ad? A NASCAR driver? A career woman? A hip-hop star? The source of a message helps determine whether consumers will accept it.
- How should we construct the message? Should it emphasize the negative consequences of being left out when others drive cool cars and you still tool around in your old clunker? Should it directly compare the car with others already on the market, or maybe present a fantasy in which a tough-minded female executive meets a dashing stranger while she cruises down the highway in her Audi?
- What media should we use? Should the ad run in a magazine? Should we air it on TV? Sell the product door-to-door? Post the material on a Web site or create a Facebook group? Convince bloggers to write about it? Reward shoppers who check in on FourSquare at an Audi dealership? If we do produce a print ad, should we run it in the pages of *Vogue*? *Good Housekeeping*? *Car and Driver*? Sometimes *where* you say something is as important as *what* you say. Ideally, we should match the attributes of the medium with those of what we sell. For example, advertising in magazines with high prestige is more effective when we want to communicate messages about overall product image and quality, whereas specialized expert magazines do a better job when we want to convey factual information.[45]
- What characteristics of the target market might lead its members to accept the ad? If targeted users are frustrated in their daily lives, they might be more receptive to a fantasy appeal. If they're status-oriented, maybe a commercial should show bystanders who swoon with admiration as the car cruises by.

OBJECTIVE 6

The communications model identifies several important components for marketers when they try to change consumers' attitudes toward products and services.

The Elements of Communication

Marketers traditionally rely on the **communications model** shown in Figure 4. This model specifies the elements they need to control in order to communicate with their customers. One of these is a *source*, where the communication originates. Another is the *message* itself. There are many ways to say something, and the structure of the message has a significant effect on how we perceive it. We must transmit the message via a *medium*, which could be TV, radio, magazines, billboards, personal contact, or even a matchbook cover. One or more *receivers* (such as Natalie) interpret the message in light of their own experiences. Finally, the source receives *feedback* so that the marketer can use receivers' reactions to modify aspects of the message as necessary.

An Updated View: Interactive Communications

Although Natalie managed to ignore most of the "junk mail" that arrived at her door, she didn't avoid every marketing message; instead, she chose which ones she wanted to see. The traditional communications model is not entirely wrong, but it also doesn't tell the whole story—especially in today's dynamic world of interactivity, where consumers

Figure 4 THE TRADITIONAL COMMUNICATIONS MODEL

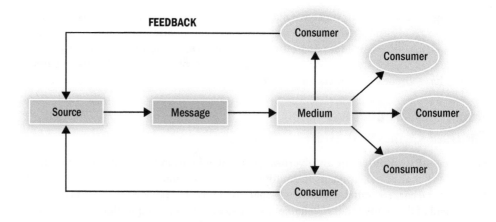

have many more choices available to them and greater control over which messages they *choose* to process.[46]

In fact, the popular strategy we call **permission marketing** acknowledges that a marketer will be much more successful when he communicates with consumers who have already agreed to listen to him; consumers who "opt out" of listening to the message probably weren't good prospects in the first place.[47] In contrast, those who say they want to learn more are likely to be receptive to marketing communications they have chosen to see or hear. As the permission marketing concept reminds us, we don't have to simply sit there and take it. We have a voice in deciding what messages we choose to see and when—and we exercise that option more and more.

Social scientists developed the traditional model to understand mass communications in which a source transmits information to many receivers at one time—typically via a *broadcast* medium such as television. This perspective essentially views advertising as the process of transferring information to the buyer before a sale. It regards a message as *perishable*—the marketer repeats the same message to a large audience and then the message "vanishes" when a new campaign takes its place. As we'll see, that model doesn't work as well now that we can *narrowcast,* or finely tune our messages to suit very small groups of receivers (sometimes even one person at a time).

Viral marketing techniques rely on consumers to spread an ad message to others in their social network because they find it cool, interesting, or just plain funny. The "subservient chicken" viral campaign for Burger King was a very successful application to promote BK's chicken sandwiches. You could type a command into the box and the "chicken" would execute it in real-time.

Source: The BURGER KING® trademarks and image are used with permission from Burger King Corporation.

OBJECTIVE 7

The consumer who processes a message is not necessarily the passive receiver of information marketers once believed him or her to be.

How long has it been since you posted to your Facebook page? Exciting technological and social developments make us rethink the picture of passive consumers as people increasingly play more proactive roles in communications. In other words, we are to a greater extent *partners*—rather than couch potatoes—in the communications process. Our input helps to shape the messages we and others like us receive, and furthermore we may seek out these messages rather than sit home and wait to see them on TV or in the paper. Figure 5 illustrates this updated approach to interactive communications.

One of the early instigators of this communications revolution was the humble handheld remote control device. As VCRs (remember them?) began to be commonplace in homes, suddenly consumers had more input into what they wanted to watch—and when. No longer did the TV networks decide when we could watch our favorite shows, and we didn't have to miss the new episode of *Mork and Mindy* because it was on at the same time as the Bears game.

Since that time, of course, our ability to control our media environment has mushroomed. Just ask some of the millions of us who use digital video recorders (DVRs) such as TiVo to watch TV shows whenever we wish—and who blithely skip over the commercials.[48] Many others have access to video-on-demand or pay-per-view TV. Home-shopping networks encourage us to call in and discuss our passion for cubic zirconium jewelry live on the air. Caller ID devices and answering machines allow us to decide if we will accept a phone call during dinner and to know if a telemarketer lurks on the other end before we pick up the phone. A bit of Web surfing allows us to identify kindred spirits around the globe, to request information about products, and even to provide suggestions to product designers and market researchers.

New Message Formats

An array of new ways to transmit information in both text and picture form offers marketers exciting alternatives to traditional advertising on TV, billboards, magazines, and so on.[49] **M-commerce** (mobile commerce), where marketers promote their goods and services via wireless devices, including cell phones, PDAs, and iPods, is red-hot. European and Asian consumers already rely on their cell phones to connect them to the world in ways we are only starting to see in the United States. In Asia, tiny cell phone screens have become electronic wallets that buy Cokes from vending machines and devices that dole out McDonald's coupons on the phone screen. Among the Chinese, cell phones have become such important status symbols that relatives at funeral rites burn paper cell phone effigies so the dead will have their mobiles in the afterlife.

If you're on Facebook, Twitter, or LinkedIn (and the odds are good that you are), you're one of the one billion people whom analysts project will use **social media** applications globally within five years.[50] This label refers to the set of technologies that enable

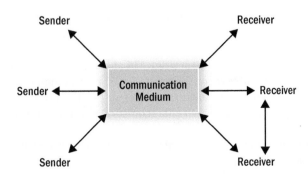

Figure 5 AN UPDATED COMMUNICATIONS MODEL

users to create content and share it with a large number of others. Social media are so widespread that in the United States and other developed countries more people use these platforms than use email—and the time people spend on these networks is growing three times faster than the rate of overall participation online.[51] Social media platforms include:

- **Blogs**—Users post messages to the Web in diary form. Blogging started as a grass-roots movement where individuals shared their thoughts on a range of topics from the mundane to the profound. Analysts estimate that two-thirds of all American Internet users will post and read blogs on a regular basis by 2012.[52]
- **Video blogging (vlogging)**—You can post video diaries on sites such as YouTube or photos on Flickr.
- **Podcasting**—You can create your own radio show that people can listen to either on their computers or iPods.
- **Virtual worlds**—Immersive 3-D digital environments (e.g., Second Life). By the beginning of 2011, already more than one billion people worldwide (yes, that's one billion) were registered with at least one virtual world.
- **Twitter**—Postings limited to 140 characters. Twitter boasts more than 175 million members and the site continues to grow exponentially as more celebrities (like Shaquille O'Neal and Oprah) post "tweets" to their followers.[53]
- **Widgets**—Small programs that users can download onto their desktops, or embed in their blogs or profile pages, that import some form of live content. For example, a football blogger can place an ESPN.com widget on his blog that displays up-to-the-minute NFL rankings.
- **Transmedia formats**—As new platforms evolve, they mix in intriguing ways because creative marketers harness multiple formats to allow consumers to express themselves and participate in campaigns. These approaches may take the form of **transmedia storytelling**; they typically include communications media that range from Web sites, blogs, and email to recorded phone calls and even graffiti messages scrawled in public spaces. Often these are **alternate reality games (ARGs)**, where thousands of people participate in a fictional story or competition to solve a mystery. One successful ARG campaign was created by the band Nine Inch Nails to publicize its Year Zero album. Players in the game found clues and received phone calls directing them to Web sites revealing images from "the future." The first clue appeared on the back of a shirt promoting Nine Inch Nails' European tour. On the back of the shirt several letters are highlighted that spell out "I am trying to believe." The words led fans to the website iamtryingtobelieve that describes a drug named "Parepin" that, in the Year Zero story, is being added to the water supply to cloud people's minds.[54] Other clues linked back to the band, such as a USB flash drive left in a bathroom stall at a concert, which in turn led fans to other Web sites that let them download printable stickers, stencils, and posters. Eventually, some players obtained special mobile phones that rang later with instructions to find a bus that took them to—drumroll—a special live performance by the band.[55]

OBJECTIVE 8

Several factors influence the effectiveness of a message source.

The Source

Regardless of whether we receive a message by "snail mail" (netheads' slang for the postal service), email, or SMS text, common sense tells us that if different people say or write the very same words, the message can affect us differently. Researchers have discussed the power of *source effects* for more than 50 years. When we attribute the same message to different sources and measure the degree of attitude change that occurs after listeners hear it, we can isolate which characteristics of a communicator cause attitude change.[56]

Under most conditions, the source of a message can have a big impact on the likelihood that receivers will accept it. Marketers can choose a spokesperson because she is an expert, attractive, famous, or even a "typical" consumer who is both likable and trustworthy. *Credibility* and *attractiveness* are two particularly important source characteristics (i.e., how much we either believe or like the communicator).[57]

How do marketing specialists decide whether to stress credibility or attractiveness when they select a message source? There should be a match between the needs of the recipient and the potential rewards the source offers. When this match occurs, the recipient is more motivated to process the message. An attractive source, for example, is more effective for receivers who tend to be sensitive about social acceptance and others' opinions, whereas a credible, expert source is more powerful when she speaks to internally oriented people.[58] However, even a credible source's trustworthiness evaporates if she endorses too many products.[59]

The choice may also depend on the type of product. A positive source can reduce risk and increase message acceptance overall, but particular types of sources are more effective to reduce different kinds of risk. Experts excel when we want to change attitudes toward utilitarian products that have high performance risk, such as vacuums, because they are complex and may not work as we expect. Celebrities work better when they focus on products such as jewelry and furniture that have high social risk, where the user is more concerned about the impression others have of him. Finally, "typical" consumers, who are appealing sources because of their similarity to the recipient, tend to be most effective when they provide real-life endorsements for everyday products that are low risk, such as cookies.[60]

Source Credibility

Source credibility refers to a communicator's expertise, objectivity, or trustworthiness. This dimension relates to consumers' beliefs that this person is competent and that she will provide the necessary information we need when we evaluate competing products. Sincerity is particularly important when a company tries to publicize its *corporate social responsibility (CSR)* activities that benefit the community in some way. When consumers believe it's genuinely doing good things, a company's image can skyrocket. But this effort can backfire if people question the organization's motivations (e.g., if they think the firm spends more to talk about its good deeds than to actually do them).[61] Not too surprisingly, people who see deceptive advertising experience a feeling of distrust that carries over to other messages from that source and even to other sources, because they are more likely to assume that advertising in general is not very credible—a true case of poisoning the well for other marketers![62]

A credible source is particularly persuasive when the consumer has yet to learn much about a product or form an opinion of it.[63] Indeed, a recent study demonstrated that simply letting consumers know a firm is profitable leads them to put more stock in what the company says in its advertising.[64]

One widely used technique to generate credibility is to pay an expert or a celebrity to tout a product—but this kind of endorsement doesn't come cheap. However, typically the investment is worth it simply because market analysts use the announcement of an endorsement contract to evaluate a firm's potential profitability, which affects its expected return. On average, then, the impact of endorsements on stock returns appears to be so positive that it offsets the cost of hiring the spokesperson.[65] Indeed, a new report on the use of celebrities in marketing reported that ads containing a celebrity endorser produced 9.4 percent higher consumer readership than ads without a celebrity endorser. In its analysis of almost 80,000 print ads that appeared in 2009–2010, Starch Advertising Research concluded that "in terms of helping with the first task in . . . getting consumers to read your ad, these data show that a celebrity endorsement moves the readership needle."[66] The drawing power of famous people may even be "wired in": One study found that compared to "ordinary" faces, our brains pay more attention to famous faces and more efficiently process information about these images.[67] Celebrities increase awareness of a firm's advertising and enhance both company image and brand attitudes.[68] A celebrity endorsement strategy can be an effective way to differentiate among similar products. This is especially important when consumers do not perceive many actual

Even actors who play doctors on TV may be credible communicators.

Source: Courtesy of Old Spice/The Procter & Gamble Company.

The Tangled Web

In recent years we've witnessed a new attempt to manipulate attitudes that some call **sock puppeting**. This term describes a company executive or other biased source who poses as someone else as he touts his organization in social media. For example, in 2007 it came to light that the CEO of Whole Foods had posted derogatory comments about rival Wild Oats without revealing his true identity. More recently,

differences among competitors, as often occurs when brands are in the mature stage of the product life cycle.

What's more, the early evidence indicates that celebrities exert the same impact on messages we receive from social media platforms. One study found that brand endorsements streamed by celebrities directly to friends and followers on platforms such as Facebook and Twitter are significantly more effective (in fact, greater than 50 percent more) than conventional display ads placed on social media pages. The celebrities in the study included Drew Brees, Snoop Dogg, Matt Hasselbeck, Enrique Iglesias, Khloe Kardashian, Nick Swisher, and Kendra Wilkinson.[69]

Although in general more positive sources tend to increase attitude change, there are exceptions to this rule. Sometimes we can think a source is obnoxious, yet it is still effective. A case in point is Mr. Whipple, the irritating but well-known TV character who scolds toilet paper shoppers, "Please don't squeeze the Charmin!" In some instances the differences in attitude change between positive sources and less positive sources become erased over time. After a while, people appear to "forget" about the negative source and change their attitudes anyway. We call this process the **sleeper effect**.[70]

What Factors Affect Credibility?

A message's credibility increases if receivers think the source's qualifications are relevant to the product he or she endorses. This linkage can overcome other objections people may have to the endorser or the product. Ronald Biggs, whose claim to fame was his 1963 role in the Great Train Robbery in the United Kingdom, successfully served as a spokesman in Brazil for a company that makes door locks—a topic about which he is presumably knowledgeable![73]

It's important to note that what is credible to one consumer segment may be a turn-off to another. Indeed, rebellious or even deviant celebrities may be attractive to some simply for that reason. Tommy Hilfiger cultivated a rebellious, street-smart image when he used rapper Snoop Doggy Dogg (who was acquitted of murder charges) to help launch his clothing line and Coolio, a former crack addict and thief, as a runway model.[74] Parents may not be thrilled by these message sources—but isn't that the point? Charlie Sheen, please report to the studio . . .

A consumer's beliefs about a product's attributes will weaken if he or she perceives that the source is biased.[75] *Knowledge bias* implies that a source's knowledge about a topic is not accurate. *Reporting bias* occurs when a source has the required knowledge but we question his willingness to convey it accurately—as when a racket manufacturer pays a star tennis player to use its products exclusively. The source's credentials might be appropriate, but the fact that consumers see the expert as a "hired gun" compromises believability. The Federal Trade Commission is considering steps to toughen the rules for testimonials by requiring advertisers to produce evidence that the results for a spokesperson are likely to be typical for others. One other possible measure will require celebrities who mention products in TV interviews to disclose any connections they have to the manufacturers of those products. Finally, bloggers who receive free products and recommend them in their blogs will have to document that they got the items at no charge.[76]

Source Attractiveness: "What Is Beautiful Is Good"

A British dairy company enlisted Johnny Rotten, the lead singer of the Sex Pistols, to appear in a commercial (or *advert*, as they say in the United Kingdom) to promote its butter. Sales went up 85 percent when the punk legend plugged the product (rotten butter?).[77] **Source attractiveness** refers to the social *value* recipients attribute to a communicator. This value relates to the person's physical appearance, personality, social status, or similarity to the receiver (we like to listen to people who are like us).

Some sources like Johnny Rotten appeal to us because they are cool, brainy, or just plain famous. However, many simply are nice to look at. Almost everywhere we turn, beautiful people try to persuade us to buy or do something. Our society places a very high premium on physical attractiveness. We assume that good-looking people are smarter, hipper, and happier than the rest of us. This is an example of a *halo effect*, which occurs when we assume that persons who rank high on one dimension excel on others as well. We can explain this effect in terms of the consistency principle discussed earlier in this chapter; we are more comfortable when all of our judgments about a person correspond.

Clearly, beauty sells—so how does this happen?[78] One explanation is that physical attractiveness is a cue that facilitates or modifies information processing because it directs our attention to the message. Some evidence indicates that consumers pay more attention to ads that contain attractive models, though not necessarily to the ad copy.[79] In other words, we're more likely to notice an ad with a beautiful person in it, but we won't necessarily read it. We may enjoy looking at a handsome person, but these positive feelings do not necessarily affect product attitudes or purchase intentions.[80]

Under the right circumstances, however, beauty can indeed be a source of information—especially when the advertised product actually (or so the marketer claims)

a nonprofit research organization called GiveWell that rates the effectiveness of charities had to discipline two of its founders who pretended to be other people on blogs and then referred people to the group's Web site.[71]

Similar problems potentially dilute the credibility of *Wikipedia*, the open-source online encyclopedia that is beloved by many students. Anyone can edit entries, so their reliability is not assured. Although other alert contributors may eventually correct false or self-serving entries, there is still room for organizations to color content in a way that serves their goals. For example, a visitor edited the *Wikipedia* entry for the SeaWorld theme parks to change all mentions of "orcas" to "killer whales" and he or she also deleted a paragraph that criticized SeaWorld's "lack of respect toward its orcas." It turns out the changes originated at a computer located in Anheuser-Busch—the company that happens to own SeaWorld. An employee of PepsiCo deleted several paragraphs of the Pepsi entry that focused on its detrimental health effects, and a person at Walmart altered an entry about how the retailer pays its employees.

Another form of sock puppeting is so-called *paid influencer programs* that attempt to start online conversations about brands when they encourage bloggers to write about them. These "sponsored conversations" can be effective, but again marketers need to be careful about the potential to distort source recommendations. For example, Kmart awarded a shopping spree to a group of bloggers who agreed to post about their experiences. Panasonic flew bloggers to the Consumer Electronics Show in Las Vegas, where they posted about the show and Panasonic products unveiled there. Mercedes gave a blogger use of an SUV for a week in exchange for posts about it.

This practice got the attention of the U.S. Federal Trade Commission, which recently updated its truth-in-advertising guidelines to require anyone paid in cash or in kind to provide an online endorsement to disclose the financial relationship to the audience. The agency jumped into action in response to the campaign by a California public relations agency hired by video game developers that had employees pose as consumers who posted positive game reviews at the iTunes store.[72]

. . . .

Marketing Pitfall

Celebrities (and their managers) don't necessarily jump at the chance to endorse just any product. After all, they have a brand image to protect as well. For years one popular strategy has been to film commercials overseas and stipulate that they are not to air at home. The practice is so widespread in Japan that one Web site even coined a term to describe it: *Japander* (a combination of Japanese and pandering)—". . . 1. a western star who uses his or her fame to make large sums of money in a short time by advertising products in Japan that they would probably never use . . . *(see sinecure [sic.], prostitute)* 2. to make an ass of oneself in Japanese media." Check out *japander.com* to see actors such as Arnold Schwarzenegger, George Clooney, and Jennifer Aniston in commercials they'd prefer their American fans don't see.[85]

enhances attractiveness or sexuality.[81] The *social adaptation perspective* assumes that the perceiver weights information more heavily if he feels it will help him to evaluate the subject of a message. We filter out irrelevant information to minimize cognitive effort. So, in these situations, a hot endorser provides appropriate information and this becomes a central, task-relevant cue. For example, attractiveness affects attitudes toward ads about perfume or cologne (where attractiveness is relevant) but not toward coffee ads (where attractiveness is not relevant).[82]

Star Power: Celebrities as Communications Sources

Celebrities hawk everything from grills (George Foreman) to perfumes (J. Lo). As our discussion about the consistency principle illustrates, these messages are more effective when there's a logical connection between the star and the product. When Bob Dylan—who wrote lyrics such as "Advertising signs that con you/Into thinking you're the one/That can do what's never been done/That can win what's never been won . . ."—pitches Victoria's Secret lingerie (yes, he really did), marketers may need to reread their consumer behavior textbook.[83] Then again, teen idol Justin Bieber has been putting his name on almost everything including . . . nail polish![84]

Star power works because celebrities embody *cultural meanings*—they symbolize important categories like status and social class (a "working-class hero," such as Kevin James of *King of Queens*), gender (a "ladies man," such as Brad Pitt), age (the boyish Michael J. Fox), and even personality types (the nerdy but earnest Andy Bernard on *The Office*). Ideally, the advertiser decides what meanings the product should convey (that is, how it should position the item in the marketplace) and then chooses a celebrity who embodies a similar meaning. The product's meaning thus moves from the manufacturer to the consumer, using the star as a vehicle.[86]

Nonhuman Endorsers

Celebrities can be effective endorsers, but there are drawbacks to using them. As we previously noted, their motives may be suspect if they plug products that don't fit their images or if consumers begin to believe the celebrities never met a product they didn't like (for a fee). They may be involved in a scandal or deviate from a brand's desired image—the Milk Processor Education Program suspended "Got Milk?" ads featuring Mary-Kate and Ashley Olsen after Mary-Kate entered a treatment facility for an undisclosed health issue.

For these reasons, some marketers seek alternative sources, including cartoon characters and mascots. As the marketing director for a company that manufactures costumed characters for sports teams and businesses points out, "You don't have to worry about your mascot checking into rehab."[87] researchers report that **spokescharacters**, such as the Pillsbury Doughboy, Chester the Cheetah, and the Snuggle Bear, do, in fact, boost viewers' recall of claims that ads make and also yield higher brand attitudes.[88] The most popular spokescharacters in 2011 included Old Spice's The Man Your Man Could Smell Like (played by former NFL athlete Isaiah Mustafa), Snoopy (who appears in commercials for MetLife), the talking M&Ms, and Allstate's Mayhem Man.[89]

An *avatar* is one increasingly popular alternative to a flesh-and-blood endorser. *Avatar* is a Hindu term for a deity that appears in superhuman or animal form. In the computing world, it means a character you can move around inside a visual, graphical world. Consumers who inhabit virtual worlds such as Second Life, Habbo Hotel, and Entropia Universe design their avatars to reflect their own unique personalities, desires, and fantasies.

The advantages of using virtual avatars compared to flesh-and-blood models include the ability to change the avatar in real time to suit the needs of the target audience. From an advertising perspective, they are likely to be more cost effective than hiring a real person. From a personal selling and customer service perspective, they handle multiple customers at one time, they are not geographically limited, and they are operational 24/7 so they free up company employees and sales personnel to perform other activities.[90]

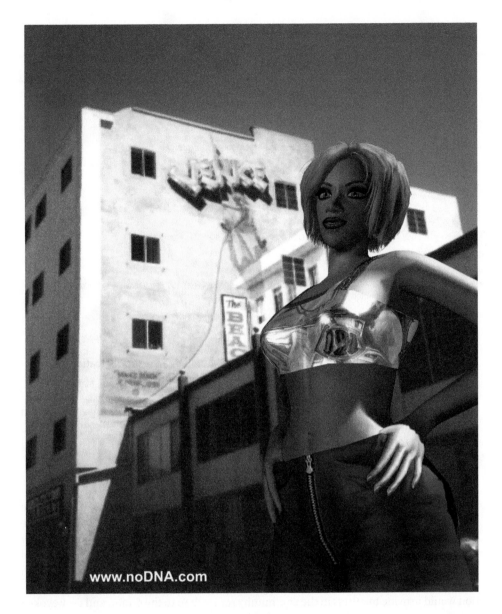

A German firm called NoDNA offers its own stable of cybermodels such as Tyra, who is shown here.
Source: Used with permission of NoDNA c/o Vierte Art.

OBJECTIVE 9

The way a marketer structures his or her message determines how persuasive it will be.

The Message

A major study of more than 1,000 commercials identified factors that determine whether a commercial message will be persuasive. The single most important feature: Does the communication stress a unique attribute or benefit of the product?[91] Table 2 lists some other good and bad elements of commercial messages.

Consumers increasingly find commercials confusing, but what's even worse is when we find them annoying. In a landmark study of irritating advertising, researchers examined more than 500 prime-time network commercials that had registered negative reactions by consumers. The most irritating commercials were for feminine hygiene products, hemorrhoid medication or laxatives, and women's underwear. The researchers identify these as prime offenders:

● The commercial shows a sensitive product (e.g., hemorrhoid medicine) and emphasizes its usage.
● The situation is contrived or overdramatized.

TABLE 2	Characteristics of Good and Bad Messages

Positive Effects	Negative Effects
Showing convenience of use	Extensive information on components, ingredients, or nutrition
Showing new product or improved features	Outdoor setting (message gets lost)
Casting background (i.e., people are incidental to message)	Large number of on-screen characters
Indirect comparison to other products	Graphic displays
Demonstration of the product in use	
Demonstration of tangible results (e.g., bouncy hair)	
An actor playing the role of an ordinary person	
No principal character (i.e., more time is devoted to the product)	

Source: Adapted from David W. Stewart and David H. Furse, "The Effects of Television Advertising Execution on Recall, Comprehension, and Persuasion," *Psychology & Marketing* 2 (Fall 1985): 135–60. Copyright © 1985 by John Wiley & Sons, Inc. Reprinted by permission.

- A person is put down in terms of appearance, knowledge, or sophistication.
- An important relationship, such as a marriage, is threatened.
- There is a graphic demonstration of physical discomfort.
- The commercial created uncomfortable tension because of an argument or an antagonistic character.
- It portrays an unattractive or unsympathetic character.
- It includes a sexually suggestive scene.
- The commercial suffers from poor casting or execution.

Characteristics of the message itself help determine its impact on attitudes. These variables include *how* we say the message as well as *what* we say. Depending on the marketer's objectives and the nature of the product, different kinds of messages product different results. For example, a recent study examined the responses of actual viewers to four televised fund-raising drives by a public television station over a two-year period. The most effective fund-raising appeals stressed the benefits that contribution to the station would provide to others in the community rather than to the donor, and they evoked negative rather than positive emotions.[92] Obviously, these results would differ in other circumstances; the point here is that the content of the message *does* matter.

A marketer faces some crucial issues when she creates a message:

- Should she convey the message in words or pictures?
- How often should she repeat the message?
- Should it draw a conclusion, or should this be left up to the listener?
- Should it present both sides of an argument?
- Should it explicitly compare the product to competitors?
- Should it include a blatant sexual appeal?
- Should it arouse negative emotions such as fear?
- How concrete or vivid should the arguments and imagery be?
- Should it be funny?

How Do We Send the Message?

Pictures or words? The saying, "One picture is worth a thousand words" captures the idea that visuals are very effective, especially when the communicator wants to influence receivers' emotional responses. For this reason, advertisers often rely on vivid illustrations or photography.[93]

This British clothing ad uses vivid (and perhaps a bit scary?) imagery to communicate.

Source: Courtesy of DDB, London.

However, a picture is not always as effective when it communicates factual information. Ads that contain the same information elicit different reactions when the marketer presents them in visual versus verbal form. The verbal version affects ratings on the utilitarian aspects of a product, whereas the visual version affects aesthetic evaluations. Verbal elements are more effective when an accompanying picture reinforces them, especially if they *frame* the illustration (the message in the picture strongly relates to the copy).[94]

Because it requires more effort to process, a verbal message is most appropriate for high-involvement situations, such as print contexts where the reader really pays attention to the advertising. Verbal material decays more rapidly in memory, so these messages require more frequent exposures to obtain the desired effect. Visual images, in contrast, allow the receiver to *chunk* information at the time of encoding. Chunking results in a stronger memory trace that aids retrieval over time.[95]

Powerful descriptions or graphics command attention and are more strongly embedded in memory. This may be because *vivid* images tend to activate mental imagery, whereas abstract stimuli inhibit this process.[96] For example major companies such as Google, Nokia, and France Telecom SA's Orange are experimenting with advertising campaigns that allow a passerby to interact with posters in bus stops, phone booths, train stations, and airports. As of now, they are using the new format to distribute wireless applications or ringtones for smartphones. But outdoor advertisers and marketers say the ads could also be used to distribute games, video ads, and coupons, and even as a way to sell physical or digital goods and services. A Google poster in Boston proclaims, "You have to wait here. You don't have to be bored," and it allows the person to download Google's mobile app through a free Wi-Fi router installed in the location.[97] Of course, this effect can cut both ways: Negative information a marketer presents in a vivid manner may result in more negative evaluations at a later time.[98]

The concrete discussion of a product attribute in ad copy also influences the importance of that attribute, because it draws more attention. For example, in a study where participants read two versions of ad copy for a watch, the version that claimed "According to industry sources, three out of every four watch breakdowns are due to water getting into the case," was more effective than the version that simply said, "According to industry sources, many watch breakdowns are due to water getting into the case."[99]

Repeat the message? Repetition can be a double-edged sword for marketers. We usually need multiple exposures to a stimulus before learning occurs. Contrary to the saying "familiarity breeds contempt," people tend to like things that are more familiar to them, even if they were not that keen on them initially.[100] Psychologists call this the *mere exposure* phenomenon.

Advertisers find positive effects for repetition even in mature product categories: Repeating product information boosts consumers' awareness of the brand, even though the marketer says nothing new.[101] However, too much repetition creates *habituation*, whereby the consumer no longer pays attention to the stimulus because of fatigue or boredom. Excessive exposure can cause advertising wear-out, which can result in negative reactions to an ad after we see it too much.[102]

The **two-factor theory** explains the fine line between familiarity and boredom; it proposes that two separate psychological processes operate when we repeatedly show an ad to a viewer. The positive side of repetition is that it increases familiarity and thus reduces uncertainty about the product. The negative side is that over time boredom increases with each exposure. At some point the amount of boredom exceeds the amount of uncertainty the message reduces, and this results in wear-out. Figure 6 depicts this pattern. Its effect is especially pronounced when each exposure is of a fairly long duration (such as a 60-second commercial).[103]

The theory implies that advertisers can overcome this problem if they limit the amount of exposure per repetition (e.g., use 15-second spots instead of longer commercials). They can also maintain familiarity but alleviate boredom if they slightly vary the content of ads over time—although each spot differs, the campaign still revolves around a common theme. Recipients who see varied ads about the product absorb more information about product attributes and experience more positive thoughts about the brand than do those who see the same information repeatedly. This additional information also allows the person to resist attempts to change his or her attitude in the face of a counterattack by a competing brand.[104]

How Do We Structure the Argument?

Many marketing messages are like debates or trials: A source presents an argument and tries to convince the receiver to shift his or her opinion. As you've no doubt guessed, the *way* we present the argument may be as important as *what* we say.

Most messages merely present one or more positive attributes about the product or reasons to buy it. These are *supportive arguments*. An alternative is to use a *two-sided message*, in which the message presents both positive and negative information. Research indicates that two-sided ads can be quite effective, yet marketers rarely use them.[105]

Why would a marketer want to devote advertising space to publicize a product's negative attributes? Under the right circumstances, **refutational arguments** that first raise a negative issue and then dismiss it can be quite effective. This approach increases source credibility because it reduces *reporting bias*. Also, people who are

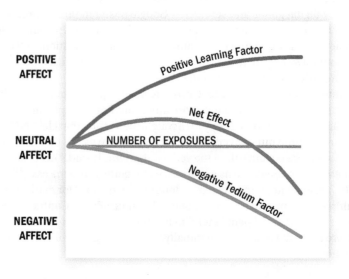

Figure 6 TWO-FACTOR THEORY OF MESSAGE REPETITION

skeptical about the product may be more receptive to a balanced argument instead of a "whitewash."[106] For example, after General Motors declared bankruptcy, an ad declared: "Let's be completely honest: No company wants to go through this."[107] Research evidence indicates that when experts have strong arguments on their side, they are actually more effective if they express some uncertainty rather than stating unequivocally that they are correct.[108]

This is not to say that the marketer should go overboard and confess to major problems with the product (though hopefully there aren't any major ones to admit to). The typical refutational strategy discusses relatively minor attributes that may present a problem or fall short when the customer compares a product to competitors. Positive, important attributes then refute these drawbacks. For example, Avis got a lot of mileage when it claimed to be only the "No. 2" car rental company, whereas an ad for Volkswagen woefully described one of its cars as a "lemon" because there was a scratch on the glove compartment chrome strip.[109] A two-sided strategy appears to be the most effective when the audience is well-educated (and presumably more impressed by a balanced argument).[110] It is also best to use when receivers are not already loyal to the product—"preaching to the choir" about possible drawbacks may raise doubts unnecessarily.

Should the argument draw conclusions, or should the marketer merely present the facts and let the consumer arrive at his own decision? On the one hand, consumers who make their own inferences instead of having ideas spoon-fed to them will form stronger, more accessible attitudes. On the other hand, leaving the conclusion ambiguous increases the chance that the consumer will not form the desired attitude.

The response to this issue depends on the consumer's motivation to process the ad and the complexity of the arguments. If the message is personally relevant, people will pay attention to it and spontaneously form inferences. However, if the arguments are hard to follow or consumers lack the motivation to follow them, it's safer for the ad to draw conclusions.[111]

Should we compare our product to our competitors'? In 1971, the FTC issued guidelines that encouraged advertisers to name competing brands in their ads. The government did this to improve the information available to consumers in ads, and indeed recent evidence indicates that, at least under some conditions, this type of presentation does result in more informed decision making.[112]

Comparative advertising refers to a strategy in which a message compares two or more recognizable brands and weighs them in terms of one or more specific attributes.[113] A recent Arby's campaign to promote its chicken sandwiches uses this approach: One commercial, set in a fictitious McDonald's boardroom, features a young man trying to convince McDonald's executives to serve a healthier type of chicken as he proclaims, "I propose that McDonald's stops putting phosphates, salt and water into its chicken. Consider replacing your chicken that is only about 70 percent chicken, with 100 percent all-natural chicken." The room erupts with laughter. At the end of the spot, a voice-over chimes in: "Unlike McDonald's, all of Arby's chicken sandwiches are made with 100 percent all-natural chicken . . . ."[114] Research indicates that this strategy is more effective for products that already have a positive brand image.[115]

This strategy can cut both ways, especially if the sponsor depicts the competition in a nasty or negative way. Although some comparative ads result in desired attitude changes, they may also be lower in believability and stir up *source derogation* (i.e., the consumer may doubt the credibility of a biased presentation).[116] Indeed, in some cultures (such as Asia), comparative advertising is rare because people find such a confrontational approach offensive.

Types of Message Appeals

A persuasive message can tug at the heartstrings or scare you, make you laugh, make you cry, or leave you yearning to learn more. In this section, we'll review the major alternatives available to communicators.

Emotional versus Rational Appeals

Colgate-Palmolive's Total brand was the first toothpaste to claim that it fights gingivitis, a benefit that let Colgate inch ahead of Procter & Gamble's Crest for the first time in decades. Colgate initially made a scientific pitch for its new entry as it emphasized Total's germ-fighting abilities. In newer ads, however, former model Brooke Shields cavorts with two children (not hers) as soft music plays in the background. She states, "Having a healthy smile is important to me. Not just as an actress but as a mom."[117]

So, which is better: to appeal to the head or to the heart? The answer often depends on the nature of the product and the type of relationship consumers have with it. It's hard to gauge the precise effects of rational versus emotional appeals. Although recall of ad content tends to be better for "thinking" ads than for "feeling" ads, conventional measures of advertising effectiveness (e.g., day-after recall) may not be adequate to assess cumulative effects of emotional ads. These open-ended measures assess cognitive responses, and they may penalize feeling ads because the reactions are not as easy to articulate.[118]

Sex Appeals

In a recent campaign that lit up the Twittersphere, vodka maker Skyy Spirits launched a print and billboard campaign that shows—from the thighs down—a woman in red tights and red heels appearing to have sex with a giant Skyy blue vodka bottle. One critic complained, "This is just ridiculous, it's porn-a-hol. Underage kids will look at this and associate sexual prowess with drinking Skyy."[119]

Echoing the widely held belief that "sex sells," many marketing communications for products from perfumes to autos feature heavy doses of erotic suggestions that range from subtle hints to blatant displays of skin. Of course, the prevalence of sexual appeals varies from country to country. Even American firms run ads elsewhere that would not go over at home. For example, a "cheeky" ad campaign designed to boost the appeal of American-made Lee jeans among Europeans features a series of bare buttocks. The messages are based on the concept that if bottoms could choose jeans, they would opt for Lee: "Bottoms feel better in Lee Jeans."[120]

Perhaps not surprisingly, female nudity in print ads generates negative feelings and tension among female consumers, whereas men's reactions are more positive—although women with more liberal attitudes toward sex are more likely to be receptive.[121] In a case of turnabout being fair play, another study found that males dislike nude males in ads, whereas females responded well to undressed males—but not totally nude ones.[122] Women also respond more positively to sexual themes when they occur in the context of a committed relationship rather than just gratuitous lust.[123]

So, does sex work? Although erotic content does appear to draw attention to an ad, its use may actually be counterproductive. In one 2010 survey, an overwhelming 61 percent of the respondents said that sexual imagery in a product's ad makes them less likely to buy it.[124] Ironically, a provocative picture can be *too* effective; it can attract so much attention as to hinder processing and recall of the ad's contents. Sexual appeals appear to be ineffective when marketers use them merely as a "trick" to grab attention. They do, however, appear to work when the product is *itself* related to sex (e.g., lingerie or Viagra).[125]

A research firm explored how men and women look at sexually themed ads and what effect, if any, what they choose to look at might have on the ads' effectiveness. One part of the study used special software to follow the visual behavior of respondents as they looked at 10 print ads. The ad sample consisted of two U.S. print ads, one sexual and one nonsexual, from each of five product categories. When the participants looked at a sexual ad, men tended to ignore the text as they focused instead on the woman in it, whereas the women participants tended first to explore the ad's text elements. Men said they liked the sexual ads more, liked the products advertised in them more, and would be more likely to buy those products. Women scored the sexual ads lower than the nonsexual ones on all three of those criteria.[126]

STOP USING REGULAR LIGHT BULBS AND WE'LL STOP RUNNING ADS LIKE THIS.

This ad from Dubai clearly appeals to the heart.
Source: Courtesy of Y&R Dubai.

Humorous Appeals

A TV commercial for Metamucil showed a National Park Service ranger who pours a glass of the laxative down Old Faithful and announces that the product keeps the famous geyser "regular." Yellowstone National Park started getting letters from offended viewers such as this one who wrote, "I suppose that in an era when people sell naming rights to sports arenas . . . that some in the National Park Service would see nothing wrong with selling the image of a National Park ranger for the marketing of a product promoting bowel regularity." Park officials also had their own concerns: They didn't want people to think that the geyser needed "help" or that it's OK to throw things down into it![127]

Does humor work? Overall, humorous advertisements do get attention. One study found that recognition scores for humorous liquor ads were better than average. However, the verdict is mixed as to whether humor affects recall or product attitudes in a significant way.[128] One reason silly ads may shift opinions is that they provide a source of *distraction*. A funny ad inhibits *counterarguing* (in which a consumer thinks of reasons why he doesn't agree with the message), so this increases the likelihood of message acceptance because he doesn't come up with arguments against the product.[129]

Humor is more likely to be effective when the ad clearly identifies the brand and the funny material does not "swamp" the message. This danger is similar to one we've already discussed about beautiful models who divert attention from copy points. Subtle humor is usually better, as is humor that does not make fun of the potential consumer. Finally, humor should be appropriate to the product's image. Hint: An undertaker or a bank might want to avoid humor, as might as a company that has accepted U.S. government bailout money.

Fear Appeals

Volkswagen's advertising campaign to promote the safety of its Jetta model really got people's attention. The spots depict graphic car crashes from the perspective of the passengers who chatter away as they drive down the street. Without warning, other vehicles come out of nowhere and brutally smash into their cars. In one spot, viewers see a passenger's head striking an airbag. The spots end with shots of stunned passengers, the damaged Jetta, and the slogan: "Safe happens." The ads look so realistic that consumers called the company to ask if any of the actors were hurt.[131]

Fear appeals emphasize the negative consequences that can occur unless the consumer changes a behavior or an attitude. Fear appeals are fairly common in advertising, although they are more common in social marketing contexts in which organizations encourage people to convert to healthier lifestyles by quitting smoking, using contraception, or relying on a designated driver. The FDA (Food and Drug Administration) is currently executing an aggressive fear appeal tactic as it releases new guidelines for cigarette advertising and packaging for the first time in more than 25 years. The agency is selecting a range of horrific images to be depicted directly on the cigarette packaging (and in the advertising) showing people who have suffered from the ravages of cigarettes. One version has a visual of a terminal cancer patient with copy that says "cigarettes cause cancer."[132]

This tactic may well scare away would-be smokers, but does a fear appeal work more generally for marketers? Most research on this topic indicates that these negative messages are most effective when the advertiser uses only a moderate threat and when the ad presents a solution to the problem. Otherwise, consumers will tune out the ad because they can do nothing to solve or avoid the threat.[133]

When a weak threat is ineffective, there may be insufficient elaboration of the harmful consequences of engaging in the behavior. When a strong threat doesn't work, there may be too much elaboration that interferes with the processing of the recommended change in behavior—the receiver is too busy thinking of reasons the message doesn't apply to her to pay attention to the offered solution.[134] A study that manipulated subjects' degree of anxiety about AIDS, for example, found that they evaluated condom ads most positively when the ads used a moderate threat. Copy that promoted use of the condom because "Sex is a risky business" (moderate threat) resulted in more attitude change than either a weaker threat that emphasized the product's sensitivity or a strong threat that discussed the certainty of death from AIDS.[135]

Similarly, scare tactics have not generally been an effective way to convince teenagers to curb their use of alcohol or drugs. Teens simply tune out the message or deny its relevance to them.[136] However, a study of adolescent responses to social versus physical threat appeals in drug prevention messages found that social threat (such as being ostracized by one's peers) is a more effective strategy.[137]

The Message as Art Form: Metaphors Be with You

Just like novelists, poets, and artists, marketers are storytellers. Their communications take the form of stories because they describe intangible product benefits. The story-teller, therefore, must express these in some concrete form so that consumers will get the message.

Advertising creatives rely (consciously or not) on well-known literary devices to communicate these meanings. For example, characters such as Mr. Goodwrench, the Jolly Green Giant, and Charlie the Tuna may personify a product or service. Many ads take the form of an **allegory**: a story about an abstract trait or concept that advertisers tell in the context of a person, animal, vegetable, or object.

A **metaphor** places two dissimilar objects into a close relationship such that "A is B," whereas a **simile** compares two objects, "A is like B." A and B, however dissimilar, share some quality that the metaphor highlights. Metaphors allow the marketer to apply meaningful images to everyday events. In the stock market, "white knights" battle "hostile raiders" with the help of "poison pills"; Tony the Tiger equates cereal with strength and "you're in good hands with Allstate" insurance.[138]

Resonance is another type of literary device advertisers frequently use. It is a form of presentation that combines a play on words with a relevant picture. Whereas metaphor substitutes one meaning for another by connecting two things that are in some way similar, resonance employs an element that has a double meaning—such as a *pun*, in which two words sound similar but have different meanings. For example, an ad for a diet strawberry shortcake dessert might bear the copy "berried treasure" so that the brand conveys qualities we associate with buried treasure such as valuable and hidden. An ad for ASICS athletic shoes proclaimed, "We believe women should be running the country" as it depicted a woman jogging, while a Bounce fabric softener ad asked "Is

This Chinese detergent ad uses a handcuff metaphor as it urges the viewer, "Free yourself from the burden of handwash."
Source: Courtesy of Saatchi & Saatchi.

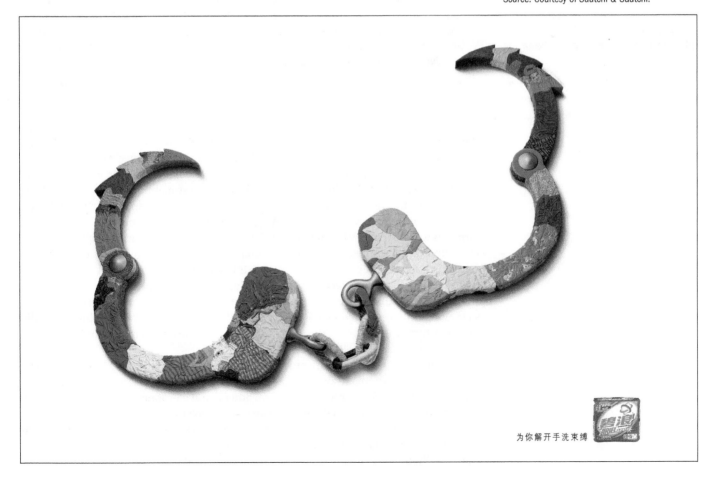

为你解开手洗束缚

CB AS I SEE IT

Professor Edward McQuarrie, *Santa Clara University*

Early in my career, I became fascinated by *wordplay* in magazine advertisements. Puns, rhymes, and much more complex figures of speech abound in advertising headlines. In fact, virtually any figure of speech catalogued by the ancient Greeks can be found in the headlines of American advertisements today. But why is that? After all, advertisers are under a lot of pressure. They have to spend tons of money in the often forlorn hope of getting a consumer to spend a second or two glancing at an ad. Why mess around with complicated wordplay and risk confusing or alienating consumers?

The answer, my colleague Professor David Mick and I discovered, goes to the heart of what makes mass-media advertising a distinctive kind of human communication.[142] The thing to remember is that no one has to look at a magazine ad, or spend much time on it. It's the exact opposite of being in school, where you have to pay attention—or flunk. And that's why advertisers put puns, rhymes, and every other rhetorical device in ad headlines: Such wordplay functions as a lure and a snare for attention. It's fun to get the joke. Result: Consumers linger a second longer, and absorb at least one point from the ad, even if they never read the rest. And a small jot of pleasure gets associated with the brand.

Traditional consumer research is tied to an experimental paradigm in which the subjects are forced to read the whole ad; within that paradigm, there is no way to discover the importance of rhetorical figures. A related problem that I believe continues to handicap consumer research is an excessive focus on persuasion by means of words. Open a contemporary magazine and look at the full-page color ads: How many words do you see? Not very many anymore. What you will see is carefully crafted photographic imagery, heavily altered by computer graphics software. In fact you will see visual puns, and visual metaphors—figures of speech in pictorial form. My colleague Professor Barbara Phillips and I have shown why it might be smart for advertisers to make their pitch in pictures rather than words; briefly, the very ambiguity of pictorial persuasion makes it more effective, because the reader has to generate more inferences to comprehend the ad.[143]

What I like about being a consumer researcher is that I get to study reality. Every ad represents an attempt by someone working very hard, under the gun to keep his or her job, to get an invisible mass of consumers to spend a second or two more with his or her creation. In my view, it's the study of these real efforts at persuasion that hold the most promise for advancing scientific understanding.

there something creeping up behind you?" as it showed a woman's dressed bunched up on her back due to static. Because the text departs from expectations, it creates a state of tension or uncertainty on the part of the viewer until he figures out the wordplay. Once the consumer "gets it," he may prefer the ad to a more straightforward message.[139] Just as a novelist or artist can tell a story in words or pictures, we can choose several ways to address our consumer audiences. Advertisers structure commercials like other art forms; as we've seen they borrow conventions from literature and art to communicate.[140] One important distinction is between a *drama* and a *lecture*.[141] A lecture is like a speech: The source speaks directly to the audience to inform them about a product or to persuade them to buy it. Because a lecture clearly implies an attempt at persuasion, the audience will regard it as such. Assuming it motivates listeners, they weigh the merits of the message along with the source's credibility. Cognitive responses occur (e.g., "How much did Coke pay him to say that?"). Consumers accept the appeal if it overcomes objections and is consistent with their beliefs.

In contrast, a drama is similar to a play or movie. Whereas a lecture holds the viewer at arm's length, a drama draws the viewer into the action. The characters indirectly address the audience: They interact with each other about a product or service in an imaginary setting. Dramas are experiential because they involve the audience emotionally. The *transformational advertising* method encourages the recipient to associate the experience of product usage with some subjective sensation—like the feeling you get when you watch a silhouetted actor on TV as he dances energetically to his iPod.

OBJECTIVE 10

Audience characteristics help to determine whether the nature of the source or the message itself will be relatively more effective.

The Source versus the Message: Do We Sell the Steak or the Sizzle?

We've discussed two major components of the communications model: the source and the message. At the end of the day, which component persuades consumers to change their attitudes? Should we worry more about *what* we say or *how* we say it and *who* says it?

Surprise! The answer is it depends. A consumer's level of involvement determines which cognitive processes will activate when she receives a message. This in turn influences which aspects of a communication she processes. Like a traveler who comes to a fork in the road, she chooses one path or the other. The direction she takes determines which aspects of the marketing communication will work and which will fall on deaf ears.

The **elaboration likelihood model (ELM)** assumes that under conditions of high involvement, we take the *central route* to persuasion. Under conditions of low involvement, we take a *peripheral route* instead. Figure 7 diagrams this model.[144]

The Central Route to Persuasion

According to the ELM, when we find the information in a persuasive message relevant or interesting, we pay careful attention to it. In this event we focus on the arguments the marketer presents and generate *cognitive responses* to this content. An expectant mother who hears a radio message that warns about drinking while pregnant might say to herself, "She's right. I really should stop drinking alcohol now that I'm pregnant." Or she might offer counterarguments, such as, "That's a bunch of baloney. My mother had a cocktail every night when she was pregnant with me, and I turned out fine." If a person generates counterarguments in response to a message, it's less likely that she will yield to the message, whereas if she generates further supporting arguments, it's more likely she'll comply.[145]

The central route to persuasion involves the standard hierarchy of effects we discussed earlier in this chapter. Recall this assumes that we carefully form and evaluate beliefs and the strong attitudes that result guide our behavior. The implication is that message factors, such as the quality of arguments an ad presents, will determine attitude change. Prior knowledge about a topic results in more thoughts about the message and also increases the number of counterarguments.[146]

Figure 7 THE ELABORATION LIKELIHOOD MODEL (ELM) OF PERSUASION

The Peripheral Route to Persuasion

In contrast, we take the peripheral route when we're not really motivated to think about the marketer's arguments. Instead, we're likely to use other cues to decide how to react to the message. These cues include the product's package, the attractiveness of the source, or the context in which the message appears. We call sources of information extraneous to the actual message *peripheral cues* because they surround the actual message.

The peripheral route to persuasion highlights the paradox of low involvement. When we *don't* care about a product, the style in which it's presented (e.g., who endorses it or the visuals that go with it) increases in importance. The implication here is that we may buy low-involvement products chiefly because the marketer designs a "sexy" package, chooses a popular spokesperson, or creates a stimulating shopping environment. To recap, the basic idea of the ELM is that highly involved consumers look for the "steak" (e.g., strong, rational arguments). Those who are less involved go for the "sizzle" (e.g., the colors and images in packaging or famous people's endorsements). It is important to remember, however, that the *same* communications variable can be both a central and a peripheral cue, depending on its relation to the attitude object. The physical attractiveness of a model might serve as a peripheral cue in a car commercial, but her beauty might be a central cue for a product such as shampoo where a major product benefit is to enhance attractiveness.[147]

CHAPTER SUMMARY

Now that you have finished reading this chapter you should understand why:

1. **It's important for consumer researchers to understand the nature and power of attitudes.**

   An *attitude* is a predisposition to evaluate an object or product positively or negatively. We form attitudes toward products and services, and these attitudes often determine whether we will purchase or not.

2. **Attitudes are more complex than they first appear.**

   Three components make up an attitude: beliefs, affect, and behavioral intentions.

3. **We form attitudes in several ways.**

   Attitude researchers traditionally assumed that we learn attitudes in a fixed sequence: First we form beliefs (*cognitions*) about an attitude object, then we evaluate that object (*affect*), and then we take some action (*behavior*). Depending on the consumer's level of involvement and the circumstances, though, his attitudes can result from other hierarchies of effects as well. A key to attitude formation is the function the attitude holds for the consumer (e.g., is it utilitarian or ego defensive?).

4. **A need to maintain consistency among all of our attitudinal components motivates us to alter one or more of them.**

   One organizing principle of attitude formation is the importance of consistency among attitudinal components—that

is, we alter some parts of an attitude to be in line with others. Such theoretical approaches to attitudes as cognitive dissonance theory, self-perception theory, and balance theory stress the vital role of our need for consistency.

5. **We use attitude models to identify specific components and combine them to predict a consumer's overall attitude toward a product or brand.**

   Multiattribute attitude models underscore the complexity of attitudes: They specify that we identify and combine a set of beliefs and evaluations to predict an overall attitude. Researchers integrate factors such as subjective norms and the specificity of attitude scales into attitude measures to improve predictability.

6. **The communications model identifies several important components for marketers when they try to change consumers' attitudes toward products and services.**

   Persuasion refers to an attempt to change consumers' attitudes. The communications model specifies the elements marketers need to transmit meaning. These include a source, a message, a medium, a receiver, and feedback.

7. **The consumer who processes a message is not necessarily the passive receiver of information marketers once believed him or her to be.**

   The traditional view of communications regards the perceiver as a passive element in the process. New developments in interactive communications highlight the need to consider the active roles a consumer plays when he or she obtains product information and builds a relationship with a company. Advocates of permission marketing argue that it's more effective to send messages to consumers who have already indicated an interest in learning about a product than trying to hit people "cold" with these solicitations.

8. Several factors influence the effectiveness of a message source.

Two important characteristics that determine the effectiveness of a source are its attractiveness and credibility. Although celebrities often serve this purpose, their credibility is not always as strong as marketers hope. Marketing messages that consumers perceive as buzz (those that are authentic and consumer generated) tend to be more effective than those they categorize as hype (those that are inauthentic, biased, and company generated).

9. The way a marketer structures his or her message determines how persuasive it will be.

Some elements of a message that help to determine its effectiveness include the following: conveyance of the message in words or pictures; employment of an emotional or a rational appeal; frequency of repetition; conclusion drawing; presentation of both sides of the argument; and inclusion of fear, humor, or sexual references. Advertising messages often incorporate elements from art or literature, such as dramas, lectures, metaphors, allegories, and resonance.

10. Audience characteristics help to determine whether the nature of the source or the message itself will be relatively more effective.

The relative influence of the source versus the message depends on the receiver's level of involvement with the communication. The elaboration likelihood model (ELM) specifies that source effects are more likely to sway a less-involved consumer, whereas a more-involved consumer will be more likely to attend to and process components of the actual message.

KEY TERMS

ABC model of attitudes
affect
allegory
alternate reality games (ARGs)
attitude
attitude object (A_o)
attitude toward the act of buying (A_{act})
balance theory
basking in reflected glory
behavior
blogs
cognition
communications model
comparative advertising
compliance
ego-defensive function
elaboration likelihood model (ELM)
experiential hierarchy of effects
fear appeals
foot-in-the-door technique

functional theory of attitudes
hierarchy of effects
identification
internalization
knowledge function
latitudes of acceptance and rejection
low-involvement hierarchy of effects
M-commerce
metaphor
multiattribute attitude models
multiple pathway anchoring and adjustment (MPAA) model
permission marketing
persuasion
podcasting
principle of cognitive consistency
refutational arguments
resonance
self-perception theory
simile

sleeper effect
social judgment theory
social media
sock puppeting
source attractiveness
source credibility
spokescharacters
standard learning hierarchy
subjective norm (SN)
theory of cognitive dissonance
theory of reasoned action
theory of trying
transmedia formats
transmedia storytelling
Twitter
two-factor theory
utilitarian function
value-expressive function
video blogging (vlogging)
virtual worlds
widgets

REVIEW

1 How can an attitude play an ego-defensive function?
2 Describe the ABC model of attitudes.
3 List the three hierarchies of attitudes, and describe the major differences among them.

4 How do levels of commitment to an attitude influence the likelihood that it will become part of the way we think about a product in the long term?

5 We sometimes enhance our attitude toward a product after we buy it. How does the theory of cognitive dissonance explain this change?

6 What is the foot-in-the-door technique? How does self-perception theory relate to this effect?

7 What are latitudes of acceptance and rejection? How does a consumer's level of involvement with a product affect his latitude of acceptance?

8 According to balance theory, how can we tell if a triad is balanced or unbalanced? How can consumers restore balance to an unbalanced triad?

9 Describe a multiattribute attitude model and list its key components.

10 "Do as I say, not as I do." How does this statement relate to attitude models?

11 What is a subjective norm, and how does it influence our attitudes?

12 What are three obstacles to predicting behavior even if we know a person's attitudes?

13 Describe the theory of reasoned action. Why might it not be equally valuable when we apply it to non-Western cultures?

14 List three psychological principles related to persuasion.

15 Describe the elements of the traditional communications model, and tell how the updated model differs.

16 What are blogs and how can marketers use them?

17 What is source credibility, and what are two factors that influence our decision as to whether a source is credible?

18 What is the difference between buzz and hype? How does this difference relate to the *corporate paradox*?

19 What is a halo effect, and why does it happen?

20 What is an avatar, and why might an advertiser choose to use one instead of hiring a celebrity endorser?

21 When should a marketer present a message visually versus verbally?

22 How does the two-factor theory explain the effects of message repetition on attitude change?

23 When is it best to present a two-sided message versus a one-sided message?

24 Do humorous ads work? If so, under what conditions?

25 Should marketers ever try to arouse fear in order to persuade consumers?

26 Why do marketers use metaphors to craft persuasive messages? Give two examples of this technique.

27 What is the difference between a lecture and a drama?

28 Describe the elaboration likelihood model, and summarize how it relates to the relative importance of *what* is said versus *how* it's said.

CONSUMER BEHAVIOR CHALLENGE

■ DISCUSS

1 Contrast the hierarchies of effects outlined in this chapter. How should marketers take these different situations into account when they choose their marketing mix?

2 Many universities use commercial companies to run campus Web sites and email services. These agreements provide Web services to colleges at little or no cost. But these actions arouse controversy because major companies pay to place advertising on the sites. That gives marketers the opportunity to influence the attitudes of thousands of students who are involuntarily exposed to product messages. University administrators argue that they could not provide the services by themselves—students expect to be able to fill out financial aid forms and register for classes online. Colleges that do not offer such services may lose their ability to attract students. How do you feel about this situation? Should companies be able to buy access to your eyeballs from the school you pay to attend if it means you get access to enhanced online services in return?

3 As more of us rely on our smartphones, advertisers are following us onto this platform. The first iAds now appear on iPhones and iPods, and the early evidence is that they work well. In one study (funded by Apple), people who were exposed to an iAd for Campbell's were more than twice as likely to recall it than those who had seen a TV ad. Recipients were also four times more likely to say they would buy the advertised product.[148] As a consumer, is this good news or bad news? How do you feel about getting ads on your smartphone? How do you think the marketplace will react to this new advertising medium as it becomes more commonplace?

4 An antismoking ad sponsored by The New York City Department of Health crossed the line for many viewers. The spot showed a young boy who cries hysterically as a crowd of adults walk by him. The voiceover says, "This is how your child feels after losing you for a minute. Just imagine if they lost you for life."

The ad aroused a lot of controversy because it wasn't clear if the child was merely acting or if the spot's producers provoked his tears for the camera. Is this genre of "scared straight" advertising an effective way to convince people to curb unhealthy behaviors like smoking?

5 The Coca-Cola company pulled a UK Internet promotion campaign after parents accused it of targeting children by using references to a notorious pornographic movie. As part of its efforts to reach young social media users for its Dr. Pepper brand, the company took over consenting users' Facebook status boxes. Then, the company would post mildly embarrassing questions such as "Lost my special blankie. How will I go sleepies?," and "What's wrong with peeing in the shower?" But, when a parent discovered

that her 14-year-old daughter's profile had been updated with a message that directly referred to a hardcore porn film, the plan backfired and Coke had to pull the promotion.[149] What does it take to get the attention of jaded young people, who get exposed to all kinds of messages in cyberspace? What guidelines (if any) should marketers follow when they try to talk to young people on social media platforms?

6 A *flog* is a fake blog a company posts to build buzz around its brand. Is this ethical?

7 The sleeper effect implies that perhaps we shouldn't worry too much about how positively people evaluate a source. Similarly, there's a saying in public relations that "any publicity is good publicity." Do you agree?

8 Discuss some conditions that would cause you to advise a marketer to use a comparative advertising strategy.

9 The American Medical Association encountered a firestorm of controversy when it agreed to sponsor a line of health-care products that Sunbeam manufactured (a decision it later reversed). Should trade or professional organizations, journalists, professors, and others endorse specific products at the expense of other offerings?

10 A marketer must decide whether to incorporate rational or emotional appeals in its communications strategy. Describe conditions that are more favorable to one or the other.

11 Many, many companies rely on celebrity endorsers as communications sources to persuade. Especially when they target younger people, these spokespeople often are "cool" musicians, athletes, or movie stars. In your opinion, who would be the most effective celebrity endorser today, and why? Who would be the least effective? Why?

12 Swiss Legend, a watch brand, gets famous people to wear its colorful timepieces. One way it does this is to give away its products at awards shows. Publicists call this common practice "gifting the talent": Companies provide stars with "goody bags" full of complimentary products.[150] What do you think about the practice of "gifting the talent" to accumulate endorsements? Is this a sound strategy? Is it ethical for celebrities to accept these gifts?

■ APPLY

1 Think of a behavior someone does that is inconsistent with his or her attitudes (e.g., attitudes toward cholesterol, drug use, or even buying things to make him or her stand out or attain status). Ask the person to elaborate on why he or she does the behavior, and try to identify the way the person resolves dissonant elements.

2 Devise an attitude survey for a set of competing automobiles. Identify areas of competitive advantage or disadvantage for each model you include.

3 Construct a multiattribute model for a set of local restaurants. Based on your findings, suggest how restaurant managers could improve their establishment's image via the strategies described in this chapter.

4 Locate foreign ads at sites like japander.com in which celebrities endorse products that they don't pitch on their home turf. Ask friends or classmates to rate the attractiveness of each celebrity, then show them these ads and ask them to rate the celebrities again. Does the star's "brand image" change after it's paired with cheesy ads? Based on these results, what advice would you give to a manager who has to choose among endorsement offers for a famous client?

5 A government agency wants to encourage people who have been drinking to use designated drivers. What advice could you give the organization about constructing persuasive communications? Discuss some factors that might be important, including the structure of the communications, where they should appear, and who should deliver them. Should it use fear appeals? If so, how?

6 Why would a marketer consider saying negative things about her product? When is this strategy feasible? Can you find examples of it?

7 Collect ads that rely on sex appeal to sell products. How often do they communicate benefits of the actual product?

8 Observe the process of counterargumentation by asking a friend to talk out loud while he watches a commercial. Ask him to respond to each point in the ad or to write down reactions to the claims the message makes. How much skepticism regarding the claims can you detect?

9 Make a log of all the commercials a network television channel shows during a 2-hour period. Assign each to a product category and decide whether each is a drama or an argument. Describe the types of messages the ads use (e.g., two-sided arguments), and keep track of the types of spokespeople who appear (e.g., TV actors, famous people, animated characters). What can you conclude about the dominant forms of persuasive tactics that marketers currently employ?

10 Collect examples of ads that rely on the use of metaphors or resonance. Do you feel these ads are effective? If you were marketing the products, would you feel more comfortable with ads that use a more straightforward, "hard-sell" approach? Why or why not?

11 Create a list of current celebrities whom you feel typify cultural categories (e.g., clown, mother figure, etc.). What specific brands do you feel each could effectively endorse?

12 Conduct an "avatar hunt" on e-commerce Web sites, online video game sites, and online communities such as *The Sims* that let people select what they want to look like in cyberspace. What seem to be the dominant figures people choose? Are they realistic or fantasy characters? Male or female? What types of avatars do you believe would be most effective for each of these different kinds of Web sites and why?

Case Study

DOMINO'S DILEMMA

Social media sites are so much part of mainstream culture that the Internet Advertising Bureau (IAB) recently reported they have exceeded the reach of television. *Social media marketing* describes the use of social media to engage with customers to meet marketing goals. It's about reaching customers via online dialogue. According to Lloyd Salmons, chairman of the IAB, it's really about brands having conversations.

But sometimes use of social media backfires for companies. This certainly was the case for Domino's, the national pizza delivery company. Two employees of a North Carolina Domino's store posted a YouTube video of themselves in the kitchen as they performed disgusting practices with pizza ingredients:

> In about five minutes it'll be sent out on delivery where somebody will be eating these, yes, eating them, and little did they know that cheese was in his nose and that there was some lethal gas that ended up on their salami . . . that how we roll at Domino's.

What steps should a company take when it faces a social media marketing disaster like this? Should Domino's just ignore the videos and assume that the buzz will die down, or should it take quick action? Domino's did nothing for the first 48 hours but eventually—after more than one million people viewed the spot—got the video removed from YouTube. Domino's also posted a YouTube clip of its CEO who stated:

> We sincerely apologize for this incident. We thank members of the online community who quickly alerted us and allowed us to take immediate action. Although the individuals in question claim it's a hoax, we are taking this incredibly seriously.

Domino's also announced that the store where the videos were taken was shut down and sanitized. In addition, the company opened a Twitter account to deal with consumer questions. The two employees involved were fired (duh!) and charged with the felony of delivering prohibited foods.

Was this a strong enough response by Domino's? Most social media marketing experts grade Domino's actions as excellent but a bit delayed. In fact, an *Advertising Age* survey revealed that 64 percent of readers believed that the company did the best it could to deal with the crisis. Still, there's no doubt this incident was a pie in the eye for the company.

DISCUSSION QUESTIONS

1 Do you think customers who saw this video changed their attitude toward Domino's?

2 Which source—the rogue employees or the company's CEO—would be more credible?

3 The video included vivid, disgusting images of the Domino's product. Was a "talking head" response by the CEO the most effective countermessage? What type of message structure and/or content might the company have used instead to push back against this depiction?

Sources: Stephanie Clifford, "Video Prank at Domino's Taints Brand," *New York Times* (April 15, 2009), www.nytimes.com, accessed June 13, 2011; Ben Levisohm and Ellen Gibson, "An Unwelcomed Delivery," *Business-Week* (May 4, 2009): 15; Emily Bryson York, "What Domino's Did Right—and Wrong—in Squelching Hubbub over YouTube Video," *Advertising Age* (April 20, 2009), http://adage.com/article?article_id=136086, accessed June 8, 2009.

NOTES

1. www.polyvore.com, accessed May 30, 2011.
2. Robert A. Baron and Donn Byrne, *Social Psychology: Understanding Human Interaction*, 5th ed. (Boston: Allyn & Bacon, 1987).
3. Daniel Katz, "The Functional Approach to the Study of Attitudes," *Public Opinion Quarterly* 24 (Summer 1960): 163–204, Richard J. Lutz, "Changing Brand Attitudes through Modification of Cognitive Structure," *Journal of Consumer Research* 1 (March 1975): 49–59.
4. Russell H. Fazio, T. N. Lenn, and E. A. Effrein, "Spontaneous Attitude Formation," *Social Cognition* 2 (1984): 214–34.
5. Sharon Shavitt, "The Role of Attitude Objects in Attitude Functions," *Journal of Experimental Social Psychology* 26 (1990): 124–48; see also J. S. Johar and M. Joseph Sirgy, "Value Expressive versus Utilitarian Advertising Appeals: When and Why to Use Which Appeal," *Journal of Advertising* 20 (September 1991): 23–34.
6. Aaron Baar, "New Subaru Campaign Takes Aim with Cupid's Arrow," *Marketing Daily* (April 28, 2008), http://publications.mediapost.com/

Index.Cfm?Fuseaction=Articles.San&S=81435&Nid=420..., accessed April 28, 2008.
7. Michael Ray, "Marketing Communications and the Hierarchy-of-Effects," in P. Clarke, ed., *New Models for Mass Communications* (Beverly Hills, CA: Sage, 1973), 147–76.
8. Herbert Krugman, "The Impact of Television Advertising: Learning without Involvement," *Public Opinion Quarterly* 29 (Fall 1965): 349–56; Robert Lavidge and Gary Steiner, "A Model for Predictive Measurements of Advertising Effectiveness," *Journal of Marketing* 25 (October 1961): 59–62.
9. Stephanie Thompson, "Bad Breakup? There, There, B&J Know Just How You Feel," *Advertising Age* (January 24, 2005): 8.
10. For some recent studies, see Andrew B. Aylesworth and Scott B. MacKenzie, "Context Is Key: The Effect of Program-Induced Mood on Thoughts about the Ad," *Journal of Advertising* 27 (Summer 1998): 17; Angela Y. Lee and Brian Sternthal, "The Effects of Positive Mood on Memory," *Journal of Consumer Research* 26 (September 1999): 115–28; Michael J. Barone,

Paul W. Miniard, and Jean B. Romeo, "The Influence of Positive Mood on Brand Extension Evaluations," *Journal of Consumer Research* 26 (March 2000): 386–401. For a study that compared the effectiveness of emotional appeals across cultures, see Jennifer L. Aaker and Patti Williams, "Empathy versus Pride: The Influence of Emotional Appeals across Cultures," *Journal of Consumer Research* 25 (December 1998): 241–61. For research that relates mood (depression) to acceptance of health-related messages, see Punam Anand Keller, Isaac M. Lipkus, and Barbara K. Rimer, "Depressive Realism and Health Risk Accuracy: The Negative Consequences of Positive Mood," *Journal of Consumer Research* 29 (June 2002): 57–69.

11. Punam Anand, Morris B. Holbrook, and Debra Stephens, "The Formation of Affective Judgments: The Cognitive–Affective Model versus the Independence Hypothesis," *Journal of Consumer Research* 15 (December 1988): 386–91; Richard S. Lazarus, "Thoughts on the Relations between Emotion and Cognition," *American Psychologist* 37, no. 9 (1982): 1019–24; Robert B. Zajonc, "Feeling and Thinking: Preferences Need No Inferences," *American Psychologist* 35, no. 2 (1980): 151–75.

12. See Sharon E. Beatty and Lynn R. Kahle, "Alternative Hierarchies of the Attitude–Behavior Relationship: The Impact of Brand Commitment and Habit," *Journal of the Academy of Marketing Science* 16 (Summer 1988): 1–10.

13. J. R. Priester, D. Nayakankuppan, M. A. Fleming, and J. Godek, "The A(2) SC(2) Model: The Influence of Attitudes and Attitude Strength on Consideration Set Choice," *Journal of Consumer Research* 30, no. 4 (2004): 574–87.

14. Chester A. Insko and John Schopler, *Experimental Social Psychology* (New York: Academic Press, 1972).

15. Ibid.

16. Robert E. Knox and James A. Inkster, "Postdecision Dissonance at Post Time," *Journal of Personality & Social Psychology* 8, no. 4 (1968): 319–23.

17. Daryl J. Bem, "Self-Perception Theory," in Leonard Berkowitz, ed., *Advances in Experimental Social Psychology* (New York: Academic Press, 1972): 1–62; cf. more recently Keisha M. Cutright, Eugenia C. Wu, Jillian C. Banfield, Aaron C. Kay, and Gavan J. Fitzsimons, "When Your World Must Be Defended: Choosing Products to Justify the System," *Journal of Consumer Research* 38, no. 1 (June 2011): 62–77.

18. Jonathan L. Freedman and Scott C. Fraser, "Compliance without Pressure: The Foot-in-the-Door Technique," *Journal of Personality & Social Psychology* 4 (August 1966): 195–202. For further consideration of possible explanations for this effect, see William DeJong, "An Examination of Self-Perception Mediation of the Foot-in-the-Door Effect," *Journal of Personality & Social Psychology* 37 (December 1979): 221–31; Alice M. Tybout, Brian Sternthal, and Bobby J. Calder, "Information Availability as a Determinant of Multiple-Request Effectiveness," *Journal of Marketing Research* 20 (August 1988): 280–90.

19. David H. Furse, David W. Stewart, and David L. Rados, "Effects of Foot-in-the-Door, Cash Incentives and Follow-ups on Survey Response," *Journal of Marketing Research* 18 (November 1981): 473–78; Carol A. Scott, "The Effects of Trial and Incentives on Repeat Purchase Behavior," *Journal of Marketing Research* 13 (August 1976): 263–69.

20. Bob Fennis, Loes Janssen, and Kathleen D. Vohs, "Acts of Benevolence: A Limited-Resource Account of Compliance with Charitable Requests," *Journal of Consumer Research* (2009): 906–25.

21. See Joan Meyers-Levy and Brian Sternthal, "A Two-Factor Explanation of Assimilation and Contrast Effects," *Journal of Marketing Research* 30 (August 1993): 359–68.

22. Mark B. Traylor, "Product Involvement and Brand Commitment," *Journal of Advertising Research* (December 1981): 51–56.

23. Fritz Heider, *The Psychology of Interpersonal Relations* (New York: Wiley, 1958).

24. Debra Z. Basil and Paul M. Herr, "Attitudinal Balance and Cause-Related Marketing: An Empirical Application of Balance Theory," *Journal of Consumer Psychology* 16, no. 4 (2006): 391–403.

25. Robert B. Cialdini, Richard J. Borden, Avril Thorne, Marcus Randall Walker, Steven Freeman, and Lloyd Reynolds Sloan, "Basking in Reflected Glory: Three (Football) Field Studies," *Journal of Personality & Social Psychology*, 34: 366–375.

26. Quoted in Jon Weinbach, "Ad Score! Major League Soccer Teams Will Sell Ad Space on Players' Jerseys," *Wall Street Journal* (September 28, 2006): B1.

27. Leslie Kaufman, "Enough Talk," *Newsweek* (August 18, 1997): 48–49.

28. Allan Wicker, "Attitudes versus Actions: The Relationship of Verbal and Overt Behavioral Responses to Attitude Objects," *Journal of Social Issues* 25 (Autumn 1969): 65.

29. M. Fishbein, "An Investigation of the Relationships between Beliefs about an Object and the Attitude toward that Object," *Human Relations* 16 (1983): 233–40.

30. Laura Bird, "Loved the Ad. May (or May Not) Buy the Product," *Wall Street Journal* (April 7, 1994): B1.

31. Icek Ajzen and Martin Fishbein, "Attitude–Behavior Relations: A Theoretical Analysis and Review of Empirical Research," *Psychological Bulletin* 84 (September 1977): 888–918.

32. Morris B. Holbrook and William J. Havlena, "Assessing the Real-to-Artificial Generalizability of Multi-Attribute Attitude Models in Tests of New Product Designs," *Journal of Marketing Research* 25 (February 1988): 25–35; Terence A. Shimp and Alican Kavas, "The Theory of Reasoned Action Applied to Coupon Usage," *Journal of Consumer Research* 11 (December 1984): 795–809.

33. R. P. Abelson, "Conviction," *American Psychologist* 43 (1988): 267–75; R. E. Petty and J. A. Krosnick, *Attitude Strength: Antecedents and Consequences* (Mahwah, NJ: Erlbaum, 1995); Ida E. Berger and Linda F. Alwitt, "Attitude Conviction: A Self-Reflective Measure of Attitude Strength," *Journal of Social Behavior & Personality* 11, no. 3 (1996): 557–72.

34. Quoted in Stephanie Clifford and Andrew Martin, "As Consumers Cut Spending, 'Green' Products Lose Allure," *New York Times* (April 21, 2011), http://www.nytimes.com/2011/04/22/business/energy-environment/22green.html?hp, accessed April 30, 2011.

35. Andy Greenfield, "The Naked Truth (Studying Consumer Behavior)," *Brandweek* (October 13, 1997): 22; Michael J. Ryan and Edward H. Bonfield, "The Fishbein Extended Model and Consumer Behavior," *Journal of Consumer Research* 2 (1975): 118–36.

36. Noah J. Goldstein, Robert B. Cialdini, and Vladas Griskevicius, "A Room with a Viewpoint: Using Social Norms to Motivate Environmental Conservation in Hotels," *Journal of Consumer Research* 35 (October 2008): 472–482.

37. Blair H. Sheppard, Jon Hartwick, and Paul R. Warshaw, "The Theory of Reasoned Action: A Meta-Analysis of Past Research with Recommendations for Modifications and Future Research," *Journal of Consumer Research* 15 (December 1988): 325–43.

38. Joseph A. Cote, James McCullough, and Michael Reilly, "Effects of Unexpected Situations on Behavior–Intention Differences: A Garbology Analysis," *Journal of Consumer Research* 12 (September 1985): 188–94.

39. Robert E. Smith and William R. Swinyard, "Attitude–Behavior Consistency: The Impact of Product Trial versus Advertising," *Journal of Marketing Research* 20 (August 1983): 257–67.

40. For a recent similar application, cf. N. T. Tavassoli and G. J. Fitzsimons, "Spoken and Typed Expressions of Repeated Attitudes: Matching Response Modes Leads to Attitude Retrieval versus Construction," *Journal of Consumer Research* 33, no. 2 (2006): 179–87.

41. Kulwant Singh, Siew Meng Leong, Chin Tiong Tan, and Kwei Cheong Wong, "A Theory of Reasoned Action Perspective of Voting Behavior: Model and Empirical Test," *Psychology & Marketing* 12, no. 1 (January 1995): 37–51; Joseph A. Cote and Patriya S. Tansuhaj, "Culture Bound Assumptions in Behavior Intention Models," in Thom Srull, ed., *Advances in Consumer Research 16* (Provo, UT: Association for Consumer Research, 1989): 105–9.

42. Joel B. Cohen and Americus Reed, "A Multiple Pathway Anchoring and Adjustment (MPAA) Model of Attitude Generation and Recruitment," *Journal of Consumer Research* 33 (June 2006): 1–15.

43. Richard P. Bagozzi and Paul R. Warshaw, "Trying to Consume," *Journal of Consumer Research* 17 (September 1990): 127–40.

44. Robert B. Cialdini and Kelton V. L. Rhoads, "Human Behavior and the Marketplace," *Marketing Research* (Fall 2001): 13.

45. Gert Assmus, "An Empirical Investigation into the Perception of Vehicle Source Effects," *Journal of Advertising* 7 (Winter 1978): 4–10. For a more thorough discussion of the pros and cons of different media, see Stephen Baker, *Systematic Approach to Advertising Creativity* (New York: McGraw-Hill, 1979).

46. Alladi Venkatesh, Ruby Roy Dholakia, and Nikhilesh Dholakia, "New Visions of Information Technology and Postmodernism: Implications for Advertising and Marketing Communications," in Walter Brenner and Lutz Kolbe, eds., *The Information Superhighway and Private Households: Case Studies of Business Impacts* (Heidelberg: Physica-Verlag, 1996): 319–37; Donna L. Hoffman and Thomas P. Novak, "Marketing in Hypermedia Computer-Mediated Environments: Conceptual Foundations," *Journal of Marketing* 60, no. 3 (July 1996): 50–68. For an early theoretical discussion of interactivity in communications paradigms, see R. Aubrey Fisher, *Perspectives on Human Communication* (New York: Macmillan, 1978).

47. Seth Godin, *Permission Marketing: Turning Strangers into Friends, and Friends into Customers* (New York: Simon & Schuster, 1999).

48. Brad Stone, "The War for Your TV," *Newsweek* (July 29, 2002): 46–47.

49. Geoffrey A. Fowler, "Asia's Mobile Ads," *Wall Street Journal* (April 25, 2005), www.wsj.com, accessed April 25, 2005; Brooks Barnes, "Coming to Your Cell: Paris Hilton," *Wall Street Journal* (March 17, 2005), www.wsj.com, accessed March 17, 2005; Alice Z. Cuneo, "Marketers Dial in to Messaging," *Advertising Age* (November 1, 2004): 18; Stephen Baker and Heather Green, "Blogs Will Change Your Business," *BusinessWeek* (May 2, 2005): 56.

50. "The People's Revolution: Implications of Web 2.0 and Social Media Applications," *Strategy Analytics* (2008).

51. "Social Nets and Blogs More Popular than E-Mail," March 17, 2009, www.emarketer.com, accessed March 17, 2009.

52. "U.S. Blog Readers 2007–2012," *Emarketer* (April 15, 2009), www.emarketer.com, accessed April 15, 2009.

53. Nicholas Carlson, "Chart of the Day: How Many Users Does Twitter REALLY Have?," *Business Insider SAI* (March 31, 2011), http://www.businessinsider.com/chart-of-the-day-how-many-users-does-twitter-really-have-2011-3, accessed May 30, 2011.

54. http://www.iamtryingtobelieve.com/, accessed May 30, 2011.

55. Jon Zahlaway, "Nine Inch Nails' Year Zero Plot Hits the Web," *SoundSpike*, February 22, 2007, http://www.livedaily.com/news/11570.html?t=102, accessed May 30, 2011.

56. Carl I. Hovland and W. Weiss, "The Influence of Source Credibility on Communication Effectiveness," *Public Opinion Quarterly* 15 (1952): 635–50; for a recent treatment, cf. Yong-Soon Kang and Paul M. Herr, "Beauty and the Beholder: Toward an Integrative Model of Communication Source Effects," *Journal of Consumer Research* 33 (June 2006): 123–30.

57. Herbert Kelman, "Processes of Opinion Change," *Public Opinion Quarterly* 25 (Spring 1961): 57–78; Susan M. Petroshius and Kenneth E. Crocker, "An Empirical Analysis of Spokesperson Characteristics on Advertisement and Product Evaluations," *Journal of the Academy of Marketing Science* 17 (Summer 1989): 217–26.

58. Kenneth G. DeBono and Richard J. Harnish, "Source Expertise, Source Attractiveness, and the Processing of Persuasive Information: A Functional Approach," *Journal of Personality & Social Psychology* 55, no. 4 (1988): 541–46.

59. Joseph R. Priester and Richard E. Petty, "The Influence of Spokesperson Trustworthiness on Message Elaboration, Attitude Strength, and Advertising Effectiveness," *Journal of Consumer Psychology* 13, no. 4 (2003): 408–21.

60. Hershey H. Friedman and Linda Friedman, "Endorser Effectiveness by Product Type," *Journal of Advertising Research* 19, no. 5 (1979): 63–71. For a study that looked at nontarget market effects—the effects of advertising intended for other market segments—see Jennifer L. Aaker, Anne M. Brumbaugh, and Sonya A. Grier, "Non-Target Markets and Viewer Distinctiveness: The Impact of Target Marketing on Advertising Attitudes," *Journal of Consumer Psychology* 9, no. 3 (2000): 127–40.

61. Yeosun Yoon, Zeynep Gurhan-Canli, and Norbert Schwarz, "The Effect of Corporate Social Responsibility (CSR) Activities on Companies with Bad Reputations," *Journal of Consumer Psychology* 16, no. 4 (2006): 377–90.

62. Peter R. Darke and Robin J. B. Ritchie, "The Defensive Consumer: Advertising Deception, Defensive Processing, and Distrust," *Journal of Marketing Research* 44 (February 2007): 114–27.

63. S. Ratneshwar and Shelly Chaiken, "Comprehension's Role in Persuasion: The Case of Its Moderating Effect on the Persuasive Impact of Source Cues," *Journal of Consumer Research* 18 (June 1991): 52–62.

64. Steven S. Posavac, Michal Herzenstein, Frank R. Kardes, and Suresh Sundaram, "Profits and Halos: The Role of Firm Profitability Information in Consumer Inference," *Journal of Consumer Psychology* 20, no. 3 (2010): 327–37.

65. Jagdish Agrawal and Wagner A. Kamakura, "The Economic Worth of Celebrity Endorsers: An Event Study Analysis," *Journal of Marketing* 59 (July 1995): 56–62.

66. "Report: Charlie Sheen May Not Shine, But Stars are Aligned as Print Ad Activists," *NYSportsJournalism.com* (February 25, 2011), http://nysportsjournalism.squarespace.com/study-stars-shine-in-print-ads/?SSScrollPosition=0&VK=94964620, accessed April 30, 2011.

67. Heather Buttle, Jane E. Raymond, and Shai Danziger, "Do Famous Faces Capture Attention?," paper presented at Association for Consumer Research Conference, Columbus, OH (October 1999).

68. Michael A. Kamins, "Celebrity and Noncelebrity Advertising in a Two-Sided Context," *Journal of Advertising Research* 29 (June–July 1989): 34; Joseph M. Kamen, A. C. Azhari, and J. R. Kragh, "What a Spokesman Does for a Sponsor," *Journal of Advertising Research* 15, no. 2 (1975): 17–24; Lynn Langmeyer and Mary Walker, "A First Step to Identify the Meaning in Celebrity Endorsers," in Rebecca H. Holman and Michael R. Solomon, eds., *Advances in Consumer Research 18* (Provo, UT: Association for Consumer Research, 1991): 364–71.

69. Joe Mandese, "Tweet This: Social Endorsements Beat Social Media Ad Buys," *Online Media Daily* (March 10, 2011), http://www.mediapost.com/publications/?fa=Articles.showArticle&art_aid=146459&nid=124651, accessed April 30, 2011.

70. Anthony R. Pratkanis, Anthony G. Greenwald, Michael R. Leippe, and Michael H. Baumgardner, "In Search of Reliable Persuasion Effects: III. The Sleeper Effect Is Dead, Long Live the Sleeper Effect," *Journal of Personality & Social Psychology* 54 (1988): 203–18.

71. Stephanie Strom, "Nonprofit Punishes a 2nd Founder for Ruse," *New York Times*, January 15, 2008, www.nytimes.com/2008/01/15/us/15givewell.html?ex=1201064400&en=97effb249, accessed January 15, 2008; Ross D. Petty and J. Craig Andrews, "Covert Marketing Unmasked: A Legal and Regulatory Guide for Practices That Mask Marketing Messages," *Journal of Public Policy & Marketing* (Spring 2008): 7–18; James B. Stewart, "Whole Foods CEO Threatens Merger, Fuels Arbitrage," *Smart Money* (July 18, 2007), www.smartmoney.com/investing/stocks/whole-foods-ceo-threatens-merger-fuels-arbitrage-21550/?hpadref=1, accessed June 4, 2009; Brian Morrissey, "'Influencer Programs' Likely to Spread," *Adweek* (March 2, 2009), http://www.adweek.com/news/advertising-branding/influencer-programs-likely-spread-98542, accessed March 2, 2009; Katie Hafner, "Seeing Corporate Fingerprints in Wikipedia Edits," *New York Times* (August 19, 2007), www.nytimes.com/2007/08/19/technology/19wikipedia.html?_r=1&oref=slogin, accessed August 19, 2007; Brian Bergstein, "New Tool Mines: Wikipedia Trustworthiness Software Analyzes Reputations of the Contributors Responsible for Entries," *MSNBC* (September 5, 2007), www.msnbc.msn.com/id/20604175, accessed September 5, 2007; http://wikiscanner.virgil.gr, accessed June 4, 2009.

72. Ameet Sachdev, "FTC Cracks Down on Fake Online Endorsements: Agency Attempts to Punish Fake Reviews, Force Disclosure," *Chicago Tribune* (October 11, 2010), http://articles.chicagotribune.com/2010-10-11/business/ct-biz-1011-web-reviews--20101011_1_ftc-cracks-endorsements-mary-engle, accessed April 15, 2011.

73. "Robber Makes It Biggs in Ad," *Advertising Age* (May 29, 1989): 26.

74. Robert LaFranco, "MTV Conquers Madison Avenue," *Forbes* (June 3, 1996): 138.

75. Alice H. Eagly, Andy Wood, and Shelly Chaiken, "Causal Inferences about Communicators and Their Effect in Opinion Change," *Journal of Personality & Social Psychology* 36, no. 4 (1978): 424–35.

76. Ira Teinowitz, "'Results May Vary' Won't Be Enough under New FTC Rules, Proposed Changes Could Put Squeeze on Ads for Diet Plans and Fitness Equipment," *Advertising Age* (March 12, 2009), www.adage.com, accessed March 12, 2009.

77. Patrick Loughran, "Sex Pistol Sends Dairy Crest Butter Sales Soaring," *Times of London* (February 3, 2009), www.timesonline.co.uk, accessed February 4, 2009.

78. Michael J. Baker and Gilbert A. Churchill, Jr., "The Impact of Physically Attractive Models on Advertising Evaluations," *Journal of Marketing Research* 14 (November 1977): 538–55; Marjorie J. Caballero and William M. Pride, "Selected Effects of Salesperson Sex and Attractiveness in Direct Mail Advertisements," *Journal of Marketing* 48 (January 1984): 94–100; W. Benoy Joseph, "The Credibility of Physically Attractive Communicators: A Review," *Journal of Advertising* 11, no. 3 (1982): 15–24; Lynn R. Kahle and Pamela M. Homer, "Physical Attractiveness of the Celebrity Endorser: A Social Adaptation Perspective," *Journal of Consumer Research* 11 (March 1985): 954–61; Judson Mills and Eliot Aronson, "Opinion Change as a Function of Communicator's Attractiveness and Desire to Influence," *Journal of Personality & Social Psychology* 1 (1965): 173–77.

79. Leonard N. Reid and Lawrence C. Soley, "Decorative Models and the Readership of Magazine Ads," *Journal of Advertising Research* 23, no. 2 (1983): 27–32.

80. Marjorie J. Caballero, James R. Lumpkin, and Charles S. Madden, "Using Physical Attractiveness as an Advertising Tool: An Empirical Test of the Attraction Phenomenon," *Journal of Advertising Research* (August–September 1989): 16–22.

81. Baker and Churchill, Jr., "The Impact of Physically Attractive Models on Advertising Evaluations"; George E. Belch, Michael A. Belch, and Angelina Villareal, "Effects of Advertising Communications: Review of Research," in *Research in Marketing 9* (Greenwich, CT: JAI Press, 1987): 59–117; A. E. Courtney and T. W. Whipple, *Sex Stereotyping in Advertising* (Lexington, MA: Lexington Books, 1983).

82. Lynn R. Kahle and Pamela M. Homer, "Physical Attractiveness of the Celebrity Endorser: A Social Adaptation Perspective," *Journal of Consumer Research* 11 (March 1985): 954–61.

83. Brian Steinberg, "Bob Dylan Gets Tangled Up in Pink: Victoria's Secret Campaign Drafts Counterculture Hero; Just Like the Rolling Stones," *Wall Street Journal* (April 2, 2004): B3.

84. Robert Klara, "Brands by Bieber," Brandweek (January 1, 2011), http://www.adweek.com/news/advertising-branding/brands-bieber-126241, accessed Feb 23, 2011.

85. Quoted in www.japander.com, accessed May 30, 2011.

86. Grant McCracken, "Who Is the Celebrity Endorser? Cultural Foundations of the Endorsement Process," *Journal of Consumer Research* 16, no. 3 (December 1989): 310–21.

87. Nat Ives, "Marketers Run to Pull the Plug When Celebrity Endorsers Say the Darnedest Things," *New York Times* (July 16, 2004), www.nytimes.com, accessed July 16, 2004.

88. Judith A. Garretson and Scot Burton, "The Role of Spokescharacters as Advertisement and Package Cues in Integrated Marketing Communications," *Journal of Marketing* 69 (October, 2005): 118–32.

89. Jeff Bercovici, "America's Most Loved Spokescharacters," *Forbes* (March 14, 2011), http://www.forbes.com/2011/03/11/old-spice-snoopy-m-and-m-most-loved-spokescharacters.html, accessed April 30, 2011.

90. Natalie T. Wood and Michael R. Solomon, eds., *Virtual Social Identity* (Newport, CA: Sage, 2010).

91. Kathy Crosett, "Consumers Confused by TV Commercials," *Adology* (October 4, 2010), http://www.marketingforecast.com/archives/7538, accessed May 30, 2011; David W. Stewart and David H. Furse, "The Effects of Television Advertising Execution on Recall, Comprehension, and Persuasion," *Psychology & Marketing* 2 (Fall 1985): 135–60.

92. Robert J. Fisher, Mark Vandenbosch, and Kersi D. Antia, "An Empathy-Helping Perspective on Consumers' Responses to Fund-Raising Appeals," *Journal of Consumer Research* 35, no. 3 (2008): 519–31.

93. R. C. Grass and W. H. Wallace, "Advertising Communication: Print vs. TV," *Journal of Advertising Research* 14 (1974): 19–23.

94. Elizabeth C. Hirschman and Michael R. Solomon, "Utilitarian, Aesthetic, and Familiarity Responses to Verbal versus Visual Advertisements," in Thomas C. Kinnear, ed., *Advances in Consumer Research 11* (Provo, UT: Association for Consumer Research, 1984): 426–31.

95. Terry L. Childers and Michael J. Houston, "Conditions for a Picture-Superiority Effect on Consumer Memory," *Journal of Consumer Research* 11 (September 1984): 643–54.

96. John R. Rossiter and Larry Percy, "Attitude Change through Visual Imagery in Advertising," *Journal of Advertising Research* 9, no. 2 (1980): 10–16.

97. Spencer E. Ante, "Billboards Join Wired Age," *Wall Street Journal* (February 4, 2011), http://professional.wsj.com/article/SB100014240527487036521045761220914750616666.html?mg=reno-wsj, accessed April 15, 2011.

98. Jolita Kiselius and Brian Sternthal, "Examining the Vividness Controversy: An Availability-Valence Interpretation," *Journal of Consumer Research* 12 (March 1986): 418–31.

99. Scott B. MacKenzie, "The Role of Attention in Mediating the Effect of Advertising on Attribute Importance," *Journal of Consumer Research* 13 (September 1986): 174–95.

100. Robert B. Zajonc, "Attitudinal Effects of Mere Exposure," *Journal of Personality & Social Psychology* 8 (1968): 1–29.

101. Giles D'Souza and Ram C. Rao, "Can Repeating an Advertisement More Frequently Than the Competition Affect Brand Preference in a Mature Market?" *Journal of Marketing* 59 (April 1995): 32–42.

102. George E. Belch, "The Effects of Television Commercial Repetition on Cognitive Response and Message Acceptance," *Journal of Consumer Research* 9 (June 1982): 56–65; Marian Burke and Julie Edell, "Ad Reactions over Time: Capturing Changes in the Real World," *Journal of Consumer Research* 13 (June 1986): 114–18; Herbert Krugman, "Why Three Exposures May Be Enough," *Journal of Advertising Research* 12 (December 1972): 11–14.

103. Robert F. Bornstein, "Exposure and Affect: Overview and Meta-Analysis of Research, 1968–1987," *Psychological Bulletin* 106, no. 2 (1989): 265–89; Arno Rethans, John Swasy, and Lawrence Marks, "Effects of Television Commercial Repetition, Receiver Knowledge, and Commercial Length: A Test of the Two-Factor Model," *Journal of Marketing Research* 23 (February 1986): 50–61.

104. Curtis P. Haugtvedt, David W. Schumann, Wendy L. Schneier, and Wendy L. Warren, "Advertising Repetition and Variation Strategies: Implications for Understanding Attitude Strength," *Journal of Consumer Research* 21 (June 1994): 176–89.

105. Linda L. Golden and Mark I. Alpert, "Comparative Analysis of the Relative Effectiveness of One- and Two-Sided Communication for Contrasting Products," *Journal of Advertising* 16 (1987): 18–25; Michael A. Kamins, "Celebrity and Noncelebrity Advertising in a Two-Sided Context," *Journal of Advertising Research* 29 (June–July 1989): 34; Robert B. Settle and Linda L. Golden, "Attribution Theory and Advertiser Credibility," *Journal of Marketing Research* 11 (May 1974): 181–85.

106. Cf. Alan G. Sawyer, "The Effects of Repetition of Refutational and Supportive Advertising Appeals," *Journal of Marketing Research* 10 (February 1973): 23–33; George J. Szybillo and Richard Heslin, "Resistance to Persuasion: Inoculation Theory in a Marketing Context," *Journal of Marketing Research* 10 (November 1973): 396–403.

107. Rupal Parekh and Jean Halliday, "New Ad Introduces Consumers to 'New GM,'" *Advertising Age* (June 1, 2009), http://adage.com/article?article_id=137010, accessed June 6, 2009.

108. Uma R. Karmarkar and Zakary L. Tormala, "Believe Me, I Have No Idea What I'm Talking About: The Effects of Source Certainty on Consumer Involvement and Persuasion," *Journal of Consumer Research* 36 (April 2009): 1033–49.

109. Golden and Alpert, "Comparative Analysis of the Relative Effectiveness of One- and Two-Sided Communication for Contrasting Products"; Gita

Venkataramani Johar and Anne L. Roggeveen, "Changing False Beliefs from Repeated Advertising: The Role of Claim-Refutation Alignment," *Journal of Consumer Psychology* 17, no. 2 (2007): 118–27.

110. George E. Belch, Michael A. Belch, and Angelina Villareal, "Effects of Advertising Communications: Review of Research," in *Research in Marketing* 9 (Greenwich, CT: JAI Press, 1987): 59–117.

111. Frank R. Kardes, "Spontaneous Inference Processes in Advertising: The Effects of Conclusion Omission and Involvement on Persuasion," *Journal of Consumer Research* 15 (September 1988): 225–33.

112. Belch, Belch, and Villareal, "Effects of Advertising Communications: Review of Research"; Cornelia Pechmann and Gabriel Esteban, "Persuasion Processes Associated with Direct Comparative and Noncomparative Advertising and Implications for Advertising Effectiveness," *Journal of Consumer Psychology* 2, no. 4 (1994): 403–32.

113. Cornelia Dröge and Rene Y. Darmon, "Associative Positioning Strategies through Comparative Advertising: Attribute vs. Overall Similarity Approaches," *Journal of Marketing Research* 24 (1987): 377–89; D. Muehling and N. Kangun, "The Multidimensionality of Comparative Advertising: Implications for the FTC," *Journal of Public Policy & Marketing* (1985): 112–28; Beth A. Walker and Helen H. Anderson, "Reconceptualizing Comparative Advertising: A Framework and Theory of Effects," in Rebecca H. Holman and Michael R. Solomon, eds., *Advances in Consumer Research 18* (Provo, UT: Association for Consumer Research, 1991): 342–47; William L. Wilkie and Paul W. Farris, "Comparison Advertising: Problems and Potential," *Journal of Marketing* 39 (October 1975): 7–15; R. G. Wyckham, "Implied Superiority Claims," *Journal of Advertising Research* (February–March 1987): 54–63.

114. Suzanne Vranica, "Arby's TV Spots Play Game of Fast-Food Chicken," *Wall Street Journal* (July 5, 2006): A16.

115. Mehmet I. Yagci, Abhijit Biswas, and Sujay Dutta, "Effects of Comparative Advertising Format on Consumer Responses: The Moderating Effects of Brand Image and Attribute Relevance," *Journal of Business Research* 62, no. 8 (August 2009): 768–74.

116. Stephen A. Goodwin and Michael Etgar, "An Experimental Investigation of Comparative Advertising: Impact of Message Appeal, Information Load, and Utility of Product Class," *Journal of Marketing Research* 17 (May 1980): 187–202; Gerald J. Gorn and Charles B. Weinberg, "The Impact of Comparative Advertising on Perception and Attitude: Some Positive Findings," *Journal of Consumer Research* 11 (September 1984): 719–27; Terence A. Shimp and David C. Dyer, "The Effects of Comparative Advertising Mediated by Market Position of Sponsoring Brand," *Journal of Advertising* 3 (Summer 1978): 13–19; R. Dale Wilson, "An Empirical Evaluation of Comparative Advertising Messages: Subjects' Responses to Perceptual Dimensions," in B. B. Anderson, ed., *Advances in Consumer Research 3* (Ann Arbor, MI: Association for Consumer Research, 1976): 53–57.

117. Louise Kramer, "In a Battle of Toothpastes, It's Information vs. Emotion," *New York Times* (January 17, 2007): C6.

118. H. Zielske, "Does Day-After Recall Penalize 'Feeling' Ads?" *Journal of Advertising Research* 22 (1982): 19–22.

119. Bruce Horovitz, "Skyy Pushes the Envelope with Sexy Ad Campaign," *USA Today* (September 28, 2010), http://www.usatoday.com/money/advertising/2010-09-28-vodka28_ST_N.htm?csp=34money&utm_source=feedburner&utm_medium=feed&utm_campaign=Feed%3A+UsatodaycomMoney-TopStories+%28Money+-+Top+Stories%29, accessed April 15, 2011.

120. Allessandra Galloni, "Lee's Cheeky Ads Are Central to New European Campaign," *Wall Street Journal* (March 15, 2002), www.wsj.com, accessed March 15, 2002.

121. Belch, Belch, and Villareal, "Effects of Advertising Communications: Review of Research"; Courtney and Whipple, *Sex Stereotyping in Advertising*; Michael S. LaTour, "Female Nudity in Print Advertising: An Analysis of Gender Differences in Arousal and Ad Response," *Psychology & Marketing* 7, no. 1 (1990): 65–81; B. G. Yovovich, "Sex in Advertising—The Power and the Perils," *Advertising Age* (May 2, 1983): M4–M5. For an interesting interpretive analysis, see Richard Elliott and Mark Ritson, "Practicing Existential Consumption: The Lived Meaning of Sexuality in Advertising," in Frank R. Kardes and Mita Sujan, eds., *Advances in Consumer Behavior 22* (1995): 740–45; Jaideep Sengupta and Darren W. Dahl, "Gender-Related Reactions to Gratuitous Sex Appeals," *Journal of Consumer Psychology* 18 (2008): 62–78.

122. Penny M. Simpson, Steve Horton, and Gene Brown, "Male Nudity in Advertisements: A Modified Replication and Extension of Gender and Product Effects," *Journal of the Academy of Marketing Science* 24, no. 3 (1996): 257–62.

123. Jaideep Sengupta and Darren W. Dahl, "Gender-Related Reactions to Gratuitous Sex Appeals," *Journal of Consumer Psychology* 18 (2008): 62–78; Darren W. Dahl, Jaideep Sengupta, and Kathleen Vohs, "Sex in Advertising: Gender Differences and the Role of Relationship Commitment," *Journal of Consumer Research* 36 (August 2009): 215–231.

124. Mark Dolliver, "Seeing Too Much Sex in Ads, or Too Little?" *Adweek* (December 6, 2010), http://teens.adweek.com/aw/content_display/data-center/research/e3i5b647315f27310efc8f6df37dcb48e9b accessed April 15, 2011.

125. Michael S. LaTour and Tony L. Henthorne, "Ethical Judgments of Sexual Appeals in Print Advertising," *Journal of Advertising* 23, no. 3 (September 1994): 81–90.

126. "Does Sex Really Sell?" *Adweek* (October 17, 2005): 17.

127. Katharine Q. Seelye, "Metamucil Ad Featuring Old Faithful Causes a Stir," *New York Times* (January 19, 2003), www.nytimes.com, accessed January 19, 2003.

128. Thomas J. Madden, "Humor in Advertising: An Experimental Analysis," working paper, no. 83-27, University of Massachusetts, 1984; Thomas J. Madden and Marc G. Weinberger, "The Effects of Humor on Attention in Magazine Advertising," *Journal of Advertising* 11, no. 3 (1982): 8–14; Weinberger and Spotts, "Humor in U.S. versus U.K. TV Commercials" Journal of Advertising 18 (2), 1989: 39-44; see also Ashesh Mukherjee and Laurette Dubé, "The Use of Humor in Threat-Related Advertising" (unpublished manuscript, McGill University, June 2002).

129. David Gardner, "The Distraction Hypothesis in Marketing," *Journal of Advertising Research* 10 (1970): 25–30.

130. Chris Abraham, "Global Web Means Your 'Fart Jokes' Can Be Heard out of Context," *Advertising Age* (June 15, 2009), http://adage.com/digitalnext/article?article_id=137273, accessed June 16, 2009.

131. Brian Steinberg, "VW Uses Shock Treatment to Sell Jetta's Safety," *Wall Street Journal* (April 19, 2006): B4.

132. Lindsay Goldwert, "FDA to Require Graphic Images on Cigarette Packages to Deter Smoking," *New York Daily News* (November 10, 2010), http://www.nydailynews.com/lifestyle/health/2010/11/10/2010-11-10_fda_proposes_putting_graphic_images_onto_package_of_cigarettes_to_deter_smoking.html, accessed April 15, 2011.

133. Michael L. Ray and William L. Wilkie, "Fear: The Potential of an Appeal Neglected by Marketing," *Journal of Marketing* 34, no. 1 (1970): 54–62.

134. Punam Anand Keller and Lauren Goldberg Block, "Increasing the Effectiveness of Fear Appeals: The Effect of Arousal and Elaboration," *Journal of Consumer Research* 22 (March 1996): 448–59.

135. Ronald Paul Hill, "An Exploration of the Relationship between AIDS-Related Anxiety and the Evaluation of Condom Advertisements," *Journal of Advertising* 17, no. 4 (1988): 35–42.

136. Randall Rothenberg, "Talking Too Tough on Life's Risks?" *New York Times* (February 16, 1990): D1.

137. Denise D. Schoenbachler and Tommy E. Whittler, "Adolescent Processing of Social and Physical Threat Communications," *Journal of Advertising* 25, no. 4 (Winter 1996): 37–54.

138. Barbara B. Stern, "Medieval Allegory: Roots of Advertising Strategy for the Mass Market," *Journal of Marketing* 52 (July 1988): 84–94.

139. Edward F. McQuarrie and David Glen Mick, "On Resonance: A Critical Pluralistic Inquiry into Advertising Rhetoric," *Journal of Consumer Research* 19 (September 1992): 180–97.

140. Cf. Linda M. Scott, "The Troupe: Celebrities as Dramatis Personae in Advertisements," in Rebecca H. Holman and Michael R. Solomon, eds., *Advances in Consumer Research 18* (Provo, UT: Association for Consumer Research, 1991): 355–63; Barbara Stern, "Literary Criticism and Consumer Research: Overview and Illustrative Analysis," *Journal of Consumer Research* 16 (1989): 322–34; Judith Williamson, *Decoding Advertisements* (Boston: Marion Boyars, 1978).

141. John Deighton, Daniel Romer, and Josh McQueen, "Using Drama to Persuade," *Journal of Consumer Research* 16 (December 1989): 335–43.

142. Edward F. McQuarrie and David Glen Mick, "On Resonance: A Critical Pluralistic Inquiry into Advertising Rhetoric," *Journal of Consumer Research* 19 (September 1992): 180–97.

143. Barbara J. Phillips and Edward F. McQuarrie, "Beyond Visual Metaphor: A New Typology of Visual Rhetoric in Advertising," *Marketing Theory* 4 (March/June 2004): 113–36.

144. Richard E. Petty, John T. Cacioppo, and David Schumann, "Central and Peripheral Routes to Advertising Effectiveness: The Moderating Role of Involvement," *Journal of Consumer Research* 10, no. 2 (1983): 135–46.

145. Jerry C. Olson, Daniel R. Toy, and Philip A. Dover, "Do Cognitive Responses Mediate the Effects of Advertising Content on Cognitive Structure?" *Journal of Consumer Research* 9, no. 3 (1982): 245–62.

146. Julie A. Edell and Andrew A. Mitchell, "An Information Processing Approach to Cognitive Responses," in S. C. Jain, ed., *Research Frontiers in Marketing: Dialogues and Directions* (Chicago, IL: American Marketing Association, 1978).

147. Richard E. Petty, John T. Cacioppo, Constantine Sedikides, and Alan J. Strathman, "Affect and Persuasion: A Contemporary Perspective," *American Behavioral Scientist* 31, no. 3 (1988): 355–71.

148. Kunur Patel, "Apple, Campbell's Say iAds Twice as Effective as TV," *Ad Age Digital* (February 3, 2011), http://adage.com/article/digital/apple-campbell-s-iads-effective-tv/148630/, accessed April 15, 2011.

149. Vikram Dodd, "Coca-Cola Forced to Pull Facebook Promotion after Porn References," *Guardian.co.uk* (July 18, 2010), http://www.guardian.co.uk/business/2010/jul/18/coca-cola-facebook-promotion-porn, accessed April 15, 2011.

150. Rob Walker, "The Gifted Ones," *New York Times Magazine* (November 14, 2004), www.nytimes.com, accessed September 29, 2007.

NIELSEN NUGGET

EXERCISE: Attitudes and Persuasion

Scenario: Healthy Clean, Inc., has a strong presence in surface disinfection under the "Germ Destructor" brand. It is important for the company to enter the hand-hygiene segment, in order to be able to provide a complete range of germ-kill solutions and to maintain the perception of category leadership. Healthy Clean company wants to investigate entering the hand-wash market with the launch of a no-touch dispensing system.

Challenge: Healthy Clean seeks to better understand consumer perceptions as they relate to various product attributes and the general acceptance of the product concept. Among other research objectives, Healthy Clean hopes to determine where it may be able to achieve competitive performance advantages. The company also seeks to identify those product attributes that may have to be adjusted or those consumer perceptions it may seek to influence.

After reviewing the data provided:

1 Identify specific attributes that Healthy Clean should emphasize in promotions if it proceeds with the new product launch.
2 Identify specific attributes, if any, that should be considered for reengineering.
3 Which of the marketing applications of the multiattribute model discussed in this chapter could be suggested by the data?

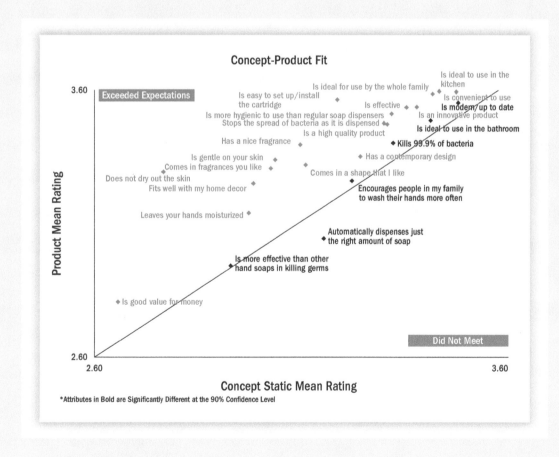

Concept-Product Fit

*Attributes in Bold are Significantly Different at the 90% Confidence Level

Decision Making

From Chapter 8 of *Consumer Behavior: Buying, Having, and Being*, Tenth Edition. Michael R. Solomon. Copyright © 2013 by Pearson Education, Inc. All rights reserved.

Decision Making

When you finish reading this chapter you will understand why:

1. Consumer decision making is a central part of consumer behavior, but the way we evaluate and choose products (and the amount of thought we put into these choices) varies widely, depending on such dimensions as the degree of novelty or risk in the decision.

2. A purchase decision actually is composed of a series of stages that results in the selection of one product over competing options.

3. Decision making is not always rational.

4. Our access to online sources changes the way we decide what to buy.

5. We often fall back on well-learned "rules-of-thumb" to make decisions.

6. Consumers rely on different decision rules when they evaluate competing options.

MyMarketingLab

Visit **www.mymktlab.com** to find activities that help you learn and review in order to succeed in this chapter.

Richard has had it. There's only so much longer he can go on watching TV on his tiny, antiquated black-and-white set. It was bad enough trying to squint at *Jersey Shore*—he can barely distinguish Snooki from The Situation on the screen. The final straw was when he couldn't tell the Titans from the Jaguars during an NFL football game. When he went next door to watch the second half on Mark's home theater setup, he finally realized what he was missing. Budget or not, it was time to act: A man has to have his priorities.

Where to start looking? The Web, naturally. Richard checks out a few comparison-shopping Web sites, including *pricegrabber.com* and *bizrate.com*. After he narrows down his options, he ventures out to scope out a few sets in person. He figures he'll probably get a decent selection (and an affordable price) at one of those huge new warehouse stores. Arriving at Zany Zack's Appliance Emporium, Richard heads straight for the Video Zone in the back—he barely notices the rows of toasters, microwave ovens, and stereos on his way. Within minutes, a smiling salesperson in a cheap suit accosts him. Even though he could use some help, Richard tells the salesperson he's only browsing. He figures these guys don't know what they're talking about, and they're simply out to make a sale no matter what.

Richard examines some of the features on the 60-inch color sets. He knew his friend Lorraine had a set by Prime Wave that she really liked, and his sister Regina warned him to stay away from the Kamashita. Although Richard finds a Prime Wave model loaded to the max with features such as a sleep timer, on-screen programming menu, cable-compatible tuner, and picture-in-picture, he chooses the less expensive Precision 2000X because it has one feature that really catches his fancy: stereo broadcast reception.

Later that day, Richard is a happy man as he sits in his easy chair and watches "JWOWW," Pauly D, and the others mixing it up on *Jersey Shore*. If he's going to be a couch potato, he's going in style.

OBJECTIVE 1
Consumer decision making is a central part of consumer behavior, but the way we evaluate and choose products (and the amount of thought we put into these choices) varies widely, depending on such dimensions as the degree of novelty or risk in the decision.

We Are Problem Solvers

A consumer purchase is a response to a problem, which in Richard's case is the need for a new TV. His situation is similar to those that we encounter virtually every day of our lives (if you decide to make no decisions on your day off, that's still a decision!). He realizes that he wants to make a purchase, and he undergoes a series of steps in order to make it. We describe these steps as (1) problem recognition, (2) information search, (3) evaluation of alternatives, and (4) product choice. Of course, after we make a decision, its outcome affects the final step in the process, in which learning occurs based on how well the choice worked out. This learning process, of course, influences the likelihood that we'll make the same choice the next time the need for a similar decision occurs. And so on and so on. . . .

Figure 1 provides an overview of this decision-making process. As we begin this chapter we'll review different approaches we might use when we need to make a purchase decision. We then focus on three of the steps in the decision process:

1 How we recognize the problem, or need for a product
2 How we search for information about product choices
3 How we evaluate alternatives to arrive at a decision

Because some purchase decisions are more important than others, the amount of effort we put into each differs. Sometimes the decision-making process is almost automatic; we seem to make snap judgments based on very little information. At other times when we decide what to buy, the process resembles a full-time job. A person may literally spend days or weeks agonizing over an important purchase such as a new home, a car, or even an iPhone versus an Android phone.

This intensive decision-making process gets even more complicated in today's environment, where we have so many options from which to choose. Ironically, for many modern consumers one of the biggest problems they face is not having *too few* choices but having *too many*. We describe this profusion of options as **consumer hyperchoice**: a condition in which the large number of available options forces us to make repeated

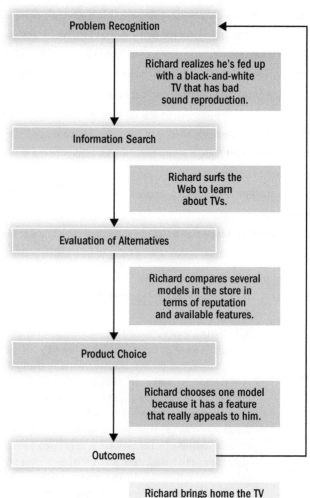

Figure 1 STAGES IN CONSUMER DECISION MAKING

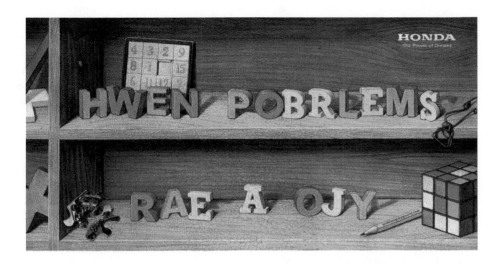

A purchase is a response to a problem.
Source: Darko Novakovic/Shutterstock.

choices that may drain psychological energy while it saps our abilities to make smart decisions.[1]

Although we tend to assume that more choice is always better, in fact this preference varies across the world. In some cultures people prefer to have hard choices made for them. For example, one study compared American and French consumers who live in different medical cultures: The U.S. norm is to emphasize patient autonomy, whereas in France it's more typical for a doctor to make important decisions on behalf of the patient. The researchers studied families that had to decide whether to take their gravely ill infants off life support. Although the American parents claimed the right to make this difficult choice, they also had greater trouble with their grief and coping processes than the French parents who left this decision to their physicians.[2]

Perspectives on Decision Making

Consumer researchers typically apply a **rational perspective** to understand decision making. In this view, we calmly and carefully integrate as much information as possible with what we already know about a product, painstakingly weigh the pluses and minuses of each alternative, and make a satisfactory decision. This traditional perspective relates the *economics of information* approach to the search process; it assumes that we collect just as much data as we need to make an informed decision. We form expectations of the value of additional information and continue to search to the extent that the rewards of doing so (what economists call the *utility*) exceed the costs. This utilitarian assumption also implies that we collect the most valuable units of information first. We absorb additional pieces only to the extent that we think they will add to what we already know.[3] In other words, we'll put ourselves out to collect as much information as we can, so long as the process isn't too onerous or time-consuming.[4]

This rational outlook implies that marketing managers should carefully study steps in decision making to understand how consumers obtain information, how they form beliefs, and what criteria they use to make product choices. Then, companies can develop products that emphasize the appropriate attributes, and marketers can tailor promotional strategies to deliver the types of information customers are most likely to desire and in the most effective formats.[5]

It all sounds good, but how valid is this perspective? Sure, we do follow these decision-making steps when we make some purchases, but this rational process doesn't accurately portray many of our purchase decisions.[6] We simply don't go through this elaborate sequence every time we buy something. If we did, we'd spend our entire lives making these decisions. This would leave us very little time to enjoy the things we eventually decide to buy. Some of our buying behaviors simply don't seem "rational" because they don't serve a logical purpose (you don't use that navel ring to hold a beach towel).

You also purchase some items with virtually no advance planning at all—have you ever impulsively thrown a fattening candy bar into your cart while you wait at the grocery checkout? (Hint: That's why candy bars and celeb magazines are placed there.)

Still other actions actually contradict what those rational models predict. For example, **purchase momentum** occurs when our initial impulse purchases actually increase the likelihood that we will buy even more (instead of less as we satisfy our needs); it's like we get "revved up" and plunge into a spending spree (we've all been there!).[7] Research also hints that people differ in terms of their **cognitive processing style**. Some of us tend to have a *rational system of cognition* that processes information analytically and sequentially using rules of logic, whereas others rely on an *experiential system of cognition* that processes information more holistically and in parallel.[8]

Researchers now realize that decision makers actually possess a *repertoire* of strategies. In a thought process we call *constructive processing,* we evaluate the effort we'll need to make a particular choice and then we tailor the amount of cognitive "effort" we expend to get the job done.[9] When the task requires a well-thought-out, rational approach, we'll invest the brainpower to do it. Otherwise, we look for shortcuts or fall back on learned responses that "automate" these choices.

We make some decisions under conditions of low involvement. In many of these situations, our decision is a learned response to environmental cues, such as when we decide to buy something on impulse because it just looks cool. We explain these types of decisions as the **behavioral influence perspective**. Under these circumstances, managers and marketers should focus on peripheral cues, such as an attention-grabbing package, rather than on factual details (i.e., sell the "sizzle" rather than the "steak").[10]

In other cases, we're highly involved in a decision, but still we can't explain our selections rationally. For example, the traditional approach is hard-pressed to account for our choice of art, music, or even a spouse ("OMG, how did she ever wind up with *him*?"). In these cases, no single quality determines the decision. Instead, the **experiential perspective** stresses the *Gestalt*, or totality, of the product or service.[11] In these contexts marketers need to assess consumers' affective responses to products or services and then develop offerings that create a positive emotional response.

Types of Consumer Decisions

To understand the decision-making process, it helps to think about the amount of effort that goes into a decision each time we must make it. Consumer researchers think in terms of a continuum, anchored on one end by *habitual decision making* and at the other extreme by *extended problem solving*. Many decisions fall somewhere in the middle, so we describe these as *limited problem solving*. Figure 2 presents this continuum.

Figure 2 A CONTINUUM OF BUYING DECISION BEHAVIOR

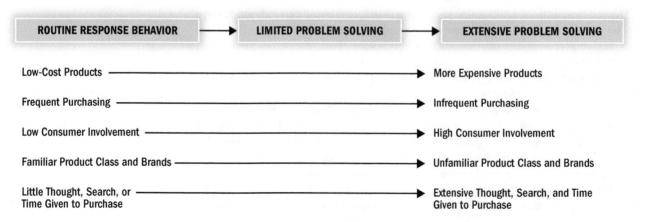

| ROUTINE RESPONSE BEHAVIOR | → | LIMITED PROBLEM SOLVING | → | EXTENSIVE PROBLEM SOLVING |

Low-Cost Products ⟶ More Expensive Products

Frequent Purchasing ⟶ Infrequent Purchasing

Low Consumer Involvement ⟶ High Consumer Involvement

Familiar Product Class and Brands ⟶ Unfamiliar Product Class and Brands

Little Thought, Search, or Time Given to Purchase ⟶ Extensive Thought, Search, and Time Given to Purchase

Extended Problem Solving

Decisions that involve **extended problem solving** correspond most closely to the traditional decision-making perspective. As Table 1 indicates, we usually initiate this careful process when the decision we have to make relates to our self-concept, and we feel that the outcome may be risky in some way. In such cases we try to collect as much information as possible, both from our memory (internal search) and from outside sources such as Google (external search). Then we carefully evaluate each product alternative; often we consider the attributes of one brand at a time and see how each brand's attributes relate to the results we hope to get from our choice.

In the past few years we've witnessed huge growth in extended problem solving in the online space, mostly due to the tremendous popularity of complex and engrossing games that people play on social media platforms. A **social game** is a multiplayer, competitive, goal-oriented activity with defined rules of engagement and online connectivity among a community of players. Because the phenomenal growth of social games is attributed largely to Facebook's game platform and the blockbuster game *FarmVille*, social games are sometimes thought of as games that people play within a social network. However, other game formats, such as Xbox Live with Kinect, also adopt social elements, including the ability to play online with other geographically dispersed players and to share game achievements on social profiles.[12]

These games, especially the so-called *core games* like *Call of Duty: Black OPS* that extend over time and involve hundreds or thousands of players, tend to morph from extended decision making to produce a kind of flow state.

Social games are built upon several layers, including platform, mode, milieu, and genre.[13] Let's briefly review the basic dimensions of social games:

- A **game platform** refers to the hardware systems on which the game is played. Platforms include *game consoles* (consoles are interactive, electronic devices used to display video games, such as Sony's PlayStation3, Microsoft's Xbox 360, and Nintendo's Wii), computers (including both online games and those that require software installation on the player's computer hard drive), and portable devices that may include smartphones or devices specifically for game play such as the Sony PSP or Nintendo DS.[14]
- **Mode** refers to the way players experience the game world. It includes aspects such as whether a player's activities are highly structured, whether the game is single-player or multiplayer, whether the game is played in close physical proximity to other players (or by virtual proximity), and whether the game is real-time or turn-based.
- **Milieu** describes the visual nature of the game, such as science fiction, fantasy, horror, and retro.

TABLE 1 Characteristics of Limited versus Extended Problem Solving

	Limited Problem Solving	Extended Problem Solving
Motivation	Low risk and involvement	High risk and involvement
Information Search	Little search	Extensive search
	Information processed passively In-store decision likely	Information processed actively Multiple sources consulted prior to visits
Alternative Evaluation	Weakly held beliefs Only most prominent criteria used Alternatives perceived as basically similar Noncompensatory strategy used	Strongly held beliefs Many criteria used Significant differences perceived among alternatives Compensatory strategy used
Purchase	Limited shopping time; may prefer self-service Choice often influenced by store displays	Many outlets shopped if needed Communication with store personnel often desirable

- The **genre** of a game refers to the method of play. Popular genres include simulation, action, and role-playing. *Simulation games* attempt to depict real-world situations as accurately as possible. There are several subgenres, including racing simulators, flight simulators, and "Sim" games that enable players to simulate the development of an environment. Among social games, simulations include the highly popular *FarmVille, Pet Resort*, and *FishVille. Action games* consist of two major subgenres: *first-person shooters (FPS)*, where you "see" the game as your avatar sees it, and third-person games. Examples of social action games are *Epic Goal*, a live-action soccer game; *Paradise Paintball*, a first-person shooter social game; and *Texas Hold 'Em*, a social gambling game. In *role-playing games* (RPGs), the players play a character role with the goal of completing some mission. Perhaps the best-known RPG started its life as a tabletop game: *Dungeons and Dragons*. Players adopt the identity of a character in the game story and go about completing tasks and collecting points and items as they strive to accomplish the intended goal. **MMORPGs**—*massively multiplayer on-line role-playing games*—are a type of RPG that truly encompass the social aspects of gaming. *World of Warcraft* is the largest of these, with more than 11 million subscribers. Social RPGs on Facebook include *Haven, Mafia Wars, Battle Stations*, and *Tennis Mania.*[15]

It's important for us to understand these new platforms for extended decision making, because many analysts feel that these will be a very important place to talk to consumers in the next few years as **game-based marketing** tactics accelerate. Brands can utilize social games for marketing in several ways—and they should! Games offer a targeted audience, a large and wide reach, a high level of engagement, low-intrusion methods of promotion, and a way to interact with brand fans. Numerous companies are already experimenting with different formats for embedding their messages into game play:

- *Display ads* are integrated in a game's environment as billboards, movie posters, and storefronts. The display advertising may be static or dynamic and may include text, images, or rich media. Rich-media advertising can run pre-roll (before the game begins), interlevel (between stages of the game), or post-roll (at the game's conclusion), though interlevel is the most common placement.
- *Static ads* are hard-coded into the game and ensure that all players view the advertising. Bing's display ad in FarmVille is an example of an in-game, static display ad. The ad offered players the chance to earn FarmVille cash by becoming a fan of Bing on Facebook. In the first day the ad ran, Bing earned 425,000 new fans.[16]
- *Dynamic ads* are variable; they change based on specified criteria. This technique is managed by networks like Google AdWords, which offers insertion technology to place ads across multiple games. The networks contract with game publishers to place advertising in their games. By combining games from several publishers, networks create a large portfolio of in-game media opportunities for advertisers. The network works with publishers to strategically embed advertising, sell the placement to advertisers, serve the ads into the games in the network, and manage the billing and accounting for the process. Advertisers can choose specific game placement or allow Google AdWords to place the ads dynamically within games in the Google Display Advertising Network. Playfish's game portfolio includes *Word Challenge, Hotel City, Who Has The Biggest Brain?,* and others. Players of these games will be exposed to commercials that run between levels of the game.

Limited Problem Solving

Limited problem solving is usually more straightforward and simple. In these instances we're not nearly as motivated to search for information or to evaluate each alternative rigorously. Instead, we're likely to use simple *decision rules* as we choose among alternatives. These cognitive shortcuts (more about these later) enable us to fall back on general guidelines, instead of having to start from scratch every time we need to decide.

This Brazilian ad for a hair-loss product appeals to men who take their impending baldness seriously.
Source: Art Director: Pedro Vargens, Creative Directors: Bruno Richter and Victor Vicente.

Habitual Decision Making

Both extended and limited problem-solving modes involve some degree of information search and deliberation. At the other end of the choice continuum, however, lies **habitual decision making**—choices we make with little to no conscious effort. Many purchase decisions are so routinized that we may not realize we've made them until we look in our shopping carts! We make these choices without conscious control, which is why researchers call this process *automaticity.*[17]

Although this kind of thoughtless activity may seem dangerous or at best stupid in many cases, it actually makes sense! When we develop these habitual, repetitive behaviors, we minimize the time and energy spent on mundane purchase decisions. However, habitual decision making poses a problem when a marketer tries to introduce a new way to do an old task. In this situation she must convince us to "unfreeze" our former habit and replace it with a new one—perhaps to use an ATM instead of a live bank teller, or switch to a self-service gas pump instead of having an attendant wait on us.

OBJECTIVE 2
A purchase decision actually is composed of a series of stages that results in the selection of one product over competing options.

Steps in the Decision-Making Process

Richard didn't suddenly wake up and crave a new TV. He went through several steps between the time he felt the need for a new boob tube and when he actually brought one home. Let's review the basic steps in this process.

MyMarketingLab
Visit **www.mymktlab.com** to test your understanding of chapter objectives.

Problem Recognition

Ford's plan to promote its Fusion hybrid model focused on people who aren't thinking about buying a new car—at least not right now. Its TV commercials targeted what the auto industry terms the "upper funnel," or potential buyers down the road. Ford's research found that a large number of U.S. drivers still are unaware of the Fusion. The company is confident that it can close sales if and when customers decide to buy a new car. But, its weak spot is to get people into the frame of mind where they want to do that. To create desire where none exists yet, visitors to a special Web site entered to win a trip and a new Fusion. Ford publicized the sweepstakes on Twitter and Facebook; during the first

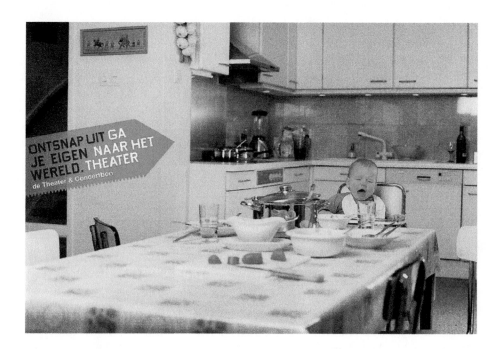

This Dutch ad encourages consumers to recognize a problem: They need to get out and go to the movies asap!

Source: © KesselsKramer, Amsterdam.

two weeks of the promotion, almost 70,000 people requested more information about the car.[18]

Problem recognition occurs at what Ford terms "the upper funnel," when we experience a significant difference between our current state of affairs and some state we desire. We realize that to get from here to there, we need to solve a problem, which may be small or large, simple or complex. A person who unexpectedly runs out of gas on the highway has a problem, as does the person who becomes dissatisfied with the image of his car, even though there is nothing mechanically wrong with it. Although the quality of Richard's TV had not changed, he altered his *standard of comparison,* and as a result he had a new problem to solve: how to improve his TV experience.

Figure 3 shows that a problem arises in one of two ways. The person who runs out of gas experiences a decline in the quality of his *actual state* (*need recognition*). In contrast, the person who craves a newer, flashier car moves his *ideal state* upward (*opportunity recognition*).[19] Either way, there is a gulf between the actual state and the ideal state. Richard perceived a problem due to opportunity recognition: He moved his ideal state upward in terms of the quality of TV reception he craved.

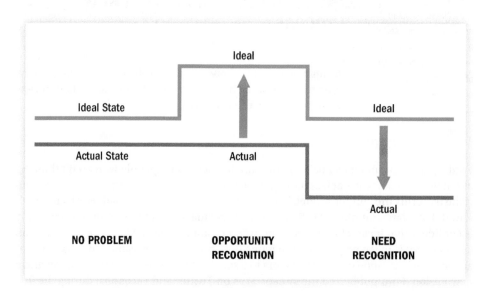

Figure 3 PROBLEM RECOGNITION: SHIFTS IN ACTUAL OR IDEAL STATES

Need recognition occurs in several ways. A person's actual state can decrease if she runs out of a product, or if she buys a product that doesn't adequately satisfy her needs, or if she realizes she has a new need or desire. For example, when you buy a house, this sets off an avalanche of other choices because now you need to buy many new things to fill it—assuming there's any money left over! In contrast, opportunity recognition often occurs when we're exposed to different or better-quality products. This happens because our circumstances change, as when we start college or land a new job, for example. As our frame of reference shifts, we make purchases to adapt to the new environment. That awesome pair of True Religion jeans you just scored somehow won't make it during a job interview.

Information Search

Once a consumer recognizes a problem, she needs the 411 to solve it. **Information search** is the process by which we survey the environment for appropriate data to make a reasonable decision. In this section we'll review some of the factors this search involves.[20]

Types of Information Search

You might recognize a need and then search the marketplace for specific information (a process we call *prepurchase search*). However, many of us, especially veteran shoppers, enjoy browsing just for the fun of it or because we like to stay up-to-date on what's happening in the marketplace. Those shopaholics engage in *ongoing search*.[21]

It helps to distinguish between internal and external search. As a result of our prior experience and the fact that we live in a consumer culture, each of us has some degree of knowledge already in memory about many products. When a purchase decision confronts us, we may engage in *internal search* as we scan our own memory banks to assemble information about different product alternatives. Usually, though, even those of us who are the most market-savvy need to supplement this knowledge with external search, so we also obtain information from advertisements, friends, or just plain people-watching. A Finnish study demonstrated that what our neighbors buy affects our own decision making. The researchers discovered that when one of a person's 10 nearest neighbors bought a car, the odds that the person would buy a car of the same make during the next week and a half jumped 86 percent.[22]

This ad from Dubai reminds consumers of a need they may not think about too often—to clean their drains.
Source: Courtesy of TBWA/RAAD, Dubai.

Deliberate versus "Accidental" Search. We may know about a product due to *directed learning:* On a previous occasion we've already searched for relevant information. A parent who bought a birthday cake for one child last month, for example, probably has a good idea of the best kind to buy for another child this month.

Other times, however, we acquire information in a more passive manner. Even though a product may not be of direct interest to us today, we still encounter advertising, packaging, and sales promotion activities that result in *incidental learning*. Mere exposure over time to conditioned stimuli and observations of others makes us learn a lot of information that we may not need for some time, if ever (think of all those advertising jingles you can't get out of your head). For marketers, this is one of the benefits of steady, "low-dose" advertising; they establish and maintain product associations until the time we need them.

In some cases, we may be so expert about a product category (or at least believe we are) that we don't conduct any additional search. Frequently, however, our own knowledge is not sufficient to make an adequate decision, so we must look elsewhere for more information. The sources we consult for advice vary: They may be impersonal and marketer-dominated sources, such as retailers and catalogs; they may be friends and family members; or they may be unbiased third parties, such as *Consumer Reports*.[24]

Online Search

When we search online for product information, we're a perfect target for advertisers because we declare our desire to make a purchase. Recognizing this, many companies pay **search engines** like Google, as well as Bing, Yahoo!, and Ask.com, to show ads to users who search for their brand names. However, when DoubleClick (an online marketing company) looked closely at what people search for, its analysts found that we rarely specify brand names in our queries. Instead, most prepurchase searches use only generic terms, such as *hard drive*. Consumers tend to make these searches early on and then conduct a small flurry of brand-name queries right before they buy.[25]

Not surprisingly, social media platforms now play a major role in the search process. Although about 60 percent of consumers now start their online process by typing queries into a search engine such as Google or Bing; 40 percent now continue their quest for more information on other social media platforms such as blogs, YouTube, Twitter, and Facebook. The goal here is not to collect more technical or performance information, but to get other people's opinions about options in the product category—and to eliminate some brands from consideration when others ding them. What's more, after they buy a brand, about three-fourths of shoppers who use social media in the process choose to follow it on the company's Facebook page so they can continue to engage with it in the future.[26]

OBJECTIVE 3

Decision making is not always rational.

Do We Always Search Rationally?

As we've seen, we don't necessarily engage in a rational search process where we carefully identify every alternative before we choose the one we want. In fact, the amount of external search we do for most products is surprisingly small, even when we would benefit if we had more information. In fact, lower-income shoppers, who have more to lose when they make a bad purchase, actually search less before they buy than do more affluent people.[27]

One widely used distinction is between a decision strategy that seeks to deliver the best possible result (**maximizing**) and one that simply tries to yield an adequate solution, often as a way to reduce the costs of the decision-making process. This is called a **satisficing** solution (economist Herbert Simon even won a Nobel Prize for this idea in 1956). Because we rarely have the resources (especially the time) to weigh every possible factor into a decision, we will often happily settle for a solution that is just good enough. This perspective on decision making is called **bounded rationality**. These two extremes have huge implications for marketing and retailing strategy, because they imply very different approaches to customers. Indeed, the maximizer strongly resembles a high-involvement consumer; she is going to go all out to explore as much information as she can before she decides. In contrast, the satisficer resembles the low-involvement consumer who will probably use some simple shortcuts (that we'll discuss shortly) to just pick something decent and get on with her life. Indeed, some recent research suggests that maximizers may be so thorough they don't even rely on their past experiences to guide their current choice. Instead, they start almost from scratch to research options for each unique decision situation. The researchers term this the **Sisyphus Effect**.[28] Sisyphus was a famous figure in Greek mythology; he was sentenced for all eternity to push a huge boulder up a hill, only to watch it roll back down just before it reached the top so that he had to start over. (Kind of like having your hard drive crash just before you finish that massive term paper. . . .)

Like our friend Richard, many consumers are satisficers; typically they visit only one or two stores and rarely seek out unbiased information sources before they make a purchase decision, especially when they have little time available to do so.[29] This pattern is especially prevalent for decisions about durable goods, such as appliances or autos, even when these products represent significant investments. One study of Australian car buyers found that more than a third had made two or fewer trips to inspect cars prior to buying one.[30]

This tendency to avoid external search is less prevalent when consumers consider the purchase of symbolic items, such as clothing. In those cases, not surprisingly, people tend to do a fair amount of external search, although most of it involves asking peers' opinions.[31] Although the stakes may be lower financially, people may see these self-expressive decisions as having dire social consequences if they make the wrong choice. The level of risk, a concept we'll discuss shortly, is high.

In addition, we often engage in *brand switching*, even if our current brand satisfies our needs. When researchers for British brewer Bass Export studied the American beer market, they discovered that many drinkers have a repertoire of two to six favorite brands rather than one clear favorite.[32]

Sometimes, it seems we simply like to try new things—we crave variety as a form of stimulation or to reduce boredom. **Variety seeking**, the desire to choose new alternatives over more familiar ones, even influences us to switch from our favorite products to ones we like less! This can occur even before we become *satiated,* or tired, of our favorite. Research supports the idea that we are willing to trade enjoyment for variety because the unpredictability *itself* is rewarding.[33] In fact, one study suggests that although consumers frequently consume items to the point where they no longer enjoy them, the marketer can counteract this **variety amnesia** simply by prompting them to recall the variety of alternative items they have consumed in the past.[34]

We're especially likely to look for variety when we are in a good mood, or when there isn't a lot of other stuff going on.[35] In the case of foods and beverages, we may decide to try new things due to *sensory-specific satiety*. Put simply, this means the pleasantness of a food item we have just eaten drops, whereas the pleasantness of uneaten foods remains unchanged.[36] So, even though we have favorites, we still like to sample other possibilities. However, when the decision situation is ambiguous, or when there is little information about competing brands, we tend to opt for the safe choice. Figure 4 shows the brand attributes consumers consider most important when they choose among alternatives, according to a survey that *Advertising Age* conducted.

Mental Accounting: Biases in the Decision-Making Process

Consider the following scenario: You've scored a free ticket to a major football game. At the last minute, though, a sudden snowstorm makes it somewhat dangerous to get to the stadium. Would you still go? Now, assume the same game and snowstorm—except this time you paid a small fortune for the ticket. Would you head out in the storm in this case?

Analyses of people's responses to this situation and to other similar puzzles illustrate principles of **mental accounting**. This process demonstrates that the way we pose a problem (we call this **framing**) and whether it's phrased in terms of gains or losses influences our decisions.[37] In this case, researchers find that people are more likely to risk their personal safety in the storm if they paid for the football ticket than if it's a freebie. Only the most die-hard fan would fail to recognize that this is an irrational choice, because the risk is the same regardless of whether you got a great deal on the ticket. Researchers call this decision-making bias the *sunk-cost fallacy:* If we've paid for something, we're more reluctant to waste it.

Behavioral Economics

In recent years, the recognition that many decisions are not based on a maximization strategy has contributed to the huge resurgence of the field of **behavioral economics**, a blend of psychology and economics that studies how consumers make economic decisions. Unlike more traditional economic approaches, this hybrid perspective recognizes that our decisions are not always based on "logical" factors such as price or quality. Rather, they are colored by our emotions and even very subtle cues in the environment that steer us toward some products and away from others. Numerous books and blogs,

Figure 4 *ADVERTISING AGE* POLL: IMPORTANCE OF BRAND ATTRIBUTES

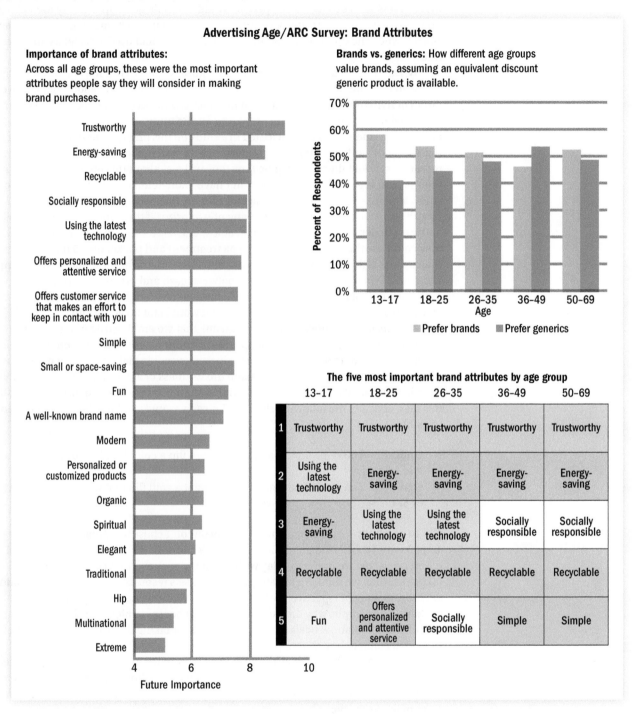

including the huge bestsellers *Freakonomics* and *Predictably Irrational,* come from and promote this view of the less-than-logical consumer.[38]

As we'll see shortly, many of the principles in behavioral economics deal with the way a choice is put into context (earlier we referred to this as *framing*), along with the bias and experience that each consumer brings to that purchase. Daniel Kahneman, the "father" of behavioral economics (he won a Nobel Prize in Economics for his seminal work) gave an example of one type of framing called **anchoring**, which refers to the fact that when people are given a number, they tend to use that number as the standard for future judgments. He noted that when he asked people if the tallest tree in the world is more or less than 900 feet, most people would correctly guess that is way too tall. Now, however, he's made you think of very tall trees, so perhaps a 500-foot-tall tree would seem small to you. The opposite would have been true if he had used 100 feet as an "anchor" number.[39]

Whether we focus on the present or the future is another example of how the way we frame an issue influences the options we choose and how we feel about them. The condition of **hyperopia** (the medical term for people who have farsighted vision) describes people who are so obsessed with preparing for the future that they can't enjoy the present. College students who participated in a study on this phenomenon reported that they regretted not working, studying, or saving money during their winter breaks. But, when researchers asked them to imagine how they will feel about this break a year from now, their biggest regrets were that they didn't have enough fun or travel enough. In another study, female subjects received a ticket for a lottery that would be held three months later. They had to choose in advance from one of two prizes if they won: either $85 in cash or an $80 voucher for a massage or facial at a spa. Even though they were reminded that they could use the $85 in cash to get a spa treatment and pocket the $5 difference, more than a third of the women chose the voucher. Researchers found similar results in other situations: When people had to choose between cash and prizes such as bottles of wine or dinners out, many of them chose the luxuries even though the cash was a better deal. One participant observed, "If I took the cash it would end up going into the rent."[40]

Loss aversion is another bias. This means that we emphasize our losses more than our gains. For example, for most people losing money is more *unpleasant* than gaining money is *pleasant*. **Prospect theory** describes how people make choices; it defines utility in terms of gains and losses. We evaluate the riskiness of a decision differently if it's put to us in terms of what we stand to gain rather than what we stand to lose.[41] To illustrate this bias, consider the following choices. For each, would you take the safe bet or choose to gamble?

- **Option 1**—You're given $30 and a chance to flip a coin: Heads you win $9, tails you lose $9.
- **Option 2**—You get $30 outright or you accept a coin flip that will win you either $39 or $21.

In one study, 70 percent of those who got option 1 chose to gamble, compared to only 43 percent of those who got option 2—yet the odds are the same for both options! The difference is that we prefer to "play with the house money"; that is, we're more willing to take risks when we think we're using someone else's resources. So, contrary to a rational decision-making perspective, we value money differently depending on its source. This explains, for example, why the same person who chooses to blow a big bonus on a $2,000 pair of Manolo Blahnik heels would never consider taking that same amount out of her savings account to buy shoes.

Finally, research in mental accounting demonstrates that extraneous characteristics of the choice situation can influence our selections, even though they wouldn't *if* we were totally rational decision makers. Researchers gave survey participants one of the two versions of this scenario:

> You are lying on the beach on a hot day. All you have to drink is ice water. For the past hour you have been thinking about how much you would enjoy a nice cold bottle of your favorite brand of beer. A companion gets up to go make a phone call and offers to bring back a beer from the only nearby place where beer is sold (either a fancy resort hotel or a small, run-down grocery store, depending on the version you're given). He says that the beer might be expensive and so asks how much you are willing to pay for it. What price do you tell him? In the survey, the median price participants who read the fancy-resort version gave was $2.65, but those who got the grocery-store version were only willing to pay $1.50. In both versions the consumption act is the same, the beer is the same, and they don't consume any "atmosphere" because they drink the beer on the beach.[42] So much for rational decision making!

Researchers continue to identify factors that bias our decisions—and many of these are factors that operate beneath the level of conscious awareness. Consider this example: During the 2010 New York Republican gubernatorial primary, one candidate (Carl Paladino) mailed out thousands of campaign ads impregnated with the smell of rotting garbage. The tagline was "Something Stinks in Albany" and the mailings included photos of scandal-tainted New York Democrats (the message had its intended effect, but the candidate lost for other reasons).

Many researchers believe that the primitive emotion of disgust evolved to protect us from contamination; we learned over the years to avoid putrid meat and other foul substances linked to pathogens. As a result, even the slight odor of something nasty elicits a universal reaction—the wrinkling of the nose, curling of the upper lips, and protrusion of the tongue. Wrinkling the nose has been shown to prevent pathogens from entering through the nasal cavity, and sticking out the tongue aids in the expulsion of tainted food and is a common precursor to vomiting. OK, now that you're sufficiently grossed out, what (you may ask in disgust) does this have to do with marketing and persuasion? Well, disgust also exerts a powerful effect on our judgments. People who experience this

CB AS I SEE IT

Professor Gavan Fitzsimmons, *Duke University*

For many years consumer researchers have thought of the consumer largely as a conscious, thinking machine. Consumers consider what is important to them, evaluate choice options on those alternatives on those dimensions, and make a decision. Recently, however, a growing group of consumer researchers has started to revisit an old idea that had been largely considered debunked: namely, that much of what goes on in the life of a consumer occurs outside of his or her conscious awareness.

The idea that consumers are influenced outside of their conscious awareness is frightening to many consumers, and has thus received considerable resistance. And yet, the data become more and more clear that consumers are influenced by stimuli they don't realize they have been exposed to, processes occur in the consumers'

minds they are unaware of, and consumers even engage in behavior that they are not conscious of (e.g., consider many habitual behaviors). These nonconscious processes are often adaptive and helpful for the consumer, but can also at times be detrimental.

One interesting recent example from our own lab involved subliminally exposing consumers to brand logos—in several studies, either an Apple or an IBM logo. Incidental brand exposures occur every day (recent estimates range between 3,000 and 10,000 times in a single day for the typical American consumer) and thus we were curious if they could influence consumer behavior in meaningful ways. Apple or IBM logos were flashed on a screen for very brief intervals—from 10 to 50 milliseconds—to mimic this real-world incidental brand exposure. Participants had no conscious experience of seeing a brand, and believed they were only seeing a box on the left or right of the screen. Our results showed that nonconscious exposure to the Apple logo led consumers to be significantly more creative than consumers similarly exposed to an IBM logo. This **incidental brand exposure** activated a goal in consumers that they actively pursued until they could satisfy it. Similar studies

have shown dramatic increases in choices of one brand versus another as a result of incidental brand exposure.

The future of research on unconscious consumer behavior is likely to continue to document domains in which the consumer is influenced outside of his or her awareness. Contexts in which consumers find themselves taxed, exhausted, or overwhelmed are all ripe for unconscious influence, which sadly have become the default rather than the exception for most consumers. Some of the most interesting questions remaining deal with exactly how nonconscious processes work, and when they may be adaptive versus harmful. If helpful, how can consumers, firms, and public policymakers embrace and encourage them? For example, many consumers might like to be more creative, or faster, for example, and thus might strategically surround themselves with Apple or Speedo logos. Over time, exposure to these logos will become incidental and they may find themselves increasingly creative or faster. If such exposures are harmful, what can these groups do to minimize their effects? Preliminary evidence suggests that warnings preceding exposure can, at least in part, dampen these nonconscious effects.

emotion become harsher in their judgments of moral offenses and offenders. In one experiment, people who sat in a foul-smelling room or at a desk cluttered with dirty food containers judged acts like lying on a résumé or keeping a wallet found on the street as more immoral than individuals who were asked to make the same judgments in a clean environment. In another study, survey respondents who were randomly asked to complete the items while they stood in front of a hand sanitizer gave more conservative responses than those who stood in another part of the hallway.[43] Scientists continue to identify other, similar effects of subtle environmental cues that carry over onto our judgments of people and products; for instance, people who hold a cold cup of water before they are asked to make ratings judge other people and objects as "colder" than do those who were given a hot cup of coffee.

How Much Do We Search?

As a general rule, we search more when the purchase is important, when we have more of a need to learn more about the purchase, or when it's easy to obtain the relevant information.[44] Consumers differ in the amount of search they tend to undertake, regardless of the product category in question. All things being equal, younger, better-educated people who enjoy the shopping/fact-finding process tend to conduct more information search. Women are more inclined to search than men are, as are those who place greater value on style and the image they present.[45]

Does knowing something about the product make it more or less likely that we will engage in search? The answer to this question isn't as obvious as it first appears: Product experts and novices use very different procedures during decision making. Novices who know little about a product should be the most motivated to find out more about it. However, experts are more familiar with the product category, so they should be better able to understand the meaning of any new product information they might acquire.

So, who searches more? The answer is neither: Search tends to be greatest among those consumers who are *moderately knowledgeable* about the product. We find an inverted-U relationship between knowledge and external search effort, as Figure 5 shows. People with very limited expertise may not feel they are competent to search extensively. In fact, they may not even know where to start. Richard, who did not spend a lot of time researching his purchase, is typical. He visited one store, and he looked only at brands with which he was already familiar. In addition, he focused on only a small number of product features.[46]

Because experts have a better sense of what information is relevant to the decision, they engage in *selective search*, which means their efforts are more focused and efficient. In contrast, novices are more likely to rely on the opinions of others and on "nonfunctional" attributes, such as brand name and price, to distinguish among alternatives. Finally, novice consumers may process information in a "top-down" rather than a

Figure 5 THE RELATIONSHIP BETWEEN AMOUNT OF INFORMATION SEARCH AND PRODUCT KNOWLEDGE

Minolta features a no-risk guarantee as a way to reduce the perceived risk in buying an office copier.

Source: Courtesy of Minolta Corporation.

"bottom-up" manner—they focus less on details than on the big picture. For instance, they may be more impressed by the sheer amount of technical information an ad presents than by the actual significance of the claims it makes.[47]

Ironically, people who have details about a product before they buy it do *not* expect to be as happy with it as do those who got only ambiguous information. The so-called **blissful ignorance effect** apparently occurs because we want to feel like we've bought the right thing—and if we know precisely how the product performs, it's not as easy to rationalize away any shortcomings. In one experiment, some subjects were told of a manufacturer's claims about a hand lotion and informed that separate research had shown that 50 percent of people in fact obtained these benefits. Another set of subjects also heard about the manufacturers' claims, but they were told that the results from independent research were not yet available. Those who were provided with less information (the latter group) actually expected the product to perform better. In other words, the less we know about something, the easier it is to persuade ourselves that we like it.[48]

Perceived Risk

As a rule, purchase decisions that involve extensive search also entail **perceived risk**, or the belief that there may be negative consequences if you use or don't use a product or service. This may occur when the product is expensive or is complex and hard to understand. Alternatively, perceived risk can be a factor when others can see what we choose, and we may be embarrassed if we make the wrong choice.[49]

Figure 6 lists five kinds of risk—including objective (e.g., physical danger) and subjective (e.g., social embarrassment) factors—as well as the products each type tends to affect. Perceived risk is less of a problem for consumers who have greater "risk capital," because they have less to lose from a poor choice. For example, a highly self-confident person might worry less than a vulnerable, insecure person who chooses a brand that peers think isn't cool.

How Do We Decide Among Alternatives?

Much of the effort we put into a purchase decision occurs at the stage where we have to put the pedal to the metal and actually choose a product from several alternatives. This may not be easy; modern consumer society abounds with choices. In some cases, there may be literally hundreds of different brands (as in cigarettes) or different variations of the same brand (as in shades of lipstick).

Ask a friend to name all the brands of perfume she can think of. The odds are she will reel off three to five names rather quickly, then stop and think awhile before she comes up with a few more. She's probably very familiar with the first set of brands, and in fact she probably wears one or more of these. Her list may also contain one or two brands that

	BUYERS MOST SENSITIVE TO RISK	PURCHASES MOST SUBJECT TO RISK
MONETARY RISK	Risk capital consists of money and property. Those with relatively little income and wealth are most vulnerable.	High-ticket items that require substantial expenditures are most subject to this form of risk.
FUNCTIONAL RISK	Risk capital consists of alternative means of performing the function or meeting the need. Practical consumers are most sensitive.	Products or services whose purchase and use requires the buyer's exclusive commitment are most sensitive.
PHYSICAL RISK	Risk capital consists of physical vigor, health, and vitality. Those who are elderly, frail, or in ill health are most vulnerable.	Mechanical or electrical goods (such as vehicles or flammables), drugs and medical treatment, and food and beverages are most sensitive.
SOCIAL RISK	Risk capital consists of self-esteem and self-confidence. Those who are insecure and uncertain are most sensitive.	Socially visible or symbolic goods, such as clothes, jewelry, cars, homes, or sports equipment are most subject to social risk.
PSYCHO-LOGICAL RISK	Risk capital consists of affiliations and status. Those lacking self-respect or attractiveness to peers are most sensitive.	Expensive personal luxuries that may engender guilt, durables, and services whose use demands self-discipline or sacrifice are most sensitive.

Figure 6 FIVE TYPES OF PERCEIVED RISK

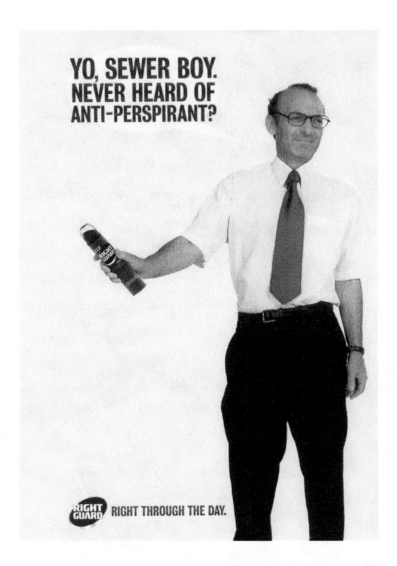

YO, SEWER BOY.
NEVER HEARD OF
ANTI-PERSPIRANT?

RIGHT GUARD RIGHT THROUGH THE DAY.

she doesn't like; to the contrary, they come to mind because she thinks they smell nasty or are unsophisticated. Note also that there are many, many more brands on the market that she did not name at all.

If your friend goes to the store to buy perfume, it is likely that she will consider buying some or most of the brands she listed initially. She might also entertain a few more possibilities if these come to her attention while she's at the fragrance counter (for example, if an employee "ambushes" her with a scent sample as she walks down the aisle).

How do we decide which criteria are important, and how do we narrow down product alternatives to an acceptable number and eventually choose one instead of others? The answer varies depending on the decision-making process we use. A person who engages in extended problem solving may carefully evaluate several brands, whereas someone who makes a habitual decision may not consider any alternatives to his normal brand. Furthermore, some evidence indicates that we do more extended processing in situations that arouse negative emotions because of conflicts we feel among the available choices. This is most likely to occur when there are difficult tradeoffs; for example, when a person has to choose between the risks involved in having a bypass operation versus the potential improvement in his life if the operation succeeds.[50]

We call the alternatives a consumer knows about his **evoked set** and the ones that he actually considers his **consideration set** (often we don't seriously consider every single brand we know about, perhaps because it's out of our price range or we've had a bad experience with it).[51] Recall that Richard did not know much about the technical aspects

This Canadian ad from Kiwi presents a solution to an everyday problem.
Source: Courtesy of Sara Lee Corporation.

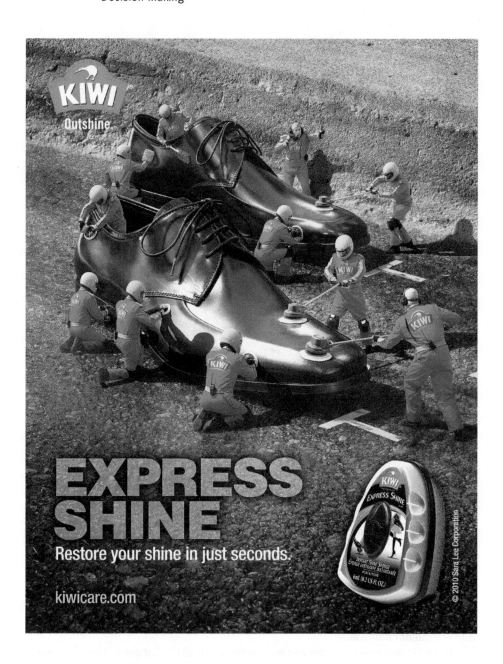

of television sets, and he had only a few major brands in memory. Of these, two were acceptable possibilities and one was not.

Consumers often consider a surprisingly small number of alternatives, especially with all the choices available to us. A cross-national study found that people generally include just a few products in their consideration, although this amount varies by product category and across countries. For example, on average American beer consumers considered only three brands, whereas Canadian consumers typically considered seven brands. In contrast, whereas auto buyers in Norway studied two alternatives, American consumers on average looked at more than eight models before they decided.[52] We seem to be a lot more picky about our wheels than our brews.

For obvious reasons, a marketer who finds that his brand is not in his target market's evoked set has cause to worry. You often don't get a second chance to make a good first impression; a consumer isn't likely to place a product in his evoked set after he has already considered it and rejected it. Indeed, we're more likely to add a new brand to the evoked set than one that we previously considered but passed over, even after a marketer has provided additional positive information about it.[53] For marketers, a consumer's

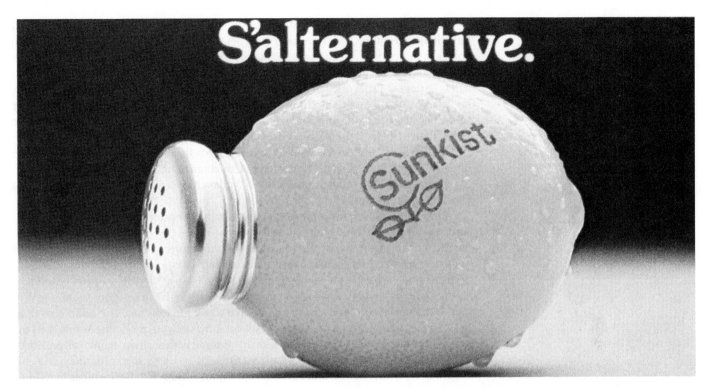

reluctance to give a rejected product a second chance underscores the importance of ensuring that it performs well from the time the company introduces it.

An advertising campaign for Hyundai illustrates how hard a company sometimes has to work to get its brand into consumers' consideration sets. Many people think of Hyundai strictly as a low-cost vehicle, even though it has received high marks for quality in recent years. The carmaker's "Think About It" campaign encouraged consumers to reconsider their long-held beliefs through frank statements like "The logo is there to tell you what the car is, not who you are" and "When a car company charges for roadside assistance, aren't they just helping themselves?" As Hyundai's vice president for marketing in America explained, "Unless we give people a compelling reason to shuffle the brand deck, they'll stand with the brands they know rather than make that switch."[54]

How Do We Put Products into Categories?

Remember that when consumers process product information, they don't do it in a vacuum. They evaluate its attributes in terms of what they already know about the item or other similar products. A person who thinks about a particular 35mm camera will most likely compare it to other 35 mm cameras rather than to a disposable camera. Because the *category* in which a consumer places a product determines the other products she will compare it to, the way we classify a brand in our minds plays a big role in how we evaluate it. These classifications derive from different product attributes, including appearance (e.g., we assume that chocolates in silver or gold wrappings are more upscale), price (we view items with price endings in .99 as cheaper than those that end in .00), or previously learned connections (if it has the name Porsche on it, it must be expensive).[55]

The products in a consumer's evoked set are likely to share some similar features. This process can either help or hurt a product, depending on what people compare it to. For example, in one survey, about 25 percent of consumers said they would be less likely to buy a product made of hemp if they know it's derived from the same plant from which marijuana comes (but without any of the latter's effects). When we come across a new product, we tend to place it into an existing category rather than create a new category.[56] Of course, that's one of the big hurdles a new form of technology has to clear: Before people will buy a microwave oven, MP3 player, or GPS, they need to make sense out of the category to which it belongs.

It is important to understand how we cognitively represent this information in a **knowledge structure**. This term refers to a set of beliefs and the way we organize these beliefs in our minds.[57] Their makeup matters to marketers because they want to ensure that customers correctly group their products. For example, General Foods brought out a new line of Jell-O flavors, such as Cranberry Orange, that it called Jell-O Gelatin Flavors for Salads. Unfortunately, the company discovered that people used the product only for salad, because the name encouraged them to put the product in their "salad" structure rather than in their "dessert" structure. General Foods dropped the product line.[58]

Typically we represent a product in a cognitive structure at one of three levels. To understand this idea, consider how someone might respond to these questions about an ice cream cone: What other products share similar characteristics, and which would you consider as alternatives to eating a cone?

These questions may be more complex than they first appear. At one level, a cone is similar to an apple because you could eat both as a dessert. At another level, a cone is similar to a piece of pie because you could eat either for dessert and both are fattening. At still another level, a cone is similar to an ice cream sundae—you could eat either for dessert, both are made of ice cream, and both are fattening. Figure 7 depicts these three levels.

It's easy to see that the foods a person associates with the category "fattening dessert" influence his or her decision about what to eat after dinner. The middle level, or *basic level category*, is typically the most useful for classifying products. At this level the items we group together tend to have a lot in common with each other, but still permit us to consider a broad enough range of alternatives. The broader *superordinate category* is more abstract, whereas the more specific *subordinate category* often includes individual brands.[59] Of course, not all items fit equally well into a category. Apple pie is a better example of the subordinate category "pie" than is rhubarb pie, even though both are types of pies. This is because it's more *prototypical*, and most people would think of apple as a pie flavor before they thought of rhubarb. In contrast, true pie experts probably know a lot about both typical and atypical category examples.[60]

Strategic Implications of Product Categorization

The way we categorize products has a lot of strategic implications. That's because this process affects which products consumers will compare to our product and also the criteria they'll use to decide if they like us or the other guys.

Position a Product. The success of a *positioning strategy* hinges on the marketer's ability to convince the consumer to consider its product within a given category. For example, the orange juice industry tried to reposition orange juice as a drink people can enjoy all day long ("It's not just for breakfast anymore"). However, soft-drink companies attempt the opposite when they portray sodas as suitable for breakfast consumption. They are trying to make their way into consumers' "breakfast drink" category, along with orange juice, grapefruit juice, and coffee. Of course, this strategy can backfire, as Pepsi-Cola

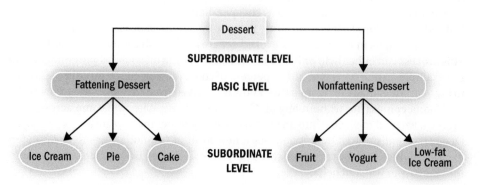

Figure 7 LEVELS OF ABSTRACTION
IN DESSERT CATEGORIES

discovered when it introduced Pepsi A.M. and positioned it as a coffee substitute. The company did such a good job of categorizing the drink as a morning beverage that customers wouldn't drink it at any other time, and the product failed.[61]

Identify Competitors. At the abstract, superordinate level, many different product forms compete for membership. The category "entertainment" might comprise both bowling and the ballet, but not many people would substitute one of these activities for the other. Products and services that on the surface are quite different, however, actually compete with each other at a broad level for consumers' discretionary dollars. Although bowling or ballet may not be a likely tradeoff for many people, a symphony might try to lure away season ticket holders to the ballet by positioning itself as an equivalent member of the superordinate category "cultural event."[62]

We're often faced with choices between noncomparable categories, where we can't directly relate the attributes in one to those in another (the old problem of comparing apples and oranges). When we can create an overlapping category that encompasses both items (e.g., entertainment, value, usefulness) and then rate each alternative in terms of that superordinate category comparison, the process is easier.[63]

Create an Exemplar Product. As we saw with the case of apple pie versus rhubarb pie, if a product is a really good example of a category it is more familiar to consumers and they more easily recognize and recall it.[64] The characteristics of **category exemplars** tend to exert a disproportionate influence on how people think of the category in general.[65] In a sense, brands we strongly associate with a category get to "call the shots": They define the criteria we use to evaluate all category members.

Being a bit less than prototypical is not necessarily a bad thing, however. Products that are moderately unusual within their product category may stimulate more information processing and positive evaluations because they are neither so familiar that we will take them for granted nor so different that we won't consider them at all.[66] A brand that is strongly discrepant (such as Zima, a clear malt beverage) may occupy a unique niche position, whereas those that are somewhat different (e.g., local microbrews) remain in a distinct position within the general category.[67]

Locate Products in a Store. Product categorization also can affect consumers' expectations regarding the places where they can locate a desired product. If products do not clearly fit into categories (e.g., is a rug furniture?), this may diminish our ability to find them or figure out what they're supposed to be once we do. For instance, a frozen dog food that pet owners had to thaw and cook before they served it to Fido failed in the market, partly because people could not adapt to the idea of buying dog food in the "frozen foods for people" section of their grocery stores.

Product Choice:
How Do We Select from the Alternatives?

Once we assemble and evaluate the relevant options in a category, eventually we have to choose one.[68] Recall that the decision rules that guide our choices range from very simple and quick strategies to complicated processes that require a lot of attention and cognitive processing.[69] Our job isn't getting any easier as companies overwhelm us with more and more features. We deal with 50-button remote controls, digital cameras with hundreds of mysterious features and book-length manuals, and cars with dashboard systems worthy of the space shuttle. Experts call this spiral of complexity **feature creep**. As evidence that the proliferation of gizmos is counterproductive, Philips Electronics found that at least half of the products buyers return have nothing wrong with them—consumers simply couldn't figure out how to use them! What's worse, on average the buyer spent only 20 minutes trying to figure out how to use the product and then gave up.

Why don't companies avoid this problem? One reason is that we often assume the more features the better. It's only when we get the product home that we realize the virtue of simplicity. In one study, consumers chose among three models of a digital device that varied in terms of how complex each was. More than 60 percent chose the one with the most features. Then, when the participants got the chance to choose from up to 25 features to customize their product, the average person chose 20 of these add-ons. But when they actually used the devices, it turns out that the large number of options only frustrated them; they ended up being much happier with the simpler product. As the saying goes, "Be careful what you wish for. . . ."[70]

Evaluative Criteria

When Richard looked at different television sets, he focused on one or two product features and completely ignored several others. He narrowed down his choices as he only considered two specific brand names, and from the Prime Wave and Precision models, he chose one that featured stereo capability.

Evaluative criteria are the dimensions we use to judge the merits of competing options. When he compared alternative products, Richard could have chosen from among many criteria that ranged from very functional attributes ("Does this TV come with remote control?") to experiential ones ("Does this TV's sound reproduction make me imagine I'm in a concert hall?").

Another important point is that criteria on which products *differ* from one another carry more weight in the decision process than do those where the alternatives are *similar*. If all brands a person considers rate equally well on one attribute (e.g., if all TVs come with remote control), Richard needs to find other reasons to choose one over another. **Determinant attributes** are the features we actually use to differentiate among our choices.

Marketers often educate consumers about which criteria they should use as determinant attributes. For example, consumer research from Church & Dwight indicated that many consumers view the use of natural ingredients as a determinant attribute. As a result, the company promoted its toothpaste made from baking soda, which the company already manufactured for Church & Dwight's Arm & Hammer brand.[71]

Sometimes a company actually invents a determinant attribute: Pepsi-Cola accomplished this when it stamped freshness dates on soda cans. It spent about $25 million on an advertising and promotional campaign to convince consumers that there's nothing quite as horrible as a stale can of soda—even though people in the industry estimate that drinkers consume 98 percent of all cans well before this could be a problem. Six months after it introduced the campaign, lo and behold, an independent survey found

This Indonesian ad shows us one of bubblegum's determinant attributes.
Source: Courtesy of draft FCB Jakarta Indonesia.

that 61 percent of respondents felt that freshness dating is an important attribute for a soft drink![72] To effectively recommend a new decision criterion, a marketer should convey three pieces of information:[73]

1 It should point out that there are significant differences among brands on the attribute.
2 It should supply the consumer with a decision-making rule, such as *if* . . . (deciding among competing brands), *then* . . . (use the attribute as a criterion).
3 It should convey a rule that is consistent with how the person made the decision on prior occasions. Otherwise, she is likely to ignore the recommendation because it requires too much mental work.

Neuromarketing: How Your Brain Reacts to Alternatives

Is there a "buy button" in your brain? Some corporations, including Google, CBS, Disney, and Frito-Lay, have teamed up with neuroscientists to find out.[75] **Neuromarketing** uses *functional magnetic resonance imaging* (or *fMRI*), a brain-scanning device that tracks blood flow as we perform mental tasks. In recent years, researchers have discovered that regions in the brain, such as the amygdala, the hippocampus, and the hypothalamus, are dynamic switchboards that blend memory, emotions, and biochemical triggers. These interconnected neurons shape the ways in which fear, panic, exhilaration, and social pressure influence our choices.

Scientists know that specific regions of the brain light up in these scans to show increased blood flow when a person recognizes a face, hears a song, makes a decision, or senses deception. Now they hope to harness this technology to measure consumers' reactions to movie trailers, automobiles, the appeal of a pretty face, and even their loyalty to specific brands. British researchers recorded brain activity as shoppers toured a virtual store. They claim they identified the neural region that becomes active when a shopper decides which product to pluck from a supermarket shelf. DaimlerChrysler took brain scans of men as they looked at photos of cars and confirmed that sports cars activated their reward centers. The company's scientists found that the most popular vehicles—the Porsche- and Ferrari-style sports cars—triggered activity in a section of the brain they call the *fusiform face area*, which governs facial recognition. A psychiatrist who ran the study commented, "They were reminded of faces when they looked at the cars. The lights of the cars look a little like eyes."

A study that took brain scans of people as they drank competing soft-drink brands illustrates how loyalty to a brand affects our reactions, even at a very basic, physiological level. When the researchers monitored brain scans of 67 people who took a blind taste test of Coca-Cola and Pepsi, each soft drink lit up the brain's reward system, and the participants were evenly split as to which drink they preferred—even though three out of four participants *said* they preferred Coke. When told they were drinking Coke, the regions of the brain that control memory lit up, and this activation drowned out the area that simply reacts to taste cues. In this case, Coke's strong brand identity trumped the sensations coming from respondents' taste receptors.

In another study, researchers reported that pictures of celebrities triggered many of the same brain circuits as did images of shoes, cars, chairs, wristwatches, sunglasses, handbags, and water bottles. All of these objects set off a rush of activity in a part of the cortex that neuroscientists know links to our sense of identity and social image. The scientists also identified types of consumers based on their responses. At one extreme were people whose brains responded intensely to "cool" products and celebrities with bursts of activity but who didn't respond at all to "uncool" images. They dubbed these participants "cool fools" who are likely to be impulsive or compulsive shoppers. At the other extreme were people whose brains reacted only to the unstylish items; this pattern fits well with people who tend to be anxious, apprehensive, or neurotic.

Many researchers remain skeptical about how helpful this technology will be for consumer research. If indeed researchers can reliably track consumers' brand preferences by seeing how their brains react, there may be many interesting potential opportunities for new research techniques that rely on what we (or at least our brains) do rather than what we say.

Marketing Pitfall

Product labels assist us with problem solving, but some are more useful than others. Here are some examples of the not-so-helpful variety:[74]

- On a Conair Pro Style 1600 hair dryer: "WARNING: Do not use in shower. Never use while sleeping."
- Instructions for folding up a portable baby carriage: "Step 1: Remove baby."
- A rest stop on a Wisconsin highway: "Do not eat urinal cakes."
- On a bag of Fritos: "You could be a winner! No purchase necessary. Details inside."
- On some Swanson frozen dinners: "Serving suggestion: Defrost."
- On Tesco's Tiramisu dessert (printed on bottom of box): "Do not turn upside down."
- On Marks & Spencer bread pudding: "Product will be hot after heating."
- On packaging for a Rowenta iron: "Do not iron clothes on body."
- On Nytol sleeping aid: "Warning: May cause drowsiness."

OBJECTIVE 4

Our access to online sources changes the way we decide what to buy.

Cybermediaries

As anyone who's ever typed a phrase such as "home theaters" into Google or another search engine knows, the Web delivers enormous amounts of product and retailer information in seconds. In fact (recall our earlier discussion of the problem of *hyperchoice*), the biggest problem Web surfers face these days is to narrow down their choices, not to beef them up. In cyberspace, simplification is key.

With the tremendous number of Web sites available and the huge number of people surfing the Web each day, how can people organize information and decide where to click? A **cybermediary** often is the answer. This is an intermediary that helps to filter and organize online market information so that customers can identify and evaluate alternatives more efficiently.[76] Many consumers regularly link to comparison-shopping sites, such as Bizrate.com or Pricegrabber.com, for example, that list many online retailers that sell a given item along with the price each charges.[77]

Cybermediaries take different forms:[78]

- *Directories* and *portals,* such as Yahoo! or The Knot, are general services that tie together a large variety of different sites.
- *Forums, fan clubs,* and *user groups* offer product-related discussions to help customers sift through options. It's clear that customer product reviews are a key driver of satisfaction and loyalty. In one large survey, about half of the respondents who bought an item from a major Web site remembered seeing customer product reviews. This group's satisfaction with the online shopping experience was 5 percent higher than for shoppers who didn't recall customer reviews.[79] Another advantage is that consumers get to experience a much wider array of options—and at the same time products such as movies, books, and CDs that aren't "blockbusters" are more likely to sell. At Netflix, the online DVD rental company, for example, fellow subscribers recommend about two-thirds of the films that people order. In fact, between 70 and 80 percent of Netflix rentals come from the company's back catalog of 38,000 films rather than recent releases.[80]

This aspect of online customer review is one important factor that's fueling a new way of thinking, which one writer calls the **long tail**.[81] The basic idea is that we no longer need rely solely on big hits (such as blockbuster movies or best-selling books) to find profits. Companies can also make money if they sell small amounts of items that only a few people want—*if* they sell enough different items. For example, Amazon.com maintains an inventory of 3.7 million books, compared to the 100,000 or so you'll find in a Barnes & Noble retail store. Most of these will sell only a few thousand copies (if that), but the 3.6 million books that Barnes & Noble *doesn't* carry make up a quarter of Amazon's revenues! Other examples of the long tail include successful microbreweries and TV networks that make money on reruns of old shows on channels such as the Game Show Network.

Intelligent agents are sophisticated software programs that use *collaborative filtering* technologies to learn from past user behavior in order to recommend new purchases.[82] When you let Amazon.com suggest a new book, the site uses an intelligent agent to propose novels based on what you and others like you have bought in the past. Collaborative filtering is still in its infancy. In the next few years, expect to see many new Web-based methods to simplify the consumer decision-making process. (Now if only someone could come up with an easier way to pay for all the great stuff you find courtesy of shopping bots!)

Researchers work hard to understand how consumers find information online, and in particular how they react to and integrate recommendations received from different kinds of online agents into their own product choices. An **electronic recommendation agent** is a software tool that tries to understand a human decision maker's multiattribute preferences for a product category as it asks the user to communicate his preferences. Based on that data, the software then recommends a list of alternatives sorted by the degree to which they fit these criteria. These agents do appear to influence consumers' decision making, though some evidence indicates that they're more effective when they recommend a product based on utilitarian attributes (functionality such as nutritional value) rather than hedonic attributes (such as design or taste).[83]

Although engineers continually improve the ability of electronic recommendation agents to suggest new things we might like, we still rely on other people to guide our search. About 80 percent of online shoppers rely on customer reviews before they buy. We call the people who supply these reviews **brand advocates.** Yahoo! estimates that 40 percent of people who spend time online are advocates and that they influence purchases two to one over nonadvocates. Marketers who adjust their strategies to acknowledge this impact find it's worth their while. For example, PETCO saw a 500 percent increase in its click-through rate when it included consumers' reviews in its online ads.[84]

The huge growth in demand for user reviews in turn fuels new opinion-based sites, such as Yelp for local businesses, TripAdvisor for travel, and Urbanspoon for restaurants. Yelp, for example, offers more than 4 million reviews of everything from corner cafés to dog groomers. People who take the time to post to these sites don't do it for money, but they do generate an income in the form of props for good recommendations. Analysts refer to this reward system as the **reputation economy**: Many thousands of consumers devote significant time to editing Wikipedia entries, serving as brand advocates, or uploading clips to YouTube simply because they enjoy the process and want to boost their reputation as knowledgeable advisors.[85]

OBJECTIVE 5

We often fall back on well-learned "rules-of-thumb" to make decisions.

Heuristics: Mental Shortcuts

Do we actually perform complex mental calculations every time we make a purchase decision? Get a life! Remember our earlier discussion about satisficing and the many times we "settle" for a choice that may not be perfect, but will be adequate? When we don't rely on a Web site to steer us to the right place, we often use other decision rules to simplify our choices. For example, Richard made certain assumptions instead of engaging in prolonged information search. In particular, he assumed that the selection at Zany Zack's was more than sufficient, so he did not bother to shop at any of Zack's competitors.[86]

Especially when limited problem solving occurs prior to making a choice, we often fall back on **heuristics**, or mental rules-of-thumb, to make a speedy decision. These rules range from the very general ("higher-priced products are higher-quality products" or "buy the same brand I bought last time") to the very specific ("buy Domino, the brand of sugar my mother always bought").[87] Sometimes these shortcuts may not be in our best interests. A car shopper who personally knows one or two people who have had problems with a particular vehicle, for example, might assume that he would have similar trouble with it rather than taking the time to find out that it actually has an excellent repair record.[88]

How Do We Rely on Product Signals?

One shortcut we often use is to *infer* hidden dimensions of products from attributes we observe. In these cases the visible element is a **product signal** that communicates some underlying quality. This explains why someone who tries to sell a used car makes sure the car's exterior is clean and shiny: Potential buyers often judge the vehicle's mechanical condition by its appearance, even though this means they may drive away in a clean, shiny clunker.[89]

When we only have incomplete product information, we often base our judgments on our beliefs about *covariation*—the associations we have among events that may or may not actually influence one another.[90] For example, a shopper may judge product quality by the length of time a manufacturer has been in business. Other signals or attributes consumers tend to believe coexist with good or bad products include well-known brand names, country of origin, price, and the retail outlets that carry the product. Unfortunately, many of us estimate covariation quite poorly, and our erroneous beliefs persist despite evidence to the contrary. In a process similar to the consistency principle, we tend to see what we're looking for. In other words, we'll look for product information that confirms our guesses and ignore or explain away information that contradicts what we already think.[91] For example, in one study, people who saw

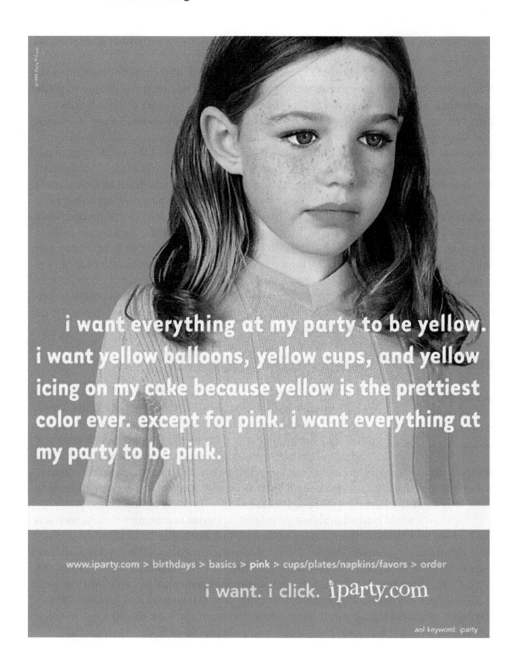

Consumers often simplify choices when they use heuristics such as automatically choosing a favorite color or brand.
Source: Courtesy of iParty Retail Store Corp.

a snack food package with a larger number of individual cookies assumed that the box actually included more product units.[92]

Market Beliefs: Is It Better if I Pay More for It?

We constantly form assumptions about companies, products, and stores. These **market beliefs** then become shortcuts that guide our decisions—as our discussion of green-washing indicates, these beliefs are not necessarily accurate.[93] Recall that Richard chose to shop at a large "electronics warehouse store" because he *assumed* that the selection would be better there than at a specialty store. Table 2 lists some market beliefs researchers have identified; how many do you share?

Do higher prices mean higher quality? The link we assume between price and quality is one of the most pervasive market beliefs.[94] In fact, novice consumers may consider price the *only* relevant product attribute. Experts also consider this information, although they tend to use price for its informational value when they evaluate products (e.g., virgin wool) that they know vary widely in quality. When this quality level is more standard

TABLE 2	Common Market Beliefs
Brand	All brands are basically the same.
	Generic products are just name brands sold under a different label at a lower price.
	The best brands are the ones that are purchased the most.
	When in doubt, a national brand is always a safe bet.
Store	Specialty stores are great places to familiarize yourself with the best brands; but once you figure out what you want, it's cheaper to buy it at a discount outlet.
	A store's character is reflected in its window displays.
	Salespeople in specialty stores are more knowledgeable than other sales personnel.
	Larger stores offer better prices than small stores.
	Locally owned stores give the best service.
	A store that offers a good value on one of its products probably offers good values on all of its items.
	Credit and return policies are most lenient at large department stores.
	Stores that have just opened usually charge attractive prices.
Prices/Discounts/Sales	Sales are typically run to get rid of slow-moving merchandise.
	Stores that are constantly having sales don't really save you money.
	Within a given store, higher prices generally indicate higher quality.
Advertising and Sales Promotion	"Hard-sell" advertising is associated with low-quality products.
	Items tied to "giveaways" are not a good value (even with the freebie).
	Coupons represent real savings for customers because they are not offered by the store.
	When you buy heavily advertised products, you are paying for the label, not for higher quality.
Product/Packaging	Largest-sized containers are almost always cheaper per unit than smaller sizes.
	New products are more expensive when they're first introduced; prices tend to settle down as time goes by.
	When you are not sure what you need in a product, it's a good idea to invest in the extra features, because you'll probably wish you had them later.
	In general, synthetic goods are lower in quality than goods made of naturals materials.
	It's advisable to stay away from products when they are new to the market; it usually takes the manufacturer a little time to work the bugs out.

Source: Adapted from Calvin P. Duncan, "Consumer Market Beliefs: A Review of the Literature and an Agenda for Future Research," in Marvin E. Goldberg, Gerald Gorn, and Richard W. Pollay eds., *Advances in Consumer Research* 17 (Provo, UT: Association for Consumer Research, 1990):729-35.

or strictly regulated (e.g., Harris Tweed sport coats), experts do not weigh price in their decisions. For the most part, this belief is justified; you do tend to get what you pay for. However, let the buyer beware: The price–quality relationship is not always justified.[95]

Country of Origin as a Product Signal

Does a shrimp have a personality? As cheap foreign imports flood the market, U.S. shrimpers hope they do. They know that consumers prefer coffee from exotic places such as Kenya and salmon from Alaska, so they hope to persuade consumers to prefer American shrimp. At the Lark restaurant in Seattle, diners can read on the menu whether the prawns come from Georgia, Florida, or Alaska. Other places get even more specific about the home address of their crustaceans. The Silverado Resort and Spa in Napa, California, serves "local West Texas white shrimp."[96]

A product's "address" matters. We Americans like to buy Italian shoes, Japanese cars, clothing imported from Taiwan, and microwave ovens built in South Korea. **Country of origin** often is a determinant attribute in the decision-making process. Consumers strongly associate certain items with specific countries, and products from those countries often attempt to benefit from these linkages. The consumer's own expertise with the product category moderates the effects of this attribute. When other information is available, experts tend to ignore country-of-origin information, whereas novices continue to rely on it. However, when other information is unavailable or ambiguous, both experts and novices will rely on a product's birthplace to make a decision.

Swadeshi describes an Indian nationalist movement that started in the 19th century in reaction to the British decision to divide the country into separate provinces. Adherents

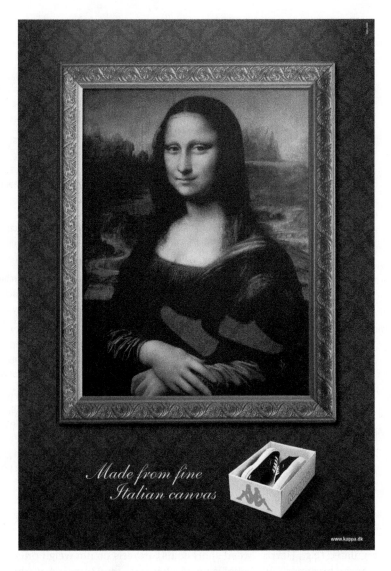

boycott multinational brands like Coca-Cola and express their ideology as they buy products made in India. Men buy Godrej or Emani shaving creams instead of Old Spice or Gillette; women make a point of shampooing with Lakme, Nirma, or Velvet instead of Western brands that are sold in India, such as Halo, All Clear, Sunsilk, Head & Shoulders, or Pantene.[97] **Ethnocentrism** is the tendency to prefer products or people of one's own culture to those of other countries. Ethnocentric consumers are likely to feel it is wrong to buy products made elsewhere, particularly because this may have a negative effect on the domestic economy.

Marketing campaigns that stress the desirability of "buying American" obviously appeal to ethnocentric consumers. The Consumer Ethnocentric Scale (CETSCALE) measures this trait. Ethnocentric consumers agree with statements such as the following:[98]

- Purchasing foreign-made products is un-American.
- Curbs should be put on all imports.
- American consumers who purchase products made in other countries are responsible for putting their fellow Americans out of work.[99]

Do We Choose Familiar Brand Names Because of Loyalty or Habit?

When you fall in love with a brand, it may be your favorite for a lifetime. In a study the Boston Consulting Group conducted of the market leaders in 30 product categories, 27 of the brands that were number one in 1930 (such as Ivory Soap and Campbell's Soup) still were at the top more than 50 years later.[100] Clearly, "choose a well-known brand name" is a powerful heuristic. As this study demonstrates, some brands in a sense are well-known *because* they are well-known—we assume that if so many people choose a product, it must be good.

Indeed, our tendency to prefer a number-one brand to the competition is so strong that it seems to mimic a pattern scientists find in other domains ranging from earthquakes to linguistics. **Zipf's Law** describes this pattern. In the 1930s, a linguist named George Kingsley Zipf found that *the*—the most-used English word—occurs about twice as often as *of* (second place), about three times as often as *and* (third), and so on. Since then, scientists have found similar relationships between the size and frequency of earthquakes and a variety of other natural and artificial phenomena.

A marketing researcher decided to apply Zipf's Law to consumer behavior. His firm asked Australian consumers to identify the brands of toilet paper and instant coffee they use and to rank them in order of preference. As the model predicted, people spend roughly twice as much of their toilet paper budget on the top choice than on the second-ranked brand, about twice as much on the number-two brand as on the third-ranked brand, and about twice as much on the number-three brand as on the number-four brand. One ramification is that a brand that moves from number two to number one in a category will see a much greater jump in sales than will, say, a brand that moves from number four to number three. Brands that dominate their markets are as much as 50 percent more profitable than their nearest competitors.[101]

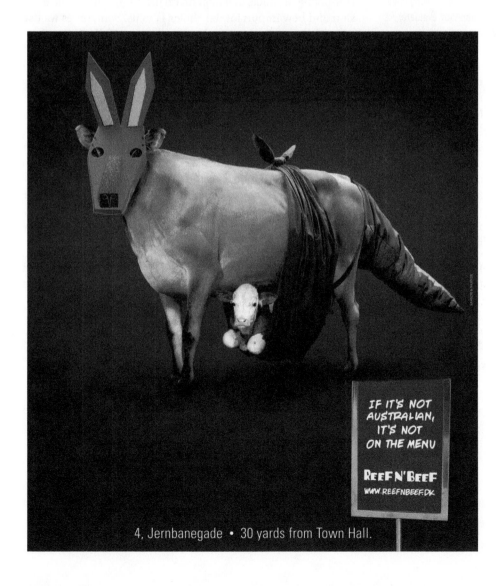

Marketers like this Danish restaurant often rely on consumers' expectations based on country-of-origin cues.
Source: Courtesy of Reef 'N Beef/Saatchi.

Inertia: The Lazy Customer

Many people tend to buy the same brand just about every time they go to the store. Often this is because of **inertia**; we buy a brand out of habit merely because it requires less effort. If another product comes along that is cheaper (or if the original product is out of stock), we won't hesitate to change our minds. A competitor who tries to encourage this switch often can do so rather easily because the shopper won't hesitate to jump to the new brand if it offers the right incentive. Indeed, one industry observer labels this variety-seeking consumer a *brand slut!* A bit harsh, but we get the point.[102]

Brand Loyalty: A "Friend," Tried-and-True

This kind of "promiscuity" will not occur if true brand loyalty exists. In contrast to inertia, **brand loyalty** describes repeat purchasing behavior that reflects a conscious decision to continue buying the same brand.[103] This definition implies that the consumer not only buys the brand on a regular basis, but also has a strong positive attitude toward it rather than simply buying it out of habit. In fact, we often find that a brand-loyal consumer has more than simply a positive attitude; frequently she is passionate about the product. Because of these emotional bonds, "true-blue" users react more vehemently when a company alters, redesigns, or (God forbid) eliminates a favorite brand.[104]

OBJECTIVE 6

Consumers rely on different decision rules when they evaluate competing options.

Decision Rules We Use When We Care

We've seen that we use different rules when we choose among competing products that depend on the complexity of the decision and how important the choice is to us. Sometimes we use a simple heuristic, but at other times we carefully weigh alternatives. We describe the processes we use when we give more thought to these decisions as we divide the rules we use into two categories: *compensatory* and *noncompensatory*. To aid in the discussion of some of these rules, Table 3 summarizes the attributes of the TV sets that Richard considered. Now, let's see how some of these rules result in different brand choices.

We use **noncompensatory decision rules** when we feel that a product with a low standing on one attribute can't compensate for this flaw even if it performs better on another attribute. In other words, we simply eliminate all options that do not meet some basic standards. A consumer like Richard who uses the decision rule, "Only buy well-known brand names," would not consider a new brand, even if it were equal or superior to existing ones. When people are less familiar with a product category or are not very motivated to process complex information, they tend to use simple, noncompensatory rules such as the ones we summarize next.[105]

The Lexicographic Rule. When a person uses the *lexicographic rule*, he selects the brand that is the best on the most important attribute. If he feels that two or more brands are

| TABLE 3 | Hypothetical Alternatives for a TV Set |

Attribute	Importance Ranking	Prime Wave	Precision	Kamashita
Size of screen	1	Excellent	Excellent	Excellent
Stereo broadcast capability	2	Poor	Excellent	Good
Brand reputation	3	Excellent	Excellent	Poor
Onscreen programming	4	Excellent	Poor	Poor
Cable-ready capability	5	Good	Good	Good
Sleep timer	6	Excellent	Poor	Good

Brand Ratings

equally good on that attribute, he then compares them on the second most important attribute. This selection process goes on until the tie is broken. In Richard's case, because both the Prime Wave and Precision models were tied on his most important attribute (a 60-inch screen), he chose the Precision because of its rating on his second most important attribute: its stereo capability.

The Elimination-by-Aspects Rule. Using the *elimination-by-aspects rule*, the buyer also evaluates brands on the most important attribute. In this case, though, he imposes specific cutoffs. For example, if Richard had been more interested in having a sleep timer on his TV (i.e., if it had a higher importance ranking), he might have stipulated that his choice "must have a sleep timer." Because the Prime Wave model had one and the Precision did not, he would have chosen the Prime Wave.

The Conjunctive Rule. Whereas the two former rules involve processing by attribute, the *conjunctive rule* entails processing by brand. As with the elimination-by-aspects procedure, the decision maker establishes cutoffs for each attribute. He chooses a brand if it meets all the cutoffs, but rejects a brand that fails to meet any one cutoff. If none of the brands meet all the cutoffs, he may delay the choice, change the decision rule, or modify the cutoffs he chooses to apply.

If Richard stipulated that all attributes had to be rated "good" or better, he would not have been able to choose any of the available options. He might then have modified his decision rule, conceding that it was not possible to attain these high standards in his price range. In this case, perhaps Richard could decide that he could live without on-screen programming, so he would reconsider the Precision model.

Compensatory Decision Rules

Unlike noncompensatory rules, **compensatory decision rules** give a product a chance to make up for its shortcomings. Consumers who employ these rules tend to be more involved in the purchase, so they're willing to exert the effort to consider the entire picture in a more exacting way.[106]

If we're willing to allow good and bad product qualities to cancel each other out, we arrive at a very different choice. For example, if Richard were not concerned about having stereo reception, he might have chosen the Prime Wave model. But because this brand doesn't feature this highly ranked attribute, it doesn't stand a chance when he uses a noncompensatory rule.

Researchers identify two basic types of compensatory rules. A person uses a *simple additive rule* if he merely chooses the alternative that has the largest number of positive attributes. This is most likely to occur when his ability or motivation to process information is limited. One drawback to this approach for the consumer is that some of these attributes may not be very meaningful or important. An ad that presents a long list of product benefits may be persuasive, despite the fact that many of the benefits it names are actually standard within the product class.

The *weighted additive rule* is a more complex version.[107] When he uses this rule, the consumer also takes into account the relative importance of positively rated attributes, essentially multiplying brand ratings by importance weights.

CHAPTER SUMMARY

Now that you have finished reading this chapter you should understand why:

1. **Consumer decision making is a central part of consumer behavior, but the way we evaluate and choose products (and the amount of thought we put into these choices) varies widely, depending on such dimensions as the degree of novelty or risk related to the decision.**

We almost constantly need to make decisions about products. Some of these decisions are very important and entail great effort, whereas we make others on a virtually automatic basis. The decision-making task is further complicated because of the sheer number of decisions we need to make in a marketplace environment characterized by consumer hyperchoice.

Perspectives on decision making range from a focus on habits that people develop over time to novel situations involving a great deal of risk in which consumers must carefully collect and analyze information before making a choice. Many of our decisions are highly automated; we make them largely by habit. This trend is accelerating as marketers begin to introduce smart products that enable silent commerce, where the products literally make their own purchase decisions (e.g., a malfunctioning appliance that contacts the repair person directly).

2. A decision is actually composed of a series of stages that results in the selection of one product over competing options.

A typical decision process involves several steps. The first is problem recognition, when we realize we must take some action. This recognition may occur because a current possession malfunctions or perhaps because we have a desire for something new.

Once the consumer recognizes a problem and sees it as sufficiently important to warrant some action, he begins the process of information search. This search may range from doing a simple scan of his memory to determine what he's done before to resolve the same problem to extensive fieldwork during which he consults a variety of sources to amass as much information as possible. In many cases, people engage in surprisingly little search. Instead, they rely on various mental shortcuts, such as brand names or price, or they may simply imitate others' choices.

In the evaluation-of-alternatives stage, the product alternatives a person considers constitute his evoked set. Members of the evoked set usually share some characteristics; we categorize them similarly. The way the person mentally groups products influences which alternatives she will consider, and usually we associate some brands more strongly with these categories (i.e., they are more prototypical).

3. Decision making is not always rational.

Research in the field of behavioral economics illustrates that decision making is not always strictly rational.

Principles of mental accounting demonstrate that the way a problem is posed (called *framing*) and whether it is put in terms of gains or losses influences what we decide.

4. Our access to online sources is changing the way we decide what to buy.

The World Wide Web has changed the way many of us search for information. Today, our problem is more likely to weed out excess detail than to search for more information. Comparative search sites and intelligent agents help to filter and guide the search process. We may rely on cybermediaries, such as Web portals, to sort through massive amounts of information as a way to simplify the decision-making process.

5. We often fall back on well-learned "rules-of-thumb" to make decisions.

Very often, we use heuristics, or mental rules-of-thumb, to simplify decision making. In particular, we develop many market beliefs over time. One of the most common beliefs is that we can determine quality by looking at the price. Other heuristics rely on well-known brand names or a product's country of origin as signals of product quality. When we consistently purchase a brand over time, this pattern may be the result of true brand loyalty or simply inertia because it's the easiest thing to do.

6. Consumers rely on different decision rules when evaluating competing options.

When the consumer eventually must make a product choice from among alternatives, he uses one of several decision rules. Noncompensatory rules eliminate alternatives that are deficient on any of the criteria we've chosen. Compensatory rules, which we are more likely to apply in high-involvement situations, allow us to consider each alternative's good and bad points more carefully to arrive at the overall best choice.

KEY TERMS

anchoring
behavioral economics
behavioral influence perspective
blissful ignorance effect
bounded rationality
brand advocates
brand loyalty
category exemplars
cognitive processing style
compensatory decision rules
consideration set
consumer hyperchoice

country of origin
cybermediary
determinant attributes
electronic recommendation agent
ethnocentrism
evaluative criteria
evoked set
experiential perspective
extended problem solving
feature creep
framing
game-based marketing

game platform
genre
habitual decision making
heuristics
hyperopia
incidental brand exposure
inertia
information search
intelligent agents
knowledge structure
limited problem solving
long tail

low-literate consumer	neuromarketing	reputation economy
market beliefs	noncompensatory decision rules	satisficing
maximizing	perceived risk	search engines
mental accounting	problem recognition	Sisyphus Effect
milieu	product signal	social game
MMORPGs (massively multiplayer online role playing games)	prospect theory	variety amnesia
	purchase momentum	variety seeking
mode	rational perspective	Zipf's Law

REVIEW

1 Why do we say that "mindless" decision making can actually be more efficient than devoting a lot of thought to what we buy?

2 List the steps in the model of rational decision making.

3 What is purchase momentum, and how does it relate (or not) to the model of rational decision making?

4 What is the difference between the behavioral influence and experiential perspectives on decision making? Give an example of the type of purchase that each perspective would most likely explain.

5 Name two ways in which a consumer problem arises.

6 Give an example of the sunk-cost fallacy.

7 What is prospect theory? Does it support the argument that we are rational decision makers?

8 Describe the relationship between a consumer's level of expertise and how much she is likely to search for information about a product.

9 List three types of perceived risk, and give an example of each.

10 "Marketers need to be extra sure their product works as promised when they first introduce it." How does this statement relate to what we know about consumers' evoked sets?

11 Describe the difference between a superordinate category, a basic level category, and a subordinate category.

12 What is an example of an exemplar product?

13 List three product attributes that consumers use as product quality signals and provide an example of each.

14 How does a brand name work as a heuristic?

15 Describe the difference between inertia and brand loyalty.

16 What is the difference between a noncompensatory and a compensatory decision rule? Give one example of each.

CONSUMER BEHAVIOR CHALLENGE

■ DISCUSS

1 This chapter argues that for many of today's consumers, it's a bigger problem to have too many choices than to not have enough choices. Do you agree? Is it possible to have too much of a good thing?

2 Commercial Alert, a consumer group, is highly critical of neuromarketing. The group's executive director wrote, "What would happen in this country if corporate marketers and political consultants could literally peer inside our brains and chart the neural activity that leads to our selections in the supermarket and voting booth? What if they then could trigger this neural activity by various means, so as to modify our behavior to serve their own ends?"[108] What do you think? Is neuromarketing dangerous?

3 If people are not always rational decision makers, is it worth the effort to study how they make purchasing decisions? What techniques might marketers employ to understand experiential consumption and translate this knowledge into marketing strategy?

4 Why is it difficult to place a product in a consumer's evoked set after the person has already rejected that product? What strategies might a marketer use to accomplish this goal?

5 Discuss two different noncompensatory decision rules and highlight the difference(s) between them. How might the use of one rule versus another result in a different product choice?

6 What is the future of social gaming? How do you evaluate the potential of these activities for marketing activities?

7 Technology has the potential to make our lives easier as it reduces the amount of clutter we need to work through to access the information on the Internet that really interests us. However, perhaps intelligent agents that make recommendations based only on what we and others like us have chosen in the past limit us, in that they reduce the chance that we will stumble on something (e.g., a book on a topic we've never heard of or a music group that's different from the style we usually listen to) through serendipity. Will the proliferation of "shopping bots" make our lives too predictable by only giving us more of the same? If so, is this a problem?

8 It's increasingly clear that many postings on blogs and product reviews on Web sites are fake or are posted there to manipulate consumers' opinions. How big a problem is this if consumers increasingly look to consumer-generated product reviews to guide their purchase decisions? What steps, if any, can marketers take to nip this problem in the bud?

9 The chapter notes that people respond to very subtle cues in the environment even when they are totally unaware of these effects. Can or should marketers exploit these influences?

■ APPLY

1 Find examples of electronic recommendation agents on the Web. Evaluate these. Are they helpful? What characteristics of the sites you locate are likely to make you buy products you wouldn't have bought on your own?

2 In the past few years, several products made in China (including toothpaste and toys) have been recalled because they are dangerous or even fatal to use. In one survey, about 30 percent of American respondents indicated that they have stopped purchasing some Chinese goods as a result of the recalls or that they usually don't buy products from China.[109] If the Chinese government hired you as a consultant to help it repair some of the damage to the reputation of products made there, what actions would you recommend?

3 Conduct a poll based on the list of market beliefs found in Table 2. Do people agree with these beliefs, and how much do they influence people's decisions?

4 Pepsi invented freshness dating and managed to persuade consumers that this was an important product attribute. Devise a similar strategy for another product category by coming up with a completely new product attribute. How would you communicate this attribute to your customers?

5 Define the three levels of product categorization the chapter describes. Diagram these levels for a health club.

6 Choose a friend or parent who grocery shops on a regular basis and keep a log of his or her purchases of common consumer products during the term. Can you detect any evidence of brand loyalty in any categories based on consistency of purchases? If so, talk to the person about these purchases. Try to determine if his or her choices are based on true brand loyalty or on inertia. What techniques might you use to differentiate between the two?

7 Form a group of three. Pick a product and develop a marketing plan based on each of the three approaches to consumer decision making: rational, experiential, and behavioral

influence. What are the major differences in emphasis among the three perspectives? Which is the most likely type of problem-solving activity for the product you have selected? What characteristics of the product make this so?

8 Locate a person who is about to make a major purchase. Ask that person to make a chronological list of all the information sources he or she consults before deciding what to buy. How would you characterize the types of sources he or she uses (i.e., internal versus external, media versus personal, etc.)? Which sources appeared to have the most impact on the person's decision?

9 Perform a survey of country-of-origin stereotypes. Compile a list of five countries and ask people what products they associate with each. What are their evaluations of the products and likely attributes of these different products? The power of a country stereotype can also be demonstrated in another way. Prepare a brief description of a product, including a list of features, and ask people to rate it in terms of quality, likelihood of purchase, and so on. Make several versions of the description, varying only the country from which it comes. Do ratings change as a function of the country of origin?

10 Ask a friend to "talk through" the process he or she used to choose one brand rather than others during a recent purchase. Based on this description, can you identify the decision rule that he or she most likely employed?

11 Give one of the scenarios described in the section on biases in decision making to 10 to 20 people. How do the results you obtain compare with those reported in this chapter?

12 Think of a product you recently shopped for online. Describe your search process. How did you become aware that you wanted or needed the product? How did you evaluate alternatives? Did you wind up buying online? Why or why not? What factors would make it more or less likely that you would buy something online versus in a traditional store?

Case Study

MAC VS. PC

"Hi, I'm a Mac . . . and I'm a PC." You probably know this successful TV campaign that features a very smart, cool Mac guy and a nerdy PC guy. These ads for Apple's Mac laptops aimed to grab a big chunk of the personal computing business, especially among younger users. Microsoft fired back as the company tried to separate itself from the undesirable PC-guy image. Its first attempt; a quirky campaign featuring comedian Jerry Seinfeld and Windows founder Bill Gates, failed to move the sales needle. Microsoft had more success with the "I'm a PC ads" that featured testimonials

claiming allegiance to PCs from all sorts of PC users, ranging from celebrities to an adorable 4½ year old. Still, it's an uphill battle: For a generation of consumers raised on cool products like the iPod and the iPad, it's a tough sell to shake Apple's spell. Although PCs still have the majority of market share, a growing number of Macs show up on college campuses every fall.

In the spring of 2011, Microsoft tried a new tactic: A student who purchased a PC for $699 or more received a free Xbox. He or she only needed to walk into Best Buy with a college ID or email address, and walk out carrying a PC along with an Xbox with a retail value of approximately $300. Compared to a Mac that starts at $999, this bundle offered an attractive value proposition to students who were also into gaming.

Is this a simple pricing promotion, or part of a more elaborate branding strategy? The Xbox represents the "fun" side of Microsoft's personality, so this bundle might help to reposition Microsoft away from the awkward office-worker stereotype and closer to Apple's cool image among members of this crucial market segment.

Microsoft is still evaluating the results of the promotion. Marketers continue to debate the effectiveness of "free" offers. Assuming that the promotion drives short-term sales of PCs, will it also influence long-term loyalty? What does this bundling mean for the Xbox, the current market leader in gaming consoles within the college market? With a free Xbox as an option in the marketplace, will college students be less willing to pay $300 for a stand-alone Xbox console? Finally, the question remains whether a free console is like a free cell phone from your wireless company, where the revenues come from add-on purchases in the form of talk minutes. Will Microsoft still profit

from those free units through game purchases, online subscriptions, accessories, and loyalty to future Xbox consoles? How will the new tablets that combine features of gaming consoles and laptops affect all of this?

DISCUSSION QUESTIONS

1 What characteristics of extended problem solving are involved in a computer purchase?
2 How might the free Xbox offer influence a consumer's mental accounting and perceived risk?
3 How might Apple be creating a heuristic for its consumers?

Sources: "Microsoft Announces New Back-to-School Offer for Students," www.microsoft.com/presspass/press/2011/may11/05-19mspcXboxpr, accessed July 1, 2011; Priya Raghubir, "Free Gift with Purchase: Promoting or Discounting the Brand?," *Journal of Consumer Psychology* 14 (2004): 181–86; "Console and PC Games—US," Mintel Reports database (October 2010), http://academic.mintel.com.ezproxy.bu.edu, accessed July 1, 2007.

NOTES

1. David Glen Mick, Susan M. Broniarczyk, and Jonathan Haidt, "Choose, Choose, Choose, Choose, Choose, Choose, Choose: Emerging and Prospective Research on the Deleterious Effects of Living in Consumer Hyperchoice," *Journal of Business Ethics* 52 (2004): 207–11; see also Barry Schwartz, *The Paradox of Choice: Why More Is Less* (New York: Ecco, 2005).
2. Simona Botti, Kristina Orfali, and Sheena S. Iyengar, "Tragic Choices: Autonomy and Emotional Responses to Medical Decisions," *Journal of Consumer Research* 36 (October 2009): 337–52; cf. also Hazel Rose Markus and Barry Schwartz, "Does Choice Mean Freedom and Well Being?" *Journal of Consumer Research* 37, no. 2 (2010): 344–55.
3. Itamar Simonson, Joel Huber, and John Payne, "The Relationship between Prior Brand Knowledge and Information Acquisition Order," *Journal of Consumer Research* 14 (March 1988): 566–78.
4. John R. Hauser, Glenn L. Urban, and Bruce D. Weinberg, "How Consumers Allocate Their Time when Searching for Information," *Journal of Marketing Research* 30 (November 1993): 452–66; George J. Stigler, "The Economics of Information," *Journal of Political Economy* 69 (June 1961): 213–25. For a set of studies focusing on online search costs, see John G. Lynch, Jr., and Dan Ariely, "Wine Online: Search Costs and Competition on Price, Quality, and Distribution," *Marketing Science* 19, no. 1 (2000): 83–103.
5. John C. Mowen, "Beyond Consumer Decision-Making," *Journal of Consumer Marketing* 5, no. 1 (1988): 15–25.
6. Richard W. Olshavsky and Donald H. Granbois, "Consumer Decision-Making—Fact or Fiction," *Journal of Consumer Research* 6 (September 1989): 93–100.
7. Ravi Dhar, Joel Huber, and Uzma Khan, "The Shopping Momentum Effect," paper presented at the Association for Consumer Research, Atlanta, GA, October 2002.
8. Thomas P. Novak and Donna L. Hoffman, "The Fit of Thinking Style and Situation: New Measures of Situation-Specific Experiential and Rational Cognition," *Journal of Consumer Research* 36 (December 2009): 56–72.
9. James R. Bettman, "The Decision Maker Who Came in from the Cold" (presidential address), in Leigh McAllister and Michael Rothschild, eds., *Advances in Consumer Research 20* (Provo, UT: Association for Consumer Research, 1993): 7–11; John W. Payne, James R. Bettman, and Eric J. Johnson, "Behavioral Decision Research: A Constructive Processing Perspective," *Annual Review of Psychology* 4 (1992): 87–131. For an overview of recent developments in individual choice models, see Robert J. Meyers and Barbara E. Kahn, "Probabilistic Models of Consumer Choice Behavior," in Thomas S. Robertson and Harold H. Kassarjian, eds., *Handbook of Consumer Behavior* (Upper Saddle River, NJ: Prentice Hall, 1991): 85–123.
10. Mowen, "Beyond Consumer Decision-Making."
11. The Fits-Like-a-Glove (FLAG) framework is a decision-making perspective that views consumer decisions as a holistic process shaped by the person's unique context; cf. Douglas E. Allen, "Toward a Theory of Consumer Choice as Sociohistorically Shaped Practical Experience: The Fits-Like-a-Glove (FLAG) Framework," *Journal of Consumer Research* 28 (March 2002): 515–32.
12. Material in this section is adapted and abridged from Tracy Tuten and Michael R. Solomon, *Social Media Marketing* (Upper Saddle River, NJ: Pearson Education, 2012).
13. Thomas Apperley, "Genre and Game Studies: Toward a Critical Approach to Video Game Genres," *Simulation & Gaming* 37, no. 1 (2006): 6–23.
14. Interactive Advertising Bureau, *IAB Game Advertising Platform Status Report*, http://www.iab.net/media/file/games-reportv4.pdf, accessed May 31, 2011.
15. Apperley, "Genre and Game Studies: Toward a Critical Approach to Video Game Genres."
16. Drew Elliott, "Opportunities for Brands in Social Games," *Ogilvy PR Blog* (May 2010), http://blog.ogilvypr.com/2010/05/opportunities-for-brands-in-social-games/, accessed July 12, 2010.
17. Joseph W. Alba and J. Wesley Hutchinson, "Dimensions of Consumer Expertise," *Journal of Consumer Research* 13 (March 1988): 411–54.
18. Jean Halliday, "With Fusion Campaign, Ford Targets 'Upper Funnel' Car Buyers: $60M to $80M Ad Blitz Aimed at Consumers Not Yet Ready to Buy New Vehicle," *Advertising Age* (March 2, 2009), www.advertisingage.com, accessed March 2, 2009.
19. Gordon C. Bruner, II, and Richard J. Pomazal, "Problem Recognition: The Crucial First Stage of the Consumer Decision Process," *Journal of Consumer Marketing* 5, no. 1 (1988): 53–63.
20. For a study that examined tradeoffs in search behavior among different channels, cf. Judi Strebel, Tulin Erdem, and Joffre Swait, "Consumer Search in High Technology Markets: Exploring the Use of Traditional Information Channels," *Journal of Consumer Psychology* 14, nos. 1 & 2 (2004): 96–104.
21. Peter H. Bloch, Daniel L. Sherrell, and Nancy M. Ridgway, "Consumer Search: An Extended Framework," *Journal of Consumer Research* 13 (June 1986): 119–26.
22. David Leonhardt, "The Neighbors as Marketing Powerhouses," *New York Times* (June 13, 2005), www.nytimes.com, accessed June 13, 2005.
23. Natalie Ross Adkins and Julie L. Ozanne, "The Low Literate Consumer," *Journal of Consumer Research* 32, no. 1 (2005): 93; Madhubalan Viswanathan, José Antonio Rosa, and James Edwin Harris, "Decision-Making and Coping of Functionally Illiterate Consumers and Some Implications for Marketing Management," *Journal of Marketing* 69, no. 1 (2005): 15.
24. Girish Punj, "Presearch Decision-Making in Consumer Durable Purchases," *Journal of Consumer Marketing* 4 (Winter 1987): 71–82.
25. Laurie Peterson, "Study Places Value on Marketing at Consumer Research Stage," *Marketing Daily* (June 27, 2007), www.mediapost.com, accessed June 27, 2007.
26. Greg Sterling, "Search + Social Media Increases CTR by 94 Percent: Report," *Search Engine Land* (February 28, 2011), http://searchengineland.com/search-social-media-increases-ctr-by-94-percent-report-66231?utm_source=feedburner&utm_medium=feed&utm_campaign=Feed%3A+searchengineland+%28Search+Engine+Land%3A+Main+Feed%29, accessed April 30, 2011.
27. Alex Mindlin, "Buyers Search Online, but Not by Brand," *New York Times* (March 13, 2006), www.nytimes.com, accessed March 13, 2006.

28. Francois A. Carrillat, Daniel M. Ladik, and Renaud Legoux, "When the Decision Ball Keeps Rolling: An Investigation of the Sisyphus Effect among Maximizing Consumers," *Marketing Letters* (September 2010): 1–14.

29. Cathy J. Cobb and Wayne D. Hoyer, "Direct Observation of Search Behavior," *Psychology & Marketing* 2 (Fall 1985): 161–79.

30. Sharon E. Beatty and Scott M. Smith, "External Search Effort: An Investigation across Several Product Categories," *Journal of Consumer Research* 14 (June 1987): 83–95; William L. Moore and Donald R. Lehmann, "Individual Differences in Search Behavior for a Nondurable," *Journal of Consumer Research* 7 (December 1980): 296–307.

31. Geoffrey C. Kiel and Roger A. Layton, "Dimensions of Consumer Information Seeking Behavior," *Journal of Marketing Research* 28 (May 1981): 233–39; see also Narasimhan Srinivasan and Brian T. Ratchford, "An Empirical Test of a Model of External Search for Automobiles," *Journal of Consumer Research* 18 (September 1991): 233–42.

32. David F. Midgley, "Patterns of Interpersonal Information Seeking for the Purchase of a Symbolic Product," *Journal of Marketing Research* 20 (February 1983): 74–83.

33. Cyndee Miller, "Scotland to U.S.: 'This Tennent's for You,'" *Marketing News* (August 29, 1994): 26.

34. Jeff Galak, Joseph P. Redden, and Justin Kruger (2009), "Variety Amnesia: Recalling Past Variety Can Accelerate Recovery from Satiation," *Journal of Consumer Research* 36, no. 4 (2009): 575–84.

35. Rebecca K. Ratner, Barbara E. Kahn, and Daniel Kahneman, "Choosing Less-Preferred Experiences for the Sake of Variety," *Journal of Consumer Research* 26 (June 1999): 1–15.

36. Harper A. Roehm and Michelle L. Roehm, "Revisiting the Effect of Positive Mood on Variety Seeking," *Journal of Consumer Research* 32 (September 2005): 330–36; Satya Menon and Barbara E. Kahn, "The Impact of Context on Variety Seeking in Product Choices," *Journal of Consumer Research* 22 (December 1995): 285–95; Barbara E. Kahn and Alice M. Isen, "The Influence of Positive Affect on Variety Seeking among Safe, Enjoyable Products," *Journal of Consumer Research* 20 (September 1993): 257–70.

37. J. Jeffrey Inman, "The Role of Sensory-Specific Satiety in Consumer Variety Seeking among Flavors" (unpublished manuscript, A. C. Nielsen Center for Marketing Research, University of Wisconsin–Madison, July 1999).

38. Steven J. Levitt and Stephen G. Dubner, *Freakonomics: A Rogue Economist Explores the Hidden Side of Everything* (New York, NY: Harper Perennial, 2009); Dan Ariely, *Predictably Irrational: The Hidden Forces That Shape Our Decisions* (New York, NY: HarperCollins, 2008).

39. Beth Snyder Bulik, "Behavioral Economics Helping Marketers Better Understand Consumers Practice Gives Advertisers Insight into Shoppers' Brand Selection," *Ad Age CMO Strategy* (July 26, 2010), http://adage.com/article/cmo-strategy/behavioral-economics-helping-marketers-understand-consumers/145091/, accessed April 17, 2011; cf. also Robin L. Soster, Ashwani Monga and William O. Bearden, "Tracking Costs of Time and Money: How Accounting Periods Affect Mental Accounting," *Journal of Consumer Research* 37, no. 4 (2010): 712–21.

40. Quoted in John Tierney, "Oversaving, a Burden for Our Times," *New York Times* (March 23, 2009), www.nytimes.com/2009/03/24/science/24tier.html?_r=1, accessed March 23, 2009.

41. Gary Belsky, "Why Smart People Make Major Money Mistakes," *Money* (July 1995): 76; Richard Thaler and Eric J. Johnson, "Gambling with the House Money or Trying to Break Even: The Effects of Prior Outcomes on Risky Choice," *Management Science* 36 (June 1990): 643–60; Richard Thaler, "Mental Accounting and Consumer Choice," *Marketing Science* (Summer 1985): 199–214.

42. Daniel Kahneman and Amos Tversky, "Prospect Theory: An Analysis of Decision under Risk," *Econometrica* 47 (March 1979): 263–91; Timothy B. Heath, Subimal Chatterjee, and Karen Russo France, "Mental Accounting and Changes in Price: The Frame Dependence of Reference Dependence," *Journal of Consumer Research* 22, no. 1 (June 1995): 90–97.

43. Peter Lieberman and David Pizarro, "All Politics Is Olfactory," *New York Times* (October 23, 2010), http://www.nytimes.com/2010/10/24/opinion/24pizarro.html?_r=1&ref=todayspaper, accessed April 29, 2011.

44. Thaler, "Mental Accounting and Consumer Choice," p. 206.

45. Girish N. Punj and Richard Staelin, "A Model of Consumer Search Behavior for New Automobiles," *Journal of Consumer Research* 9 (March 1983): 366–80. For recent work on online search that decomposes search strategies in terms of type of good, cf. Peng Huang, Nicholas H. Lurie, and Sabyasachi Mitra, "Searching for Experience on the Web: An Empirical Examination of Consumer Behavior for Search and Experience Goods," *Journal of Marketing*, 73 (March 2009), 55–69.

46. Cobb and Hoyer, "Direct Observation of Search Behavior"; Moore and Lehmann, "Individual Differences in Search Behavior for a Nondurable"; Punj and Staelin, "A Model of Consumer Search Behavior for New Automobiles"; Brian T. Ratchford, M. S. Lee, and D. Toluca, "The Impact of the Internet on Information Search for Automobiles," *Journal of Marketing Research* 40, no. 2 (2003): 193–209.

47. James R. Bettman and C. Whan Park, "Effects of Prior Knowledge and Experience and Phase of the Choice Process on Consumer Decision Processes: A Protocol Analysis," *Journal of Consumer Research* 7 (December 1980): 234–48.

48. Alina Tugend, "Some Blissful Ignorance Can Cure Chronic Buyer's Remorse," *New York Times* (March 15, 2008), www.nytimes.com/2008/03/15/Business/15shortcuts.Html?Scp=1&Sq=Tugend&St=Nyt, accessed March 15, 2008.

49. Alba and Hutchinson, "Dimensions of Consumer Expertise"; Bettman and Park, "Effects of Prior Knowledge and Experience and Phase of the Choice Process on Consumer Decision Processes"; Merrie Brucks, "The Effects of Product Class Knowledge on Information Search Behavior," *Journal of Consumer Research* 12 (June 1985): 1–16; Joel E. Urbany, Peter R. Dickson, and William L. Wilkie, "Buyer Uncertainty and Information Search," *Journal of Consumer Research* 16 (September 1989): 208–15.

50. For an interpretive treatment of risk, cf. Craig J. Thompson, "Consumer Risk Perceptions in a Community of Reflexive Doubt," *Journal of Consumer Research* 32, no. 2 (2005): 235.

51. Mary Frances Luce, James R. Bettman, and John W. Payne, "Choice Processing in Emotionally Difficult Decisions," *Journal of Experimental Psychology: Learning, Memory, & Cognition* 23 (March 1997): 384–405; example provided by Professor James Bettman, personal communication (December 17, 1997).

52. Some research suggests that structural elements of the information available, such as the number and distribution of attribute levels, will influence how items in a consideration set are processed; cf. Nicholas H. Lurie, "Decision-Making in Information-Rich Environments: The Role of Information Structure," *Journal of Consumer Research* 30 (March 2004): 473–86.

53. John R. Hauser and Birger Wernerfelt, "An Evaluation Cost Model of Consideration Sets," *Journal of Consumer Research* 16 (March 1990): 393–408.

54. Robert J. Sutton, "Using Empirical Data to Investigate the Likelihood of Brands Being Admitted or Readmitted into an Established Evoked Set," *Journal of the Academy of Marketing Science* 15 (Fall 1987): 82.

55. Cf., for example, Kenneth C. Manning and David E. Sprott, "Price Endings, Left-Digit Effects, and Choice," *Journal of Consumer Research* 36, no. 2 (2009): 328–35; Sandra J. Milberg, Francisca Sinn, and Ronald C. Goodstein, "Consumer Reactions to Brand Extensions in a Competitive Context: Does Fit Still Matter?" *Journal of Consumer Research* 37, no. 3 (2010): 543–53; David Sleeth-Keppler and Christian S. Wheeler, "A Multidimensional Association Approach to Sequential Consumer Judgments," *Journal of Consumer Psychology* 21, no. 1 (2011): 14–23; Aner Sela, Jonah Berger, and Wendy Liu, "Variety, Vice, and Virtue: How Assortment Size Influences Option Choice," *Journal of Consumer Research* 35, no. 6 (2009): 941–51.

56. Stuart Elliott, "A Brand Tries to Invite Thought," *New York Times* (September 7, 2007), www.nytimes.com, accessed September 7, 2007.

57. Cyndee Miller, "Hemp Is Latest Buzzword," *Marketing News* (March 17, 1997): 1.

58. Alba and Hutchison, "Dimensions of Consumer Expertise"; Joel B. Cohen and Kunal Basu, "Alternative Models of Categorization: Toward a Contingent Processing Framework," *Journal of Consumer Research* 13 (March 1987): 455–72.

59. Robert M. McMath, "The Perils of Typecasting," *American Demographics* (February 1997): 60.

60. Eleanor Rosch, "Principles of Categorization," in E. Rosch and B. B. Lloyd, eds., *Recognition and Categorization* (Hillsdale, NJ: Erlbaum, 1978); cf. also Joseph Lajos, Zsolt Katona, Amitava Chattopadhyay, and Miklos Savary, "Category Activation Model: A Spreading Activation Network Model of Subcategory Positioning when Categorization Uncertainty Is High," *Journal of Consumer Research* 36, no. 1 (June 2009): 122–36.

61. Michael R. Solomon, "Mapping Product Constellations: A Social Categorization Approach to Symbolic Consumption," *Psychology & Marketing* 5, no. 3 (1988): 233–58.

62. McMath, "The Perils of Typecasting."

63. Elizabeth C. Hirschman and Michael R. Solomon, "Competition and Cooperation among Culture Production Systems," in Ronald F. Bush and Shelby D. Hunt, eds., *Marketing Theory: Philosophy of Science Perspectives* (Chicago: American Marketing Association, 1982): 269–72.

64. Michael D. Johnson, "The Differential Processing of Product Category and Noncomparable Choice Alternatives," *Journal of Consumer Research* 16 (December 1989): 300–39.

65. Mita Sujan, "Consumer Knowledge: Effects on Evaluation Strategies Mediating Consumer Judgments," *Journal of Consumer Research* 12 (June 1985): 31–46.

66. Rosch, "Principles of Categorization."

67. Joan Meyers-Levy and Alice M. Tybout, "Schema Congruity as a Basis for Product Evaluation," *Journal of Consumer Research* 16 (June 1989): 39–55.

68. Mita Sujan and James R. Bettman, "The Effects of Brand Positioning Strategies on Consumers' Brand and Category Perceptions: Some Insights from Schema Research," *Journal of Marketing Research* 26 (November 1989): 454–67.

69. See William P. Putsis, Jr., and Narasimhan Srinivasan, "Buying or Just Browsing? The Duration of Purchase Deliberation," *Journal of Marketing Research* 31 (August 1994): 393–402.

70. Robert E. Smith, "Integrating Information from Advertising and Trial: Processes and Effects on Consumer Response to Product Information," *Journal of Marketing Research* 30 (May 1993): 204–19.

71. Ronald Alsop, "How Boss's Deeds Buff a Firm's Reputation," *Wall Street Journal* (January 31, 2007): B1.

72. Jack Trout, "Marketing in Tough Times," *Boardroom Reports* 2 (October 1992): 8.

73. Stuart Elliott, "Pepsi-Cola to Stamp Dates for Freshness on Soda Cans," *New York Times* (March 31, 1994): D1; Emily DeNitto, "Pepsi's Gamble Hits Freshness Dating Jackpot," *Advertising Age* (September 19, 1994): 50.

74. Examples provided by Dr. William Cohen, personal communication, October 1999.

75. Natasha Singer, "Making Ads That Whisper to the Brain," *New York Times* (November 13, 2010), http://www.nytimes.com/2010/11/14/business/14stream.html?_r=1&ref=technology, accessed April 17, 2011; Martin Reimann, Andreas Aholt, Carolin Neuhaus, Thorsten Teichert, and Bernd Weber, "On the Use of Functional Magnetic Resonance Imaging in Consumer Research: Review, Procedures and Own Empirical Results" (unpublished manuscript, 2009); Robert Lee Hotz, "Searching for the Why of Buy," *Los Angeles Times Online* (February 27, 2005), www.latimes.com/news/science/la-sci-brain27feb27,0,3899978.story?coll=la-home-headlines; Sandra Blakeslee, "If You Have a 'Buy Button' in Your Brain, What Pushes It?" *New York Times* (October 19, 2004), www.nytimes.com, accessed October 19, 2004; Clive Thompson, "There's a Sucker Born in Every Medial Prefrontal Cortex," *New York Times* (October 26, 2003), www.nytimes.com, accessed September 29, 2007.

76. www.neurosciencemarketing.com/blog, accessed June 7, 2009; Hotz, "Searching for the Why of Buy"; Blakeslee, "If You Have a 'Buy Button' in Your Brain, What Pushes It?"; Thompson, "There's a Sucker Born in Every Medial Prefrontal Cortex."

77. Michael Porter, *Competitive Advantage* (New York: Free Press, 1985).

78. Linda Stern, "Wanna Deal? Click Here," *Newsweek* (March 22, 2004): 65.

79. Material in this section was adapted from Michael R. Solomon and Elnora W. Stuart, *Welcome to Marketing.com: The Brave New World of E-Commerce* (Upper Saddle River, NJ: Prentice Hall, 2001).

80. "Customer Product Reviews Drive Online Satisfaction and Conversion," *Marketing Daily* (January 24, 2007), www.mediapost.com, accessed January 24, 2007.

81. Chris Anderson, *The Long Tail: Why the Future of Business Is Selling Less of More* (New York: Hyperion, 2006).

82. Jeffrey M. O'Brien, "You're Soooooooo Predictable," *Fortune* (November 27, 2006): 230.

83. Joseph Lajos, Amitava Chattopadhyay, and Kishore Sengupta, "When Electronic Recommendation Agents Backfire: Negative Effects on Choice Satisfaction, Attitudes, and Purchase Intentions," *INSEAD Working Paper Series* (2009).

84. Emily Burg, "Leverage User-Generated Content to Boost Brands," *Marketing Daily* (March 13, 2007), www.mediapost.com, accessed March 13, 2007.

85. Sangkil Moon, Paul K. Bergey, and Dawn Iacobucci, "Dynamic Effects among Movie Ratings, Movie Revenues, and Viewer Satisfaction," *Journal of Marketing* 74 (January 2010): 108–21; http://www.yelp.com/search?find_desc=restaurants&find_loc=Philadelphia%2C+PA&action_search=Search, accessed May 31, 2011; Anya Kamenetz, "The Perils and Promise of the Reputation Economy," *Fast Company* (December 3, 2008), www.fastcompany.com/magazine/131/on-the-internet-everyone-knows-youre-a-dog.html, accessed December 3, 2008.

86. Laurie J. Flynn, "Like This? You'll Hate That (Not All Web Recommendations Are Welcome)," *New York Times* (January 23, 2006), www.nytimes.com, accessed January 23, 2006. For fairly recent work that uses consumers' self-reported need for cognition as a moderator of heuristic usage, cf. Aimee Drolet, Mary Frances Luce, and Itamar Simonson, "When Does Choice Reveal Preference? Moderators of Heuristic vs. Goal Based Choice," *Journal of Consumer Research* (June 2009): 137–47.

87. Robert A. Baron, *Psychology: The Essential Science* (Boston: Allyn & Bacon, 1989); Valerie S. Folkes, "The Availability Heuristic and Perceived Risk," *Journal of Consumer Research* 15 (June 1989): 13–23; Kahneman and Tversky, "Prospect Theory: An Analysis of Decision under Risk."

88. Wayne D. Hoyer, "An Examination of Consumer Decision-Making for a Common Repeat Purchase Product," *Journal of Consumer Research* 11 (December 1984): 822–29; Calvin P. Duncan, "Consumer Market Beliefs: A Review of the Literature and an Agenda for Future Research," in Marvin E. Goldberg, Gerald Gorn, and Richard W. Pollay, eds., *Advances in Consumer Research 17* (Provo, UT: Association for Consumer Research, 1990): 729–35; Frank Alpert, "Consumer Market Beliefs and Their Managerial Implications: An Empirical Examination," *Journal of Consumer Marketing* 10, no. 2 (1993): 56–70.

89. Michael R. Solomon, Sarah Drenan, and Chester A. Insko, "Popular Induction: When Is Consensus Information Informative?" *Journal of Personality* 49, no. 2 (1981): 212–24.

90. Beales et al., "Consumer Search and Public Policy," *Journal of Consumer Research* 8 (1981), 1 (June): 11–22.

91. Gary T. Ford and Ruth Ann Smith, "Inferential Beliefs in Consumer Evaluations: An Assessment of Alternative Processing Strategies," *Journal of Consumer Research* 14 (December 1987): 363–71; Deborah Roedder John, Carol A. Scott, and James R. Bettman, "Sampling Data for Covariation Assessment: The Effects of Prior Beliefs on Search Patterns," *Journal of Consumer Research* 13 (June 1986): 38–47; Gary L. Sullivan and Kenneth J. Berger, "An Investigation of the Determinants of Cue Utilization," *Psychology & Marketing* 4 (Spring 1987): 63–74.

92. Adriana V. Madzharov and Lauren G. Block, "Effects of Product Unit Image on Consumption of Snack Foods," *Journal of Consumer Psychology* 20, no. 4 (2010): 398–409.

93. John, Scott, and Bettman, "Sampling Data for Covariation Assessment."

94. Duncan, "Consumer Market Beliefs."

95. Chr. Hjorth-Andersen, "Price as a Risk Indicator," *Journal of Consumer Policy* 10 (1987): 267–81; David M. Gardner, "Is There a Generalized Price-Quality Relationship?," *Journal of Marketing Research* 8 (May 1971): 241–43; Kent B. Monroe, "Buyers' Subjective Perceptions of Price," *Journal of Marketing Research* 10 (1973): 70–80.

96. Katy McLaughlin, "Shrimp Gets a Makeover, As Foreign Imports Rise U.S. Fishermen Try Giving Prawns Regional Identities," *Wall Street Journal* (August 19, 2004): D1.

97. Rohit Varman and Russell W. Belk, "Nationalism and Ideology in an Anti-Consumption Movement," *Journal of Consumer Research* 36 (December 2009): 686–700.

98. Items excerpted from Terence A. Shimp and Subhash Sharma, "Consumer Ethnocentrism: Construction and Validation of the CETSCALE," *Journal of Marketing Research* 24 (August 1987): 282.

99. See Sung-Tai Hong and Dong Kyoon Kang, "Country-of-Origin Influences on Product Evaluations: The Impact of Animosity and Perceptions of Industriousness Brutality on Judgments of Typical and Atypical Products," *Journal of Consumer Psychology* 16, no. 3, (2006): 232–39; Richard Jackson Harris, Bettina Garner-Earl, Sara J. Sprick, and Collette Carroll, "Effects of Foreign Product Names and Country-of-Origin Attributions on Advertisement Evaluations," *Psychology & Marketing* 11 (March–April 1994): 129–45; Terence A. Shimp, Saeed Samiee, and Thomas J. Madden, "Countries and Their Products: A Cognitive Structure Perspective," *Journal of the Academy of Marketing Science* 21 (Fall 1993): 323–30; Durairaj Maheswaran, "Country of Origin as a Stereotype: Effects of Consumer Expertise and Attribute Strength on Product Evaluations," *Journal of Consumer Research* 21 (September 1994): 354–65; Ingrid M. Martin and Sevgin Eroglu, "Measuring a Multi-Dimensional Construct: Country Image," *Journal of Business Research* 28 (1993): 191–210; Richard Ettenson, Janet Wagner, and Gary Gaeth, "Evaluating the Effect of Country of Origin and the 'Made in the U.S.A.' Campaign: A Conjoint Approach," *Journal of Retailing* 64 (Spring 1988): 85–100; C. Min Han and Vern Terpstra, "Country-of-Origin Effects for Uni-National and Bi-National Products," *Journal of International Business* 19 (Summer 1988): 235–55; Michelle A. Morganosky and Michelle M. Lazarde, "Foreign-Made Apparel: Influences on Consumers' Perceptions of Brand and Store Quality," *International Journal of Advertising* 6 (Fall 1987): 339–48.

100. Adam Bryant, "Message in a Beer Bottle," *Newsweek* (May 29, 2000): 43.

101. Richard W. Stevenson, "The Brands with Billion-Dollar Names," *New York Times* (October 28, 1988): A1; Eric Pfanner, "Zipf's Law, or the Considerable Value of Being Top Dog, as Applied to Branding," *New York Times* (May 21, 2007); Ronald Alsop, "Enduring Brands Hold Their Allure by Sticking Close to Their Roots," *Wall Street Journal*, centennial ed. (1989): B4.

102. Greg Morago, "The Brand Sluts—Many Who Covet Their Retailers' Garb No Longer Look at the Logo," *Hartford Courant on the Web* (January 1, 2007). http://articles.courant.com/2007-01-01/features/0701010538_1_brand-envy-trend, accessed September 10, 2011.

103. Jacob Jacoby and Robert Chestnut, *Brand Loyalty: Measurement and Management* (New York: Wiley, 1978).

104. Ibid.

105. C. Whan Park, "The Effect of Individual and Situation-Related Factors on Consumer Selection of Judgmental Models," *Journal of Marketing Research* 13 (May 1976): 144–51.

106. For an examination of cultural differences in analytical versus holistic attribute evaluation, cf. Alokparna Basu Monga and Deborah Roedder John. "Cultural Differences in Brand Extension Evaluation: The Influence of Analytic versus Holistic Thinking." *Journal of Consumer Research* 33 (March 2007): 529–36.

107. Joseph W. Alba and Howard Marmorstein, "The Effects of Frequency Knowledge on Consumer Decision-Making," *Journal of Consumer Research* 14 (June 1987): 14–25.

108. Blakeslee, "If You Have a 'Buy Button' in Your Brain, What Pushes It?"

109. "Americans Are Open to Chinese Goods, Poll Finds," *New York Times* (October 22, 2007), www.nytimes.com/2007/10/22/business/22bizpoll.html?ex=1350705600&en=1615df5334b6437f&ei=5088&partner=rssnyt&emc=rss, accessed October 22, 2007.

Buying and Disposing

Buying and Disposing

When you finish reading this chapter you will understand why:

1. Many factors at the time of purchase dramatically influence the consumer's decision-making process.

2. The information a store or Web site provides strongly influences a purchase decision, in addition to what a shopper already knows or believes about a product.

3. A salesperson often is the crucial connection to a purchase.

4. Marketers need to be concerned about a consumer's evaluations of a product after he or she buys it as well as before.

5. Getting rid of products when consumers no longer need or want them is a major concern both to marketers and to public policymakers.

MyMarketingLab

Visit **www.mymktlab.com** to find activities that help you learn and review in order to succeed in this chapter.

Source: MANDY GODBEHEAR/Shutterstock.

Kyle is really psyched. The big day has actually arrived: He's going to buy a car! He's had his eye on that silver 2005 Oldsmobile Alero parked in the lot of Jon's Auto-Rama for weeks now. Although the sticker says $2,999, Kyle figures he can probably get this baby for a cool $2,000; now that GM has discontinued the Oldsmobile mark as part of its efforts to remake itself as a lean, mean car company, many people will figure that parts will be hard to find. Besides, Jon's dilapidated showroom and seedy lot make it look like just the kind of place that's hungry to move some cars.

Kyle did his homework on the Web. First he found out the wholesale value of similar used Aleros from the Kelley Blue Book (*kbb.com*), and then he scouted out some cars for sale in his area at *cars .com*. So, Kyle figures he's coming in loaded for bear—he's going to show these guys they're not dealing with some rube.

Unlike some of the newer, flashy car showrooms he's been in lately, this place is a real nuts-and-bolts operation; it's so dingy and depressing he can't wait to get out of there and take a shower. Kyle dreads the prospect of haggling over the price, but he hopes to convince the salesperson to take his offer because he knows the real market value of the car he wants. At the Auto-Rama lot, big signs on all the cars proclaim that today is Jon's Auto-Rama Rip Us Off Day! Things look better than Kyle expected—maybe he can get the car for even less than he hoped. He's a bit surprised when a salesperson comes over to him and introduces herself as Rhoda. He expected to deal with a middle-aged man in a loud sport coat (a stereotype he has about used-car salespeople), but this is more good luck: He reasons that he won't have to be so tough if he negotiates with a woman his age.

Rhoda laughs when he offers her $1,800 for the Olds; she points out that she can't take such a low bid for such a sweet car to her boss or she'll lose her job. Rhoda's enthusiasm for the car convinces Kyle all the more that he has to have it. When he finally writes a check for $2,700, he's exhausted from all the haggling. What an ordeal! In any case, Kyle reminds himself that he at least convinced Rhoda to sell him the car for less than the sticker price, and maybe he can fix it up and sell it for even more in a year or two. That Web surfing really paid off: He's a tougher negotiator than he thought.

OBJECTIVE 1

Many factors at the time of purchase dramatically influence the consumer's decision-making process.

Situational Effects on Consumer Behavior

Even in today's buyer's market, many consumers dread the act of buying a car. In fact, a survey by Yankelovich Partners found that this transaction is the most anxiety-provoking and least satisfying of any retail experience.[1] But change is in the wind, as dealers transform the car showroom. Car shoppers like Kyle log onto Internet buying services, call auto brokers who negotiate for them, buy cars at warehouse clubs, and visit giant auto malls where they can easily comparison-shop.

Kyle's experience when he bought a car illustrates some of the concepts we'll discuss in this chapter. Making a purchase is often not a simple, routine matter where you just pop into a store and make a quick choice. As Figure 1 illustrates, many contextual factors affect our choice, such as our mood, whether we feel time pressure to make the purchase, and the particular reason we need the product. In some situations, such as when we buy a car or a home, the salesperson or realtor plays a pivotal role in our final selection. Also, people today often use the Web to arm themselves with product and price information before they even enter a dealership or a store; this puts more pressure on retailers to deliver the value their customers expect.

But the sale doesn't end at the time of purchase. A lot of important consumer activity occurs after we bring a product home. Once we use a product, we have to decide whether we're satisfied with it. The satisfaction process is especially important to savvy marketers who realize that the key to success is not to sell a product *one* time, but rather to forge a relationship with the consumer so that he will come back for more. Finally, just as Kyle thought about the resale value of his car, we must also consider how consumers dispose of products and how we often rely on secondary markets (e.g., used-car dealers) to obtain what we want. We'll consider these issues in this chapter.

A *consumption situation* includes a buyer, a seller, and a product or service—but also many other factors, such as the reason we want to make a purchase and how the physical environment makes us feel.[2] Common sense tells us that we tailor our purchases to specific occasions and that the way we feel at a specific point in time affects what we want to do—or buy. Smart marketers understand these patterns and plan their efforts to coincide with situations in which we are most prone to purchase. For example, book clubs invest heavily in promotional campaigns in June because many people want to stock up on "beach books" to read during the summer; for the same reason, we get tons of featured fun fiction books for our Kindles and Nooks in April and May. Our moods even change radically during the day, so at different times we might be more or less interested in what a marketer offers. Social media platforms also are looking at ways to adapt quickly to situational changes. Facebook is testing ads targeted in real time based on users' status updates ("What's on your mind?") and wall posts. Theoretically, a user who posts near the end of his workday that "It's Miller time" could immediately be served a promotion from MillerCoors or another beer company.[3]

A study used a technique researchers call the *day reconstruction method* to track these changes. More than 900 working women kept diaries of everything they did during the day, from reading the paper in the morning to falling asleep in front of the TV at night. The next day they relived each diary entry and rated how they felt at the time (annoyed, happy, etc.). Overall, researchers found that the study participants woke up a little grumpy but soon entered a state of mild pleasure. This mood increased by degrees through the day, though it was punctuated by occasional bouts of anxiety, frustration, and anger. Not surprisingly, the subjects were least happy when they engaged in mundane activities

Figure 1 ISSUES RELATED TO PURCHASE AND POSTPURCHASE ACTIVITIES

like commuting to work and doing housework, whereas they rated sex, socializing with friends, and relaxing as most enjoyable. Contrary to prior findings, however, the women were happier when they watched television than when they shopped or talked on the phone. They ranked taking care of children low, below cooking and not far above housework. The good news: Overall, people seem to be pretty happy, and these ratings aren't influenced very much by factors such as household income or job security. By far, the two factors that most upset daily moods were a poor night's sleep and tight work deadlines.[4]

In addition to the functional relationships between products and usage situation, another reason to take environmental circumstances seriously is that a person's *situational self-image*—the role she plays at any one time—helps to determine what she wants to buy or consume.[5] A guy who tries to impress his date as he plays the role of "man-about-town" may spend more lavishly, order champagne instead of beer, and buy flowers—purchases he would never consider when he hangs out with his friends, slurps beer, and plays the role of "one of the boys." Let's see how these dynamics affect the way people think about what they buy.

If we systematically identify important usage situations, we can tailor market segmentation strategies to ensure that our offerings meet the specific needs these situations create. For example, we often tailor our furniture choices to specific settings. We prefer different styles for a city apartment, a beach house, or an executive suite. Similarly, we distinguish motorcycles in terms of how riders use them, including commuting, riding them as dirt bikes, or on a farm versus highway travel.[6]

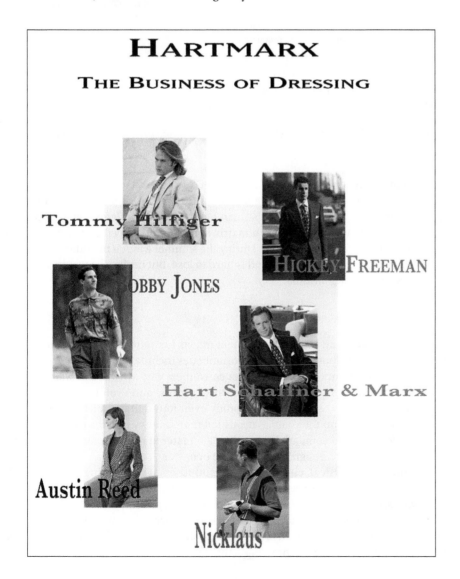

Clothing choices are often heavily influenced by the situation in which we need to wear them.

Source: Courtesy of Hart Schaffner Marx/Hartmarx.

TABLE 1 A Person-Situation Segmentation Matrix for Suntan Lotion

Situation	Young Children		Teenagers		Adult Women		Adult Men		Benefits/Features
	Fair Skin	Dark Skin	Fair Skin	Dark Skin	Fair Skin	Dark Skin	Fair Skin	Dark Skin	
Beach/boat sunbathing	Combined insect repellent				Summer perfume				a. Product serves as windburn protection b. Formula and container can stand heat c. Container floats and is distinctive (not easily lost)
Home-poolside sunbathing					Combined moisturizer				a. Product has large pump dispenser b. Product won't stain wood, concrete, furnishings
Sunlamp bathing					Combined moisturizer and massage oil				a. Product is designed specifically for type of lamp b. Product has an artificial tanning ingredient
Snow skiing					Winter perfume				a. Product provides special protection from special light rays and weather b. Product has antifreeze formula
Person benefit/ features	Special protection a. Protection is critical b. Formula is non-poisonous		Special protection a. Product fits in jean pocket b. Product used by opinion leaders		Special protection Female perfume		Special protection Male perfume		

Source: Adapted from Peter R. Dickson, "Person-Situation: Segmentation's Missing Link," *Journal of Marketing* 46 (Fall 1982): 62. By permission of American Marketing Association.

Table 1 gives one example of how a marketer fine-tunes its segmentation strategy to the usage situation. When we list the major contexts in which people use a product (e.g., snow skiing and sunbathing for a suntan lotion) and the different types of people who use the product, we can construct a matrix that identifies specific product features we should emphasize for each situation. During the summer a lotion manufacturer might promote the fact that the bottle floats and is hard to lose, but during the winter season it could tout its nonfreezing formula.

Our Social and Physical Surroundings

A consumer's physical and social environment affects her motives to use a product, as well as how she will evaluate the item. Important cues include her immediate environment as well as the amount and type of other consumers who are there as well. Dimensions of the physical environment, such as decor, odors, and even temperature, can significantly influence consumption. One study even found that if a Las Vegas casino pumped certain odors into the room, patrons fed more money into the slot machines![7] We'll take a closer look at some of these factors a bit later in this chapter when we consider how important store design is to consumer behavior.

In addition to physical cues, though, groups or social settings significantly affect many of our purchase decisions. In some cases, the sheer presence or absence of **co-consumers**, the other patrons in a setting, actually is a product attribute; think about an exclusive resort or boutique that promises to provide privacy to privileged customers. At other times, the presence of others can have positive value. A sparsely attended ball game or an empty bar can be a depressing sight.

Have you ever experienced a panicky feeling if you're trapped in the middle of a big crowd? The presence of large numbers of people in a consumer environment increases *physiological arousal levels*, so our experiences are more intense. This boost, however, can be positive or negative; the experience depends on how we *interpret* this arousal. It is important to distinguish between *density* and *crowding* for this reason. The former term refers to the actual number of people who occupy a space; whereas the unpleasant psychological state of crowding exists only if a negative affective state occurs as a result of this density.[8] For example, 100 students packed into a classroom designed for 75 may result in an unpleasant situation for all, but the same number of people jammed together at a party—and who occupy a room of the same size—might just make for a great time. Indeed, one recent study even suggests that crowded consumers react by making more varied and unique choices in a store setting, perhaps as a way to rebel against feeling confined.[9]

In addition, the *type* of consumers who patronize a store or service or who use a product affects our evaluations. We often infer something about a store when we examine its customers. For this reason, some restaurants require men to wear jackets for dinner (and supply rather tacky ones if they don't), and bouncers at some "hot" nightspots handpick people who wait in line based on whether they have the right "look" for the club. To paraphrase the comedian Groucho Marx, "I would never join a club that would have me as a member!"

Net Profit

Geospatial applications such as Foursquare and Gowalla now make patronizing a place repeatedly into a sport. Avid users compete to check in as many times as they can to earn the title of "Mayor." Now, some smart retailers are figuring out that it makes sense to reward others who check in, even if they don't win this coveted honor. Recently 60 merchants, including Whole Foods and Starwood Hotels, partnered with American Express to offer cash rewards to customers who check in on Foursquare and buy something at the store. Although these platforms have yet to catch on among most of the mainstream public, certainly other location-aware mobile services (such as GPS navigation, weather alerts, and store locators) are already widely accepted. Indeed, already more than half of American consumers who own devices with GPS capability use them for these purposes—and already a third of this group have already applied them for purchasing and e-coupons. One app, ShopKick, has been adopted by retailers such as American Eagle, Macy's, Sports Authority, and Target, and it already boasts more than 1 million active users.[10]

Temporal Factors

Time is one of consumers' most precious resources. We talk about "making time" or "spending time" and we frequently remind others that "time is money." Common sense tells us that we think more about what we want to buy when we have the luxury to take our time. Even a normally meticulous shopper who never buys before she compares prices might sprint through the mall at 9:00 P.M. on Christmas Eve to scoop up anything left on the shelves if she needs a last-minute gift. The same logic applies to online marketing; **open rates** (the percentage of people who open an email message from a marketer) vary throughout the day. The peak time for high open rates: mid-day on weekdays (presumably when all those people at work take a lunch break).[11]

Economic Time

Time is an economic variable; it is a resource that we must divide among our activities.[12] We try to maximize satisfaction when we allocate our time to different tasks. Of course, people's allocation decisions differ; we all know people who seem to play all of the time, and others who are workaholics. An individual's priorities determine his **timestyle**.[13] People in different countries also "spend" this resource at different rates. A social scientist compared the pace of life in 31 cities around the world as part of a study on timestyles.[14]

He and his assistants timed how long it takes pedestrians to walk 60 feet and the time postal clerks take to sell a stamp. Based on these responses, he claims that the fastest and slowest countries are:

Fastest countries—(1) Switzerland, (2) Ireland, (3) Germany, (4) Japan, (5) Italy

Slowest countries—(31) Mexico, (30) Indonesia, (29) Brazil, (28) El Salvador, (27) Syria

Many consumers believe they are more pressed for time than ever before; marketers label this feeling **time poverty**. The problem appears to be more perception than fact. The reality is that we simply have more options for spending our time, so we feel pressured by the weight of all of these choices. The average working day at the turn of the 19th century was 10 hours (6 days per week), and women did 27 hours of housework per week, compared to less than 5 hours weekly now. Of course, there are plenty of husbands who share these burdens more, and in some families it's not as important as it used to be to maintain an absolutely spotless home as our values change. Ironically, though husbands do help out a lot more than they used to, married women spend a lot more time on housework than do single women (having kids to take care of figures in there). Married men and single women do roughly the same amount each week and (surprise!) single men average the least time of anyone (about 7 to 8 hours per week). Still, about a third of Americans report always feeling rushed, up from 25 percent of the population in 1964.[15]

Psychological Time

"Time flies when you're having fun," but other situations (like some classes?) seem to last forever. Our experience of time is very subjective; our immediate priorities and needs determine how quickly time flies. It's important for marketers to understand the fluidity of time because we're more likely to be in a consuming mood at some times than at others.

A study examined how the timestyles of a group of American women influence their consumption choices.[16] The researchers identified four dimensions of time: (1) the *social dimension* refers to individuals' categorization of time as either "time for me" or "time with/for others"; (2) the *temporal orientation dimension* depicts the relative significance individuals attach to past, present, or future; (3) the *planning orientation dimension* alludes to different time management styles varying on a continuum from analytic to spontaneous; and (4) the *polychronic orientation dimension* distinguishes between people who prefer to do one thing at a time from those who have multitasking timestyles. After they interviewed and observed these women, the researchers identified a set of five metaphors that they say capture the participants' perspectives on time:

- **Time is a pressure cooker**—These women are usually analytical in their planning, other-oriented, and monochronic in their timestyles. They treat shopping in a methodical manner and they often feel under pressure and in conflict.
- **Time is a map**—These women are usually analytical planners; they exhibit a future temporal orientation and a polychronic timestyle. They often engage in extensive information search and comparison-shop.
- **Time is a mirror**—Women in this group are also analytic planners and have a polychronic orientation. However, they have a past temporal orientation. Because of their risk averseness in time use, these women are usually loyal to products and services they know and trust. They prefer convenience-oriented products.
- **Time is a river**—These women are usually spontaneous in their planning orientation and have a present focus. They go on unplanned, short, and frequent shopping trips.
- **Time is a feast**—These women are analytical planners with a present temporal orientation. They view time as something they consume to pursue sensory pleasure and gratification, and for this reason they value hedonic consumption and variety-seeking.

Our experience of time is largely a result of our culture, because people around the world think about the passage of time very differently. To most Western consumers, time is a neatly

Too busy to eat? Help is at hand.

Introducing Campbell's® Soup at Hand.™
A whole new way to eat right when you're on the run.

Now you can enjoy sippable soup, anytime, anywhere, with new Campbell's Soup at Hand. Four deliciously satisfying soups in sippable, heat-and-go microwavable cups. Sure your hands are full, but it's amazing what you can do with new Soup at Hand from Campbell's.

M'm! M'm! Good!®

© 2002 Campbell Soup Company

MANUFACTURER'S COUPON	EXPIRES 12/31/02

Save 50¢ on 1 Campbell's® Soup at Hand™

CONSUMER: One coupon per purchase. Good only on product indicated. Consumer pays any sales tax. Void if sold, exchanged or transferred.
RETAILER: Redeem on terms stated for consumer upon purchase of product indicated. ANY OTHER USE CONSTITUTES FRAUD. If submitted in compliance with Campbell Soup Company's Coupon Redemption Policy (copies available upon request), you will be reimbursed face value plus 8¢. Mail to: **CAMPBELL SOUP COMPANY, CMS DEPT. #51000, ONE FAWCETT DRIVE, DEL RIO, TX 78840.** Failure to produce on request invoices proving purchase of stock covering coupons may void all coupons submitted. Void if taxed, restricted, prohibited or presented by other than retailers of our products. Cash value 1/100¢.

07041

5 51000 15350 5 (8101)0 07041 1202

Time poverty is creating opportunities for many new products (like portable soups) that let people multitask.
Source: Courtesy of Campbell Soup Company.

compartmentalized thing: We wake up in the morning, go to school or work, come home, eat dinner, go out, go to sleep, wake up, and do it all over again. We call this perspective *linear separable time*—events proceed in an orderly sequence and "There's a time and a place for everything." There is a clear sense of past, present, and future. We perform many activities as the means to some end that will occur later, such as when we "save for a rainy day."

This perspective seems natural to us, but not all others share it. Some cultures run on *procedural time* and ignore the clock completely; people simply decide to do something "when the time is right." For example, in Burundi people might arrange to meet when the cows return from the watering hole. If you ask someone in Madagascar how long it takes to get to the market, you will get an answer such as, "in the time it takes to cook rice."

Alternatively, in *circular* or *cyclic* time, natural cycles such as the regular occurrence of the seasons govern people's sense of time (a perspective many Hispanic cultures share). To these consumers, the notion of the future does not make sense; that time will be much like the present. Because the concept of future value does not exist, these consumers often prefer to buy an inferior product that is available now rather than wait for a better one that may become available later. Also, it is hard to convince people who function on circular time to buy insurance or save for a rainy day when they don't think in terms of a linear future.

To appreciate all the different ways people think about time, consider those who speak Aymara, an Indian language of the high Andes. They actually see the future as behind them and the past ahead of them! Aymara call the future *qhipa pacha/timpu*, meaning back or behind time, and the past *nayra pacha/timpu*, meaning front time. And they gesture ahead of them when remembering things past and backward when talking about the future. Anthropologists explain that people in this culture distinguish primarily between what they know and what they don't—and they know what they see in front of them with their own eyes. So, because they know the past, it lies ahead of them. The future is unknown, so it lies behind them where they can't see it.[17] Just imagine trying to sell them life insurance!

The sketches in Figure 2 illustrate what happened when a researcher asked college students to draw pictures of time. The drawing at the top left represents procedural time; there is lack of direction from left to right and little sense of past, present, and future. The three drawings in the middle denote cyclical time, with markers that designate regular cycles. The bottom drawing represents linear time, with a segmented time line moving from left to right in a well-defined sequence.[18]

The psychological dimension of time—how we actually experience it—is an important factor in **queuing theory**, the mathematical study of waiting lines. As we all know, our experience when we wait has a big effect on our evaluations of what we get at the end of the wait. Although we assume that something must be pretty good if we have to wait for it, the negative feelings that long waits arouse can quickly turn people off.[19] In a survey, NCR Corp. found that standing around the local Department or Division of Motor Vehicles is the most dreaded wait of all. Waiting in line at retail outlets came in a close second, followed by registering at clinics or hospitals, checking in at airports, and ordering at fast-food restaurants or deli counters. On average, consumers estimate that they spend more than 2 days per year waiting in line for service, and half believe they waste between 30 minutes and 2 hours each week on lines.[20]

Figure 2 DRAWINGS OF TIME
Source: Esther S. Page-Wood, Carol J. Kaufman, and Paul M. Lane, (1990) "The Art of Time." *Proceedings of the 1990 Academy of Marketing Science* conference, ed B. J. Dunlap, Vol. xiii, Cullowhee, NC: Academy of Marketing Science, 56–61. Copyright © 1990 Academy of Marketing Science. Used with permission.

Marketers use "tricks" to minimize psychological waiting time. These techniques range from altering customers' perceptions of a line's length to providing distractions that divert attention from waiting:[21]

● One hotel chain received excessive complaints about the wait for elevators, so it installed mirrors near the elevator banks. People's natural tendency to check their appearance reduced complaints, even though the actual waiting time was unchanged.

● Airline passengers often complain about the wait to claim their baggage. In one airport, they would walk 1 minute from the plane to the baggage carousel and then wait 7 minutes for their luggage. When the airport changed the layout so that the walk to the carousel took 6 minutes and bags arrived 2 minutes after that, complaints disappeared.[22]

● Restaurant chains are scrambling to put the "fast" back into fast food, especially for drive-through lanes, which now account for 65 percent of revenues. In a study that ranked the speed of 25 fast-food chains, cars spent an average of 203.6 seconds from the menu board to departure. Wendy's was clocked the fastest at 150.3 seconds. To speed things up and eliminate spills, McDonald's created a salad that comes in a container to fit into car cup holders. Arby's is working on a "high viscosity" version of its special sauce that's less likely to spill. Burger King is testing see-through bags so customers can quickly check their orders before speeding off.[23]

Queuing theory must take cultural differences into account, because these affect how we behave while in line. One Hong Kong researcher maintains, for example, that Asians and others in more collective cultures compare their situation with those around them. This means they're more likely to stand patiently in a long line: They are likely to compare their situation to the number of people *behind* them rather than to the number ahead of them. By contrast, Americans and others in more individualistic societies don't make these "social comparisons." They don't necessarily feel better that more people are behind them, but they feel bad if too many people are in front of them. A Disney executive claims that Europeans also exhibit different behaviors depending on their nationality. He notes that at the Disneyland Resort Paris, British visitors are orderly but the French and Italians "never saw a line they couldn't be in front of."[25]

OBJECTIVE 2

The information a store or Web site provides strongly influences a purchase decision, in addition to what a shopper already knows or believes about a product.

The Shopping Experience

Our mood at the time of purchase can really affect what we feel like buying.[26] We direct our behavior to satisfy certain goal states. If you don't believe it, try grocery shopping on an empty stomach! Or make a decision when you're stressed, and you'll understand how a physiological state impairs information-processing and problem-solving abilities.[27]

Two basic dimensions, *pleasure* and *arousal*, determine whether we will react positively or negatively to a consumption environment.[28] What it boils down to is that you can either enjoy or not enjoy a situation, and you can feel stimulated or not. As Figure 3 indicates, different combinations of pleasure and arousal levels result in a variety of emotional states. An arousing situation can be either distressing or exciting, depending on whether the context is positive or negative (e.g., a street riot versus a street festival). So, a specific mood is some combination of pleasure and arousal. The state of happiness is high in pleasantness and moderate in arousal, whereas elation is high on both dimensions.[29] A mood state (either positive or negative) biases our judgments of products and services in that direction.[30] Put simply, we give more positive evaluations when we're in a good mood (this explains the popularity of the business lunch!).

Many factors, including store design, the weather, and whether you just had a fight with your significant other, affect your mood. Music and television programming do as well.[31] When we hear happy music or watch happy programs, we experience more

Figure 3 DIMENSIONS OF EMOTIONAL STATES

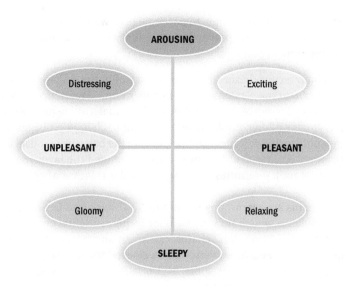

positive reactions to commercials and products.[32] And when we're in a good mood, we process ads with less elaboration. We pay less attention to the specifics of the message and we rely more on heuristics.[33]

Our emotional reactions to marketing cues are so powerful that some high-tech companies study mood in very small doses (in 1/30 of a second increments) as they analyze people's facial reactions when they see ads or new products. They measure happiness as they look for differences between, for example, a *true smile* (which includes a relaxation of the upper eyelid) and a *social smile* (which occurs only around the mouth). Whirlpool used this technique to test consumers' emotional reactions to a yet-to-be-launched generation of its Duet washers and dryers. The company's goal: To design an appliance that will actually make people happy. Researchers discovered that even though test subjects said they weren't thrilled with some out-of-the-box design options, such as unusual color combinations, their facial expressions said otherwise.[34]

When the Going Gets Tough, the Tough Go Shopping

We all know some people who shop simply for the sport of it, and others whom we have to drag to a mall. Shopping is how we acquire needed products and services, but social motives for shopping also are important. Thus, shopping is an activity that we can perform for either utilitarian (functional or tangible) or hedonic (pleasurable or intangible) reasons.[35]

So, do people hate to shop or love it? We segment consumers in terms of their **shopping orientation**, or general attitudes about shopping. These orientations vary depending on the particular product categories and store types we consider. Rob hates to shop for a car, but he may love to browse in music stores. A shopper's motivation influences the type of shopping environment that will be attractive or annoying; for example, a person who wants to locate and buy something quickly may find loud music, bright colors, or complex layouts distracting, whereas someone who is there to browse may enjoy the sensory stimulation.[36]

Some scale items that researchers use to assess our shopping motivations illustrate the diverse reasons we may shop. One item that measures hedonic value is "During the trip, I felt the excitement of the hunt." When we compare that type of sentiment to a functional statement, "I accomplished just what I wanted to on this shopping trip," there's a clear contrast between these two dimensions.[37] Hedonic shopping motives include the following:[38]

- **Social experiences**—The shopping center or department store replaces the traditional town square or county fair as a community gathering place. Many people (especially in suburban or rural areas) have almost no other places to spend their leisure time. That probably explains the popularity of late-night games college students in some rural areas play at their local Walmart. In addition to sports such as scavenger hunts, aisle football, and a relay race limbo under the shopping-cart stand, "10 in 10" is a big attraction. To play this game, students form into teams; each team has 10 minutes to put 10 items from anywhere in the store in a shopping cart. Then they turn their cart over to the opposing team, which has to figure out where the items came from and return them to the shelves where they belong (not so easy in a store stocked with more than 100,000 different items). The first team back to the checkout counters with an empty cart wins.[39] Note: If you get busted for playing this game, you did NOT learn about it here.

- **Sharing of common interests**—Stores frequently offer specialized goods that allow people with shared interests to communicate.
- **Interpersonal attraction**—Shopping centers are a natural place to congregate. The shopping mall is a favorite "hangout" for teenagers. It also represents a controlled, secure environment for the elderly, and many malls now feature "mall walkers' clubs" for early morning workouts.
- **Instant status**—As every salesperson knows, some people savor the experience of being waited on, even though they may not necessarily buy anything. One men's clothing salesman offered this advice: "Remember their size, remember what you sold them last time. Make them feel important! If you can make people feel important, they are going to come back. Everybody likes to feel important!"[40] When a team of researchers conducted in-depth interviews with women to understand what makes shopping a pleasurable experience, they found one motivation was role-playing. For example, one respondent dressed up for shopping excursions to upscale boutiques because she likes to pretend she is wealthy and have salespeople fall all over her.[41]
- **The thrill of the hunt**—Some people pride themselves on their knowledge of the marketplace. Unlike our car-buying friend Kyle, they may love to haggle and bargain.

E-Commerce: Clicks versus Bricks

As more and more Web sites pop up to sell everything from refrigerator magnets to Mack trucks, marketers continue to debate how the online world affects their business.[42] In particular, many lose sleep as they wonder whether e-commerce will replace traditional retailing, work in concert with it, or perhaps even fade away to become another fad your kids will laugh about someday (OK, that's not real likely).

One thing to keep in mind is that the experience of acquiring the good may be quite different offline versus online. This aspect of the transaction can provide value added over and above the good or service you buy. We clearly see this difference between the two worlds when we compare how people gamble in casinos versus online. When researchers interviewed 30 gamblers to explore these experiences, they found sharp contrasts. Those who enjoy casino gambling have a strong sense of connection to fellow gamblers, so it's very much a social experience. Online gamblers enjoy the anonymity of the Internet. Casino gamblers get turned on by the sensual experiences and excitement of the casino, whereas online gamblers gravitate more to the feeling of safety and control they get because they stay at home. Casino gamblers talked about the friendly atmosphere, while those who stayed online reported behaviors that a real casino wouldn't tolerate, such as taunts and bullying.[43] Although both groups aim to have fun and hope to make money, it's a safe bet that their experiences are quite different.

For marketers, the growth of online commerce is a sword that cuts both ways. On the one hand, they reach customers around the world even if they're physically located 100 miles from nowhere. On the other hand, they now compete not only with the store across the street but also with thousands of Web sites that span the globe. Also, when consumers obtain products directly from the manufacturer or wholesaler, this eliminates the intermediary—the loyal, store-based retailers that carry the firm's products and sell them at a marked-up price.[44]

So what makes e-commerce sites successful? Some e-tailers take advantage of technology to provide extra value to their customers that their land-locked rivals can't. eBay offers a feature within its Fashion app called "See It On" that allows the user to

E-commerce sites like Bluefly give shoppers the option of shopping without leaving home.
Source: Courtesy of Bluefly.com.

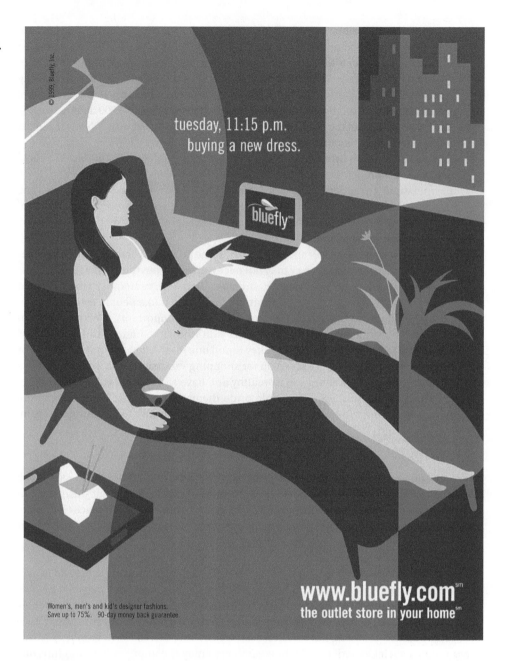

virtually try on sunglasses in real time using an iPhone 4 or iPod Touch. He or she can adjust the fit, choose different styles, frames, lenses, and colors to find the perfect look, and then browse through eBay to find the perfect price.[45] Other new fashion sites, such as Net-a-Porter and Gilt Groupe, directly connect buyers and sellers so that designers can be more nimble and react quickly to changing consumer tastes. Others like Threadless, ModCloth, Lookk, and Fabricly go a step further: They crowdsource fashion to determine what styles they will actually produce based on what customers tell them they will buy. Indeed, the high-fashion site ModaOperandi bills itself as a **pretailer**; it provides exclusive styles by prodding manufacturers to produce runway pieces they wouldn't otherwise make because store buyers weren't sure anyone would pay the money for them.[46]

More generally, online shoppers value these aspects of a Web site:

- The ability to click on an item to create a pop-up window with more details about the product, including price, size, colors, and inventory availability.
- The ability to click on an item and add it to your cart without leaving the page you're on.

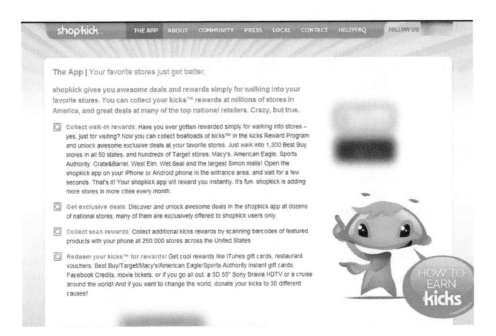

Shopkick is a location-based smartphone application that unlocks deals and rewards when shoppers enter participating stores.
Source: Courtesy of shopkick.

- The ability to "feel" merchandise through better imagery, more product descriptions, and details.
- The ability to enter all data related to your purchase on one page, rather than going through several checkout pages.
- The ability to mix and match product images on one page to determine whether they look good together.[47]

Table 2 summarizes some of the pros and cons of e-commerce. It's clear that traditional shopping isn't quite dead yet, but brick-and-mortar retailers do need to work harder to give shoppers something they can't get (yet anyway) in the virtual world: a stimulating or pleasant environment. Now let's check out how they're doing that.

TABLE 2   Pros and Cons of E-Commerce

Benefits of E-Commerce	Limitations of E-Commerce
For the Consumer	**For the Consumer**
Shop 24 hours a day	Lack of security
Less traveling	Fraud
Can receive relevant information in seconds from any location	Can't touch items
More choices of products	Exact colors may not reproduce on computer monitors
More products available to less-developed countries	Expensive to order and then return
Greater price information	Potential breakdown of human relationships
Lower prices so that less affluent can purchase	
Participate in virtual auctions	
Fast delivery	
Electronic communities	
For the Marketer	**For the Marketer**
The world is the marketplace	Lack of security
Decreases costs of doing business	Must maintain site to reap benefits
Very specialized business can be successful	Fierce price competition
Real-time pricing	Conflicts with conventional retailers
	Legal issues not resolved

Source: Adapted from Michael R. Solomon and Elnora W. Stuart, *Welcome to Marketing.com: The Brave New World of E-Commerce* (Upper Saddle River, NJ: Prentice Hall, 2001).

Retailing as Theater

At several U.S. malls, shoppers show up in shorts and flip-flops. They're turning out to ride a Flowrider, a huge wave-making machine.[48] Shopping center developers turn to attractions like this to lure reluctant customers back to malls. The competition for customers becomes even more intense as nonstore alternatives, from Web sites and print catalogs to TV shopping networks and home shopping parties, continue to multiply.

With all of these shopping alternatives available, how can a traditional store compete? Many malls are giant entertainment centers, almost to the point that their traditional retail occupants seem like an afterthought. Today, it's commonplace to find carousels, miniature golf, skating rinks, or batting cages in a suburban mall. Hershey opened a make-believe factory smack in the middle of Times Square. It features four steam machines and 380 feet of neon lighting, plus a moving message board that lets visiting chocoloholics program messages to surprise their loved ones.[49]

The quest to entertain means that many stores go all out to create imaginative environments that transport shoppers to fantasy worlds or provide other kinds of stimulation. We call this strategy **retail theming**. Innovative merchants today use four basic kinds of theming techniques:

1 *Landscape themes* rely on associations with images of nature, Earth, animals, and the physical body. Bass Pro Shops, for example, creates a simulated outdoor environment, including pools stocked with fish.
2 *Marketscape themes* build on associations with manmade places. An example is The Venetian hotel in Las Vegas, which lavishly recreates parts of the real Italian city.
3 *Cyberspace themes* build on images of information and communications technology. eBay's retail interface instills a sense of community among its vendors and traders.
4 *Mindscape themes* draw on abstract ideas and concepts, introspection and fantasy, and often possess spiritual overtones. The Kiva day spa in downtown Chicago offers health treatments based on a theme of Native American healing ceremonies and religious practices.[50]

One popular theming strategy is to convert a store into a **being space**. This environment resembles a commercial living room where we can go to relax, be entertained, hang out with friends, escape the everyday, or even learn. When you think of *being spaces*, Starbucks probably comes to mind. The coffee chain's stated goal is to become our "third place" where we spend the bulk of our time, in addition to home and work. Starbucks led the way when it outfitted its stores with comfy chairs and Wi-Fi. But there are many other marketers who meet our needs for exciting commercial spaces—no matter what those needs are. In Asia, venues such as Manboo and Fujiyama Land provide havens where gamers can do their thing 24/7—and even take a shower on-site during a break. Other spaces cater to the needs of **minipreneurs** (one-person businesses) as they offer work-centered being spaces. At New York's Paragraph, writers who need a quiet place to ruminate can hang out in a loft that's divided into a writing room and a lounge area. TwoRooms ("You Work, They Play") provides office space and child care for home-based workers.[51]

Reflecting the ever-quickening pace of our culture, many of these *being spaces* come and go very rapidly—on purpose. **Pop-up stores** appear in many forms around the world. Typically, these are temporary installations that do business only for a few days or weeks and then disappear before they get old. The Swatch Instant Store sells limited-edition watches in a major city until the masses discover it; then it closes and moves on to another "cool" locale. The Dutch beer brand Dommelsch organized pop-up concerts: Fans entered barcodes they found on cans, beer bottles, and coasters on the brewer's Web site to discover dates and locations. You may even run into a pop-up store on your campus; several brands, including the Brazilian flip-flop maker Havaianas, Victoria's Secret's Pink, and sustainable-clothing brand RVL7, run pop-up projects around the United States.[52]

CB AS I SEE IT

Professor Cele Otnes, *University of Illinois at Urbana-Champaign*

Bow can retailers make consumers' in-store experiences more meaningful in order to positively influence key attitudinal and behavioral measures, such as brand loyalty and likelihood of repeat purchasing? One research topic that relates to this question is how retailers use in-store rituals to shape consumers' experiences. *Rituals* are expressive, dramatic events we repeat over time.

Our research explores whether and how these types of rituals actually affect customers' experience with a brand. We have interviewed more than 20 retailers and service providers who identify themselves as using rituals designed for their employees or customers in order to enhance their relationships with these stakeholders, to improve efficiency, and to differentiate themselves from their competitors. We're exploring such issues as how consumers resist rituals, how consumers help co-create rituals with other shoppers and with retailers (as is the case at Build-A-Bear, when consumers engage in grooming rituals with the toys they've just created), and whether and how these rituals actually enhance consumers' retail experiences. From a strategic perspective, we will also explore whether ritualizing the shopping experience allows retailers to charge premium prices, to be forgiven more easily if they make mistakes with consumers, and to allocate less of their money to marketing communications. So next time you stand in line at Marble Slab Creamery or wear a "birthday sombrero" on your head at your favorite Mexican restaurant, remember—you've been ritualized!

Store Image

As so many stores compete for customers, how do we ever pick one over others? Just like products, stores have "personalities." Some shops have very clearly defined images (either good or bad). Others tend to blend into the crowd. What factors shape this personality, or **store image**? Some of the important dimensions of a store's image are location, merchandise suitability, and the knowledge and congeniality of the sales staff.[53]

These design features typically work together to create an overall impression. When we think about stores, we don't usually say, "Well, that place is fairly good in terms of convenience, the salespeople are acceptable, and services are good." We're more likely to proclaim, "That place gives me the creeps," or "It's so much fun to shop there." We quickly get an overall impression of a store, and the feeling we get may have more to do with intangibles, such as interior design and the types of people we find in the aisles, than with the store's return policies or credit availability. As a result, some stores routinely pop up in our consideration sets, whereas we never consider others ("Only geeks shop there!").[54]

Atmospherics

Retailers want you to come in—and stay. Careful store design increases the amount of space the shopper covers, and stimulating displays keep them in the aisles longer. This "curb appeal" translates directly to the bottom line: Researchers tracked grocery shopper's movements by plotting the position of their cell phones as they moved about a store. They found that when people lingered just 1 percent longer, sales rose by 1.3 percent.

Of course, grocers know a lot of tricks after years of observing shoppers. For example, they call the area just inside a supermarket's entrance the "decompression zone": People tend to slow down and take stock of their surroundings when they enter the store, so store designers use this space to promote bargains rather than to sell. Similarly, Walmart's "greeters" help customers to settle in to their shopping experience. Once they get a serious start, the first thing shoppers encounter is the produce section. Fruits and vegetables can easily be damaged, so it would be more logical to buy these items at the end of a shopping trip. But fresh, wholesome food makes people feel good (and righteous) so they're less guilty when they throw the chips and cookies in the cart later.[55]

Because marketers recognize that a store's image is a very important part of the retailing mix, store designers pay a lot of attention to **atmospherics**, the "conscious designing of space and its various dimensions to evoke certain effects in buyers."[56] These dimensions include colors, scents, and sounds. For example, stores with red interiors tend to make people tense, whereas a blue decor imparts a calmer feeling.[57] Some preliminary evidence also indicates that odors (olfactory cues) influence our evaluations of a store's environment.[58]

A store's atmosphere in turn affects what we buy. In one study, researchers asked shoppers how much pleasure they felt five minutes after they entered a store. Those who enjoyed their experience spent more time and money.[59] To boost the entertainment value of shopping (and to lure online shoppers back to brick-and-mortar stores), some retailers offer **activity stores** that let consumers participate in the production of the products or services they buy there. One familiar example is the Build-A-Bear Workshop chain, where customers dress bear bodies in costumes.[60]

Retailers cleverly engineer their store designs to attract customers. Light colors impart a feeling of spaciousness and serenity; signs in bright colors create excitement. When the fashion designer Norma Kamali replaced fluorescent lights with pink ones in department store dressing rooms to flatter shoppers' faces and banish wrinkles, women were more willing to try on (and buy) the company's bathing suits.[61] Walmart found that sales were higher in areas of a prototype store lit in natural daylight compared to the artificial light in its regular stores.[62] One study found that shoppers in stores with brighter in-store lighting examined and handled more merchandise.[63]

In addition to visual stimuli, all sorts of sensory cues influence us in retail settings.[64] For example, patrons of country-and-western bars drink more when the jukebox music is slower. According to a researcher, "Hard drinkers prefer listening to slower-paced, wailing, lonesome, self-pitying music."[65] Music also can affect eating habits. Another study found that diners who listened to loud, fast music ate more food. In contrast, those who listened to Mozart or Brahms ate less and more slowly. The researchers concluded that diners who choose soothing music at mealtimes can increase weight loss by at least 5 pounds a month![66]

In-Store Decision Making

Despite all their efforts to "pre-sell" consumers through advertising, marketers increasingly recognize that the store environment exerts a strong influence on many purchases. Women tell researchers, for example, that store displays are one of the major information sources they use to decide what clothing to buy.[67] This influence is even stronger when we shop for food: Analysts estimate that shoppers decide on about two out of every three supermarket purchases while they walk through the aisles.[68] Research evidence indicates that consumers have **mental budgets** for grocery trips that are typically composed of both an itemized portion and *in-store slack*. This means they typically decide beforehand on an amount they plan to spend, but then they have an additional amount in mind (slack) they are willing to spend on unplanned purchases—if they come across any they really want to have. Thus stores should encourage consumers to spend all of their mental budgets by offering samples or posting reminder placards as they approach the checkout lines to remind them of things they may have forgotten.[69]

Mobile shopping apps on smartphones provide imaginative new ways for retailers to guide shoppers through the experience, as they do everything from locate merchandise, identify the nearest restroom in a mall, or scout out sales. Some help you remember where you parked your car; others actually provide reward points when you visit certain stores. The apps also promise to provide a solution to the major hassles that drive consumers away from bricks-and-mortar stores, especially long checkout times and incompetent (or MIA) sales associates. One survey reported that nearly 3 in 10 store visits ended with an average of $132 unspent because shoppers gave up in frustration and abandoned their carts. The study also found that more than 40 percent of shoppers who received guidance from a retail associate armed with a handheld mobile computer reported an improved shopping experience. To rub salt into the wound, more than half of store employees agreed that because use of online shopping tools is escalating, their customers were more knowledgeable about their products than the salespeople are![70]

Marketers work hard to engineer purchasing environments that allow them to connect with consumers at the exact time they make a decision. This strategy even applies to drinking behavior: Diageo, the world's largest liquor company, discovered that 60 percent of bar customers don't know what they will drink until seconds before they place their orders. To make it more likely that the customer's order will include Smirnoff vodka, Johnnie Walker Scotch, or one of its other brands, Diageo launched its Drinks Invigoration Team to increase what it calls its "share of throat." The Dublin-based team experiments with bar "environments" and bottle-display techniques, and comes up with drinks to match customers' moods. For example, the company researchers discovered that bubbles stimulate the desire for spirits, so it developed bubble machines it places in back of bars. Diageo even categorizes bars into types and identifies types of drinkers—and the drinks they prefer—who frequent each. These include "style bars," where cutting-edge patrons like to sip fancy fresh-fruit martinis, and "buzz bars," where the clientele likes to drink Smirnoff mixed with energy brew Red Bull.[71]

Spontaneous Shopping

When a shopper suddenly decides to buy something in the store, one of two different processes explains this:

1 She engages in **unplanned buying** when she's unfamiliar with a store's layout or perhaps she's under some time pressure. Or, if she sees an item on a store shelf, this might remind her she needs it. About one-third of all unplanned buying occurs because a shopper recognizes a new need while she's in the store.[72]

2 She engages in **impulse buying** when she experiences a sudden urge she simply can't resist.[73] A consumer whom researchers asked to sketch a typical impulse purchaser drew Figure 4.

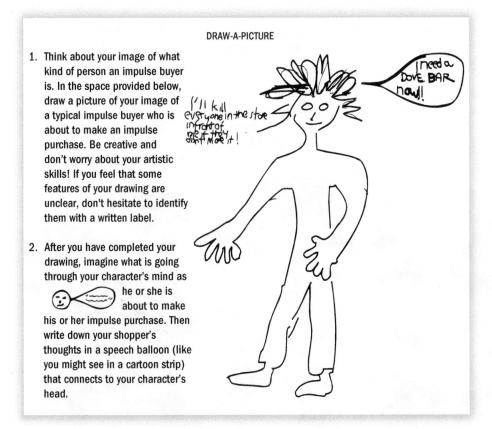

Figure 4 ONE CONSUMER'S IMAGE OF AN IMPULSE BUYER

Source: Dennis Rook, "Is Impulse Buying (Yet) a Useful Marketing Concept?" (unpublished manuscript, University of Southern California, Los Angeles, 1990): Fig. 7-A.

Retailers typically place so-called *impulse items*, such as candy and gum, near the checkout to cater to these urges. Similarly, many supermarkets install wider aisles to encourage browsing, and the widest tend to feature products with the highest profit margins. They stack low markup items that shoppers purchase regularly in narrower aisles to allow shopping carts to speed through. Starbucks encourages impulse purchasing when it charges customers who want to download songs they hear over the store's speakers directly onto their iPhones.[74] A hint to policymakers who want to discourage impulse purchases of unhealthy snack items or fast food: Limit the use of credit cards. A study that analyzed the actual shopping behavior of 1,000 households over a period of 6 months reported that shopping baskets have a larger proportion of food items rated as impulsive and unhealthy when shoppers use credit or debit cards to pay for the purchases.[75] Also, don't feel so righteous when you decide to pass up that tempting candy bar: Another study found that shoppers who refrain now are more likely to reward themselves later with an indulgent purchase![76]

Point-of-Purchase Stimuli

A well-designed in-store display boosts impulse purchases by as much as 10 percent. That explains why U.S. companies spend about $19 billion each year on **point-of-purchase (POP) stimuli**.[77]

A POP can be an elaborate product display or demonstration, a coupon-dispensing machine, or an employee who gives out free samples of a new cookie in the grocery aisle. Now the pace of POP spending will probably pick up even more: An alliance of major marketers, including Procter & Gamble, Coca-Cola, 3M, Kellogg, Miller Brewing, and Walmart, is using infrared sensors to measure the reach of in-store marketing efforts. Retailers have long counted the number of shoppers who enter and exit their stores, and they use product barcode data to track what shoppers buy. But big consumer-products companies also need to know how many people actually walk by their promotional displays, so that they can evaluate how effective these are. Although it's possible to fool these sensors (they still can't tell if someone simply cuts through to reach the other end of the store), this sophisticated measurement system is a valuable first step that many advertisers eagerly await.[78]

The importance of POP in shopper decision making explains why product packages increasingly play a key role in the marketing mix as they evolve from the functional to the fantastic:

NXT body wash/moisturizer cans light up on the store shelf.

Source: Courtesy of NXT/Clio Designs Incorporated.

● In the past 100 years, Pepsi changed the look of its can, and before that its bottles, only 10 times. Now the company switches designs every few weeks. It's also testing cans that spray an aroma when you open one to match the flavor of the drink, such as a wild cherry scent misting from a Wild Cherry Pepsi can.

- Coors Light bottles sport labels that turn blue when the beer is chilled to the right temperature.
- Huggies' Henry the Hippo hand soap bottles have a light that flashes for 20 seconds to show children how long they should wash their hands.
- Evian's "palace bottle" turns up in restaurants and luxury hotels. The bottle has an elegant swanlike neck and sits on a small silver tray.
- Unilever North America sells Axe shower gel bottles shaped like video game joysticks.
- Some companies are considering the insertion of a computer chip and tiny speaker inside a package. This gimmick might be useful for cross-promotion. For example, a package of cheese could say "I go well with Triscuit crackers" when a shopper takes it off the shelf. Of course, this attention-getting trick could backfire if everyone starts to do it. As one ad executive commented, "If you're walking down a row in a supermarket and every package is screaming at you, it sounds like a terrifying, disgusting experience."[79]

OBJECTIVE 3

A salesperson often is the crucial connection to a purchase.

The Salesperson: A Lead Role in the Play

The salesperson is one of the most important players in the retailing drama—as Kyle learned in his interaction with Rhoda.[80] Exchange theory stresses that every interaction involves a trade of value. Each participant gives something to the other and hopes to receive something in return.[81] A (competent) salesperson offers a lot of value because his or her expert advice makes the shopper's choice easier.

Marketing Pitfall

Not all sales interactions are positive, but some *really* stand out. Here are a few incidents that make the rest of them easier to swallow:

- A woman sued a car dealer in Iowa, claiming that a salesperson persuaded her to climb into the trunk of a Chrysler Concorde to check out its spaciousness. He then slammed the trunk shut and bounced the car several times, apparently to the delight of his coworkers. The manager had offered a prize of $100 to the salesperson who could get a customer to climb in.[88]

- A Detroit couple filed a $100 million lawsuit against McDonald's, alleging that three McDonald's employees beat them after they tried to return a watery milkshake.

- In Alabama, a McDonald's employee was arrested on second-degree assault charges after she stabbed a customer in the forehead with a ballpoint pen.[89]

Consumers aren't the only ones who get angry about frustrating service interactions. Many employees have an axe to grind as well. At a Web site put up by a disgruntled former employee of a certain fast-food franchise, we share the pain of this ex-burger flipper: "I have seen the creatures that live at the bottom of the dumpster. I have seen the rat by the soda machine. I have seen dead frogs in the fresh salad lettuce." Fries with that?

At the *customerssuck.com* Web site, restaurant and store workers who have to grin and bear it all day go to vent. Once off the clock, they share their frustrations about the idiocy, slovenliness, and insensitivity of their customers. Some contributors to the Web site share stupid questions their customers ask, such as "How much is a 99-cent cheeseburger?" whereas others complain about working conditions and having to be nice to not-so-nice people. The slogan of the site is "the customer is never right."[90]

A buyer–seller situation is like many other *dyadic encounters* (two-person groups); it's a relationship in which both parties must reach some agreement about the roles of each participant during a process of *identity negotiation*.[82] For example, if Rhoda immediately establishes herself as an expert, she is likely to have more influence over Kyle through the course of the relationship. Some of the factors that help to define a salesperson's role (and effectiveness) are her age, appearance, educational level, and motivation to sell.[83] Another variable is similarity between the seller and the buyer. In fact, even **incidental similarity,** such as a shared birthday or growing up in the same place, can be enough to boost the odds of a sale.[84]

In addition, more effective salespersons usually know their customers' traits and preferences better than do ineffective salespersons, and they adapt their approach to meet the needs of each specific customer.[85] The ability to be adaptable is especially vital when customers and salespeople have different *interaction styles*.[86] We each vary in the degree of assertiveness we bring to interactions. At one extreme, *nonassertive* people believe it's not socially acceptable to complain, and sales situations may intimidate them. *Assertive* people are more likely to stand up for themselves in a firm but nonthreatening way. *Aggressives* may resort to rudeness and threats if they don't get their way (we've all run into these folks).[87]

OBJECTIVE 4
Marketers need to be concerned about a consumer's evaluations of a product after he or she buys it as well as before.

Postpurchase Satisfaction

In a survey of 480 chief marketing officers (CMOs), 58 percent reported that their companies do not reward their employees if customer satisfaction improves. More than one-third said they have no way to track word of mouth among customers, and less than three in ten said their firms are good at resolving customers' complaints.[91] What's wrong with this picture?

Our overall feelings about a product after we've bought it—what researchers call **consumer satisfaction/dissatisfaction (CS/D)**—obviously play a big role in our future behavior. It's a lot easier to sell something once than to sell it again if it bombed the first time. We evaluate the things we buy as we use them and integrate them into our daily consumption activities.[92] In a sense, each of us is a product reviewer, whether or not we bother to talk or blog about our experiences.

Companies that score high in customer satisfaction often have a big competitive advantage—especially when so many firms skimp on the attention they pay to customers. A 5-year study of customer satisfaction in the Canadian banking industry provides typical results: Banks that provided better service commanded a larger "share of wallet" than did others (i.e., their customers entrusted them with a larger proportion of their money).[93]

Good marketers constantly look for reasons why their customers might be dissatisfied so that they can try to improve.[94] For example, United Airlines' advertising agency wanted to identify specific aspects of air travel that ticked people off. Researchers gave frequent flyers crayons and a map that showed different stages in a long-distance trip. Respondents colored in these stages, using hot hues to symbolize areas that cause stress and anger and cool colors for parts of the trip they associate with satisfaction and calm feelings. Although many of them painted jet cabins in a serene aqua, they colored the ticket counters orange and terminal waiting areas fire-red. As a result, United focused more on improving its overall operations instead of only the in-flight experience.[95]

Just What *Is* Quality?

What do consumers look for in products? That's easy: They want quality and value.[96] However, these terms have slippery meanings that are hard for us to pin down. We infer quality when we rely on cues as diverse as brand name, price, product warranties, and even our estimate of how much money a company invests in its advertising.[97]

In the book *Zen and the Art of Motorcycle Maintenance*, a cult hero of college students in an earlier generation literally went crazy as he tried to figure out the meaning of quality.[98] Marketers appear to use the word *quality* as a catchall term for *good*. Because of its wide and imprecise usage, the attribute of *quality* threatens to become a meaningless claim. If everyone has it, what good is it?

To muddy the waters a bit more, satisfaction or dissatisfaction is more than a reaction to how well a product or service performs. According to the **expectancy disconfirmation model**, we form beliefs about product performance based on prior experience with the product or communications about the product that imply a certain level of quality.[99] When something performs the way we thought it would, we may not think much about it. If it fails to live up to expectations, this may create negative feelings. However, if performance happens to exceed our expectations, we're happy campers.

To understand this perspective, think about how you decide if a restaurant is good or bad depending on the type of place it is. You expect sparkling clear glassware at a fancy eating establishment, and you're not happy if you discover a grimy glass. However, you may not be surprised if you see fingerprints on your beer mug at a local greasy spoon; you may even shrug off this indiscretion because it's part of the place's "charm."

This perspective underscores how important it is to *manage expectations.* We often trace a customer's dissatisfaction to his erroneous expectations of the company's ability to deliver a product or service. NO company is perfect. It's just not realistic to think that everything will always turn out perfectly (although some firms don't even come close!).

There are various strategies a firm can choose when customers expect too much. The organization can either accommodate these demands as it improves the range or quality of products it offers, alter these expectations, or perhaps choose to "fire the customer" if it is not feasible to meet his needs (banks and credit card companies often do this when they identify customers who don't make them enough money to justify keeping their accounts).[100] How can a marketer alter expectations? For example, a waiter can tell a diner in advance that the portion size she ordered isn't very big, or a car salesperson can warn a buyer that he may smell some strange odors during the break-in period. A firm also can *underpromise*, as Xerox routinely does when it inflates the time it will take for a service rep to visit. When the rep arrives a day earlier than expected, this impresses the customer.

When a product doesn't work as we expect or turns out to be unsafe (like the recent spate of hazardous products from China, ranging from toothpaste to dog food), it's the understatement of the year to say we're not satisfied. In these situations, marketers must immediately take steps to reassure us or risk losing a customer for life. If the company confronts the problem truthfully, we are often willing to forgive and forget; we've seen this happen in incidents over the years when a firm suffers a negative incident. Examples include Tylenol (product tampering), Chrysler (the company disconnected the odometers on executives' cars and resold them as new—well before the carmaker declared bankruptcy!), or Perrier (traces of the chemical benzene turned up in the drink). But if the firm seems to be dragging its heels or covering up, our resentment grows. This is what happened during the BP oil spill and corporate scandals such as the collapse of Enron and AIG.

What Can We Do When We're Dissatisfied?

Fifty-four million dollars for a pair of missing pants? A judge in Washington, D.C., made headlines when he filed a $54 million lawsuit against his neighborhood dry cleaner because it lost a pair of his pinstriped suit pants. He claimed that a local consumer protection law entitled him to thousands of dollars for each day over nearly four years in which signs at the shop promised "same day service" and "satisfaction guaranteed." The suit dragged on for several months, but at the end of the day the plaintiff went home with empty pockets.[101] And some people claim we have too many lawsuits in this country!

This ad for Ford relies on a common claim about quality.
Source: Courtesy of Ford Motor Co.

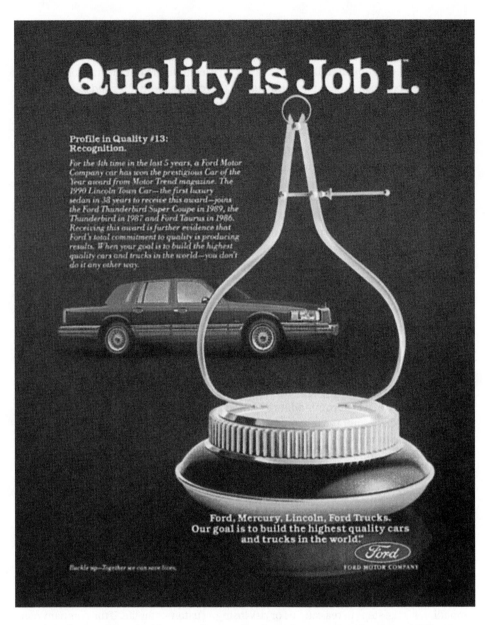

Quality is Job 1.

**Profile in Quality #13:
Recognition.**

For the 4th time in the last 5 years, a Ford Motor Company car has won the prestigious Car of the Year award from Motor Trend magazine. The 1990 Lincoln Town Car—the first luxury sedan in 38 years to receive this award—joins the Ford Thunderbird Super Coupe in 1989, the Thunderbird in 1987 and Ford Taurus in 1986. Receiving this award is further evidence that Ford's total commitment to quality is producing results. When your goal is to build the highest quality cars and trucks in the world—you don't do it any other way.

Ford, Mercury, Lincoln, Ford Trucks.
Our goal is to build the highest quality cars
and trucks in the world."

Buckle up—Together we can save lives.

FORD MOTOR COMPANY

If you're not happy with a product or service, what can you do about it? You have three possible courses of action (though sometimes you can take more than one):[102]

1 **Voice response**—You can appeal directly to the retailer for redress (e.g., a refund).
2 **Private response**—You can express your dissatisfaction to friends and boycott the product or the store where you bought it.
3 **Third-party response**—Like the pantless judge, you can take legal action against the merchant, register a complaint with the Better Business Bureau, or write a letter to the newspaper.

In one study, business majors wrote complaint letters to companies. When the firm sent a free sample in response, this action significantly improved how they felt about it. This didn't happen, however, when they *only* received a letter of apology—but no swag. Even worse, students who got no response reported an even more negative image than before. This shows that *any* kind of response is better than none.[103]

A number of factors influence which route we choose. People are more likely to take action if they're dissatisfied with expensive products such as household durables, cars, and clothing than for problems with inexpensive products.[104] Ironically, consumers who are satisfied with a store in general are more likely to complain if they experience something bad; they take the time to complain because they feel connected to the store. Older people are more likely to complain, and they are much more likely to believe that the store will actually resolve the problem. And, if a company resolves the problem, a customer feels even better about it than if she hadn't complained in the first place![105]

However, if the consumer does not believe that the store will respond to her complaint, she will be more likely to simply switch than fight, as she just takes her business elsewhere.[107] The moral: Marketers should actually *encourage* consumers to complain to them: People are more likely to spread the word about unresolved negative experiences to their friends than they are to boast about positive occurrences.[108]

TQM: Going to the Gemba

Many analysts who study consumer satisfaction, or those who design new products or services to increase it, recognize that it is crucial to understand how people actually interact with their environment to identify potential problems. To do so, they typically conduct *focus groups,* in which a small set of consumers comes into a facility to try a new item while company personnel observe them from behind a mirror. However, some researchers advocate a more up-close-and-personal approach that allows them to watch people in the actual environment where they consume the product. This perspective originated in the Japanese approach to **total quality management (TQM)**—a complex set of management and engineering procedures that aims to reduce errors and increase quality.

To help them achieve more insight, researchers go to the **gemba**, which to the Japanese means "the one true source of information." According to this philosophy, it's essential to send marketers and designers to the precise place where consumers use the product or service rather than to ask laboratory subjects to use it in a simulated environment.

Figure 5 illustrates this idea in practice. Host Foods, which operates food concessions in major airports, sent a team to the *gemba*—in this case, an airport cafeteria—to identify problem areas. Employees watched as customers entered the facility, and then followed them as they inspected the menu, procured silverware, paid, and found a table. The findings were crucial to Host's redesign of the facility. For example, the team identified a common problem that many people traveling solo experience: the need to put down one's luggage to enter the food line and the feeling of panic you get because you're not able to keep an eye on your valuables when you get your meal. This simple insight allowed Host to modify the design of its facilities to improve a patron's line-of-sight between the food area and the tables.[109]

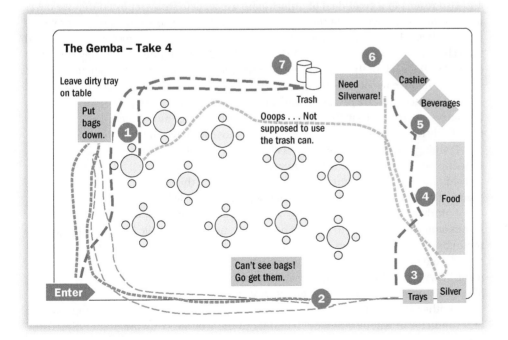

Figure 5 GOING TO THE GEMBA
Source: © Quality Function Deployment Institute. Used with permission.

367

OBJECTIVE 5

Getting rid of products when consumers no longer need or want them is a major concern both to marketers and to public policymakers.

Product Disposal

Because we do form strong attachments to some products, it can be painful to dispose of some of our things. Our possessions anchor our identities; our past lives on in our things.[110] Some Japanese ritually "retire" worn-out sewing needles, chopsticks, and even computer chips when they burn them in a ceremony to thank them for years of good service.[111]

Still, we all have to get rid of our "stuff" at some point, either because it has served its purpose or perhaps because it no longer fits with our view of ourselves (as when newlyweds "upgrade" to a real place). Concern about the environment, coupled with a need for convenience, makes ease of product disposal a key attribute in categories from razors to diapers. Furthermore, our demand for sustainable products that don't harm the environment when we're done with them creates new markets and new opportunities for entrepreneurs who find a better alternative.

For example, Terra Cycle sells an "exotic" product: A key ingredient on its label is "liquefied worm poop." A 25-year-old college dropout founded the company. (Company literature confesses that he was trying to grow "certain plants" in a worm bin inside his college apartment in order to "harvest the buds" when he stumbled on the idea. Inspiration comes from many sources!) Terra Cycle makes fertilizer products that it packages in used plastic bottles, many of which the company itself collects through a nationwide recycling program it organized. Terra Cycle claims that waste packaged in waste makes it the "ultimate eco-friendly" product. The fertilizer comes from containers filled with shredded newspaper, food scraps—and worms that eat this waste and digest it. The resulting "poop" happens to make great plant food.[112]

Disposal Options

In many cases we acquire a new product even though the old one still functions—perhaps that's one of the hallmarks of our materialistic society. Some reasons to replace an item include a desire for new features, a change in the individual's environment (e.g., a refrigerator is the wrong color for a freshly painted kitchen), or a change in the person's role or self-image.[113]

The issue of product disposition is vital because of its enormous public policy implications. We live in a throwaway society, which creates problems for the environment and also results in a great deal of unfortunate waste. One study reported that we never use as much as 12 percent of the grocery products we buy; consumers buy nearly two-thirds of these **abandoned products** for a specific purpose such as a particular recipe and then change their plans. Because we don't use these items immediately, they slowly get pushed to the back of the cupboard and forgotten.[114] Some of those "science projects" that grow in the back of your refrigerator might qualify. In another survey, 15 percent of adults admitted they are *pack rats,* and another 64 percent said they are selective savers. In contrast, 20 percent say they throw out as much garbage as they can. The consumers most likely to save things are older people and those who live alone.[115]

Training consumers to recycle has become a priority in many countries. In Japan, residents sort their garbage into as many as 44 different categories; for example, if they discard one sock, it goes into a bin for burnables, but if they throw out a pair it goes into used cloth, though only if the socks "are not torn, and the left and right sock match."[116]

A study examined the relevant goals consumers have when they recycle. It used a means–end chain analysis to identify how consumers link specific instrumental goals to more abstract terminal values. Researchers identified the most important lower-order goals to be "avoid filling up landfills," "reduce waste," "reuse materials," and "save the environment." They linked these to the terminal values of "promote health/avoid sickness," "achieve life-sustaining ends," and "provide for future generations."

Another study reported that the perceived effort involved in recycling was the best predictor of whether people would go to the trouble. This pragmatic dimension outweighed general attitudes toward recycling and the environment in predicting intention to recycle.[117] When researchers apply these techniques to study recycling and other product disposal behaviors, it will be easier for social marketers to design advertising copy and other messages that tap into the underlying values that will motivate people to increase environmentally responsible behavior.[118] Of course, one way to ease the pain is to reward consumers for recycling. Gap tried this when it teamed up with Cotton Incorporated to collect old denim, which will be turned into insulation and donated to communities to help them build new houses. The sweetener in the deal: Those who donated got a 30 percent discount on new jeans purchases and a 40 percent discount to those who buy the pants on Gap's Facebook page.[119]

Lateral Cycling: Junk versus "Junque"

During **lateral cycling**, one consumer exchanges something she owns with someone else for something the other person owns. Reusing other people's things is especially important in our throwaway society because, as one researcher put it, "there is no longer an 'away' to throw things to."[120] Although traditional marketers don't pay much attention to used-product sellers, factors such as concern about the environment, demands for quality, and cost and fashion consciousness make these "secondary" markets more important.[121] In fact, economic estimates of this **underground economy** range from 3 to 30 percent of the gross national product of the United States and up to 70 percent of the gross domestic product of other countries. Trade publications such as *Yesteryear, Swap Meet Merchandising, Collectors Journal, The Vendor Newsletter*, and *The Antique Trader* offer reams of practical advice to consumers who want to bypass formal retailers and swap merchandise.

In the United States alone, there are more than 3,500 flea markets—including at least a dozen huge operations such as the 60-acre Orange County Marketplace in California—that operate nationwide to produce upward of $10 billion in gross sales.[122] Other growth areas include student markets for used computers and textbooks, as well as ski swaps, at which consumers exchange millions of dollars worth of used ski equipment. A new generation of secondhand store owners is developing markets for everything from used office equipment to cast-off kitchen sinks. Many are nonprofit ventures started with government funding. A trade association called the Reuse Development Organization (redo.org) encourages them.[123]

Again, social media platforms offer new ways to recycle. Numerous **sharing sites** like SnapGoods, NeighborGoods.com, and ShareSomeSugar base their business models around allowing people to share, exchange, and rent goods in a local setting. In fact, some research indicates that people who participate in these sites also benefit because they feel they are part of a community. One study found that when people post messages on Twitter (also part of a community), this releases oxytocin, a neurotransmitter that evokes feelings of contentment and is thought to help induce a sense of positive social bonding. The researcher observed that this interaction "reduces stress hormones, even through the Web. You're feeling a real physiological relationship to that person, even if they are online."[124]

Lateral cycling is literally a lifestyle for some people with an anticonsumerist bent who call themselves **freegans** (this label is a takeoff on *vegans*, who shun all animal products). Freegans are modern-day scavengers who live off discards as a political statement against corporations and consumerism. They forage through supermarket trash and eat the slightly bruised produce or just-expired canned goods that we routinely throw out, and negotiate gifts of surplus food from sympathetic stores and restaurants. Freegans dress in castoff clothes and furnish their homes with items they find on the street. They get the word on locations where people throw out a lot of stuff (end-of-semester dorm cleanouts are a prime target) as they check out postings at freecycle.org, where users post unwanted items and at so-called *freemeets* (flea markets where no one exchanges money).[125]

If our possessions do indeed come to be a part of us, how do we bring ourselves to part with these precious items? The way we divest ourselves of our things may make a statement (think about throwing out things an ex-partner gave you). One study found that people who are very attached to their "stuff" may engage a *professional organizer* to help them declutter and simplify their lives; in essence, the organizer is an intermediary who helps the person to detach from reminders of his former life so that he can move on.[126]

Some researchers examined how consumers practice **divestment rituals**, in which they take steps to gradually distance themselves from things they treasure so that they can sell them or give them away. Anthropomorphic beliefs about objects lead people to treat them as if they were alive. In one study, consumers who were encouraged to think about their car in anthropomorphic terms were less willing to replace it. So, as many of us know, when it's finally time to get rid of a valued item, this can be a very painful process; sort of like saying goodbye to an old friend.[127]

How do we ease the pain? As they observed people getting items ready to be sold at garage sales, a set of researchers identified these rituals:

- **Iconic transfer ritual**—Taking pictures and videos of objects before we sell them.
- **Transition-place ritual**—Putting items in an out-of-the way location such as a garage or attic before we dispose of them.
- **Ritual cleansing**—Washing, ironing, and/or meticulously wrapping the item.[128]

CHAPTER SUMMARY

Now that you have finished reading this chapter you should understand why:

1. Many factors at the time of purchase dramatically influence the consumer's decision-making process.

Many factors affect a purchase. These include the consumer's antecedent state (e.g., his or her mood, time pressure, or disposition toward shopping). Time is an important resource that often determines how much effort and search will go into a decision. Our moods are influenced by the degree of pleasure and arousal a store environment creates.

The usage context of a product is a segmentation variable; consumers look for different product attributes depending on the use to which they intend to put their purchase. The presence or absence of other people (co-consumers)—and the types of people they are—can also affect a consumer's decisions.

The shopping experience is a pivotal part of the purchase decision. In many cases, retailing is like theater: The consumer's evaluation of stores and products may depend on the type of "performance" he witnesses. The actors (e.g., salespeople), the setting (the store environment), and the props (e.g., store displays) influence this evaluation. Like a brand personality, a number of factors, such as perceived convenience, sophistication, and expertise of salespeople, determine store image. With increasing competition from non-store alternatives, creating a positive shopping experience has never been more important. Online shopping is growing in importance, and this new way to acquire products has both good (e.g., convenience) and bad (e.g., security) aspects.

2. The information a store or Web site provides strongly influences a purchase decision, in addition to what a shopper already knows or believes about a product.

Because we don't make many purchase decisions until we're actually in the store, point-of-purchase (POP) stimuli are very important sales tools. These include product samples, elaborate package displays, place-based media, and in-store promotional materials such as "shelf talkers." POP stimuli are particularly useful in promoting impulse buying, which happens when a consumer yields to a sudden urge for a product. Increasingly, mobile shopping apps are also playing a key role.

3. A salesperson often is the crucial link to a purchase.

The consumer's encounter with a salesperson is a complex and important process. The outcome can be affected by such factors as the salesperson's similarity to the customer and his or her perceived credibility.

4. Marketers need to be concerned about a consumer's evaluations of a product after he or she buys it as well as before.

A person's overall feelings about the product after he buys determine consumer satisfaction/dissatisfaction. Many factors influence our perceptions of product quality, including price, brand name, and product performance. Our degree of satisfaction often depends on the extent to which a product's performance is consistent with our prior expectations of how well it will function.

5. Getting rid of products when consumers no longer need or want them is a major concern to both marketers and public policymakers.

Product disposal is an increasingly important problem. Recycling is one option that will become more crucial as consumers' environmental awareness grows. Lateral cycling occurs when we buy, sell, or barter secondhand objects.

KEY TERMS

abandoned products
activity stores
atmospherics
being space
co-consumers
consumer satisfaction/
    dissatisfaction (CS/D)
divestment rituals
expectancy disconfirmation model
freegans
gemba

impulse buying
incidental similarity
lateral cycling
mental budgets
minipreneurs
mobile shopping apps
open rates
point-of-purchase (POP) stimuli
pop-up stores
pretailer
queuing theory

retail theming
sharing sites
shopping orientation
store image
time poverty
timestyle
total quality management (TQM)
underground economy
unplanned buying

REVIEW

1 What do we mean by situational self-image? Give an example of this phenomenon.
2 Describe the difference between density and crowding. Why is this difference relevant in purchase environments?
3 What is time poverty, and how can it influence our purchase decisions?
4 What are the two dimensions that determine whether we will react positively or negatively to a purchase environment?
5 List three separate motivations for shopping, and give an example of each.

6 What are some important pros and cons of e-commerce?
7 List three factors that help to determine store image.
8 What is the difference between unplanned buying and impulse buying?
9 How do a consumer's prior expectations about product quality influence his satisfaction with the product after he buys it?
10 List three actions a consumer can take if she is dissatisfied with a purchase.
11 What is the underground economy and why is it important to marketers?

CONSUMER BEHAVIOR CHALLENGE

■ DISCUSS

1 Is the customer always right? Why or why not?
2 Are pop-up stores simply a fad, or a retailing concept that's here to stay?
3 Discuss some of the shopping motivations the chapter describes. How might a retailer adjust its strategy to accommodate these motivations?
4 What are some positive and negative aspects of a policy that requires employees who interact with customers to wear a uniform?
5 Think about exceptionally good and bad salespeople you have encountered as a shopper. What qualities seem to differentiate them from others?
6 Discuss the concept of "timestyle." Based on your own experiences, how might we segment consumers in terms of their timestyles?
7 Several men's clothing retailers nationwide now provide free booze to their male clientele to encourage them to hang out in their stores.[129] Is it ethical to encourage customers to get wasted before they shop?

8 Compare and contrast different cultures' conceptions of time. What are some implications for marketing strategy within each of these frameworks?
9 The movement away from a "disposable consumer society" toward one that emphasizes creative recycling creates many opportunities for marketers. Can you identify some?
10 Some retailers work hard to cultivate a certain look or image, and they may even choose employees who fit this look. Abercrombie & Fitch, for example, seems to link itself to a clean-cut, all-American image. At one point a lawsuit claimed that Abercrombie & Fitch systematically "refuses to hire qualified minority applicants as brand representatives to work on the sales floor and discourages applications from minority applicants" (Abercrombie replied that it has "zero tolerance for discrimination").[130] We know that the Hooters restaurant chain is notorious for its attractive female waitresses. Should a retailer have the right to recruit employees who are consistent with its image even if this means excluding certain types of people (e.g., non-Caucasians, men) from the sales floor?

11 The mall of the future will most likely be less about purchasing products than about exploring them in a physical setting. This means that retail environments will have to become places to build brand images, rather than simply places to sell products. What are some strategies stores can use to enhance the emotional/sensory experiences they give to shoppers?

12 The store environment is heating up as more and more companies put their promotional dollars into point-of-purchase efforts. Some stores confront shoppers with videos at the checkout counter, computer monitors attached to their shopping carts, and ads stenciled on the floors. We're also increasingly exposed to ads in nonshopping environments. A health club in New York was forced to remove TV monitors that showed advertising on the Health Club Media Networks, after exercisers claimed that the programming interfered with their workouts. Do you feel that these innovations are overly intrusive? At what point might shoppers rebel and demand some peace and quiet when they shop? Do you see any market potential in the future for stores that "countermarket" by promising a "hands-off" shopping environment?

13 Courts often prohibit special-interest groups from distributing literature in shopping malls. Mall managements claim that these centers are private property. However, these groups argue that the mall is the modern-day version of the town square and as such is a public forum. Find some recent court cases involving this free-speech issue, and examine the arguments pro and con. What is the current status of the mall as a public forum? Do you agree with this concept?

■ APPLY

1 Conduct naturalistic observation at a local mall. Sit in a central location and observe the activities of mall employees and patrons. Keep a log of the nonretailing activity you observe (e.g., special performances, exhibits, socializing, etc.). Does this activity enhance or detract from business the mall conducts? As malls become more like high-tech game rooms, how valid is the criticism that shopping areas only encourage more loitering by teenage boys, who don't spend a lot in stores and simply scare away other customers?

2 Select three competing clothing stores in your area and conduct a store image study for them. Ask a group of consumers to rate each store on a set of attributes and plot these ratings on the same graph. Based on your findings, are there any areas of competitive advantage or disadvantage you could bring to the attention of store management?

3 Using Table 1 as a model, construct a person–situation segmentation matrix for a brand of perfume.

4 What applications of queuing theory can you find that local services use? Interview consumers as they wait in line to determine how their experience affects their satisfaction with the service.

5 Many retailers believe that when they pile a lot of stuff around their store, this cluttered look encourages shoppers to hunt for items and eventually buy more. Dollar General recently raised the height of its shelves to more than six feet; J. C. Penney transformed empty walls into jewelry and accessory displays; Old Navy added lanes lined with items like water bottles, candy, and lunchboxes. Best Buy is even testing the impact of filling aisles with bulky items like Segways and bicycles to compensate for the smaller space that thin TVs and smaller speakers take up. Notably, Walmart recently did an abrupt about-face: The company only recently remodeled its stores by eliminating the pallets of items it used to stack in the centers of aisles, and it reduced overall inventory by about 9%. Customers loved the leaner, cleaner look. Only one problem: They bought less stuff. As a senior Walmart executive commented, "They loved the experience. They just bought less. And that generally is not a good long-term strategy." Now, Walmart is adding inventory back in and is once again piling stacks of merchandise in aisles.[131] What's your take on these store stocking strategies? Visit several "big-box" stores in your area, such as Walmart, Target, Best Buy, Costco, and so on. If possible, interview shoppers about their experiences. Do they have trouble navigating around the store? Do they enjoy the clutter? Does it feel like a "treasure hunt" when they have to pick their way around piles and pallets? If you were designing a store, how would you craft a stocking strategy that would make it easy to shop there?

6 Interview people who are selling items at a flea market or garage sale. Ask them to identify some items to which they had a strong attachment. Then, see if you can prompt them to describe one or more divestment rituals they went through as they prepared to offer these items for sale.

7 Identify three people who own electric coffeemakers. Then, "go to the gemba" by observing them as they actually prepare coffee in the appliance at home. Based on these experiences, what recommendations might you make to the designer of a new coffeemaker model that would improve customers' experiences with the product?

Case Study

GIVING AND RECEIVING ON FREECYCLE.ORG

Like it or not, we live in a disposable society. And it isn't just paper products and fast-food containers we throw away. We use our televisions, computers, cell phones, furniture, clothing, and other products until something better comes along, and then we toss them. Landfills everywhere reel under the onslaught of the trash we create.

But what if people could find someone to take their old junk off their hands? Or what if individuals could find a needed item that someone else just happens to be throwing away? *Freecycle.org* meets this need. This Web site came into being as a recycling concept to reduce the strain on landfills and cut down on consumer wastefulness. Freecycle, which uses a bulletin board structure, works so well because it's so simple. It connects people who have items to give away with others who need them, and vice versa. It's basically like an "eBay for free." Indeed, many users call the site by its nickname of "Freebay."

From its humble beginnings in the Tucson, Arizona, area in 2003, today there are millions of members who constitute thousands of user communities in more than 75 countries; they say they are "changing the world one gift at a time." *Freecycle.org* is one of the most popular nonprofit destinations in cyberspace; *Time* dubbed it "one of the 50 coolest" Web sites. This notoriety comes within a few short years and with no promotion other than word of mouth and plenty of free publicity.

Anyone can join this 24/7 virtual garage sale, and membership is free. In fact, the main rule of *Freecycle.org* is that you can only offer free items. Givers and receivers contact each other via email and then arrange for delivery. The site's founder estimates that the average freecycled item weighs 1 pound. That means that the Freecycle movement keeps 400 tons of "garbage" out of landfills every day.

This is certainly a sign of success. But other measures of success have become apparent as well, like the satisfaction of all those involved. What one person doesn't want, someone else will take off their hands. In this exchange everyone wins. "It's become a huge gift economy and very life affirming for everyone who has given away something. You can't help but get a good feeling when you've helped another person," the founder said.

As long as people want to get rid of or acquire an old couch, a six-year-old husky, a storm door, a van that needs a transmission, or even horse manure, Freecycle has a bright future. "When it comes to the Internet and connecting with one another, there are no limitations," Beal said. "We'll continue growing and experiencing the goodness that comes from giving."

DISCUSSION QUESTIONS

1 Why do you think Freecycle.org has achieved such high levels of growth in such a short period of time?

2 Freecycle created an alternative disposal option that is rapidly growing. Discuss ways that freecycling might affect the purchase habits of consumers.

3 Should for-profit businesses like eBay get into the freecycling business? Should companies motivate more consumers to give things away that they might otherwise be able to sell or auction? Can they still make a profit while they help to eliminate waste?

Sources: "A Brief History," *www.freecycle.org*, accessed June 13, 2011; "Cleanup Idea Keeps up with the Times," *NG News* (June 11, 2011), http://Newswire.Freecycle.Org/2011/06/11/Ng-News-Cleanup-Idea-Keeps-Up-With-The-Times/, accessed June 13, 2011; Tamsin Kelly, "Multi-Bargain Swap Shop," *Daily Telegraph* (July 7, 2007): 13; "Free Swap Program Finds Homes for Recycled Goods," *Wall Street Journal* (January 2, 2008); Mac McLean, "Don't Throw Unwanted Items Away," *Bristol Herald Courier* (January 13, 2009): http://www2.tricities.com/m/news/2009/jan/13/freecycling_strikes_the_right_note-ar-249741/, accessed September 11, 2011.

NOTES

1. Keith Naughton, "Revolution in the Showroom," *BusinessWeek* (February 19, 1996): 70.
2. Pradeep Kakkar and Richard J. Lutz, "Situational Influence on Consumer Behavior: A Review," in Harold H. Kassarjian and Thomas S. Robertson, eds., *Perspectives in Consumer Behavior*, 3rd ed. (Glenview, IL: Scott, Foresman, 1981): 204–14.
3. Christopher Heine, "Will Facebook Ads Soon Reflect 'What's On Your Mind?,'" *ClickZ* (March 23, 2011), http://www.clickz.com/clickz/news/2036901/facebook-ads-soon-reflect-whats-mind, accessed April 17, 2011.
4. Benedict Carey, "TV Time, Unlike Child Care, Ranks High in Mood Study," *New York Times* (December 3, 2004), www.nytimes.com, accessed December 3, 2004.
5. Carolyn Turner Schenk and Rebecca H. Holman, "A Sociological Approach to Brand Choice: The Concept of Situational Self-Image," in Jerry C. Olson, ed., *Advances in Consumer Research 7* (Ann Arbor, MI: Association for Consumer Research, 1980): 610–14.
6. Peter R. Dickson, "Person–Situation: Segmentation's Missing Link," *Journal of Marketing* 46 (Fall 1982): 56–64.
7. Alan R. Hirsch, "Effects of Ambient Odors on Slot-Machine Usage in a Las Vegas Casino," *Psychology & Marketing* 12 (October 1995): 585–94.
8. Daniel Stokols, "On the Distinction between Density and Crowding: Some Implications for Future Research," *Psychological Review* 79 (1972): 275–77.
9. Jonathan Levav and Rui (Juliet) Zhu, "Seeking Freedom through Variety," *Journal of Consumer Research* 36, no. 4 (2009): 600–10.
10. "Are Location-Based Shopping Apps Catching On?," *eMarketer* (March 15, 2011), http://www.emarketer.com/Article.aspx?R=1008280&AspxAutoDetectCookieSupport=1, accessed April 17, 2011.
11. Tanya Irwin, "ReachMail: Email Marketers Should Focus on Mid-Day," *Marketing Daily* (March 17, 2011), http://www.mediapost.com/publications/?fa=Articles.showArticle&art_aid=146883&nid=124807, accessed April 18, 2011.
12. Carol Felker Kaufman, Paul M. Lane, and Jay D. Lindquist, "Exploring More Than 24 Hours a Day: A Preliminary Investigation of Polychronic Time Use," *Journal of Consumer Research* 18 (December 1991): 392–401.
13. Laurence P. Feldman and Jacob Hornik, "The Use of Time: An Integrated Conceptual Model," *Journal of Consumer Research* 7 (March 1981): 407–19; see also Michelle M. Bergadaa, "The Role of Time in the Action of the Consumer," *Journal of Consumer Research* 17 (December 1990): 289–302.
14. Alan Zarembo, "What If There Weren't Any Clocks to Watch?" *Newsweek* (June 30, 1997): 14; based on research reported in Robert Levine, *A*

Geography of Time: The Temporal Misadventures of a Social Psychologist, or How Every Culture Keeps Time Just a Little Bit Differently (New York: Basic Books, 1997).

15. Deborah Kotz, "Wives Do More Housework, Study Shows," *U.S. News & World Report* (April 7, 2008), http://health.usnews.com/blogs/on-women/2008/04/07/wives-do-more-housework-study-shows.html, accessed June 8, 2009; John P. Robinson, "Time Squeeze," *Advertising Age* (February 1990): 30-33.

16. June S. Cotte, S. Ratneshwar, and David Glen Mick, "The Times of Their Lives: Phenomenological and Metaphorical Characteristics of Consumer Timestyles," *Journal of Consumer Research* 31 (September 2004): 333-45.

17. James Gorman, "Does This Mean People Turned Off, Tuned Out and Dropped In?" *New York Times* (June 27, 2006), www.nytimes.com, accessed June 27, 2006.

18. Robert J. Graham, "The Role of Perception of Time in Consumer Research," *Journal of Consumer Research* 7 (March 1981): 335-42; Esther S. Page-Wood, Paul M. Lane, and Carol J. Kaufman, "The Art of Time," in B. J. Dunlap, ed., *Proceedings of the 1990 Academy of Marketing Science Conference 13* (Cullowhee, NC: Academy of Marketing Science, 1990): 56-61.

19. Dhruv Grewal, Julie Baker, Michael Levy, and Glenn B. Voss, "The Effects of Wait Expectations and Store Atmosphere Evaluations on Patronage Intentions in Service-Intensive Retail Store," *Journal of Retailing* 79 (2003): 259-68; cf. also Shirley Taylor, "Waiting for Service: The Relationship Between Delays and Evaluations of Service," *Journal of Marketing* 58 (April 1994): 56-69.

20. "We're Hating the Waiting; 43% Prefer Self-Service," *Marketing Daily* (January 23, 2007), www.mediapost.com, accessed January 23, 2007.

21. David H. Maister, "The Psychology of Waiting Lines," in John A. Czepiel, Michael R. Solomon, and Carol F. Surprenant, eds., *The Service Encounter: Managing Employee/Customer Interaction in Service Businesses* (Lexington, MA: Lexington Books, 1985): 113-24.

22. David Leonhardt, "Airlines Using Technology in a Push for Shorter Lines," *New York Times* (May 8, 2000), www.nytimes.com, accessed May 8, 2000.

23. Jennifer Ordonez, "An Efficiency Drive: Fast-Food Lanes, Equipped with Timers, Get Even Faster," *Wall Street Journal* (May 18, 2000), www.wsj.com, accessed May 18, 2000.

24. Quoted in A. Pawlowski, "Queuing Psychology: Can Waiting in Line Be Fun?" *CNN* (November 26, 2008), www.cnn.com/2008/TECH/science/11/20/queuing.psychology/index.html?eref=rss, accessed November 26, 2008; Sarah Tully, "What Are the Best Disneyland Phone Apps?," *Orange County Register* (March 18, 2010), http://ocresort.ocregister.com/2010/03/18/what-are-the-best-disneyland-phone-apps/38003/, accessed June 4, 2011; Dawn C. Chmielewski, "Disney, Verizon to Turn the Cellphone into a Theme-Park Visitor's Tool," *Los Angeles Times*, November 12, 2008, www.latimes.com/business/La-Fi-Disney12-2008nov12,0,4711602.Story?Track=Rss, accessed November 12, 2008.

25. Henry Fountain, quoted in "The Ultimate Body Language: How You Line Up for Mickey," *New York Times* (September 18, 2005), www.nytimes.com, accessed September 18, 2005.

26. Laurette Dube and Bernd H. Schmitt, "The Processing of Emotional and Cognitive Aspects of Product Usage in Satisfaction Judgments," in Rebecca H. Holman and Michael R. Solomon, eds., *Advances in Consumer Research 18* (Provo, UT: Association for Consumer Research, 1991): 52-56; Lalita A. Manrai and Meryl P. Gardner, "The Influence of Affect on Attributions for Product Failure," in Rebecca H. Holman and Michael R. Solomon, eds., *Advances in Consumer Research 18* (Provo, UT: Association for Consumer Research, 1991): 249-54.

27. Kevin G. Celuch and Linda S. Showers, "It's Time to Stress Stress: The Stress-Purchase/Consumption Relationship," in Rebecca H. Holman and Michael R. Solomon, eds., *Advances in Consumer Research 18* (Provo, UT: Association for Consumer Research, 1991): 284-89; Lawrence R. Lepisto, J. Kathleen Stuenkel, and Linda K. Anglin, "Stress: An Ignored Situational Influence," in Rebecca H. Holman and Michael R. Solomon, eds., *Advances in Consumer Research 18* (Provo, UT: Association for Consumer Research, 1991): 296-302.

28. Velitchka D. Kaltcheva and Barton A. Weitz, "When Should a Retailer Create an Exciting Store Environment?" *Journal of Marketing* 70 (January 2006): 107-18.

29. John D. Mayer and Yvonne N. Gaschke, "The Experience and Meta-Experience of Mood," *Journal of Personality & Social Psychology* 55 (July 1988): 102-11.

30. Meryl Paula Gardner, "Mood States and Consumer Behavior: A Critical Review," *Journal of Consumer Research* 12 (December 1985): 281-300; Scott Dawson, Peter H. Bloch, and Nancy M. Ridgway, "Shopping Motives, Emotional States, and Retail Outcomes," *Journal of Retailing* 66 (Winter 1990): 408-27; Patricia A. Knowles, Stephen J. Grove, and W. Jeffrey Burroughs, "An Experimental Examination of Mood States on Retrieval and Evaluation of Advertisement and Brand Information," *Journal of the Academy of Marketing Science* 21 (April 1993): 135-43; Paul W. Miniard, Sunil Bhatla, and Deepak Sirdeskmuhk, "Mood as a Determinant of Postconsumption Product Evaluations: Mood Effects and Their Dependency on the Affective Intensity of the Consumption Experience," *Journal of Consumer Psychology* 1, no. 2 (1992): 173-95; Mary T. Curren and Katrin R. Harich, "Consumers' Mood States: The Mitigating Influence of Personal Relevance on Product Evaluations," *Psychology & Marketing* 11 (March-April 1994): 91-107; Gerald J. Gorn, Marvin E. Goldberg, and Kunal Basu, "Mood, Awareness, and Product Evaluation," *Journal of Consumer Psychology* 2, no. 3 (1993): 237-56.

31. Gordon C. Bruner, "Music, Mood, and Marketing," *Journal of Marketing* 54 (October 1990): 94-104; Basil G. Englis, "Music Television and Its Influences on Consumers, Consumer Culture, and the Transmission of Consumption Messages," in Rebecca H. Holman and Michael R. Solomon, eds., *Advances in Consumer Research 18* (Provo, UT: Association for Consumer Research, 1991): 111-14.

32. Marvin E. Goldberg and Gerald J. Gorn, "Happy and Sad TV Programs: How They Affect Reactions to Commercials," *Journal of Consumer Research* 14 (December 1987): 387-403; Gorn, Goldberg, and Basu, "Mood, Awareness, and Product Evaluation"; Curren and Harich, "Consumers' Mood States."

33. Rajeev Batra and Douglas M. Stayman, "The Role of Mood in Advertising Effectiveness," *Journal of Consumer Research* 17 (September 1990): 203; John P. Murry, Jr., and Peter A. Dacin, "Cognitive Moderators of Negative-Emotion Effects: Implications for Understanding Media Context," *Journal of Consumer Research* 22 (March 1996): 439-47; see also Curren and Harich, "Consumers' Mood States"; Gorn, Goldberg, and Basu, "Mood, Awareness, and Product Evaluation."

34. Jeffrey Zaslow, "Happiness Inc.," *Wall Street Journal* (March 18, 2006): P1.

35. For a scale to assess these dimensions of the shopping experience, see Barry J. Babin, William R. Darden, and Mitch Griffin, "Work and/or Fun: Measuring Hedonic and Utilitarian Shopping Value," *Journal of Consumer Research* 20 (March 1994): 644-56.

36. Kaltcheva and Weitz, "When Should a Retailer Create an Exciting Store Environment?"

37. Babin, Darden, and Griffin, "Work and/or Fun."

38. Edward M. Tauber, "Why Do People Shop?" *Journal of Marketing* 36 (October 1972): 47-48.

39. Ann Zimmerman and Laura Stevens, "Attention, Shoppers: Bored College Kids Competing in Aisle 6," *Wall Street Journal* (February 23, 2005). http://professional.wsj.com/article/SB110911598024661430-H9jfYNkla-F4oJ2sZ32IaqiAm5.html?mg=reno-wsj, accessed September 11, 2011.

40. Robert C. Prus, *Making Sales: Influence as Interpersonal Accomplishment* (Newbury Park, CA: Sage Publications, 1989): 225.

41. Michael-Lee Johnstone and Denise M Conroy, "Dressing for the Thrill: An Exploration of Why Women Dress Up to Go Shopping," *Journal of Consumer Behaviour* 4, no. 4 (2005): 234.

42. Some material in this section was adapted from Michael R. Solomon and Elnora W. Stuart, *Welcome to Marketing.com: The Brave New World of E-Commerce* (Upper Saddle River, NJ: Prentice Hall, 2001).

43. June Cotte and Kathryn A. Latour, "Blackjack in the Kitchen: Understanding Online versus Casino Gambling," *Journal of Consumer Research* 35 (February 2009): 742-58.

44. Rebecca K. Ratner, Barbara E. Kahn, and Daniel Kahneman, "Choosing Less-Preferred Experiences for the Sake of Variety," *Journal of Consumer Research* 26 (June 1999): 1-15.

45. "Total Immersion and eBay Bring Virtual 'See It On' Feature to eBay's Fashion App," *Business Wire* (February 1, 2011), http://www.businesswire.com/news/home/20110201006053/en/Total-Immersion-eBay-Bring-Virtual-%E2%80%98See-On%E2%80%99, accessed June 3, 2011.

46. Alisa Gould-Simon, "How Fashion Retailers Are Redefining E-Commerce with Social Media," *Mashable.com* (March 7, 2011), http://mashable.com/2011/03/07/fashion-retailers-social-e-commerce/, accessed April 17, 2011.

47. www.allurent.com/newsDetail.php?newsid=20, accessed January 29, 2007. No – but can we leave it without a cite as it's common sense (or because I say so?)....

48. Stephanie Rosenbloom, "Malls Test Experimental Waters to Fill Vacancies," *New York Times* (April 4, 2009), www.nytimes.com/2009/04/05/business/05mall.html?_r=1, accessed April 4, 2009.

49. Vanessa O'Connell, "Fictional Hershey Factory Will Send Kisses to Broadway," *Wall Street Journal* (August 5, 2002), www.wsj.com, accessed August 5, 2002.

50. Millie Creighton, "The Seed of Creative Lifestyle Shopping: Wrapping Consumerism in Japanese Store Layouts," in John F. Sherry Jr., ed., *Servicescapes: The Concept of Place in Contemporary Markets* (Lincolnwood, IL: NTC Business Books, 1998): 199-228; also cf. Robert V. Kozinets, John F. Sherry, Diana Storm, Adam Duhachek, Krittinee Nuttavuthisit, and Benet DeBerry-Spence, "Ludic Agency and Retail Spectacle," *Journal of Consumer Research* 31 (December 2004): 658-72.

51. http://www.paragraphny.com/, accessed June 3, 2011.

52. Jennifer Saranow, "Retailers Give It the Old College Try," *Wall Street Journal* (August 28, 2008): B8; *March 2007 Trend Briefing*, www.trendwatching.com/briefing, accessed March 30, 2007.

53. Most measures of store image are quite similar to other attitude measures discussed in Chapter 7. For an excellent bibliography of store image studies, see Mary R. Zimmer and Linda L. Golden, "Impressions of Retail Stores: A Content Analysis of Consumer Images," *Journal of Retailing* 64 (Fall 1988): 265–93.

54. Spiggle and Sewall, "A Choice Sets Model of Retail Selection."

55. "The Science of Shopping: The Way the Brain Buys," *The Economist* (December 18, 2008), www.economist.com, accessed February 2, 2009.

56. Philip Kotler, "Atmospherics as a Marketing Tool," *Journal of Retailing* (Winter 1973–74): 10; Anna Mattila and Jochen Wirtz, "Congruency of Scent and Music as a Driver of In-Store Evaluations and Behavior," *Journal of Retailing* 77, no. 2 (2001): 273–89; J. Duncan Herrington, "An Integrative Path Model of the Effects of Retail Environments on Shopper Behavior," in Robert L. King, ed., *Marketing: Toward the Twenty-First Century* (Richmond, VA: Southern Marketing Association, 1991): 58–62; see also Ann E. Schlosser, "Applying the Functional Theory of Attitudes to Understanding the Influence of Store Atmosphere on Store Inferences," *Journal of Consumer Psychology* 7, no. 4 (1998): 345–69.

57. Joseph A. Bellizzi and Robert E. Hite, "Environmental Color, Consumer Feelings, and Purchase Likelihood," *Psychology & Marketing* 9 (September–October 1992): 347–63.

58. See Eric R. Spangenberg, Ayn E. Crowley, and Pamela W. Henderson, "Improving the Store Environment: Do Olfactory Cues Affect Evaluations and Behaviors?" *Journal of Marketing* 60 (April 1996): 67–80, for a study that assessed olfaction in a controlled, simulated store environment.

59. Robert J. Donovan, John R. Rossiter, Gilian Marcoolyn, and Andrew Nesdale, "Store Atmosphere and Purchasing Behavior," *Journal of Retailing* 70, no. 3 (1994): 283–94.

60. www.buildabear.com, accessed June 9, 2009.

61. Deborah Blumenthal, "Scenic Design for In-Store Try-ons," *New York Times* (April 9, 1988): N9.

62. John Pierson, "If Sun Shines in, Workers Work Better, Buyers Buy More," *Wall Street Journal* (November 20, 1995): B1.

63. Charles S. Areni and David Kim, "The Influence of In-Store Lighting on Consumers' Examination of Merchandise in a Wine Store," *International Journal of Research in Marketing* 11, no. 2 (March 1994): 117–25.

64. Charles S. Areni and David Kim, "The Influence of In-Store Lighting on Consumers' Examination of Merchandise in a Wine Store," *International Journal of Research in Marketing* 11, no. 2 (March 1994): 117–25.

65. "Slow Music Makes Fast Drinkers," *Psychology Today* (March 1989): 18.

66. Brad Edmondson, "Pass the Meat Loaf," *American Demographics* (January 1989): 19.

67. "Through the Looking Glass," *Lifestyle Monitor* 16 (Fall–Winter 2002).

68. Jennifer Lach, "Meet You in Aisle Three," *American Demographics* (April 1999): 41.

69. Karen M. Stilley, J. Jeffrey Inman, and Kirk L. Wakefield, "Planning to Make Unplanned Purchases? The Role of In-Store Slack in Budget Deviation," *Journal of Consumer Research* 37, no. 2 (2010): 264–78.

70. "Motorola Survey: Shoppers Better Connected to Information than Store Associates," *Chain Store Age* (January 17, 2011), http://www.chainstoreage.com/article/motorola-survey-shoppers-better-connected-information-store-associates, accessed April 30, 2011; Kris Hudson, "Malls Test Apps to Aid Shoppers," *Wall Street Journal* (April 26, 2011), http://online.wsj.com/article/SB10001424052748704336504576258740640080926.html?mod=dist_smartbrief, accessed April 29, 2011.

71. Ernest Beck, "Diageo Attempts to Reinvent the Bar in an Effort to Increase Spirits Sales," *Wall Street Journal* (February 23, 2001), www.wsj.com, accessed October 1, 2007.

72. Easwar S. Iyer, "Unplanned Purchasing: Knowledge of Shopping Environment and Time Pressure," *Journal of Retailing* 65 (Spring 1989): 40–57; C. Whan Park, Easwar S. Iyer, and Daniel C. Smith, "The Effects of Situational Factors on In-Store Grocery Shopping," *Journal of Consumer Research* 15 (March 1989): 422–33.

73. Iyer, "Unplanned Purchasing"; Park, Iyer, and Smith, "The Effects of Situational Factors on In-Store Grocery Shopping."

74. Matt Richtel, "At Starbucks, Songs of Instant Gratification," *New York Times* (October 1, 2007), www.nytimes.com, accessed October 1, 2007.

75. Manoj Thomas, Kalpesh Kaushik Desai, and Satheeshkumar Seenivasan, "How Credit Card Payments Increase Unhealthy Food Purchases: Visceral Regulation of Vices," *Journal of Consumer Research* 38, no. 1 (June 2011): _126-139.

76. Mukhopadhyay Anirban and Gita Venkataramani Johar, "Indulgence as Self-Reward for Prior Shopping Restraint: A Justification-Based Mechanism," *Journal of Consumer Psychology* 19, no. 3 (2009): 334–45.

77. Emily Steel, "Luring Shoppers to Stores," *Wall Street Journal* (August 26, 2010), http://online.wsj.com/article/SB10001424052748704540904575451841980063132.html, accessed April 18, 2011.

78. Ellen Byron and Suzanne Vranica, "Scanners Check Out Who's Browsing Marketers, Retailers Test Sensors to Weigh Reach of In-Store Promotions," *Wall Street Journal* (September 27, 2006): B2; cf. also www.popai.com/index.php?option=com_content&view=frontpage&Itemid=1, accessed June 9, 2009.

79. Quoted in Louise Story, "Product Packages Now Shout to Get Your Attention," *New York Times* (August 10, 2007), www.nytimes.com, accessed August 10, 2007.

80. Cf. Robert B. Cialdini, *Influence: Science and Practice*, 2nd ed. (Glenview, IL: Scott, Foresman, 1988).

81. Richard P. Bagozzi, "Marketing as Exchange," *Journal of Marketing* 39 (October 1975): 32–39; Peter M. Blau, *Exchange and Power in Social Life* (New York: Wiley, 1964); Marjorie Caballero and Alan J. Resnik, "The Attraction Paradigm in Dyadic Exchange," *Psychology & Marketing* 3, no. 1 (1986): 17–34; George C. Homans, "Social Behavior as Exchange," *American Journal of Sociology* 63 (1958): 597–606; Paul H. Schurr and Julie L. Ozanne, "Influences on Exchange Processes: Buyers' Preconceptions of a Seller's Trustworthiness and Bargaining Toughness," *Journal of Consumer Research* 11 (March 1985): 939–53; Arch G. Woodside and J. W. Davenport, "The Effect of Salesman Similarity and Expertise on Consumer Purchasing Behavior," *Journal of Marketing Research* 8 (1974): 433–36.

82. Mary Jo Bitner, Bernard H. Booms, and Mary Stansfield Tetreault, "The Service Encounter: Diagnosing Favorable and Unfavorable Incidents," *Journal of Marketing* 54 (January 1990): 7–84; Robert C. Prus, *Making Sales* (Newbury Park, CA: Sage Publications, 1989); Arch G. Woodside and James L. Taylor, "Identity Negotiations in Buyer–Seller Interactions," in Elizabeth C. Hirschman and Morris B. Holbrook, eds., *Advances in Consumer Research* 12 (Provo, UT: Association for Consumer Research, 1985): 443–49.

83. Barry J. Babin, James S. Boles, and William R. Darden, "Salesperson Stereotypes, Consumer Emotions, and Their Impact on Information Processing," *Journal of the Academy of Marketing Science* 23, no. 2 (1995): 94–105; Gilbert A. Churchill, Jr., Neil M. Ford, Steven W. Hartley, and Orville C. Walker, Jr., "The Determinants of Salesperson Performance: A Meta-Analysis," *Journal of Marketing Research* 22 (May 1985): 103–18.

84. Jiang Lan, Joandrea Hoegg, Darren W. Dahl, and Amitava Chattopadhyay, "The Persuasive Role of Incidental Similarity on Attitudes and Purchase Intentions in a Sales Context," *Journal of Consumer Research* 36, no. 5 (2010): 778–91.

85. Siew Meng Leong, Paul S. Busch, and Deborah Roedder John, "Knowledge Bases and Salesperson Effectiveness: A Script-Theoretic Analysis," *Journal of Marketing Research* 26 (May 1989): 164; Harish Sujan, Mita Sujan, and James R. Bettman, "Knowledge Structure Differences Between More Effective and Less Effective Salespeople," *Journal of Marketing Research* 25 (February 1988): 81–86; Robert Saxe and Barton Weitz, "The SOCCO Scale: A Measure of the Customer Orientation of Salespeople," *Journal of Marketing Research* 19 (August 1982): 343–51; David M. Szymanski, "Determinants of Selling Effectiveness: The Importance of Declarative Knowledge to the Personal Selling Concept," *Journal of Marketing* 52 (January 1988): 64–77; Barton A. Weitz, "Effectiveness in Sales Interactions: A Contingency Framework," *Journal of Marketing* 45 (Winter 1981): 85–103.

86. Jagdish N. Sheth, "Buyer-Seller Interaction: A Conceptual Framework," in *Advances in Consumer Research 3* (Cincinnati, OH: Association for Consumer Research, 1976): 382–86; Kaylene C. Williams and Rosann L. Spiro, "Communication Style in the Salesperson-Customer Dyad," *Journal of Marketing Research* 22 (November 1985): 434–42.

87. Marsha L. Richins, "An Analysis of Consumer Interaction Styles in the Marketplace," *Journal of Consumer Research* 10 (June 1983): 73–82.

88. Calmetta Y. Coleman, "A Car Salesman's Bizarre Prank May End Up Backfiring in Court," *Wall Street Journal* (May 2, 1995): B1.

89. "Woman Stabbed over McDonald's Meal Dispute," *Opelika/Auburn News* (April 13, 2002).

90. www.customerssuck.com, accessed June 4, 2011; Keith Naughton, "Tired of Smile-Free Service," *Newsweek* (March 6, 2000): 44–45; www.protest.net, accessed June 4, 2011.

91. "Voice of the Consumer Not Leveraged," Center for Media Research (February 3, 2009), www.mediapost.com, accessed February 3, 2009.

92. Rama Jayanti and Anita Jackson, "Service Satisfaction: Investigation of Three Models," in Rebecca H. Holman and Michael R. Solomon, eds., *Advances in Consumer Research 18* (Provo, UT: Association for Consumer Research, 1991): 603–10; David K. Tse, Franco M. Nicosia, and Peter C. Wilton, "Consumer Satisfaction as a Process," *Psychology & Marketing* 7 (Fall 1990): 177–93. For a treatment of satisfaction issues from a more interpretive perspective, see Susan Fournier and David Mick, "Rediscovering Satisfaction," *Journal of Marketing* 63 (October 1999): 5–23.

93. Bruce Cooil, Timothy L. Keiningham, Lerzan Aksoy, and Michael Hsu, "A Longitudinal Analysis of Customer Satisfaction and Share of Wallet: Investigating the Moderating Effect of Customer Characteristics," *Journal of Marketing* 71 (January 2007): 67–83. For a study that looks at consumer variables moderating this relationship, cf. Kathleen Seiders, Glenn B. Voss, Dhruv Grewal, and Andrea L. Godfrey, "Do Satisfied Customers Buy

More? Examining Moderating Influences in a Retailing Context," *Journal of Marketing* 69 (October 2005): 26–43.

94. Constance L. Hayes, "Service Takes a Holiday," *New York Times* (December 23, 1998): C1.

95. Leslie Kaufman, "Enough Talk," *Newsweek* (August 18, 1997): 48–49.

96. Robert Jacobson and David A. Aaker, "The Strategic Role of Product Quality," *Journal of Marketing* 51 (October 1987): 31–44. For a review of issues regarding the measurement of service quality, see J. Joseph Cronin, Jr., and Steven A. Taylor, "Measuring Service Quality: A Reexamination and Extension," *Journal of Marketing* 56 (July 1992): 55–68.

97. Amna Kirmani and Peter Wright, "Money Talks: Perceived Advertising Expense and Expected Product Quality," *Journal of Consumer Research* 16 (December 1989): 344–53; Donald R. Lichtenstein and Scot Burton, "The Relationship Between Perceived and Objective Price-Quality," *Journal of Marketing Research* 26 (November 1989): 429–43; Akshay R. Rao and Kent B. Monroe, "The Effect of Price, Brand Name, and Store Name on Buyers' Perceptions of Product Quality: An Integrative Review," *Journal of Marketing Research* 26 (August 1989): 351–57; Shelby Hunt, "Post-Transactional Communication and Dissonance Reduction," *Journal of Marketing* 34 (January 1970): 46–51; Daniel E. Innis and H. Rao Unnava, "The Usefulness of Product Warranties for Reputable and New Brands," in Rebecca H. Holman and Michael R. Solomon, eds., *Advances in Consumer Research* 18 (Provo, UT: Association for Consumer Research, 1991): 317–22; Terence A. Shimp and William O. Bearden, "Warranty and Other Extrinsic Cue Effects on Consumers' Risk Perceptions," *Journal of Consumer Research* 9 (June 1982): 38–46.

98. Morris B. Holbrook and Kim P. Corfman, "Quality and Value in the Consumption Experience" in *Consumer Perception of Merchandise and Store Quality*, eds. J. Jacoby and J.C. Olson, Lexington, MA: Heath, 1983: 31–57.; Robert M. Pirsig, *Zen and the Art of Motorcycle Maintenance: An Inquiry into Values* (New York: Bantam Books, 1974).

99. Gilbert A. Churchill, Jr., and Carol F. Surprenant, "An Investigation into the Determinants of Customer Satisfaction," *Journal of Marketing Research* 19 (November 1983): 491–504; John E. Swan and I. Frederick Trawick, "Disconfirmation of Expectations and Satisfaction with a Retail Service," *Journal of Retailing* 57 (Fall 1981): 49–67; Peter C. Wilton and David K. Tse, "Models of Consumer Satisfaction Formation: An Extension," *Journal of Marketing Research* 25 (May 1988): 204–12. For a discussion of what may occur when customers evaluate a new service for which comparison standards do not yet exist, see Ann L. McGill and Dawn Iacobucci, "The Role of Post-Experience Comparison Standards in the Evaluation of Unfamiliar Services," in John F. Sherry, Jr., and Brian Sternthal, eds., *Advances in Consumer Research* 19 (Provo, UT: Association for Consumer Research, 1992): 570–78; William Boulding, Ajay Kalra, Richard Staelin, and Valarie A. Zeithaml, "A Dynamic Process Model of Service Quality: From Expectations to Behavioral Intentions," *Journal of Marketing Research* 30 (February 1993): 7–27.

100. Jagdish N. Sheth and Banwari Mittal, "A Framework for Managing Customer Expectations," *Journal of Market Focused Management* 1 (1996): 137–58.

101. Ariel Sabar, "In Case of Missing Trousers, Aggrieved Party Loses Again," *New York Times* (June 26, 2007), www.nytimes.com, accessed June 26, 2007.

102. Mary C. Gilly and Betsy D. Gelb, "Post-Purchase Consumer Processes and the Complaining Consumer," *Journal of Consumer Research* 9 (December 1982): 323–28; Diane Halstead and Cornelia Droge, "Consumer Attitudes Toward Complaining and the Prediction of Multiple Complaint Responses," in Rebecca H. Holman and Michael R. Solomon, eds., *Advances in Consumer Research* 18 (Provo, UT: Association for Consumer Research, 1991): 210–16; Jagdip Singh, "Consumer Complaint Intentions and Behavior: Definitional and Taxonomical Issues," *Journal of Marketing* 52 (January 1988): 93–107.

103. Gary L. Clark, Peter F. Kaminski, and David R. Rink, "Consumer Complaints: Advice on How Companies Should Respond Based on an Empirical Study," *Journal of Services Marketing* 6 (Winter 1992): 41–50.

104. Alan Andreasen and Arthur Best, "Consumers Complain—Does Business Respond?" *Harvard Business Review* 55 (July–August 1977): 93–101.

105. Tibbett L. Speer, "They Complain Because They Care," *American Demographics* (May 1996): 13–14; cf. also Yany Grégoire, Thomas M. Tripp, and Renaud Legoux, "When Customer Love Turns into Lasting Hate: The Effects of Relationship Strength and Time on Customer Revenge and Avoidance," *Journal of Marketing* 73 (November 2009): 18–32.

106. Emily Steel, "How to Handle 'IHateYourCompany.com': Some Firms Buy Up Negative Domain Names to Avert 'Gripe Sites,'" *Wall Street Journal* (September 5, 2008), http://online.wsj.com/article_email/SB122057760688302147-lMyQjAxMDI4MjAwNTUw . . . http://webreprints.djreprints.com/2574430594663.html, accessed September 11, 2011, accessed September 5, 2008.

107. Ingrid Martin, "Expert-Novice Differences in Complaint Scripts," in Rebecca H. Holman and Michael R. Solomon, eds., *Advances in Consumer Research* 18 (Provo, UT: Association for Consumer Research, 1991):

225–31; Marsha L. Richins, "A Multivariate Analysis of Responses to Dissatisfaction," *Journal of the Academy of Marketing Science* 15 (Fall 1987): 24–31.

108. John A. Schibrowsky and Richard S. Lapidus, "Gaining a Competitive Advantage by Analyzing Aggregate Complaints," *Journal of Consumer Marketing* 11 (1994): 15–26; Clay M. Voorhees, Michael K. Brady, and David M. Horowitz, "A Voice from the Silent Masses: An Exploratory and Comparative Analysis of Noncomplainers," *Journal of the Academy of Marketing Science* 34 (Fall 2006): 514–27.

109. Material adapted from a presentation by Glenn H. Mazur, QFD Institute, 2002.

110. Russell W. Belk, "The Role of Possessions in Constructing and Maintaining a Sense of Past," in Marvin E. Goldberg, Gerald Gorn, and Richard W. Pollay, eds., *Advances in Consumer Research* 17 (Provo, UT: Association for Consumer Research, 1989): 669–76.

111. David E. Sanger, "For a Job Well Done, Japanese Enshrine the Chip," *New York Times* (December 11, 1990): A4.

112. Rob Walker, "The Worm Turns," *New York Times Magazine* (May 20, 2007), accessed May 20, 2007; www.terracycle.net, accessed June 4, 2011.

113. Jacob Jacoby, Carol K. Berning, and Thomas F. Dietvorst, "What about Disposition?" *Journal of Marketing* 41 (April 1977): 22–28.

114. Brian Wansink, S. Adam Brasel, and Steven Amjad, "The Mystery of the Cabinet Castaway: Why We Buy Products We Never Use," *Journal of Family & Consumer Sciences* 92, no. 1 (2000): 104–7.

115. Jennifer Lach, "Welcome to the Hoard Fest," *American Demographics* (April 2000): 8–9.

116. Norimitsu Onishi, "How Do Japanese Dump Trash? Let Us Count the Myriad Ways," *New York Times* (May 12, 2005), www.nytimes.com, accessed May 12, 2005.

117. Debra J. Dahab, James W. Gentry, and Wanru Su, "New Ways to Reach Non-Recyclers: An Extension of the Model of Reasoned Action to Recycling Behaviors," in *Advances in Consumer Research* Volume 22, eds. Frank R. Kardes and Mita Sujan, Provo, UT: Association for Consumer Research, Pages: 251–256.

118. Richard P. Bagozzi and Pratibha A. Dabholkar, "Consumer Recycling Goals and Their Effect on Decisions to Recycle," *Psychology & Marketing* 11, no. 4 (1994): 313–40; see also L. J. Shrum, Tina M. Lowrey, and John A. McCarty, "Recycling as a Marketing Problem: A Framework for Strategy Development," *Psychology & Marketing* 11 (July–August 1994): 393–416; Dahab, Gentry, and Su, "New Ways to Reach Non-Recyclers."

119. "Gap Asks Consumers to Recycle Their Jeans," *RetailingToday.com* (October 5, 2010), http://www.retailingtoday.com/article/gap-asks-consumers-recycle-their-jeans, accessed April 18, 2011.

120. John F. Sherry, Jr., "A Sociocultural Analysis of a Midwestern American Flea Market," *Journal of Consumer Research* 17 (June 1990): 13–30.

121. Allan J. Magrath, "If Used Product Sellers Ever Get Organized, Watch Out," *Marketing News* (June 25, 1990): 9; Kevin McCrohan and James D. Smith, "Consumer Participation in the Informal Economy," *Journal of the Academy of Marketing Science* 15 (Winter 1990): 62.

122. John F. Sherry, Jr., "Dealers and Dealing in a Periodic Market: Informal Retailing in Ethnographic Perspective," *Journal of Retailing* 66 (Summer 1990): 174.

123. www.redo.org, accessed June 4, 2011.

124. Quoted in Jenna Wortham, "Neighborly Borrowing, Over the Online Fence," *New York Times* (August 28, 2010), http://www.nytimes.com/2010/08/29/business/29ping.html?_r=1&scp=1&sq=collaborative%20consumption&st=cse, accessed April 18, 2011; www.snapgoods.com, accessed June 4, 2011; www.neighborgoods.com, accessed June 4, 2011; www.sharesomesugar.com, accessed June 4, 2011.

125. http://freegan.info/?page_id=2, accessed June 9, 2009; Steven Kurutz, "Not Buying It," *New York Times* (June 21, 2007), www.nytimes.com, accessed June 21, 2007.

126. Russell W. Belk, Joon Yong Seo, and Eric Li. "Dirty Little Secret: Home Chaos and Professional Organizers," *Consumption, Markets and Culture* 10 (June 2007): 133–40.

127. Jesse Chandler and Norbert Schwarz, "Use Does Not Wear Ragged the Fabric of Friendship: Thinking of Objects as Alive Makes People Less Willing to Replace Them," *Journal of Consumer Psychology* 20, no. 2 (2010): 138–45.

128. John L. Lastovicka and Karen V. Fernandez, "Three Paths to Disposition: The Movement of Meaningful Possessions to Strangers," *Journal of Consumer Research* 31 (March 2005): 813–23.

129. Ray A. Smith, "Belly Up to the Bar and Buy Some Jeans," *Wall Street Journal* (April 2, 2009), http://online.wsj.com/article/SB123862311574879951.html, accessed April 2, 2009.

130. Shelly Branch, "Maybe Sex Doesn't Sell, A&F Is Discovering," *Wall Street Journal* (December 12, 2003), www.wsj.com, accessed December 12, 2003.

131. Quoted in Stephanie Clifford, "Stuff Piled in the Aisle? It's There to Get You to Spend More," *New York Times* (April 7, 2011), http://www.nytimes.com/2011/04/08/business/08clutter.html?_r=1&hp=&adxnnl=1&adxnlx=1302264052-gF+9E6s92AG9nsm5jbylpg, accessed April 18, 2011.

NIELSEN NUGGET

EXERCISE: Buying and Disposing

Scenario: Bubbles is a well-established premium brand in the soft drinks category. The brand is being negatively impacted by both the economic climate and increasing promotional pressure from its key competitor, Squeeze. If the trend continues, Bubbles will face a loss of more than $2.5M next year.

Challenge: Bubbles seeks to understand how to better utilize its promotional spending more effectively and efficiently to stem the sales decline and stabilize the brand's business. The key question is which promotions Bubbles

should focus on, and with which retailers, to achieve this objective.

After reviewing the data provided:

1 Analyze the relative successes of Bubble promotions at each of the four retailers.
2 Do you think either of the forms of spontaneous shopping described in this chapter could be at work in this case? Why or why not?
3 Why do you think point-of-purchase stimuli are so strongly associated with this product category?

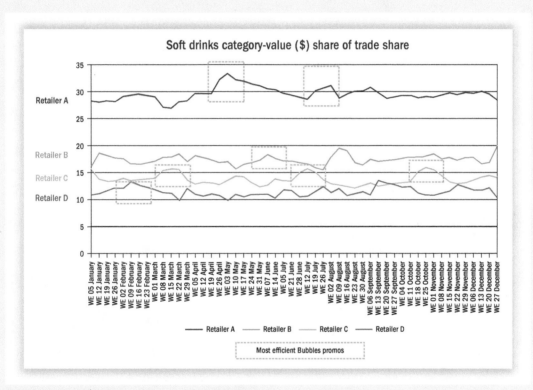

Retailer Value ($) Share of Trade—Soft Drinks
Retailer share of trade peaks during Bubble promotions. The continuous Squeeze promotions do not have as strong an impact for retailers.

Organizational and Household Decision Making

Organizational and Household Decision Making

Chapter
Objectives

When you finish reading this chapter you will understand why:

1. Marketers often need to understand *consumers'* behavior rather than *a* consumer's behavior.

2. Companies as well as individuals make purchase decisions.

3. Our traditional notions about families are outdated.

4. Many important demographic dimensions of a population relate to family and household structure.

5. Members of a family unit play different roles and have different amounts of influence when the family makes purchase decisions.

6. Children learn over time what and how to consume.

MyMarketingLab

Visit **www.mymktlab.com** to find activities that help you learn and review in order to succeed in this chapter.

Amanda is about as nervous as she can be. Tonight she and her partner Orlando are throwing their first party in their new apartment, and it's really coming down to the wire. Some of her friends and family who were skeptical about Amanda's plan to move out of her parents' house to live with a man will have the chance to say "I told you so" if this debut of her new living arrangement self-destructs.

Life hasn't exactly been a bed of roses since she and Orly moved in together. It's a bit of a mystery: Although his desk is tidy and organized at the publishing company where they both work, his personal habits are another story. Orly's really been making an effort to clean up his act, but Amanda has taken on more than her share of cleaning duties—partly out of self-defense, because they have to share a bathroom! And she's learned the hard way not to trust Orly to do the grocery shopping; he goes to the store with a big list of staples and returns with beer and junk food. You would think that a man who negotiates major computer purchases for his company would have a bit more sense when it comes to sticking to a budget and picking out the right household supplies. What's even more frustrating is that although Orly can easily spend a week digging up information about the new big-screen TV they're buying (with her bonus!), she has to virtually drag him by the ear to look at dining room furniture. Then, to add insult to injury, he's quick to criticize her choices—especially if they cost too much.

So, how likely is it that while she's at work Orlando has been home cleaning up the apartment and making some hors d'oeuvres as he promised? Amanda did her part by downloading a recipe for crabmeat salad and wasabi caviar from the entertaining section on epicurious.com. She even jotted down some adorable table setting ideas, such as napkin holders made out of homegrown bamboo at Martha Stewart's Web site.[1] And, of course she totally coordinated the guest list on Evite and has carefully kept track of who has said they're coming. The rest is up to him. At this point she'd be happy if Orly remembers to pick up his underwear from the living room couch. This *soiree* could turn out to be a real proving ground for their relationship. Amanda sighs as she walks into an editors' meeting. She sure has learned a lot about relationships since she set up a new household; living together is going to be a lot bumpier than romance novels make it out to be.

OBJECTIVE 1
Marketers often need to understand *consumers'* behavior rather than *a consumer's* behavior.

Organizational Decision Making

Amanda's trials and tribulations with Orlando illustrate the joint nature of many consumer decisions. In many situations, more than one person participates in the problem-solving sequence—from initial problem recognition and information search to evaluation of alternatives and product choice. To further complicate matters, these decisions often include two or more people who may not have the same level of investment in the outcome, the same tastes and preferences, or the same consumption priorities. If you've ever debated where to go out to eat with your friends, or perhaps bickered about whose turn it is to do the dishes, you get the picture. You can read 50 restaurant reviews on Yelp! and still it's like pulling teeth to reach a consensus.

In this chapter we examine *collective decision making*—situations in which more than one person chooses the products or services that multiple consumers use. In the first part of the chapter we look at organizational decision making, in which one person or a group decides on behalf of a larger group. We then move on to focus more specifically on one of the most important organizations to which we belong: the family unit. We'll consider how members of a family negotiate among themselves and how important changes in modern family structure affect this process. We conclude with a look at how "new employees"—children—learn to be consumers.

Why do we lump together big corporations and small families? One important similarity is that in both cases individuals or groups play a number of specific roles when they choose products or services for their organizational unit.[2] Depending on the decision, the choice may include some or all of the group members, and different group members play important roles in what can be a complicated process. These roles include the following:

- **Initiator**—The person who brings up the idea or identifies a need.
- **Gatekeeper**—The person who conducts the information search and controls the flow of information available to the group. In organizational contexts, the gatekeeper identifies possible vendors and products for the rest of the group to consider.
- **Influencer**—The person who tries to sway the outcome of the decision. Some people may be more motivated than others to get involved, and participants also possess different amounts of power to get their point across.
- **Buyer**—The person who actually makes the purchase. The buyer may or may not actually use the product.
- **User**—The person who actually consumes the product or service.

OBJECTIVE 2
Companies as well as individuals make purchase decisions.

Organizational Buyers and Decision Making

Many employees of corporations or other organizations make purchase decisions on a daily basis. **Organizational buyers** are people like Orlando who purchase goods and services on behalf of companies for the companies' use in manufacturing, distribution, or resale. These individuals buy from **business-to-business (B2B) marketers** who must satisfy the needs of organizations such as corporations, government agencies, hospitals, and retailers. In terms of sheer volume, B2B is where the action is: Roughly $2 trillion worth of products and services change hands among organizations, which is actually *more* than end consumers purchase.

Organizational buyers have a lot of responsibility. They decide on the vendors with whom they want to do business and what specific items they require from these suppliers. The items they consider range in price and significance from paper clips (by the case, not the box) to Orlando's multimillion-dollar computer system. Obviously, there's a lot of good reasons (about 2 trillion, to be exact) for marketers to understand how these organizational consumers make these important decisions.

A number of factors influence the organizational buyer's perception of the purchase situation. These include his *expectations* of the supplier (e.g., product quality, the competence and behavior of the firm's employees, and prior experiences in dealing with that supplier), the *organizational climate* of his own company (i.e., how the company rewards performance and what it values), and the buyer's *assessment* of his own performance (e.g., whether he believes in taking risks).[3]

Like other consumers, organizational buyers engage in a learning process in which employees share information with one another and develop an "organizational memory"

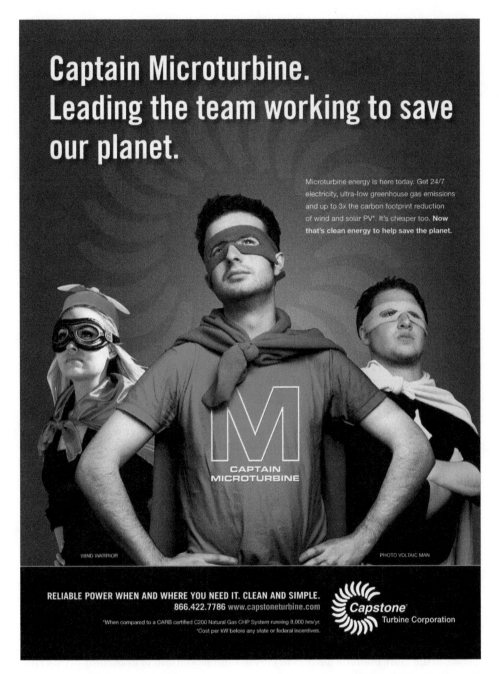

that consists of shared beliefs and assumptions about the best choices to make.[4] Just as our "market beliefs" influence him when he goes shopping with the family on the weekend, the same thing happens at the office. He (perhaps with fellow employees) solves problems as he searches for information, evaluates alternatives, and makes decisions.[5] There are, of course, some important differences between the two situations.

How Does Organizational Decision Making Compare to Consumer Decision Making?

Let's summarize the major differences between organizational and industrial purchase decisions versus individual consumer decisions:[6]

- The purchase decisions that companies make frequently involve many people, including those who do the actual buying, those who directly or indirectly influence this decision, and the employees who will actually use the product or service.

- Organizations and companies often use precise technical specifications that require a lot of knowledge about the product category.
- Impulse buying is rare (industrial buyers do not suddenly get an "urge to splurge" on lead pipe or silicon chips). Because buyers are professionals, they base their decisions on past experience and they carefully weigh alternatives.
- Decisions often are risky, especially in the sense that a buyer's career may ride on his judgment.
- The dollar volume of purchases is often substantial—it dwarfs most individual consumers' grocery bills or mortgage payments. One hundred to two hundred fifty organizational customers typically account for more than half of a supplier's sales volume, which gives the buyers a lot of influence over the supplier.
- Business-to-business marketing often emphasizes personal selling more than advertising or other forms of promotion. Dealing with organizational buyers typically requires more face-to-face contact than when marketers sell to end consumers.

We must consider these important features when we try to understand the purchasing decisions organizations make. Having said that, however, there are actually more similarities between organizational buyers and ordinary consumers than many people realize. True, organizational purchase decisions do tend to have a higher economic or functional component compared to individual consumer choices, but emotional aspects do play a role. Organizational buyers may appear to the outsider to be models of rationality, but at times they base their decisions on brand loyalty, on long-term relationships with particular suppliers or salespeople, or even on aesthetic preferences. Even investors, who are supposed to make cold, calculated judgments about the worth of companies based on financial indicators, sometimes are influenced instead by other concerns; for instance, they may be biased toward companies that provide better working conditions for employees or that are unusual in some other way.[7]

How Do Organizational Buyers Operate?

Like end consumers, both internal and external stimuli influence organizational buyers. Internal stimuli include the buyer's unique psychological characteristics, such as his willingness to make risky decisions, job experience, and training. External stimuli include the nature of the organization for which he works as well as the overall economic and technological environment in which the industry operates. Another set of factors is cultural: We find vastly different norms for doing business in different countries. For example, Americans tend to be less formal in their interactions than are many of their European or Asian counterparts.

As you'd expect, the organizational buyer's decision-making process depends on just what he needs to buy. As with consumer purchases, the more complex, novel, or risky the decision, the more effort he devotes to information search and to evaluating his alternatives. However, if he relies on a fixed set of suppliers for routine purchases, he greatly reduces his information search and effort.[8] Typically, a group of people (members of a **buying center**) play different roles in more complex organizational decisions. As we will see later on, this joint involvement is somewhat similar to family decision making, where family members are likely to participate in more important purchases.

The Buyclass Framework

When we apply the **buyclass theory of purchasing**, we divide organizational buying decisions into three types ranging from the least to the most complex. Three decision-making dimensions describe the purchasing strategies of an organizational buyer:[9]

1 The level of information he must gather before he makes a decision.
2 The seriousness with which he must consider all possible alternatives.
3 The degree to which he is familiar with the purchase.

Call the experts© for more power at high reach.

Reach further with Komatsu's telescopic handlers. With lifting heights from 9 to over 16 metres and lifting capacities from 3500 to 4500 kg, the range includes machines to suit every application. The state-of-the-art hydraulic system and single PPC joystick let you get the most from the huge power available and deliver precise control of the working equipment even during simultaneous operations. To complete the package, each of these highly versatile machines offers exceptional stability, high travel speed, superb manoeuvrability and best-in-class all-round visibility. Not bad for a telescopic.

KOMATSU

Komatsu Europe International nv - Mechelsesteenweg 586 - B-1800 Vilvoorde - Belgium

Industrial marketers can be creative when they want to be, as this European ad for a heavy equipment manufacturer demonstrates.
Source: Used courtesy of Komatsu Europe.

In practice, these three dimensions relate to how much cognitive effort the buyer expends when he decides. Three types of "buyclasses," or strategies determined by these dimensions, encompass most organizational decision situations.[10] Each type of purchase corresponds to one of the three types of decisions: habitual decision making, limited problem solving, and extensive problem solving. Table 1 summarizes these strategies.

- A **straight rebuy** is a habitual decision. It's an automatic choice, as when an inventory level reaches a preestablished reorder point. Most organizations maintain an

TABLE 1 Types of Organizational Buying Decisions

Buying Situation	Extent of Effort	Risk	Buyer's Involvement
Straight rebuy	Habitual decision making	Low	Automatic reorder
Modified rebuy	Limited problem solving	Low to moderate	One or a few
New task	Extensive problem solving	High	Many

Source: Adapted from Patrick J. Robinson, Charles W. Faris, and Yoram Wind, *Industrial Buying and Creative Marketing* (Boston: Allyn & Bacon, 1967).

approved vendor list, and as long as experience with a supplier is satisfactory, there is little or no ongoing information search or evaluation.

- A **modified rebuy** situation involves limited decision making. It occurs when an organization wants to repurchase a product or service but also wants to make some minor modifications. This decision might involve a limited search for information among a few vendors. One or a few people will probably make the final decision.
- A **new task** involves extensive problem solving. Because the company hasn't made a similar decision already, there is often a serious risk that the product won't perform as it should or that it will be too costly. The organization designates a buying center with assorted specialists to evaluate the purchase, and they typically gather a lot of information before they come to a decision.

B2B E-Commerce

Business-to-business (B2B) e-commerce refers to Internet interactions between two or more businesses or organizations. This includes exchanges of information, products, services, or payments. The Web revolutionized the way companies communicate with other firms and even the way they share information with their own people. Roughly half of B2B e-commerce transactions take the form of auctions, bids, and exchanges in which numerous suppliers and purchasers interact.[11] For example, more than 50 major corporations that belong to The Worldwide Retail Exchange (WWRE), such as CVS Corporation, Best Buy, Target, Tesco, JCPenney, and The Gap, participate in an online exchange community to complete their commercial transactions. This collaboration allows the members to work together on product development, production planning, and inventory replenishment.[12]

The Open-Source Revolution

In the simplest form of B2B e-commerce, the Internet provides an online catalog of products and services businesses need. Companies like Dell Computer use their Internet site to deliver online technical support, product information, order status information, and customer service to corporate customers. Early on, Dell discovered that it could serve the needs of its customers more effectively if it tailored its Internet presence to different customer segments. Today Dell's Internet site allows shoppers to get recommendations based on their customer segment (home, home office, government, small business, and education). The company saves millions of dollars a year as it replaces hard-copy manuals with electronic downloads. For its larger customers, Dell provides customer-specific, password-protected pages that allow business customers to obtain technical support or to place an order.[13]

As social networking technologies proliferate among end users, businesses adopt these approaches also. In fact, a 2010 survey reported that fully 86 percent of businesses use social media as part of their B2B marketing communications—even though most are just using these technologies very sporadically until they figure out the best ways to take advantage of these emerging platforms.[15]

The advertising agency Avenue A Razorfish adopted an open-source **wiki** platform as its intranet; this lets several people change a document on a Web page and then track those changes (of course, the most famous wiki is Wikipedia). High-tech companies like Intel and SAP are experimenting with recording meetings that get downloaded to iPods, blogs where employees can talk back to their bosses, and internal Web pages like GoogleDocs that allow people to read their colleagues' meeting notes and add their own. A few companies even use Facebook as an intranet site for their employees.[16]

Prediction Markets

Are all of us smarter than each of us? A **prediction market** is one of the hottest new trends in organizational decision-making techniques. This approach asserts that groups of people with knowledge about an industry are, collectively, better predictors of the future than are any of them as individuals.

In a prediction market framework, companies from Microsoft to Eli Lilly and Hewlett-Packard empower their employees as "traders." Like a stock market, traders place bets on what they think will happen regarding future sales, the success of new products, or how other firms in a distribution channel will behave—and they often receive a cash reward if their "stock picks" pan out. For example, the pharmaceutical giant Eli Lilly routinely places multimillion-dollar bets on drug candidates that face overwhelming odds of failure. The relatively few new compounds that do succeed have to make enough money to cover the losses the others incur. Obviously, the company will benefit if it can separate the winners from the losers earlier in the process. Lilly ran an experiment in which about 50 of its employees involved in drug development, including chemists, biologists, and project managers, traded six mock drug candidates through an internal market. The group correctly predicted the three most successful drugs.[17] At the publicly accessible prediction market Intrade (*intrade.com*) participants bet on the outcomes of political races, financial activities, or even the market value of rare wines and artwork. Or, surf over to the Hollywood Stock Exchange (*hsx.com*) to check out which celebrities and new movie releases traders think will succeed or bomb; you can bet Hollywood executives do![18]

Crowdsourcing

In another emerging application, many companies find that it's both cost efficient and productive to call on outsiders from around the world to solve problems their own scientists can't handle. Just as firms might outsource production to subcontractors, they are **crowdsourcing**. Dell's Ideastorm site solicits solutions and new product ideas from geeks worldwide, as does NineSigma, where companies solicit technical contributions to allow them to accelerate their rate of product innovation.[19]

OBJECTIVE 3
Our traditional notions about families are outdated.

The Family

In 2010, our culture marked a milestone: Married couples represented just 48 percent of American households. In contrast, back in 1950 78 percent of households were occupied by married couples. New Census data also revealed that just a fifth of households were composed of traditional families—married couples with children—compared to 43 percent in 1950.[20] Does this mean that families are obsolete?

Hardly. The reality is that many other *types* of families continue to grow rapidly. Indeed, some experts argue that as traditional family living arrangements wane, we place even greater emphasis on siblings, close friends, and other relatives who provide companionship and social support.[21] Some people join *intentional families*; groups of unrelated people who meet regularly for meals and who spend holidays together.[22] Indeed, for some the act of meeting together to consume homemade food plays a central role in defining family: It is a symbolic way to separate a family unit from other social groups by allowing the cook(s) to personalize the meal and express affection via the effort that went into preparing the feast.[23]

OBJECTIVE 4
Many important demographic dimensions of a population relate to family and household structure.

The Modern Family

The **extended family** used to be the most common family unit. It consists of three generations who live together, and it often includes grandparents, aunts, uncles, and cousins. Like the Cleavers of *Leave It to Beaver* and other TV families of the 1950s, the **nuclear family**—a mother, a father, and one or more children (perhaps with a sheepdog thrown in for good measure)—largely replaced the extended family, at least in American society. However, we've witnessed many changes since the days of Beaver Cleaver. Although many people continue to base their image of the typical family on old TV shows, demographic data tell us that this "ideal" image of the family is no longer realistic. The U.S. Census Bureau regards

Marketing Opportunity

The open-source revolution is part of a seismic shift in the way some cutting-edge companies think about their business model. One label for this new approach is **freemium**—you distribute a free version of your product that's supported by a paid premium version. The idea is to encourage the maximum number of people to use your product and eventually convert a small fraction of them to paying customers. In the process you accumulate a sizable customer base that has value to advertisers (Exhibit A: Google). This also creates a **network effect**, whereby each person who uses the product or service benefits as more people participate. For example, if you check out restaurant reviews on Zagat, you'd rather know what 1,000 diners thought of a place than to settle for feedback from just 10 cranky people.

The freemium model pops up in all sorts of places: People play free online games, they listen to free music on Pandora (legally), they trash their cable service and watch free TV shows and movies on Hulu, and they cancel their landlines in favor of free international calls on Skype. The new and booming market for iPhone apps follows the freemium principle also when you download a program like *Tap Tap Revenge* (like the popular game *Guitar Hero*, you have to hit notes that stream down your screen). Millions of people downloaded the app, and then some of them forked over cash when the creator offered paid versions built around real bands like Weezer and Nine Inch Nails.[14] In the wacky world of Web 2.0, you give something away to make money. Go figure.

• • • • • • • • • • • • • • • •

American Girl produces historical-period characters complete with books, dolls, and accessories, as well as modern-period dolls. The company also operates The American Girl Place, where young girls who own the dolls drag their parents and grandparents to attractions including dioramas and a doll hair salon. Consumer researchers who studied the American Girl phenomenon concluded that part of the brand's huge popularity is due to its multigenerational appeal. After they interviewed numerous girls, mothers, and grandmothers, they found that consumers of all ages valued the opportunities for family connection and also learning about their heritage and those of other cultures.[24]

Source: Reprinted with permission of American Girl Inc.

any occupied housing unit as a **household**, regardless of the relationships among the people who live there. Thus, one person living alone, three roommates, or two lovers (whether straight or gay) constitute a household.

Furthermore, as we've already seen, marriage as an institution is evolving. A 2011 report released by the U.S. Census Bureau said that nearly half of all women between the ages of 25 and 29 have never been married, up from about a quarter of that age group in 1986. In 1950, the median age of first marriages was 23 for men and 20 for women. In 2009, it was 28 for men and 26 for women.[25] The recession is also taking its toll on families: The Census Bureau report a sharp rise in the number of children living with their grandparents as mothers increasingly take jobs outside the home. Overall, 6.5 percent of children in the United States live with their grandparents, which is double the rate from 1970.[26]

The ways people get into (and out of) relationships also continues to evolve, as people increasingly rely on dating sites and social networks to find mates. A survey by the dating site Match.com reported that one in six couples who got married in the last year met online.[27] Another study by the dating Web site OK Cupid, however, found that the romantic relationships of active Twitter users don't last as long as those of the rest of the population.[28] Maybe people who meet up in cyberspace are just used to clicking at will to find other options.

Also, due in part to harsh economic conditions, children are more likely to live at home after graduating from college rather than taking their own places. Demographers call these returnees **boomerang kids** (you throw them out . . . they keep coming back). In today's shrinking job market (and in some cases the lucky few who do initially get job offers find out the offers have been rescinded!), many young people are forced to redefine the assumption that college graduation automatically means living on their own. Even before the recession we saw this trend quickening. As of 2007, 55 percent of men and

48 percent of women ages 18 to 24 lived with their parents.[29] In addition, many adults care for their own parents as well as for their children. In fact, Americans on average spend 17 years caring for children, but 18 years assisting aged parents.[30] Some label middle-aged people the **Sandwich Generation**, because they must support both the generation above them and the one below them.

Young adults who do leave the nest to live by themselves are relatively unlikely to return, whereas those who move in with roommates are more likely to come back. Young people who move in with a romantic partner are more likely than average to end up back home if the relationship fails![31] If the dismal economic environment continues, it will affect a variety of markets, as boomerang kids spend less on housing and staples and more on discretionary purchases such as entertainment.

Family Size

Family size depends on such factors as educational level, the availability of birth control, and religion. Demographers define the **fertility rate** as the number of births per year per 1,000 women of childbearing age. Marketers keep a close eye on the population's birth rate to gauge how the pattern of births will affect demand for products in the future. The U.S. fertility rate increased dramatically in the late 1950s and early 1960s, when the

Edinburgh from £9.50 one way.   national express

Many boomerang kids today return home to live with their parents–voluntarily or not.
Source: Copyright Cdp-Travissully Ltd.

389

parents of so-called *baby boomers* began to reach childbearing age. It declined in the 1970s and began to climb again in the 1980s as baby boomers began to have their own children in a new "baby boomlet."

Worldwide, surveys show that many women want smaller families today. This trend is a problem for European countries whose fertility rates have plummeted during past decades. Ironically, while populations boom in many underdeveloped parts of the world, industrialized countries face future crises because there will be relatively fewer young people to support their elders. For population levels to remain constant, the fertility rate has to be 2.0 so that the two children can replace their parents. That's not happening in places such as Spain, Sweden, Germany, and Greece, where the fertility rate is 1.4 or lower. As a benchmark, the U.S. rate is 2.1. More babies were born in the United States in 2007 than in any other year in American history—but this figure mostly reflects a greater number of women of childbearing age.[32]

Some countries are weighing measures to encourage people to have more children. For example, Spain is looking at cheaper utility bills for large families, assisting young couples who are trying to buy homes, and creating hundreds of thousands of new pre-schools and nursery schools. The Italian government provides mothers with nearly full salary compensation for about half a year of maternity leave, but many women still refuse to have more kids. There are many reasons for this shift from past eras when heavily Catholic countries tended to have large families: Contraception and abortion are more readily available, divorce is more common, and older people who used to look after grandchildren now pursue other activities such as travel. Some experts also cite the fact that many Italian men live with their mothers into their 30s, so when they do get married they're not prepared to help out at home. One analyst commented, "Even the most open-minded guy—if you scratch with the nail a little bit, there's the mother who did everything for him."[33]

In the United States, the National Center of Health Statistics confirms that the percentage of women of childbearing age who define themselves as *voluntarily childless* is rising. Twenty percent of women ages 40 to 44 have no children, double the level of 30 years ago. Women with advanced degrees are more likely to be childless, the study found. Of women who gave birth in 2006, 36 percent were separated, widowed, divorced, or never married.[34]

Childless couples are an attractive market segment for some companies (but obviously not for others, such as Gerber Baby Food). So-called **DINKS** (double income, no kids) couples are better educated on average than are two-income couples with children. According to the U.S. Census Bureau, 30 percent of childless couples consist of two college graduates, compared with 17 percent of those with kids. The childless are more likely to have professional or managerial occupations (24 percent versus 16 percent of dual-employed couples with children). Dave and Buster's, a Dallas-based restaurant chain, caters to this group as it enforces strict policies to deter families with small children. However, many childless couples feel snubbed by a child-oriented society. In recent years they have formed networking organizations such as Childfree by Choice to support this lifestyle decision.[35]

Animals Are People Too! Nonhuman Family Members

Almost one-third of all U.S. households have at least one pet, and 92 percent of pet owners consider their furry friends members of the family—83 percent call themselves "Mommy" or "Daddy" when they talk to their pets.[39] Many of us assume that pets share our emotions; perhaps that helps to explain why more than three-quarters of domestic cats and dogs receive presents on holidays and birthdays.[40] We've doubled our spending on our pets in the past decade, and today the pet industry pulls in more revenue (almost $40 billion annually) than either the toy or candy industries. Even in the recession, consumers don't make their pets pay the price, although we pay more for pet food, supplies, and services than ever. Here are a few examples of pet-smart marketing:[41]

● Kennels look a lot more like spas for the furry. At some of them, dogs can hike, swim, listen to music, watch TV, and even get a pedicure—complete with nail polish. Heated

The author's pug, Kelbie Rae.

tile floors and high-tech ventilation systems are common. When a dog stays in the "ambassador suite" at Club Bow-Wow, a staff member sleeps overnight in the room. PetSmart, the largest U.S. pet-store chain, opened a chain of PetsHotels, where furry guests lounge on hypoallergenic lambskin blankets and snack on lactose-free, fat-free ice cream. The suites feature raised dog beds and a television that plays videos, such as *Lady and the Tramp* and *101 Dalmatians*.

- Companies that make human products, such as Gucci, Juicy Couture, Harley-Davidson, IKEA, Lands' End, Paul Mitchell, and Ralph Lauren, also sell products for pets, ranging from shampoos to nail polish to gold-plated bowls. Harley-Davidson started its pet collection after it noticed that customers at rallies and other events bring along their dogs; some ride shotgun in the motorcycles' saddle bags or side cars. Customers can buy denim and leather jackets for their pets, as well as riding goggles, bandanas, spiked leather collars, and even squeaky toys shaped like oil cans.

- Designer water for dogs? A California company started things off when it introduced a vitamin-enriched water product for dogs. A Florida company sells "DogWater" in containers that double as throwing toys. Then there's K9 Water Inc., a company whose catalog lists products such as "Gutter Water" and chicken-flavored "Toilet Water." Make that a double.

- What happens when our four-legged companion goes to the great kennel in the sky? One trend is to freeze-dry the departed pet rather than bury it or cremate it. The bereaved say that turning furry friends into perma-pets helps them deal with loss and maintains a connection to their former companions. Once dried, the animal's body doesn't decay, so it can continue to occupy that special place on the couch.

The Family Life Cycle

Many factors affect what a family spends, including the number of people (children and adults) in the family, their ages, and whether one, two, or more adults work outside of the home. Two especially important factors that determine how a couple spends time and money are (1) whether they have children and (2) whether the woman works.

Family Life-Cycle Models

Because they recognize that family needs and expenditures change over time, marketers apply the **family life cycle (FLC)** concept to segment households. The FLC combines

Pet Airways is the first pets-only airline. The "pawsengers" fly in pet carriers aboard Beechcraft planes along with a pet attendant. There are separate sections for cats and dogs—but no first-class cabin.[42]

Source: Pet Airways, Inc.

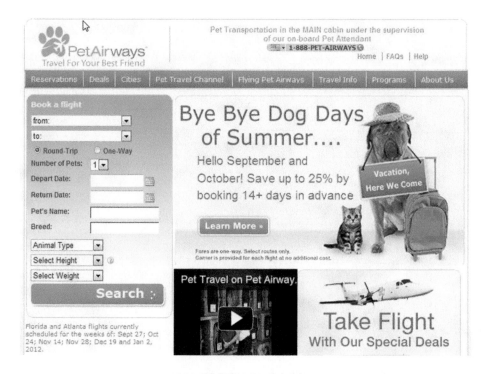

trends in income and family composition with the changes these demands place on this income. As we age, our preferences and needs for products and activities tend to change. Twenty-somethings spend less than average on most products and services because their households are small and their incomes are low (especially today!). Income levels tend to rise (at least until retirement), so that people can afford more over time. Older consumers spend more per capita on luxury items such as gourmet foods and upscale home furnishings.[43] In addition, we don't need to repeat many purchases we make when we start out. For example, we tend to accumulate durable goods such as large appliances and replace them only as necessary.

As Amanda and Orlando discovered when they moved in together, a life-cycle approach to the study of the family assumes that pivotal events alter role relationships and trigger new stages of life that alter our priorities. In addition to the birth of a first child, other pivotal events include the departure of the last child from the house, the death of a spouse, retirement of the principal wage earner, and divorce. At Web sites like The Bump, women find tools such as an Ovulation Calculator and lists of baby names; The Knot offers a range of wedding-related services when those babies grow up and get hitched. As people move through these life stages, we observe significant changes in expenditures in leisure, food, durables, and services, even after we adjust the figures to reflect changes in income.[44] We can simply attribute some of these changes to variations in functional needs, whereas others reflect deeper motivations as we transition from one role to another. For example, researchers find that new mothers undergo profound changes in self-concept during pregnancy and after delivery; these changes influence the types of products they consume to reflect their new identities.[45]

Life-Cycle Effects on Buying

It's particularly useful to get a handle on longitudinal changes in priorities when we want to predict demand for specific product categories over time. For example, the money a couple with no children spends on dinners out and vacations will go to quite different purchases after the birth of a child, when a night on the town becomes a distant memory. Ironically, although the entertainment industry focuses on winning the hearts and wallets of young consumers, it's the senior citizens who have become America's true party

Pets are as important to people in South Africa as they are here.
Source: Courtesy of Euro RSCG South Africa.

animals. The average household headed by a 65- to 74-year-old spends more on entertainment than does the average household in which the primary wage earner is under age 25.[46]

Over the years, researchers have proposed several models to describe family life-cycle stages, but with limited effect because most failed to take into account such important social trends as the changing role of women, the acceleration of alternative lifestyles, childless and delayed-child marriages, and single-parent households. We need to focus on four variables to adequately describe these changes: (1) age, (2) marital status, (3) the presence or absence of children in the home, and (4) the ages of children, if present. In addition, we have to relax our definition of marital status to include *any* couple living together in a long-term relationship. Thus, although we might not consider roommates "married," for marketing purposes a man and woman who have established a household would be, as would two homosexual men or lesbian women who have a similar understanding. When we update our outlook, we identify a set of categories that includes many more types of family situations.[47] Consumers we classify into these categories show marked differences in consumption patterns:

- Young bachelors and newlyweds are the most likely to exercise; to go out to bars, concerts, movies, and restaurants; and to drink alcohol. Although people in their 20s account for less than 4 percent of all household spending in the United States, their expenditures are well above average in such categories as apparel, electronics, and gasoline.[48]
- Families with young children are more likely to consume health foods such as fruit, juice, and yogurt; those made up of single parents and older children buy more junk foods. The dollar value of homes, cars, and other durables is lowest for bachelors and single parents but increases as people go through the full-nest and childless-couple stages.
- Partly because they score wedding gifts, newlyweds are the most likely to own appliances such as toaster ovens and electric coffee grinders. Babysitter and day-care usage is, of course, highest among single-parent and full-nest households, whereas older couples and bachelors are most likely to employ home maintenance services (e.g., lawn mowing).

The Intimate Corporation: Family Decision Making

The decision process within a household unit resembles a business conference. Certain matters go on the table for discussion, different members advocate different actions based on their differing priorities and agendas, and there may be power struggles to rival any tale of corporate intrigue. In just about every living situation, whether it's a conventional family or students who share a sorority house or apartment, group members assume different roles just as purchasing agents, engineers, account executives, and others do within a company.

When Chevrolet wanted to win drivers over to its Venture minivan, the company sent teams of anthropologists out to observe families in their natural habitats. Conventional wisdom says that minivan buyers are practical; they care about affordability, lots of features, and plenty of room. But these researchers discovered a different story: People see the vehicles as part of the family. When they asked consumers to identify the best metaphor for a minivan, many picked a photo of a hang glider because it represents freedom and families on the go. The advertising slogan for the Venture became, "Let's go."[49]

Families make two basic types of decisions:[50]

1 In a **consensual purchase decision**, members agree on the desired purchase; they disagree only in terms of how they will make it happen. In these circumstances, the family will most likely engage in problem solving and consider alternatives until they find a way to satisfy everyone in the group. For example, in a family that decides to get a dog, some of the members (you can guess who) voice concerns about who will take care of it. The solution is to draw up a chart that assigns family members to specific duties.

2 In an **accommodative purchase decision**, however, group members have different preferences or priorities and can't agree on a purchase that satisfies everyone's needs. It is here that they use bargaining, coercion, and compromise to achieve agreement on what to buy or who gets to use it. Conflict occurs when there is incomplete correspondence in family members' needs and preferences. Although household spending and budgeting is the most common source of conflict in these disputes, TV-viewing choices come in a close second![51]

Decisions create conflict among family members to the extent that the issue is somehow important or novel, or if individuals have strong opinions about good and bad alternatives. The degree to which these factors generate conflict determines the type of decision the family will make.[52] Some specific factors that determine how much family decision conflict there will be include:[53]

- **Interpersonal need**—(a person's level of investment in the group): A teenager may care more about what her family buys for the house than will a college student who lives in a dorm.
- **Product involvement and utility**—(the degree to which a person will use the product to satisfy a need): A mother who is an avid coffee drinker will obviously be more interested in the purchase of a new coffeemaker than will her teenage son who swigs Coke by the gallon.
- **Responsibility**—(for procurement, maintenance, payment, and so on): People are more likely to have disagreements about a decision if it entails long-term consequences and commitments. For example, a family decision about getting a dog may involve conflict over who will be responsible for walking and feeding it.
- **Power**—(or the degree to which one family member exerts influence over the others): In traditional families, the husband tends to have more power than the wife, who in turn has more than the oldest child, and so on. Conflict can arise when one person

continually uses the power he has within the group to satisfy his own priorities. For example, if a child believed that his life would end if he did not receive a Kinect for his birthday, he might be more willing to "cash in some chips" and throw a tantrum.

One analysis of family decision making took a closer look at the idea that family members mutually construct a **family identity** that defines the household both to members and to insiders.[54] According to this perspective, family rituals, narratives (stories the members tell about the family), and everyday interactions help families maintain their structure, maintain their family character (day-to-day characteristics of family life), and clarify members' relationships to one another. The value of this approach to marketers is that it reminds us of how often products and services help to define the family identity. For example, a father might take his young children out for ice cream every Saturday afternoon, so this becomes a predictable ceremony that defines their relationship. Or, a mom might seek the comfort of her iPod to shield her from the noise when her kids play after school, while a TiVo "saves marriages" because it allows family members to compromise when they decide who gets access to the TV.

The Family as Customer Network

Earlier we noted that companies are a lot like families (though some are more dysfunctional than others!). A 2011 perspective comes at this idea from the other direction, as it compares families to companies. The researchers looked at the family unit as a set of **customer networks**; in the commercial space, these are structures that invest in products and services to help them reach collective identity goals, recognizing that these pursuits may compete with rather than complement individual interests. They applied this concept to the context of family vacations to understand how marketers can succeed by reconciling the goals of different family members (especially when some of these are individual goals and others involve cooperation with other members).

Anyone who has "endured" a family vacation understands that the process of maximizing everyone's fun can be more complicated than a United Nations resolution. So, the goal here is to customize product and service offerings to make it more likely that all members' goals will be fulfilled. For example, one solution is to structure the situation so that members can engage in parallel activity; they can participate in similar activities concurrently to achieve goals that overlap in character but occur at different levels. Nike could help members build collective, relational, and individual identities grounded in running experiences and enhance network satisfaction through flexible online tools for coordinating group runs, uploading times to a community Web site, and mapping out individual routes. By participating in the same activity as coalitions or individuals, members can address goals at different levels while solidifying the character elements that unite them. These approaches tend to work better than "something-for-everyone" packages that wind up satisficing everyone but making no one really happy (maximizing).[55]

Sex Roles and Decision-Making Responsibilities

When the Indian composer A. R. Rahman accepted two Oscars for his work on the hit movie *Slumdog Millionaire*, he thanked his mother . . . as an afterthought he also remembered to thank his wife. India's culture strongly encourages a doting relationship between mothers and sons. It's common for many successful men to consult their mothers for advice daily, and some tycoons put their mothers on their boards of directors. Hinduism stresses powerful female gods, and many citizens refer to the country as Mother India. Clearly, older decision makers in the family unit carry a lot of weight, both in the house and out: Young people often take their parents to their first job interview.[56] Americans may not lag far behind if the number of **helicopter moms** continues to swell: These are overprotective mothers who "hover" around their kids and insert themselves into virtually all aspects of their lives—including, in some cases, job interviews![57]

The Tangled Web

Johnson & Johnson encountered a firestorm of protest from irate mothers (not a smart group to mess with) after the company ran an online advertisement for its over-the-counter pain pill Motrin. The spot intended to target mothers who get back pain when they carry their babies in slings, but many women felt the ad was an insensitive portrayal of women's pain as well as of their preferred method of carrying their babies. Within days after the launch, calls for a boycott began to gather on blogs, YouTube, and Twitter. J&J quickly pulled the ad—but it learned the hard way how mothers tune into social media today.[62]

So, who "wears the pants" in the family? Sometimes it's not obvious which spouse makes the decisions. Indeed, although many men literally wear the pants, it's women who buy them. Haggar's research showed that nearly half of married women bought pants for their husbands without the husbands being present, so the firm started to advertise its menswear products in women's magazines. When one family member chooses a product, we call this an **autonomic decision**. In traditional households, for example, men often have sole responsibility to select a car, whereas decorating choices fall to women. **Syncretic decisions**, such as a vacation destination, might involve both partners. These choices are common for vacations, homes, appliances, furniture, home electronics, and long-distance phone services. As the couple's educational level increases, they are more likely to make decisions together.[58] Roper sees signs of a shift in marital decision making toward more compromise and turn-taking. For example, the survey finds that wives tend to win out in arguments about how the house is kept, whereas husbands get control of the remote.[59]

The proportion of autonomic decisions is steadily tipping toward women. It's not news to claim that women hold the purse strings in many families. However, this dominance is accelerating because, in a departure from the past, many women are not just the spenders, they are also the earners. Today the U.S. workforce is almost 50 percent female, and a majority of high-paying management and professional jobs are held by women. For every two males who graduate from college or get a higher degree, three women do. Although overall women still earn less than men, about a third of them earn more than their husbands. This shift is occurring around the world; some analysts argue that we are entering a **sheconomy** where women will dominate emerging markets.

Here in the United States a study of 30- to 44-year-olds showed that when a husband is the primary or sole breadwinner, household spending decisions are divided roughly equally. He makes about a third of them, she makes a third, and they make a third jointly. But, in the 22 percent of households in which the wife earned more, she made more than twice as many decisions as her husband about where the money would go. The more money women earn, the exponentially more money they manage. These shifts even occur in areas where men have dominated. Women make up almost half of the $200 billion consumer-electronics business, and $105 billion of the $256 billion home-improvement market. Even 44 percent of NFL fans are women![60] In contrast, single men remain a powerful and often ignored force in the marketplace. Right now, 3 out of 10 men are single, and more than 80 percent of them make the sole or key big-ticket decisions in their households—at least for now.[61]

To what degree are traditional sex roles changing? Recent evidence says quite a bit; men and women increasingly express similar attitudes about how they prefer to balance home life and work. Some experts argue that the gender revolution is developing into **gender convergence**. A comprehensive view of current research reported more similarities than differences between American men and women. Most people recognize that mothers work more and do less housework, and that men work less and do more housework and childcare than their fathers, although they still shoulder significantly less of the burden than do women.[63]

In any case, spouses typically exert significant influence on decision making, even after one of them has died. An Irish study found that many widows claim to sense the continued presence of their dead husbands and to regularly conduct "conversations" with them about household matters![64] Comments from married women who participated in focus groups conducted by *Redbook* magazine illustrate some of the dynamics of autonomic versus syncretic decision making:

- "We just got our steps done and that was a big project. The contractor would talk (to my husband) and not talk to me. And I said, 'Excuse me, I'm here, too.'"
- "We are looking for a house now, and we're making decisions on which side of town we want it on, what size house do we want, and it's a together decision. That's never how my mother did it."
- "My husband did not want a van, because we have just one child, but I said, 'I want a van. And it's not because everyone else has a van. I want comfort.' He wanted a convertible. And we got a van."[65]

Marketers need to figure out who makes the buying decisions in a family because this information tells them who to target and whether they need to reach both spouses to influence a choice. For example, marketing research in the 1950s indicated that women were beginning to play a larger role in household purchasing decisions. In response, lawn mower manufacturers emphasized the rotary mower over other power mowers to downplay women's fears of injury. Rotary models, which conceal the cutting blades and engine, began to pop up in ads that depicted young women and smiling grandmothers as they cut the grass.[66]

Researchers pay special attention to which spouse plays the role of the **family financial officer (FFO)**—the individual who keeps track of the family's bills and decides how to spend any surplus funds. Newlyweds tend to share this role, and then over time one spouse or the other takes over these responsibilities.[67] In traditional families (and especially those with low educational levels), women are primarily responsible for family financial management: The man makes it and the woman spends it. Each spouse "specializes" in certain activities.[68]

The pattern is different among families where more modern sex-role norms operate. These couples believe that both people should participate in family maintenance activities. In these cases, husbands assume more responsibility for laundering, housecleaning, grocery shopping, and so on, in addition to such traditionally "male" tasks as home maintenance and garbage removal.[69] Shared decision making is the norm for most American couples today: A Roper poll reported that 94 percent of partnered women say they make the decision or share equally in home furnishing selections (not a huge surprise), but in addition, 81 percent said the same for financial savings/investments, and 74 percent participate when the couple decides what car to buy.[70]

Working mothers often struggle with what one researcher calls the **juggling lifestyle**: a frenzied, guilt-ridden compromise between conflicting cultural ideals of motherhood and professionalism.[71] This frantic way of life isn't surprising in light of a survey by the U.S. Department of Labor showing that the average working woman spends about twice as much time as the average working man on household chores and the care of children. She also gets about an hour less sleep each night than the average stay-at-home mom.[72]

Cultural background plays a big role in determining whether husbands or wives control purchase decisions. For example, husbands tend to dominate decision making among couples with a strong Hispanic ethnic identification. Vietnamese Americans also are more likely to adhere to the traditional model: The man makes the decision regarding any large purchase, whereas the woman gets a budget to manage the home. In a study that compared marital decision making in the United States and China, American women reported more "wife decides" situations than did the Chinese. Advertising and marketing strategies often reflect assumptions about "who's the boss." These examples illustrate some cross-cultural differences:[73]

- The Coca-Cola Company developed a campaign to appeal to Latin American women based on a big research project the company conducted in Brazil. It found that a motherly female kangaroo was most likely to appeal to women who shop for their families—and who happen to account for 80 percent of Coke's $3.5 billion in Brazilian sales. Coke used the theme "Mom knows everything," after women in focus groups said they felt the media neglected them even though they purchased virtually every product in their households.

- Butterfly, an Indian program, enlists village medicine men to convince local women to take birth control pills. A big obstacle is that women are not accustomed to making these decisions. The response of one village resident is typical: "I have never taken contraceptives. My husband is my master—he will decide."

- Traditional sex-role norms also influenced a commercial that Procter & Gamble produced for its Ariel laundry detergent in India. It shows a man named Ravi doing the laundry, which is highly unusual there. A female voice questions, "Where's the wife? Are you actually going to wash them? . . . [A] man should not wash clothes . . . [He is] sure to fail."

Mothers take on many responsibilities as they care for the family unit.

Source: Courtesy KidCare TV.

● Ads showing men doing housework are risky in Asia as well, even though today more Asian women work outside the home. A South Korean vacuum cleaner ad flashed to a woman who lies on the floor; she gives herself a facial with slices of cucumber while her husband vacuums around her. Women there didn't appreciate this ad. As a local ad executive put it, they regarded the ad as a challenge to "the leadership of women in the home."

In general, four factors appear to determine the degree to which one or the other spouse or both jointly will decide what to buy:[74]

1 **Sex-role stereotypes**—Couples who believe in traditional sex-role stereotypes tend to make individual decisions for sex-typed products (i.e., those they consider "masculine" or "feminine.")

2 **Spousal resources**—The spouse who contributes more resources to the family has the greater influence.

3 **Experience**—Couples who have gained experience as a decision-making unit make individual decisions more frequently.

4 **Socioeconomic status**—Middle-class families make more joint decisions than do either higher- or lower-class families.

Despite recent changes in decision-making responsibilities, women are still primarily responsible for the continuation of the family's **kin-network system**: They maintain ties among family members, both immediate and extended. Women are more likely to coordinate visits among relatives, stay in touch with family members, send greeting cards, and arrange social engagements.[75] This organizing role means that women often make important decisions about the family's leisure activities, and they are more likely to decide with whom the family will socialize.

Heuristics in Joint Decision Making

The **synoptic ideal** calls for the husband and wife to take a common view and to act as joint decision makers. According to this view, they would very thoughtfully weigh alternatives, assign one another well-defined roles, and calmly make mutually beneficial consumer decisions. The couple would act rationally and analytically, and use as much information as possible to maximize joint utility. Do you know anyone who does that? In reality, spousal decision making may be more about choosing whatever option will result in less conflict. A couple "reaches" rather than "makes" a decision. Researchers simply describe this process as "muddling through."[76]

One common technique to simplify the decision-making process uses *heuristics*. The following decision-making patterns, which realtors frequently observe when a couple decides on a new house, illustrate how couples use heuristics.

The couple defines their areas of common preference on obvious, objective dimensions rather than subtler, hard-to-define cues. For example, they may easily agree on the

CB AS I SEE IT

Professor Alladi Venkatesh, *University of California, Irvine*

As new technologies diffuse into the home, new terminology has begun to emerge as, for example, *smart homes, home automation, digital home, digital living, networked home, home of the future, smart appliances*, and so on. To further complicate the technological scene, we are witnessing enormous growth of social media (Facebook, MySpace, YouTube, etc.). We will use the term *smart home technologies* to describe these and other similar technologies. Although smart home technologies have developed in different directions because of the types of industry players involved, some common themes underlie these developments. For example, family shopping behavior—from online product information search to payments, vacation planning, and communication—are some of the many activities that families undertake using these new technologies. They all seem to point to a great sense of anticipation that home life as we have understood it in the past 50 or 60 years will

undergo some fundamental changes. It is claimed that some of these changes may be the result of advances at the technological frontier.

Embedded in the concept of the smart home are smart appliances, multimedia systems, energy devices, sensors, lighting systems, sensors and control systems, and home robots that manifest basic qualities of programmable machine intelligence. However, their implementation has not been very successful and has been a little slow. Recent developments, however, seem to suggest that smart home concepts are closer to reality and must be taken seriously.

To put these developments in a historical perspective, one can trace all such advances to the early 1980s when the PC was introduced into the home. This was also the period when various electronic gadgets entered the domestic space: VCRs, microwave ovens, answering machines, and cable TV, to name an important few. A lot has happened since then. In the 1990s, the technological scene changed dramatically with the arrival of the Internet, connecting the household to the external environment in some fundamental views. In the beginning of the 21st century, the introduction of mobile phones and wireless technologies has further expanded the technological boundaries. The possibilities seem endless. In this

ever-increasing technological frenzy, some caution must be exercised as new technologies knock on the door to gain acceptance by families. Our previous studies show that families are reluctant to "overtechnologize" their homes, but at the same time are quite open to technologies that fit with their current patterns of behaviors and possibly add value to the family life. It is this balance between too much and too little technology that one must seek.

Given the developments described previously, technology diffusion into the home remains an unexplored area in the field of consumer research. For consumer researchers, the challenging questions are:

- How are smart home technologies diffusing into the home?
- How is the family changing as a result of new technologies coming into the home?
- Who are the innovators? And what are the characteristics of their products and services?
- What are the models of technology and appropriate adoption and use?
- How are the family roles transformed in light of these new changes?
- What are the implications for product advertising in light of social media?

number of bedrooms they need in the new home, but they have a harder time when they need to agree on how the home should look.

The couple negotiates a system of *task specialization* in which each is responsible for certain duties or decision areas and does not intrude on the other's "turf." For many couples, sex roles often dictate just what these territories are. For example, the wife may do advance scouting for houses that meet their requirements, and the husband determines whether the couple can obtain a mortgage.

The likelihood of one partner conceding to the wishes of the other depends on how passionately each person desires a specific outcome. One spouse yields to the influence of the other in many cases simply because his or her preference for a certain attribute is not particularly intense. In other situations he is more willing to fight for what he wants (in other words, "choose your battles").[77] In cases where intense preferences for different attributes exist, rather than attempting to influence each other, spouses will "trade off" a less-intense preference for a more strongly felt desire. For example, a husband who is somewhat indifferent about kitchen design may give in to his wife in exchange for permission to design his own garage workshop.

OBJECTIVE 6

Children learn over time what and how to consume.

Children as Decision Makers: Consumers-in-Training

As they struggle to convince us to buy new cars, carmakers also take time out to woo some people who are still too young to drive. Many advertise in child-oriented areas such as gyms that cater to kids, social networking sites that young people visit frequently, and the Saturday morning cartoons. In Whyville.net, a virtual world where nearly 2 million children aged 8 to 15 hang out, kids can buy virtual Scion xBs if they have enough "clams" (Whyville's monetary unit). If not, they can meet with Eric, a virtual Toyota Financial Services advisor, to finance an xB replica they can use to tool around while in-world. Small wonder: A study Nickelodeon conducted reported that almost two-thirds of parents now say their children "actively participate" in car-buying decisions.[78]

This early involvement in decision making helps to explain why Disney works so hard to reach parents and *really* young kids—that is, so young they're not even born yet. Disney estimates the North American baby market, including staples like formula, to be worth $36.3 billion annually. A representative of the Disney Baby program that operates in 580 maternity hospitals in the United States visits a new mother and offers a free Disney Cuddly Bodysuit, a variation of the classic Onesie. The rep provides bedside demonstrations and asks mothers to sign up for e-mail alerts fromDisneyBaby.com. As one company executive observes, "To get that mom thinking about her family's first park experience before her baby is even born is a home run."[79]

Anyone who has had the "delightful" experience of grocery shopping with children in tow knows that kids often have a say (sometimes a loud, whiny one) in what their parents buy. Children make up three distinct markets:[80]

1 **Primary Market**—Kids spend a lot on their own wants and needs, which include toys, apparel, movies, and games. When marketers at M&Ms candy figured out who actually buys a lot of their products, they redesigned vending machines with coin slots lower to the ground to accommodate shorter people, and sales rose dramatically.[81]

2 **Influence Market**—**Parental yielding** occurs when a parental decision maker "surrenders" to a child's request.[82] Yielding drives many product selections because about 90 percent of these requests are for a specific brand. Researchers estimate that children directly influence about $453 billion worth of family purchases in a year. They report that on average children weigh in with a purchase request every 2 minutes when they shop with parents.[83] In recognition of this influence, Mrs. Butterworth's Syrup created a $6 million campaign to target kids directly with humorous ads that show the lengths to which adults will go to get the syrup bottle

to talk to them. An executive who worked on the campaign explained, "We needed to create the *nag factor* [where kids demand that their parents buy the product]."[84]

The likelihood of yielding depends partly on the dynamics within a particular family. As we all know, parental styles range from permissive to strict, and they also vary in terms of the amount of responsibility parents give their children.[85] Income level also comes into play; kids at the lower end of the spectrum have a greater say in brand purchases than those from high-income families. Parents whom children can most easily influence also tend to be highly receptive to advertising; according to a major research firm, these "child influenced shoppers" are twice as likely as the average U.S. adult to agree that if they see a brand-name product on a TV show, this reassures them it's a good product. They're also twice as likely to say that they'll probably try a new product if they see a character in a movie use it.

One study documented the strategies kids use to request purchases. Although most children simply ask for things, some other common tactics included saying they had seen it on TV, saying that a sibling or friend has it, or offering to do chores in exchange. Other actions—which included directly placing the object in the cart and continuous pleading—were less innocuous, but no less "persuasive" behaviors![86] In addition, the amount of influence children have over consumption is culturally determined. Children who live in individualistic cultures such as the United States have more direct influence, whereas kids in collective cultures such as Japan get their way more indirectly.[87]

3 **Future Market**—Kids have a way of growing up to be adults, so savvy marketers try to lock in brand loyalty at an early age. That explains why Kodak encourages kids to become photographers. Currently, only 20 percent of children aged 5 to 12 own cameras, and they shoot an average of only one roll of film a year. The company produces ads that portray photography as a cool pursuit and as a form of rebellion. It packages cameras with an envelope to mail the film directly back so parents can't see the photos.

Consumer Socialization

We've seen that kids are responsible for a lot of marketplace activity, but how do they know what they like and want? Children do not spring from the womb with consumer skills in place. **Consumer socialization** is the process "by which young people acquire skills, knowledge, and attitudes relevant to their functioning in the marketplace."[88] From where does this knowledge come? Friends and teachers certainly participate in this process. For instance, children talk to one another about consumer products, and this tendency increases as the kids age.[89] Especially for young children, though, the two primary socialization sources are the family and the media.

Parents' Influence

Parents influence consumer socialization both directly and indirectly. They deliberately try to instill their own values about consumption in their children ("You're going to learn the value of a dollar!"). Parents also determine the degree to which their children come into contact with other information sources, such as television, salespeople, and peers.[91] Cultural expectations regarding children's involvement in purchase decisions influence when and how parents socialize their kids as consumers. For example, parents in traditional cultures such as Greece and India rely on later development timetables for consumer-related skills and understanding of advertising practices than do American and Australian parents.[92]

Grown-ups also serve as significant models for observational learning. Children learn about consumption as they watch their parents' behaviors and imitate them. Marketers encourage this process when they package adult products in child versions. This "passing down" of product preferences helps to create brand loyalty; researchers find evidence of intergenerational influence when they study the product choices of mothers and their daughters.[93]

Marketing Pitfall

Toys are fun to play with, but often a hidden agenda is that they're also socialization agents that teach kids about life. Sometimes, perhaps, they can be a bit *too* realistic. Some critics objected to a new doll called Baby Alive Learns to Potty. She comes with a pink plastic toilet. When a child presses the doll's bracelet, she chirps, "Sniff sniff. I made a stinky!" The doll also comes with "green beans" and "bananas" that the child feeds to the doll—then they come out the other end. Put Baby Alive on her toilet and a magnet triggers a change in the bowl: The "water" is replaced with "potty waste," which the child can flush (with appropriate sound effects). Critics charge that some things are better left to the land of make-believe. Indeed, most child psychologists agree that the best toys encourage children to use their imaginations.[90]

The process of consumer socialization begins with infants; within the first 2 years, children request products they want. By about age 5, most kids make purchases with the help of parents and grandparents, and by age 8 most buy things on their own.[94] Figure 1 summarizes the sequence of stages as kids turn into consumers.

Parents exhibit different styles when they socialize their children:[95]

- *Authoritarian parents* are hostile, restrictive, and emotionally uninvolved. They do not have warm relationships with their children, they censor the types of media their children see, and they tend to have negative views about advertising.
- *Neglecting parents* also are detached from their children, and the parents don't exercise much control over what their children do.
- *Indulgent parents* communicate more with their children about consumption-related matters and are less restrictive. They believe that children should be allowed to learn about the marketplace without much interference.

Television and the Web: Electric Babysitters

Advertising starts to influence us at a very early age. As we've seen, many marketers push their products on kids to encourage them to build a lifelong habit. One controversial exception occurred in France. An ad McDonald's placed in the magazine *Femme Actuelle* actually encouraged parents to limit kids' visits to its outlets when it proclaimed, "There is no reason to eat excessive amounts of junk food, nor go more than once a week to McDonald's." A spokesperson for McDonald's in the United States said the company did not agree with the views the ad expressed.[96] That's unfortunate: One study funded by the National Institutes of Health projected that a ban on fast-food advertising to children would cut the national obesity rate by as much as 18 percent.[97]

In two studies, British researchers compared the effects of television advertising on the eating habits of 152 kids between the ages of 5 and 11. In both studies, the kids watched 10 ads followed by a cartoon. In one session, the kids saw ads for toys before they watched a video. In another session, the researchers replaced the toy ads with food ads that commonly run during children's programs. After both viewings, held 2 weeks apart, the kids were allowed to snack as much as they wanted from a table of low-fat and high-fat snacks, including grapes, cheese-flavored rice cakes, chocolate buttons, and

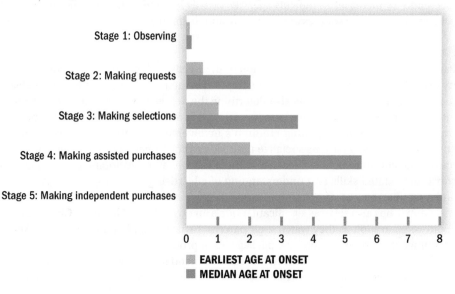

A CONSUMER IS BORN

Children start accompanying parents to the marketplace as early as one month old and begin to make independent purchases as early as four years old.

Figure 1 FIVE STAGES OF CONSUMER DEVELOPMENT BY EARLIEST AGE AT ONSET AND MEDIAN AGE AT ONSET potato chips. The 5- to 7-year-old kids who saw the food ads ate 14 to 17 percent more calories than those who saw the toy ads. The results were even more dramatic among 9- to 11-year-olds. Those in the food ad condition ate from 84 to 134 percent more calories than did those in the toy ad condition.[98]

As we've already seen, a lot of kids divide their time between the TV set and the computer (and their cell phones as well). In the United States, about 80 percent of children age 5 and under use the Internet at least once a week. What's more, like their older brothers and sisters, little kids are avid multitaskers: A Nielsen study reported that 36 percent of kids ages 2 to 11 watch online content and TV at the same time.[99] Now, to hasten kids' introduction to social media, a team of Finnish designers invented a block-sorting toy that also works like Twitter. It allows preverbal kids to grab colorful blocks with icons for sleeping, eating, or brushing their teeth; fit them into slots to indicate what they're up to; then the device transmits the "status update" to light up the corresponding block-shape on the same toy in another household.[100]

Sex-Role Socialization

Children pick up on the concept of gender identity at an earlier age than researchers previously believed—by as young as age 1 in some cases. By the age of 3, most U.S. children categorize driving a truck as masculine and cooking and cleaning as feminine.[101] Even characters that cartoons portray as helpless are more likely to wear frilly or ruffled dresses.[102]

One function of child's play is to rehearse for adulthood. Children act out different roles they might assume later in life and learn about the expectations others have of them. The toy industry provides the props that children use to perform these roles.[103] Depending on which side of the debate you're on, these toys either reflect or teach children about what society expects of males and females. Preschool boys and girls do not exhibit many differences in toy preferences, but after the age of 5 they part company: Girls tend to stick with dolls, whereas boys gravitate toward "action figures" and high-tech diversions.

At *Barbie.com*, a girl can customize her avatar and her room.[104]
Source: Courtesy of Mattel.

Marketing Pitfall

Do marketers try to turn girls into women before they should? Adult products and practices increasingly trickle down to the younger set. Analysts estimate that girls 11 to 14 see about 500 advertisements a day. We read about elementary school students who spend the afternoon at the beauty salon and even 5-year-olds who have spa days and pedicure parties. In 2005, the NPD group reported that the average age at which women began to use beauty products was 17. By 2009, that average had dropped to 13. Another study by Experian found that 43 percent of 6- to 9-year-olds use lipstick or lip gloss, and 38 percent use hairstyling products. In addition to adult shows like *Extreme Makeover*, youngsters learn about makeup from the girls of *Toddlers & Tiaras*, and *Little Miss Perfect*.[108]

Now, even feminine hygiene products target young girls. A Kotex Web site designed for mothers asks, "Some girls get their period as young as 8. Have you had the talk?" The company designed a pad specifically for 8- to 12-year-olds that is shorter and narrower than other Kotex pads; it's sold in glittery boxes decorated with hearts, stars, and swirls (which are also printed on the pads themselves). Kotex reports research showing that one out of three girls has no idea what is happening when her first period arrives, while four out of five mothers feel ill-prepared to educate their daughters about menstruation.[109]

Industry critics charge that this is because males dominate the toy industry, but toy company executives counter that they simply respond to kids' natural preferences.[105] Indeed, after two decades of trying to avoid boy-versus-girl stereotypes, many companies seem to have decided that differences are inevitable. Toys "R" Us unveiled a new store design after it interviewed 10,000 kids; the chain now has separate sections it calls Girls' World and Boys' World. According to the president of Fox Family Channels, "Boys and girls are different, and it's great to celebrate what's special about each." Boys tend to be more interested in battle and competition; girls are more interested in creativity and relationships. This is what experts refer to as "male and female play patterns."[106]

Some doll manufacturers recognize the powerful role toys play in consumer socialization, so they create characters they hope will teach little girls about the real world—not the fantasy "bimbo" world that many dolls represent. Barbie's rebirth as a career woman illustrates how a firm takes concerns about socialization to heart. Although Mattel introduced a Barbie doll astronaut in 1964 and an airline pilot in 1999, it never provided much detail about the careers themselves. Today girls can choose to play with Working Woman Barbie. She comes with a miniature computer and cell phone as well as a CD-ROM about understanding finances. She dresses in a gray suit, but the skirt reverses to a red dress for her to wear with red platform shoes when she goes on after-work adventures with Ken.[107]

Cognitive Development

A child's ability to make mature, "adult" consumer decisions obviously increases with age (not that grown-ups always make mature decisions). Marketers segment kids in terms of their **stage of cognitive development**, or their ability to comprehend concepts of increasing complexity. Some evidence indicates that very young children learn consumption-related information surprisingly well.[110]

The Swiss psychologist Jean Piaget was the foremost proponent of the idea that children pass through distinct stages of cognitive development. He believed that a certain cognitive structure characterizes each stage as the child learns to process information.[111] In one classic demonstration of cognitive development, Piaget poured the contents of a short, squat glass of lemonade into a taller, thinner glass that actually held the same amount of liquid. Five-year-olds, who still believed that the shape of the glass determined its contents, thought this glass held more liquid than the first glass. They are in what Piaget termed a *preoperational stage of development*. In contrast, 6-year-olds tended to be unsure, but 7-year-olds knew the amount of lemonade had not changed.

Many developmental specialists no longer believe that children necessarily pass through these fixed stages at the same time. An alternative view proposes that they differ in information-processing capability, or ability to store and retrieve information from memory. Researchers who advocate this approach identify three developmental stages:[112]

1 **Limited**—Children who are younger than age 6 do not employ storage and retrieval strategies.
2 **Cued**—Children between the ages of 6 and 12 employ these strategies but only when prompted to do so.
3 **Strategic**—Children 12 and older spontaneously employ storage and retrieval strategies.

This sequence of development underscores the notion that children do not think in the same way adults do, and we can't expect them to use information the same way either. It also reminds us that they do not necessarily form the same conclusions as adults when they encounter product information. Kids are not as likely to realize that something they see on TV is not "real," and as a result they are more vulnerable to persuasive messages. Younger kids aren't able to distinguish media depictions from reality, so the more a child watches MTV's *Laguna Beach* or *SpongeBob SquarePants*, the more he will accept the images it depicts as real.[113] Kids also see idealized images of what it is like to be an adult.

Because children over the age of six do about a quarter of their television viewing during prime time, adult programs and commercials have a big effect on them. For example, young girls who see adult lipstick commercials associate lipstick with beauty.[114]

Research underscores the idea that children's understanding of brand names evolves as they age. Kids learn to relate to brand names at an early age; they recognize brand names in stores, develop preferences for some brands over others, and request branded items by name. However, brand names function as simple perceptual cues for these children that let them identify a familiar object with particular features. *Conceptual brand meanings*, which specify the nonobservable abstract features of the product, enter into the picture in middle childhood (about age 8); children incorporate them into their thinking and judgments a few years later. By the time a child reaches 12 years of age, she thinks about brands on a conceptual or symbolic level and she's likely to incorporate these meanings into brand-related judgments.[115]

Several business ventures illustrate that using sound principles of consumer psychology can also make good financial sense. The trend started a long time ago with public television's *Sesame Street*, but today the for-profit networks are in the game as well. The first successful foray into the preschool market was *Blue's Clues* in 1996, which turned into a huge hit as viewers abandoned the smarmy *Barney & Friends*.

Now, when millions of preschoolers tune in to Nickelodeon's hit show *Dora the Explorer*, they don't realize that they view content based on **multiple-intelligence theory**. This influential perspective argues for other types of intelligence, such as athletic prowess or musical ability, beyond the traditional math and verbal skills psychologists use to measure IQ. Thus, when Dora consults her map, she promotes "spatial" skills. And when she asks her young viewers to help her count planks to build a bridge, Dora builds "interpersonal intelligence."[116]

Marketing Research and Children

The Walt Disney Co. recently assembled a team of anthropologists who spent 18 months studying 6- to 14-year-old boys. The company, which has tended toward girl-friendly fare like *Hannah Montana* and *The Little Mermaid* in recent years, wanted to get a better handle on a market segment that spends about $50 billion every year (it recently bought Marvel Comics to expand its reach to boys). After team members observed boys in their natural habitats, they recommended subtle but important changes to programs that better capture this world:

- The central character on the show *Aaron Stone* is a mediocre basketball player. The team learned that boys identify more with characters who try to improve than with those who easily win.
- Actors on the show now carry their skateboards with the bottoms facing outward, because boys in real life do that to show off how they have personalized their boards.
- The games section of the Disney XD Web site includes trophy cases, because the researchers found that players like to share their achievements with others.[117]

Compared to adults, kids are difficult subjects for market researchers. They tend to be unreliable reporters of their own behavior, they have poor recall, and they often do not understand abstract questions.[118] Some European countries restrict marketers' ability to interview children, so it's even harder to collect this kind of data there. Still, as Disney discovered, market research can pay off.[119]

Product Testing

A particularly helpful type of research with children is product testing. Young subjects provide a valuable perspective on what products will succeed with other kids. Marketers obtain these insights as they watch kids play with toys or talk to them in focus groups. The Fisher-Price Company maintains a nursery it calls the Playlab. Children (whom it chooses from a waiting list of 4,000) play with new toys while staff members watch from behind a one-way mirror.[120]

Message Comprehension

Because children differ in their abilities to process product-related information, advertisers' direct appeals to them raise many serious ethical issues.[121] Children's advocacy groups argue that kids younger than age 7 do not understand the persuasive intent of commercials, and (as we've seen) younger children cannot readily distinguish between a commercial and programming. Kids' cognitive defenses are not yet sufficiently developed to filter out commercial appeals, so in a sense, altering their brand preferences may be likened to "shooting fish in a barrel," as one critic put it.[122] Figure 2 shows one attempt to assess whether kids can tell that a commercial is trying to persuade them.

Beginning in the 1970s, the Federal Trade Commission (FTC) took action to protect children. The agency limited commercials during "children's" programming (most often Saturday morning television) and required "separators" to help children discern when a program ended and a commercial began (e.g., "We'll be right back after these commercial messages"). The FTC reversed itself in the early 1980s during the deregulatory, probusiness climate of the Reagan administration. The 1990 Children's Television Act restored some of these restrictions. Still, critics argue that rather than sheltering children from marketplace influences, the dominant way that marketers view them is as what one calls "kid customer."[123]

On the bright side, however, it seems that food companies are finally taking action to combat the growing problem of childhood obesity that they helped to create. Numerous corporations, including Sara Lee, Burger King, Campbell Soup Company, Coca-Cola, Pepsi, Dannon, General Mills, Hershey, Kellogg, Kraft Foods, Mars, McDonald's, and Nestlé, have joined the Council of Better Business Bureau's Children's Food and Beverage Initiative. They have pledged to market to kids 11 and under only products that meet government or American Heart Association standards for "healthy" foods. In addition, this agreement restricts the use of third-party licensed characters in ads targeted to child audiences, and sharply limits the usage of product images in places like elementary schools and video games.[124] As we continue to witness pushback from parents and consumer groups, we can probably expect that other industries will follow suit in adopting more responsible guidelines as attitudes toward materialism and childhood socialization continue to evolve.

Figure 2 EAMPLES OF SKETCHES RESEARCHERS USE TO MEASURE CHILDREN'S PERCEPTIONS OF COMMERCIAL INTENT

CHAPTER SUMMARY

Now that you have finished reading this chapter you should understand why:

1. Marketers often need to understand *consumers'* behavior rather than *a* consumer's behavior.

More than one person actually makes many purchasing decisions. Collective decision making occurs whenever two or more people evaluate, select, or use a product or service. In organizations and in families, members play several different roles during the decision-making process. These roles include gatekeeper, influencer, buyer, and user.

2. Companies as well as individuals make purchase decisions.

Organizational buyers are people who make purchasing decisions on behalf of a company or other group. Although many of the same factors that affect how they make decisions in their personal lives influence these buyers, their organizational choices tend to be more rational. Their decisions are also likely to involve more financial risk, and as the choices become more complex, it is probable that a greater number of people will be involved in making the decision. The amount of cognitive effort that goes into organizational decisions relates to internal factors, such as the individuals' psychological characteristics, and external factors, such as the company's willingness to tolerate risk. One of the most important determinants is the type of purchase the company wants to make: The extent of problem solving required depends on whether the product or service it procures is simply a reorder (a straight rebuy), a reorder with minor modifications (modified rebuy), or something it has never bought before or something complex and risky (new task). Online purchasing sites revolutionize the way organizational decision makers collect and evaluate product information in business-to-business (B2B) e-commerce.

3. Our traditional notions about families are outdated.

The number and type of U.S. households is changing in many ways, including delays in getting married and having children, and in the composition of family households, which are increasingly headed by a single parent. New perspectives on the family life cycle, which focuses on how people's needs change as they move through different stages in their lives, are forcing marketers to more seriously consider consumer segments such as gays and lesbians, divorced persons, and childless couples when they develop targeting strategies.

4. Many important demographic dimensions of a population relate to family and household structure.

Demographics are statistics that measure a population's characteristics. Some of the most important of these relate to family structure (e.g., the birth rate, the marriage rate, and the divorce rate). A *household* is an occupied housing unit.

5. Members of a family unit play different roles and have different amounts of influence when the family makes purchase decisions.

Marketers have to understand how families make decisions. Spouses in particular have different priorities and exert varying amounts of influence in terms of effort and power. Children are also increasingly influential in a widening range of purchase decisions.

6. Children learn over time what and how to consume.

Children undergo a process of socialization, during which they learn how to be consumers. Parents and friends instill some of this knowledge, but a lot of it comes from exposure to mass media and advertising. Because it's so easy to persuade children, consumers, academics, and marketing practitioners hotly debate the ethical aspects of marketing to them.

KEY TERMS

accommodative purchase decision
autonomic decision
boomerang kids
business-to-business (B2B) e-commerce
business-to-business (B2B) marketers
buyclass theory of purchasing
buyer
buying center

consensual purchase decision
consumer socialization
crowdsourcing
customer networks
DINKS (double income, no kids)
extended family
family financial officer (FFO)
family identity
family life cycle (FLC)
fertility rate

freemium
gatekeeper
gender convergence
helicopter moms
household
influencer
initiator
juggling lifestyle
kin-network system
modified rebuy

multiple-intelligence theory	parental yielding	straight rebuy
network effect	prediction market	syncretic decisions
new task	Sandwich Generation	synoptic ideal
nuclear family	sheconomy	user
organizational buyers	stage of cognitive development	wiki

REVIEW

1 What are some factors that influence how an organizational buyer evaluates a purchase decision?

2 What is a prediction market?

3 Summarize the buyclass model of purchasing. How do decisions differ within each class?

4 What are some of the ways in which organizational decisions differ from individual consumer decisions? How are they similar?

5 List at least three roles employees play in the organizational decision-making process.

6 What is a nuclear family, and how is it different from an extended family?

7 How do we calculate a nation's fertility rate? What fertility rate is required to ensure that population size does not decline?

8 What are boomerang kids?

9 What is the FLC, and why is it important to marketers?

10 List some variables we must consider when we try to understand different stages in the FLC.

11 What is the difference between a consensual and an accommodative purchase decision? What are some factors that help to determine how much conflict the family will experience when it makes a decision?

12 What is the difference between an autonomic and a syncretic decision?

13 What are some differences between "traditional" and "modern" couples in terms of how they allocate household responsibilities?

14 What factors help to determine if decisions will be made jointly or by only one spouse?

15 What is a kin-network system?

16 Describe a heuristic a couple might use when they make a decision, and provide an example of it.

17 What are three reasons why children are an important segment to marketers?

18 What is consumer socialization? Who are some important players in this process? How do toys contribute?

19 Discuss stages of cognitive development and how these relate to the comprehension of marketing messages.

20 Why is it difficult to conduct marketing research with children?

CONSUMER BEHAVIOR CHALLENGE

■ DISCUSS

1 Is the family unit dead?

2 Discuss the pros and cons of the voluntarily childless movement. Are followers of this philosophy selfish?

3 The chapter mentions various marketing practices, such as sales of specially designed feminine hygiene products to 8- to 12-year-old girls. Do marketers rob kids of their childhood?

4 The Defense Department shut down a controversial research program following a public outcry. Its intent was to create a prediction market to forecast terrorist activities. Was the decision to terminate the program warranted? Why or why not?

5 Do kids spend too much time online? Why or why not?

6 Do you think market research should be performed with children? Give the reasons supporting your answer.

7 Marketers have been criticized when they donate products and services to educational institutions in exchange for free promotion. In your opinion, is this a fair exchange, or should corporations be prohibited from attempting to influence youngsters in school?

8 For each of the following five product categories—groceries, automobiles, vacations, furniture, and appliances—describe the ways in which you believe having children or not affects a married couple's choices.

9 When they identify and target newly divorced couples, do you think marketers exploit these couples' situations? Are there instances in which you think marketers may actually be helpful to them? Support your answers with examples.

10 Industrial purchase decisions are totally rational. Aesthetic or subjective factors don't—and shouldn't—play a role in this process. Do you agree?

11 We can think of college students who live away from home as having a substitute "family." Whether you live with your parents, with a spouse, or with other students, how are decisions made in your college residence "family"? Do some

people take on the role of mother or father or child? Give a specific example of a decision that had to be made and the roles members played.

12 The promotional products industry thrives on corporate clients that order $19 billion per year of T-shirts, mugs, pens, and other branded items that are intended to keep their organizations at the forefront of their customers' minds. This has caused a lot of backlash, especially in the medical/pharmaceutical industry where critics worry about the undue influence of these advertising messages. Stanford University Medical Center prohibits its physicians from accepting even small gifts, such as pens and mugs, from pharmaceutical sales representatives, under a new policy that it hopes will limit industry influence on patient care and doctor education. The new policy is part of a small but growing movement among medical centers (Yale and the University of Pennsylvania have similar policies). The policy also prohibits doctors from accepting free drug samples and from publishing articles ghostwritten by industry contractors in medical journals (a fairly common practice). These changes come at a time when many of us are concerned about the safety and rising cost of drugs and medical devices. About 90 percent of the pharmaceutical industry's $21 billion marketing budget targets physicians. Some studies have shown that even small gifts create a sense of obligation; one critical study charged that free drug samples are "a powerful inducement for physicians and patients to rely on medications that are expensive but not more effective." Indeed, some industry documents from a civil lawsuit show that big pharmaceutical companies sometimes calculate to the penny the profits that doctors could make from their drugs. Sales representatives shared those profit estimates with doctors and their staffs, the documents show.[125] In response to pressure in the market, the pharmaceutical industry is largely banning the use of promotional products. One result is that the businesses that supply these premiums will lose around $1 billion per year in sales. What do you think about this initiative? Is it fair to deprive an industry of its livelihood in this way? Why or why not? Where is the line between legitimate promotion of one's products and unethical practice? Should professionals engage in organizational decision making that has such far-reaching medical and financial ramifications?

■ APPLY

1 Arrange to interview two married couples, one younger and one older. Prepare a response form that lists five product categories—groceries, furniture, appliances, vacations, and automobiles—and ask each spouse to indicate, without consulting the other, whether purchases in each category are made by joint or unilateral decisions, and to indicate whether the unilateral decisions are made by the husband or the wife. Compare each couple's responses for agreement between husbands and wives relative to who makes the decisions, and compare both couples' overall responses for differences relative to the number of joint versus unilateral decisions. Report your findings and conclusions.

2 Collect ads for three different product categories that target families. Find another set of ads for different brands of the same items that don't feature families. Prepare a report comparing the probable effectiveness of the two approaches. Which specific categories would most likely benefit from a family emphasis?

3 Pick three married couples and ask each husband and wife to list the names of all cousins, second cousins, and so on for both sides of the family. Based on the results, what can you conclude about the relative role of men and women in maintaining the kin-network system?

4 Observe the interactions between parents and children in the cereal section of a local grocery store (remember to take earplugs with you). Prepare a report on the number of children who expressed preferences, how they expressed their preferences, and how parents responded, including the number who purchased the child's choice.

5 Watch 3 hours of children's programming on commercial television stations. Evaluate the marketing techniques used in the commercials in terms of the ethical issues raised in the final section of this chapter. Report your findings and conclusions.

6 Select a product category and, using the life-cycle stages this chapter describes, list the variables likely to affect a purchase decision for the product by consumers in each stage of the cycle.

7 Consider three important changes in the modern family structure. For each, find an example of a marketer who seems to be conscious of this change in its product communications, retailing innovations, or other aspects of the marketing mix. If possible, also try to find examples of marketers who have failed to keep up with these developments.

Case Study

CHILDREN: THE FINAL FRONTIER . . . FOR CELL PHONES

With the adult and even teen markets for cell phones quickly becoming saturated (more than 65 percent of U.S. teens have them now), the industry looks to other segments. The growth market for the cell phone industry in the near future is children aged 8 to 12—or even younger. Many in the industry see grade-school children as the final frontier if phone manufacturers are to continue to grow. Already, parents give children as young as 5 years old their own cell phones.

A host of companies make phones for the younger market. Disney, Hasbro, Mattel, and Firefly Mobile offer models in bright colors that feature graphics of favorite characters such as SpongeBob SquarePants and Barbie. They designed these phones for smaller hands, and many lack traditional keypads. Parents can program what the phones do, control incoming and outgoing calls, and prepay minutes.

But does such a young child really need a cell phone? There are many child advocates, including Ralph Nader, Canadian kids' entertainer Raffi, and various politicians, who say that they do not. Some critics claim that cell phone makers have declared "open season" on children with their aggressive marketing tactics. In addition, there is some evidence (mixed, so far) that cell phone usage can be carcinogenic and may be especially risky for young children.

The cell phone companies defend their actions. Many have released statements saying that they don't market their products (even the kid-friendly ones) to children, but rather to their parents. Disney said it developed Disney Mobile as a service to address the needs of a family audience, and that its products and services are available to all members of the family, including adults. Marketers claim that they simply answer the demands of consumers for services such as the five-key, parent-programmable Firefly.

Of course, children want the phones because they're cool, because their friends have them, and because they want to be more grown-up. In fact, many tweens reject the kiddie versions and demand real adult-style cell phones. According to a spokesman for Verizon Wireless, kids "don't want what we call 'Fisher Price' phones. They want the real deal, with the camera and the QWERTY keyboard for text messaging." Coolness and prestige alone are usually not good enough for parents to give in and buy one of the gadgets for their kids. However, marketers position the phones to Mom and Dad on a different basis: The phones provide an extra layer of security to anxious parents who want to be able to locate their kids at all times. Many of the children's phones offer GPS tracking as well as all the parental control features. When parents are convinced that the increased ability to stay connected with their children enhances safety, the purchase decision is simple. Whether due to safety concerns or simply because parents give in to their kids' demands, the efforts of cell phone marketers appear to be paying off. Already, 55 percent of children ages 9 to 11 and 35 percent of children ages 7 years and younger carry their own mobiles. If companies can get younger children in the habit of using phones, the kids will probably be consumers for life.

DISCUSSION QUESTIONS

1 When it comes to cell phones for kids, who is the customer? Discuss the dynamics of the decision to buy a cell phone for a young child.
2 How do current trends in the family life cycle affect the marketing of cell phones to children?

Sources: Jaclyn Bruntfield, "What Risks Are Posed by Kids' Cell Phone Use?," *Green Parenting* (June 6, 2011), http://harrison.patch.com/articles/what-risks-are-posed-by-kids-cell-phone-use, accessed June 14, 2011; Madhusmita Bora, "Must-Have for Tweens: Cell Phone," *St. Petersburg Times* (August 26, 2007): 1A; Allison Ross, "Fast Texting—Tween Market Pumps Cellphone Sales," *McClatchy Tribune Business News* (December 14, 2008); Louise Lee, "Mom, Let's Talk: A Brand New Batch of Cell Phones Takes Aim at Kids as Young as 5," *BusinessWeek* (August 13, 2007): 82.

NOTES

1. www.epicurious.com, accessed June 4, 2011; www.marthastewart.com, accessed June 4, 2011.
2. Fred E. Webster and Yoram Wind, *Organizational Buying Behavior* (Upper Saddle River, NJ: Prentice Hall, 1972).
3. See J. Joseph Cronin, Jr., and Michael H. Morris, "Satisfying Customer Expectations: The Effect on Conflict and Repurchase Intentions in Industrial Marketing Channels," *Journal of the Academy of Marketing Science* 17 (Winter 1989): 41–49; Thomas W. Leigh and Patrick F. McGraw, "Mapping the Procedural Knowledge of Industrial Sales Personnel: A Script-Theoretic Investigation," *Journal of Marketing* 53 (January 1989): 16–34; William J. Qualls and Christopher P. Puto, "Organizational Climate and Decision Framing: An Integrated Approach to Analyzing Industrial Buying," *Journal of Marketing Research* 26 (May 1989): 179–92.
4. James M. Sinkula, "Market Information Processing and Organizational Learning," *Journal of Marketing* 58 (January 1994): 35–45.
5. Allen M. Weiss and Jan B. Heide, "The Nature of Organizational Search in High Technology Markets," *Journal of Marketing Research* 30 (May 1993): 220–33; Jennifer K. Glazing and Paul N. Bloom, "Buying Group Information Source Reliance," *Proceedings of the American Marketing Association Educators' Conference* (Summer 1994): 454.
6. B. Charles Ames and James D. Hlaracek, *Managerial Marketing for Industrial Firms* (New York: Random House Business Division, 1984); Edward F. Fern and James R. Brown, "The Industrial/Consumer Marketing Dichotomy: A Case of Insufficient Justification," *Journal of Marketing* 48 (Spring 1984): 68–77.
7. Jaakko Aspara, "Aesthetics of Stock Investments," *Consumption Markets & Culture* 12 (June 2009): 99–131.
8. Daniel H. McQuiston, "Novelty, Complexity, and Importance as Causal Determinants of Industrial Buyer Behavior," *Journal of Marketing* 53 (April 1989): 66–79.

9. Patrick J. Robinson, Charles W. Faris, and Yoram Wind, *Industrial Buying and Creative Marketing* (Boston: Allyn & Bacon, 1967).

10. Erin Anderson, Wujin Chu, and Barton Weitz, "Industrial Purchasing: An Empirical Examination of the Buyclass Framework," *Journal of Marketing* 51 (July 1987): 71–86.

11. Steven J. Kafka, Bruce D. Temkin, Matthew R. Sanders, Jeremy Sharrard, and Tobias O. Brown, "eMarketplaces Boost B2B Trade," *The Forrester Report* (Cambridge, MA: Forrester Research, Inc., February 2000).

12. http://wwre.globalsources.com/, accessed June 14, 2011; http://company.monster.com/wre, accessed June 16, 2009.

13. http://www.dell.com/us/business/p/, accessed June 14, 2011.

14. Chris Anderson, "The Economics of Giving It Away," *Wall Street Journal* (January 31, 2009), http://online.wsj.com/article/SB123335678420235003.html, accessed January 31, 2009.

15. "New Survey Finds B2B Marketers Gaining Ground in Social Media," *White Horse* (May 18, 2010), http://www.whitehorse.com/_templates/t_press_release.aspx?id=1523, accessed April 19, 2011.

16. Sean Silverthorne, "Facebook as Corporate Intranet—It's Starting to Happen," *The View from Harvard Business* (December 18, 2007), http://blogs.bnet.com/harvard/?p=158, accessed June 15, 2009; Vauhini Vara, "Offices Co-Opt Consumer Web Tools Like 'Wikis' and Social Networking," *Wall Street Journal* (September 12, 2006), www.wsj.com, accessed September 12, 2006.

17. Barbara Kiviat, "The End of Management," *Time Inside Business* (July 12, 2004), www.time.com/time/magazine/article/0,9171,994658,00.html, accessed October 5, 2007.

18. www.intrade.com, accessed June 4, 2011; www.hsx.com, accessed June 4, 2011.

19. www.ideastorm.com, accessed June 4, 2011; www.ninesigma.com, accessed June 4, 2011.

20. Sabrina Tavernise, "Married Couples Are No Longer a Majority, Census Finds," *New York Times* (May 26, 2011), http://www.nytimes.com/2011/05/26/us/26marry.html?_r=2&scp=1&sq=marriage%20rate&st=cse, accessed June 4, 2011.

21. Robert Boutilier, "Targeting Families: Marketing to and Through the New Family," in *American Demographics Marketing Tools* (Ithaca, NY: American Demographics Books, 1993): 4–6; W. Bradford Fay, "Families in the 1990s: Universal Values, Uncommon Experiences," *Marketing Research: A Magazine of Management & Applications* 5 (Winter 1993): 47.

22. Ellen Graham, "Craving Closer Ties, Strangers Come Together as Family," *Wall Street Journal* (March 4, 1996): B1.

23. Risto Moisio, Eric J. Arnould, and Linda L. Price, "Between Mothers and Markets: Constructing Family Identity through Homemade Food," *Journal of Consumer Culture* 4, no. 3 (2004): 361–84.

24. Nina Diamond, John F. Sherry, Jr., Albert M. Muniz, Jr., Mary Ann McGrath, Robert V. Kozinets, and Stefania Borghini, "American Girl and the Brand Gestalt: Closing the Loop on Sociocultural Branding Research," *Journal of Marketing* 73 (May 2009): 118–34.

25. Sabrina Tavernise, "Study Finds Women Slower to Wed, and Divorce Easing," *New York Times* (May 18, 2011), http://www.nytimes.com/2011/05/19/us/19marriage.html?_r=1&scp=1&sq=age%20of%20marriage&st=cse, accessed June 4, 2011.

26. Sabrina Tavernise, "Grandparents' Role Grows as the Economy Struggles," *New York Times* (November 10, 2010), http://www.nytimes.com/2010/11/11/us/11marriage.html?_r=1&scp=2&sq=grandparent&st=cse, accessed April 19, 2011.

27. "Match.com Releases Study on Trends in Online Dating," *Dating Site Reviews* (April 30, 2010), http://www.datingsitesreviews.com/article.php?story=Match-Releases-Study-Trends-Online-Datin, accessed June 14, 2011.

28. Ben Parr, "Twitter Users Have Shorter Relationships," *Mashable* (April 20, 2011), http://mashable.com/2011/04/19/active-twitter-users-have-shorter-relationships-stats/?utm_source=feedburner&utm_medium=email&utm_campaign=Feed%3A+Mashable+%28Mashable%29, accessed April 30, 2011.

29. Bella English, "The Boomerang Kids," *Boston Globe* (January 13, 2009), www.boston.com/lifestyle/family/articles/2009/01/13/the_boomerang_kids/?page=2, accessed June 16, 2009.

30. "Mothers Bearing a Second Burden," *New York Times* (May 14, 1989): 26.

31. Marcia Mogelonsky, "The Rocky Road to Adulthood," *American Demographics* (May 1996): 26.

32. Erik Eckholm, "'07 U.S. Births Break Baby Boom Record," *New York Times* (March 18, 2009), www.nytimes.com/2009/03/19/health/19birth.html?_r=1, accessed March 18, 2009.

33. Frank Bruni, "Persistent Drop in Fertility Reshapes Europe's Future," *New York Times* (December 26, 2002), www.nytimes.com, accessed December 26, 2002.

34. Katie Zezima, "More Women Than Ever Are Childless, Census Finds," *New York Times* (August 18, 2008), www.nytimes.com, accessed August 19, 2008.

35. P. Paul, "Childless by Choice," *American Demographics* (November 2001): 45–48, 50; www.childfreebychoice.com, accessed June 16, 2009.

36. Emily Friedman, "Does Virtual Cheating Still Count?," *ABC News* (August 13, 2007), http://abcnews.go.com/Technology/story?id=3473291&page=1, accessed August 13, 2007; Regina Lynn, "Virtual Rape Is Traumatic, but Is It a Crime?," *Wired* (May 4, 2007); www.wired.com/culture/lifestyle/commentary/sexdrive/2007/05/sexdrive_0504, accessed June 16, 2009; "Representative Kirk Wants to Ban Second Life's 'Rape Rooms' from Schools," *Virtual Worlds News* (May 7, 2008), www.virtualworldsnews.com/2008/05/representative.html?cid=113790134, accessed June 16, 2009.

37. Erik Sass, "Facebook Is Now Leading Source of Evidence in Divorce Cases," *Social Media & Marketing Daily* (March 10, 2011), http://www.mediapost.com/publications/?fa=Articles.showArticle&art_aid=146421&nid=124595, accessed April 19, 2011.

38. Amy Harmon, "Grandma's on the Computer Screen," *New York Times* (November 26, 2008), www.nytimes.com/2008/11/27/us/27minicam.html?emc=eta1, accessed November 27, 2008.

39. Rebecca Gardyn, "Animal Magnetism," *American Demographics* (May 2002): 31–37.

40. For a review, cf. Russell W. Belk, "Metaphoric Relationships with Pets," *Society & Animals* 4, no. 2 (1996): 121–46.

41. "Pets Win Prizes as Recession Bites," *Virgin Money* (April 23, 2009), http://uk.virginmoney.com/virgin/news-centre/press-releases/2009/Pets_win_prizes_as_recession_bites.jsp, accessed June 16, 2009; Carla Baranauckas, "A Dog's Life, Upgraded," *New York Times* (September 24, 2006), www.nytimes.com, accessed September 24, 2006; Thom Forbes, "PetSmart's Hotels Offer Doggies the Lap of Luxury," *Marketing Daily* (December 28, 2006), http://www.mediapost.com/publications/?fa=Articles.printFriendly&art_aid=53099, accessed December 28, 2006; Stephanie Thompson, "What's Next, Pup Tents in Bryant Park?" *Advertising Age* (January 29, 2007): 4; Maryann Mott, "Catering to the Consumers with Animal Appetites," *New York Times on the Web* (November 14, 2004), http://www.nytimes.com/2004/11/14/business/yourmoney/14pet.html, accessed September 9, 2011; www.k9waterco.com/, accessed June 14, 2011; Jim Carlton, "For Finicky Drinkers, Water from the Tap Isn't Tasty Enough," *Wall Street Journal* (March 11, 2005), www.wsj.com, accessed March 11, 2005.

42. http://petairways.com/, accessed June 14, 2011.

43. Brad Edmondson, "Do the Math," *American Demographics* (October 1999): 50–56.

44. www.thebump.com, accessed June 4, 2011; www.theknot.com, accessed June 4, 2011; Edmondson, "Do the Math."

45. The VOICE Group, "Buying into Motherhood? Problematic Consumption and Ambivalence in Transitional Phases," *Consumption Markets & Culture* 13, no. 4 (2010): 373–97.

46. Cheryl Russell, "The New Consumer Paradigm," *American Demographics* (April 1999): 50.

47. These categories are an adapted version of an FLC model proposed by Gilly and Enis (1982). Based on a recent empirical comparison of several competing models, Schaninger and Danko found that this framework outperformed others, especially in terms of its treatment of nonconventional households, though they recommend several improvements to this model as well. See Gilly and Enis, "Recycling the Family Life Cycle" Mary C. Gilly, Ben M. Enis (1982), "Recycling The Family Life Cycle: A Proposal For Redefinition", in Advances in Consumer Research Volume 09, eds. Andrew Mitchell, Ann Abor : Association for Consumer Research, Pages: 271–276.; Schaninger and Danko, "A Conceptual and Empirical Comparison of Alternate Household Life Cycle Models" *Journal of Consumer Research.* 19, 4 (March1993): 580–94; Scott D. Roberts, Patricia K. Voli, and Kerenami Johnson, "Beyond the Family Life Cycle: An Inventory of Variables for Defining the Family as a Consumption Unit," in Victoria L. Crittenden, ed., *Developments in Marketing Science 15* (Coral Gables, FL: Academy of Marketing Science, 1992): 71–75; George P. Moschis. "Life Course Perspectives on Consumer Behaviour," *Journal of the Academy of Marketing Science* 35 (2007): 295–307.

48. Edmondson, "Do the Math."

49. Jennifer Lach, "Intelligence Agents," *American Demographics* (March 1999): 52–60; for a detailed ethnographic study of how households assimilate products, cf. Jennifer Chang Coupland, "Invisible Brands: An Ethnography of Households and the Brands in Their Kitchen Pantries," *Journal of Consumer Research* 33, no. 2 (2005): 106.

50. Harry L. Davis, "Decision-Making Within the Household," *Journal of Consumer Research* 2 (March 1972): 241–60; Michael B. Menasco and David J. Curry, "Utility and Choice: An Empirical Study of Wife/Husband Decision-Making," *Journal of Consumer Research* 16 (June 1989): 87–97; Conway Lackman and John M. Lanasa, "Family Decision-Making Theory: An Overview and Assessment," *Psychology & Marketing* 10 (March–April 1993): 81–94.

51. Shannon Dortch, "Money and Marital Discord," *American Demographics* (October 1994): 11.

52. For research on factors affecting how much influence adolescents exert in family decision making, see Ellen Foxman, Patriya Tansuhaj, and Karin M. Ekstrom, "Family Members' Perceptions of Adolescents' Influence in Family Decision-Making," *Journal of Consumer Research* 15 (March 1989): 482–91; Sharon E. Beatty and Salil Talpade, "Adolescent Influence in Family Decision-Making: A Replication with Extension," *Journal of Consumer Research* 21 (September 1994): 332–41; for a recent study that compared the influence of parents versus siblings, cf. June Cotte and S. L. Wood, "Families and Innovative Consumer Behavior: A Triadic Analysis of Sibling and Parental Influence," *Journal of Consumer Research* 31, no. 1 (2004): 78–86.

53. Daniel Seymour and Greg Lessne, "Spousal Conflict Arousal: Scale Development," *Journal of Consumer Research* 11 (December 1984): 810–21.

54. Amber M. Epp and Linda L. Price, "Family Identity: A Framework of Identity Interplay in Consumption Practices," *Journal of Consumer Research* 35 (June 2008): 50–70; Robert Lohrer, "Haggar Targets Women with $8M Media Campaign," *Daily News Record* (January 8, 1997): 1.

55. Amber M. Epp and Linda L. Price, "Designing Solutions around Customer Network Identity Goals," *Journal of Marketing* 75, no. 2 (March 2011): 36–54.

56. Heather Timmons, "The Hand That Rocks the Cradle Can Call the Shots," *New York Times* (April 3, 2009), http://www.nytimes.com/2009/04/04/business/global/04indiamom.html?scp=113&sq=&st=nyt, accessed April 3, 2009.

57. www.urbanbaby.com/talk/posts/51108366, accessed June 16, 2009; "Helicopter Moms vs. Free-Range Kids," *Newsweek.com* (April 21, 2008), www.newsweek.com/id/133103, accessed June 16, 2009.

58. Diane Crispell, "Dual-Earner Diversity," *American Demographics* (July 1995): 32–37.

59. "Marriage: The Art of Compromise," *American Demographics* (February 1998): 41.

60. Belinda Luscombe, "Woman Power: The Rise of the Sheconomy," *Time Magazine* (November 22, 2010), http://www.time.com/time/magazine/article/0,9171,2030913-3,00.html, accessed April 19, 2011; Sarah Mahoney, "New Rules of Mama Marketing: Older, Greener," *Marketing Daily* (July 12, 2010), http://www.mediapost.com/publications/?fa=Articles.showArticle&art_aid=131754, accessed April 19, 2011.

61. Tanya Irwin, "Study: Men Defy Marketing Stereotypes," *Marketing Daily* (April 25, 2011), http://www.mediapost.com/publications/?fa=Articles.showArticle&art_aid=149272&nid=126106, accessed April 30, 2011.

62. Shirley S. Wang, "J&J Pulls Online Motrin Ad after Social-Media Backlash," *Wall Street Journal* (November 18, 2008): B4.

63. Patricia Cohen, "Signs of Détente in the Battle Between Venus and Mars," *New York Times* (May 31, 2007), www.nytimes.com, accessed May 31, 2007; for a detailed look at couples' goal-setting with regard to artificial reproductive technologies, cf. Eileen Fisher, Cele C. Otnes, and Linda Tuncay, "Pursuing Parenthood: Integrating Cultural and Cognitive Perspectives on Persistent Goal Striving," *Journal of Consumer Research* 34, no. 4 (2007): 425–40.

64. Darach Turley, "Dialogue with the Departed," *European Advances in Consumer Research* 2 (1995): 10–13.

65. "Wives and Money," *American Demographics* (December 1997): 34; for a more recent study of decision making among lesbian couples, cf. Robert Wilkes and Debra A. Laverie, "Purchasing Decisions in Non-Traditional Households: The Case of Lesbian Couples," *Journal of Consumer Behaviour* 6, no. 1 (2007): 60–73.

66. Thomas Hine, *Populuxe* (New York: Knopf, 1986).

67. Boutilier, "Targeting Families: Marketing to and Through the New Family."

68. Karlene Lukovitz, "Women in Wealthy Homes Make 2 of 3 Buying Decisions," *Marketing Daily* (May 15, 2008), www.mediapost.com, accessed May 15, 2008; Dennis L. Rosen and Donald H. Granbois, "Determinants of Role Structure in Family Financial Management," *Journal of Consumer Research* 10 (September 1983): 253–58; Robert F. Bales, *Interaction Process Analysis: A Method for the Study of Small Groups* (Reading, MA: Addison-Wesley, 1950). For a cross-gender comparison of food shopping strategies, see Rosemary Polegato and Judith L. Zaichkowsky, "Family Food Shopping: Strategies Used by Husbands and Wives," *Journal of Consumer Affairs* 28, no. 2 (1994): 278–99.

69. Alma S. Baron, "Working Parents: Shifting Traditional Roles," *Business* 37 (January–March 1987): 36; William J. Qualls, "Household Decision Behavior: The Impact of Husbands' and Wives' Sex Role Orientation," *Journal of Consumer Research* 14 (September 1987): 264–79; Charles M. Schaninger and W. Christian Buss, "The Relationship of Sex-Role Norms to Household Task Allocation," *Psychology & Marketing* 2 (Summer 1985): 93–104.

70. Jennifer Steinhauer, "Mars and Venus: Who Is 'the Decider'?" *New York Times* (April 26, 2006), www.nytimes.com, accessed April 26, 2006; "Tailor-Made," *Advertising Age* (September 23, 2002): 14.

71. Craig J. Thompson, "Caring Consumers: Gendered Consumption Meanings and the Juggling Lifestyle," *Journal of Consumer Research* 22 (March 1996): 388–407.

72. Edmund L. Andrews, "Survey Confirms It: Women Outjuggle Men," *New York Times* (September 15, 2004), www.nytimes.com, accessed September 15, 2004.

73. Miriam Jordan, "India's Medicine Men Market an Array of Contraceptives," *Wall Street Journal Interactive Edition* (September 21, 1999); Patricia Winters Lauro, "Sports Geared to Parents Replace Stodgy with Cool," *New York Times* (January 3, 2000), www.nytimes.com, accessed January 3, 2000; Cynthia Webster, "Effects of Hispanic Ethnic Identification on Marital Roles in the Purchase Decision Process," *Journal of Consumer Research* 21 (September 1994): 319–31. For a study that examined the effects of family depictions in advertising among Hispanic consumers, see Gary D. Gregory and James M. Munch, "Cultural Values in International Advertising: An Examination of Familial Norms and Roles in Mexico," *Psychology & Marketing* 14 (March 1997): 99–120; John Steere, "How Asian-Americans Make Purchase Decisions," *Marketing News* (March 13, 1995): 9; John B. Ford, Michael S. LaTour, and Tony L. Henthorne, "Perception of Marital Roles in Purchase Decision Processes: A Cross-Cultural Study," *Journal of the Academy of Marketing Science* 23 (Spring 1995): 120–31; Chankon Kim and Hanjoon Lee, "A Taxonomy of Couples Based on Influence Strategies: The Case of Home Purchase," *Journal of Business Research* 36 (June 1996): 157–68; Claudia Penteado, "Coke Taps Maternal Instinct with New Latin American Ads," *Advertising Age International* (January 1997): 15.

74. Gary L. Sullivan and P. J. O'Connor, "The Family Purchase Decision Process: A Cross-Cultural Review and Framework for Research," *Southwest Journal of Business & Economics* (Fall 1988): 43; Marilyn Lavin, "Husband-Dominant, Wife-Dominant, Joint," *Journal of Consumer Marketing* 10, no. 3 (1993): 33–42.

75. Micaela DiLeonardo, "The Female World of Cards and Holidays: Women, Families, and the Work of Kinship," *Signs* 12 (Spring 1942): 440–53.

76. C. Whan Park, "Joint Decisions in Home Purchasing: A Muddling-Through Process," *Journal of Consumer Research* 9 (September 1982): 151–62; see also William J. Qualls and Francoise Jaffe, "Measuring Conflict in Household Decision Behavior: Read My Lips and Read My Mind," in John F. Sherry Jr. and Brian Sternthal, eds., *Advances in Consumer Research* 19 (Provo, UT: Association for Consumer Research, 1992): 522–31.

77. Kim P. Corfman and Donald R. Lehmann, "Models of Cooperative Group Decision-Making and Relative Influence: An Experimental Investigation of Family Purchase Decisions," *Journal of Consumer Research* 14 (June 1987): 1–13.

78. http://whyville.net/smmk/nice, accessed June 14, 2011; Jennifer Saranow, "'This Is the Car We Want, Mommy'—Car Makers Direct More Ads at Kids (And Their Parents)," *Wall Street Journal* (November 9, 2006): D1.

79. Quoted in Brooks Barnes, "Disney Looking into Cradle for Customers," *New York Times* (February 6, 2011), http://www.nytimes.com/2011/02/07/business/media/07disney.html?_r=1&ref=business#, accessed April 19, 2011.

80. James U. McNeal, "Tapping the Three Kids' Markets," *American Demographics* (April 1998): 3, 737–41.

81. Harris Curtis, "Making Kids Street Smart," *Newsweek* (September 16, 2002): 10.

82. Kay L. Palan and Robert E. Wilkes, "Adolescent-Parent Interaction in Family Decision-Making," *Journal of Consumer Research* 24 (September 1997): 159–69; cf. also Tiffany Meyers, "Kids Gaining Voice in How Home Looks," *Advertising Age* (March 29, 2004): S4.

83. Russell N. Laczniak and Kay M. Palan, "Under the Influence," *Marketing Research* (Spring 2004): 34–39.

84. Stephanie Thompson, "Mrs. Butterworth's Changes Her Target," *Advertising Age* (December 20, 1999): 44.

85. Adrienne W. Fawcett, "Kids Sway One in Three Parents to Buy Stuff (Duh)," http://www.mediapost.com/publications/?fa=Articles.showArticle&art_aid=55549&passFuseAction=PublicationsSearch.showSearchReslts&art_searched=&page_number=0, accessed February 15, 2007; Les Carlson, Ann Walsh, Russell N. Laczniak, and Sanford Grossbart, "Family Communication Patterns and Marketplace Motivations, Attitudes, and Behaviors of Children and Mothers," *Journal of Consumer Affairs* 28, no. 1 (1994): 25–53; see also Roy L. Moore and George P. Moschis, "The Role of Family Communication in Consumer Learning," *Journal of Communication* 31 (Autumn 1981): 42–51.

86. Leslie Isler, Edward T. Popper, and Scott Ward, "Children's Purchase Requests and Parental Responses: Results from a Diary Study," *Journal of Advertising Research* 27 (October–November 1987): 28–39.

87. Gregory M. Rose, "Consumer Socialization, Parental Style, and Development Timetables in the United States and Japan," *Journal of Marketing* 63, no. 3 (1999): 105–19; Gregory M. Rose, Vassilis Dalakis, and Fredric Kropp, "Consumer Socialization and Parental Style across Cultures: Findings from Australia, Greece, and India," *Journal of Consumer Psychology* 13, no. 4 (2003): 366–76.

88. Scott Ward, "Consumer Socialization," in Harold H. Kassarjian and Thomas S. Robertson, eds., *Perspectives in Consumer Behavior* (Glenview, IL: Scott, Foresman, 1980), 380; cf. also Patricia Robinson and Steven Maxwell Kates, "Children and Their Brand Relationships," *Advances in Consumer Research* 32, no. 1 (2005); Terry O'Sullivan, "Advertising and Children: What Do the Kids Think?," *Qualitative Market Research* 8, no. 4 (2005): 371.

89. Thomas Lipscomb, "Indicators of Materialism in Children's Free Speech: Age and Gender Comparisons," *Journal of Consumer Marketing* (Fall 1988): 41–46.

90. Brigid Schulte, "Baby Dolls Raise a Stink in More Ways than One," *Washington Post* (December 21, 2008): A1.

91. George P. Moschis, "The Role of Family Communication in Consumer Socialization of Children and Adolescents," *Journal of Consumer Research* 11 (March 1985): 898–913.

92. Gregory M. Rose, Vassilis Dalakas, and Fredric Kropp, "A Five-Nation Study of Developmental Timetables, Reciprocal Communication and Consumer Socialization," *Journal of Business Research* 55 (2002): 943–49.

93. Elizabeth S. Moore, William L. Wilkie, and Richard J. Lutz, "Passing the Torch: Intergenerational Influences as a Source of Brand Equity," *Journal of Marketing* 66 (April 2002): 17–37.

94. James U. McNeal and Chyon-Hwa Yeh, "Born to Shop," *American Demographics* (June 1993): 34–39.

95. Kari Greenberg, "Study: Kids Influence Family's Use of Media," *Marketing Daily* (June 10, 2010), http://www.mediapost.com/publications/?fa=Articles.showArticle&art_aid=129877, accessed April 19, 2011; Les Carlson, Sanford Grossbart, and J. Kathleen Stuenkel, "The Role of Parental Socialization Types on Differential Family Communication Patterns Regarding Consumption," *Journal of Consumer Psychology* 1, no. 1 (1992): 31–52; cf. also Sonya A. Grier, Janell Mensinger, Shirley H. Huang, Shiriki K. Kumanyika, and Nicolas Stettler, "Fast-Food Marketing and Children's Fast-Food Consumption: Exploring Parents' Influences in an Ethnically Diverse Sample," *Journal of Public Policy & Marketing* 26 (Fall 2007): 221–235.

96. Marian Burros, "McDonald's France Puts Its Mouth Where Its Money Is," *New York Times* (October 30, 2002), www.nytimes.com, accessed October 30, 2002.

97. Emily Bryson York, "NIH: Banning Fast Food Ads Will Make Kids Less Fat," *Advertising Age* (November 19, 2008), http://adage.com/results.php?endeca=1&return=endeca&search_offset=0&search_order_by=score&search_advanced=1&searchprop=AdAgeAll&search_phrase=banning+fast+food+ads+will+make+kids+less+fat&searchmode=matchall&sortby=date&range=adage&variable=90&date_range=specific&date_begin=11%2F19%2F08&date_end=&x=42&y=20, accessed November 24, 2008.

98. Andrew Martin, "Kellogg to Curb Marketing of Foods to Children," *New York Times* (June 14, 2007), www.nytimes.com, accessed June 14, 2007; Tara Parker-Pope, "Watching Food Ads on TV May Program Kids to Overeat," *Wall Street Journal* (July 10, 2007): D1.

99. Erik Sass, "Four Out of Five Kids Ages Five and Under Are on the Web," *Marketing Daily* (March 17, 2011), http://www.mediapost.com/publications/?fa=Articles.showArticle&art_aid=146941&nid=124844, accessed April 19, 2011.

100. http://passiripatti.com/2010/11/social-media-for-toddlers/, accessed June 14, 2011; "Sign of the Times: Toy Blocks That Teach Toddlers Social Networking," *Fast Company* (November 30, 2010), http://www.fastcodesign.com/1662781/toy-blocks-become-twitter-for-toddlers?partner=homepage_newsletter, accessed April 19, 2011.

101. Glenn Collins, "New Studies on 'Girl Toys' and 'Boy Toys,'" *New York Times* (February 13, 1984): D1.

102. Susan B. Kaiser, "Clothing and the Social Organization of Gender Perception: A Developmental Approach," *Clothing & Textiles Research Journal* 7 (Winter 1989): 46–56.

103. Lori Schwartz and William Markham, "Sex Stereotyping in Children's Toy Advertisements," *Sex Roles* 12 (January 1985): 157–70.

104. http://www.barbie.com/activities/friends/, accessed June 14, 2011.

105. Joseph Pereira, "Oh Boy! In Toyland, You Get More if You're Male," *Wall Street Journal* (September 23, 1994): B1; Joseph Pereira, "Girls' Favorite Playthings: Dolls, Dolls, and Dolls," *Wall Street Journal* (September 23, 1994): B1.

106. Lisa Bannon, "More Kids' Marketers Pitch Number of Single-Sex Products," *Wall Street Journal* (February 14, 2000), www.wsj.com, accessed February 14, 2000.

107. www.amazon.com/Mattel-Working-Woman-Barbie-Doll/dp/B001871UEO, accessed June 16, 2009; Constance L. Hayes, "A Role Model's Clothes: Barbie Goes Professional," *New York Times* (April 1, 2000), www.nytimes.com, accessed April 1, 2000.

108. Jessica Bennett, "Generation Diva: How Our Obsession with Beauty Is Changing Our Kids," *Newsweek* (March 30, 2009), www.newsweek.com/id/191247, accessed April 8, 2009.

109. Andrew Adam Newman, "A Younger Group for Feminine Products," *New York Times* (April 14, 2011), http://www.nytimes.com/2011/04/15/business/media/15adco.html?_r=1, accessed April 19, 2011.

110. Laura A. Peracchio, "How Do Young Children Learn to Be Consumers? A Script-Processing Approach," *Journal of Consumer Research* 18 (March 1992): 425–40; Laura A. Peracchio, "Young Children's Processing of a Televised Narrative: Is a Picture Really Worth a Thousand Words?," *Journal of Consumer Research* 20 (September 1993): 281–93; see also M. Carole Macklin, "The Effects of an Advertising Retrieval Cue on Young Children's Memory and Brand Evaluations," *Psychology & Marketing* 11 (May–June 1994): 291–311.

111. Jean Piaget, "The Child and Modern Physics," *Scientific American* 196, no. 3 (1957): 46–51; see also Kenneth D. Bahn, "How and When Do Brand Perceptions and Preferences First Form? A Cognitive Developmental Investigation," *Journal of Consumer Research* 13 (December 1986): 382–93.

112. Deborah L. Roedder, "Age Differences in Children's Responses to Television Advertising: An Information-Processing Approach," *Journal of Consumer Research* 8 (September 1981): 144–53; see also Deborah Roedder John and Ramnath Lakshmi-Ratan, "Age Differences in Children's Choice Behavior: The Impact of Available Alternatives," *Journal of Marketing Research* 29 (May 1992): 216–26; Jennifer Gregan-Paxton and Deborah Roedder John, "Are Young Children Adaptive Decision Makers? A Study of Age Differences in Information Search Behavior," *Journal of Consumer Research* 21, no. 4 (1995): 567–80.

113. For a study on the effects of commercial programming on creative play, cf. Patricia M. Greenfield, Emily Yut, Mabel Chung, Deborah Land, Holly Kreider, Maurice Pantoja, and Kris Horsley, "The Program-Length Commercial: A Study of the Effects of Television/Toy Tie-Ins on Imaginative Play," *Psychology & Marketing* 7 (Winter 1990): 237–56.

114. Gerald J. Gorn and Renee Florsheim, "The Effects of Commercials for Adult Products on Children," *Journal of Consumer Research* 11 (March 1985): 962–67. For a study that assessed the impact of violent commercials on children, see V. Kanti Prasad and Lois J. Smith, "Television Commercials in Violent Programming: An Experimental Evaluation of Their Effects on Children," *Journal of the Academy of Marketing Science* 22, no. 4 (1994): 340–51.

115. Gwen Bachmann Achenreiner and Deborah Roedder John, "The Meaning of Brand Names to Children: A Developmental Investigation," *Journal of Consumer Psychology* 13, no. 3 (2003): 205–19.

116. Paula Lyon Andruss, "'Dora' Translates Well," *Marketing News* (October 13, 2003): 8.

117. Brooks Barnes, "Disney Expert Uses Science to Draw Boy Viewers," *New York Times* (April 13, 2009), www.nytimes.com/2009/04/14/arts/television/14boys.html?scp=1&sq=Brooks%20Barnes,%2093Disney%20Expert%20Uses%20Science%20to%20Draw%20Boy%20Viewers,%94%20&st=cse, accessed April 13, 2009.

118. Janet Simons, "Youth Marketing: Children's Clothes Follow the Latest Fashion," *Advertising Age* (February 14, 1985): 16.

119. For details regarding the design of research on children, see Laura A. Peracchio, "Designing Research to Reveal the Young Child's Emerging Competence," *Psychology & Marketing* 7 (Winter 1990): 257–76.

120. Laura Shapiro, "Where Little Boys Can Play with Nail Polish," *Newsweek* (May 28, 1990): 62.

121. Gary Armstrong and Merrie Brucks, "Dealing with Children's Advertising: Public Policy Issues and Alternatives," *Journal of Public Policy & Marketing* 7 (1988): 98–113.

122. Bonnie Reece, "Children and Shopping: Some Public Policy Questions," *Journal of Public Policy & Marketing* (1986): 185–94.

123. Daniel Cook, University of Illinois, personal communication, December 2002; Daniel Cook, "Contradictions and Conundrums of the Child Consumer: The Emergent Centrality of an Enigma in the 1990s," paper presented at the Association for Consumer Research, October 2002.

124. http://www.bbb.org/us/children-food-beverage-advertising-initiative/, accessed June 14, 2011; John Eggerton, "Sara Lee Agrees to Limit Food Marketing to Kids," *Broadcasting & Cable* (September 23, 2010), http://www.broadcastingcable.com/article/457541-Sara_Lee_Agrees_to_Limit_Food_Marketing_to_Kids.php, accessed April 19, 2011.

125. Natasha Singer, "No Mug? Drug Makers Cut Out Goodies for Doctors," *New York Times* (December 30, 2008), www.nytimes.com, accessed December 30, 2008; Alex Berenson, "Cancer Drug Representatives Spelled Out the Way to Profit," *New York Times* (June 12, 2007), www.nytimes.com, accessed June 12, 2007; Andrew Pollack, "Stanford to Ban Drug Makers' Gifts to Doctors, Even Pens," *New York Times* (September 12, 2006), www.nytimes.com, accessed September 12, 2006.

Groups and Social Media

Groups and Social Media

Chapter Objectives

When you finish reading this chapter you will understand why:

1. Other people and groups, especially those who possess some kind of social power, often influence our decisions about what to buy.

2. We seek out others who share our interests in products or services.

3. We are motivated to buy or use products in order to be consistent with what other people do.

4. Certain people are especially likely to influence others' product choices.

5. The things other consumers tell us about products (good and bad) often are more influential than the advertising we see.

6. Online technologies accelerate the impact of word-of-mouth communication.

7. Social media are changing the way companies and consumers interact.

MyMarketingLab

Visit **www.mymktlab.com** to find activities that help you learn and review in order to succeed in this chapter.

Source: Ljupco Smokovski/Shutterstock.

Zachary leads a secret life. During the week, he is a straitlaced stock analyst for a major investment firm. He spends a big chunk of the week worrying about whether he'll have a job, so work is pretty stressful these days. However, his day job only pays the bills to finance his real passion: cruising on his Harley-Davidson Road Glide Custom. His Facebook posts are filled with lunchtime laments about how much he'd rather be out on the road (hopefully his boss won't try to friend him). Actually, Zach feels it's worth the risk: He's participating in Harley's free country social media promotion that encourages riders to post their stories ("freedom statements") on Facebook and Twitter to see if they'll include one of his posts on a Harley banner ad.[1] His girlfriend worries a bit about his getting totaled in an accident, but Zach knows if he stays alert the only way that will probably happen is if he can't kick his habit of texting her while he's driving the bike.

Come Friday evening, it's off with the Brooks Brothers suit and on with the black leather, as he trades in his Lexus for his treasured Harley. A dedicated member of HOG (Harley Owners Group), Zachary belongs to the "RUBs" (rich urban bikers) faction of Harley riders. Everyone in his group wears expensive leather vests with Harley insignias and owns customized "low riders." Just this week, Zach finally got his new Harley perforated black leather jacket at the company's Motorclothes Merchandise web page.[2] As one of the Harley web pages observed, "it's one thing to have people buy your products. It's another thing to have them tattoo your name on their bodies." Zach had to restrain himself from buying more Harley stuff; there were vests, eyewear, belts, buckles, scarves, watches, jewelry, even housewares ("home is the road") for sale. He settled for a set of Harley salt-and-pepper shakers that would be perfect for his buddy Dan's new crib.

Zachary's experiences on social media platforms make him realize the lengths to which some of his fellow enthusiasts go to make sure others know they are hog riders. Two of his riding buddies are in a lively competition to be "mayor" of the local Harley dealership on foursquare, while many others tweet to inform people about a group ride that will occur later in the day—kind of a flashmob on wheels.

Zach spends a lot of money to outfit himself to be like the rest of the group, but it's worth it. He feels a real sense of brotherhood with his fellow RUBs. The group rides together in two-column formation to bike rallies that sometimes attract up to 300,000 cycle enthusiasts. What a sense of power he feels when they all cruise together—it's them against the world!

Of course, an added benefit is the business networking he's accomplished during his jaunts with his fellow professionals who also wait for the weekend to "ride on the wild side—these days it would be professional suicide to let your contacts get cold, and you can't just count on LinkedIn to stay in the loop."[3]

Reference Groups

Humans are social animals. We belong to groups, try to please others, and look to others' behavior for clues about what we should do in public settings. In fact, our desire to "fit in" or to identify with desirable individuals or groups is the primary motivation for many of our consumption behaviors. We may go to great lengths to please the members of a group whose acceptance we covet.[4]

Zachary's biker group is an important part of his identity, and this membership influences many of his buying decisions. He has spent many thousands of dollars on parts and accessories since he became a RUB. His fellow riders bond via their consumption choices, so total strangers feel an immediate connection with one another when they meet. The publisher of *American Iron*, an industry magazine, observed, "You don't buy a Harley because it's a superior bike, you buy a Harley to be a part of a family."[5]

Zachary doesn't model himself after just *any* biker—only the people with whom he really identifies can exert that kind of influence on him. For example, Zachary's group doesn't have much to do with outlaw clubs whose blue-collar riders sport big Harley tattoos. The members of his group also have only polite contact with "Ma and Pa" bikers, whose rides are the epitome of comfort and feature such niceties as radios, heated handgrips, and floorboards. Essentially, only the RUBs comprise Zachary's *reference group*.

A **reference group** is "an actual or imaginary individual or group conceived of [as] having significant relevance upon an individual's evaluations, aspirations, or behavior."[6] Reference groups influence us in three ways: *informational, utilitarian*, and *value-expressive*. Table 1 describes these influences. In this chapter we'll focus on how other people, whether fellow bikers, coworkers, friends, family, or simply casual acquaintances, influence our purchase decisions. We'll consider how our group memberships shape our preferences because we want others to accept us or even because we mimic the actions of famous people we've never met. We'll also explore why some people in particular affect our product preferences and how marketers find those people and enlist their support to persuade consumers to jump on the bandwagon.

When Are Reference Groups Important?

Recent research on smoking cessation programs powerfully illustrates the impact of reference groups. The study found that smokers tend to quit in groups: When one person quits, this creates a ripple effect that motivates others in his social network to give up the death sticks also. The researchers followed thousands of smokers and nonsmokers for more than 30 years, and they also tracked their networks of relatives, coworkers, and friends. They discovered that over the years, the smokers tended to cluster together (on average in groups of three). As the overall U.S. smoking rate declined dramatically during this period, the number of clusters in the sample decreased, but the remaining clusters stayed the same size; this indicated that people quit in groups rather than as individuals. Not surprisingly, some social connections were more powerful than others. A spouse who quit had a bigger impact than did a friend, whereas friends had more influence than siblings. Coworkers had an influence only in small firms where everyone knew one another.[7]

Reference group influences don't work the same way for all types of products and consumption activities. For example, we're not as likely to take others' preferences into account when we choose products that are not very complex, that are low in perceived risk, or that we can try before we buy.[8] In addition, knowing what others prefer may influence us at a general level (e.g., owning or not owning a computer, eating junk food versus health food), whereas at other times this knowledge guides the specific

TABLE 1	Three Forms of Reference Group Influence

Informational Influence	• The individual seeks information about various brands from an association of professionals or independent group of experts. • The individual seeks information from those who work with the product as a profession. • The individual seeks brand-related knowledge and experience (such as how Brand A's performance compares to Brand B's) from those friends, neighbors, relatives, or work associates who have reliable information about the brands. • The brand the individual selects is influenced by observing a seal of approval of an independent testing agency (such as Good Housekeeping). • The individual's observation of what experts do (such as observing the type of car that police drive or the brand of television that repairmen buy) influences his or her choice of a brand.
Utilitarian Influence	• So that he or she satisfies the expectations of fellow work associates, the individual's decision to purchase a particular brand is influenced by their preferences. • The individual's decision to purchase a particular brand is influenced by the preferences of people with whom he or she has social interaction. • The individual's decision to purchase a particular brand is influenced by the preferences of family members. • The desire to satisfy the expectations that others have of him or her has an impact on the individual's brand choice.
Value-Expressive Influence	• The individual feels that the purchase or use of a particular brand will enhance the image others have of him or her. • The individual feels that those who purchase or use a particular brand possess the characteristics that he or she would like to have. • The individual sometimes feels that it would be nice to be like the type of person that advertisements show using a particular brand. • The individual feels that the people who purchase a particular brand are admired or respected by others. • The individual feels that the purchase of a particular brand would help show others what he or she is or would like to be (such as an athlete, successful business person, good parent, etc.).

Source: Adapted from C. Whan Park and V. Parker Lessig, "Students and Housewives: Differences in Susceptibility to Reference Group Influence," *Journal of Consumer Research* 4 September 1977): 102. Copyright © 1977 JCR, Inc. Reprinted with permission of The University of Chicago Press.

brands we desire within a product category (e.g., if we wear Levi's jeans versus Diesel jeans, or smoke Marlboro cigarettes rather than Virginia Slims).

Why are reference groups so persuasive? The answer lies in the potential power they wield over us. **Social power** is "the capacity to alter the actions of others."[10] To the degree to which you are able to make someone else do something, regardless of whether they do it willingly, you have power over that person. The following classification of power bases helps us to distinguish among the reasons a person exerts power over another, the degree to which the influence is voluntary, and whether this influence will continue to have an effect even when the source of the power isn't around.[11]

● **Referent power**—If a person admires the qualities of a person or a group, he tries to copy the referent's behaviors (e.g., choice of clothing, cars, leisure activities), just as Zack's fellow bikers affected his preferences. Prominent people in all walks of life affect our consumption behaviors by virtue of product endorsements (e.g., Lady Gaga for Polaroid), distinctive fashion statements (e.g., Kim Kardashian's displays of high-end designer clothing), or championing causes (e.g., Brad Pitt for UNICEF). **Referent power** is important to many marketing strategies because consumers voluntarily modify what they do and buy in order to identify with a referent.

● **Information power**—A person possesses **information power** simply because she knows something others would like to know. Editors of trade publications such as *Women's Wear Daily* often possess tremendous power because of their ability to compile and disseminate information that can make or break individual designers or companies. People with information power are able to influence consumer opinion by virtue of their (assumed) access to the "truth."

A recent real-life experiment demonstrates the potential social value of harnessing reference group power. For years the Sacramento, California, Municipal Utility District tried various tactics to goad people into using less energy, such as awarding rebates to residents who buy energy-saving appliances. These efforts weren't working too well, so the district tried something new: It told people how their energy consumption compared to their neighbors' energy consumption. Thirty-five thousand randomly selected customers received statements that rated their energy use compared to 100 of their neighbors who lived in homes of a similar size. The relatively energy-efficient customers earned two smiley faces on their statements, and those whose usage was higher than average opened their envelopes to see frowns (they had to delete the frown part after customers got too upset with this criticism). After six months, the utility found that customers who had gotten the "frown" report cards reduced energy use by 2 percent compared to the rest of the district.

Some colleges employ a similar technique when they create a competition among dormitories to identify which residence hall does the best job of conserving resources. At Central College in Pella, Iowa, students who live in a "green dorm" can access a Web site that tells them how much power their specific suite uses compared to the other suites in the building. Peer pressure is powerful.[9]

- **Legitimate power**—Sometimes we grant power by virtue of social agreements, such as the authority we give to police officers, soldiers, and yes, sometimes even professors. The **legitimate power** a uniform confers wields authority in consumer contexts, including teaching hospitals where medical students don white coats to enhance their standing with patients.[12] Marketers "borrow" this form of power to influence consumers. For example, an ad that shows a model who wears a white doctor's coat adds an aura of legitimacy or authority to the presentation of the product ("I'm not a doctor, but I play one on TV").
- **Expert power**—To attract the casual Internet user, U.S. Robotics signed up British physicist Stephen Hawking to endorse its modems. A company executive commented, "We wanted to generate trust. So we found visionaries who use U.S. Robotics technology, and we let them tell the consumer how it makes their lives more productive." Hawking, who has Lou Gehrig's disease and speaks via a synthesizer, said in one TV spot, "My body may be stuck in this chair, but with the Internet my mind can go to the end of the universe."[13] Hawking's **expert power** derives from the knowledge he possesses about a content area. This helps to explain the weight many of us assign to professional critics' reviews of restaurants, books, movies, and cars—even though, with the advent of blogs and open-source references such as Wikipedia, it's getting a lot harder to tell just who is really an expert![14]
- **Reward power**—A person or group with the means to provide positive reinforcement has **reward power**. The reward may be the tangible kind, such as the contestants on *Survivor* experience when their comrades vote them off the island. Or it can be more intangible, such as the approval the judges on *American Idol* deliver to contestants.
- **Coercive power**—We exert **coercive power** when we influence someone because of social or physical intimidation. A threat is often effective in the short term, but it doesn't tend to stick because we revert to our original behavior as soon as the bully leaves the scene. Fortunately, marketers rarely try to use this type of power (unless you count those annoying calls from telemarketers!). However, we can see elements of this power base in fear appeals, as well as in intimidating salespeople who try to succeed with a "hard sell."

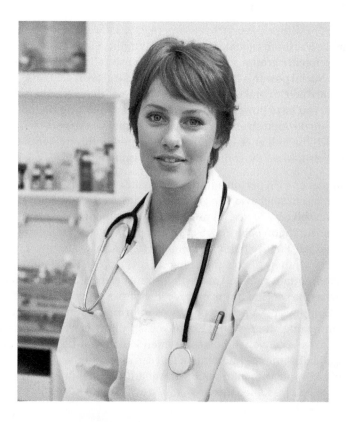

A physician has expert power, and a white coat reinforces this expertise by conferring legitimate power.
Source: Jupiterimages/Thinkstock.

Types of Reference Groups

Although two or more people normally form a group, we often use the term *reference group* a bit more loosely to describe *any* external influence that provides social cues.[15] The referent may be a cultural figure who has an impact on many people (e.g., Michelle Obama) or a person or group whose influence operates only in the consumer's immediate environment (e.g., Zachary's biker club). Reference groups that affect consumption can include parents, fellow motorcycle enthusiasts, the Tea Party, or even the Chicago Bears, the Dave Matthews Band, or Spike Lee.

Some people influence us simply because we feel similar to them. Have you ever experienced a warm feeling when you pull up at a light next to someone who drives the exact car as yours? One reason that we feel a bond with fellow brand users may be that many of us are a bit narcissistic (not you, of course); we feel an attraction to people and products that remind us of ourselves. That may explain why we feel a connection to others who happen to share our name. Research on the **name-letter effect** finds that, all things equal, we like others who share our names or even initials better than those who don't. When researchers look at large databases like Internet phone directories or Social Security records, they find that Johnsons are more likely to wed Johnsons, women named Virginia are more likely to live in (and move to) Virginia, and people whose surname is Lane tend to have addresses that include the word *lane*, not *street*. During the 2000 presidential campaign, people whose surnames began with B were more likely to contribute to George Bush, whereas those whose surnames began with G were more likely to contribute to Al Gore.[16]

Obviously, some groups and individuals are more powerful than others and affect a broader range of our consumption decisions. For example, our parents may play a pivotal role as we form our values on many important issues, such as attitudes about marriage or where to go to college. We call this **normative influence**—that is, the reference group helps to set and enforce fundamental standards of conduct. In contrast, a Harley-Davidson club exerts **comparative influence** because it affects members' decisions about specific motorcycle purchases.[17]

Brand Communities and Consumer Tribes

Before it released the popular Xbox game *Halo 2*, Bungie Studios put up a Web site to explain the story line. However, there was a catch: The story was written from the point of view of the Covenant (the aliens who are preparing to attack Earth in the game)—and in *their* language. Within 48 hours, avid gamers around the world shared information in gaming chat rooms to crack the code and translate the text. More than 1.5 million people preordered the game before its release.[18] This cooperative effort illustrates a major trend in consumer behavior.

A **brand community** is a group of consumers who share a set of social relationships based on usage of or interest in a product. Unlike other kinds of communities, these members typically don't live near each other—except when they may meet for brief periods at organized events or **brandfests** that community-oriented companies such as Jeep or Harley-Davidson sponsor. These events help owners to "bond" with fellow enthusiasts and strengthen their identification with the product as well as with others they meet who share their passion. In virtually any category, you'll find passionate brand communities (in some cases devoted to brands that don't even exist anymore); examples include the 3Com Ergo Audrey (discontinued Internet appliance), Apple Newton (discontinued personal digital assistant), BMW MINI (car), Garmin (GPS device), Jones Soda (carbonated beverage), Lomo and Holga (cameras), Tom Petty and the Heartbreakers (musical group), StriVectin (cosmeceutical), and *Xena: Warrior Princess* (TV program).

Researchers find that people who participate in these events feel more positive about the products as a result, and this enhances brand loyalty. They tend to forgive product failures or lapses in service quality, and they're less likely to switch brands even if they learn that competing products are as good or better. Furthermore, these community members become emotionally involved in the company's welfare, and they often serve as brand missionaries as they carry its marketing message to others.[19] Researchers find that brand community members do more than help the product build buzz; their inputs actually create added value for themselves and other members as they develop better ways to use and customize products. For example, it's common for experienced users to coach "newbies" in ways to maximize their enjoyment of the product so that more and more people benefit from a network of satisfied participants. In other cases members benefit because their communities empower them to learn; for example, a study that looked at people who suffered from thyroid problems and who indicated they were uninformed and ill prepared to make decisions about their treatment later exhibited more active involvement and informed decision making after they participated in an online community with others who shared their health issues.[20] Figure 1 demonstrates this process of **collective value creation**.[21]

The notion of a **consumer tribe** is similar to the idea of a brand community; it is a group of people who share a lifestyle and can identify with each other because of a shared allegiance to an activity or a product. Although these tribes are often unstable and short-lived, at least for a time members identify with others through shared emotions, moral beliefs, styles of life, and of course the products they jointly consume as part of their tribal affiliation.

Some companies, especially those that are more youth-oriented, use a **tribal marketing strategy** that links their product to, say, a group of shredders. However, there also are plenty of tribes with older members, such as car enthusiasts who gather to celebrate such cult products as the Citroën in Europe and the Ford Mustang in the United States, or "foodies" who share their passion for cooking with other Wolfgang Puck wannabes around the world.[22]

Membership versus Aspirational Reference Groups

A **membership reference group** consists of people we actually know, whereas we don't know those in an **aspirational reference group**, but we admire them anyway. These people are likely to be successful businesspeople, athletes, performers, or whoever rocks our world. Not surprisingly, many marketing efforts that specifically adopt a reference group appeal concentrate on highly visible, widely admired figures (such as well-known athletes or performers); they link these people to brands so that the products they use or endorse also take on this aspirational quality. For example, an amateur basketball player who

Figure 1 THE PROCESS OF COLLECTIVE VALUE CREATION IN BRAND COMMUNITIES

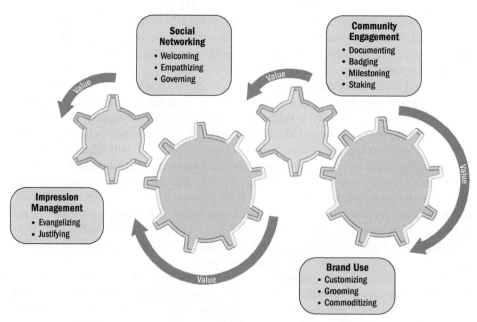

Source: Reprinted with permission from *Journal of Marketing,* published by the American Marketing Association, Schau, Hope Jensen, Albert M. Muñiz, and Eric J. Arnould, September 2009, 73, 30–51.

CB AS I SEE IT

Professor John Schouten, *University of Portland*

There is no such thing as purely personal significance. To the extent that we create individual meaning at all, we do so from a shared language of objects, words, feelings, and experiences whose meanings have already been constructed by social groups. Similarly, there is no such thing as an individual consumer decision. We make our choices from assortments that society has provided, based on values and expectations that we have learned, questioned, embraced, or rejected as members of social groups.

Some groups or communities we choose. Others choose us. Ultimately, the character of our membership in any group is a matter of constant negotiation. Communities of any kind often coincide with or create markets.

In response to shared needs and desires, humans come together, harness creativity and labor, and produce new goods and services. In the best cases, the creative power of community can accomplish tremendous good through cultural change. The LOHAS (Lifestyles of Health and Sustainability) community is one such social group, made up of both consumers and businesses. See lohas.com for more about the community's goals and impact.

Our biggest challenge today, in my view, is the collision between escalating human consumption and the rapidly declining capacity of the earth's natural systems to support it. I believe the best real hope for a tolerable human future lies in the ability of communities to redefine acceptable modes of consumer behavior and to participate actively and creatively in making them not only possible but also preferable to those practices that currently undermine the foundation of our existence.

For me, the most exciting aspects of communities are their dynamism and their power to effect change at levels ranging from individual purchases to global movements for social and environmental justice. Recently my studies have turned to such "communities of purpose." For example, for more than three years now Diane Martin and I have been engaged with groups of people determined to make Walmart more environmentally sustainable. Self-selecting community members include Walmart executives and associates, key members of its supply chain, environmental activists, academics, and others. Uniting these diverse participants are shared goals of carbon neutrality, zero waste, and products that support the sustainable use of the earth's finite resources. So far these groups have achieved impressive results, helping Walmart to divert millions of tons of waste from landfills, radically reduce its use of fossil fuels, develop more sustainable products, and (true to Walmart's mission) continue to profit, even in times of economic recession, with low prices to its customers. Explore walmartstores.com/sustainability and its link to Sustainable Value Networks for more about the results of these ongoing efforts.

---

idolizes Miami Heat star Dwyane Wade might drool over a pair of Air Jordan 12 Dwyane Wade PE shoes.[23] One study of business students who aspired to the "executive" role found a strong relationship between products they associated with their *ideal selves* and those they assumed that real executives own.[24] Of course, it's worth noting that as social media usage increases, the line between those we "know" and those we "friend" gets blurrier. Still, whether offline or online, we tend to seek out others who are similar. Indeed, one study even found that people on Twitter tend to follow others who share their mood: People who are happy tend to re-tweet or reply to others who are happy, while those who are sad or lonely tend to do the same with others who also post negative sentiments.[25]

Because we tend to compare ourselves to similar others, many promotional strategies include "ordinary" people whose consumption activities provide informational social influence. How can we predict which people you know will be part of your membership reference group? Several factors make it more likely:

- **Propinquity**—As physical distance between people decreases and opportunities for interaction increase, they are more likely to form relationships. We call this physical nearness **propinquity**. An early study on friendship patterns in a housing complex showed the strong effects of this factor: All things equal, residents were much more likely to be friends with the people next door than with those who lived only two doors away. Furthermore, people who lived next to a staircase had more friends than those at the ends of a hall (presumably, they were more likely to "bump into" people as they used the stairs).[26]

- **Mere exposure**—We come to like persons or things if we see them more often. Social scientists call this tendency the **mere exposure phenomenon**.[27] Greater frequency of contact, even if unintentional, may help to determine one's set of local referents. The same effect holds when we evaluate works of art or even political candidates.[28] One study predicted 83 percent of the winners of political primaries solely by the amount of media exposure each candidate received.[29]

- **Group cohesiveness**—**Cohesiveness** refers to the degree to which members of a group are attracted to each other and how much each values his or her membership in this group. As the value of the group to the individual increases, so too does the likelihood that the group will influence that individual's consumption decisions. Smaller groups tend to be more cohesive because in larger groups the contributions of each member are usually less important or noticeable. By the same token, groups often try to restrict membership to a select few, which increases the value of membership to those who do get in.

Positive versus Negative Reference Groups

Reference groups impact our buying decisions both positively and negatively. In most cases, we model our behavior to be in line with what we think the group expects us to do. Sometimes, however, we also deliberately do the *opposite* if we want to distance ourselves from **avoidance groups**. You may carefully study the dress or mannerisms of a group you dislike (e.g., "nerds," "druggies," or "preppies") and scrupulously avoid buying anything that might identify you with that group. For example, rebellious adolescents do the opposite of what their parents desire to make a statement about their independence. In one study, college freshman reported consuming less alcohol and restaurant patrons selected less fattening food when drinking alcohol and eating junk food linked to members of avoidance groups.[31]

Your motivation to distance yourself from a negative reference group can be as powerful or more powerful than your desire to please a positive group.[32] That's why advertisements occasionally show an undesirable person who uses a competitor's product. This kind of execution subtly makes the point that you can avoid winding up like *that* kind of person if you just stay away from the products he buys. As a once-popular book reminded us, "Real men *don't* eat quiche!"[33]

We Like to Do It in Groups

We get away with more when we do it in a group. One simple reason: The more people who are together, the less likely it is that any one member will get singled out for attention. That helps to explain why people in larger groups have fewer restraints on their behavior. For example, we sometimes behave more wildly at costume parties or on Halloween than we do when others can easily identify us. We call this phenomenon **deindividuation**—a process whereby individual identities become submerged within a group.

Social loafing is a similar effect; it happens when we don't devote as much to a task because our contribution is part of a larger group effort.[37] You may have experienced this if you've worked on a group project for a class! Waitpersons are painfully aware of social loafing: People who eat in groups tend to tip less per person than when they eat alone.[38] For this reason, many restaurants automatically tack on a fixed gratuity for groups of six or more.

Furthermore, the decisions we make as part of a group tend to differ from those each of us would choose on our own. The **risky shift effect** refers to the observation that group members tend to consider riskier alternatives after the group discusses an issue than they would if each member made his or her own decision without talking about it with others.[39] Psychologists propose several explanations for this increased riskiness. One possibility is that something similar to social loafing occurs. As more people are involved in a decision, each individual is less accountable for the outcome, so this results in *diffusion* *of responsibility.*[40] The practice of placing blanks in at least one of the rifles a firing squad uses diffuses each soldier's responsibility for the death of a prisoner, because it's never certain who actually shot him. Another explanation is the *value hypothesis*, which states that our culture values risky behavior, so when people make decisions in groups they conform to this expectation.[41]

Research evidence for the risky shift is mixed. A more general finding is that group discussion tends to increase **decision polarization**. This means that the direction the group members leaned before discussion began (whether a risky choice or a conservative choice) becomes even more extreme in that direction after the group talks about it. Group discussions regarding product purchases tend to create a risky shift for low-risk items, but they yield even more conservative group decisions for high-risk products.[42]

Even shopping behavior changes when people do it in groups. For example, people who shop with at least one other person tend to make more unplanned purchases, buy more, and cover more areas of a store than do those who browse solo.[43] Both normative and informational social influence explains this. A group member may buy something to gain the approval of the others, or the group may simply expose her to more products and stores. Either way, retailers are well advised to encourage group-shopping activities.

The famous Tupperware party is a successful example of a **home shopping party** that capitalizes on group pressures to boost sales.[44] In this format a company representative makes a sales presentation to a group of people who gather at the home of a friend or acquaintance. The shopping party works due to informational social influence: Participants model the behavior of others who provide them with information about how to use certain products, especially because a relatively homogeneous group (e.g., neighborhood homemakers) attends the party. Normative social influence also operates because others can easily observe our actions. Pressures to conform may be particularly intense and may escalate as more and more group members "cave in" (we call this process the *bandwagon effect*).

In addition, these parties may activate deindividuation or the risky shift. As consumers get caught up in the group, they may agree to try new products they would not normally consider. These same dynamics underlie the latest wrinkle on the Tupperware home-selling technique: the Botox party. The craze for Botox injections that paralyze facial nerves to reduce wrinkles (for 3 to 6 months, anyway) is fueled by gatherings where dermatologists or plastic surgeons redefine the definition of house calls. For patients, mixing cocktail hour with cosmetic injections takes some of the anxiety out of the procedure. Egged on by the others at the party, a doctor can dewrinkle as many as 10 patients in

Costumes hide our true identities and encourage deindividuation.
Source: Sergei Bachlakov/Shutterstock.

The Tangled Web

The Web encourages the rise of a new kind of avoidance group: **antibrand communities.** These groups also coalesce around a celebrity, store, or brand—but in this case they're united by their disdain for it. The Rachael Ray Sucks Community on the blogging and social-networking site *LiveJournal* claims more than 1,000 members who don't hesitate to post their latest thoughts about the various shortcomings, flaws, and disagreeable traits of the (otherwise popular) television food personality. They criticize Ray's overuse of chicken stock, her kitchen hygiene, her smile (posters like to compare it to The Joker's of Batman fame), her penchant for saying "Yum-o!" and so on. The community has a basic rule for membership: "You must be anti-Rachael!"[34]

One team of researchers that studies these communities observes that they tend to attract social idealists who advocate non-materialistic lifestyles. After they interviewed members of online communities who oppose Walmart, Starbucks, and McDonald's, they concluded that these antibrand communities provide a meeting place for those who share a moral stance; a support network to achieve common goals; a way to cope with workplace frustrations (many members actually work for the companies they bash!); and a hub for information, activities, and related resources.[35] Another study chronicles the level of opposition the Hummer inspires. For example, whereas brand enthusiasts celebrate the Hummer's road safety because of its size and weight, antibranders who drive smaller cars slam the vehicle's bulk. One driver posted this message: "The H2 is a death machine. You'd better hope that you don't collide with an H2 in your economy car. You can kiss your ass goodbye thanks to the H2's massive weight and raised bumpers. Too bad you couldn't afford an urban assault vehicle of your own."[36]

an hour. An advertising executive who worked on the Botox marketing strategy explained that the membership reference group appeal is more effective than the traditional route that uses a celebrity spokesperson to tout the injections in advertising: "We think it's more persuasive to think of your next-door neighbor using it."[45] The only hitch is that after you get the injections, your face is so rigid your friends can't tell if you're smiling!

OBJECTIVE 3

We are motivated to buy or use products in order to be consistent with what other people do.

Conformity

The early Bohemians who lived in Paris around 1830 made a point of behaving, well, differently from others. One flamboyant figure of the time earned notoriety because he walked a lobster on a leash through the gardens of the Royal Palace. His friends drank wine from human skulls, cut their beards in strange shapes, and slept in tents on the floors of their garrets.[46] Sounds a bit like some frats we've visited.

Although in every age there certainly are those who "march to their own drummers," most people tend to follow society's expectations regarding how they should act and look (with a little improvisation here and there, of course). **Conformity** is a change in beliefs or actions as a reaction to real or imagined group pressure. In order for a society to function, its members develop **norms**, or informal rules that govern behavior. Without these rules, we would have chaos. Imagine the confusion if a simple norm such as stopping for a red traffic light did not exist.

We conform in many small ways every day, even though we don't always realize it. Unspoken rules govern many aspects of consumption. In addition to norms regarding appropriate use of clothing and other personal items, we conform to rules that include gift-giving (we expect birthday presents from loved ones and get upset if they don't materialize), sex roles (men often pick up the check on a first date), and personal hygiene (our friends expect us to shower regularly). We also observe conformity in the online world; research supports the idea that consumers are more likely to show interest in a product if they see that it is already very popular.

One study analyzed how millions of Facebook users adopted apps to personalize their pages. Researchers tracked, on an hourly basis, the rate at which 2,700 apps were installed by 50 million Facebook users. They discovered that once an app had reached a rate of about 55 installations a day, its popularity started to soar. Facebook friends were notified when one of their online buddies adopted a new app, and they could also see a list of the most popular ones. Apparently this popularity feedback was the key driver that determined whether still more users would download the software.[47]

Still, we don't mimic others' behaviors all the time, so what makes it more likely that we'll conform? These are some common culprits:[48]

- **Cultural pressures**—Different cultures encourage conformity to a greater or lesser degree. The American slogan "Do your own thing" in the 1960s reflected a movement away from conformity and toward individualism. In contrast, Japanese society emphasizes collective well-being and group loyalty over individuals' needs.
- **Fear of deviance**—The individual may have reason to believe that the group will apply *sanctions* to punish nonconforming behaviors. It's not unusual to observe adolescents shunning a peer who is "different" or a corporation or university passing over a person for promotion because she is not a "team player."
- **Commitment**—The more people are dedicated to a group and value their membership in it, the greater their motivation to conform to the group's wishes. Rock groupies and followers of TV evangelists may do anything their idols ask of them, and terrorists willingly die for their cause. According to the **principle of least interest**, the person who is *least* committed to staying in a relationship has the most power because that party doesn't care as much if the other person rejects him.[49] Remember that on your next date.
- **Group unanimity, size, and expertise**—As groups gain in power, compliance increases. It is often harder to resist the demands of a large number of people than only a few, especially when a "mob mentality" rules.

- **Susceptibility to interpersonal influence**—This trait refers to an individual's need to have others think highly of him or her. Consumers who don't possess this trait are *role-relaxed*; they tend to be older, affluent, and to have high self-confidence. Subaru created a communications strategy to reach role-relaxed consumers. In one of its commercials, a man proclaims, "I want a car. . . . Don't tell me about wood paneling, about winning the respect of my neighbors. They're my neighbors. They're not my heroes."[50]

OBJECTIVE 4
Certain people are especially likely to influence others' product choices.

Opinion Leadership

As Cold Stone Creamery expands to Japan, the ice cream store projects a somewhat different image than it has in the United States. The chain wants to be ultracool as it generates a buzz among fashion-conscious "office ladies"—as the Japanese call young, single, female professionals. These women are very influential in Japan; their reactions to a new product can make or break it. To woo this group, Cold Stone sponsored a fashion show for young women (assuming the models can fit into the dresses after sampling a few of the chain's caloric creations), and fashion magazines staged photo shoots at the stores.[52]

Although consumers get information from personal sources, they do not usually ask just *anyone* for advice about purchases. If you decide to buy a new stereo, you will most likely seek advice from a friend who knows a lot about sound systems. This friend may own a sophisticated system, or she may subscribe to specialized magazines such as *Stereo Review* and spend her free time browsing through electronics stores. However, you may have another friend who has a reputation for being stylish and who spends his free time reading *Gentleman's Quarterly* and shopping at trendy boutiques. You might not bring up your stereo problem with him, but you may take him with you to shop for a new fall wardrobe.

Everyone knows people who are knowledgeable about products and whose advice others take seriously. Like one of the Japanese office ladies, this individual is an **opinion leader**, a person who is frequently able to influence others' attitudes or behaviors.[53] Clearly, some people's recommendations carry more weight than others. Opinion leaders are extremely valuable information sources because they possess the social power we discussed earlier in the chapter:

- They are technically competent, so they possess expert power.[54]
- They prescreen, evaluate, and synthesize product information in an unbiased way, so they possess knowledge power.[55]
- They are socially active and highly interconnected in their communities.[56]
- They are likely to hold offices in community groups and clubs and to be active outside of the home. As a result, opinion leaders often wield legitimate power by virtue of their social standing.
- They tend to be similar to the consumer in terms of their values and beliefs, so they possess referent power. Note that although opinion leaders are set apart by their interest or expertise in a product category, they are more convincing to the extent that they are *homophilous* rather than *heterophilous*. **Homophily** refers to the degree to which a pair of individuals is similar in terms of education, social status, and beliefs.[57] Effective opinion leaders tend to be slightly higher in terms of status and educational attainment than those they influence, but not so high as to be in a different social class.
- Opinion leaders are often among the first to buy new products, so they absorb much of the risk. This experience reduces uncertainty for the rest of us who are not as courageous. Furthermore, whereas company-sponsored communications tend to focus exclusively on the positive aspects of a product, the hands-on experience of opinion leaders makes them more likely to impart *both* positive and negative information about product performance. Thus, they are more credible because they have no "axe to grind."

Marketing Pitfall

One criticism of focus groups that provide feedback from consumers is that participants who listen to what others say in the group may change their opinions based on this temporary group influence. Some recent experiments underscore how powerful this effect can be. These studies replicated the live feedback graphs that networks sometimes use to report audience responses during political debates; marketing research firms also use this dial-testing format when they ask focus groups to evaluate TV shows and commercials. In one study that mimicked *American Idol*, several hundred college students watched performances as fake audience feedback appeared on the screen. When the feedback was negative, their evaluations of the contestants dipped also. In a similar study, participants watched an excerpt of a 1984 debate between presidential candidates Ronald Reagan and Walter Mondale (presumably these subjects were just a glimmer in their fathers' eyes when this election happened). Respondents who saw screen feedback that favored Reagan were 2.8 times more likely to say they would have voted for him, whereas those who saw similar feedback in favor of Mondale were 1.8 times more likely to say they would have voted for the Democratic candidate.[51]

How Influential Is an Opinion Leader?

Ford's prelaunch campaign for its crossover SUV Flex model aimed to get buzz going as it gave opinion leaders an exclusive look at the new car. In five cities, the company invited radio deejays, musicians, and other creative people to take a tour of the Flex. These influentials went on an urban odyssey as fleets of the vehicles took them to art galleries, nightclubs, and other hot spots. In a separate campaign to plug its Fiesta model, the carmaker selected 100 young people who got free use of a car for six months in return for blogging about it.[58]

When social scientists initially developed the concept of the opinion leader, they assumed that certain influential people in a community would exert an overall impact on group members' attitudes. Later work, however, questioned the assumption that there is such a thing as a *generalized opinion leader* whose recommendations we seek for all types of purchases. Very few people are capable of being expert in a number of fields (even though they believe otherwise). Sociologists distinguish between those who are *monomorphic*, or expert in a limited field, and those who are *polymorphic*, or expert in several fields.[59] Even opinion leaders who are polymorphic, however, tend to concentrate on one broad domain, such as electronics or fashion. For example, Mediamark Research & Intelligence estimates that 10.5 percent of the U.S. adult population, whom it labels "Big Circle Influentials," are the key influencers for personal finance decisions.[60]

Research on opinion leadership generally indicates that although opinion leaders do exist for multiple product categories, expertise tends to overlap across similar categories. It is rare to find a generalized opinion leader. An opinion leader for home appliances is likely to serve a similar function for home cleaners but not for cosmetics. In contrast, we may consult a fashion opinion leader whose primary influence is on clothing choices for recommendations on cosmetics purchases but not necessarily for her opinions on microwave ovens.[61]

A reexamination of the traditional perspective on opinion leadership reveals that the process isn't as clear-cut as some researchers thought.[62] The original framework is called the **two step flow model of influence**. It proposes that a small group of *influencers* disseminate information because they can modify the opinions of a large number of other people. When the authors ran extensive computer simulations of this process, they found that the influence is driven less by influentials and more by the interaction among those who are easily influenced; they communicate the information vigorously to one another and they also participate in a two-way dialogue with the opinion leader as part of an **influence network**. These conversations create **information cascades**, which occur when a piece of information triggers a sequence of interactions (much like an avalanche).

It's worth noting that consumer researchers and other social scientists continue to debate the dynamics of these networks. For example, the jury is still out about just how influential it is when different people tweet about a product. On the one hand, an online service called Klout claims to precisely measure just how influential each of us is. It awards pop sensation Justin Bieber, with his 6.4 million Twitter followers, a perfect score of 100; go there and see how influential you are.[63] Although many marketers today focus on identifying key influencers and motivating them to spread the word about a brand, another camp believes that it's more productive simply to get your message out to as many people as possible. They argue that it's very difficult to predict what will trigger a cascade, so it's better to hedge your bets by simply getting the word out as widely as possible.[64] Stay tuned, as the science of understanding online influence races to keep up with the mushrooming usage of these new platforms.

Types of Opinion Leaders

We've seen that early conceptions of the opinion leader role assumed a static, one-way process: The opinion leader absorbs information from the mass media and in turn transmits data to opinion receivers. This view also confuses the functions of several different types of consumers.

Opinion leaders may or may not be purchasers of the products they recommend. Early purchasers also tend to be *innovators*; they like to take risks and try new things. Researchers call opinion leaders who also are early purchasers *innovative communicators*. One study identified characteristics of college men who were innovative communicators for fashion products. These men were among the first to buy new fashions, and other students were likely to follow their lead when they made their own purchases. Other characteristics of the men included the following:[65]

- They were socially active.
- They were appearance conscious and narcissistic (i.e., they were quite fond of themselves and self-centered).
- They were involved in rock culture.
- They were heavy readers of magazine like *Playboy* and *Sports Illustrated*.
- They were likely to own more clothing, and a broader range of styles, than other students.

Opinion leaders also are likely to be *opinion seekers*. They are generally more involved in a product category and actively search for information. As a result, they are more likely to talk about products with others and to solicit others' opinions as well.[66] Contrary to the older, static view of opinion leadership, most product-related conversation does not take place in a "lecture" format where one person does all the talking. A lot of product-related conversation occurs in the context of a casual interaction rather than as formal instruction.[67] One study, which found that opinion seeking is especially high for food products, revealed that two-thirds of opinion seekers also view themselves as opinion leaders.[68]

The Market Maven

To publicize Clinical Therapy, a new lotion from Vaseline, an advertising campaign mapped the social network of a small town in Alaska. In Kodiak, reps took over a storefront and gave away free bottles. In return, the recipients had to identify the person in town who recommended the product to them. Through this process they found a woman whom many of the townspeople named as their source.[69]

The Alaskan woman Vaseline found (no, she isn't Sarah Palin) is a **market maven**— she is a person who likes to transmit marketplace information of all types. These shopaholics are not necessarily interested in certain products and they may not necessarily be early purchasers; they're simply into staying on top of what's happening in the marketplace. They come closer to the function of a generalized opinion leader because they tend to have a solid overall knowledge of how and where to procure products. They're also more confident in their own ability to make smart purchase decisions. Researchers use the following scale items, to which respondents indicate how much they agree or disagree, to identify market mavens:[70]

1 I like introducing new brands and products to my friends.
2 I like helping people by providing them with information about many kinds of products.
3 People ask me for information about products, places to shop, or sales.
4 If someone asked me where to get the best buy on several types of products, I could tell him or her where to shop.
5 My friends think of me as a good source of information when it comes to new products or sales.

The Surrogate Consumer

In addition to everyday consumers who influence others' purchase decisions, a class of marketing intermediary we call the *surrogate consumer* often guides what we buy. A **surrogate consumer** is a person whom we retain to provide input into our purchase decisions. Unlike the opinion leader or market maven, we usually compensate the surrogate for his or her advice. Interior decorators, stockbrokers, professional shoppers, and college consultants are surrogate consumers.

Regardless of whether they actually make the purchase on behalf of the consumer, their recommendations can be enormously influential. The consumer, in essence, relinquishes control over several or all decision-making functions, such as information search, the evaluation of alternatives, or the actual purchase. For example, a client may commission an interior decorator to redo her house, and we may entrust a broker to make crucial buy/sell decisions on our behalf. Marketers tend to overlook surrogates when they try to convince consumers to buy their goods or services. This can be a big mistake, because they may mistarget their communications to end consumers when they should focus on the surrogates who actually sift through product information and recommend a purchase to their clients.[71]

How Do We Find Opinion Leaders?

Unfortunately, because most opinion leaders are everyday consumers rather than celebrities, they are hard to find. A celebrity or an influential industry executive is by definition easy to locate. That person has national or at least regional visibility or is listed in published directories. In contrast, opinion leaders tend to operate at the local level and may influence only a small group of consumers rather than an entire market segment. When PepsiCo recently launched its Sierra Mist Ruby Splash flavor, the company hired a firm to identify local people in different cities who could help it recruit a select group of "influencers" to spread the word by offering the soft drink at events they hosted or attended. The requirements were specific: Influencers had to love lemon-lime beverages, be ages 18 to 34, and be musicians, skateboard shop owners, people who love to throw backyard barbeques, or others who had laid-back lifestyles and who were well-known in their communities. One influencer, for example, was a musician who hosted a backyard jam session for 20 friends; before the event, a crew dropped off ice-cold cans of the soft drink as well as branded sunglasses, misters, and car fresheners with a Ruby Splash scent. Another opinion leader owned a skateboard store; he hosted an outdoor movie night to debut a new surf film. In all, the company sponsored more than 300 of these minievents in a 2-month period. Nice job if you can get it.[72]

Because it's difficult to identify specific opinion leaders in a large market, most attempts to do so focus instead on *exploratory studies*. In these efforts, researchers identify the profile of a representative opinion leader and then generalize these insights to a larger market. For example, one company that sought out financial opinion leaders found that these consumers were more likely to manage their own finances and tended to use a computer to do so. They also were more likely to follow their investments on a daily basis and to read books and watch television shows devoted to financial issues.[73]

Self-Designation

The most commonly used technique to identify opinion leaders is simply to ask individual consumers whether they consider themselves to be opinion leaders. Although respondents who report a greater degree of interest in a product category are more likely to be opinion leaders, we must view the results of surveys that discover self-designated opinion leaders with some skepticism. Some people have a tendency to inflate their own importance and influence, whereas others who really are influential might not admit to this quality or be conscious of it if they are.[74]

Here's the problem: The fact that we transmit advice about products does not mean other people *take* that advice. For someone to be considered a bona fide opinion leader, opinion seekers must actually heed his advice. An alternative is to select certain group members (*key informants*) whom we ask to identify opinion leaders. The success of this approach hinges on locating those who have accurate knowledge of the group.

The self-designating method is not as reliable as a more systematic analysis (where we can verify an individual's self-designation by asking others if they agree), but the advantage is that we can easily apply it to a large group of potential opinion leaders. Figure 2 shows one of the measurement scales researchers use for this kind of self-designation.

Figure 2   OPINION LEADER SCALE

Please rate yourself on the following scales relating to your interactions with friends and neighbors regarding _____.

1. In general, do you talk to your friends and neighbors about _____:

very often				never
5	4	3	2	1

2. When you talk to your friends and neighbors about _____ do you:

give a great deal of information				give very little information
5	4	3	2	1

3. During the past six months, how many people have you told about a new _____?

told a number of people				told no one
5	4	3	2	1

4. Compared with your circle of friends, how likely are you to be asked about new _____?

very likely to be asked				not at all likely to be asked
5	4	3	2	1

5. In discussion of new _____, which of the following happens most?

you tell your friends about _____				your friends tell you about _____
5	4	3	2	1

6. Overall in all of your discussions with friends and neighbors are you:

often used as a source of advice				not used as a source of advice
5	4	3	2	1

Sociometry

The play *Six Degrees of Separation* is based on the premise that everyone on the planet indirectly knows everyone else—or at least knows people who in turn know them. Indeed, social scientists estimate that the average person has 1,500 acquaintances and that five to six intermediaries could connect any two people in the United States.[75] A popular game challenges players to link the actor Kevin Bacon with other actors in much the same way.

Sociometric methods trace communication patterns among members of a group. These techniques allow researchers to systematically map out the interactions among group members. Like the Vaseline campaign in Alaska described earlier, this means we interview consumers and find out who they ask for product information. In many cases one or a few people emerge as the "nodes" in a map—and *voilá*, we've found our opinion leaders. This method is the most precise, but it is very difficult and expensive to implement because it involves very close study of interaction patterns in small groups. For this reason, it's best to apply a sociometric technique in a closed, self-contained social setting, such as in hospitals, in prisons, and on army bases, where members are largely isolated from other social networks.

A recent sociometric study on obesity (similar to the one we read about earlier regarding clusters of smokers) provides a striking example of how our social networks influence what we do. The researchers analyzed a sample of more than 12,000 people who participated in the Framingham Heart Study, which closely documented their health from 1971 to 2003. They discovered that obesity can spread from person to person, much like a virus (we'll talk more about how consumer trends spread in this fashion later in this chapter). The investigators knew who was friends with whom, as well as who was a spouse or sibling or neighbor, and they knew how much each person weighed at various times over 3 decades so they could reconstruct what happened over the years if study participants became obese. Guess what? When one person gains weight, close friends

The Tangled Web

The Whopper Sacrifice was an advertising campaign Burger King launched to promote its new Angry Whopper sandwich. You could earn a free burger, but to get it you had to sacrifice 10 of your Facebook friends. After you delete these names, you get a coupon in the mail. Your ex-friends get a note informing them that they were dumped for a freebie sandwich. The burger costs $3.69, so when you do the math, each former friend is worth about 37 cents. Although it sounds cruel to give up a friend for this amount, many Facebookers jumped at the chance to purge their friend lists. As one student with several hundred friends commented, "It's a good excuse to get rid of old girlfriends and their families on my account and get a Whopper out of it."[80]

tend to gain weight, too: A person's chances of becoming obese if a close friend put on the pounds increased by 57 percent! The friend's influence remained even if he lived hundreds of miles away. The researchers speculated that the reason for this *social contagion* effect is that when our best buds get fat, this alters our perception of normal body weight so we aren't as concerned when we put on a few pounds as well. The moral of the story: Hang out with thin people![76]

Many professionals, such as doctors, accountants, and lawyers, as well as services marketers like lawn-care companies and cleaning services, depend primarily on word of mouth to generate business. In many cases, consumers recommend a service provider to a friend or coworker, and in other cases businesspeople make recommendations to their customers. For example, only 0.2 percent of respondents in one study reported that they choose a physician based on advertising. Instead, they rely primarily on advice from family and friends.[77]

We use sociometric analyses to better understand *referral behavior* and to locate strengths and weaknesses in terms of how one's reputation flows through a community.[78] *Network analysis* focuses on communication in social systems, considers the relations among people in a *referral network*, and measures the *tie strength* among them. To understand how a network guides what we buy, consider a study researchers conducted among women who lived together in a sorority house. They found evidence that subgroups, or *cliques*, within the sorority were likely to share preferences for various products. In some cases, the sisters even shared their choices of "private" (i.e., socially inconspicuous) products (probably because of shared bathrooms in the sorority house).[79]

Tie strength refers to the nature of the bond between people. It can range from *strong primary* (e.g., one's spouse) to *weak secondary* (e.g., an acquaintance whom one rarely sees). Although strong ties are important, weak ties are too because they perform a *bridging function*. This type of connection allows a consumer access between subgroups. For example, you might have a regular group of friends that is a primary reference group (strong ties). If you have an interest in tennis, one of these friends might introduce you to a group of people in her dorm who play on the tennis team. As a result, you gain access to their valuable expertise through this bridging function. This referral process demonstrates the *strength of weak ties*.

Online Opinion Leaders

The Internet makes opinion leaders even more powerful—it's like giving a baseball player steroids (only legal). Instead of reaching only those within earshot, now an influential person can sway the opinions of thousands or even millions of people around the world. In online groups, opinion leaders sometimes are called **power users**. They have a strong communication network that gives them the ability to affect purchase decisions for a number of other consumers, directly and indirectly.[81]

Much like their offline counterparts, power users are active participants at work and in their communities. Their social networks are large and well developed. Others trust them and find them to be credible sources of information about one or more specific topics. They tend to have a natural sense of intellectual curiosity, which may lead them to new sources of information. And they post an awful lot of brand-related content: Forrester Research has dubbed these brand-specific mentions **influence impressions**. In advertising lingo, an *impression* refers to a view or an exposure to an advertising message. Forrester estimates that each year, American consumers generate 256 billion influence impressions as people talk about their lives with each other, telling stories and experiences that invariably include brands.[82] These influence impressions are primarily delivered by—you guessed it—power users: Only 6.2 percent of social media users are responsible for about 80 percent of these brand mentions. Forrester calls these influencers **Mass Connectors**.

As Mass Connectors spread influence impressions, the impact of the message grows due to the **momentum effect**.[83] Influencers publish the message on blogs, share widgets, place a brand logo on their Facebook pages, and so on. Friends share with friends who

Travelocity enlisted its Roaming Gnome to boost online consumer engagement and trigger a momentum effect. The spokescharacter was (supposedly) outraged that the Aflac Duck had more friends on Facebook, and so Travelocity created International Gnome Day. On his page, the gnome implored fans to share his plea with their friends in the hopes that he could achieve his goal by the big day.
Source: ©2011 Travelocity.com LP.

share with friends. If a brand is well-liked, relevant, and buzz-worthy, the media value originating from nonpaid, word-of-mouth referrals for the brand can be enormous.

Word-of-Mouth Communication

OBJECTIVE 5
The things other consumers tell us about products (good and bad) often are more influential than the advertising we see.

Altoids breath mints have been around for 200 years, but only recently have they become a big hit. How did this happen? The revival began when the mint started to attract a devoted following among smokers and coffee drinkers who hung out in the blossoming Seattle club scene during the 1980s. Until 1993, when Kraft bought manufacturer Callard & Bowser, only those "in the know" sucked the mints. The brand's marketing manager persuaded Kraft to hire advertising agency Leo Burnett to develop a modest promotional campaign. The agency decided to publicize the candy with subway posters sporting retro imagery and other "low-tech" media to avoid making the product seem mainstream—that would turn off the original audience.[84] As young people started to tune into this "retro" treat, its popularity skyrocketed.

As the Altoids success story illustrates, "buzz" makes a hit product. **Word-of-mouth (WOM)** is product information that individuals transmit to other individuals. Because we get the word from people we know, WOM tends to be more reliable and trustworthy than messages from more formal marketing channels. And, unlike advertising, WOM often comes with social pressure to conform to these recommendations.[85]

Ironically, despite all the money marketers pump into lavish ads, WOM is far more powerful: It influences two-thirds of all consumer-goods sales.[87] In one survey, 69 percent of interviewees said they relied on a personal referral at least once over the course of a year to help them choose a restaurant, 36 percent reported that they used referrals to decide on computer hardware and software, and 22 percent got help from friends and associates to decide where to travel.[88]

Varsity Brands is a leading supplier to cheerleaders. The company sponsored a big survey of teenage girls to learn how they decide what to buy. No surprises here: Half of the respondents spend an hour or more each day texting, and another third spend an hour socializing online. In contrast, 44 percent spend less than 15 minutes actually talking on the phone (who uses the phone to talk anymore?). When these girls discover a brand they like, three-quarters say they are likely to recommend it to a friend. About half become online fans of the brand, and 55 percent agree that "[i]f I see a favorable post online about an item, it will likely influence me to buy it." A Varsity marketing executive commented, "When it comes to spreading ideas via social media, teen girls lead the pack. They are more likely to use online time for connecting, self-expression, and relationship building. They are more likely to have used e-mail and are almost twice as likely as boys to have shared photos through a website, posted a comment on a blog or community, blogged themselves or kept an online journal."[86]

Source: Andrew Rich/istockphoto.com

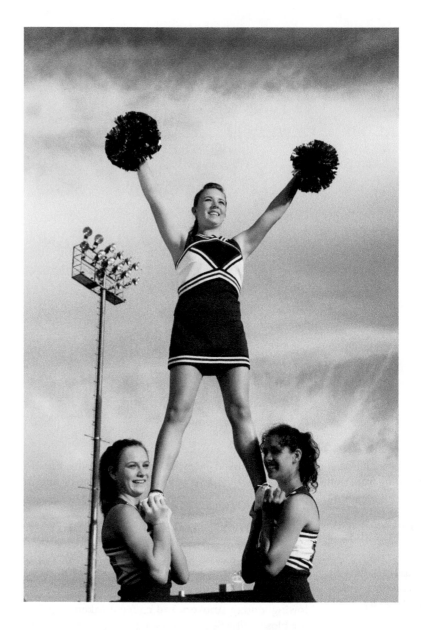

If you think carefully about the content of your own conversations in the course of a normal day, you will probably agree that much of what you discuss with friends, family members, or coworkers is product-related: When you compliment someone on her dress and ask her where she bought it, recommend a new restaurant to a friend, or complain to your neighbor about the shoddy treatment you got at the bank, you engage in WOM. Recall, for example, that comments and suggestions his fellow RUBs made drove many of Zachary's biker purchases. Marketers have been aware of the power of WOM for many years, but recently they've been more aggressive about trying to promote and control it instead of sitting back and hoping people will like their products enough to talk them up. Companies like BzzAgent enlist thousands of "agents" who try new products and spread the word about those they like.[89] Many sophisticated marketers today also precisely track WOM. For example, the ongoing TalkTrack study reports which brands consumers mention the most in different categories. Based on online surveys of 14,000 women, it reports that middle-aged (baby boomer) women talk about Kraft more than any other packaged-goods food brand, and they discuss Olay the most among beauty products.[90]

As far back as the Stone Age (well, the 1950s, anyway), communications theorists challenged the assumption that advertising primarily determines what we buy. As a rule, advertising is more effective when it reinforces our existing product preferences than when it tries to create new ones.[91] Studies in both industrial and consumer purchase settings underscore the idea that although information from impersonal sources is important to create brand awareness, consumers rely on WOM in the later stages of evaluation and adoption.[92] Quite simply, the more positive information consumers get about a product from peers, the more likely they will be to adopt the product.[93]

The influence of others' opinions is at times even more powerful than our own perceptions. In one study of furniture choices, consumers' estimates of how much their friends would like the furniture was a better predictor of purchase than what they thought of it.[94] In addition, consumers may find their own reasons to push a brand that take the manufacturer by surprise. That's what happened with Mountain Dew: Its popularity among younger consumers is due to the "buzz" about the soda's high caffeine content. As an advertising executive explained, "The caffeine thing was not in any of Mountain Dew's television ads. This drink is hot by word-of-mouth."[95]

WOM is especially powerful when the consumer is relatively unfamiliar with the product category. We would expect such a situation in the case of new products (e.g., medications to prevent hair loss) or those that are technologically complex (e.g., smartphones). One way to reduce uncertainty about the wisdom of a purchase is to talk about it. Talking gives the consumer an opportunity to generate supporting arguments for the purchase and to garner support for this decision from others. For example, the strongest predictor of a person's intention to buy a residential solar water-heating system is the number of solar-heat users the person knows.[96]

You talk about products for several reasons:[97]

- You might be highly involved with a type of product or activity and enjoy talking about it. Computer hackers, avid football fans, and "fashion plates" seem to share the ability to steer a conversation toward their particular interests.
- You might be knowledgeable about a product and use conversations as a way to let others know it. Thus, word-of-mouth communication sometimes enhances the ego of the individual who wants to impress others with her expertise.
- You might initiate a discussion out of genuine concern for someone else. We like to ensure that people we care about buy what is good for them or that they do not waste their money.

As its name suggests, BzzAgent recruits consumers to create a "buzz" for clients. You can sign up at bzzagent.com.
Source: © 2009 Bzzagent.

CB AS I SEE IT

Prof. Praveen Aggarwal, *University of Minnesota Duluth*

Though most of us would like to believe that we act independently while making our purchase decisions, the fact of the matter remains that our decisions are heavily influenced by others. The traditional literature on interpersonal influences examines the role of word of mouth (WOM) in decision making. We routinely turn to our friends and family members for advice and information. Many of us even serve as opinion leaders who help others with their decision making.

In the context of WOM communications, does it matter if the message being exchanged has specific details or is of a generic nature? For instance, if someone wanted to communicate to you that a particular cell phone's battery was better than average, would it make a difference if they gave a generic advice that "the cell phone's battery lasts longer than average" rather than giving you more specific information such as "the cell phone's battery lasts an additional five hours per charge"? Our research indicates that WOM communications are more effective if they contain more specific information. Interestingly, this advantage disappears when the sender of the message is seen as an expert or has strong social ties with the receiver.

In a related area of research on interpersonal influences, my colleagues and I examine situations in which people knowingly delegate the task of decision making to someone else. This is different from seeking others' opinions, in the sense that they decide not to decide and instead let someone else make their decisions for them. The individuals to whom the decision-making task is delegated are called *surrogate buyers*. Wardrobe consultants, interior decorators, stock brokers, and wine stewards are some common examples where the end user delegates the choice decision to someone else. What kinds of conditions promote decision delegation? Our research indicates higher levels of delegation when the differential between the user's and surrogate's expertise is high, and when the surrogate is seen as trustworthy and accountable. It also helps if the surrogate customizes recommendations to the individual's needs and wants.

How can companies find out what kinds of things are being said about their products by their buyers and end users? Although it was difficult to gauge the general sentiment of people's opinions in the pre-Internet era, the vast repository of opinions, reviews, and recommendations available online provides a tantalizing opportunity for managers to gain a summary assessment of the WOM shaping up around their brands. The problem, however, is that the volume of information available is so vast that it is extremely difficult to sift through it and draw summary conclusions. Our research addresses this vexing problem. Drawing on research in lexical text analysis and computational linguistics, we were able to develop a simple mechanism to take massive amounts of information and convert them into simple indices that managers can use to track how the WOM around their brands is evolving![98]

OBJECTIVE 6

Online technologies accelerate the impact of word-of-mouth communication.

Negative WOM: The Power of Rumors

WOM is a two-edged sword that cuts both ways for marketers. Informal discussions among consumers can make or break a product or store. Furthermore, consumers weigh **negative word-of-mouth** more heavily than they do positive comments. According to a study by the White House Office of Consumer Affairs, 90 percent of unhappy customers will not do business with a company again. Each of these people is likely to share her grievance with at least nine other people, and 13 percent of these disgruntled customers tell more than 30 people about their negative experience.[99]

Especially when we consider a new product or service, we're likely to pay more attention to negative information than to positive information and to tell others about our nasty experience.[100] Research shows that negative WOM reduces the credibility of a firm's advertising and influences consumers' attitudes toward a product as well as their intention to buy it.[101] Dell found this out the hard way when bloggers denounced the computer maker's quality and service levels; then the popular media picked up this discontent and magnified it.[102]

As Dell discovered, it's incredibly easy to spread negative WOM online. Many dissatisfied customers and disgruntled former employees create Web sites simply to share their tales of woe with others. For example, a Web site for people to complain about the Dunkin' Donuts chain got to be so popular that the company bought it in order to control the bad press it got. A man created the site because he couldn't get skim milk for his coffee.[103] An in-depth study of 40 complaint Web sites such as walmartsucks.com identified three basic themes:[104]

1. **Injustice**—Consumer protestors frequently talk about their fruitless attempts to contact the company.
2. **Identity**—Posters characterize the violator (often top management) as evil, rather than simply incompetent.
3. **Agency**—Individual Web site creators try to create a collective identity for those who share their anger with a company. They evoke themes of crusade and heroism to rally others to believe that they have the power to change a status quo in which companies can wrong consumers without retribution.

In the 1930s, some companies hired "professional rumormongers" to organize word-of-mouth campaigns that pushed their clients' products and criticized competitors'.[105] More recently, Bio Business International, a small Canadian company that markets 100 percent cotton nonchlorine-bleached tampons under the name Terra Femme, encouraged women to spread a message that the tampons its American competitors make contain dioxin. There is very little evidence to support the claim that these products are dangerous, but as a result of this rumor, Procter & Gamble received thousands of complaints about its feminine hygiene products.[106]

As we transmit information to one another, it tends to change. The resulting message usually does not resemble the original at all. The British psychologist Frederic Bartlett used the method of *serial reproduction* to examine how content mutates. Like the game of "Telephone" many of us played as kids, he asked a subject to reproduce a stimulus,

Hoaxkill.com is a Web site dedicated to tracking hoaxes and debunking product rumors.
Source: Courtesy of Joroen Siking Hoaxkill.com.

The Tangled Web

There is a long tradition of inventing fake stories to see who will swallow them. For instance, in 1824 a man convinced 300 New Yorkers to sign up for a construction project. He claimed that all the new building in the lower part of Manhattan (what is now the Wall Street area) was making the island bottom-heavy. So, they needed to saw off this section of town and tow it out to sea to prevent New York City from tipping over!

The Web is a perfect medium for spreading rumors and hoaxes, and we can only guess how much damage this "project" would cause today if the perpetrator recruited construction crews via email! Modern-day hoaxes abound; many of these are in the form of email chain letters promising instant riches if you pass the message on to 10 friends. Your professor will love one variation of this hoax: In a scam called "Win Tenure Fast," academics were told to add their names to a document and then cite it in their own research papers. The idea is that everyone who gets the letter cites the professor's name, and with so many citations you're guaranteed to get tenure! If only it were that easy.

Some hoaxes involve major corporations. A popular one promised that if you tried Microsoft products, you would win a free trip to Disneyland. Nike received several hundred pairs of old sneakers a day after the rumor spread that you would get a free pair of new shoes in exchange for your old, smelly ones (pity the delivery people who had to cart these packages to the company!). Procter & Gamble received more than 10,000 irate calls after a rumor began to spread on newsgroups that its Febreze fabric deodorant kills dogs. In a preemptive strike, the company registered numerous Web site names such as febrezekillspet.com, febrezesucks.com, and ihateprocterandgamble.com to be sure angry consumers didn't use them.

A new form of malicious rumor is **cyberbullying**, which occurs when one or more people post malicious comments online about someone else in a coordinated effort to harass the targeted individual. In South Korea, a famous actress named Choi Jinsil hung herself after online rumors claimed she had driven another actor to take his life. A Korean singer killed herself because rumors claimed she had had plastic surgery. In the United States, the most high-profile case involved the suicide of a 13-year-old girl after

such as a drawing or a story. He then gave another subject this reproduction and asked him to copy it, and repeated this process several times. Figure 3 illustrates how a message changes as people reproduce it. Bartlett found that distortions almost inevitably follow a pattern: They tend to change from ambiguous forms to more conventional ones as subjects try to make them consistent with their preexisting schemas. He called this process *assimilation* and he noted that it often occurs as people engage in *leveling,* when they omit details to simplify the structure; or *sharpening,* when they exaggerate prominent details.

Buzz Building

In the "old days" (i.e., a few years ago), here's how a toy company would launch a new product: Unveil a hot holiday toy during a spring trade fair, run a November–December saturation television ad campaign during cartoon prime time to sell the toy to kids, sit back and watch as desperate parents scrambled through the aisles at Toys "R" Us, and then wait for the resulting media coverage to drive still more sales.

Fast-forward to a recent toy story: A Hong Kong company called Silverlit Toys makes the $30 Picoo Z helicopter. At one point a Google search for the term Picoo produced more than 109,000 URLs, with many of those links pointed to major online global gift retailers like Hammacher-Schlemmer and Toys "R" Us. Do you think this huge exposure was the result of a meticulously planned promotional strategy? Think again. By most accounts, a 28-year-old tech worker in Chicago started the Picoo Z buzz; he bought his helicopter after he read about it on a hobbyist message board. A few months later he uploaded his homemade video of the toy on YouTube. Within 2 weeks, 15 of his friends

Figure 3 THE TRANSMISSION OF MISINFORMATION

had also bought the toy, and they in turn posted their own videos and pointed viewers to the original video. Internet retailers who troll online conversations for fresh and exciting buzz identified the toy and started to add their own links to the clips. Within a few short months, there were hundreds of Picoo Z videos and more than a million people viewed them.[107]

To promote their hip-hop albums, Def Jam and other labels start building a buzz months before a release as they leak advance copies to deejays who put together "mix tapes" they sell on the street. If the kids seem to like a song, *street teams* then push it to club deejays. As the official release date nears, these groups of fans start to slap up posters around the inner city. They plaster telephone poles, sides of buildings, and car windshields with promotions that announce the release of new albums.[108] These streetwise strategies started in the mid-1970s, when pioneering deejays like Kool DJ Herc and Afrika Bambaataa promoted their parties through graffiti-style flyers. As Ice Cube observed, "Even though I'm an established artist, I still like to leak my music to a kid on the street and let him duplicate it for his homies before it hits radio."[109]

This type of grassroots effort epitomizes *guerrilla marketing*: promotional strategies that use unconventional means and venues to push products. The term implies that the marketer "ambushes" the unsuspecting recipient. These campaigns often recruit legions of real consumers who agree to engage in some kind of street theater or other activity to convince others to use the product or service. Scion, for example, often reaches out to its young buyers with street teams that distribute merchandise and hang wild posters wherever they can to encourage twentysomethings to check out the carmaker's videos and multiplayer games on its Web site.[110]

Today, big companies buy into guerrilla marketing strategies big time, especially to snag younger consumers who they don't reach with more traditional advertising. Here are some guerrilla campaigns that built buzz:

- Procter & Gamble's Tremor division spreads the word about its products among young people. It recruits almost 300,000 kids between the ages of 13 and 19 to deliver endorsements in school cafeterias, at sleepovers, by cell phone, and by email. It taps these "Tremorites" to talk up just about everything, from movies and music (such as new releases by artists like Lenny Kravitz and Coldplay) to milk and motor oil—and they do it free. Tremor looks for kids with a wide social circle and a gift of gab. To register, kids fill out a questionnaire, which asks them, among other things, to report how many friends, family members, and acquaintances they communicate with every day. (Tremorites have an average of 170 names on their buddy lists; a typical teen has 30.) P&G rewards the kids for their help with exclusive music mixes and other trinkets such as shampoo and cheap watches.[112]
- Kayem Foods, which makes Al Fresco chicken sausage, hired a company to organize a guerrilla campaign called the Great Sausage Fanout. On a July 4 weekend, legions of people who went to cookouts showed up with packages of Al Fresco chicken sausage for their hosts to throw on the grill. The company sent the "agents" coupons for free sausage and a set of instructions for the best ways to talk up the product.[113]
- The train line CSX launched a safety-awareness campaign when it hired people to throw eggs at the company's outdoor billboards. The billboards carry the stark black-on-white words "Cars hitting trains." Eggs smashing against the billboard demonstrate the impact of a car hitting a train. The idea is to get people to be careful when they cross railroad tracks.[114]
- *Brand ambassadors* pop up in eye-catching outfits to announce a new brand or service. AT&T sent its ambassadors to high-traffic areas of California and New Jersey, where they did random favors such as handing dog biscuits to people as they walked their dogs and providing binoculars to concertgoers to promote its new AT&T Local Service. Hyatt Hotels unleashed 100 bellhops in Manhattan: They opened doors, carried packages, and handed out pillow mints to thousands of consumers.[115]

classmates created a fake boy online who first flirted with the girl and then taunted her with the claim that the world would be better off without her. The hoax allegedly began because the mother of one of the classmates wanted to find out what the victim was saying about her daughter online.

Have you gotten one of those adorable lap giraffes yet? Thousands of people started to look for these novel pets after an online message circulated about them and Sokoblovsky Farms, the place that breeds these petite versions of the gentle creatures we see in zoos. One hitch: There is no such thing as a lap giraffe. The scam was part of a marketing campaign for DirecTV, America's biggest satellite cable TV provider. It started with a TV commercial that starred a rich Russian who "also likes saving zee money." At the end of the spot, he gives a little kiss to a giraffe that's the size of a small lap dog. The company followed up with a fake Web site that included photos of the pets and even a "live camera feed" from the farm, which shows a tiny giraffe grazing. More than half a million people put their names on a waiting list to receive one of the tiny animals. It's not clear if they're still waiting for their pets to arrive, but DirecTV certainly hooked a lot of exposures.[116]
Source: Courtesy of DIRECTV.

Marketing Pitfall

Is any publicity good publicity? One of the most widely publicized guerrilla marketing stunts in recent years illustrates the potential for a good idea to go bad in a hurry. To promote its *Aqua Teen Hunger Force* show on the Adult Swim segment of its Cartoon Network, Turner Broadcasting hired a company to plant flashing light boards in public areas such as bridges around several cities. Observers in Boston thought they saw terrorist bombs instead, and the city essentially shut down as officials dealt with what they thought was a national security issue. Turner had to pay hefty fines and endure a lot of criticism for this stunt. However, the Adult Swim Web site boosted its traffic by 77 percent on the day after the story broke.[111]

Viral marketing refers to the strategy of getting visitors to a Web site to forward information on the site to their friends in order to make still more consumers aware of the product. It usually takes off when an organization creates online content that is entertaining or just plain weird.

The Social Media Revolution

The odds are that you've interacted with social media today. If you checked into your Facebook page (of course not in class!), fired off a tweet, read a restaurant review on Yelp!, or maybe even killed off some nasty orcs on World of Warcraft, you're part of the social media revolution that is changing how consumers interact with the marketplace and with one another. Sometimes people define social media in terms of hardware (like Android smartphones) or software (like Wikipedia), but really it's first and foremost about *community*: the collective participation of members who together build and maintain a site.[117]

Social Media and Community

The Skittles candy brand changed its Web site into a social media hub and in the process significantly boosted consumers' awareness of the product. Instead of seeing corporate-produced content, a visitor to the site finds links to Twitter to read tweets about Skittles (good and bad). Another link guides her to Skittles videos and photos on YouTube and Flickr, and if she clicks "Friends," she'll go directly to the brand's Facebook area.[118]

Marketers like Skittles are stumbling over one another to adapt their strategies to a Web 2.0 environment. These new communications platforms can be as varied as a social networking site like Facebook, a social shopping site like Groupon, or a virtual world like MTV's Virtual Laguna Beach. Nonetheless, they share some basic characteristics:

- They improve as the number of users increase. For example, Amazon's ability to recommend books to you based on what other people with similar interests buy gets better as it tracks more and more people who enter search queries.
- Their currency is eyeballs. Google makes money as it charges advertisers according to the number of people who see their ads after they type in a search term.
- They are free and in perpetual beta. Wikipedia, the online encyclopedia, gets updated constantly by volunteer editors who "correct" others' errors.
- They categorize entries according to a **folksonomy** rather than a *taxonomy* (a pre-established labeling hierarchy). Instead, sites rely on users to sort contents. Listeners at Pandora.com create their own "radio stations" that play songs by artists they choose, as well as other similar artists.[119] People who upload their photos to Flickr tag them with the labels *they* think best describe the pictures.

In some ways, online communities are not much different from those we find in our physical environment. The *Merriam-Webster Dictionary* (online version, of course) defines **community** as "a unified body of individuals, unified by interests, location, occupation, common history, or political and economic concerns." In fact, one social scientist refers to an online community as a **cyberplace** where "people connect online with kindred spirits, engage in supportive and sociable relationships with them, and imbue their activity online with meaning, belonging, and identity."[120]

OBJECTIVE 7

Social media are changing the way companies and consumers interact.

Social Networks

Let's take a closer look at the social fabric of social media. Each application consists of a **social network**, a set of socially relevant nodes connected by one or more relations.[121] **Nodes** are members of the network (e.g., the 600-million-plus Facebook users). Members (whom we also refer to as **network units**) are connected by their relationships with (or **ties** to) each other. Relationships are based on various affiliations, such as kinship, friendship and affective ties, shared experiences, and shared hobbies and interests. When we think of community, we tend to think of people, but in principle members of a network can be organizations, articles, countries, departments, or any other definable unit. A good example is your university alumni association. The association is a community of networked individuals and organizations. Social networks are sometimes called **social graphs**, though this term may also refer to a diagram of the interconnections of units in a network.

Nodes in a network experience **interactions**; these are behavior-based ties like talking with each other, attending an event together, or working together. If you chat online with a prospective dating partner on Match.com, you are a node engaging in an interaction with another node (hopefully a node, but not a nerd . . .). And, if that actually works out and you participate in an online forum that shares experiences about wedding photographers in your area, you engage in interactions with other nodes who are also getting hitched. Interactions are participative in nature; they are shared activities among members in the network.

Flows occur between nodes. Flows are exchanges of resources, information, or influence among members of the network. On Facebook you share news, updates about your life, opinions on favorite books and movies, photos, videos, and notes. As you share content, you create flows from among those in your network. In social media, these flows of communication go in many directions at any point in time and often on multiple platforms—a condition we term **media multiplexity**. Flows are not simply two-way or three-way; they may go through an entire community, a list or group within a network, or several individuals independently. Flows of communication also occur outside the community platform. Whereas the online community may exist entirely within a Web space, the flows of communication may extend to other domains as well, like emails, text messages, virtual worlds, and even face-to-face **meetups** in which members of an online network arrange to meet in a physical location.

For marketers, flows are especially important because they are the actionable components of any social network system in terms of the sharing of information, delivery of promotional materials, and sources of social influence. The extent of this social influence (where one person's attitudes or behavior change as a result of others' attempts) varies depending upon the power or attractiveness of other nodes.

Social object theory suggests that social networks will be more powerful communities if there is a way to activate relationships among people and objects. In this perspective, an *object* is something of common interest and its primary function is to mediate the interactions between people. All relationships have social objects embedded in the relationship. In the online world, a site like Facebook provides venues for several object formats to ensure that relationships can thrive within the site's framework. One factor that drives Facebook's stunning success is that it offers so many objects for users to share; these include events, family and friends, quizzes, and so on. Other social networking sites (SNSs) provide a more specialized or focused set of objects. For example, consider how each of these SNSs incorporates objects as part of its mission. On Flickr, users participate because they want to share photos. These images are the objects that give meaning to the platform and motivate people to visit. Video is the social object around which YouTube centers. On Diigo, the objects are URLs. On Foursquare, the objects are places. On Dogster, the objects are our canine companions.

Object sociality, the extent to which an object can be shared in social media, is clearly related to an audience's unique interests, by virtue of tying the site relationships to a specific object such as photos of people's dogs or bookmarked websites that provide details about the history of alternative music. The audience becomes specialized at least to a degree. Importantly, though, SNSs oriented around object sociality are likely to be **passion-centric**. That is, the people who join those communities not only share an interest in the object in question, but chances are also high that they are obsessed with it. We all know people who devote countless hours to a hobby or who (to an outsider) seem insanely obsessed about the fine details of Star Wars characters, vintage wines, or warring guilds in World of Warcraft.

Characteristics of Online Communities

All communities, whether they are online or in the physical world, share important characteristics: Participants experience a feeling of membership, a sense of proximity to one another (even though in online groups other members' physical selves may be thousands of miles away), and in most cases some interest in the community's activities. Members may identify with one another due to a common mission (e.g., a Twitter campaign to donate money for oil spill relief) or simply because they come from the same neighborhood or belong to the same sorority (e.g., Classmates.com connects people who attended the same high school).

Communities help members meet their needs for affiliation, resource acquisition, entertainment, and information. Above all else, communities are social! Whether online or offline, they thrive when the members participate, discuss, share, and interact with others as well as recruit new members to the community. Members do vary in their degree of participation, but the more active the membership, the healthier the community.

Social media provide the fuel that fans the fires of online communities. In the Web 1.0 era, people visited a lot of Web sites to get content that interested them. But these really weren't communities, because the flow of information was all one way. In today's Web 2.0 environment, all that has changed as interactive platforms enable online communities to exhibit the following basic characteristics:[122]

- **Conversations**—Communities thrive on communication among members. These conversations are not based on talking or writing but on a hybrid of the two. If you communicate with a friend via AIM or Facebook chat, you may feel that you actually "talked" to her.

- **Presence**—Though online communities exist virtually rather than at a physical location, the better ones supply tangible characteristics that create the sensation of actually being in a place. This is particularly true for virtual-world communities that include three-dimensional depictions of physical spaces, but it also applies to visually simplistic online communities like message board groups. **Presence** is defined as the effect that people experience when they interact with a computer-mediated or computer-generated environment.[123] Social media sites can enhance a sense of presence by enabling interactions among visitors and making the environment look and feel real.[124]

- **Collective Interest**—Just as your offline communities are based on family, religious beliefs, social activities, hobbies, goals, place of residence, and so on, your online communities also need commonalities to create bonds among the members. These groups come together to allow people to share their passions, whether these are for indie bands, white wines, or open-source apps.

- **Democracy**—The political model of most online communities is democratic (that's with a small d, not the Democratic Party); leaders emerge due to the reputation they earn among the general membership. In this context, **democracy** is a descriptive term that refers to rule by the people. The leaders are appointed or elected by the community based on their demonstrated ability to add value to the group. For instance, in the online community 4chan, an online bulletin board devoted to the sharing of images related to and discussion of Japanese *anime*, members widely acknowledge that the person who posts under the name of "moot" is a leader. His leadership comes from his role in the creation of the community as well as from his ongoing participation and the quality of his contributions.

  Because of the horizontal structure of social media, we typically find that control over what appears on the platform shifts from a small elite to the larger mass. **Media democratization** means that the members of social communities, not traditional media publishers like magazines or newspaper companies, control the creation, delivery, and popularity of content.

- **Standards of Behavior**—Virtual communities need rules that govern behavior in order to operate. Some of these rules are spelled out explicitly (e.g., if you buy an item on eBay, you agree that you have entered into a legal contract to pay for it), but many of them are unspoken. A simple example is discouragement of the practice of **flaming**, when a POST CONTAINS ALL CAPITAL LETTERS TO EXPRESS ANGER.

- **Level of Participation**—For an online community to thrive, a significant proportion of its members must participate. Otherwise the site will fail to offer fresh material and ultimately traffic will slow. Participation can be a challenge, though. Most users are **lurkers**: They absorb content that others post, but they don't usually contribute their own. Researchers estimate that only 1 percent of a typical community's users regularly participate, and another 9 percent do so only intermittently. The remaining 90 percent just observe what's on the site, so they don't add a lot of value—other than adding to the number of "eyeballs" the site can claim when it tries to convince advertisers to buy space. How can a site convert lurkers into active users? The easier it is to participate, the more likely it is that the community can generate activity among a larger proportion of visitors. In part this means ensuring that there are several ways to participate that vary in ease of use. Facebook is an example of an online community that has figured out how to offer several forms of participation. Members can post status updates (very easy), make comments, upload pictures, share notes and links, play social games, answer quizzes, decorate their profiles, upload videos, and create events (a bit harder), among other forms of participation.

- **Crowd Power**—Social media change the fundamental relationship between marketers and consumers: Companies no longer market to customers, they market *with* them. Although many organizations resist this change, others build new business models on the **wisdom of crowds** perspective (from a book by that name). This argues that under the right circumstances, groups are smarter than the smartest people in them. If this is true, it implies that large numbers of consumers can predict successful products.[125] For example, at Threadless, customers rank T-shirt designs

Be Square
by Justin White

Really Exist
by Chow Hon Lam

Puppet In Love
by Lim Heng Swee

At *threadless.com*, users vote on which T-shirt designs the company will print and sell.

Source: © Threadless.com, 2009.

ahead of time, and the company prints the winning ideas. Every week, contestants upload T-shirt designs to the site, where about 700 compete to be among the 6 that are printed during that time. Threadless visitors score designs on a scale of 0 to 5, and the staff members select winners from the most popular entrants. The six lucky artists each get $2,000 in cash and merchandise. *Threadless sells out of every shirt it offers.* This business model has made a small fortune for a few designers "the crowd" particularly likes. One pair of Chicago-based artists sold $16 million worth of T-shirts. To keep the judges and buyers coming back, the owners offer rewards: Upload a photo of yourself wearing a Threadless T-shirt and you get a store credit of $1.50. Refer a friend who buys a T-shirt and you get $3. The site sells more than 1,500 T-shirts in a typical day.[126]

Here are some more crowd-based sites to watch:

- At Quirky, people submit ideas for innovative products like a Boil Buoy that floats in a pot and rings when it's hot, or Cordies that organize your power cords. Quirky's users choose the products they like; if the company gets a sufficient number of purchase commitments, the items are manufactured and sent.[127]
- Sermo is a social network for physicians. It has no advertising, job listings, or membership fees. It makes its money (about $500,000 a year so far) by charging institutional investors for the opportunity to listen in as approximately 15,000 doctors chat among themselves. Say, for example, a young patient breaks out in hives after he takes a new prescription. A doctor might post whether she thinks this is a rare symptom or a drug side effect. If other doctors feel it's the latter, this negative news could affect the drug manufacturer's stock, so their opinions have value to analysts. Doctors who ask or answer a question that paying observers deem especially valuable receive bonuses of $5 to $25 per post.[128]
- How about social networking sites that "create" a concert as they persuade an artist to perform in a certain city or country? At Eventful.com, fans demand events and performances in their town and spread the word to make them happen. Or how about actually buying a piece of the bands you like? Go to SellaBand, where fans ("believers") buy "parts" in a band for $10 per share. Once the band sells 5,000 parts, SellaBand arranges a professional recording, including top studios, A&R (Artists & Repertoire) managers (industry talent scouts), and producers. Believers receive a limited-edition CD of the recording. Believers get a piece of the profits, so they're likely to promote the band wherever they can.[129]
- The St. Louis Cardinals invited fans to send the team scouting reports on promising college players. The idea is to collect intelligence on talent at small colleges that scouts don't routinely visit. One of the team's executives explained, "We don't have a monopoly on baseball knowledge. Just looking at the fan sites and posting boards, you see an amazing amount of energy. Why not harness it?"[130]

Thousands of in-world residents design, create, and purchase clothing, furniture, houses, vehicles, and other products their avatars need—and many do it in style as they acquire the kind of "bling" they can only dream about in real life. Some forward-thinking marketers understand that these platforms are the next stage they can use to introduce their products into people's lives, whether real or virtual. Today, for example, people who play *The Sims* can import actual pieces of furniture from IKEA into their virtual homes; the use of this sort of platform to accelerate purchases for real homes is unplowed ground. With more than 150 of these immersive 3-D environments now live or in development, we may well see other social networks like Facebook migrate to these platforms in the near future. Whether via your computer or even your cell phone, you and your "friends" will hang out together (or at least your avatars will), and you'll shop and compare your choices wherever you are (hopefully not in class!). This is *not* a fad: As of 2011, more than 1 billion people worldwide were registered in at least one virtual world.

CHAPTER SUMMARY

Now that you have finished reading this chapter you should understand why:

1. **Other people and groups, especially those who possess some kind of social power, often influence our decisions about what to buy.**

We belong to or admire many different groups, and a desire for them to accept us often drives our purchase decisions. Individuals or groups whose opinions or behavior are particularly important to consumers are reference groups. Both formal and informal groups influence the individual's purchase decisions, although such factors as the conspicuousness of the product and the relevance of the reference group for a particular purchase determine how influential the reference group is.

Individuals have influence in a group to the extent that they possess social power. Types of social power include information power, referent power, legitimate power, expert power, reward power, and coercive power.

2. **We seek out others who share our interests in products or services.**

Brand communities unite consumers who share a common passion for a product. Brandfests, which companies organize to encourage this kind of community, can build brand loyalty and reinforce group membership.

3. **We are motivated to buy or use products in order to be consistent with what other people do.**

We conform to the desires of others for two basic reasons: (1) People who model their behavior after others because they take others' behavior as evidence of the correct way to act are conforming because of informational social influence; and (2) those who conform to satisfy the expectations of others or to be accepted by the group are affected by normative social influence. Group members often do things they would not do as individuals because their identities become merged with the group; they become deindividuated.

4. **Certain people are especially likely to influence others' product choices.**

Opinion leaders who are knowledgeable about a product and whose opinions are highly regarded tend to influence others' choices. Specific opinion leaders are somewhat hard to identify, but marketers who know their general characteristics can try to target them in their media and promotional strategies. Other influencers include market mavens, who have a general interest in marketplace activities; and surrogate consumers, who are compensated for their advice about purchases.

5. **The things other consumers tell us about products (good and bad) often are more influential than the advertising we see.**

Much of what we know about products we learn through word-of-mouth (WOM) communication rather than formal advertising. We tend to exchange product-related information in casual conversations. Guerrilla marketing strategies try to accelerate the WOM process when they enlist consumers to help spread the word. Although WOM often is helpful to make consumers aware of products, it can also hurt companies when damaging product rumors or negative WOM occur.

6. **Online technologies accelerate the impact of word-of-mouth communication.**

The Web greatly amplifies our exposure to numerous reference groups. Virtual consumption communities unites those who share a common bond—usually enthusiasm about or knowledge of a specific product or service. Emerging marketing strategies try to leverage the potential of the Web to spread information from consumer to consumer extremely quickly. Viral marketing techniques enlist individuals to tout products, services, Web sites, and so on to others on behalf of companies. Blogging allows consumers to easily post their thoughts about products for others to see.

7. **Social media are changing the way companies and consumers interact.**

Social networking, where members post information and make contact with others who share similar interests and opinions, changes the way we think about marketing. As Web 2.0 continues to develop, companies and consumers increasingly interact directly. The wisdom-of-crowds perspective argues that under the right circumstances, groups are smarter than the smartest people in them. If this is true, it implies that large numbers of consumers can predict successful products.[132] In a sense, a lot of social networking sites let their members dictate purchase decisions.

KEY TERMS

antibrand communities
aspirational reference group
avoidance groups
brand community
brandfests
coercive power
cohesiveness
collective value creation
community
comparative influence
conformity
consumer tribe
cyberbullying
cyberplace
decision polarization
deindividuation
democracy
digital virtual consumption (DVC)
expert power
flaming
flows
folksonomy
home shopping party
homophily
influence impressions

influence network
information cascades
information power
interactions
legitimate power
lurkers
market maven
Mass Connectors
media democratization
media multiplexity
meetups
membership reference group
mere exposure phenomenon
MMOGS (massive multiplayer online games)
momentum effect
name-letter effect
negative word-of-mouth
network units
nodes
normative influence
norms
object sociality
opinion leader
passion-centric

power users
presence
principle of least interest
propinquity
reference group
referent power
reward power
risky shift effect
social graphs
social loafing
social network
social object theory
social power
sociometric methods
surrogate consumer
tie strength
ties
tribal marketing strategy
two step flow model of influence
urban myth
viral marketing
virtual goods
virtual worlds
wisdom of crowds
word-of-mouth (WOM)

REVIEW

1 Name two dimensions that influence whether reference groups affect an individual's purchase decisions.
2 List three types of social power, and give an example of each.
3 Which tend to influence our behavior more: large formal groups or small informal groups? Why?
4 What is a brand community, and why is it of interest to marketers?
5 Describe the difference between a membership and an aspirational reference group and give an example of each kind.
6 Name one factor that makes it more likely a person will become part of a consumer's membership reference group.
7 Define *deindividuation* and give an example of this effect.
8 What is the risky shift, and how does it relate to shopping with friends?
9 What is the difference between normative and informational social influence?

10 Define *conformity* and give an example of it. Name three reasons why people conform.
11 How does the Principle of Least Interest relate to your success in a romantic relationship?
12 What is *social comparison*? To what type of person do we usually choose to compare ourselves?
13 What is the difference between independence and anticonformity?
14 What is word-of-mouth, and how can it be more powerful than advertising?
15 Which is more powerful: positive or negative word of mouth?
16 Describe some ways in which marketers use the Internet to encourage positive WOM.
17 What is viral marketing? Guerrilla marketing? Give an example of each.

18 What is an opinion leader? Give three reasons why they are powerful influences on consumers' opinions. What are some characteristics of opinion leaders?

19 Is there such a thing as a generalized opinion leader? Why or why not?

20 What is the relationship between an opinion leader and an opinion seeker?

21 What is the difference between a market maven and a surrogate consumer?

22 How can marketers use opinion leaders to help them promote their products or services?

23 What are sociometric techniques? Under what conditions does it make sense to use them?

CONSUMER BEHAVIOR CHALLENGE

■ DISCUSS

1 Although social networking is red-hot, could its days be numbered? Many people have concerns about privacy issues. Others feel that platforms like Facebook are too overwhelming. As one media executive comments, "Nobody has 5,000 real friends. At the end of the day it just becomes one big cauldron of noise." What's your stand on this: Can we have too much of a good thing? Will people start to tune out all of these networks?[133]

2 The average American teenager spends well over 8 hours a day in front of a screen, whether smartphone, PC, TV, or tablet. One study reported increasing physical isolation among Internet users; it created a controversy and drew angry complaints from some users who insisted that time they spent online did not detract from their social relationships. However, the researchers said they had now gathered further evidence showing that Internet use has lowered the amount of time people spend socializing with friends and even sleeping. According to the study, an hour of time spent using the Internet reduces face-to-face contact with friends, coworkers, and family by 23.5 minutes; lowers the amount of time spent watching television by 10 minutes; and reduces sleep time by 8.5 minutes.[134] What's your perspective on this issue? Does increasing use of the Internet have positive or negative implications for interpersonal relationships in our society?

3 The Word-of-Mouth Marketing Association announced a set of rules and guidelines for word-of-mouth advertising. The trade group maintains that marketers must make sure that people talking up products or services disclose for whom they work. They also must use real consumers, not actors, who discuss what they really believe about a product.[135] The rules were prompted by several controversial incidents, such as a campaign the U.S. arm of Sony Ericsson Mobile Communications created for a camera phone. The company hired 60 actors to hang out at tourist attractions and ask unsuspecting passersby to take their pictures with the Sony Ericsson devices. It told the actors to identify themselves only when asked directly. What do you think about "stealth" campaigns such as this? Should marketers be required to disclose their true intentions when they try to initiate positive word-of-mouth?

4 Do you agree that deindividuation encourages binge drinking on campus? What can or should a college do to discourage this behavior?

5 The adoption of a certain brand of shoe or apparel by athletes can be a powerful influence on students and other fans. Should high school and college coaches be paid to determine what brand of athletic equipment their players wear?

6 The strategy of viral marketing gets customers to sell a product to other customers on behalf of the company. That often means convincing your friends to climb on the bandwagon, and sometimes you get a cut if they buy something.[136] Some might argue that that means you're selling out your friends (or at least selling to your friends) in exchange for a piece of the action. Others might say you're simply sharing the wealth with your buddies. Have you ever passed along names of your friends or sent them to a Web site such as hotmail.com? If so, what happened? How do you feel about this practice?

7 Are home shopping parties that put pressure on friends and neighbors to buy merchandise ethical?

8 The high-profile stunt to publicize *Aqua Teen Hunger Force* created a massive public disruption. When does a guerrilla marketing tactic go too far—or is anything fair game in the heated competition to capture jaded consumers' attention?

9 Mobile social networking is the next frontier in technology, as companies race to adapt platforms like Facebook to our cell phones. Marketers are not far behind, especially because there are 3.3 billion cell phone subscribers worldwide; that number is far greater than the number of Internet users. One report says that about 2 percent of all mobile users already use their cell phones for social networking, such as chat and multimedia sharing; it forecasts that this proportion will zoom to at least 12.5 percent in a few years. Mobile social networks are appealing in part because companies can identify precisely where users are in the physical world. For example, the SpaceMe service from GyPSii displays a map that identifies your friends' locations as well as photos, videos, and other information about them. A Dutch network called Bliin lets users update their location every 15 seconds.[137] This enhanced capability creates some fascinating marketing possibilities—but perhaps it also raises some ethical red flags. What do you see as the opportunities and the threats as we inevitably move to a world where our whereabouts are known to others?

10 Walmart contended with a widespread text-messaging hoax that warned women to stay away from its stores or risk death. The digital rumor apparently originated in an **urban myth** (an unsubstantiated "fact" that many people accept as true) that circulated via email several years ago. As a reflection of how widespread this myth became, at one point Walmart was number 5 on Twitter's list of trending topics.[138] If you were a Walmart communications executive, how might you deal with this kind of public relations nightmare?

■ APPLY

1 The power of unspoken social norms often becomes obvious only when we violate them. To witness this result firsthand, try one of the following: Stand facing the back wall in an elevator, serve dessert before the main course, offer to pay cash for dinner at a friend's home, wear pajamas to class, or tell someone *not* to have a nice day.

2 Identify a set of avoidance groups for your peers. Can you identify any consumption decisions that you and your friends make with these groups in mind?

3 Identify fashion opinion leaders on your campus. Do they fit the profile the chapter describes?

4 Conduct a sociometric analysis within your dormitory or neighborhood. For a product category such as music or cars, ask each individual to identify other individuals with whom they share information. Systematically trace all of these avenues of communication, and identify opinion

leaders by locating individuals whom others say provide helpful information.

5 See if you can demonstrate the risky shift. Get a group of friends together and ask each to privately rate the likelihood, on a scale from 1 to 7, that they would try a controversial new product (e.g., a credit card that works with a chip implanted in a person's wrist). Then ask the group to discuss the product and rate the idea again. If the average rating changes, you've just observed a risky shift.

6 Trace a referral pattern for a service provider such as a hair stylist; track how clients came to choose him or her. See if you can identify opinion leaders who are responsible for referring several clients to the businessperson. How might the service provider take advantage of this process to grow his or her business?

Case Study

AN OPINION LEADER MIRACLE?

How does a sandwich spread that's been around since the 1930s engage a younger generation? Miracle Whip took this challenge in 2010 with its "We are Miracle Whip and we will not tone it down" campaign. The brand secured product placement in the Lady Gaga music video *Telephone* as well as the video game *Skate 3*. It also ran television advertising targeted to the 18- to 35-year-old market that advised, "Don't go unnoticed, don't blend in, don't be ordinary, boring or bland: In other words, don't be so mayo."

Miracle Whip's public relations bonanza began quickly after the campaign was launched. After Stephen Colbert of Comedy Central's *The Colbert Report* aired the new television ad, he stated that he was offended by the statement "Don't be so mayo," and that he has had it with the "mayo-nay-sayers." Colbert then

ran a mayonnaise parody ad that featured similar characters and a voiceover that proclaimed, "Don't be a miracle wimp."

The ball was squarely in Miracle Whip's court. The brand responded by buying ad time on Colbert's next show; it ran new ads directed to Stephen Colbert, "mayo-lover," who "viciously" attacked the product on his show. Colbert, wanting to get the last word, went on the night after the Miracle Whip ads aired and thanked the company for their advertising. He noted, "I could certainly use the money to buy more delicious mayonnaise."

Miracle Whip continued to create more controversy as it moved to its "Love us or Hate us" campaign. This initiative launched with television ads featuring everyday people and celebrities as they talked about their feelings toward Miracle Whip. Some of the reviews weren't very complimentary;

comments like "Miracle Whip tastes like lotion but sweet" and "I could never date anyone who likes Miracle Whip" don't sell a lot of jars. Pauly from the reality television show *Jersey Shore* even claimed, "I would never eat it, I would never put it in my hair." Consumers are directed through the ads to Miracle Whip's YouTube channel. If they click over, in addition to scoring a free sample, they can vote to "love us or hate us." It seems that Whip lovers were motivated to tune in, as more than 50,000 voted to love the brand while only a small fraction of that number said they hate the spread.

DISCUSSION QUESTIONS

1 In what way is Miracle Whip using reference groups and opinion leaders?

2 Do you think these groups will influence other consumers to purchase a low-involvement product like sandwich spread?

3 What would you guess was Miracle Whip's rationale for airing negative comments about the product on television?

4 Is Miracle Whip trying to build a brand community?

Sources: T. L. Stanley, "Miracle Whip Ads: Love Them or Hate Them?," *Adweek* (February 24, 2011), *http://www.adweek.com/adfreak/miracle-whip-ads-love-them-or-hate-them-127028*, accessed June 15, 2011; Emily Bryson York, "Miracle Whip Ad Campaign to Spread 'Boring' Mayo Message," *Advertising Age* (March 22, 2010), *http://adage.com/article/news/miracle-whip-campaign-spread-boring-mayo-message/142914/*, accessed June 15, 2011.

NOTES

1. http://freecountry.harley-davidson.com/landing.php, accessed June 15, 2011.
2. http://www.harley-davidson.com/browse/browse_categories. jsp?WebLogicSession=N3ErFgFyvT2Aiw6MWlyasMkqO sqqZrbOvNQIoR4HpGugrh1zxE0o!-36114594!hiwpbmsp04. ihd.hd!7005!8005&FOLDER%3C%3Efolder_id= 1408474395439177&locale=en_US&bmUID=1308066867683&bmLocale =en_US, accessed June 15, 2011.
3. Details adapted from John W. Schouten and James H. McAlexander, "Market Impact of a Consumption Subculture: The Harley-Davidson Mystique," in Fred van Raaij and Gary Bamossy, eds., *Proceedings of the 1992 European Conference of the Association for Consumer Research* (Amsterdam, 1992); John W. Schouten and James H. McAlexander, "Subcultures of Consumption: An Ethnography of the New Bikers," *Journal of Consumer Research* 22 (June 1995): 43–61. See also Kelly Barron, "Hog Wild," *Forbes* (May 15, 2000), http://www.forbes.com/forbes/2000/0515/6511068a.html.
4. Joel B. Cohen and Ellen Golden, "Informational Social Influence and Product Evaluation," *Journal of Applied Psychology* 56 (February 1972): 54–59; Robert E. Burnkrant and Alain Cousineau, "Informational and Normative Social Influence in Buyer Behavior," *Journal of Consumer Research* 2 (December 1975): 206–15; Peter H. Reingen, "Test of a List Procedure for Inducing Compliance with a Request to Donate Money," *Journal of Applied Psychology* 67 (1982): 110–18.
5. Dyan Machan, "Is the Hog Going Soft?," *Forbes* (March 10, 1997): 114–19.
6. C. Whan Park and V. Parker Lessig, "Students and Housewives: Differences in Susceptibility to Reference Group Influence," *Journal of Consumer Research* 4 (September 1977): 102–10.
7. Gina Kolata, "Study Finds Big Social Factor in Quitting Smoking," *New York Times* (May 22, 2008), www.nytimes.com/2008/05/22/science/22smoke .html?ex=1369195200&en=0a10910fcde1a1ac&ei=5124&partner=perm alink&exprod=permalink, accessed May 22, 2008.
8. Jeffrey D. Ford and Elwood A. Ellis, "A Re-examination of Group Influence on Member Brand Preference," *Journal of Marketing Research* 17 (February 1980): 125–32; Thomas S. Robertson, *Innovative Behavior and Communication* (New York: Holt, Rinehart & Winston, 1980), ch. 8.
9. Leslie Kaufman, "Utilities Turn Their Customers Green, With Envy," *New York Times* (January 30, 2009), http://www.nytimes.com/2009/01/31/ science/earth/31compete.html?scp=1&sq=Utilities%20Turn%20 their%20customers%20green&st=cse, accessed January 31, 2009.
10. Kenneth J. Gergen and Mary Gergen, *Social Psychology* (New York: Harcourt Brace Jovanovich, 1981): 312.
11. J. R. P. French, Jr., and B. Raven, "The Bases of Social Power," in D. Cartwright, ed., *Studies in Social Power* (Ann Arbor, MI: Institute for Social Research, 1959): 150–67.
12. Michael R. Solomon, "Packaging the Service Provider," *The Service Industries Journal* 5 (March 1985): 64–72.
13. Tamar Charry, "Unconventional Spokesmen Talk up U.S. Robotics' Fast Modems in a New TV Campaign," *New York Times* (February 6, 1997), http://www.nytimes.com/1997/02/06/business/

unconventional-spokesmen-talk-up-us-robotics-fast-modems-in-a-new-tv-campaign.html?scp=44&sq=Tamar+Charry&st=nyt, accessed September 13, 2011.
14. Patricia M. West and Susan M. Broniarczyk, "Integrating Multiple Opinions: The Role of Aspiration Level on Consumer Response to Critic Consensus," *Journal of Consumer Research* 25 (June 1998): 38–51.
15. Gergen and Gergen, *Social Psychology*.
16. Stephanie Rosenbloom, "Names That Match Forge a Bond on the Internet," *New York Times*, (April 10, 2008), www.nytimes.com/2008/04/10/ us/10names.html?ref=us, accessed April 10, 2008.
17. Harold H. Kelley, "Two Functions of Reference Groups," in Harold Proshansky and Bernard Siedenberg, eds., *Basic Studies in Social Psychology* (New York: Holt, Rinehart & Winston, 1965): 210–14.
18. http://halo.xbox.com/en-us/intel/titles/halo2, accessed June 15, 2011; Kris Oser, "Microsoft's Halo 2 Soars on Viral Push," *Advertising Age* (October 25, 2004): 46.
19. Hope Jensen Schau, Albert M. Muñiz, Jr., and Eric J. Arnould, "How Brand Community Practices Create Value," *Journal of Marketing* 73 (September 2009), 30–51; John W. Schouten, James H. McAlexander, and Harold F. Koenig. "Transcendent Customer Experience and Brand Community." *Journal of the Academy of Marketing Science* 35 (2007): 357–68; James H. McAlexander, John W. Schouten, and Harold F. Koenig, "Building Brand Community," *Journal of Marketing* 66 (January 2002): 38–54; Albert Muñiz and Thomas O'Guinn, "Brand Community," *Journal of Consumer Research* (March 2001): 412–32; Scott A. Thompson and Rajiv K. Sinha, "Brand Communities and New Product Adoption: The Influence and Limits of Oppositional Loyalty," *Journal of Marketing* 72 (November 2008): 65–80.
20. Rama K. Jayanti and Jagdip Singh, "Framework for Distributed Consumer Learning in Online Communities," *Journal of Consumer Research* 36, no. 6 (2010): 1058–81.
21. Schau, Muñiz, and Arnould, "How Brand Community Practices Create Value."
22. Veronique Cova and Bernard Cova, "Tribal Aspects of Postmodern Consumption Research: The Case of French In-Line Roller Skaters," *Journal of Consumer Behavior* 1 (June 2001): 67–76.
23. http://www.sneakerfiles.com/2011/06/15/air-jordan-xii-12-dwyane-wade-player-exclusive/, accessed June 15, 2011; Jennifer Edson Escalas and James R. Bettman, "You Are What You Eat: The Influence of Reference Groups on Consumers' Connections to Brands," *Journal of Consumer Psychology* 13, no. 3 (2003): 339–48.
24. A. Benton Cocanougher and Grady D. Bruce, "Socially Distant Reference Groups and Consumer Aspirations," *Journal of Marketing Research* 8 (August 1971): 79–81.
25. Nick Bilton, "Twitter Users Congregate Based on Mood, Study Says," *New York Times* (March 16, 2011), http://bits.blogs.nytimes.com/2011/03/16/twitter-users-congregate-based-on-mood-study-says/, accessed April 29, 2011.
26. A. Benton Cocanougher and Grady D. Bruce, "Socially Distant Reference Groups and Consumer Aspirations," *Journal of Marketing Research* 8 (August 1971): 79–81.

27. R. B. Zajonc, H. M. Markus, and W. Wilson, "Exposure Effects and Associative Learning," *Journal of Experimental Social Psychology* 10 (1974): 248–63.

28. D. J. Stang, "Methodological Factors in Mere Exposure Research," *Psychological Bulletin* 81 (1974): 1014–25; R. B. Zajonc, P. Shaver, C. Tavris, and D. Van Kreveid, "Exposure, Satiation and Stimulus Discriminability," *Journal of Personality & Social Psychology* 21 (1972): 270–80.

29. J. E. Grush, K. L. McKeogh, and R. F. Ahlering, "Extrapolating Laboratory Exposure Research to Actual Political Elections," *Journal of Personality & Social Psychology* 36 (1978): 257–70.

30. Barry Rehfeld, "At These Camps, Everybody Is a Star (If Only for a Day)," *New York Times* (June 12, 2005), http://www.nytimes.com/2005/06/12/business/yourmoney/12fantasy.html?scp=1&sq=Barry%20Rehfeld,%20%E2%80%9CAt%20These%20Camps,%20Everybody%20Is%20a%20Star%20(If%20Only%20for%20a%20Day)&st=cse, accessed June 12, 2005.

31. Jonah Berger and Lindsay Rand, "Shifting Signals to Help Health: Using Identity Signaling to Reduce Risky Health Behaviors," *Journal of Consumer Research* 35, no. 3 (2008): 509–18.

32. Basil G. Englis and Michael R. Solomon, "To Be and Not to Be: Reference Group Stereotyping and the Clustering of America," *Journal of Advertising* 24 (Spring 1995): 13–28; Michael R. Solomon and Basil G. Englis, "I Am Not, Therefore I Am: The Role of Anti-Consumption in the Process of Self-Definition" (special session at the Association for Consumer Research meetings, October 1996, Tucson, Arizona; cf. also Brendan Richardson and Darach Turley, "Support Your Local Team: Resistance, Subculture and the Desire for Distinction," *Advances in Consumer Research* 33, no. 1 (2006): 175–80.

33. Bruce Feirstein, *Real Men Don't Eat Quiche* (New York: Pocket Books, 1982); www.auntiefashions.com, accessed December 31, 2002; Katherine White and Darren W. Dahl, "Are All Out-Groups Created Equal? Consumer Identity and Dissociative Influence," *Journal of Consumer Research* 34 (December 2007): 525–36.

34. http://boardoutmind.livejournal.com/, accessed June 15, 2011; Rob Walker, "Anti-Fan Club," *New York Times* (November 26, 2006), www.nytimes.com, accessed November 26, 2006.

35. Candice R. Hollenbeck and George M. Zinkhan, "Consumer Activism on the Internet: The Role of Anti-Brand Communities," *Advances in Consumer Research* 33, no. 1 (2006): 479–85.

36. Marius K. Luedicke, "Brand Community under Fire: The Role of Social Environments for the Hummer Brand Community," *Advances in Consumer Research* 33, no. 1 (2006): 486–93.

37. B. Latane, K. Williams, and S. Harkins, "Many Hands Make Light the Work: The Causes and Consequences of Social Loafing," *Journal of Personality & Social Psychology* 37 (1979): 822–32.

38. S. Freeman, M. Walker, R. Borden, and B. Latane, "Diffusion of Responsibility and Restaurant Tipping: Cheaper by the Bunch," *Personality & Social Psychology Bulletin* 1 (1978): 584–87.

39. Nathan Kogan and Michael A. Wallach, "Risky Shift Phenomenon in Small Decision-Making Groups: A Test of the Information Exchange Hypothesis," *Journal of Experimental Social Psychology* 3 (January 1967): 75–84; Nathan Kogan and Michael A. Wallach, *Risk Taking* (New York: Holt, Rinehart & Winston, 1964); Arch G. Woodside and M. Wayne DeLozier, "Effects of Word-of-Mouth Advertising on Consumer Risk Taking," *Journal of Advertising* (Fall 1976): 12–19.

40. Kogan and Wallach, *Risk Taking*.

41. Roger Brown, *Social Psychology* (New York: Free Press, 1965).

42. David L. Johnson and I. R. Andrews, "Risky Shift Phenomenon Tested with Consumer Product Stimuli," *Journal of Personality & Social Psychology* 20 (1971): 382–85; see also Vithala R. Rao and Joel H. Steckel, "A Polarization Model for Describing Group Preferences," *Journal of Consumer Research* 18 (June 1991): 108–18.

43. Donald H. Granbois, "Improving the Study of Customer In-Store Behavior," *Journal of Marketing* 32 (October 1968): 28–32; Tamara F. Mangleburg, Patricia M. Doney, and Terry Bristol, "Shopping with Friends and Teens' Susceptibility to Peer Influence," *Journal of Retailing* 80 (2004): 101–16.

44. Len Strazewski, "Tupperware Locks in New Strategy," *Advertising Age* (February 8, 1988): 30.

45. Melanie Wells, "Smooth Operator," *Forbes* (May 13, 2002): 167–68.

46. Luc Sante, "Be Different! (Like Everyone Else!)," *New York Times Magazine* (October 17, 1999), www.nytimes.com, accessed October 3, 2007.

47. Tanya Irwin, "Study: Facebook Users Show 'Herding Instinct,'" *Marketing Daily* (October 12, 2010), http://www.mediapost.com/publications/?fa=Articles.showArticle&art_aid=137340&nid=119587, accessed April 29, 2011.

48. For a study that attempted to measure individual differences in proclivity to conformity, see William O. Bearden, Richard G. Netemeyer, and Jesse E. Teel, "Measurement of Consumer Susceptibility to Interpersonal Influence," *Journal of Consumer Research* 15 (March 1989): 473–81.

49. John W. Thibaut and Harold H. Kelley, *The Social Psychology of Groups* (New York: Wiley, 1959); W. W. Waller and R. Hill, *The Family, a Dynamic Interpretation* (New York: Dryden, 1951).

50. Bearden, Netemeyer, and Teel, "Measurement of Consumer Susceptibility to Interpersonal Influence"; Lynn R. Kahle, "Observations: Role-Relaxed Consumers: A Trend of the Nineties," *Journal of Advertising Research* (March–April 1995): 66–71; Lynn R. Kahle and Aviv Shoham, "Observations: Role-Relaxed Consumers: Empirical Evidence," *Journal of Advertising Research* (May–June 1995): 59–62.

51. Sam Schechner, "When Your Political Opinion Isn't Yours Alone: Broadcasts of Political Debates That Include Live Audience Feedback Can Influence What You're Thinking—Hecklers Can, Too," *Wall Street Journal* (October 10, 2008), http://online.wsj.com/article/SB122359949981721549.html, accessed October 11, 2008.

52. Amy Chozick, "Cold Stone Aims to Be Hip in Japan Ice-Cream Chain, Uses Word-of-Mouth as Part of Bid for an Urban Image," *Wall Street Journal* (December 14, 2006): B10.

53. Everett M. Rogers, *Diffusion of Innovations*, 3rd ed. (New York: Free Press, 1983); cf. also Duncan J. Watts and Peter Sheridan Dodds, "Influentials, Networks, and Public Opinion Formation," *Journal of Consumer Research* 34 (December 2007): 441–58; Morris B. Holbrook and Michela Addis, "Taste versus the Market: An Extension of Research on the Consumption of Popular Culture," *Journal of Consumer Research* 34 (October 2007): 415–24.

54. Dorothy Leonard-Barton, "Experts as Negative Opinion Leaders in the Diffusion of a Technological Innovation," *Journal of Consumer Research* 11 (March 1985): 914–26; Rogers, *Diffusion of Innovations*; cf. also Jan Kratzer and Christopher Lettl, "Distinctive Roles of Lead Users and Opinion Leaders in the Social Networks of Schoolchildren," *Journal of Consumer Research* 36 December (2009): 646–59.

55. Herbert Menzel, "Interpersonal and Unplanned Communications: Indispensable or Obsolete?," in Edward B. Roberts, ed., *Biomedical Innovation* (Cambridge, MA: MIT Press, 1981), 155–63.

56. Meera P. Venkatraman, "Opinion Leaders, Adopters, and Communicative Adopters: A Role Analysis," *Psychology & Marketing* 6 (Spring 1989): 51–68.

57. Rogers, *Diffusion of Innovations*.

58. Karl Greenberg, "Ford Puts Trendsetters Behind Wheel in VIP Events," *Marketing Daily* (November 11, 2008), www.mediapost.com/publications/?fa=Articles.san&s=94582&Nid=49281&p=407, accessed November 11, 2008.

59. Robert Merton, *Social Theory and Social Structure* (Glencoe, IL: Free Press, 1957).

60. Center for Media Research, "Inconspicuous, But Influential" (December 26, 2008), www.mediapost.com, accessed December 26, 2008.

61. Charles W. King and John O. Summers, "Overlap of Opinion Leadership across Consumer Product Categories," *Journal of Marketing Research* 7 (February 1970): 43–50.; see also Ronald E. Goldsmith, Jeanne R. Heitmeyer, and Jon B. Freiden, "Social Values and Fashion Leadership," *Clothing & Textiles Research Journal* 10 (Fall 1991): 37–45; J. O. Summers, "Identity of Women's Clothing Fashion Opinion Leaders," *Journal of Marketing Research* 7 (1970): 178–85.

62. Duncan J. Watts and Peter Sheridan Dodds, "Influentials, Networks, and Public Opinion Formation," *Journal of Consumer Research* 34 (December 2007): 441–58.

63. http://klout.com/home, accessed June 15, 2011.

64. Matthew Creamer, "Your Followers Are No Measure of Your Influence," *Advertising Age* (January 3, 2011), http://adage.com/article/special-report-influencers-2010/facebook-followers-measure-influence/147957/, accessed April 30, 2011.

65. Steven A. Baumgarten, "The Innovative Communicator in the Diffusion Process," *Journal of Marketing Research* 12 (February 1975): 12–18.

66. Laura J. Yale and Mary C. Gilly, "Dyadic Perceptions in Personal Source Information Search," *Journal of Business Research* 32 (1995): 225–37.

67. Russell W. Belk, "Occurrence of Word-of-Mouth Buyer Behavior as a Function of Situation and Advertising Stimuli," in Fred C. Allvine, ed., *Combined Proceedings of the American Marketing Association*, series no. 33 (Chicago: American Marketing Association, 1971): 419–22.

68. Lawrence F. Feick, Linda L. Price, and Robin A. Higie, "People Who Use People: The Other Side of Opinion Leadership," in Richard J. Lutz, ed., *Advances in Consumer Research 13* (Provo, UT: Association for Consumer Research, 1986): 301–5.

69. Stephanie Clifford, "Spreading the Word (and the Lotion) in Small-Town Alaska," *New York Times* (October 8, 2008), www.nytimes.com/2008/10/09/business/media/09adco.html, accessed October 9, 2008.

70. For discussion of the market maven construct, see Lawrence F. Feick and Linda L. Price, "The Market Maven," *Managing* (July 1985): 10; scale items adapted from Lawrence F. Feick and Linda L. Price, "The Market Maven: A Diffuser of Marketplace Information," *Journal of Marketing* 51 (January 1987): 83–87; Ronald A. Clark, Ronald E. Goldsmith, and Elizabeth B. Goldsmith,

"Market Mavenism and Consumer Self-Confidence," *Journal of Consumer Behavior* 7 (2008): 239–48.

71. Michael R. Solomon, "The Missing Link: Surrogate Consumers in the Marketing Chain," *Journal of Marketing* 50 (October 1986): 208–18.

72. Patricia Odell, "Pepsi Uses 'Influencers' to Launch a New Product," *PROMO* (June 18, 2009), www.promomagazine.com, accessed June 18, 2009.

73. Barbara Stern and Stephen J. Gould, "The Consumer as Financial Opinion Leader," *Journal of Retail Banking* 10 (1988): 47–49.

74. William R. Darden and Fred D. Reynolds, "Predicting Opinion Leadership for Men's Apparel Fashions," *Journal of Marketing Research* 1 (August 1972): 324–28. A modified version of the opinion leadership scale with improved reliability and validity appears in Terry L. Childers, "Assessment of the Psychometric Properties of an Opinion Leadership Scale," *Journal of Marketing Research* 23 (May 1986): 184–88.

75. Dan Seligman, "Me and Monica," *Forbes* (March 23, 1998): 76.

76. Gina Kolata, "Find Yourself Packing It On? Blame Friends," *New York Times* (July 26, 2007), *www.nytimes.com*, accessed July 26, 2007.

77. "Referrals Top Ads as Influence on Patients' Doctor Selections," *Marketing News* (January 30, 1987): 22.

78. Peter H. Reingen and Jerome B. Kernan, "Analysis of Referral Networks in Marketing: Methods and Illustration," *Journal of Marketing Research* 23 (November 1986): 370–78.

79. Peter H. Reingen, Brian L. Foster, Jacqueline Johnson Brown, and Stephen B. Seidman, "Brand Congruence in Interpersonal Relations: A Social Network Analysis," *Journal of Consumer Research* 11 (December 1984): 771–83; see also James C. Ward and Peter H. Reingen, "Sociocognitive Analysis of Group Decision-Making among Consumers," *Journal of Consumer Research* 17 (December 1990): 245–62.

80. Jenna Wortham, "What's the Value of a Facebook Friend? About 37 Cents," *New York Times* (January 9, 2009), www.nytimes.com, accessed January 9, 2009.

81. Ed Keller and Jon Berry. *The Influentials* (New York: Simon & Schuster, 2003).

82. "Introducing Peer Influence Analysis: 500 Billion Peer Impressions Each Year," *Empowered*, (April 20, 2010), http://forrester.typepad.com/groundswell/2010/04/introducing-peer-influence-analysis.html, accessed December 31, 2010.

83. "MySpace, Isobar & Carat, Never Ending Friending: A Journey into Social Networking," http://creative.myspace.com/groups/_ms/nef/images/40161_nef_onlinebook.pdf, accessed December 31, 2010; cf. also Malcolm Gladwell, *The Tipping Point* (New York: Little, Brown, 2000).

84. Pat Wechsler, "A Curiously Strong Campaign," *BusinessWeek* (April 21, 1997): 134.

85. Johan Arndt, "Role of Product-Related Conversations in the Diffusion of a New Product," *Journal of Marketing Research* 4 (August 1967): 291–95.

86. Quoted in Sheila Shayon, "Teen Girls: Shopping and Texting, Texting and Shopping," *BrandChannel* (November 26, 2010), http://www.brandchannel.com/home/post/2010/11/26/Teen-Girls-Snapshot-Shopping-and-Social-Media.aspx, accessed February 23, 2011.

87. John Gaffney, "The Cool Kids Are Doing It. Should You?" *Asiaweek* (November 23, 2001): 1.

88. Douglas R. Pruden and Terry G. Vavra, "Controlling the Grapevine," *MM* (July–August 2004): 23–30.

89. www.bzzagent.com, accessed June 15, 2011.

90. Les Luchter, "Kraft, Folgers, Olay Top Baby Boomer Gals' WOM," *Marketing Daily*, (November 18, 2008), www.mediapost.com/publications/?fa=Articles.showArticle&art_aid=95000, accessed November 18, 2008.

91. Elihu Katz and Paul F. Lazarsfeld, *Personal Influence* (Glencoe, IL: Free Press, 1955).

92. John A. Martilla, "Word-of-Mouth Communication in the Industrial Adoption Process," *Journal of Marketing Research* 8 (March 1971): 173–78; see also Marsha L. Richins, "Negative Word-of-Mouth by Dissatisfied Consumers: A Pilot Study," *Journal of Marketing* 47 (Winter 1983): 68–78.

93. Arndt, "Role of Product-Related Conversations in the Diffusion of a New Product."

94. James H. Myers and Thomas S. Robertson, "Dimensions of Opinion Leadership," *Journal of Marketing Research* 9 (February 1972): 41–46.

95. Ellen Neuborne, "Generation Y," *BusinessWeek* (February 15, 1999): 86.

96. Leonard-Barton, "Experts as Negative Opinion Leaders in the Diffusion of a Technological Innovation."

97. James F. Engel, Robert J. Kegerreis, and Roger D. Blackwell, "Word-of-Mouth Communication by the Innovator," *Journal of Marketing* 33 (July 1969): 15–19; cf. also Rajdeep Growl, Thomas W. Cline, and Anthony Davies, "Early-Entrant Advantage, Word-of-Mouth Communication, Brand Similarity, and the Consumer Decision Making Process," *Journal of Consumer Psychology* 13, no. 3 (2003): 187–97.

98. Sung-Youl Jun, Taihoon Cha, and Praveen Aggarwal, "How Much Better? The Effect of Tensile Information on Word-of-Mouth Effectiveness," *Journal of Marketing Theory & Practice* 19, no. 3 (2011): 263–77; Praveen Aggarwal, Rajiv Vaidyanathan, and Alladi Venkatesh, "Using Lexical-Semantic Analysis to Derive Online Brand Perceptions: An Application to Retail Marketing Research," *Journal of Retailing* 85, no. 2 (2009): 145–58; Praveen Aggarwal and Tridib Mazumdar, "Delegation of Purchase Tasks: An Empirical Investigation," *Psychology & Marketing* 25, no. 1 (2008): 73–95.

99. Chip Walker, "Word-of-Mouth," *American Demographics* (July 1995): 38–44; Albert M. Muñiz, Jr., Thomas O'Guinn, and Gary Alan Fine, "Rumor in Brand Community," in Donald A. Hantula, ed., *Advances in Theory and Methodology in Social and Organizational Psychology: A Tribute to Ralph Rosnow* (Mahwah, NJ: Erlbaum, 2005); cf. also Gaby A. C. Schellekens, Peeter W. J. Verlegh, and Ale Smidts, "Language Abstraction in Word of Mouth," *Journal of Consumer Research* 37, no. 2 (2010): 207–23.

100. Richard J. Lutz, "Changing Brand Attitudes through Modification of Cognitive Structure," *Journal of Consumer Research* 1 (March 1975): 49–59. For some suggested remedies to bad publicity, see Mitch Griffin, Barry J. Babin, and Jill S. Attaway, "An Empirical Investigation of the Impact of Negative Public Publicity on Consumer Attitudes and Intentions," in Rebecca H. Holman and Michael R. Solomon, eds., *Advances in Consumer Research* 18 (Provo, UT: Association for Consumer Research, 1991): 334–41; Alice M. Tybout, Bobby J. Calder, and Brian Sternthal, "Using Information Processing Theory to Design Marketing Strategies," *Journal of Marketing Research* 18 (1981): 73–79; see also Russell N. Laczniak, Thomas E. DeCarlo, and Sridhar N. Ramaswami, "Consumers' Responses to Negative Word-of-Mouth Communication: An Attribution Theory Perspective," *Journal of Consumer Psychology* 11, no. 1 (2001): 57–73.

101. Robert E. Smith and Christine A. Vogt, "The Effects of Integrating Advertising and Negative Word-of-Mouth Communications on Message Processing and Response," *Journal of Consumer Psychology* 4, no. 2 (1995): 133–51; Paula Fitzgerald Bone, "Word-of-Mouth Effects on Short-Term and Long-Term Product Judgments," *Journal of Business Research* 32 (1995): 213–23.

102. Keith Schneider, "Brands for the Chattering Masses," *New York Times* (December 17, 2006), *www.nytimes.com*, accessed October 3, 2007.

103. "Dunkin' Donuts Buys Out Critical Web Site," *New York Times* (August 27, 1999), *www.nytimes.com*, accessed August 27, 1999. For a discussion of ways to assess negative WOM online, cf. David M. Boush and Lynn R. Kahle, "Evaluating Negative Information in Online Consumer Discussions: From Qualitative Analysis to Signal Detection," *Journal of EuroMarketing* 11, no. 2 (2001): 89–105.

104. James C. Ward and Amy L. Ostrom, "Complaining to the Masses: The Role of Protest Framing in Customer-Created Complaint Web Sites," *Journal of Consumer Research* 33, no. 2 (2006): 220.

105. King and Summers, "Overlap of Opinion Leadership across Consumer Product Categories."

106. Michael Fumento, "Tampon Terrorism," *Forbes* (May 17, 1999): 170.

107. youtube.com/watch?v=y6t1R3yB-cs, accessed June 15, 2011.

108. Sonia Murray, "Street Marketing Does the Trick," *Advertising Age* (March 20, 2000): S12.

109. "Taking to the Streets," *Newsweek* (November 2, 1998): 70–73.

110. Karl Greenberg, "Scion's Web-Based Pre-Launch Scorns Tradition," *Marketing Daily* (March 6, 2007), www.mediapost.com, accessed March 6, 2007.

111. David Goetzl, "Boston Bomb Stunt Drove Online Traffic to Cartoon Network," *Marketing Daily* (February 5, 2007), www.mediapost.com, accessed February 5, 2007.

112. Melanie Wells, "Wabbing," *Forbes* (February 2, 2004): 84–88; Jeff Leeds, "The Next Hit Song? Ask P&G," *New York Times* (November 8, 2004), www.nytimes.com, accessed November 8, 2004.

113. Rob Walker, "The Hidden (in Plain Sight) Persuaders," *New York Times* (December 5, 2004), www.nytimes.com, accessed December 5, 2004.

114. Suzanne Vranica, "Guerrilla Marketing Takes a Soft-Boiled Approach: Public-Service Campaigns Are Now Using the Tactic; Smashing Eggs for Safety," *Wall Street Journal* (July 8, 2004): B4.

115. Kate Fitzgerald, "Branding Face to Face," *Advertising Age* (October 21, 2002): 47.

116. Michael Waltzer, "Petite Lap Giraffe: A Tiny Viral Marketing Success," Brandchannel (April 5, 2011), http://www.brandchannel.com/home/post/2011/04/05/Petite-Lap-Giraffe.aspx, accessed June 15, 2011.

117. The material in this section is adapted from Tracy Tuten and Michael R. Solomon, *Social Media Marketing* (Englewood Cliffs, NJ: Pearson, 2012).

118. Karlene Lukovitz, "Marketers Praise Skittles' Gutsy Site Move," *Marketing Daily* (March 3, 2009), www.mediapost.com, accessed March 3, 2009.

119. www.pandora.com, accessed June 15, 2011.

120. Barry Wellman, "Physical Place and Cyberplace: The Rise of Personalized Networking," *International Journal of Urban & Regional Research* 24, no. 2 (2001): 227–52.

121. Alexandra Marin and Barry Wellman, "Social Network Analysis: An Introduction," in *Handbook of Social Network Analysis* (London: Sage, 2010).

122. John Coate, "Cyberspace Innkeeping: Building Online Community" (1998), http://www.cervisa.com/innkeeping, accessed December 31, 2010.

123. T. B. Sheridan, "Further Musings on the Psychophysics of Presence," *Presence: Teleoperators and Virtual Environments* 5 (1994): 241–46.

124. Matthew Lombard and Theresa Ditton, "At the Heart of It All: The Concept of Presence," *Journal of Computer Mediated Communication* 3, no. 2 (1973), http://jcmc.indiana.edu/vol3/issue2/lombard.html, accessed December 31, 2010.

125. James Surowiecki, *The Wisdom of Crowds* (New York: Anchor, 2005); Jeff Howe, "The Rise of Crowdsourcing," *Wired* (June 2006), www.wired.com/wired/archive/14.06/crowds.html, accessed October 3, 2007.

126. Mark Weingarten, "Designed to Grow," *Business 2.0* (June 2007): 35–37. For a contrarian view, cf. Joseph P. Simmons, Leif D. Nelson, Jeff Galak, and Shane Frederick, "Intuitive Biases in Choice versus Estimation: Implications for the Wisdom of Crowds," *Journal of Consumer Research* 38, 1 (June 2011): 1–15.

127. www.quirky.com, accessed June 15, 2011.

128. www.sermo.com, accessed June 15, 2011; Susanna Hamner, "Cashing in on Doctors' Thinking," *Business 2.0* (June 2006): 40.

129. www.eventful.com, accessed June 15, 2011; www.sellaband.com, accessed June 15, 2011.

130. Quoted in Darren Everson, "Baseball Taps Wisdom of Fans," *Wall Street Journal* (March 7, 2008): W4.

131. Janice Denegri-Knot and Mike Molesworth, "Concepts and Practices of Digital Virtual Consumption," *Consumption Markets & Culture* 13, no. 2 (2010): 109–32; Natalie T. Wood and Michael R. Solomon, "Adonis or Atrocious: Spokesavatars and Source Effects in Immersive Digital Environments," in Matthew S. Eastin, Terry Daugherty, and Neal M. Burns, eds., *Handbook of Research on Digital Media and Advertising: User Generated Content Consumption* (Hershey, PA IGI Global, 2011): 521–34.

132. Surowiecki, *The Wisdom of Crowds*; Howe, "The Rise of Crowdsourcing."

133. Quoted in Suzanne Vranica, "Ad Houses Will Need to Be More Nimble, Clients Are Demanding More and Better Use of Consumer Data, Web," *Wall Street Journal* (January 2, 2008): B3.

134. John Markoff, "Internet Use Said to Cut into TV Viewing and Socializing," *New York Times on the Web* (December 30, 2004), http://www.nytimes.com/2004/12/30/technology/30internet.html?_r=1&scp=1&sq=John%20Markoff,%20%E2%80%9CInternet%20Use%20Said%20to%20Cut%20into%20TV%20Viewing%20and%20Socializing&st=cse, accessed September 13, 2011.

135. Suzanne Vranica, "Getting Buzz Marketers to Fess Up," *Wall Street Journal* (February 9, 2005): B9.

136. Thomas E. Weber, "Viral Marketing: Web's Newest Ploy May Make You an Unpopular Friend," *Wall Street Journal* (September 13, 1999), *www.wsj.com*, accessed September 13, 1999.

137. Victoria Shannon, "Social Networking Moves to the Cellphone," *New York Times* (March 6, 2008), www.nytimes.com/2008/03/06/technology/06wireless.html?ex=1362459600&en=571b090085db559d&ei=5088&partner=rssnyt&emc=rss, accessed March 6, 2008.

138. Jack Neff, "Will Text Rumor Scare Off Wal-Mart Customers? Messaging Hoax in at Least 16 States Warns Women They Could Be Killed," *Advertising Age* (March 19, 2009), www.adage.com; accessed March 19, 2009; Choe Sang-Hun, "Web Rumors Tied to Korean Actress's Suicide," *New York Times* (October 2, 2008), http://www.nytimes.com/2008/10/03/world/asia/03actress.html?scp=1&sq=web%20rumors%20tied%20to%20Korean%20actress&st=cse, accessed October 3, 2008; The Associated Press, "Fighting the Web Bullying That Led to a Suicide," *New York Times* (June 1, 2008), http://www.nytimes.com/2008/06/01/us/01internet.html?scp=1&sq=Fighting%20the%20Web%20Bullying%20That%20Led%20to%20a%20Suicide&st=cse, accessed June 1, 2008.

454

ABC model of attitudes a multidimensional perspective stating that attitudes are jointly defined by affect, behavior, and cognition

Abandoned products grocery items that shoppers buy but never use

Absolute threshold the minimum amount of stimulation that can be detected on a given sensory channel

Acceptance cycles a way to differentiate among fashions in terms of their longevity

Accommodative purchase decision the process of using bargaining, coercion, compromise, and the wielding of power to achieve agreement among group members who have different preferences or priorities

Acculturation the process of learning the beliefs and behaviors endorsed by another culture

Acculturation agents friends, family, local businesses, and other reference groups that facilitate the learning of cultural norms

Activation models of memory approaches to memory stressing different levels of processing that occur and activate some aspects of memory rather than others, depending on the nature of the processing task

Activity stores a retailing concept that lets consumers participate in the production of the products or services being sold in the store

Actual self a person's realistic appraisal of his or her qualities

Adaptation the process that occurs when a sensation becomes so familiar that it no longer commands attention

Advergaming online games merged with interactive advertisements that let companies target specific types of consumers

Advertising wear-out the condition that occurs when consumers become so used to hearing or seeing a marketing stimulus that they no longer pay attention to it

Affect the way a consumer feels about an attitude object

Affluenza well-off consumers who are stressed or unhappy despite of or even because of their wealth

Age cohort a group of consumers of approximately the same age who have undergone similar experiences

Agentic goals an emphasis on self-assertion and mastery, often associated with traditional male gender roles

AIOs (activities, interests, and opinions) the psychographic variables researchers use to group consumers

Allegory a story told about an abstract trait or concept that has been personified as a person, animal, or vegetable

Alternate-reality game (ARG) an application that blends online and off-line clues and encourages players to collaborate to solve a puzzle

Anchoring a concept in behavioral economics that refers to a number that people use as a standard for future judgments

Androgyny the possession of both masculine and feminine traits

Animism cultural practices whereby inanimate objects are given qualities that make them somehow alive

Antibrand communities groups of consumers who share a common disdain for a celebrity, store, or brand

Anticonsumption the actions taken by consumers involving the deliberate defacement or mutilation of products

Antifestival an event that distorts the symbols associated with other holidays

Approach–approach conflict a person must choose between two desirable alternatives

Approach–avoidance conflict a person desires a goal but wishes to avoid it at the same time

Archetypes a universally shared idea or behavior pattern, central to Carl Jung's conception of personality; archetypes involve themes—such as birth, death, or the devil—that appear frequently in myths, stories, and dreams

Art product a creation viewed primarily as an object of aesthetic contemplation without any functional value

Aspirational reference group high-profile athletes and celebrities used in marketing efforts to promote a product

Associative network a memory system that organizes individual units of information according to some set of relationships; may include such concepts as brands, manufacturers, and stores

Asynchronous interactions message posts that don't require all participants to respond immediately

Atmospherics the use of space and physical features in store design to evoke certain effects in buyers

Attention the assignment of processing activity to selected stimuli

Attentional gate a process whereby information retained for further processing is transferred from sensory memory to short-term memory

Attitude a lasting, general evaluation of people (including oneself), objects, or issues

Attitude object (A_o) anything toward which one has an attitude

Attitude toward the act of buying (A_{act}) the perceived consequences of a purchase

Audio watermarking a technique where composers and producers weave distinctive sound/motif into a piece of music that sticks in people's minds over time

Augmented reality technology applications that layer digital information over a physical space to add additional information for users

Autonomic decision when one family member chooses a product for the whole family

Avatar manifestation of a Hindu deity in superhuman or animal form. In the computing world it has come to mean a cyberspace presence represented by a character that you can move around inside a visual, graphical world

Avoidance-avoidance conflict a choice situation where both alternatives are undesirable

Avoidance groups reference groups that exert a negative influence on individuals because they are motivated to distance themselves from group members

B2C e-commerce businesses selling to consumers through electronic marketing

Baby Boomer a large cohort of people born between the years of 1946 and 1964 who are the source of many important cultural and economic changes

Badges evidence of some achievement consumers display either in the physical world or on social platforms

Balance theory a theory that considers relations among elements a person might perceive as belonging together, and people's tendency to change relations among elements in order to make them consistent or "balanced"

Basking in reflected glory the practice of publicizing connections with successful people or organizations to enhance one's own standing

Beacon a code that companies embed in people's hard drives that captures what they type on Web sites to assist in behavioral targeting

Behavior a consumer's actions with regard to an attitude object

Behavioral economics the study of the behavioral determinants of economic decisions

Behavioral influence perspective the view that consumer decisions are learned responses to environmental cues

Behavioral learning theories the perspectives on learning that assume that learning takes place as the result of responses to external events

Behavioral pricing research that looks at how consumers respond to and use price in their perceptual processes

Behavioral targeting e-commerce marketers serve up customized ads on Web sites or cable TV stations based on a customer's prior activity

Being space a retail environment that resembles a residential living room where customers are encouraged to congregate

Binary opposition a defining structural characteristic of many myths in which two opposing ends of some dimension are represented (e.g., good versus evil, nature versus technology)

Bioterrorism a strategy to disrupt the nation's food supply with the aim of creating economic havoc

Blissful ignorance effect states that people who have details about a product before they buy it do not expect to be as happy with it as do those who got only ambiguous information

Blogs messages posted online in diary form

Body cathexis a person's feelings about aspects of his or her body

Body dysmorphic disorder an obsession with perceived flaws in appearance

Body image a consumer's subjective evaluation of his or her physical self

Boomerang kids grown children who return to their parents' home to live

Bounded rationality a concept in behavioral economics that states since we rarely have the resources (especially the time) to weigh every possible factor into a decision, we settle for a solution that is just good enough

Brand advocates consumers who supply product reviews online

Brand community a set of consumers who share a set of social relationships based on usage or interest in a product

Brand equity a brand that has strong positive associations in a consumer's memory and commands a lot of loyalty as a result

Brand loyalty repeat purchasing behavior that reflects a conscious decision to continue buying the same brand

Brand-name imprinting linking a brand to a category in memory

Brand personality a set of traits people attribute to a product as if it were a person

Brand prominence the display of blatant status symbols to insure that others recognize one's luxury brands

Brandfests a corporate-sponsored event intended to promote strong brand loyalty among customers

BRIC the bloc of nations with very rapid economic development: Brazil, Russia, India, and China

Bromance a relationship characterized by strong affection between two straight males

Business ethics rules of conduct that guide actions in the marketplace

Business-to-business (B2B) e-commerce internet interactions between two or more businesses or organizations

Business-to-business (B2B) marketers specialists in meeting the needs of organizations such as corporations, government agencies, hospitals, and retailers

Buyclass theory of purchasing a framework that characterizes organizational buying decisions in terms of how much cognitive effort is involved in making a decision

Buyer the person who actually makes the purchase

Buying center the part of an organization charged with making purchasing decisions

C2C e-commerce consumer-to-consumer activity through the Internet

Category exemplars brands that are particularly relevant examples of a broader classification

Chavs British term that refers to young, lower-class men and women who mix flashy brands and accessories from big names such as Burberry with track suits

Chunking a process in which information is stored by combining small pieces of information into larger ones

Classic a fashion with an extremely long acceptance cycle

Classical conditioning the learning that occurs when a stimulus eliciting a response is paired with another stimulus that initially does not elicit a response on its own but will cause a similar response over time because of its association with the first stimulus

Closure principle the *Gestalt* principle that describes a person's tendency to supply missing information in order to perceive a holistic image

Co-branding strategies linking products together to create a more desirable connotation in consumer minds

Co-consumers other patrons in a consumer setting

Coercive power influence over another person due to social or physical intimidation cohesiveness

Cognition the beliefs a consumer has about an attitude object

Cognitive learning theory approaches that stress the importance of internal mental processes. This perspective views people as problem solvers who actively use information from the world around them to master their environment

Cognitive processing style a predisposition to process information. Some of us tend to have a *rational system of cognition* that processes information analytically and sequentially using roles of logic, while others rely on an *experiential system of cognition* that processes information more holistically and in parallel

Cohesiveness the degree to which members of a group are attracted to each other and how much each values their membership in this group

Collecting the systematic acquisition of a particular object or set of objects

Collective value creation the process whereby brand community members work together to develop better ways to use and customize products

Communal goals an emphasis on affiliation and the fostering of harmonious relations, often associated with traditional female gender roles

Communications model a framework specifying that a number of elements are necessary for communication to be achieved, including a source, message, medium, receivers, and feedback

Community in a digital context, a group of people who engage in supportive and sociable relationships with others who share one or more common interests

Comparative advertising a strategy in which a message compares two or more specifically named or recognizably presented brands and makes a comparison of them in terms of one or more specific attributes

Comparative influence the process whereby a reference group influences decisions about specific brands or activities

Compatibility in the context of diffusion of innovations, the extent to which a new product fits with a consumer's preexisting lifestyle

Compensatory decision rules a set of rules that allows information about attributes of competing products to be averaged in some way; poor standing on one attribute can potentially be offset by good standing on another

Complexity in the context of diffusion of innovation, the extent to which a new product is difficult to use or to integrate into a person's daily life

Compliance we form an attitude because it helps us to gain rewards or avoid punishment

Compulsive consumption the process of repetitive, often excessive, shopping used to relieve tension, anxiety, depression, or boredom

Computer-mediated environment immersive virtual worlds

Conditioned response (CR) a response to a conditioned stimulus caused by the learning of an association between a conditioned stimulus (CS) and an unconditioned stimulus (UCS)

Conditioned stimulus (CS) a stimulus that produces a learned reaction through association over time

Conformity a change in beliefs or actions as a reaction to real or imagined group pressure

Connexity a lifestyle term coined by the advertising agency Saatchi & Saatchi to describe young consumers who place high value on being both foot-loose and connected

Conscientious consumerism a new value that combines a focus on personal health with a concern for global health

Consensual purchase decision a decision in which the group agrees on the desired purchase and differs only in terms of how it will be achieved

Consideration set the products a consumer actually deliberates about choosing

Conspicuous consumption the purchase and prominent display of luxury goods to provide evidence of a consumer's ability to afford them

Consumed consumers those people who are used or exploited, whether willingly or not, for commercial gain in the marketplace

Consumer a person who identifies a need or desire, makes a purchase, and/or disposes of the product

Consumer addiction a physiological and/or psychological dependency on products or services

Consumer behavior the processes involved when individuals or groups select, purchase, use, or dispose of products, services, ideas, or experiences to satisfy needs and desires

Consumer confidence the state of mind of consumers relative to their optimism or pessimism about economic conditions; people tend to make more discretionary purchases when their confidence in the economy is high

Consumer confusion in legal contexts, the likelihood that one company's logo, product design, or package is so similar to another that the typical shopper would mistake one for the other

Consumer hyperchoice a condition where the large number of available options forces us to make repeated choices that drain psychological energy and diminish our ability to make smart decisions

Consumer identity renaissance the redefinition process people undergo when they retire

Consumer satisfaction/dissatisfaction (CS/D) the overall attitude a person has about a product after it has been purchased

Consumer socialization the process by which people acquire skills that enable them to function in the marketplace

Consumerspace marketing environment where customers act as partners with companies to decide what the marketplace will offer

Consumer style a pattern of behaviors, attitudes, and opinions that influences all of a person's consumption activities—including attitudes toward advertising, preferred channels of information and purchase, brand loyalty, and price consciousness

Consumer tribe group of people who share a lifestyle and who can identify with each other because of a shared allegiance to an activity or a product

Consumption communities Web groups where members share views and product recommendations online

Consumption constellation a set of products and activities used by consumers to define, communicate, and perform social roles

Contamination when a place or object takes on sacred qualities because of its association with another sacred person or event

Contemporary Young Mainstream Female Achievers (CYMFA) modern women who assume multiple roles

Continuous innovation a modification of an existing product

Contrast stimuli that differ from others around them

Conventions norms that regulate how we conduct our everyday lives

Co-optation a cultural process by which the original meanings of a product or other symbol associated with a subculture are modified by members of mainstream culture

Core values common general values held by a culture

Cosmopolitanism a cultural value that emphasizes being open to the world and striving for diverse experiences

Cosplay a form of performance art in which participants wear elaborate costumes that represent a virtual world avatar or other fictional character

Cougars older women who date younger men

Country of origin original country from which a product is produced. Can be an important piece of information in the decision-making process

Craft product a creation valued because of the beauty with which it performs some function; this type of product tends to follow a formula that permits rapid production, and it is easier to understand than an art product

Creolization foreign influences are absorbed and integrated with local meanings

Crescive norms unspoken rules that govern social behavior

Crowdsourcing similar to a firm that outsources production to a subcontractor; companies call upon outsiders from around the world to solve problems their own scientists can't handle

Cult products items that command fierce consumer loyalty and devotion

Cultural capital a set of distinctive and socially rare tastes and practices that admits a person into the realm of the upper class

Cultural formula a sequence of media events in which certain roles and props tend to occur consistently

Cultural gatekeepers individuals who are responsible for determining the types of messages and symbolism to which members of mass culture are exposed

Cultural selection the process by which some alternatives are selected over others by cultural gatekeepers

Culture the values, ethics, rituals, traditions, material objects, and services produced or valued by the members of a society

Culture jamming the defacement or alteration of advertising materials as a form of political expression

Culture of participation the driving philosophy behind social media that includes a belief in democracy, the ability to freely interact with other people, companies and organization, open access to venues that allows users to share content from simple comments to reviews, ratings, photos, stories, and more, and the power to build on the content of others from your own unique point of view

Culture production system (CPS) the set of individuals and organizations responsible for creating and marketing a cultural product

Custom a norm that controls basic behaviors, such as division of labor in a household

Customer networks groups in companies and families that customer networks invest in products and services to help them reach collective identity goals

Cyberbullying when one or more people post malicious comments online about someone else in a coordinated effort to harass them

Cybermediary intermediary that helps to filter and organize online market information so that consumers can identify and evaluate alternatives more efficiently

Cyberplace an online social community

Database marketing tracking consumers' buying habits very closely, and then crafting products and messages tailored precisely to people's wants and needs based on this information

Decay structural changes in the brain produced by learning decrease over time

Decision polarization the process whereby individuals' choices tend to become more extreme (polarized), in either a conservative or risky direction, following group discussion of alternatives

Deethnicization process whereby a product formerly associated with a specific ethnic group is detached from its roots and marketed to other subcultures

Deindividuation the process whereby individual identities get submerged within a group, reducing inhibitions against socially inappropriate behavior

Democracy in a social media context, a term that refers to rule by the people; community leaders are appointed or elected based on their demonstrated ability to add value to the group

Demographics the observable measurements of a population's characteristics, such as birthrate, age distribution, and income

Desacralization the process that occurs when a sacred item or symbol is removed from its special place, or is duplicated in mass quantities, and becomes profane as a result

Determinant attributes the attributes actually used to differentiate among choices

Differential threshold the ability of a sensory system to detect changes or differences among stimuli

Diffusion of innovations the process whereby a new product, service, or idea spreads through a population

Digital divide the gulf between wealthy and poor people in terms of online access

Digital native young people who have grown up with computers and mobile technology; multitaskers with cell phones, music downloads, and instant messaging on the Internet. Who are comfortable communicating online and by text and IM rather than by voice

Digital virtual consumption (DVC) purchases of virtual goods for use in online games and social communities

DINKS acronym for Double Income, No Kids; a consumer segment with a lot of disposable income

Discontinuous innovation a new product or service that radically changes the way we live

Discretionary income the money available to a household over and above that required for necessities

Divestment rituals the steps people take to gradually distance themselves from things they treasure so that they can sell them or give them away

Doppelgänger brand image a parody of a brand posted on a Web site that looks like the original but is in fact a critique of it

Drive the desire to satisfy a biological need in order to reduce physiological arousal

Drive theory concept that focuses on biological needs that produce unpleasant states of arousal

Dynamically continuous innovation a significant change to an existing product

Early adopters people who are receptive to new products and adopt them relatively soon, though they are motivated more by social acceptance and being in style than by the desire to try risky new things

Echo boomers people born between 1986–2002, also known as Gen Y and Millennials

Economics of information perspective in which advertising is an important source of consumer information emphasizing the economic cost of the time spent searching for products

Ego the system that mediates between the id and the superego

Ego-defensive function attitudes we form to protect ourselves either from external threats or internal feelings

80/20 rule a rule-of-thumb in volume segmentation, which says that about 20 percent of consumers in a product category (the heavy users) account for about 80 percent of sales

Elaborated codes the ways of expressing and interpreting meanings that are more complex and depend on a more sophisticated worldview, which tend to be used by the middle and upper classes

Elaboration likelihood model (ELM) the approach that one of two routes to persuasion (central versus peripheral) will be followed, depending on the personal relevance of a message; the route taken determines the relative importance of the message contents versus other characteristics, such as source attractiveness

Elaborative rehearsal a cognitive process that allows information to move from short-term memory into long-term memory by thinking about the meaning of a stimulus and relating it to other information already in memory

Electronic recommendation agent a software tool that tries to understand a human decision maker's multiattribute preferences for a product category by asking the user to communicate his or her preferences. Based on that data, the software then recommends a list of alternatives sorted by the degree that they fit with the person's preferences

Embeds tiny figures inserted into magazine advertising by using high-speed photography or airbrushing. These hidden figures, usually of a sexual nature, supposedly exert strong but unconscious influences on innocent readers

Emic perspective an approach to studying for (or marketing to) cultures that stresses the unique aspects of each culture

Encoding the process in which information from short-term memory enters into long-term memory in a recognizable form

Enculturation the process of learning the beliefs and behaviors endorsed by one's own culture

Episodic memories memories that relate to personally relevant events; this tends to increase a person's motivation to retain these memories

Ethnic subculture a self-perpetuating group of consumers held together by common cultural ties

Ethnocentrism the belief in the superiority of one's own country's practices and products

Etic perspective an approach to studying (or marketing to) cultures that stresses commonalities across cultures

Evaluative criteria the dimensions used by consumers to compare competing product alternatives

Evoked set those products already in memory plus those prominent in the retail environment that are actively considered during a consumer's choice process

Exchange a transaction in which two or more organizations or people give and receive something of value

Expectancy disconfirmation model states that we form beliefs about product performance based on prior experience with the product and/or communications about the product that imply a certain level of quality; when something performs the way we thought it would, we may not think much about it. If it fails to live up to expectations, this may create negative feelings. On the other hand, we are satisfied if performance exceeds our initial expectations

Expectancy theory the perspective that behavior is largely "pulled" by expectations of achieving desirable outcomes, or positive incentives, rather than "pushed" from within

Experience the result of acquiring and processing stimulation over time

Experiential hierarchy of effects an attitude is initially formed on the basis of a raw emotional reaction

Experiential perspective an approach stressing the *Gestalt* or totality of the product or service experience, focusing on consumers' affective responses in the marketplace

Expert power influence over others due to specialized knowledge about a subject

Exposure an initial stage of perception during which some sensations come within range of consumers' sensory receptors

Extended family traditional family structure in which several generations live together

Extended problem solving an elaborate decision-making process, often initiated by a motive that is fairly central to the self-concept and accompanied by perceived risk; the consumer tries to collect as much information as possible, and carefully weighs product alternatives

Extended self the external objects we consider a part of our self-identity

Extinction the process whereby a learned connection between a stimulus and response is eroded so that the response is no longer reinforced

Fad a very short-lived fashion

Family branding an application of stimulus generalization when a product capitalizes on the reputation of its manufacturer's name

Family financial officer (FFO) the individual in the family who is in charge of making financial decisions

Family identity the definition of a household by family members that it presents to members and to those outside the family unit

Family life cycle (FLC) a classification scheme that segments consumers in terms of changes in income and family composition and the changes in demands placed on this income

Fantasy a self-induced shift in consciousness, often focusing on some unattainable or improbable goal; sometimes fantasy is a way of compensating for a lack of external stimulation or for dissatisfaction with the actual self

Fashion the process of social diffusion by which a new style is adopted by some group(s) of consumers

Fashion system those people and organizations involved in creating symbolic meanings and transferring these meanings to cultural goods

Fattism a preference for thin people and/or discrimination against overweight people gender-bending products

Fear appeals an attempt to change attitudes or behavior through the use of threats or by highlighting negative consequences of noncompliance with the request

Feature creep the tendency of manufacturers to add layers of complexity to products that make them harder to understand and use

Fertility rate a rate determined by the number of births per year per 1,000 women of childbearing age

Figure-ground principle the *Gestalt* principle whereby one part of a stimulus configuration dominates a situation whereas other aspects recede into the background

Fixed-interval reinforcement after a specified time period has passed, the first response an organism makes elicits a reward

Fixed-ratio reinforcement reinforcement occurs only after a fixed number of responses

Flaming a violation of digital etiquette to express when a post is written in all capital letters

Flashmobs a group of people who converge on a physical location to perform some act "spontaneously" and then disperse

Flows exchanges of resources, information, or influence among members of an online social network

Flow state situation in which consumers are truly involved with a product, an ad, or a Web site

Folksonomy an online posting system where users categorize entries themselves rather than relying upon a pre-established set of labels

Food desert a geographic area where residents are unable to obtain adequate food and other products to maintain a healthy existence

Foot-in-the-door technique based on the observation that a consumer is more likely to comply with a request if he or she has first agreed to comply with a smaller request

Fortress brands brands that consumers closely link to rituals; this makes it unlikely they will be replaced

Framing a concept in behavioral economics that the way a problem is posed to consumers (especially in terms of gains or losses) influences the decision they make

Freegans a takeoff on *vegans*, who shun all animal products; anticonsumerists who live off discards as a political statement against corporations and materialism

Freemium a free version of a product that's supported by a paid premium version. The idea is to encourage the maximum number of people to use the product and eventually convert a small fraction of them to paying customers

Frequency marketing a marketing technique that reinforces regular purchasers by giving them prizes with values that increase along with the amount purchased

Frugalistas fashion-conscious consumers who pride themselves on achieving style on a limited budget

Functional theory of attitudes states that attitudes exist *because* they serve some function for the person. Consumers who expect that they will need to deal with similar situations at a future time will be more likely to start to form an attitude in anticipation

Gadget lovers enthusiastic early adopters of high-tech products

Game-based marketing a strategy that involves integrating brand communications in the context of an online group activity

Game platform an online interface that allows users to engage in games and other social activities with members of a community

Gatekeeper the person who conducts the information search and controls the flow of information available to the group

Gemba Japanese term for the one true source of information

Gen X people born between 1965–1985

Gen Y people born between 1986–2002; also known as Echo Boomers and Millennials

Gender-bending product a traditionally sex-typed item adapted to the opposite gender

Gender convergence blurring of sex roles in modern society; men and women increasingly express similar attitudes about balancing home life and work

Genre in the context of social gaming, the method of play such as simulation, action, and role-playing

Geodemography techniques that combine consumer demographic information with geographic consumption patterns to permit precise targeting of consumers with specific characteristics

Geospatial platforms online applications that use smartphones to identify consumers' physical locations

Gestalt meaning derived from the totality of a set of stimuli, rather than from any individual stimulus

Gift-giving ritual the events involved in the selection, presentation, acceptance, and interpretation of a gift

Global consumer culture a culture in which people around the world are united through their common devotion to brand name consumer goods, movie stars, celebrities, and leisure activities

Globalized consumption ethic the global sharing of a material lifestyle including the valuing of well-known multinational brands that symbolize prosperity

Goal a consumer's desired end state

Golden triangle the portion of a Web site that a person's eyes naturally gravitate to first, which makes it more likely that search results located in that area will be seen

Goth subculture a lifestyle group inspired by vampire myths that illustrates an androgynous approach to gender identity

Gray market the economic potential created by the increasing numbers of affluent elderly consumers

Green marketing a marketing strategy involving an emphasis on protecting the natural environment

Greenwashing inflated claims about a product's environmental benefits

Grooming rituals sequences of behaviors that aid in the transition from the private self to the public self or back again

Guerrilla marketing promotional strategies that use unconventional locations and intensive word-of-mouth campaigns

Habitual decision making choices made with little or no conscious effort

Habitus ways in which we classify experiences as a result of our socialization processes

Halal food and other products whose usage is permissible according to the laws of Islam

Halo effect a phenomenon that occurs when people react to other, similar stimuli in much the same way they responded to the original stimulus

Haptic touch-related sensations

Heavy users a name companies use to identify their customers who consume their products in large volumes

Hedonic adaptation in order to maintain a fairly stable level of happiness we tend to become used to positive and negative events in our lives

Hedonic consumption the multisensory, fantasy, and emotional aspects of consumers' interactions with products

Helicopter moms overprotective mothers who "hover" around their kids and insert themselves into virtually all aspects of their lives

Heuristics the mental rules of thumb that lead to a speedy decision

Hierarchy of effects a fixed sequence of steps that occurs during attitude formation; this sequence varies depending on such factors as the consumer's level of involvement with the attitude object

Hierarchy of Needs (Maslow's) a framework that specifies different levels of motives that depends upon the consumer's personal situation

High-context culture group members tend to be close-knit and are likely to infer meanings that go beyond the spoken word

Highlighting effect the order in which consumers learn about brands determines the strength of association between these brands and their attributes

Hispanic people whose geographic and/or cultural origins are in Latin American countries

Hoarding unsystematic acquisition of objects (in contrast to collecting)

Homeostasis the state of being in which the body is in physiological balance; goal-oriented behavior attempts to reduce or eliminate an unpleasant motivational state and return to a balanced one

Home shopping party a selling format where a company representative makes a sales presentation to a group of people who gather at the home of a friend or acquaintance

Homogamy the tendency for individuals to marry others similar to themselves

Homophily the degree to which a pair of individuals is similar in terms of education, social status, and beliefs

Horizontal revolution a fundamental change in how consumers communicate via social media whereby information doesn't just flow from big companies and governments; information flows *across* people as well

Host culture a new culture to which a person must acculturate

Household according to the U.S. Census Bureau, an occupied housing unit

Hybrid ad a marketing communication that explicitly references the context (e.g., TV show) in which it appears

Hyperopia the medical term for people who have farsighted vision; describes people who are so obsessed with preparing for the future that they can't enjoy the present

Hyperreality the becoming real of what is initially simulation or "hype"

Icon a sign that resembles the product in some way

Id the Freudian system oriented toward immediate gratification

Ideal of beauty a model, or exemplar, of appearance valued by a culture

Ideal self a person's conception of how he or she would like to be

Identification the process of forming an attitude to conform to another person's or group's expectations

Identity marketing a practice whereby consumers are paid to alter some aspects of their selves to advertise for a branded product

Illusion of truth effect telling people that a consumer claim is false can make them misremember it as true

Impression management our efforts to "manage" what others think of us by strategically choosing clothing and other cues that will put us in a good light

Impulse buying a process that occurs when the consumer experiences a sudden urge to purchase an item that he or she cannot resist

Incidental brand exposure an experimental technique that involves showing product logos to respondents without their conscious awareness

Incidental learning unintentional acquisition of knowledge

Incidental similarity points of commonality between a buyer and a seller such as a shared birthday

Index a sign that is connected to a product because they share some property

Individualism one of Hofstede's cultural dimensions: The extent to which the culture values the welfare of the individual versus that of the group

Inertia the process whereby purchase decisions are made out of habit because the consumer lacks the motivation to consider alternatives

Influence impressions brand-specific mentions on social media posts

Influence network a two-way dialogue between participants in a social network and opinion leaders

Influencer the person who tries to sway the outcome of the decision

Information cascades an online communication process where one piece of information triggers a sequence of interactions

Information power influence over others due to the possession of inside knowledge

Information search the process by which the consumer surveys his or her environment for appropriate data to make a reasonable decision

Initiator the person who brings up the idea or identifies a need

Innovation a product or style that is perceived as new by consumers

Innovators people who are always on the lookout for novel developments and will be the first to try a new offering

Instrumental conditioning also known as operant conditioning, occurs as the individual learns to perform behaviors that produce positive outcomes and to avoid those that yield negative outcomes

Instrumental values goals endorsed because they are needed to achieve desired end states, or terminal values

Intelligent agents software programs that learn from past user behavior in order to recommend new purchases

Interactions in a social media context, behavior-based ties between participants such as talking with each other, attending an event together, or working together

Interference one way that forgetting occurs; as additional information is learned, it displaces the earlier information

Internalization deep-seated attitudes become part of our value system

Interpretant the meaning derived from a sign or symbol

Interpretation the process whereby meanings are assigned to stimuli

Interpretivism as opposed to the dominant positivist perspective on consumer behavior, instead stresses the importance of symbolic, subjective experience and the idea that meaning is in the mind of the person rather than existing "out there" in the objective world

Invidious distinction the use of status symbols to inspire envy in others through display of wealth or power

Involvement the motivation to process product-related information

j.n.d. (just noticeable difference) the minimum difference between two stimuli that can be detected by a perceiver

Juggling lifestyle working mothers' attempts to compromise between conflicting cultural ideals of motherhood and professionalism

Kansei engineering a Japanese philosophy that translates customers' feelings into design elements

Kin-network system the rituals intended to maintain ties among family members, both immediate and extended

Knowledge function the process of forming an attitude to provide order, structure, or meaning

Knowledge structure organized system of concepts relating to brands, stores, and other concepts

Laddering a technique for uncover consumers' associations between specific attributes and general values

Laggards consumers who are exceptionally slow to adopt innovations

Late adopters the majority of consumers who are moderately receptive to adopting innovations

Lateral cycling a process in which already-purchased objects are sold to others or exchanged for other items

Latitudes of acceptance and rejection in the social judgment theory of attitudes, the notion that people differ in terms of the information they will find acceptable or unacceptable. They form latitudes of acceptance and rejection around an attitude standard. Ideas that fall within a latitude will be favorably received, but those falling outside of this zone will not

Learning a relatively permanent change in a behavior caused by experience

Legitimate power influence over others due to a position conferred by a society or organization

Leisure class wealthy people for whom work is a taboo

Licensing popular marketing strategy that pays for the right to link a product or service to the name of a well-known brand or designer

Life course paradigm this perspective views behavior at any stage in life or given point in time as the product of one's actions or responses to earlier life conditions and the way the individual has adapted to social and environmental circumstances

Lifestyle a pattern of consumption that reflects a person's choices of how to spend his or her time and money.

Lifestyle marketing perspective strategy based on the recognition that people sort themselves into groups on the basis of the things they like to do, how they like to spend their leisure time, and how they choose to spend their disposable income

Limited problem solving a problem-solving process in which consumers are not motivated to search for information or to rigorously evaluate each alternative; instead they use simple decision rules to arrive at a purchase decision

List of Values (LOV) scale identifies consumer segments based on the values members endorse and relates each value to differences in consumption behaviors

LOHAS an acronym for "lifestyles of health and sustainability"; a consumer segment that worries about the environment, wants products to be produced in a sustainable way, and who spend money to advance what they see as their personal development and potential

Long tail states that we need no longer rely solely on big hits (such as blockbuster movies or best-selling books) to find profits. Companies can also make money if they sell small amounts of items that only a few people want—if they sell enough different items

Long-term memory (LTM) the system that allows us to retain information for a long period of time

Long-term orientation one of the five basic dimensions that characterize cultures in Hofstede's framework of cross-cultural values

Look-alike packaging putting a generic or private label product in a package that resembles a popular brand to associate the brand with the popular one

Looking-glass self the process of imagining the reaction of others toward oneself

Low-context culture in contrast to high-context cultures that have strong oral traditions and that are more sensitive to nuance, low-context cultures are more literal

Low-involvement hierarchy of effects the process of attitude formation for products or services that carry little risk or self-identity

Low-literate consumer people who read at a very low level; tend to avoid situations where they will have to reveal their inability to master basic consumption decisions such as ordering from a menu

Lurkers passive members of an online community who do not contribute to interactions

M-commerce the practice of promoting and selling goods and services via wireless devices including cell phones, PDAs, and iPods

Market beliefs a consumer's specific beliefs or decision rules pertaining to marketplace phenomena

Market maven a person who often serves as a source of information about marketplace activities

Market segmentation strategies targeting a brand only to specific groups of consumers who share well-defined and relevant characteristics

Masculinism study devoted to the male image and the cultural meanings of masculinity

Masculinity according to Hofstede's framework of cross-cultural values the extent to which a culture emphasizes male vs. female distinctions

Mass class a term analysts use to describe the millions of global consumers who now enjoy a level of purchasing power that's sufficient to let them afford many high-quality products

Mass connectors highly influential members of social media networks

Mass customization the personalization of products and services for individual customers at a mass-production price

Materialism the importance consumers attach to worldly possessions

Maximizing a decision strategy that seeks to deliver the best possible result

Means-end chain model assumes that people link very specific product attributes (indirectly) to terminal values such as freedom or safety

Media democratization in a social media context, members of social communities, not traditional media publishers like magazines or newspaper companies, control the creation, delivery, and popularity of content

Media multiplexity in a social media context, when flows of communication go in many directions at any point in time and often on multiple platforms

Meetups members of an online network arrange to meet in a physical location

Megachurches very large churches that serve between 2,000 and 20,000 congregants

Membership reference group ordinary people whose consumption activities provide informational social influence

Meme theory a perspective that uses a medical metaphor to explain how an idea or product enters the consciousness of people over time, much like a virus

Memory a process of acquiring information and storing it over time so that it will be available when needed

Mental accounting principle that states that decisions are influenced by the way a problem is posed

Mental budgets consumers' pre-set expectations of how much they intend to spend on a shopping trip

Mere exposure phenomenon the tendency to like persons or things if we see them more often

Metaphor the use of an explicit comparison ("A" is "B") between a product and some other person, place, or thing

Metrosexual a straight, urban male who exhibits strong interests and knowledge regarding product categories such as fashion, home design, gourmet cooking, and personal care that run counter to the traditional male sex role

Microcultures groups that form around a strong shared identification with an activity or art form

Milieu in the context of social gaming, the visual nature of the game such as science fiction, fantasy, horror, and retro

Millennials people born between 1986–2002; also known as Echo Boomers and Gen Y

Minipreneurs one-person businesses

Mixed emotions affect with positive and negative components

MMOGS (massively multiplayer online games) an online, interactive experience in which people around the world participate in the form of avatars

MMORPGs (massively multiplayer online role playing games) online role-playing games that typically involve thousands of players

Mobile shopping apps smartphone applications that retailers provider to guide shoppers in stores and malls

Mode in the context of social gaming, the way players experience the game world

Modeling imitating the behavior of others

Modified rebuy in the context of the buy-class framework, a task that requires a modest amount of information search and evaluation, often focused on identifying the appropriate vendor

Momentum effect an accelerating diffusion of a message in social media due to the contributions of influential members

Monomyth a myth with basic characteristics that are found in many cultures

More a custom with a strong moral overtone

Motivation an internal state that activates goal-oriented behavior

Motivational research a qualitative research approach, based on psychoanalytic (Freudian) interpretations, with a heavy emphasis on unconscious motives for consumption

Multiattribute attitude models those models that assume that a consumer's attitude (evaluation) of an attitude object depends on the beliefs he or she has about several or many attributes of the object; the use of a multiattribute model implies that an attitude toward a product or brand can be predicted by identifying these specific beliefs and combining them to derive a measure of the consumer's overall attitude

Multiple-intelligence theory a perspective that argues for other types of intelligence, such as athletic prowess or musical ability, beyond the traditional math and verbal skills psychologists use to measure IQ

Multiple pathway anchoring and adjustment (MPAA) model a model that emphasizes multiple pathways to attitude formation

Multitasking processing information from more than one medium at a time

Myth a story containing symbolic elements that expresses the shared emotions and ideals of a culture

Name-letter effect all things equal we like others who share our names or even initials better than those who don't

Narrative product information in the form of a story

Narrative transportation the result of a highly involving message where people become immersed in the storyline

Natural user interface a philosophy of computer design that incorporates habitual human movements

Need a basic biological motive

Negative reinforcement the process whereby the environment weakens responses to stimuli so that inappropriate behavior is avoided

Negative word of mouth the passing on of negative experiences involved with products or services by consumers to other potential customers to influence others' choices

Network effect each person who uses a product or service benefits as more people participate

Network units members of a social network

Neuromarketing a new technique that uses a brain scanning device called functional magnetic resonance imaging (fMRI), that tracks blood flow as people perform mental tasks. Scientists know that specific regions of the brain light up in these scans to show increased blood flow when a person recognizes a face, hears a song, makes a decision, senses deception, and so on. Now they are trying to harness this technology to measure consumers' reactions to movie trailers, choices about automobiles, the appeal of a pretty face, and loyalty to specific brands

New task in the context of the buyclass framework, a task that requires a great degree of effort and information search

Nodes members of a social network connected to others via one or more shared relationships

Noncompensatory decision rules decision shortcuts a consumer makes when a product with a low standing on one attribute cannot make up for this position by being better on another attribute

Normative influence the process in which a reference group helps to set and enforce fundamental standards of conduct

Norms the informal rules that govern what is right or wrong

Nostalgia a bittersweet emotion; the past is viewed with sadness and longing; many "classic" products appeal to consumers' memories of their younger days

Nouveau riches affluent consumers whose relatively recent acquisition of income rather than ancestry or breeding accounts for their enhanced social mobility

Nuclear family a contemporary living arrangement composed of a married couple and their children

Object in semiotic terms, the product that is the focus of a message

Object sociality the extent to which an object (text, image, video) is shared among members of online social networks

Objectification when we attribute sacred qualities to mundane items

Observability in the context of diffusion of innovations, the extent to which a new product is something that is easy for consumers to see in use in order to motivate others to try it

Observational learning the process in which people learn by watching the actions of others and noting the reinforcements they receive for their behaviors

Online gated communities digital social networks that selectively allow access to people who possess criteria such as wealth or physical attractiveness

Open data partnership a group of companies working together to allow consumers to choose if they want their online behaviors to be tracked and to give them the opportunity to edit the interests, demographics and other profile information collected about them

Open rates the percentage of people who open an email message from a marketer

Opinion leader person who is knowledgeable about products and who frequently is able to influence others' attitudes or behaviors with regard to a product category

Organizational buyers people who purchase goods and services on behalf of companies for use in the process of manufacturing, distribution, or resale

Paradigm a widely accepted view or model of phenomena being studied; the perspective that regards people as rational information processors is currently the dominant paradigm, although this approach is now being challenged by a new wave of research that emphasizes the frequently subjective nature of consumer decision making

Parental yielding the process that occurs when a parental decision maker is influenced by a child's product request

Parody display deliberately avoiding status symbols; to seek status by mocking it

Passion-centric members of a social network share an intense interest in some topic

Pastiche mixture of images

Perceived age how old a person feels as compared to his or her true chronological age

Perceived risk belief that a product has potentially negative consequences

Perception the process by which stimuli are selected, organized, and interpreted

Perceptual defense the tendency for consumers to avoid processing stimuli that are threatening to them

Perceptual filters past experiences that influence what stimuli we decide to process

Perceptual selection process by which people attend to only a small portion of the stimuli to which they are exposed

Perceptual vigilance the tendency for consumers to be more aware of stimuli that relate to their current needs

Permission marketing popular strategy based on the idea that a marketer will be much more successful in persuading consumers who have agreed to let them try

Personality a person's unique psychological makeup, which consistently influences the way the person responds to his or her environment

Personality traits identifiable characteristics that define a person

Personalized retargeting a sophisticated form of behavioral targeting that provides messages that refer to the exact product a person views on a website

Persuasion an active attempt to change attitudes

Phonemes vowel and consonant sounds

Pleasure principle the belief that behavior is guided by the desire to maximize pleasure and avoid pain

Plinking™ act of embedding a product or service link in a video

Plutonomy an economy that a small number of rich people control

Podcasting an audio broadcast that people listen to on portable MP3 players or laptops

Point-of-purchase (POP) stimuli the promotional materials that are deployed in stores or other outlets to influence consumers' decisions at the time products are purchased

Popular culture the music, movies, sports, books, celebrities, and other forms of entertainment consumed by the mass market

Pop-up stores temporary locations that allow a company to test new brands without a huge financial commitment

Positioning strategy an organization's use of elements in the marketing mix to influence the consumer's interpretation of a product's meaning vis-à-vis competitors

Positive reinforcement the process whereby rewards provided by the environment strengthen responses to stimuli and appropriate behavior is learned

Positivism a research perspective that relies on principles of the "scientific method" and assumes that a single reality exists; events in the world can be objectively measured; and the causes of behavior can be identified, manipulated, and predicted

Power distance one of Hofstede's cultural dimensions: The way members perceive differences in power when they form interpersonal relationships

Power users opinion leaders in online networks

Prediction market an approach based on the idea that groups of people with knowledge about an industry are jointly better predictors of the future than are any individuals

Presence the effect that people experience when they interact with a computer-mediated environment

Pretailer an e-commerce site that provides exclusive styles by prodding manufacturers to produce runway pieces they wouldn't otherwise make to sell in stores

Priming properties of a stimulus that evoke a schema that leads us to compare the stimulus to other similar ones we encountered in the past

Principle of cognitive consistency the belief that consumers value harmony among their thoughts, feelings, and behaviors and that they are motivated to maintain uniformity among these elements

Principle of least interest the person who is least committed to staying in a relationship has the most power

Principle of similarity the *Gestalt* principle that describes how consumers tend to group objects that share similar physical characteristics

PRIZM (Potential Rating Index by Zip Market) clustering technique that classifies every zip code in the United States into one of 66 categories, ranging from the most affluent "Blue-Blood Estates" to

the least well off "Public Assistance," developed by Claritas, Inc

Problem recognition the process that occurs whenever the consumer sees a significant difference between his or her current state of affairs and some desired or ideal state; this recognition initiates the decision-making process

Product complementarity the view that products in different functional categories have symbolic meanings that are related to one another

Product line extension related products to an established brand

Product placement the process of obtaining exposure for a product by arranging for it to be inserted into a movie, television show, or some other medium

Product signal communicates an underlying quality of a product through the use of aspects that are only visible in the ad

Productivity orientation a continual striving to use time constructively

Profane consumption the process of consuming objects and events that are ordinary or of the everyday world

Progressive learning model the perspective that people gradually learn a new culture as they increasingly come in contact with it; consumers assimilate into a new culture, mixing practices from their old and new environments to create a hybrid culture

Propinquity as physical distance between people decreases and opportunities for interaction increase, they are more likely to form relationships

Prospect theory a descriptive model of how people make choices

Psychographics the use of psychological, sociological, and anthropological factors to construct market segments

Psychophysics the science that focuses on how the physical environment is integrated into the consumer's subjective experience

Punishment the learning that occurs when a response is followed by unpleasant events

Purchase momentum initial impulses to buy in order to satisfy our needs increase the likelihood that we will buy even more

Queuing theory the mathematical study of waiting lines

Rational perspective a view of the consumer as a careful, analytical decision maker who tries to maximize utility in purchase decisions

Reality engineering the process whereby elements of popular culture are

appropriated by marketers and become integrated into marketing strategies

Reality principle principle that the ego seeks ways that will be acceptable to society to gratify the id

Recall the process of retrieving information from memory; in advertising research the extent to which consumers can remember a marketing message without being exposed to it during the study

Reciprocity norm a culturally learned obligation to return the gesture of a gift with one of equal value

Recognition in advertising research the extent to which consumers say they are familiar with an ad the researcher shows them

Reference group an actual or imaginary individual or group that has a significant effect on an individual's evaluations, aspirations, or behavior

Reference price a figure a consumer uses to determine if a selling price is too high or low

Referent power influence over others because they are motivated to imitate or affiliate with a person or group

Refutational arguments calling attention to a product's negative attributes as a persuasive strategy where a negative issue is raised and then dismissed; this approach can increase source credibility

Relationship marketing the strategic perspective that stresses the long-term, human side of buyer-seller interactions

Relative advantage in the context of diffusion of innovations, the extent to which a new product or service is an improvement over alternatives that are already available in the market

Repetition multiple exposures to a stimulus

Reputation economy a reward system based on recognition of one's expertise by others who read online product reviews

Resonance a literary device, frequently used in advertising that uses a play on words (a double meaning) to communicate a product benefit

Response bias a form of contamination in survey research in which some factor, such as the desire to make a good impression on the experimenter, leads respondents to modify their true answers

Restricted codes the ways of expressing and interpreting meanings that focus on the content of objects, which tend to be used by the working class

Retail theming strategy where stores create imaginative environments that transport shoppers to fantasy worlds or provide other kinds of stimulation

Retrieval the process whereby desired information is recovered from long-term memory

Retro brand an updated version of a brand from a prior historical period

Reverse product placement fictional products that appear in TV shows or movies become popular in the real world

Reward power a person or group with the means to provide positive reinforcement

Rich media elements of an online ad that employ movement to gain attention

Risky shift the tendency for individuals to consider riskier alternatives after conferring with a group than if members made their own decisions with no discussion

Rites of passage sacred times marked by a change in social status

Ritual a set of multiple, symbolic behaviors that occur in a fixed sequence and that tend to be repeated periodically

Ritual artifacts items (consumer goods) used in the performance of rituals

Role theory the perspective that much of consumer behavior resembles actions in a play

Sacralization a process that occurs when ordinary objects, events, or people take on sacred meaning to a culture or to specific groups within a culture

Sacred consumption the process of consuming objects and events that are set apart from normal life and treated with some degree of respect or awe

Salience the prominence of a brand in memory

Sandwich Generation a description of middle-aged people who must care for both children and parents simultaneously

Satisficing a decision strategy that aims to yield an adequate solution rather than the best solution in order to reduce the costs of the decision-making process

Schema an organized collection of beliefs and feelings represented in a cognitive category

Script a learned schema containing a sequence of events an individual expects to occur

Search engines software (such as Google) that helps consumers access information based upon their specific requests

Self-concept the beliefs a person holds about his or her own attributes and how he or she evaluates these qualities

Self-esteem the positivity of a person's self-concept

Self-image congruence models research that suggests we choose products when their attributes match some aspect of the self

Self-perception theory an alternative (to cognitive dissonance) explanation of dissonance effects; it assumes that people use observations of their own behavior to infer their attitudes toward some object

Semiotics a field of study that examines the correspondence between signs and symbols and the meaning or meanings they convey

Sensation the immediate response of sensory receptors (eyes, ears, nose, mouth, fingers) to such basic stimuli as light, color, sound, odors, and textures

Sensory marketing marketing strategies that focus on the impact of sensations on our product experiences

Sensory memory the temporary storage of information received from the senses

Sensory overload a condition where consumers are exposed to far more information than they can process

Sensory signature a unique characteristic of a brand conveyed on a perceptual channel (e.g., fragrance)

Sentiment analysis a process (sometimes also called *opinion mining*) that scours the social media universe to collect and analyze the words people use when they describe a specific product or company

Serial wardrobers shoppers who buy an outfit, wear it once, and return it

Sex roles a culture's expectations about how members of the male or female gender should act, dress, or speak

Sexting the growing trend of young people posting sexually suggestive photos of themselves online

Sex-typed traits characteristics that are stereotypically associated with one gender or the other

Shaping the learning of a desired behavior over time by rewarding intermediate actions until the final result is obtained

Sharing sites e-commerce sites that allow users to share, exchange and rent goods in a local setting

Sheconomy developing countries where analysts predict women will be a dominant force in the local economy

Shopping orientation a consumer's general attitudes and motivations regarding the act of shopping

Short-term memory (STM) the mental system that allows us to retain information for a short period of time

Shrinkage the loss of money or inventory from shoplifting and/or employee theft

Sign the sensory imagery that represents the intended meanings of the object

Simile comparing two objects that share a similar property

Sisyphus effect decision makers who are so thorough they don't even rely on their past experiences to guide their current choice. Instead they start almost from scratch to research options for each unique decision situation

Sleeper effect the process whereby differences in attitude change between positive and negative sources seem to diminish over time

Social capital organizational affiliations and experiences that provide access to desirable social networks

Social class the overall rank of people in a society; people who are grouped within the same social class are approximately equal in terms of their income, occupations, and lifestyles

Social comparison the basic human tendency to compare ourselves to others

Social game a multi-player, competitive, goal-oriented activity with defined rules of engagement and online connectivity among a community of players

Social graphs social networks; relationships among members of online communities

Social judgment theory the perspective that people assimilate new information about attitude objects in light of what they already know or feel; the initial attitude acts as a frame of reference, and new information is categorized in terms of this standard

social game A multi-player, competitive, goal-oriented activity with defined rules of engagement and online connectivity among a community of players

Social loafing the tendency for people not to devote as much to a task when their contribution is part of a larger group effort

Social marketing the promotion of causes and ideas (social products), such as energy conservation, charities, and population control

Social media the set of technologies that enable users to create content and share it with a large number of others

Social mobility the movement of individuals from one social class to another

Social network a group of people who connect with one another online due to some shared interest or affiliation

Social object theory proposes that social networks will be more powerful communities if there is a way to activate relationships among people and objects within them

Social power the capacity of one person to alter the actions or outcome of another

Social stratification the process in a social system by which scarce and valuable resources are distributed unequally to status positions that become more or less permanently ranked in terms of the share of valuable resources each receives

Sociometric methods the techniques for measuring group dynamics that involve tracing communication patterns in and among groups

Sock puppeting a company executive or other biased source poses as someone else to tout his organization in social media

Sound symbolism the process by which the way a word sounds influences our assumptions about what it describes and attributes such as size

Source attractiveness the dimensions of a communicator that increase his or her persuasiveness; these include expertise and attractiveness

Source credibility a communications source's perceived expertise, objectivity, or trustworthiness

Spacing effect the tendency to recall printed material to a greater extent when the advertiser repeats the target item periodically rather than presenting it over and over at the same time

Spectacles a marketing message that takes the form of a public performance

Spendthrifts consumers who derive pleasure from large-scale purchasing

Spiritual-therapeutic model organizations that encourage behavioral changes such as weight loss that are loosely based on religious principles

Spokescharacters the use of animated characters or fictional mascots as product representatives

Spontaneous recovery ability of a stimulus to evoke a weakened response even years after the person initially perceived it

Spreading activation meanings in memory are activated indirectly; as a node is activated, other nodes linked to it are also activated so that meanings spread across the network

Stage of cognitive development the ability to comprehend concepts of increasing complexity as a person matures

Standard learning hierarchy the traditional process of attitude formation that starts with the formation of beliefs about an attitude object

State-dependent retrieval people are better able to access information if their internal state is the same at the time of recall as when they learned the information

Status crystallization the extent to which different indicators of a person's status (income, ethnicity, occupation) are consistent with one another

Status hierarchy a ranking of social desirability in terms of consumers' access to resources such as money, education, and luxury goods

Status symbols products whose primary function is to communicate one's social standing to others

Stimulus discrimination the process that occurs when behaviors caused by two stimuli are different, as when consumers learn to differentiate a brand from its competitors

Stimulus generalization the process that occurs when the behavior caused by a reaction to one stimulus occurs in the presence of other, similar stimuli

Storage the process that occurs when knowledge in long-term memory is integrated with what is already in memory and "warehoused" until needed

Store image a store's "personality," composed of such attributes as location, merchandise suitability, and the knowledge and congeniality of the sales staff

Straight rebuy in the context of the buyclass framework, the type of buying decision that is virtually automatic and requires little deliberation

Subculture a group whose members share beliefs and common experiences that set them apart from other members of a culture

Subjective norm an additional component to the multiattribute attitude model that accounts for the effects of what we believe other people think we should do

Subliminal perception the processing of stimuli presented below the level of the consumer's awareness

Superego the system that internalizes society's rules and that works to prevent the id from seeking selfish gratification

Superstitions beliefs that run counter to rational thought or are inconsistent with known laws of nature

Surrogate consumer a professional who is retained to evaluate and/or make purchases on behalf of a consumer

Symbol a sign that is related to a product through either conventional or agreed-on associations

Symbolic interactionism a sociological approach stressing that relationships with other people play a large part in forming the self; people live in a symbolic environment, and the meaning attached to any situation or object is determined by a person's interpretation of these symbols

Symbolic self-completion theory the perspective that people who have an incomplete self-definition in some context will compensate by acquiring symbols associated with a desired social identity

Synchronous interactions a conversation that requires participants to respond in real-time

Syncretic decision purchase decision that is made jointly by both spouses

Synoptic ideal a model of spousal decision making in which the husband and wife take a common view and act as joint decision makers, assigning each other well-defined roles and making mutually beneficial decisions to maximize the couple's joint utility

Taste culture a group of consumers who share aesthetic and intellectual preferences

Terminal values end states desired by members of a culture

The Values and Lifestyles System (VALS2™) a psychographic segmentation system

Theory of cognitive dissonance theory based on the premise that a state of tension is created when beliefs or behaviors conflict with one another; people are motivated to reduce this inconsistency (or dissonance) and thus eliminate unpleasant tension

Theory of reasoned action an updated version of the Fishbein multiattribute attitude theory that considers factors such as social pressure and A_{act} (the attitude toward the act of buying a product), rather than simply attitudes toward the product itself

Theory of trying states that the criterion of behavior in the reasoned action model of attitude measurement should be replaced with *trying* to reach a goal

Tie strength the nature and potency of the bond between members of a social network

Ties connections between members of a social network

Tightwads consumers who experience emotional pain when they make purchases

Time poverty a feeling of having less time available than is required to meet the demands of everyday living

Timestyle an individual's priorities regarding how or she spends time as influenced by personal and cultural factors

Tipping point moment of critical mass

Torn self a condition where immigrants struggle to reconcile their native identities with their new cultures

Total quality management (TQM) management and engineering procedures aimed at reducing errors and increasing quality; based on Japanese practices

Trade dress color combinations that become strongly associated with a corporation

Transactional advertising an advertising message in a social game that transactional advertising rewards players if they respond to a request

Transformative Consumer Research (TCR) promotes research projects that include the goal of helping people or bringing about social change

Transitional economies a country that is adapting from a controlled, centralized economy to a free-market system

Transmedia formats social media platforms such as alternative reality games that allow consumers to participate in an advertising campaign

Transmedia storytelling the use of a mix of social media platforms to create a plot that involves consumers who try to solve puzzles or mysteries in the narrative

Trialability in the context of diffusion of innovations, the extent to which a new product or service can be sampled prior to adoption

Tribal marketing strategy linking a product's identity to an activity-based "tribe" such as basketball players

Trickle-down theory the perspective that fashions spread as the result of status symbols associated with the upper classes "trickling down" to other social classes as these consumers try to emulate those with greater status

Tweens a marketing term used to describe children aged 8 to 14

Twitter a popular social media platform that restricts the poster to a 140 word entry

Two-factor theory the perspective that two separate psychological processes are operating when a person is repeatedly exposed to an ad: repetition increases familiarity and thus reduces uncertainty about the product but over time boredom increases with each exposure, and at some point the amount of boredom incurred begins to exceed the amount of uncertainty reduced, resulting in wear-out

Two step flow model of influence proposes that a small group of *influencers* disseminate information since they can modify the opinions of a large number of other people

Uncertainty avoidance one of Hofstede's cultural dimensions: The degree to which people feel threatened by ambiguous situations and have beliefs and institutions that help them to avoid this uncertainty

Unconditioned stimulus (UCS) a stimulus that is naturally capable of causing a response

Underground economy secondary markets (such as flea markets) where transactions are not officially recorded

Unipolar emotions emotional reactions that are either wholly positive or wholly negative

Unplanned buying when a shopper buys merchandise she did not intend to purchase, often because she recognizes a new need while in the store

Urban myth an unsubstantiated "fact" that many people accept as true

User the person who actually consumes a product or service

User-generated content consumers voice their opinions about products, brands, and companies on blogs, podcasts, and social networking sites such as Facebook and Twitter, and film their own commercials that they post on sites such as YouTube

Utilitarian function states that we develop some attitudes toward products simply because they provide pleasure or pain

Value a belief that some condition is preferable to its opposite

Value-expressive function states we develop attitudes toward products because of what they say about him or her as a person

Value system a culture's ranking of the relative importance of values

Variable-interval reinforcement the time that must pass before an organism's response is reinforced varies based on some average

Variable-ratio reinforcement you get reinforced after a certain number of responses, but you don't know how many responses are required

Variety amnesia a condition where people consume products to the point where they no longer enjoy them

Variety seeking the desire to choose new alternatives over more familiar ones

Video blogging (vlogging) posting video diaries on sites such as YouTube or photos on Flickr

Viral marketing the strategy of getting customers to sell a product on behalf of the company that creates it

Virtual goods digital items that people buy and sell online

Virtual identity the appearance and personality a person takes on as an avatar in a computer-mediated environment like Second Life

Virtual worlds immersive 3D virtual environments such as Second Life

Voluntary simplifiers people who believe that once basic material needs are satisfied, additional income does not lead to happiness

Von Restorff effect techniques like distinctive packaging that increase the novelty of a stimulus also improve recall

Want the particular form of consumption chosen to satisfy a need

Warming process of transforming new objects and places into those that feel cozy, hospitable, and authentic

Web 2.0 the current version of the Internet as a social, interactive medium from its original roots as a form of one-way transmission from producers to consumers

Weber's Law the principle that the stronger the initial stimulus, the greater its change must be for it to be noticed

Widgets small programs that users can download onto their desktops, or embed in their blogs or profile pages, that import some form of live content

Wiki online program that lets several people change a document on a Web page and then track those changes

Wisdom of crowds a perspective that argues under the right circumstances, groups are smarter than the smartest people in them; implies that large numbers of consumers can predict successful products

Word of mouth (WOM) product information transmitted by individual consumers on an informal basis

Word-phrase dictionary in sentiment analysis, a library that codes data so that the program can scan the text to identify whether the words in the dictionary appear

Worldview a perspective on social norms and behaviors that tends to differ among social classes

Zipf's Law pattern that describes the tendency for the most robust effect to be far more powerful than others in its class; applies to consumer behavior in terms of buyers' overwhelming preferences for the market leader in a product category

Index

8

80/20 Rule, 8, 33, 237, 248, 458

A

Abilities, 59, 75, 101, 150, 158, 160, 284, 305, 353, 406
Abstract, 84, 95, 99, 161, 178, 281, 287, 324-325, 358, 368, 405, 455
Abstraction, 100, 110, 144, 268, 324, 452
Abuse, 207, 245, 247
Account executive, 255
Accountability, 18, 22
Accountants, 6, 432
Accounting, 3, 163, 219, 308, 314, 316, 336-337, 339-340, 462
   future of, 337
Acculturation, 142, 158-159, 455
accuracy, 107, 114, 170, 214, 265, 267, 295
   of information, 114, 295
Achievement, 129, 131, 139, 142, 188, 229, 239, 455
action verbs, 184
Actual products, 71
Adaptation, 64, 66, 75, 149, 159, 278, 296, 455, 460
   advertising, 64, 66, 159, 278, 296, 455
Addictive consumption, 243
addresses, 421, 436
adjustments, 169
Administrators, 88, 292
Advanced economies, 160
Advances, 38, 114-115, 162-164, 212-213, 215, 250, 295-298, 331, 339, 341, 373-376, 399, 411-413, 451-452
Advantages, 77, 226, 278, 299
Advergaming, 455
Advertising, 4, 7, 20-25, 28-29, 31, 34-35, 37-39, 42-43, 47, 52, 58-61, 63-66, 71, 74, 76-79, 86-87, 92, 98, 101, 103, 106-107, 110-115, 119-120, 123-124, 136, 138, 140, 142, 144, 146, 152, 154, 159-164, 174, 186, 189, 197, 200, 202, 207-215, 219, 224, 229, 232-233, 236-238, 240, 242, 246-247, 249-251, 258-259, 266, 268, 271-273, 275, 277-284, 286-288, 291-298, 308, 312, 314-315, 323, 326, 331, 339, 341, 360, 364-365, 369, 372, 374, 376, 384, 386, 394, 397, 399, 401-402, 407, 409, 411-413, 416, 426, 429, 432-436, 439, 445-453, 455, 457-458, 464, 467
   corporate, 23-24, 34, 38, 79, 112, 114, 163, 174, 212, 249, 275, 292, 296, 365, 386, 394, 409, 411
   creation of, 209
   defined, 4, 31, 103, 399, 455
   e-mail, 35, 161, 296, 434
   ethics in, 37
   evaluating, 38, 79, 339, 341, 384, 452
   local, 39, 52, 58, 77, 140, 152, 154, 163-164, 266, 293, 331, 365, 369, 372, 397, 409, 439, 451, 455, 457
   mobile, 7, 58, 138, 146, 186, 249-251, 273, 281, 295, 360, 399, 448, 458
   mystery, 103, 115, 119, 376
   online, 4, 7, 20, 22, 35, 37-38, 58, 63, 65, 77-79, 112-113, 115, 119, 138, 162-164, 174, 213-214, 219, 242, 246-247, 249, 251, 277, 292-294, 296, 308, 312, 339, 341, 360, 369, 374, 376, 386, 399, 407, 411-412, 416, 426, 432-434, 436, 439, 446-448, 450-453, 455, 457-458, 464, 467
   product, 4, 7, 20, 22, 28-29, 34-35, 37, 42, 47, 52, 64, 71, 74, 76-79, 86-87, 92, 101, 103, 106-107, 110-112, 114-115, 120, 123-124, 136, 142, 144, 152, 154, 160-163, 174, 197, 209-210, 212-214, 229, 232-233, 236-238, 242, 247, 249-250, 258-259, 266, 268, 271, 273, 275, 277-284,
286-288, 291-297, 312, 315, 323, 326, 331, 341, 364-365, 369, 372, 374, 376, 384, 386, 394, 397, 399, 401, 407, 409, 416, 426, 429, 433-436, 439, 446, 448-452, 455, 457-458, 464, 467
   reminder, 360
   retail, 22, 34, 210, 246-247, 250-251, 360, 372, 374, 376, 386, 452, 464
   teaser, 63
   types of, 28, 35, 98, 111-112, 123, 146, 159, 208, 214, 247, 259, 275, 283, 293, 394, 399, 402, 429, 446-447, 455, 458
Advertising agencies, 21, 29, 38, 77, 146, 238
Advertising campaign, 22, 43, 52, 112, 119, 186, 233, 236, 271, 286, 323, 429, 432, 467
Advertising wear-out, 87, 110, 282, 455
Affect, 6, 23, 29, 47, 49, 52, 77, 83, 87-88, 96, 103, 112-113, 115, 123-124, 143, 150, 158, 160-161, 169, 214, 256-257, 274, 277, 282, 290-292, 297-298, 320, 325, 339-340, 346-348, 353, 359-360, 370, 373-375, 382, 389, 391, 407, 409-410, 418-419, 421, 432, 445, 447, 455, 462
Africa, 7, 150, 172, 198, 393
African American consumers, 7
African Americans, 10, 19
Age, 3, 8-9, 11, 16, 23, 29, 33, 35, 37-38, 49, 55, 58, 65, 78-79, 99, 113, 115, 137, 139, 148, 150, 160-164, 183, 186, 188-189, 194, 200, 202, 207, 209, 212-214, 223, 226, 237, 242, 246, 250-251, 261, 278, 294-298, 314-315, 339-341, 345, 364, 374-375, 388-390, 392-393, 401-406, 411-413, 426, 434, 450-453, 455, 458-459, 463
Agencies, 9, 21-22, 29, 38, 77, 79, 113, 146, 154, 219, 222, 224, 231, 238, 250, 382, 456
agenda, 78, 331, 341, 401
   hidden, 78, 401
Agent, 6, 142, 328, 336, 458
Agents, 142, 328-329, 336-338, 341, 394, 401, 411, 434, 439, 455, 461
   report, 411, 439
aggression, 77, 93
agreement, 74, 238, 364, 394, 406, 409, 455
Agreements, 22, 292, 420
AIDS, 159, 198, 281, 286, 298, 317
AIG, 24, 365
Aircraft, 51, 148
Alabama, 364
ALE, 139, 452
Alternative evaluation, 307
Anger, 38, 103, 227, 244, 346, 364, 437, 443
Animals, 84, 89, 119, 127, 197, 205, 233, 241, 358, 390, 393, 411, 418, 440
antecedents, 132, 164, 295
anticipate, 63
Anticonsumption, 247-248, 341, 455
appearance, 4, 94, 137, 139, 145-146, 153, 160, 168-171, 178, 186, 188, 194-198, 200, 202-203, 207-208, 214, 277, 280, 323, 329, 353, 364, 429, 456, 460, 467
Application, 20, 38, 53, 70, 87, 113, 131, 226, 250-251, 272, 295, 357, 387, 441, 452, 455, 459
Applications, 4, 17, 58, 76, 86-88, 92, 94, 112, 135, 139, 143, 160, 163, 220, 222, 266, 273, 281, 296, 299, 313, 349, 371-372, 411, 455, 460, 462
Arbitrage, 296
archive, 161, 177, 453
Argentina, 7, 157, 182
arguments, 37, 132, 270, 280, 282-283, 286, 289-291, 293, 372, 396, 435, 464
   logical, 270
ARM, 266, 288, 326, 346, 448
Arousal, 47, 51, 85, 102, 120, 122, 297-298, 349, 353, 370, 412, 458

Art, 9, 13, 31, 68, 105, 114, 137, 147, 160-163, 186, 205-206, 212-215, 219, 251, 279, 287-288, 291, 296, 306, 309, 352, 365, 373-374, 376, 411-413, 424, 428, 451-452, 455, 457, 462
Asia, 77, 151, 153-154, 163-164, 213-215, 267, 273, 283, 295, 358, 398, 453
Asian Americans, 10, 204
Assertiveness, 364
Assimilation effect, 262
Atmospherics, 359-360, 371, 375, 455
attachments, 35, 182, 207, 368
attention, 4, 13, 19, 36, 42, 44, 46-47, 49, 52, 59-66, 74-77, 87, 93-94, 96, 99, 101-104, 107, 109, 113-115, 131-133, 135-137, 141, 147, 162, 165, 203-204, 210, 242, 257, 260, 275, 277, 281-284, 286, 288-289, 293, 296-298, 306, 321, 325, 353-354, 360, 363-364, 369, 372, 374-375, 397, 424, 436, 448, 455, 464-465
Attitudes, 6, 19, 29, 35, 37, 47, 78, 100, 113, 142, 146, 154, 192-193, 207, 212-213, 236-237, 247, 251, 253-299, 341, 354, 369, 375-376, 396, 401, 406, 412, 421, 427-428, 436, 442, 452, 455, 457-461, 463, 465-467
   components of, 256, 264, 289, 291, 442
Attorneys, 390
Attribute, 49, 73, 99, 102, 113, 210, 229, 232, 264-266, 274, 277, 279, 281, 295, 297, 326-327, 330-331, 334-335, 338, 340-341, 348, 365, 368, 392, 400, 456-457, 463
attributes, 20, 31, 50, 52, 72, 74, 79, 89, 94, 99-100, 102, 112, 123, 129, 132, 144, 155, 170, 179, 185, 196, 198, 238, 257-258, 264-265, 271, 277, 282-283, 299, 305, 307, 314-315, 318, 323, 325-326, 329, 334-338, 370, 372, 400, 457-458, 460-462, 464-466
Attribution theory, 297, 452
audience, 9, 39, 59, 62, 68, 77, 96, 115, 162, 214, 254, 272, 277-278, 283, 288-289, 291, 308, 410, 427, 433, 442, 451
   feedback from, 427
   global, 162
   in social media, 442
   needs of, 278, 410
   primary, 68, 442
   size of, 9, 39
Augmented reality, 58, 75-76, 78, 455
Australia, 7, 97, 151, 154, 184, 190, 202, 412
Austria, 246
Authority, 227, 247, 250, 270, 349, 420
   express, 349
availability, 20, 295, 297, 341, 356, 359, 389
Available, 26, 56, 73, 79, 94-95, 104, 106, 129, 151, 193-194, 204, 210, 232, 235, 242, 259, 261, 270-272, 283, 304, 313, 315, 319, 321-322, 328, 331, 335, 340, 352, 357-358, 382, 390, 410, 413, 436, 457-458, 460, 462, 464, 466
Avatars, 112-113, 174-175, 208, 211, 213, 278, 293, 390, 444-445, 462
avoidance, 91, 127, 143, 158-159, 161, 376, 424-425, 447, 449, 455, 467
Awareness, 20, 36, 58-59, 67, 87, 102, 108, 113, 150, 193, 199, 212, 245, 249, 260, 275, 282, 317, 370, 374, 435, 439-440, 461, 466

B

Baby boomers, 151, 390
Back-translation, 154
bad news, 292
Bait-and-switch, 19
Balance sheet, 23
Bankruptcy, 18, 210, 283, 365
Banks, 311, 353, 364-365
Bargaining, 375, 394, 455
   integrative, 375
Barter, 370
Basic form, 85
Behavior, 1-3, 5-7, 14, 16, 20, 25-35, 38, 41, 47, 51,

469

53, 59, 75, 77, 79, 81-84, 89-94, 96, 99-100, 109-115, 117, 121-122, 125, 127, 129, 142-143, 146-147, 153, 158-159, 162-163, 167-169, 174, 176, 184-185, 190, 195, 197, 207, 209-214, 217, 220-224, 227-229, 238-239, 242, 245-248, 250-251, 253, 255-257, 259, 261-264, 266-269, 278, 284, 286, 289-293, 295, 297, 301-303, 306, 317, 328, 333-335, 337, 339-340, 343, 345, 348, 353, 361-362, 364, 369, 371, 373-376, 379-382, 399, 405, 407-408, 410, 412-413, 415, 418, 420-421, 423-426, 432, 441-443, 446-448, 450-452, 455-467
   consistency in, 127
   in groups, 129, 418, 424-425
Behavioral learning theories, 84, 109-110, 456
Behavioral targeting, 241-242, 248, 456, 463
Belgium, 139
belief system, 140, 239
Believability, 277, 283
Benefits, 33, 67, 87, 107, 120, 122-123, 127, 129, 150, 160-161, 192, 237, 256, 280, 287, 293, 312, 319, 335, 348, 357, 387, 460, 463
   extended, 387
   service, 237, 287, 387, 463
Benevolence, 295
Better Business Bureau, 366, 406
biases, 44, 69, 163, 314, 338, 353, 453
   cultural, 44, 163, 353
bibliography, 375
Bicycles, 185, 372
Bid, 248, 345, 451
billing, 308
blogging, 274, 291, 425, 428, 446, 467
blogs, 17, 79, 131, 162-163, 214, 274, 277, 291-292, 295-296, 312, 314, 337, 374, 386, 396, 411, 420, 432, 450, 456, 467
   business, 79, 162-163, 295-296, 374, 386, 396, 411, 432, 450, 456
   company, 162, 214, 277, 291-292, 312, 386, 396, 411, 420, 467
   fake, 296, 337
   product reviews on, 337
Boards of directors, 395
body art, 205
Body language, 374
Bonds, 4, 14, 19, 34, 158, 179, 334, 443
   attachment, 14
   contract, 443
   performance, 14
Boomers, 151, 390, 458, 460, 462
Borrowing, 150, 376
bots, 328, 337
Bounded rationality, 312, 336, 456
Boycotts, 38
Brand, 4-5, 7-8, 14-16, 19-20, 23, 44-45, 47, 50, 52-53, 67, 71-76, 78, 83-89, 93-97, 99-104, 106, 108, 110-115, 124, 131-133, 135-141, 143, 151, 153-155, 157, 160-164, 177, 179-180, 182, 185, 200, 203, 210, 212-215, 224, 226-229, 231-233, 237, 246-250, 254, 256-259, 262, 264-267, 275-276, 278, 282-284, 286-288, 290, 292-295, 297, 299, 307-308, 311-312, 314-318, 320-323, 325-327, 329-341, 358-359, 365, 370-374, 376-377, 384, 388, 400-401, 405-406, 410-411, 413, 419, 421-422, 425, 428, 432-435, 439-440, 446-452, 455-458, 460-462, 464-466
   brand equity, 19, 87, 110, 113, 231, 250, 413, 456
   brand extension, 112, 295, 341
   brand personality, 67, 163, 179, 229, 231-233, 248-250, 370, 456
   co-branding, 456
   decisions about, 335, 421-422, 446, 457
   licensing, 88, 110, 112, 264, 461
   managing, 113, 164, 250, 374, 376, 451
   overview, 45, 78, 162, 297, 339, 411
   packaging, 4, 47, 73, 76, 88, 103, 110, 164, 229, 232, 249, 286, 290, 312, 327, 331, 450, 462
   positioning, 72-73, 75, 210, 213, 250, 297, 325, 340, 464
   public relations, 161, 293, 449
   sales promotions, 135
   value proposition, 339
Brand ambassadors, 177, 439
Brand communities, 16, 421-422, 446, 450-451
Brand equity, 19, 87, 110, 113, 231, 250, 413, 456

Brand extensions, 88, 340
Brand loyalty, 4, 83, 103, 154, 163, 212, 231, 334, 336-338, 341, 359, 384, 401, 421, 446, 456-457
Brand management, 212, 232
Brand managers, 151, 232
Brand meaning, 114-115
Brand names, 52, 71, 78, 83-86, 95-96, 99, 101-102, 108, 114-115, 258, 312, 326, 329, 332, 334, 336, 405, 413
Brand personality, 67, 163, 179, 229, 231-233, 248-250, 370, 456
Brandfests, 421, 446-447, 456
Branding, 4, 77-78, 88, 110, 113, 115, 138, 164, 178, 212, 250, 296, 339, 341, 411, 452, 456, 459
   generic, 88
   licensing, 88, 110
   strategies, 4, 88, 110, 341, 452, 456
Branding strategies, 456
Brands, 4, 8, 11, 14, 17-20, 37, 46, 52, 56, 58, 67, 72-74, 76-77, 82, 86, 88-89, 96, 99-104, 110-115, 123, 139, 142-143, 146, 148-151, 153, 155-156, 162-164, 179, 208, 210, 212-213, 224-226, 228-229, 231, 236, 238, 240, 249-250, 257, 259, 262, 264-266, 276-277, 283, 293-294, 296, 306, 308, 312, 314-315, 318, 320-327, 331, 333-336, 339-341, 358, 361, 376, 405, 409, 411, 419, 421-422, 429, 432, 434, 436, 450, 452, 455-457, 459-461, 463-464, 467
   defined, 4, 14, 103, 139, 226, 455
   family, 77, 88, 103, 110, 115, 142-143, 148, 210, 231, 264, 312, 376, 409, 411, 419, 432, 434, 436, 455, 459, 461, 463
   generic, 88, 231, 312, 315, 331, 436
   importance of, 112, 115, 143, 155, 265-266, 315, 323, 335, 456, 461, 467
   individual, 82, 99-101, 110, 142, 148, 150, 163, 208, 213, 224, 226, 250, 264, 324, 339-341, 419, 436, 455, 459-461, 464, 467
   manufacturer, 19, 72, 88, 153, 228, 277, 331, 459
   national, 20, 77, 113, 150, 153, 155-156, 164, 208, 213, 266, 294, 322, 331, 341
   private-label, 88
   store, 11, 19, 46, 52, 56, 58, 72, 77, 89, 96, 100, 102, 110, 139, 212-213, 277, 294, 318, 321, 325, 331, 334, 358, 361, 376, 409, 436, 455, 467
Brazil, 28, 148, 153-154, 215, 277, 350, 397, 456
Breakdown, 20, 357
Bribery, 19
Brick-and-mortar retailers, 357
Bridges, 243, 440
Britain, 35, 52
Broker, 430
Brokers, 26, 345, 436
Budget, 7, 303, 333, 375, 381, 397, 409, 460
Budgeting, 394
Bullying, 355, 453
Bundling, 339
Burglary, 178
Burundi, 351
business books, 374
Business ethics, 18, 33, 37, 215, 339, 456
   definition of, 33
   responsibility in, 18
business intelligence, 251
Business model, 249, 387, 445
Business review, 38, 79, 164, 376
Business services, 233
Business-to-business marketing, 384
Buttons, 11, 95, 152, 183, 215, 402
Buyclass, 384, 407-408, 411, 456, 462-463, 466
Buyers, 39, 56, 68, 78, 234, 256, 262, 309, 314, 320, 322, 325, 329, 339, 341, 356, 360, 375-376, 382, 384, 394, 407-408, 436, 439, 445, 455, 463, 467
   Buying center, 384, 407
   Culture, 376, 455, 463, 467
   Modified rebuy, 407
   Product, 56, 68, 78, 234, 256, 309, 320, 322, 325, 329, 341, 356, 375-376, 382, 384, 394, 407-408, 436, 439, 455, 463, 467
   Rational, 256, 339, 407-408, 463
   Reference group, 455, 463
   Role, 56, 78, 375-376, 384, 408, 436
   Social classes, 467
   Transactional, 376, 467

Buying center, 384, 386, 407, 456
Buzz, 72, 149, 155, 291-294, 361, 422, 427-428, 433, 435, 438-439, 453
buzzwords, 209

C
Call centers, 226
Campers, 365
Canada, 7, 47, 154, 161, 164
Capabilities, 17, 161, 220
Capacity, 63, 96, 114, 205, 419, 423, 466
Capital, 124, 231, 233, 320, 443, 457, 459, 465
   customer, 233
   definition of, 459
   fixed, 459, 465
   human, 233, 465
   working, 233
capital letters, 443, 459
Capitalism, 156
Career, 176, 185-186, 239, 271, 288, 384, 404
Careers, 151, 404
Caribbean, 45, 76-77
Case Studies, 295
Case study, 36, 76, 79, 112, 160, 164, 210, 249, 294, 338, 373, 410, 449
Cash cows, 37
Catalogs, 240, 312, 358
Cause-related marketing, 295
Celebrity endorsements, 263
Celebrity endorser, 263, 275, 292-293, 296
Cell phones, 62, 96, 148, 181, 241, 273, 353, 359, 373, 403, 410, 448, 458, 462
Censorship, 34
Census data, 387
Central Europe, 164
Certainty, 286, 297
Channel, 20, 47, 55, 59, 76, 104, 185-186, 192, 214, 222, 233, 241, 289, 293, 387, 450, 455, 465
Channels, 7, 45, 55, 59, 154, 186, 222, 328, 339, 404, 410, 433, 457
   Industrial, 410
Character, 9, 31-32, 45, 49, 57, 63, 72, 98, 104, 140, 151, 153, 164, 173-174, 192, 232, 243, 276, 278, 280, 308, 331, 361, 395, 401, 405, 423, 455, 457
   Development, 308, 401
Cheating, 411
Checkout, 306, 355, 357, 360, 362, 372
Child labor, 21
Child Protection Act, 22
   1966, 22
Children, 9, 23, 25-26, 28-29, 34, 36, 38, 68, 74, 76, 93, 100, 112, 114, 140, 142, 148, 150, 152, 154-155, 163, 171, 178, 184, 193, 202, 204, 212-213, 223, 242, 244-245, 248, 284, 292, 347-348, 363, 380, 382, 387-393, 395, 397, 400-410, 412-413, 456, 463, 465, 467
   minor, 154, 407
Chile, 109
China, 7, 14, 37, 72, 142, 149, 152-153, 156-157, 164, 195-196, 200, 203, 214-215, 338, 365, 397, 456
   material culture, 156
Chinese, 72, 79, 141-142, 150, 152-153, 155-157, 163-164, 196, 200, 215, 248, 273, 287, 338, 341, 397
Christianity, 157
CIF, 141-142
citations, 438
Civil rights, 19
Claims, 20, 22-24, 35, 47, 77-78, 89, 100, 102, 107, 115, 119, 129, 142, 148, 163, 185, 190, 210, 224, 226, 229, 231, 269, 277-278, 293, 297, 319, 350, 353, 368, 425, 428, 460
   inflated, 460
   investigation, 77-78, 297
Classical conditioning, 84-87, 89, 109-111, 113-114, 259, 456
Classification, 161, 419, 456, 459
Click-through rate, 329
Climate, 20, 24, 377, 382, 406, 410
Climate change, 20, 24
clothing, 4, 9, 13, 49, 58, 88, 93, 113, 129-130, 141, 157, 160, 172, 174, 176, 178, 181, 191, 194, 197, 199, 204-205, 209-212, 242, 263, 277, 281, 314, 331, 347, 355, 358, 360, 366, 371-373, 413, 419, 426, 428-429, 445, 451, 461
   for job interviews, 174

Clustering, 240-241, 251, 451, 464
Clusters, 106, 154, 240-241, 418, 431
CMS, 214
Coalitions, 395
Co-branding, 456
codes of ethics, 19
Coercion, 394, 455
Coercive power, 420, 446-447, 456
Cognition, 77, 114, 211, 228, 250, 256-257, 291, 294-295, 306, 339, 341, 455-456
Cognitive dissonance, 127, 159, 260-261, 290-292, 465-466
Cognitive learning theory, 92, 110, 456
collaboration, 17, 386
Collapse, 365
Collections, 219
Colleges, 27, 233, 264, 292, 420, 445
Collision, 423
Columbia, 77, 133
Commitment, 34, 120, 162, 212, 259, 291, 295, 297, 320, 426, 464
Commodities, 212, 214, 245
Common market, 331
Communication, 17, 29, 37, 42, 55, 74, 87, 98, 113, 132, 160, 163-164, 211, 226, 251, 270-271, 273, 279, 288-289, 291, 295-297, 307, 341, 375-376, 399, 412-413, 416, 431-433, 435-436, 441-443, 446, 449-450, 452-453, 456, 460-462, 466
    grapevine, 452
Communication model, 226
Communication process, 461
communication style, 226, 375
    American, 375
Communism, 156
community building, 146
Companies, 8, 13, 15-20, 23-24, 33, 35, 39, 45-47, 51, 55, 72-73, 86, 88-89, 95-96, 107-108, 112, 119, 125, 131, 137, 141, 146-148, 151, 153, 155-156, 160, 164, 174, 179, 191, 203-205, 210, 231, 234, 238, 242-243, 247, 281, 292-294, 296, 305, 308, 312, 324-325, 328, 330, 354, 362-367, 372-373, 376, 380, 382-384, 386-387, 391, 395, 404, 406-407, 409-410, 416, 419, 421-422, 425, 432, 434, 436-437, 439, 441, 443-444, 446, 448, 455-458, 460, 462-463, 467
company image, 275
Comparative advertising, 266, 283, 291, 293, 297, 457
Comparative analysis, 297, 376
compatibility, 457
Compensation, 390
Compete, 13, 36, 62, 74, 120, 151, 164, 192, 325, 349, 355, 358-359, 395, 445
Competition, 7, 45, 61, 64, 72, 114, 139, 160, 198, 214, 232, 274, 283, 297, 333, 339-340, 357-358, 370, 404, 417, 420, 448
    perfect, 404, 417
Competitive advantage, 46, 293, 341, 364, 372, 376
Competitive environment, 114
Competitors, 4, 48, 60, 73-74, 86-87, 89, 101, 233, 266, 276, 280, 283, 325, 329, 333, 359, 437, 464, 466
complaints, 137, 152, 353, 364, 376, 437, 448
    customer, 364, 376
Complementarity, 241, 464
Compliance, 259, 268, 291, 295, 426, 450, 457
Compliments, 84, 89, 91, 93
compromise, 179, 222, 394-395, 397, 412, 455, 461
Conditions, 11, 22, 49, 59, 90-91, 93, 106, 115, 149, 178, 209, 228-229, 258, 274, 283, 289, 292-293, 297, 306, 364, 384, 388, 436, 448, 457, 461
Conference Board, 18
Confidence, 24, 53, 59, 107, 115, 123, 150, 156, 161, 171, 176, 233, 266, 299, 320, 427, 452, 457
Configuration, 68-69, 96, 459
Conflict, 55, 103, 126-127, 148, 158, 174, 184, 213, 221, 261, 350, 394, 399, 408, 410, 412, 455
connotation, 95, 456
Consideration, 55, 67, 114, 155, 295, 312, 321-323, 336, 340, 359, 457
Consistency, 127, 179, 254, 260-261, 264, 267, 270, 277-278, 290-291, 295, 329, 338, 464
Construction, 64, 96, 155, 233, 295, 341, 438
Consumed consumers, 245, 247-248, 457
Consumer addiction, 243, 248, 457
Consumer behavior, 1-3, 5-7, 14, 16, 20, 25, 27-34, 38, 41, 47, 53, 59, 75, 77, 79, 81, 83, 100,
    111, 113-115, 117, 129, 142-143, 158-159, 162-163, 167-169, 174, 176, 195, 207, 209, 211-214, 217, 220-221, 227-228, 238, 242, 247-248, 250-251, 253, 261-263, 278, 292, 295, 297, 301-303, 317, 333, 335, 337, 339-340, 343, 345, 348, 371, 373-374, 379, 408, 412-413, 415, 421, 423, 448, 450, 452, 455, 457, 461, 465, 467
    cultural factors, 467
    models of, 339-340, 412, 455
Consumer choice, 113-115, 212, 339-340
    branding and, 115
Consumer goods, 15, 22, 30, 156-157, 460, 465
Consumer groups, 33, 406
Consumer knowledge, 114, 250, 340
Consumer preferences, 108, 115, 214, 250
Consumer Product Safety Commission, 22
Consumer products, 22, 137, 148, 338, 401
Consumer Products Safety Act, 22
Consumer protection, 22, 38, 365
Consumer satisfaction/dissatisfaction, 364, 370, 457
Consumer search, 339-341
    economics of, 339
Consumer spending, 157, 211
Consumer trends, 431
Consumer-generated content, 136
Consumerism, 21, 24, 38, 146, 158, 369, 374, 457
Consumers, 2-13, 16-27, 29, 32-39, 42, 44-47, 49-50, 52, 54-56, 58-59, 61-64, 67-68, 70-78, 82-92, 94-98, 100-103, 105-115, 118-120, 122, 124, 126-127, 129-133, 135-138, 140, 142, 144, 146, 148-151, 153-160, 162-165, 169-171, 173, 176-182, 185, 189, 192, 194, 197, 202-203, 205, 207-210, 212, 220, 222-223, 226, 228-231, 233-234, 236-250, 254-264, 266, 268-275, 277-279, 282-284, 286-292, 295, 297, 302, 304-306, 308, 310-314, 317-318, 320, 322-341, 344-346, 348-352, 354-355, 359-361, 364, 366-376, 380-382, 384, 388, 390, 392-394, 400-402, 407, 409-413, 416, 418-421, 423-441, 444, 446, 448, 450-452, 455-467
    lifestyles, 11, 146, 148, 153, 155, 189, 234, 238, 248, 286, 393, 423, 425, 430, 461, 465-466
Consumption, 4, 6, 13-14, 25-27, 30-31, 33-34, 37-38, 43, 45, 71, 75, 77, 107, 113, 115, 119, 122-123, 126, 129, 131-132, 137, 140, 142-143, 149, 154, 156, 159, 161-164, 169, 176-179, 182, 187, 193, 210-213, 215, 222-223, 229, 236, 238, 240-241, 243-245, 247-251, 255, 257, 264, 297, 316, 324, 337, 340-341, 346, 348, 350, 353, 364, 374, 376, 382, 393, 401-402, 410-413, 418-421, 423-424, 426, 444, 446-447, 450-451, 453, 457-458, 460-462, 464-465, 467
    consumer, 4, 6, 14, 25-27, 30-31, 33-34, 37-38, 71, 75, 77, 107, 113, 115, 119, 122-123, 129, 131-132, 137, 140, 142-143, 149, 154, 156, 159, 161-164, 169, 176, 178-179, 182, 193, 211-213, 215, 222-223, 229, 236, 238, 240, 243-245, 247-251, 255, 257, 264, 297, 324, 337, 340-341, 346, 348, 364, 374, 376, 401-402, 410-413, 419-421, 423, 446-447, 450-451, 453, 457-458, 460-462, 464-465, 467
Contacts, 139, 154, 266, 336, 417
Content, 4, 16-18, 20, 22, 33-34, 63, 87, 100, 105, 113, 132, 135-137, 141, 145, 151, 162-163, 170, 189, 212, 214, 219-220, 274, 277, 280, 282, 284, 289, 294, 298, 341, 375, 403, 405, 420, 432, 434-435, 437, 440-443, 453, 458, 462, 464-465, 467
    e-commerce, 16, 33-34, 113, 341, 464-465
Contract, 156, 275, 308, 443
contractions, 204
Contracts, 249
Contrast effect, 262
Control, 22, 28, 37, 50, 53, 59, 87, 92, 113-114, 129, 133, 135, 170, 179, 184, 207, 220, 244, 268-269, 271-273, 309, 326-327, 355, 389, 396-397, 399, 402, 410, 430, 434, 437, 443, 462-463, 465
Control processes, 114
Control systems, 399
    external, 399
Controllers, 175
Controlling, 119, 220, 452
Conventions, 153-154, 170, 288, 457

Convergence, 407, 460
Conversation, 55, 171, 429, 435, 466
conversations, 4, 133, 277, 294, 396, 428, 434-435, 439, 443, 446, 452
conversion, 341
cookies, 43, 68, 120, 133, 204, 223, 270, 275, 330, 359
Cooperation, 19, 268, 340, 395
Copyright, 1, 31, 41, 81, 117, 126, 167, 217, 241, 253, 280, 301, 343, 352, 379, 389, 415, 419, 455
Core competency, 72
Corporate social responsibility, 275, 296
    CSR, 275, 296
Corporate web sites, 112
corporation, 5, 45, 49, 72, 138, 177, 190, 242, 272, 319, 322, 383, 386, 394, 426, 467
    definition of, 190
Corporations, 18-19, 151, 154, 193, 247, 327, 369, 382, 386, 406, 408, 438, 456, 459
    domestic, 369
    foreign, 19, 151, 154
    professional, 369
Cosmopolitanism, 149, 158, 163, 457
Costs, 22, 45, 203, 223, 246, 305, 312, 339-340, 357, 432, 465
    distribution, 339-340
Countries, 7, 15, 19, 26, 36-37, 39, 49, 112, 118, 133, 138, 141-142, 144-145, 148-149, 151-156, 158, 160, 170, 183, 185, 189, 194, 274, 322, 331-332, 338, 341, 349-350, 357, 368-369, 373, 384, 390, 405, 441, 460, 465
Country of origin, 329, 331, 336, 338, 341, 457
Country-of-origin, 331, 333, 338, 341
Coupons, 53, 58, 124, 273, 281, 331, 349, 439
courtesy, 5, 8, 10-12, 15, 17, 23-25, 27-28, 46, 50, 52, 54, 62, 69, 84-85, 88, 90, 95, 97, 104-105, 107, 109, 128, 130, 133-134, 138-139, 153, 164, 171-173, 175, 177, 180, 183, 187, 189-190, 195-196, 199, 202, 227, 232, 236, 245, 258, 260, 267, 276, 281, 285, 287, 311, 319, 322-323, 326, 328, 330, 332-333, 347, 351, 356-357, 362-363, 366, 383, 385, 393, 398, 403, 437, 440
CPSC, 22
Creativity, 92, 295, 404, 423
credibility, 229, 275, 277, 282-283, 288, 291-292, 296-297, 370, 436, 464, 466
Credit, 6, 22, 85, 113, 127, 130, 136, 165, 205, 228, 246, 255, 331, 359, 362, 365, 375, 445, 449
Credit cards, 85, 113, 130, 362
Creolization, 157-159, 457
criticism, 20, 29-30, 72, 128, 141, 298, 372, 420, 427, 440
Crowdsourcing, 387, 407, 453, 457
CSR, 275, 296
    corporate social responsibility, 275, 296
cultural context, 31
Cultural differences, 19, 49, 154, 161, 164, 170, 269, 341, 353, 397
    in motivation, 161
Cultural factors, 54, 120, 467
Cultural identity, 144
Cultural sensitivity, 152
Cultural values, 4, 118, 141-144, 149, 158, 163, 412, 462
Culture, 4, 7, 13-14, 18, 24, 29-31, 33-34, 37-38, 48-49, 71, 79, 106, 118, 120-122, 131, 140-143, 145, 149, 151-156, 158-159, 161, 163-164, 168, 174, 182, 184, 186, 190-191, 194-195, 198-200, 202-205, 208, 211-213, 215, 219, 224, 229, 237, 248-250, 294-295, 311, 332, 340, 352, 358, 374, 376, 387, 395, 410-411, 425, 429, 451, 453, 455, 457-467
    colors and, 184
    consumption and, 38, 149, 212, 250, 411
    definition of, 33, 190, 425, 459
    national, 13, 34, 49, 153, 155-156, 164, 202, 208, 211, 213, 294
    research on, 149, 451, 453
    sports and, 149
    status and, 149
Culture shock, 164
Currency, 38, 140, 441
Cursor, 63
Curves, 196
    supply, 196
Customer orientation, 375
Customer satisfaction, 113, 364, 375-376
Customer service, 226, 278, 315, 386

Customer service representative, 226
customer support, 250
Customers, 7-8, 11, 14-15, 18-20, 35, 37, 47, 51-53,
  56, 58, 76, 91-92, 135-138, 141, 151,
  153-154, 159, 174, 183, 209-210, 215, 223,
  229, 233, 235-238, 247, 249, 258, 261, 267,
  271, 278, 294-295, 305, 309, 312, 324-325,
  328, 331, 338, 346, 348-349, 353, 355-356,
  358-362, 364-365, 367, 371-372, 375-376,
  384, 386-387, 391, 409, 412, 420, 423, 432,
  436-437, 444, 448, 450, 453, 456-457,
  459-463, 467
  as partners, 457
  business-to-business, 384, 386, 456
Customs, 19, 152, 154, 157

D
Damage, 338, 438
data, 7, 9, 11, 20, 33, 35, 37-39, 45, 72, 94-95, 99,
  104, 106, 110, 125, 154, 162, 165, 180, 193,
  200, 223, 226, 229, 234, 237-238, 240-242,
  248, 250, 266, 275, 298-299, 305, 311, 317,
  328, 340-341, 357, 362, 377, 387, 405, 428,
  453, 458, 461, 463, 467
Data collection, 223
data storage, 72
Database, 11, 33-35, 339, 458
  characteristics of, 339
  examples of, 33-34
  uses, 11, 34
Database marketing, 11, 33-34, 458
databases, 107, 139, 421
dates, 72, 173, 326, 341, 358
Deadlines, 347
Death, 13, 27, 119, 185, 204-205, 224, 242, 244, 251,
  286, 392, 418, 425, 455
  premature, 185
Debit cards, 362
Debt, 228, 245
deception, 56, 296, 327, 463
  in advertising, 296
Deceptive practices, 22, 56
Decider, 412
Decision makers, 226, 242, 306, 316, 337, 395,
  399-400, 407, 413, 465-466
Decision making, 98, 161, 283, 301-341, 360,
  362-363, 379-413, 422, 436, 452, 460, 463,
  466
Decision-making, 77, 95, 250, 304-307, 309, 312, 314,
  316, 321, 327-328, 331, 335-336, 339, 341,
  344-345, 370, 384, 386, 390, 395, 398-399,
  407-408, 411-412, 430, 436, 451-452, 457,
  459, 464-465
  biases in, 314
  group, 95, 250, 328, 384, 390, 395, 407, 411-412,
    430, 451-452, 457, 459, 464-465
  in organizations, 407
Decision-making process, 95, 304, 306, 309, 312, 314,
  321, 328, 331, 336, 344-345, 370, 384, 399,
  407-408, 457, 459, 464-465
Decoding, 298
Delegation, 436, 452
  effective, 436
Demand, 20, 24, 60, 211, 273, 329, 368, 372, 389,
  392, 401, 410, 445
  change in, 368, 401
  elastic, 211
  for money, 329
Demand for products, 389
Democracy, 5, 18, 443, 447, 458
Demographics, 4, 9, 20, 33, 37, 77-79, 115, 210, 215,
  218, 233, 236-237, 241, 247, 250-251, 340,
  375-376, 407, 411-413, 452, 458, 463
Denmark, 145, 211
Department of Agriculture, 22
Department of Labor, 397
Department stores, 198, 331
Depression, 178, 244-245, 295, 457
design, 29, 42, 44-47, 49, 53, 55, 57-58, 73-74, 76-77,
  89, 98, 112, 131, 137, 141, 146, 160, 191,
  205, 209, 219, 230, 258, 278, 299, 329, 348,
  353-354, 359, 367, 369, 375, 400, 404, 413,
  445, 452, 455, 457, 461-463
  elements of, 73
  principles of, 74, 77, 258
Determinant, 115, 295, 326, 331, 336, 374, 458
Developed countries, 26, 151, 274, 357
  World Bank, 151
Developing countries, 112, 148, 151, 465

defined, 465
diagrams, 71, 289
Differentiation, 132
  product, 132
Diffusion, 155, 399, 424, 451-452, 457-459, 462-464,
  467
Digital divide, 458
Digital marketing, 78
Digital media, 113, 453
Direct mail, 240, 296
Direct marketing, 143, 267
Directories, 64, 328, 421, 430
disabilities, 26
Disability, 55
Discipline, 29-30, 277, 320
Discount stores, 73
Discounts, 35, 52, 165, 331
Discouragement, 443
Discretionary income, 203, 458
Discrimination, 64, 86, 89, 111, 371, 459, 466
Disease, 36, 202, 211, 214, 242, 251, 420
Display ads, 64, 276, 308
Disposable income, 210, 458, 461
Disposal, 106, 111, 346, 368-370, 373
Distance, 35, 59, 65, 78, 122, 143, 159, 233, 364, 370,
  423-424, 455, 458, 464
  cultural, 78, 122, 143, 423, 455, 458, 464
Distinctiveness, 296
distractions, 353
Distribution, 9-10, 73, 143, 232, 250, 339-340, 382,
  387, 458, 463
Distribution channel, 387
Diversity, 5, 29, 204, 240, 412
Division of labor, 458
documents, 409
Dollar, 5, 23, 39, 251, 341, 372, 382, 384, 387, 393,
  401
Dollars, 13-14, 50, 115, 205, 246, 264, 325, 365, 369,
  372, 386, 418
Dominance, 156, 212, 396
Draft, 70, 326
drawings, 202, 352
Drugs, 119, 140, 215, 243-244, 286, 320, 387, 409
Dubai, 5, 120, 285, 311
Durable goods, 313, 392
Duties, 381, 394, 400
Duty, 307
Dynamic effects, 341
Dynamics, 33, 149, 151-152, 209, 214, 220, 347, 396,
  401, 410, 425, 428, 466

E
Early adopters, 458, 460
Eastern Europe, 156
E-commerce, 16, 33-34, 37, 72, 113, 241-242, 293,
  341, 355-357, 371, 374, 386, 407, 455-456,
  464-465
  benefits of, 293, 357
Economic cost, 20, 458
Economic development, 456
Economic environment, 8, 130, 389
Economics, 20, 33-34, 37, 212, 237, 251, 305,
  314-315, 336, 339-340, 411-412, 455-456,
  458-459
Economies of scale, 151
Economy, 37, 45, 55, 63, 75, 107, 148, 153, 156, 159,
  165, 215, 228, 256, 329, 332, 337, 339, 341,
  369, 371, 373, 376, 411, 425, 457, 463-465,
  467
  team, 425
Education, 1, 22, 36-37, 41, 77, 81, 117, 130, 161-163,
  167, 203, 217, 237, 239, 251, 253, 278, 301,
  339, 343, 379, 386, 409, 415, 427, 455, 460,
  466
Efficiency, 100, 359, 374
Egypt, 172, 215
El Salvador, 350
Elections, 170, 451
electronic media, 115, 149
email, 7, 17, 35, 38, 62, 113, 149, 161, 174, 246, 274,
  292, 338, 349, 373, 376, 411, 438-439, 449,
  463
E-mail, 35, 161, 296, 400, 434
  advertising, 35, 161, 296, 434
email
  for job interviews, 174
Embassies, 50
EMC, 78, 161, 211, 213-215, 251, 341, 411, 453
Emerging markets, 396

emotional appeals, 142, 284, 293, 295
emotions, 47, 51, 100, 103, 107, 110-111, 115,
  123-125, 161, 258, 280, 311, 314, 321, 327,
  375, 390, 422, 462-463, 467
  color and, 161
Empathy, 229, 295, 297
emphasis, 6, 31, 33, 143, 169, 198-199, 211, 222-224,
  227, 269, 338, 387, 409, 455-456, 460, 462
Employee theft, 246, 465
Employees, 18-19, 24, 91, 99, 112, 170, 192, 246,
  277-278, 294, 359, 361, 364, 367, 371-372,
  382-384, 386-387, 408, 437
  loyalty, 18-19, 359, 384
  stress and, 364
Employment, 291
Empowerment, 179
Encoding, 94, 110, 114, 214, 281, 459
Endorsements, 263, 275-276, 290, 293, 296, 419, 439
  necessary, 275
England, 7, 131, 145
English, 49, 154-157, 164, 251, 333, 411
English language, 155, 164
Enhancement, 160, 204
Enron, 24, 365
Entertainment industry, 392
Entities, 125
Entrepreneur, 187, 248
  serial, 248
Entrepreneurs, 45, 65, 368
Environment, 8, 19-20, 22, 26, 30, 44-45, 55, 74,
  76-77, 89-90, 101-102, 112, 114, 119, 122,
  129-130, 146, 148, 155, 159, 175, 178, 210,
  212, 219, 223, 242, 247, 266, 268, 273, 290,
  304, 308, 311, 314, 318, 335, 337, 346,
  348-349, 353-355, 357-358, 360, 367-372,
  374-375, 384, 389, 399, 421, 440-441, 443,
  456-457, 459-461, 463-464, 466-467
  natural, 26, 55, 178, 210, 212, 266, 353, 355, 360,
    460, 463
Environmental Protection Agency, 22
Equity, 19, 87, 110, 113, 231, 250, 413, 456
  internal, 456
Esteem needs, 131
E-tailers, 355
ETC, 194, 209, 211, 269, 293, 338, 346, 372, 399,
  419, 444
ethical aspects, 407
Ethical behavior, 147
Ethical issues, 20, 406, 409
Ethics, 18-19, 33, 37-38, 212, 215, 339, 456, 458
  Bribery, 19
  Business ethics, 18, 33, 37, 215, 339, 456
  Gifts, 19
  Internet, 18, 33, 38, 456, 458
  Laws, 38
  Social media, 18, 33, 37, 339, 458
Ethnicity, 10, 466
Ethnocentrism, 163, 332, 336, 341, 459
Ethnography, 411, 450
etiquette, 215, 459
  business, 215
  online, 459
Euro, 62, 152, 155, 393
Europe, 43, 77, 151, 154-156, 164, 182, 188, 203,
  213, 228, 233, 242, 246, 251, 385, 411, 422
Evaluation, 44, 73, 78-79, 194, 255, 257, 264-265,
  268-269, 297-298, 303-304, 307, 336,
  340-341, 370, 374, 376, 381, 386, 413, 430,
  435, 450, 455-456, 462
Evaluation of alternatives, 303-304, 381, 430
Evaluative criteria, 326, 336, 459
evidence, 38, 46-47, 51, 59, 74, 78, 92, 101-102, 104,
  129, 135, 143, 149, 171, 194, 196-197, 226,
  246, 249, 251, 269, 276-277, 283, 292, 317,
  321, 325, 328-329, 338, 360, 390, 401, 404,
  410-411, 425, 432, 437, 446, 448, 451, 455,
  457
exaggeration, 262
Exchange, 6, 16, 19, 22, 33-35, 97, 147, 177, 247,
  277, 363, 369, 373, 375, 386-387, 400-401,
  408, 438, 446, 448, 451, 459, 465
Exchanges, 242, 369, 386, 441, 459
Exclusive distribution, 232
Expansion, 95, 210
expect, 18, 86, 91, 100, 122, 142-143, 148, 170, 176,
  184, 201, 228, 232, 256, 275, 292, 319, 328,
  346, 365, 384, 404, 406, 426, 435, 456, 460
Expectancy theory, 122, 158, 459
Expectations, 42, 44, 49, 66, 69, 73-74, 93, 122,

168-169, 176, 182-183, 186, 188-189, 193, 198, 202, 208, 259, 288, 299, 305, 325, 333, 365, 370-371, 374, 376, 382, 401, 403, 410, 419, 423, 426, 446, 459-460, 462, 465
Expected product, 376
Expected return, 275
Expenditures, 37, 240, 245, 320, 391-392
Experience, 5-7, 15, 23, 31, 33, 44-45, 47, 51, 53-55, 58, 62-63, 66, 68, 74-76, 83, 89, 91, 93, 95, 98, 100, 102-103, 109, 113-115, 126, 132-133, 135, 137-139, 141, 148, 153, 162, 170, 173, 179, 193-194, 200, 202, 220, 244-245, 258, 262-263, 268, 275, 282, 288, 307, 310-311, 315, 317, 321, 328, 339-340, 345-346, 349-350, 352-353, 355, 359-360, 363-367, 370, 372, 374, 376, 384, 386, 398, 400, 408, 419-420, 427, 436, 441-443, 450, 459, 461-462, 464, 466
  expertise, 94, 98, 115, 275, 296, 318, 331, 337, 339-341, 375, 420, 426-428, 432, 435-436, 464, 466
Explanations, 35, 122, 224, 228, 295, 424
Explosion, 16-17, 137, 169
Exports, 157
  China, 157
Extended family, 387, 407-408, 459
Extended problem solving, 306-307, 321, 336, 339, 459
External environment, 45, 399
External stakeholders, 26
Eye contact, 174

F
Facebook, 3, 17-18, 20, 36-37, 72, 83, 87-88, 99, 105, 115, 124, 131, 135, 137, 139, 151, 159, 169, 172-174, 176, 209, 213, 244, 251, 255, 261, 271, 273, 276, 292, 298, 307-309, 312, 346, 369, 373, 386, 390, 399, 411, 417, 426, 432-433, 440-443, 445, 448, 451-452, 467
Facial expressions, 354
Failure, 21, 42, 45, 74, 170, 210, 226, 270, 374, 387
Fair Packaging and Labeling Act, 22
  1966, 22
  fairness, 18
Family, 6, 9, 29, 35, 43, 77, 88, 103, 105-106, 110, 115, 142-145, 148, 152, 159, 171, 182, 187, 190-191, 193, 210, 227, 231, 237, 244, 246, 264, 299, 312, 376, 380-382, 384, 387-401, 404, 407-413, 418-419, 432, 434, 436, 439, 442-443, 448, 451, 455, 459, 461, 463
  extended family, 387, 407-408, 459
  nuclear family, 387, 408, 463
Family life cycle, 391, 407, 410-411, 459
FAST, 8-9, 16, 37-38, 44, 62-63, 71, 76, 78, 92, 95, 98, 113, 115, 136, 138, 150, 157, 162, 164, 176, 203-204, 207, 209, 215, 249-250, 297, 341, 352-353, 357, 360, 362, 364, 373-375, 402, 410, 413, 438, 450
Fatalism, 269
Favors, 439
Feature, 3, 59, 78, 86, 93, 161, 192, 198, 210, 219, 245, 266, 279, 284, 303-304, 325, 335-336, 355, 362, 374, 391, 409-410, 418, 459
Federal Cigarette Labeling and Advertising Act, 22
  1967, 22
Federal Trade Commission, 22, 277, 406
Federal Trade Commission (FTC), 406
  FTC, 406
feedback, 83-84, 93, 129, 144, 208, 271-272, 290, 387, 426-427, 451, 456
  giving, 426
Field studies, 295
Fields, 29-30, 33, 64, 186, 197, 428
Fiji, 203
Filtering, 328
Finance, 203, 229, 250, 400, 417, 428
Financial issues, 430
Financial management, 397, 412
Financial risk, 407
Financial services, 22, 400
Fines, 440
Fire, 20, 22, 63, 137, 161, 178, 194, 203, 210, 212, 214, 364-365, 451
  apartment, 210
Firms, 7, 9, 15, 18-20, 26-27, 37, 50, 113, 149, 151, 155, 214, 231, 251, 284, 317, 364-365, 367, 376, 386-387, 410, 418, 427
  case study, 410
first impressions, 111

Flammable Fabrics Act, 22
Flattery, 113, 210
Flexibility, 100
Flickr, 7, 105, 115, 274, 440-442, 467
Flood, 105, 178, 331
Focus group, 14
Focus groups, 28, 44, 53, 111, 204, 232, 367, 396-397, 405, 427
Folksonomy, 441, 447, 459
Food, 7-9, 13, 15, 21-24, 26, 30, 37, 44, 47, 53-54, 63, 67, 71, 78, 84, 92, 95, 98, 105, 107, 119-120, 122, 127, 130, 137-138, 143, 145, 147, 150-151, 154, 157, 163-164, 171, 176, 178, 182, 190, 198, 209, 211, 229, 237, 242, 244, 251, 258, 286, 297, 314, 317-318, 320, 325, 330, 352-353, 359-360, 362, 364-365, 367-369, 373-375, 381, 387, 390, 392, 402-403, 406, 411-413, 418, 424-425, 429, 434, 456, 459-460
  production, 164, 360, 387
Food and Drug Administration, 22, 286
Forecasts, 50, 142, 448
Foreign Corrupt Practices Act, 19
Forrester Research, 411, 432
Foundations, 114, 162, 267, 295-296
Foursquare, 159, 171, 211, 271, 349, 417, 442
Fragmentation, 163
France, 7, 27, 145, 151, 154, 179, 203, 209, 213, 246, 281, 305, 340, 402, 413
  economies of, 151
Franchises, 18
fraud, 18, 242, 246-247, 251, 357
  employee, 246
Freedom, 22, 140, 142-145, 158, 174, 179, 223, 339, 373, 394, 417, 462
Freezing, 123
Frequency, 55, 92, 110-111, 114, 139, 264, 270, 291, 333, 341, 424, 459
FTC, 78, 283, 296-297, 406
Fund, 36, 71, 96, 161, 196, 255, 280, 297

G
Gambling, 13, 18, 26, 98, 238, 245, 251, 308, 340, 355, 374
  contract, 308
Gatekeeper, 382, 407, 460
Gatekeepers, 458
Gay consumers, 209
Gender, 3, 9, 11, 35, 65, 76, 78, 112, 139, 173, 182-185, 188-191, 204, 208, 213, 215, 226, 242, 249, 278, 297, 403, 407, 412-413, 455-456, 459-460, 465
Gender identity, 191, 213, 403, 460
Gender roles, 455-456
Generation Y, 452
Generic product, 315
Geodemography, 240, 248, 460
Geography, 10, 237, 374
Georgia, 251, 331
Geospatial platforms, 171, 208, 460
Germany, 7, 19, 134, 154, 246, 286, 350, 390
Ghana, 112, 204
Gifts, 19, 140, 160, 223, 293, 369, 393, 409, 413
Global culture, 4, 151
Global marketing, 15, 154, 158
Global Positioning System, 142
  GPS, 142
Global recession, 8
Global village, 164
Global warming, 13, 24
Globalization, 37, 158-159, 214
  summary, 158
Goals, 98, 102-103, 113, 121-122, 125, 129, 142, 161, 163, 184, 208, 220, 269, 277, 294, 368, 376, 395, 412, 423, 425, 443, 455-456, 458, 461
  broad-based, 142
  definition of, 425
Goal-setting, 412
  traditional, 412
Gold, 205, 241, 251, 323, 391
Goods, 8, 14-15, 19-20, 22, 26, 30, 37, 39, 129, 140, 149-150, 155-157, 160, 162, 164, 193, 223, 240, 244, 273, 281, 313, 320, 331, 338, 340-341, 355, 369, 373, 382, 392, 423, 430, 444, 447, 457-460, 462-463, 465-467
  free, 26, 140, 156, 162, 164, 281, 338, 341, 373, 459, 467
  inferior, 19
  intermediate, 465

nondurable, 340
  normal, 160, 465
  private, 20, 460, 462
  public, 19, 26, 150, 162, 240, 341, 460, 466
Gossip, 171
Government, 22, 56, 153, 156-157, 182, 198, 203-204, 206, 242, 244, 248, 283, 286, 293, 338, 369, 382, 386, 390, 406, 456
  roles of, 182, 456
Government agencies, 382, 456
GPS, 20, 26, 53, 58, 142, 323, 349, 410, 421
GPS navigation, 349
Grapevine, 452
Graphs, 427, 441, 447, 465
Gray market, 460
Grease money, 19
Great Britain, 35
Great Recession, 149, 228, 266
Greece, 246, 390, 401, 412
Green marketing, 26, 33, 460
Greenwashing, 148, 159, 330, 460
grooming, 130, 159, 178, 188, 191, 194, 359, 422, 460
Gross domestic product, 369
  real, 369
Gross national product, 156, 369
Gross sales, 369
Groundswell, 452
Group, 4, 6, 9, 14, 16, 23, 29, 34-35, 39, 44, 66, 68, 87, 92, 95, 99, 112, 122, 131, 138, 144, 146, 148, 160-161, 169-170, 178, 182-186, 192-194, 200, 204-205, 207-209, 214, 226, 229, 231, 236-239, 243, 246, 249-250, 259, 268, 271, 277, 315, 317, 319, 324, 328, 332, 337-338, 349-350, 372, 382, 384, 387-388, 390, 394-396, 404, 407, 410-413, 417-428, 430-432, 441, 443, 446-452, 455-467
  behavior in, 268, 317, 328, 443, 461, 466-467
Group cohesiveness, 424
Group decision-making, 412, 452
  group dynamics, 466
Group influences, 418, 457
Group membership, 446
groups, 4-7, 9-10, 17, 19-20, 24, 26, 28-29, 32-33, 39, 44, 53, 111, 113, 129, 139, 143, 150, 182, 192, 196, 204-205, 207, 220, 229, 232-233, 235-241, 245, 248, 251, 272, 315, 317, 328, 336, 348, 355, 364, 367, 372, 382, 386-387, 396-397, 405-406, 412, 415-416, 418-453, 455, 457-458, 461-462, 464-467
Guerrilla marketing, 33, 36, 243, 439-440, 446-448, 452, 460
Guidelines, 23, 38, 78, 160, 182, 277, 283, 286, 293, 308, 406, 448
  Ethics, 38
  Networking, 448

H
Habitual decision making, 306, 309, 336, 385, 460
hairstyles, 139, 194
Halo effect, 86, 110-111, 277, 292, 460
headlines, 288, 365
Health care, 13, 36
Health issues, 422
helping others, 150
Heuristics, 329-330, 336, 354, 399, 460
Hierarchy, 129-131, 146, 158-160, 257-259, 289, 291, 294, 441, 459-460, 462, 466
Hierarchy of effects, 257-259, 289, 291, 459-460, 462
Hierarchy of needs, 129-131, 158-160, 460
High-context culture, 460
Hinduism, 395
Hispanic Americans, 10, 157, 204
Holding company, 210
Home shopping parties, 358, 448
Hong Kong, 47, 152, 154, 164, 197, 353, 438
Hospitals, 53, 352, 382, 400, 420, 431, 456
HTML, 37-38, 77-79, 113-115, 161-164, 211-215, 250-251, 295-298, 340-341, 374-376, 390, 411-413, 450-453
HTTP, 37-38, 77-79, 113-115, 161-164, 211-215, 250-251, 294-298, 339-341, 373-376, 410-413, 450-453
humor, 34, 87, 286, 291, 298
Humorous ads, 292, 400
Hurricanes, 210
hypothesis, 214, 295, 298, 425, 451

I

Ice, 43, 45, 47, 87, 123, 153, 155, 164, 197-198, 223, 316, 324, 391, 395, 427, 430, 439, 451
  dam, 198
III, 212, 251, 296
IKEA, 148, 153-154, 391, 445
Illegal activities, 246
illustration, 281, 452
Image, 4, 7, 10, 14, 24, 31-32, 50, 54, 58, 67, 69, 71-72, 74, 77, 79, 86, 88-89, 94, 96, 105, 114, 123, 143, 149, 154, 171, 174, 176, 179, 187, 194, 203, 206-215, 226-227, 229, 231, 233, 238, 248, 250, 256, 264, 266, 271-272, 275, 277-278, 283, 285-286, 293, 297, 310, 318, 327, 338-339, 341, 347, 359-361, 366, 368, 370-373, 375, 387, 419, 427, 451, 456, 458, 462-463, 465-466
  country, 10, 24, 50, 143, 154, 213, 227, 338, 341, 360
  national, 10, 77, 208, 211, 213-214, 266, 285, 341
Immediate action, 294
Implementation, 22, 399
Imports, 331-332, 341
  India, 332
Impression, 47, 106, 172, 176, 208, 275, 322, 359, 422, 432, 461, 464
Impulse purchase, 361
Inc., 1, 15, 31, 34, 41, 50, 57, 65, 79, 81, 90, 108, 117, 125, 165, 167, 175, 192, 205, 210, 217, 240, 251, 253, 280, 299, 301, 343, 374, 379, 388, 391-392, 411, 415, 419, 455
Incentives, 122, 161, 270, 295, 459
Income, 3, 9, 19, 29, 77, 122, 146, 186, 203, 210, 226, 228, 233, 237, 239-240, 242, 246, 312, 320, 329, 347, 390, 392, 401, 407, 458-459, 461, 463, 465-467
  differences in, 9, 19, 77, 210, 240, 461, 465
  disposable, 210, 458, 461
  increase in, 210, 329
  market, 9, 146, 203, 210, 233, 237, 240, 347, 401, 458, 467
  national, 77, 390
  per capita, 392
  permanent, 461
  personal, 146, 210, 320, 390, 407, 458, 461, 467
Indexes, 200
Index.html, 79, 162, 374
  creating, 162
India, 54, 69, 124, 148, 150, 157, 164, 182, 212-213, 332, 395, 397, 401, 412, 456
Individual brands, 324
Individualism, 143, 159, 426, 461
Indonesia, 151, 326, 350
Industrial sales, 410
Industry, 8, 15, 21-23, 39, 43, 45, 47, 52-53, 64, 75, 77-78, 92, 96, 119, 149, 160-161, 178, 191, 193, 198, 202, 204-205, 210-211, 219, 233, 242, 245-247, 249, 251, 255, 261, 266, 281, 309, 324, 326, 334, 364, 384, 386, 390, 392, 399, 403-404, 409-410, 418, 424, 430, 445, 464
infer, 6, 121, 230, 261, 329, 349, 364, 465
Inflated claims, 460
Inflation, 78
Influencer, 6, 277, 296, 382, 407, 430, 461
Informal economy, 376
Information, 4, 6, 11, 16, 18, 20, 22-25, 33-35, 37-39, 44, 50, 55-56, 58, 61-63, 67, 78-79, 82, 89, 92-104, 106-107, 110-111, 114-115, 131-132, 135-136, 140, 154, 160-162, 178, 189, 193, 210, 212, 218-219, 228-229, 235, 237-238, 240, 242, 247-251, 254, 257-259, 262, 271-273, 275, 277-278, 280-283, 289-290, 295-298, 303-314, 318-319, 322-325, 327-331, 334-341, 344, 346, 350, 353, 357-358, 360, 367, 370, 374-375, 381-384, 386, 390, 397, 399, 401, 404, 406-407, 410, 413, 419, 421, 425, 427-433, 435-437, 440-442, 446-447, 449, 451-452, 455-467
  about consumer products, 401
Information and communications technology, 358
Information processing, 44, 78-79, 111, 114-115, 132, 257, 277, 298, 325, 375, 410, 452
Information search, 132, 303-304, 307, 309, 311, 318, 336, 340, 350, 381-382, 384, 386, 399, 413, 430, 451, 460-463
Information technology, 295
Initial public offering, 249
  IPO, 249
Initiative, 36, 406, 409, 413, 449

Initiator, 382, 407, 461
Injury, 154, 176, 267, 381, 397
  advertising, 154, 397
  personal, 176, 381
Innovation, 155, 239, 387, 451-452, 457-458, 461
  importance of, 155, 458, 461
Innovations, 100, 149, 372, 409, 451, 457-458, 461, 463-464, 467
  continuous, 457-458
  discontinuous, 458
  dynamically continuous, 458
Innovators, 239, 399, 429, 461
Installations, 28, 358, 426
instant messaging, 458
Insults, 24
Insurance, 34-35, 72, 74, 92, 130, 242, 246, 249, 287, 352
  applications, 92
  contracts, 249
  gap, 72
  option, 35
  types of, 35
Integrity, 18, 142
intelligence, 251, 399, 405, 408, 411, 428, 445, 462
Intelligent agents, 328, 336-337, 461
interactive media, 220
Interdependence, 14, 98
Interest, 9-10, 24, 26, 33-34, 50, 59, 62, 87, 119, 125, 131-132, 135-136, 146, 149-150, 158, 176, 204, 229, 240, 242, 291, 312, 372, 421, 426-427, 430, 432, 442-443, 446-447, 456, 463-465
  credit, 136
Intermediaries, 431
Internalization, 214, 259, 291, 461
International business, 341
International marketing, 164, 211
Internet, 16-18, 22, 33, 35, 38, 62, 99, 149, 162, 174, 176-177, 184, 193, 219, 244, 246, 274, 292, 294, 337, 340-341, 345, 355, 373, 386, 399, 403, 420-421, 432, 436, 439, 447-448, 450-451, 453, 456, 458, 467
  defined, 399
  ethics and, 18
  public policy issues, 33, 38
  search engines, 337
Internet advertising, 294
interrupting, 251
Interviews, 35, 146, 174, 178, 222-223, 231, 235, 268, 277, 355, 395
Intimidation, 420, 456
Intranet, 386, 411
Inventory, 43, 127, 246, 249, 328, 356, 372, 385-386, 411, 465
Investment, 196, 212, 275, 382, 394, 417
  government, 382
  private, 212
Investments, 71, 130, 313, 397, 410, 430
Investors, 249, 384, 445
Iraq, 185, 213
Ireland, 350
IRIS, 34-35, 38
Islam, 156, 164, 460
Islamic law, 179
Italy, 7, 130, 141, 163, 244, 350

J

Japan, 7, 19, 49, 58, 142, 151, 153, 162, 164, 189, 195, 197-198, 203-206, 215, 251, 278, 350, 368, 401, 412, 427, 451
  culture in, 7, 142
Jargon, 78, 162
Jingles, 83-84, 97, 112, 312
job interviews, 174, 395
job market, 203, 388
job offer, 209, 255
Jobs, 38, 45, 127, 192, 388, 396
Jordan, 164, 269, 412, 423, 450
journals, 191, 409
  record, 191
Junk mail, 271

K

Kenya, 331
Kiosks, 58
Knockoffs, 155
Knowledge, 4, 7, 30-31, 83, 92-94, 98-100, 102, 110, 112-114, 132, 143, 163, 220, 223, 234, 248,

250, 256-257, 277, 280, 289, 291, 297, 311-312, 318, 324, 336-337, 339-341, 355, 359, 375, 384, 386, 401, 407, 410, 418-420, 427, 429-430, 445-446, 459, 461-462, 464, 466
  sharing, 99, 355
  specialized, 7, 355, 459
Korea, 7, 151, 244, 250-251, 331, 438

L

Labeling, 22, 34, 441
Labor, 18, 21, 24, 141, 397, 423, 458
Laggards, 461
Language, 49, 53, 154-155, 164, 197-198, 226, 352, 374, 421, 423, 452
  online, 53, 164, 226, 374, 423, 452
  style, 154, 164, 226
Latin America, 49, 151, 164
Lawsuits, 89, 365
Layoffs, 18
  layout, 29, 353, 361
Leader, 156, 339, 427-431, 443, 447-449, 452, 463, 467
Leadership, 39, 73, 299, 398, 427-429, 443, 451-452
  communication in, 452
Learning, 26, 29, 81-115, 122, 142, 149, 162, 173, 251, 257-259, 281-282, 291, 294, 303, 312, 340, 382, 388, 401, 410, 412, 450-451, 455-459, 461, 463-466
Learning perspective, 84
Learning theories, 84, 109-110, 456
Legal issues, 357
  e-commerce, 357
Legislation, 22, 34
Legitimate power, 420, 427, 446-447, 461
Less-developed countries, 357
letters, 16, 68, 77, 87, 96, 113, 138, 162, 274, 285, 340, 366, 438, 443, 459
  application, 87, 113, 459
Leverage, 19, 211, 341, 446
Licenses, 10, 183
Licensing, 88, 110, 112, 264, 461
Life insurance, 92, 352
  buying, 352
  group, 92
Lifestyle, 4, 11, 14, 33, 73, 104, 119, 156, 158-159, 161, 213-215, 233-239, 241-242, 249-251, 259, 298, 369, 374-375, 390, 397, 407, 411-412, 422, 457, 460-461
  consumer behavior and, 251
  lifestyles of health and sustainability, 461
  market segmentation, 4, 33, 214
Limited problem solving, 306-308, 329, 336, 385, 461
Line extensions, 232, 311
LinkedIn, 18, 273, 417
listening, 7, 66, 205, 272, 360
  process of, 272
Literacy, 25, 241
Lithuania, 50, 77
Loans, 26, 196, 203, 242
Local marketing, 39
Locals, 157, 164
Locus of control, 220
Logos, 71-73, 79, 88-89, 138, 311, 317, 461
London, 25, 37, 64, 66, 77, 135, 138, 155, 161, 163, 215, 233, 236, 281, 296, 321, 453
Long tail, 328, 336, 341, 462
long-term memory, 96-97, 101, 110, 458-459, 462, 465-466
Loss, 33, 51, 127, 156, 178, 203, 207, 210, 242, 309, 316, 377, 391, 435, 465-466
  control, 207, 309, 465
  direct, 156
  expected, 203
  income, 203, 210, 242, 465-466
  known, 156, 466
  reduction, 127
Low-context cultures, 462
Lying, 269, 316, 318

M

Macroeconomics, 29-30
Mad cow disease, 251
Madagascar, 351
Magazine advertising, 59, 214, 298, 458
Magazines, 4, 7, 13, 16, 29, 64, 76, 100, 190, 199, 214, 271, 273, 306, 396, 427, 443, 462
Malaria, 36

Malaysia, 15, 184, 197
Management, 29, 162-163, 172, 208, 212, 214, 232, 339, 341, 350, 367, 371-372, 376, 396-397, 411-412, 422, 437, 461, 467
  activities of, 372
  functions of, 212
Managers, 7, 38, 47, 70, 77, 98, 102, 151, 220, 226, 228, 232-233, 278, 293, 305-306, 387, 436, 445
Manufacturers, 22-23, 27, 29, 39, 43, 50-51, 67, 86, 99, 141, 160, 165, 183, 210, 237, 277, 319, 356, 397, 404, 410, 455, 459, 464
Manufacturing, 45, 88, 242, 382, 463
Margins, 362
Marijuana, 323
Market effects, 296
Market leader, 339, 467
Market position, 73, 233, 297
Market potential, 10, 204, 372
Market research, 146, 161, 163, 212, 233, 250, 405, 408, 413
  theory, 163, 250, 405, 408
Market segment, 204, 339, 405, 430
Market segmentation, 4, 33, 115, 185, 214, 347, 462
  branding, 4, 115
  defined, 4, 462
Market share, 94, 96, 338
Market value, 231, 345, 387
Marketing, 3-4, 6-9, 11-20, 25-39, 42, 46-47, 51, 55, 58-59, 62, 67-69, 71, 73-79, 83-84, 86-88, 92, 94-95, 98, 100-101, 103, 105-108, 110-111, 113-115, 118, 120, 122-123, 131-132, 135-136, 138-139, 143, 148, 150-151, 154, 156, 158-164, 173, 177, 179, 185, 189, 191-192, 202, 204, 208-209, 211-215, 218-220, 222-224, 226, 228-231, 233, 235, 241-243, 245, 247-248, 250-251, 256, 258-259, 264, 266-272, 275, 278, 280, 282, 284-286, 289, 291-299, 305, 308, 311-312, 317, 323, 327, 332-333, 336-341, 348-349, 352, 354, 357, 359, 361-362, 364, 371, 373-376, 384-387, 390, 393, 397, 401, 404-405, 407-413, 419-420, 422, 424, 426-427, 429, 433-434, 439-440, 444, 446-453, 455, 457-461, 463-467
  business-to-business, 384, 386, 407
  dark side of, 77, 242
  defined, 4, 14, 31, 103, 139, 226, 352, 359, 455, 465-466
  global, 4, 7-8, 13-15, 26, 33-36, 113, 118, 120, 122-123, 131-132, 135-136, 138-139, 143, 148, 150-151, 154, 156, 158-164, 231, 298, 412, 453, 457, 460
  Guerrilla, 33, 36, 243, 439-440, 446-448, 452, 460
  ideas, 4, 9, 32, 154, 191, 209, 219, 222, 224, 250, 387, 434, 457, 461, 465
  needs and, 9, 19, 32, 39, 161, 220, 223, 457
  of places, 75, 387
  of value, 6, 459
  people, 3-4, 6-9, 11, 13-20, 25-30, 32-39, 47, 51, 55, 58-59, 62, 67-68, 74-77, 79, 83-84, 86-88, 92, 94-95, 98, 101, 103, 105-107, 118, 120, 122-123, 131-132, 135-136, 138, 143, 148, 150-151, 154, 156, 158-160, 164, 173, 177, 179, 185, 189, 192, 202, 204, 208-209, 214, 219-220, 222-224, 226, 228-229, 231, 233, 235, 241-243, 245, 247-248, 256, 258-259, 264, 266-271, 275, 280, 282, 285-286, 291-294, 296, 299, 305, 311-312, 317, 323, 327, 332-333, 336-338, 340, 348-349, 352, 354, 359, 362, 364, 371, 373-374, 376, 384, 386-387, 390, 393, 397, 401, 407, 409, 419-420, 422, 424, 426-427, 429, 433-434, 439-440, 444, 446-449, 451, 455, 457-461, 463-467
  place, 4, 14, 26, 31, 51, 76, 84, 95, 101, 106, 118, 143, 150, 154, 158, 191, 204, 211, 233, 242, 272, 292, 308, 323, 333, 337, 349, 354, 359, 361-362, 364, 374, 386-387, 401, 429, 440, 453, 457-458
  utility and, 411
  value and, 78
Marketing channels, 410, 433
Marketing concept, 7, 215, 272, 361
Marketing environment, 457
Marketing management, 339
marketing messages, 32, 69, 92, 101, 106, 138, 158, 224, 282, 291, 296, 408

Marketing mix, 73, 292, 362, 409, 464
  Place, 292, 362
  Price, 73, 464
  Product, 73, 292, 362, 409, 464
  Promotion, 292, 409
Marketing plan, 7, 338
Marketing research, 27, 38-39, 78-79, 111, 113-115, 163, 212-213, 250-251, 295-297, 339-341, 375-376, 397, 405, 408, 410-413, 427, 450-452
  ethics, 38, 212, 339
Marketing strategies, 4, 14, 25, 34, 37, 68, 87, 110, 158, 160, 220, 247, 397, 419, 439, 446, 452, 464-465
Marketing strategy, 7-8, 38, 76, 143, 151, 209, 233, 256, 337, 371, 422, 426, 447, 460-461, 467
Marketplace, 3, 18, 24, 29, 33, 39, 46, 73, 86, 95, 162, 193, 226, 242, 245, 251, 278, 292, 295, 311, 335, 339, 355, 357, 369, 375, 396, 401-402, 406, 412, 429, 440, 446, 456-457, 459, 462
Markets, 9, 11, 79, 142, 149, 151, 153-154, 160-162, 164, 191, 211-213, 228, 296, 333, 339, 346, 368-369, 374, 376, 386, 389, 396, 400, 410-412, 423, 437, 453, 467
  development of, 212
  thin, 160, 211
Markup, 362
Markups, 246
Mass customization, 135, 159, 162, 462
Mass market, 13, 37, 298, 464
Mass media, 163, 197, 407, 428
Massachusetts, 192, 249, 298
Mass-media advertising, 288
Material culture, 156, 212
Materialism, 25, 37, 142, 148-150, 155, 158-159, 163, 211, 227, 250, 406, 413, 459, 462
Maternity leave, 390
Mature consumers, 49
M-commerce, 273, 291, 462
meaning, 29, 31-34, 37, 42-44, 56, 63, 67-69, 71, 73-74, 78-79, 86-87, 95-98, 100, 102, 113-115, 132, 158, 175, 204-205, 214, 224, 256, 278, 287, 290, 296-297, 318, 352, 365, 413, 423, 441-442, 458, 460-461, 464-466
  understanding of, 33, 256
Means-end chain, 144, 159, 368, 462
Measurement, 39, 115, 150, 162-163, 212-213, 226, 250, 268, 341, 362, 376, 430, 451, 466
measurements, 228, 294, 458
Mecca, 95, 156
Media, 7, 16-18, 20, 33, 36-39, 58, 62-63, 72, 75-78, 83-84, 86, 99, 103, 105, 113-115, 124, 126, 135, 137, 139, 142-143, 149-150, 154, 161-164, 184, 191, 193, 197, 202, 207-211, 213-214, 220, 226, 237-238, 244, 247, 251, 259, 271, 273-274, 276, 278, 288, 291-296, 307-308, 312, 338-339, 346, 369-370, 372, 374-375, 386, 396-397, 399, 401-404, 407, 411-413, 415-453, 457-458, 460-462, 465-467
  communication process, 461
median, 186, 316, 388, 402
Mediation, 295
medium, 17, 38, 55, 62, 77, 86, 100, 107, 135, 161-163, 235, 271-273, 290, 292, 297, 339, 411, 438, 456, 463-464, 467
  electronic, 273
  visual, 297
  written, 55
meetings, 112-113, 386, 451
  online, 112-113, 386, 451
  types of, 112
  virtual, 112-113
Memory, 7, 29, 45, 50, 67-68, 77, 81-82, 84-115, 231, 269, 281, 294, 297, 307, 311, 322, 327, 336, 340, 382, 392, 404, 413, 455-456, 458-459, 462, 464-466
Merchant, 248, 366
message, 23, 34-36, 38-39, 55, 59-60, 64-65, 67-69, 71, 75, 87, 90, 92, 100-102, 104, 114, 118, 131-132, 134-139, 158, 160-161, 176-177, 187, 189, 195, 203, 209-210, 213, 236, 250, 254, 258, 271-275, 277-283, 286-294, 296-297, 317, 341, 349, 353-354, 358, 406, 422, 425, 428, 432, 436-438, 440, 443, 450, 452, 455-458, 462-464, 466-467
  competing, 36, 87, 100, 102, 236, 275, 282-283, 293, 457
  distribution of, 250

  ethical, 75, 209, 293, 406
  follow-up, 35, 92
  informative, 341
  marketing, 34-36, 38-39, 55, 59, 67-69, 71, 75, 87, 92, 100-101, 114, 118, 131-132, 135-136, 138-139, 158, 160-161, 177, 189, 209, 213, 250, 258, 271-272, 275, 278, 280, 282, 286, 289, 291-294, 296-297, 317, 341, 349, 354, 422, 440, 450, 452, 455, 457-458, 463-464, 466-467
  negative, 59, 90, 100, 160, 271, 277, 279-283, 286, 293, 341, 349, 353, 436-437, 450, 452, 455, 462-464, 466
  positive, 38, 68, 87, 90, 100, 209-210, 275, 277, 280, 282-283, 294, 297, 349, 353-354, 436, 456, 462, 464, 467
  purpose of, 160
  sales, 39, 67-68, 114, 135, 161, 209-210, 277-278, 296, 425, 438, 458, 466
  scope of, 203
Message sources, 277
metaphors, 287-288, 291-293, 350
Me-too product, 86
Metrosexual, 208-209, 462
Mexico, 7, 34, 153-154, 164, 170, 350, 412
Microcultures, 143, 462
Microeconomics, 29-30
Middle class, 156, 203
Middle East, 55, 154, 156
Millennials, 458, 460, 462
Minimum wage, 24
mobile phones, 274, 399
Modernization, 155
Modified rebuy, 385-386, 407, 462
Mold, 202
Monetary risk, 320
Money, 6-7, 11, 19, 27, 29, 34-35, 56, 71, 85, 92, 96, 106-107, 112, 115, 127, 144-146, 149, 160, 163-164, 170, 172, 192, 194, 214-215, 228, 233, 240-242, 245-246, 248, 250, 266, 270, 278, 286, 288, 296-297, 299, 311, 316, 320, 328-329, 331, 340, 348-349, 355-356, 359-360, 364-365, 369, 376, 387, 391-392, 396, 411-413, 417, 433, 435, 440-442, 445, 449-450, 458, 461-462, 465-466
  demand for, 329, 392
Monopoly, 445
Mortgage, 180, 268, 384, 400
Motivation, 39, 94, 96, 114, 117-165, 211, 220, 222-224, 239, 250, 261, 268, 283, 307, 335, 354-355, 364, 418, 424, 426, 459, 461-462
  theories of, 161, 224, 250
Motor vehicles, 352
Motorcycles, 16, 241, 347, 391
multimedia, 101, 134, 137, 399, 448
Multinational company, 149
Multitasking, 62, 75, 78, 350, 463
Museums, 29
Music, 4-5, 7-9, 13, 16, 24, 35, 37, 44, 52, 63, 72, 87, 101, 113, 126, 136, 138, 154, 157, 160, 177, 214, 232, 241-242, 255, 259, 263, 284, 306, 337, 353-354, 360, 374-375, 387, 390, 439, 442, 449, 455, 458, 463
  and culture, 24, 37
Muslims, 150, 172
Myths, 155, 191, 224, 455-456, 460

N
NAFTA, 37
National brands, 113
National Environmental Policy Act, 22
  1969, 22
National identity, 164
National security, 144, 440
National Traffic and Safety Act, 22
  1958, 22
Nationalism, 341
Nations, 163, 395, 456
  economic development, 456
Natural disasters, 55, 178, 210
Natural environment, 26, 460
navigation, 349
Need for achievement, 129
Need for affiliation, 129
Need for power, 129
negative information, 281-282, 427, 436, 452
negative messages, 286
Negotiation, 364, 423
  Process, 364

Questions, 364
Net profit, 45, 87, 96, 131, 149, 349, 353, 444
Netherlands, 7, 151, 157, 188
Networking, 17, 34, 37, 169, 184, 241, 386, 390, 400, 411, 413, 417, 422, 441-442, 444-446, 448, 452-453, 467
Neuromarketing, 327, 337, 463
New products, 21, 50, 88, 331, 351, 354, 367, 387, 425, 427, 429, 434-435, 458
New York Times, 37-38, 77-79, 113-115, 161-164, 211-215, 250-251, 270, 294-298, 339-341, 373-376, 411-413, 450-453
New Zealand, 177
Newspapers, 35
Nielsen, 39, 103-104, 145, 165, 244, 299, 340, 377, 403
Nigeria, 198
Nonprofit organizations, 27, 34, 38
Norms, 141, 158-159, 174, 193, 200, 214, 269, 290, 295, 384, 397, 412, 426, 447, 449, 455, 457, 463, 467
North America, 137, 151, 177, 204-205, 363
Norway, 150, 246, 322
Nostalgic attachment, 14
Nuclear family, 387, 408, 463
Nutrition Labeling and Education Act, 22
    1990, 22

O
Obama administration, 22-23
Objectives, 2, 5, 42, 45, 82, 84, 115, 118, 131, 168, 178, 218, 226, 242, 254, 256, 280, 299, 302, 309, 344, 353, 380, 382, 416, 418
objectivity, 33, 275, 466
Obligation, 409, 464
Observability, 463
Observational learning, 93-94, 110, 401, 463
Occurrence, 91, 351, 451
Oceans, 149
OECD, 19
    Organization for Economic Cooperation and
        Development, 19
Offer, 27, 35, 45, 47, 53, 58, 70, 77, 101, 112, 119, 123, 137, 140, 151, 173, 180, 204, 207, 209, 220, 226, 238, 246, 251, 255, 289, 292, 308, 313, 328, 331, 339, 345, 349, 355, 358, 360, 369, 372-373, 410-411, 443, 445, 449, 457
Offset, 413, 457
Offsets, 275
Oil, 144-145, 147, 150, 348, 365, 391, 439, 442
One-to-one marketing, 162
Online advertising, 65
Online marketing, 312, 349
    catalogs, 312
Online media, 213, 296
Online research, 99
Online shopping, 328, 361, 370
online video, 13, 72, 293, 390
Operant conditioning, 89, 113, 461
Operations, 28, 114, 150, 198, 204, 242, 364, 369
Opinion leader, 427-431, 447-449, 452, 463
Opinion leaders, 348, 427-432, 436, 446, 448-452, 461, 464
Opportunities, 7, 10, 26, 76, 101, 112, 151, 162, 186, 193, 205, 238, 264, 308, 339, 351, 368, 371, 388, 390, 423, 449, 464
    e-commerce, 371, 464
Optimism, 457
Oracle, 72
Organization, 6, 18-19, 23-24, 36, 68, 74, 146, 151, 162, 164, 182, 200, 203-204, 208, 214, 224, 263, 275-277, 293, 365, 369, 384, 386, 413, 440, 456, 458, 461, 464, 466
Organization for Economic Cooperation and
    Development, 19
    OECD, 19
Organizations, 6-7, 14, 17-18, 27, 34, 36, 38-39, 77, 101, 112, 143, 146, 163, 203, 248, 264, 277, 286, 293, 382-386, 390, 407, 409, 441, 444, 456, 458-459, 466
Orientation, 118, 123, 143, 148, 158-159, 170, 184, 188-189, 220, 224, 239, 250, 346, 350, 354, 371, 375, 412, 462, 464-465
    future, 350, 464
    performance, 375, 465
Outdoor advertising, 64
Output, 94
Ownership, 242

P
PACE, 349, 358, 362
Packaging, 4, 22, 26, 38, 47, 49, 55, 68, 73, 76, 88, 103, 110, 147, 150, 164, 229, 232, 249, 286, 290, 312, 327, 331, 450, 462, 467
Paradigm shift, 30
paragraphs, 277
Partnership, 20, 33-34, 156, 241, 390, 463
Paternalistic, 19
Peer pressure, 29, 420
Perceived risk, 319-320, 337, 339, 341, 418, 459, 463
Perception, 29, 41-79, 160, 193, 212, 222, 226, 233, 261, 290-291, 295, 297, 299, 350, 374, 376, 382, 412-413, 432, 459, 463, 465-466
    attribution theory, 297
    influences on, 59, 374
Perceptual map, 74, 76
Performance, 14, 39, 65, 73, 86, 137-138, 162, 210, 234, 264, 269, 274-275, 299, 312, 365, 370, 375, 382, 419, 427, 457, 459, 465-466
Perils, 192, 297, 340-341
Permission marketing, 272, 291, 295, 463
Permits, 154, 457
Personal communication, 113, 164, 251, 341, 413
Personal property, 210
Personal selling, 278, 375, 384
Personality, 4, 14, 29, 67, 77, 79, 113-114, 128, 153, 161, 163-164, 178-179, 210-215, 217-251, 277-278, 295-297, 331, 341, 359, 370, 374, 425, 451, 455-456, 463, 466-467
    cultural differences in, 161, 341
personality tests, 128, 228
Personality traits, 226, 228-230, 247-248, 250, 463
Persuasion, 59, 74-75, 114, 163, 212, 250, 253-254, 256-299, 317, 458, 463
    personal, 114, 163, 212, 256, 268-269, 271, 278, 458
persuasive messages, 271, 292, 404
    examples of, 292
Peru, 157
Pharmaceutical industry, 409
Philippines, 15, 157, 170
photographs, 160, 248
PHP, 37, 163, 374-375, 411, 413, 450
Physical cues, 229, 348
Physical environment, 55, 346, 348, 441, 464
Physiological needs, 131, 158
piercings, 95, 139, 205
Piggybacking, 86
Place, 4, 14, 26, 31, 44, 51, 63, 76, 84, 89, 95, 101, 106, 118, 127, 129, 137, 142-144, 150, 154, 158, 174, 178, 182, 186, 191, 203-204, 211, 233, 242, 272, 274, 292, 308, 316, 318, 322-323, 329, 333, 337, 345, 349, 351, 354-355, 358-359, 361-362, 364-365, 367-368, 370, 374, 386-388, 391-392, 401, 425, 429, 432, 440, 443, 453, 456-458, 462
    as product, 337
    marketing mix, 292, 362
Place-based media, 370
Plaintiff, 365
Plans, 27, 83, 88, 127, 150-151, 161-162, 203, 215, 219, 249-250, 271, 296, 368
    business, 27, 88, 150-151, 161-162, 215, 219, 249-250, 296
podcasting, 274, 291, 463
podcasts, 17, 467
    video, 467
Point-of-purchase displays, 258
Policies, 20, 25, 247, 331, 359, 390, 409
Political spectrum, 20
Politics, 212, 237, 247, 340
Polychronic orientation, 350
Popular culture, 13, 33-34, 79, 151, 155, 158-159, 229, 451, 463-464
Population, 4, 9, 29, 33, 119, 150-151, 158, 192, 204-205, 209, 214, 228, 238, 244, 311, 350, 380, 387-390, 407-408, 428, 458, 465
Pop-up stores, 358, 371, 464
Portfolio, 95, 157, 308
Portugal, 156
Positioning, 35, 72-73, 75, 142, 210, 213, 250, 297, 324-325, 340, 464
    brand positioning, 340
    product positioning, 213, 250
positive messages, 209
Poverty, 26, 198, 350-351, 371, 466
Power, 10, 18, 20, 24, 31, 49, 51-53, 78, 93, 108, 111, 114, 122, 129, 136, 143, 150, 159, 161, 209, 211, 222-224, 229, 244, 248, 254-255, 257, 267, 274-275, 278, 290, 297, 338, 375, 382, 394-395, 397, 407, 412, 416-420, 423, 426-427, 432, 434, 436-437, 442, 444-447, 449-450, 455-456, 458-459, 461-462, 464-466
Power distance, 143, 159, 464
preaching, 283
Prediction market, 386-387, 408, 464
Premium, 39, 55, 76, 86, 129, 146, 148, 277, 359, 377, 387, 459
    forward, 76
Premiums, 35, 409
Price, 4, 13, 22, 29, 45, 52, 55-56, 58, 72-75, 78, 86, 130, 132, 135, 145, 154, 165, 232-233, 235, 247, 249-250, 266, 303, 314, 316, 318, 321, 323, 328-331, 335-336, 339-341, 345-346, 355-357, 365, 370, 376, 382, 390, 405, 410-412, 451, 456-457, 462, 464
    defined, 4, 462
    marketing mix, 73, 464
    public policy and, 78
Price leadership, 73
Price range, 321, 335
Price wars, 165
Prices, 22, 35, 52, 55-56, 78, 97, 114, 165, 246, 330-331, 349, 357, 359, 423
    auction, 246
    minimum, 55
    retail, 22, 246, 330, 359
Pricing, 22, 56, 75, 78, 357, 456
    deceptive, 22, 56, 78
    strategy, 56, 75, 78, 456
    value, 56, 78, 456
Principal, 280, 392
Principles, 68, 74, 76-77, 84, 86, 92, 94, 113, 147, 179, 240, 256, 258, 270, 292, 314-315, 336, 340, 405, 464, 466
Print advertising, 101, 297-298
Print media, 86
privacy, 20, 33, 35, 178, 248, 251, 348, 448
    of information, 20, 33, 248
Private-label brands, 88
Probability, 93, 95, 103, 265
    objective, 93
Problem recognition, 303-304, 309-310, 336-337, 339, 381, 464
problem solving, 306-308, 321, 327, 329, 336, 339, 385-386, 394, 407, 459, 461
Procurement, 394
Product adoption, 450
Product advertising, 399
Product choice, 64, 84, 214, 303-304, 325, 336, 381
product design, 73, 89, 457
Product development, 386
Product life cycle, 276
Product line, 77, 88, 110, 324, 464
Product or service, 4, 237, 243, 258, 261, 264, 287-288, 306, 320, 346, 365-367, 382-383, 386-387, 407, 436, 439, 446, 458-459, 461, 463-464, 467
Product placement, 72, 75, 79, 449, 464-465
Product positioning, 213, 250
Product quality, 329, 336-337, 370-371, 376, 382
Product sampling, 269
Product strategy, 238
Production, 94, 101, 135, 164, 340, 360, 386-387, 455, 457-458, 462
    national, 164
Production planning, 386
Productivity, 123, 159, 464
Products, 2-7, 9-25, 28-29, 31-34, 37, 42, 45-47, 50-56, 60, 63-64, 67, 70-72, 74-76, 78-79, 82-83, 86-89, 93-95, 97, 99, 101-102, 104-112, 118-127, 129-133, 135-144, 146-151, 154-155, 157-165, 168-169, 171-174, 176, 178-179, 181-182, 184-188, 191, 193-194, 197, 200-202, 204-205, 207-209, 211-213, 215, 222-224, 227-229, 231, 233-234, 236-237, 239-240, 242-244, 246-247, 249, 254, 256, 259, 266, 270-271, 273, 275, 277-280, 283-284, 290, 293, 295, 297, 302-303, 305-306, 311-315, 318, 320, 322-332, 334-336, 338, 340-341, 344, 346-347, 350-351, 353-355, 357, 359-362, 364-373, 376, 382, 386-387, 389, 391-392, 395-396, 398-402, 404-406, 408-411, 413, 416-418, 421-427, 429-430, 432-439,

476

444-446, 448, 455-467
attributes of, 89, 123, 271, 334, 338, 457, 462
branding, 4, 78, 88, 110, 138, 164, 178, 212, 341, 411, 456, 459
consumer products, 22, 137, 148, 338, 401
defined, 4, 14, 31, 139, 188, 359, 399, 455, 462, 465-466
development of, 212, 266
labeling, 22, 34
levels of, 129, 131-132, 136, 160-161, 181, 193, 244, 259, 324, 338, 373, 436, 455, 460
marketing mix, 362, 409, 464
packaging, 4, 22, 47, 55, 76, 88, 110, 147, 150, 164, 229, 249, 290, 312, 327, 331, 462, 467
professionalism, 397, 461
Professionals, 7, 146, 384, 409, 417, 419, 427, 432
Profit, 30, 45, 87, 96, 131, 147, 149, 243, 264, 339, 349, 353, 362, 373, 405, 409, 413, 423, 444
Profits, 161, 231, 250, 296, 328, 409, 445, 462
Programmer, 133
Promotion, 113, 140, 162, 164-165, 202, 292-293, 298, 308, 310, 312, 331, 339, 346, 363, 373, 384, 408-409, 417, 426, 465
costs of, 312, 465
marketing mix, 292, 409
Promotional products, 409
Promotional strategies, 160, 305, 423, 439, 446, 460
prompting, 314
Property, 71, 97-98, 210, 212, 223, 320, 372, 461, 465
Prosperity, 151-152, 156, 164, 198, 460
Protection, 19, 22, 38, 49, 88, 130, 199, 236, 348, 365
Prototype, 360
Psychographics, 4, 33, 217-218, 220-251, 464
Psychology, 29-31, 37, 68, 77-79, 93, 113-115, 161-163, 211-215, 224, 247, 250-251, 280, 294-297, 314, 339-341, 373-376, 405, 411-413, 450-452
Public health, 112
Public offering, 249
Public opinion, 29, 162, 211, 294, 296, 451
Public policies, 25
Public policy, 18, 21, 26, 28, 33, 38, 56, 78, 150, 212, 296-297, 341, 368, 413
pricing and, 78
Public relations, 161, 277, 293, 449
campaign, 161, 277, 449
Publicity, 17, 37-38, 120, 213, 243, 293, 373, 440, 452
Purchasing, 6, 20, 53, 150, 193, 228, 236, 258, 306, 332, 334, 337-338, 349, 359, 361-362, 372, 375, 383-384, 394, 397, 407-408, 411-412, 456, 462, 466
Purchasing agents, 394
Purchasing power, 150, 462
purpose, 22, 141, 160, 205, 291, 305, 358, 368, 423
general, 22
specific, 368

Q

Qualitative research, 98, 462
Quality, 22, 24, 26, 34, 45, 54, 56, 74, 78, 86, 88, 91, 95, 114, 145, 149, 155, 162, 207, 240-241, 266, 270-271, 287, 289, 299, 310-311, 314, 323, 329-331, 336-339, 341, 364-367, 369-371, 376, 382, 421-422, 430, 436, 443, 459, 462, 464, 467
Quality management, 367, 371, 467
query, 176

R

Race, 10, 64, 138, 182, 195, 213, 251, 261, 355, 448
Radio-frequency identification, 139
RFID, 139
Rates, 35, 92, 141, 203, 224, 241, 246, 266, 277, 349, 371, 390, 463
Rating, 240, 265, 299, 335, 449, 464
Rational appeals, 284
Rational decision making, 316, 337
Rationalization, 127
Ratios, 196
Raw materials, 55
Reach, 7, 9, 18, 20, 39, 51, 53, 59, 62, 76, 78, 113, 121-122, 125, 160, 172, 209, 213, 218, 233, 238, 240, 242, 247, 269, 292, 294, 308, 355, 362, 364, 375-376, 382, 390, 395, 397, 400, 405, 427, 439, 458, 466
Real estate, 77
Rebates, 92, 420

Recency, 270
Recession, 8, 22, 55, 148-149, 214, 228, 266, 388, 390, 411, 423
Reciprocity, 270, 464
recommendations, 4, 6, 33, 76, 115, 139, 165, 277, 295, 328-329, 337, 341, 372, 386, 427-428, 430, 432-433, 436, 457
placement of, 76
Records, 72, 99, 193, 421
Recruiting, 18
Recruitment, 295
Reference group, 418-424, 426, 432, 446-447, 450-451, 455, 457, 462-464
Reference prices, 55-56, 78
Referrals, 433, 452
Reform, 22
Regulation, 375
Regulations, 22, 56, 153
global, 153
Relationship marketing, 11, 33, 464
Relationships, 11, 14, 19, 29, 35, 71-72, 74, 91, 103, 131, 144, 149, 170, 175, 178-179, 184, 189, 192, 212, 224, 244, 250, 255, 295, 333, 347, 357, 359, 381, 384, 388, 390, 392, 395, 402, 404, 411, 413, 421, 423, 441-442, 448, 455-457, 463-466
preferences, 14, 29, 178, 250, 295, 384, 392, 404, 413, 455, 466
Relative advantage, 266, 464
Religion, 122, 247, 263, 311, 389
reorder point, 385
Repetition, 86-87, 107, 111, 113, 281-282, 291-292, 297, 464, 467
Replication, 250, 297, 412
reports, 16, 77, 103, 107, 125, 188, 192, 198, 203, 242, 312, 339, 341, 390, 404, 434, 445
accuracy of, 107
online, 16, 77, 192, 242, 312, 339, 341, 390, 434
Repositioning, 323
Representations, 96, 214
Resale, 346, 382, 463
research, 7, 25-27, 29-31, 33-34, 37-39, 45-47, 53, 56, 59, 67, 77-79, 84, 86-87, 96-99, 103, 107, 111-115, 123, 131, 135, 137, 141-144, 146, 149-150, 161-164, 179, 184-185, 189, 191-194, 196, 200, 204, 211-215, 220, 222-224, 226, 228-229, 231, 233, 235-238, 246, 248-251, 261, 264, 267, 275, 277, 282-284, 286, 288, 294-299, 306, 309, 311, 313-314, 316-317, 319, 326-327, 331, 336, 339-341, 359-360, 369, 373-376, 390, 396-397, 399, 401, 404-405, 408, 410-413, 418-419, 421, 425-428, 432, 436, 438, 450-453, 456, 462-465, 467
conducting, 191, 237
planning, 192-193, 231, 306, 375, 399
primary, 34, 193, 220, 264, 317, 390, 396, 401, 418, 428, 432
secondary, 77, 193, 369, 432, 467
Resellers, 22
Resource acquisition, 442
Resources, 26, 29, 91, 119, 239-240, 261, 312, 316, 349, 398, 420, 423, 425, 441, 456, 459, 466
Responsibility, 18, 38, 155, 193, 275, 296, 382, 394, 397, 401, 425, 451
Restricted, 464
Restrictions, 406
Retail prices, 22
Retail stores, 375
Retailers, 23, 27, 39, 50, 52, 56, 91, 106, 165, 173, 183, 198, 210-211, 246, 251, 312, 328, 341, 346, 349, 355, 357, 359-360, 362, 369, 371-372, 374-375, 377, 382, 425, 438-439, 456, 462
Retailing, 17, 211-212, 251, 312, 341, 355, 358, 360, 363, 370-371, 374-376, 409, 451-452, 455
Retention, 94, 98, 160
Retirement, 130, 137, 392
Retro brand, 108, 111, 465
Reuters, 162, 251
Revenue, 35, 46, 88, 210, 390
Revenues, 77, 156, 245, 264, 328, 339, 341, 353
Reward power, 420, 446-447, 465
Rewards, 84, 88-89, 92-93, 140, 259, 275, 305, 349, 357, 382, 439, 445, 457, 464, 467
RFID, 139
Radio-frequency identification, 139
RIMS, 58
Riot, 176, 353

Risk, 25, 192, 205, 209, 239, 244, 249, 275, 288, 295, 302-303, 307, 314, 319-321, 335-337, 339-341, 350, 365, 376, 385-386, 407, 417-418, 425, 427, 451, 459, 462-463
business, 249, 295, 339-341, 376, 386, 407, 417, 451
classification, 459
commercial, 337, 386
definition of, 209, 425, 459
financial, 407, 459
fire, 365, 451
market, 192, 205, 249, 275, 314, 321, 336-337, 339, 341, 376, 386, 451, 462
objective, 303, 320, 376, 418, 427
personal, 209, 314, 320, 341, 407, 427, 451, 462
political, 249, 337, 339, 427, 451, 459
property, 320
strategic, 376
subjective, 288, 320, 341, 350, 463
Risk taking, 451
Risks, 113, 214, 298, 316, 321, 382, 410, 429
Risk-taking, 192
Robbery, 277
Rokeach Value Survey, 143, 163
Role, 4, 6, 13-14, 25, 29, 32-34, 37, 45, 49, 53, 56, 64, 78-79, 92, 96, 101, 110, 114-115, 140, 148, 150, 158, 162-163, 168, 173-174, 176, 178, 183-185, 188-191, 193, 197, 204-205, 207-208, 210-213, 220, 250, 268, 277, 280, 290, 294, 296-298, 308, 312, 323, 337, 340, 346-347, 355, 362-364, 368, 370, 374-376, 384, 387, 392-393, 397-398, 403-404, 408-409, 411-413, 421, 423, 427-428, 436, 443, 450-452, 460, 462, 465
informational, 423, 450, 462
interpersonal, 250, 340, 355, 374, 427, 436, 451-452
managerial, 212
Romania, 156, 162, 164
Rules of thumb, 460
Rumors, 436-438, 446, 453
Russia, 170, 456

S

Salary, 219, 390
Sales, 6, 8, 11, 18, 39, 49, 52-53, 67-68, 77, 79, 114, 124, 135, 142, 146, 161, 164, 209-210, 240, 246, 266, 277-278, 296, 309, 312, 331, 333, 338-339, 346, 359-360, 364, 369-371, 374-375, 377, 384, 387, 397, 400, 408-410, 425, 429, 438, 458, 460, 466
Sales presentation, 425, 460
Sales promotion, 312, 331
Salespeople, 18, 185, 261, 331, 345, 355, 359, 361, 364, 370-371, 375, 384, 401, 420
Inside, 359
Motivation, 261, 355, 364
Outside, 18
Samples, 174, 228, 237, 247, 360, 362, 370, 409
Sampling, 269, 341, 427
Sanctions, 426
SAP, 386
Saudi Arabia, 140, 156, 170
Saving, 141, 144, 214, 228, 269, 315-316, 420, 440
saving face, 214
Scanning, 35, 184, 327, 463
Scarcity, 270
Schema, 67-68, 75, 79, 100, 111, 213, 250, 340, 464-465
scope, 30, 203, 251, 264, 303
SEA, 26, 68, 152, 438
Search costs, 339
Search engines, 312, 337, 465
Second Life, 16, 18, 112, 174, 274, 390, 411, 444, 467
Securities, 22
Securities and Exchange Commission, 22
Security, 35, 76, 130, 142, 144-145, 178, 205, 208, 223, 242, 246, 248, 251, 347, 357, 370, 410, 421, 440
of e-commerce, 357
Segmentation, 4, 10, 33, 39, 115, 163, 185, 192, 213-214, 236, 238, 251, 347-348, 370, 372-373, 458, 462, 466
age, 33, 115, 163, 213-214, 251, 458
behavioral, 214, 466
defined, 4, 462, 466
ethnicity, 10, 466
gender, 185, 213
psychographics, 4, 33, 236, 238, 251

Selection, 27, 63-64, 75, 78, 212, 302-303, 309, 330, 335-336, 340-341, 346, 375, 458, 460, 463
Selection process, 335, 463
Self-actualization, 131, 146, 160
Self-concept, 14, 168-170, 177-178, 180, 182, 194, 202, 204, 207-209, 211-212, 256, 307, 392, 459, 465
   Expert power, 459
   Positive attitude, 256
Self-concept attachment, 14
self-consciousness, 176, 212, 227
Self-esteem, 148, 161, 168, 170-171, 194, 197, 207-208, 210-211, 220, 244-245, 320, 465
Self-improvement, 142
   Strategies, 142
Self-monitoring, 176, 212, 250
Self-reliance, 142
Sellers, 56, 356, 369, 376
Selling concept, 375
Sensitivity, 152, 286
   culture and, 152
Sensory marketing, 46-47, 51, 75, 465
sensory memory, 96, 110-111, 455, 465
sentiment analysis, 124-125, 159, 161, 465, 467
Service benefits, 387, 463
Service businesses, 374
Service encounter, 114, 374-375
Service industries, 450
Service provider, 432, 449-450
Services, 3-7, 9, 14, 16, 18, 22, 28, 32, 34, 39, 45, 47, 74, 82-83, 95, 105, 109, 118, 120, 123, 127, 129, 131, 135, 140-141, 146, 148, 157-158, 169, 173-174, 193-194, 202, 208, 226, 233-234, 239, 242-243, 247, 254, 271, 273, 281, 290, 292, 306, 320, 325, 328, 345, 349-350, 353, 359-360, 367, 372, 376, 382, 386, 390, 392-393, 395-396, 399-400, 408, 410, 416, 418, 423, 430, 432, 446, 448, 455, 457-458, 462-463
   attributes of, 123, 271, 457, 462
   branding, 4
   defined, 4, 14, 226, 359, 399, 455, 462
   levels of, 129, 131, 193, 455
   quality management, 367
sexting, 181, 208-209, 465
Sexual orientation, 189
Ships, 148
Shoplifting, 242, 246, 248, 251, 465
Shopping center, 354, 358
Shopping centers, 14, 355
Shortage, 5
short-term memory, 96-97, 110-111, 114, 455, 458-459, 465
Shrinkage, 246, 248, 465
Signaling, 451
Silence, 45
SIMPLE, 14, 18, 20, 27, 29, 47, 58, 64, 76, 83-84, 87, 89, 92, 94, 109, 123, 132, 163, 175, 179, 192, 218, 233, 237, 241, 247, 249, 257-258, 264, 268, 308, 310, 313, 315, 325, 334-336, 346, 367, 373, 405, 410, 424, 426, 436, 443, 458, 461
Singapore, 7, 47, 62, 184, 243, 269
SIR, 49
Size, 9, 17, 31, 35, 39, 47, 52, 55-56, 64, 74-75, 97, 114, 139, 160, 197, 199-200, 204-205, 207, 210-211, 214-215, 237, 247, 333-334, 340, 349, 355-356, 365, 389, 396, 408, 418, 420, 425-426, 440, 466
Skills, 53, 133, 150, 209, 361, 401, 405, 457, 462
Slang, 154, 185, 274
slide shows, 14
Slogans, 86, 97, 207
Small business, 386
Smartphones, 76, 171, 281, 292, 307, 360, 435, 440, 460
Smoke, 114, 241, 261, 419
SOAP, 45, 112, 123, 130, 142, 156-157, 161, 179, 187, 194, 198, 223, 299, 363
Social activities, 443, 460
Social anxiety, 212
Social behavior, 211, 255, 295, 375, 457
Social class, 9-10, 37, 240, 278, 427, 465
Social class segmentation, 10
Social environment, 348
Social group, 29, 34, 170, 423
Social influences, 251
Social loafing, 424, 447, 451, 465
Social marketing, 25, 27, 33-34, 107, 286, 465

Social media, 16-18, 20, 33, 36-37, 72, 83-84, 99, 105, 115, 124, 139, 161-162, 184, 220, 244, 251, 273-274, 276, 291-294, 296, 307, 312, 339, 346, 369, 374, 386, 396, 399, 403, 411, 415-453, 458, 460-462, 465-467
   consumer behavior, 16, 20, 33, 83, 115, 162, 220, 251, 292, 339, 374, 415, 421, 423, 448, 450, 452, 461, 465, 467
   ethics and, 18
   product life cycle, 276
   public relations, 161, 293, 449
Social mobility, 463, 465
Social network, 20, 272, 307, 418, 429, 441-442, 445, 447, 452-453, 459, 461, 463, 465-466
Social networking, 17, 34, 169, 184, 241, 386, 400, 411, 413, 422, 441-442, 445-446, 448, 452-453, 467
Social networking sites, 17, 184, 400, 442, 445-446, 467
social networking technologies, 386
social networks, 3, 20, 131, 140, 149, 159, 162, 388, 431-432, 441-442, 445, 448, 451, 463, 465-466
   business, 3, 162, 432, 445, 451
   private, 20, 432
Social norms, 295, 449, 467
Social responsibility, 18, 38, 155, 275, 296
   consumerism, 38
   marketing research, 38, 296
   packaging, 38
   target marketing, 296
Social Security, 421
Social status, 277, 427, 460, 465
Social stratification, 466
Socialization, 142, 150, 182-183, 401-404, 406-408, 412-413, 457, 460
Societies, 20, 141, 162-163, 170, 182, 184, 353
Society, 4, 7, 10, 14, 16, 19-20, 29, 31, 33, 37, 61, 74, 140, 143, 150, 159, 163-164, 168-169, 171, 175, 179, 182-183, 185, 198, 200, 202-205, 208-212, 218, 221, 231, 242, 245, 247-248, 250, 269, 277, 320, 368-369, 371, 373, 387, 390, 403, 411, 423, 426, 448, 458, 460-461, 464-466
   summary, 74, 247
Society for Consumer Psychology, 29
software, 20, 65, 72, 112, 125, 133, 151, 170, 247, 284, 288, 296, 307, 328, 426, 433, 440, 458, 461, 465
   acquisition of, 461
   custom, 458
   malicious, 458
   purchasing, 20
   tracking, 20, 65, 458
South Africa, 7, 172, 393
South America, 77, 204-205
South Korea, 151, 244, 331, 438
Sovereignty, 163
Spain, 7, 203, 206, 390
   culture in, 7
Specialization, 400
Specialized knowledge, 459
Specialty products, 205
Specialty stores, 331
specific purpose, 368
speeches, 226, 444
Sponsorships, 38
Stakeholders, 26, 359
Standardization, 158
Standards of living, 148
statistics, 9, 37, 238, 390, 407
Status, 5, 9, 29, 93, 121-122, 129-131, 149, 156, 170, 197, 204-205, 208, 219, 223, 242, 271, 273, 277-278, 292-293, 320, 339, 346, 355, 372, 386, 393, 398, 403, 427, 437, 444, 456, 460-461, 463, 465-467
Status quo, 437
Status symbols, 121, 129, 273, 456, 461, 463, 466-467
status updates, 346, 444
Steam, 160, 358
Stereotyping, 185, 213, 296-297, 413, 451
Stock, 11-12, 16, 50, 165, 198, 231, 242, 249, 275, 287, 334, 346, 359, 387, 410, 417, 425, 436, 445
Store image, 212, 359, 370-372, 375, 466
Store personnel, 307
Storefront, 183, 429
Stories, 18, 70, 83, 101, 108, 114, 141, 163, 180, 182,

222, 224, 256, 287, 297, 395, 417, 432, 438, 455, 458
storytelling, 274, 291, 467
Straight rebuy, 385, 407-408, 466
Strategies, 4, 8, 14, 25, 33-34, 37, 39, 68, 87-88, 108, 110, 142, 158-160, 165, 213, 220, 238, 247, 249, 269, 293, 297, 305-306, 325, 329, 337, 340-341, 347, 365, 372, 384-385, 397, 401, 404, 407, 412, 419, 423, 439-440, 446, 452, 456, 460, 462, 464-465
   competitive, 249, 293, 340-341, 372, 465
   corporate, 34, 88, 249, 337, 365, 440, 456
   functional, 341, 347, 384, 460, 464
Strategy, 7-8, 19, 24, 34, 38, 56, 73, 75-76, 78, 86-89, 92, 95-96, 111-112, 135, 143, 151-153, 156-157, 160, 177, 209-210, 231, 233, 235, 238, 246, 250-251, 256, 261, 263, 266, 272, 275, 278, 283, 286, 293, 296, 298, 307, 312, 314, 324, 337-340, 348, 358, 361, 371-372, 376, 422, 426-427, 438, 440, 447-448, 451, 456-457, 460-465, 467
   combination, 86, 278
   corporate social responsibility, 275, 296
   CSR, 275, 296
   defined, 307, 462, 465
   focus, 56, 95, 111, 143, 151-152, 238, 250-251, 275, 427, 457, 463-465
   global, 7-8, 24, 34, 135, 143, 151-153, 156-157, 160, 231, 298, 438, 457, 460, 462
   multinational, 151, 153, 460
   pull, 210, 233, 293, 296, 298
   push, 38, 160
Stress, 31, 62, 92, 127, 142, 152, 156, 170, 184, 223, 226, 256, 264, 266, 275, 279, 290, 311, 332, 364, 369, 374, 456
   environmental, 456
Students, 3, 35, 51, 59, 66, 69-70, 93, 101, 112, 120, 130, 159, 171, 174, 177-178, 181-182, 184, 197, 207, 212, 224, 233, 264, 266, 268-270, 277, 292, 316, 339, 349, 352, 365-366, 394, 404, 408, 419-420, 423, 427, 429, 448, 450
style manuals, 170
Subculture, 30, 191, 208, 214, 450-451, 457, 459-460, 466
Subgroups, 200, 432
Subliminal advertising, 42, 58-60, 74, 78
Success, 11, 20, 42, 45, 74, 77, 87, 108, 127, 129, 151, 154-155, 158, 170, 187-188, 210-211, 228-229, 242, 247, 249, 261, 266, 270, 324, 338, 346, 373, 387, 430, 433, 442, 447, 452
Supermarkets, 362
Supply, 55, 95, 171, 196, 242, 261, 274, 327, 329, 349, 409, 423, 443, 456
Supply chain, 423
Support, 11, 26, 34, 87, 92, 95, 127, 160, 171, 179, 184, 196, 240, 243, 250, 261, 305, 337, 386-387, 389-390, 408, 418, 423, 425, 435, 437, 451
Surgeons, 203, 425
Surplus, 369, 397
   consumer, 369
Survey questions, 39
Survey research, 39, 235, 464
surveys, 56, 107, 146, 155, 235, 270, 390, 430, 434, 461
Sustainability, 146, 423, 461
Swag, 366
Sweden, 7, 151, 154, 203, 390
Sweepstakes, 309
Switzerland, 7, 246, 350
system, 3, 5, 20, 22, 27, 51, 55, 94, 96-97, 114, 132, 135, 140, 142, 148, 153, 156, 159, 173, 175, 194, 205, 219, 221, 226, 238-240, 242, 248, 250, 259, 295, 299, 306, 327, 329, 362, 382, 398, 400, 407-409, 435, 442, 455-456, 458-462, 464-467

T
Tables, 367
Taiwan, 197, 331
Tapes, 59, 146, 439
Target market, 4, 19, 223, 237, 271, 322
Target marketing, 296
   branding, 296
Tattoos, 44, 205, 208-209, 212, 215, 418
Taxation, 22
taxonomy, 79, 412, 441
teams, 49, 88, 182, 207, 278, 295, 383, 394, 439
   advantages of, 278

conflict in, 394
effective, 278
types of, 394
Technological environment, 384
Technology, 16, 20, 31, 35, 62, 76, 78, 135, 137, 139,
 151, 159-160, 162, 173, 184, 242, 244, 251,
 295-296, 308, 315, 323, 327, 337, 339, 341,
 355, 358, 374, 390, 399, 410-411, 420, 448,
 453, 455-456, 458, 463
 advances in, 162, 295-296, 339, 341, 374, 411
 information technology, 295
Teens, 4, 7, 62, 141, 163, 181, 191-192, 203-204, 207,
 211, 214, 286, 298, 410, 451
Telemarketers, 420
telephone, 49, 64, 148, 437, 439, 449
Television advertising, 86, 114, 161-163, 211, 280,
 294, 297, 402, 413, 449
 product placement, 449
 public relations, 161, 449
 trends, 163
templates, 411
Tenure, 195, 438
Terminology, 399
Territory, 212
Terrorism, 242, 247, 452
Text messaging, 410
Thailand, 15, 50, 198, 269
 marketing, 15, 269
The Economist, 20, 214, 375
The New Yorker, 161
Theft, 246-247, 465
 employee, 246, 465
Threats, 7, 256, 364, 449, 458-459
TIC, 35
Time management, 350
Time poverty, 350-351, 371, 466
Timing, 228
Tipping point, 452, 467
tone, 193-194, 449
 objective, 194
Total quality management, 367, 371, 467
 TQM, 367, 371, 467
Total quality management (TQM), 367, 371, 467
Trade, 22, 35, 49, 75, 77, 113, 142, 147, 160, 165,
 214, 277, 293, 314, 363, 369, 377, 400, 406,
 411, 419, 438, 448, 467
 domestic, 369
 surplus, 369
Trade dress, 49, 75, 77, 467
Trade promotion, 165
Trademark, 14, 45, 88, 177, 191
Trademarks, 57, 272
Trade-offs, 214
traditionalists, 227
Trailers, 327, 463
Training, 28-29, 98, 119, 368, 384, 400
Transactions, 311, 386, 467
Transfers, 87, 96
transitions, 37, 114, 174
Translation, 72, 154, 164
 language, 154, 164
Transnational organization, 164
Transparency, 22
Transportation, 4, 22, 135, 159, 162, 249, 463
 advances in, 162
 costs, 22
 networks, 159, 162, 463
Trends, 9, 49, 136, 146, 163, 215, 386, 392-393,
 410-411, 431
Trialability, 467
TRIPS, 26, 249, 314, 350, 353, 360
Trucks, 12, 178, 250, 355
Trust, 19, 88, 141, 155, 213, 350, 381, 420, 432
Turkey, 141, 156-157, 164, 179
 middle class, 156
Tweens, 410, 467
Twitter, 17-18, 83, 105, 115, 124, 161, 169, 185, 211,
 273-274, 276, 291, 294, 296, 309, 312, 369,
 388, 396, 403, 411, 413, 417, 423, 428, 440,
 442, 449, 467
Two-factor theory, 282, 291-292, 467

U
Uncertainty avoidance, 143, 159, 467
Underground economy, 369, 371, 467
underscores, 323, 365, 404-405
Unemployment, 29
Unions, 192
United Arab Emirates, 120

United Kingdom, 154, 203, 233, 246, 277
United Nations, 395
United States, 4, 7, 10, 12, 18-19, 22-23, 43, 49, 55,
 97, 141-143, 146, 154-156, 158-159, 163,
 184, 188, 192, 204, 208, 222, 240, 242, 245,
 248, 250, 269, 273-274, 358, 369, 388, 390,
 396-397, 400-403, 412, 422, 427, 431, 438,
 464
Universities, 27, 29, 88, 264, 292
U.S, 7, 9, 18-19, 22, 36, 43-44, 51-52, 99, 122, 130,
 141-142, 146, 148, 150-151, 153, 155, 160,
 163-164, 186, 188, 192, 198-199, 203-205,
 239-240, 243-244, 246, 249, 277, 284, 286,
 296, 298, 305, 309, 311, 331, 340-341, 358,
 362, 374, 387, 389-391, 396-397, 401, 403,
 407, 410-411, 418, 420, 424, 428, 448, 450,
 460
U.S., 7, 9, 18-19, 22, 36, 43-44, 51-52, 99, 122, 130,
 141-142, 146, 148, 150-151, 155, 160,
 163-164, 186, 188, 192, 198-199, 203-205,
 239-240, 243-244, 246, 249, 277, 284, 286,
 298, 305, 309, 311, 331, 340-341, 358, 362,
 374, 387, 389-391, 396-397, 401, 403, 407,
 410-411, 418, 420, 424, 428, 448, 450, 460
U.S. Census Bureau, 9, 387, 390, 460
U.S. Department of Labor, 397
U.S. Federal Trade Commission, 277
user-generated content, 17-18, 33-34, 341, 467
Utilities, 450
Utility, 17, 75, 233, 240, 297, 305, 316, 390, 394, 399,
 411, 420, 464, 466

V
Validity, 104, 212, 223, 228-229, 250, 452
Value, 6, 11, 13, 20, 30-31, 39, 45, 56, 74, 78, 88, 105,
 110, 112, 124-125, 129, 131, 136-137,
 140-146, 148-150, 153, 156, 158-163, 169,
 184, 231, 239-240, 242, 250, 256, 259-260,
 266, 269-270, 277, 291, 294, 299, 305,
 315-316, 318, 325, 329-331, 338-339, 341,
 345-346, 348, 350-351, 354-356, 360,
 363-364, 374, 376-377, 387, 393, 395, 399,
 401, 418-420, 422-425, 433, 443, 445, 447,
 450, 452, 455-459, 461, 464, 467
 building, 11, 105, 129, 146, 161, 184, 231, 240,
 420, 450
 consumer-generated, 136
 defined, 31, 399, 443, 455
 market value, 231, 345, 387
 marketing and, 163, 242
 of marketing, 6, 20, 30, 78, 148, 161-163, 250, 266,
 270, 294, 339, 341, 348, 374, 376, 422,
 450, 452
Value added, 355
Value creation, 422, 447, 456
Value proposition, 339
Vandalism, 179, 247
Variability, 114
Variables, 9, 39, 226, 228, 234, 236-237, 247, 250,
 280, 375, 393, 408-409, 411, 455
Venezuela, 170, 203, 215
verbs, 184
 action, 184
videos, 17, 20, 87, 105, 113, 233, 294, 370, 372, 391,
 439-441, 444, 449
 digital, 20, 113, 444, 449
 online, 17, 20, 105, 113, 294, 370, 439-441, 444
Vietnam, 157, 164
Violence, 24, 93, 140
Viral marketing, 272, 440, 446-448, 452-453, 467
Viral marketing techniques, 272, 446
virtual communities, 443
Virtual goods, 140, 162, 444, 447, 458, 467
Virtual worlds, 16, 18, 35, 79, 112-113, 174, 211, 244,
 274, 278, 291, 390, 411, 442, 444, 447, 457,
 467
virus, 431, 462
Vision, 47, 49, 96, 148, 214, 316, 460
Visualize, 95
visuals, 280, 290
 effective, 280
 power of, 290
VoIP, 390, 444
Volume, 8, 237, 376, 382, 384, 411, 436, 458
Volumes, 460

W
Wages, 36

Wall Street Journal, 37-38, 77-79, 113-115, 162-164,
 212-215, 242, 250-251, 295-298, 341,
 373-376, 411-413, 451-453
War, 141, 148, 164, 215, 295
Warehouse clubs, 346
Warranties, 22, 365, 376
Warranty, 232
Water, 36, 38, 44, 95, 98-99, 112, 122, 130, 154, 157,
 193, 212, 235, 250, 274, 281, 283, 316, 318,
 327, 372, 391, 401, 411, 435
Weaknesses, 232, 432
Wealth, 10, 197, 215, 320, 448, 455, 461, 463
Web, 2, 4, 7, 14, 16-17, 20, 23, 33, 35, 38, 46-47, 58,
 62-63, 72, 76, 78, 87, 99-100, 111-114, 119,
 124, 131-137, 139, 149, 151, 164, 169,
 171-175, 181, 184, 187, 191-192, 206-207,
 209, 211, 213, 219, 231, 241-242, 248-249,
 251, 271, 273-274, 276-278, 292-293, 296,
 298, 303-304, 309, 328-329, 336-338,
 340-341, 344-346, 353, 355-356, 358, 364,
 367, 369-370, 373, 381, 386-388, 390, 392,
 395-396, 402, 404-405, 411, 413, 417,
 420-421, 425, 432, 437-440, 442-444, 446,
 448, 452-453, 456-457, 459-460, 467
Web 2.0, 17, 33, 296, 387, 440, 443, 446, 467
Web site, 4, 7, 23, 46-47, 63, 87, 112-113, 119,
 132-134, 136-137, 151, 169, 171-172, 175,
 187, 191, 209, 219, 242, 248-249, 271,
 277-278, 309, 328-329, 344, 353, 356, 358,
 364, 370, 373, 381, 388, 395, 404-405,
 420-421, 437-440, 448, 452, 459-460
 credibility, 277, 370
 design, 46-47, 112, 137, 191, 209, 219, 278, 329,
 353, 404, 452
 privacy, 248, 448
 security, 242, 248, 370, 421, 440
Web sites, 4, 7, 14, 62-63, 76, 87, 112, 135, 173, 192,
 206-207, 209, 231, 241-242, 248-249, 274,
 292-293, 303, 328, 337, 355, 358, 373, 392,
 437, 442, 444, 446, 452, 456
websites, 442
Welsh language, 49
Widgets, 274, 291, 432, 467
Wiki, 77, 211, 386, 408, 467
wikis, 411
Wireless communications, 16
Wisdom of crowds, 444, 447, 453, 467
Women, 3, 7, 9, 13, 23, 28-29, 37, 48-51, 63, 76-77,
 92-93, 95, 99, 119, 129, 131, 141-142, 151,
 157, 160-161, 163, 169-171, 175, 179-187,
 189, 191, 193-215, 219, 222-224, 236, 238,
 244-245, 265, 268, 279, 284, 287, 316, 318,
 346-348, 350, 355, 360, 374, 388-390,
 392-393, 396-398, 404, 409, 411-412, 419,
 421, 424, 427, 432, 434, 437, 451, 453,
 456-457, 459-460, 465
Won, 35, 42, 46, 55, 74, 135-136, 139, 141, 152, 154,
 162, 178, 227, 251, 264, 277-278, 296,
 311-312, 315-316, 325, 334, 345, 348, 386,
 390, 417
word of mouth, 364, 373, 432, 436, 447, 452, 463, 467
Word-of-mouth advertising, 448, 451
Word-of-mouth communication, 416, 433, 435-436,
 452
Word-of-mouth marketing, 448
Work, 9, 19, 25-28, 30-31, 34, 36, 43, 47, 59, 62, 64,
 68, 75-76, 89, 92, 98-99, 101-103, 107,
 111-112, 114, 121-123, 126, 129, 131, 141,
 148, 150-151, 154, 156, 158, 162, 172, 176,
 179, 191, 205, 214, 222, 224, 226, 228-229,
 232, 237, 248, 256, 262, 264, 272, 275, 284,
 286, 289, 292, 315, 317, 323, 327-328,
 331-332, 337, 340-341, 347, 349, 355,
 357-359, 361, 365, 371, 374-375, 377, 381,
 386, 391, 395-396, 398, 404, 412, 417-419,
 425, 428, 432, 448, 451, 456, 460-461
 attitudes toward, 154, 237, 256, 264, 275, 284
Workers, 24, 63, 151, 197, 248, 251, 358, 364, 375
workforce, 141, 396
 women in, 141
workplace, 425
World, 3-4, 7, 9, 12-14, 16-20, 24, 26, 30-31, 33,
 35-38, 43-44, 47, 52, 55, 63, 72, 74, 76-78,
 83-84, 92, 99, 105, 110, 112-113, 118, 133,
 137, 140-142, 144, 146, 148-156, 158, 160,
 162-164, 173-175, 182, 184-185, 189, 191,
 196, 198, 200, 204, 206, 209-211, 213, 215,
 222-223, 233, 237, 244, 249, 251, 271,
 273-274, 278, 286, 295, 297, 305, 307-308,

316-317, 336, 341, 349, 353, 355, 357-358,
361, 373-374, 387, 390, 396, 400, 404-405,
412, 417, 421-422, 426, 432, 439-445, 449,
453, 455-457, 460-462, 464-465
World Bank, 151
World Health Organization, 200
World War, 141, 148
World Wide Web, 99, 336
worm, 368, 376
WWW, 2, 5, 10, 35-38, 42, 45, 76-79, 82, 84, 112-115,
118, 131, 160-164, 168, 178, 210-215, 218,
240, 242, 249-251, 254, 256, 294-298, 302,
309, 338-341, 344, 353, 372-376, 380, 382,
409-413, 416, 418, 449-453

Y
Young entrepreneurs, 45
YouTube, 5, 7, 17-18, 36-37, 138, 192, 231, 233, 264,
274, 294, 312, 329, 396, 399, 438, 440, 442,
450, 452, 467

Z
ZIP codes, 240